Ancient Egypt

THE LIGHT OF THE
WORLD

A Work of

Reclamation and Restitution

in Twelve Books

Gerald Massey

AUTHOR OF
"A BOOK OF BEGINNINGS" AND "THE NATURAL GENESIS"

VOLUME 2

ISBN 1-56459-103-4

3/03

Kessinger Publishing Company
Montana, U.S.A.

CONTENTS

VOL. II

LIST OF ILLUSTRATIONS

VOL. II

THE ARK, THE DELUGE, AND THE WORLD'S GREAT YEAR.

Book IX

At first sight the general effect of the innumerable deluge-legends is to suggest the existence of a primitive kind of catastrophobia resulting from fear of the water-flood. The arkite symbolism originated in the mount and tree, the cave or enclosure being a natural place of refuge when the waters were out upon the earth; and these were followed by the raft, the boat, or ark that swam the waters as a means of human safety. Before the legends of a deluge could have been formulated, the deluge as an overwhelming flood of water had become a figure used in sign-language to express the natural fact in a variety of phenomena to which the type might be and was applied. It is expressed in English still by what is termed "a flooding." But a deluge is not only an overflow of water. There is a deluge of blood (both Egyptian and Polynesian). Night brings its deluge of darkness, and dawn lets loose the floods of day. The so-called deluge-legend comprises a hundred legends and a hundred applications of the same type, from one single origin in sign-language as the primitive mode of representing a fact in nature. The deluge is universal because it was *not* local. The human race spread out over all the earth would not have been greatly troubled about an excessive overflow of water once upon a time in Mesopotamia. The legend is coeval with all time, and current amongst all people, because the deluge did not occur "once upon a time." On the grand scale it was the mythical representation of the ending and submergence of an old order of things in the astronomical mythology; but there were various distinct deluges with that meaning, and not merely one. The Egyptian deluge in the so-called "destruction of mankind" is described as continuing for three nights and days. The time is measured by three days' length in navigation through a deluge of blood (*Records of the Past*, 6, 103). Now, three nights and days is the length of time that was computed for the monthly absence of the moon in the nether-world. Hence there was a deluge of darkness on that scale in mythology. But the deluge occurred in at least four categories of phenomena. There was a deluge of blood and a deluge of darkness, as well as a deluge of water. There is also the deluge that was a type of periodic time; and by no black art of bibliolatry can these four kinds of deluge be combined in one.

A deluge being an ending of a cycle in time, we can understand the

N N

language of the Codex Chimalpopoca (translated by the Abbé Brasseur de Bourbourg) concerning the flood, when it says, " Now the water was tranquil for forty years plus twelve." " All was lost. Even the mountains sank into the water, and the water remained tranquil for fifty-two springs." In this account, the well-known Mexican cycle of fifty-two years is measured by means of a deluge at the end of the period. In Inner Africa the year was reckoned by the periodic great rain ; in Egypt by the inundation ; and a deluge, we repeat, became the natural type of an ending in time in the uranographic representation. In India, a solar pralaya, in which *the waters rise till they reach the seven Rishis in the region of the pole*, is of necessity kronian, and applies solely to the keeping of time and period astronomically. The Assyrian deluge is described as lasting seven days. This agrees with the seven days' silence in the Wisdom of Esdras, by which the consummation of the age, or ending of the period, was to be commemorated " like as in the former judgments," deluges, or endings of the cycle or age in time. The flood of Noah is on the scale of the year or thereabouts. The deluge of time, as it was called by the Chaldean magi, is a breach of continuity, a phase of dissolution. It was a period of negation that was filled in with a festival as a mode of memorialising the *dies non* or *no time*. It was a condition of the lawlessness of misrule, of promiscuous intercourse, of drunkenness, that characterized the saturnalia by which it was celebrated.

There is a Kamite prototype in " the destruction of mankind" for the woman who is the reputed cause of a deluge in the Egyptian mythos. This is Sekhet the avenger. She is *the very great one of the liquid domain*. No one is master of the water of Sekhet, which she lets loose as an element of death and destruction. She was the great mistress of terror in fire and flood. In " the destruction of mankind" it is said, " There was Sekhet, during several nights, trampling the blood under her feet as far as Heracleopolis." Ra, the solar god, " ordered the goddess to *slay the evil race* in three days of navigation." " And the fields were entirely covered with water through the will of the majesty of the god ; and there came the goddess (Hathor) in the morning, and she found the fields covered with water, and she was pleased with it, and she went away satisfied and saw no men " (*i.e.*, none of the exterminated evil race). This is a form of the Egyptian deluge designated a great destruction, but with no earthly application to the human race. In the African legend relating to the origin of Lake Tanganyika, that was told to Stanley by the Wagigi fishermen, it was a woman, to whom the secret of the water-spring had been entrusted, who was the cause of the deluge. Possibly this woman was the earth as mother of the waters, seeing that Scomalt is the earth-mother of the Okanagaus, and that she also was charged with letting in the deluge. Scomalt is a form of the primordial genetrix, equivalent to Apt in Egypt. Long ago, they say, when the sun was no bigger than a star, this strong medicine-woman ruled over what appears to have become a lost continent. Her subjects rose against her in rebellion. Whereupon she broke up the land, and all the people but two met with their death by drowning. A man and a woman escaped in a canoe and arrived on the mainland, and from this pair the Okanagaus are descended (Bancroft, vol. iii, 149).

A starting-point in various deluge-legends is from the world all water. This originated with the firmament as the celestial water that was called the Nnu, or Nun. Now one meaning of the word Nun in Egyptian is the flood. Thus the water of heaven is synonymous with the deluge. In one aspect the deluge, as a figure in the sign-language of the astronomical mythology, was a mode of representing the sinking of the pole in the celestial ocean which was figured as the world of water. This is the world all water in the legendary lore. The flood upon which Jehovah sat as king was no other than the firmamental Nun (Ps. xxix. 10). So the throne of Osiris was based upon the flood, that is upon the Nun. In the vignettes to the Ritual Osiris sits upon the throne in Amenta as the great judge and ruler, and his throne is "balanced" as it is described, upon the flood. Water being the primary element of life, it was also based on figuratively ; and Osiris with his throne resting on the water takes the place of the earlier Nnu, or later Noah, resting in his ark as master of the deep. Nnu was god of the celestial water. The wateress in one form was the goddess Nut. This, then, and nothing short of it, is the root of the matter when, as in the Navajo-Indian legend, certain persons, who are so often one female and one male, make their escape from the over-whelming waters by climbing up a reed to the land of life which, as a land of reeds, was the primal paradise, or the fields where the papyrus was in flower above the waters of a universal deluge, as represented in the veriest dawning of mythology.

We have to learn the sign-language before we can understand the nature of mythology. When it is said that Horus inundates the world like the sun each morning, that is with the light as the deluge of day. There is a white water and a black, equivalent to the white bird of light and the black bird of night, as opposite figures of Sut and Horus for the dark and the day. The evil Apap, who drinks the water cubit by cubit at each gulp as the sun goes down, is slain by Horus at daybreak, when he once more sets free the waters of light which are designated the waters of dawn. In like manner, the waters of day rush forth when Indra slays the serpent of darkness, who was thought of as the swallower of the light = water of heaven. Osiris is called the "overflower," the "great extender," the "shoreless one," who in this imagery of the deluge "brings to its fulness the divine force which is hidden within him" (Rit., ch. 64, 13-15, Renouf). Thus, in continuing the primitive mode of thinging the concept, Osiris is the water-force personified, instead of being represented as a crocodile, which was also one of the primal types of water.

"The deluge" is only *single* as a type. There are various deluges known to mythology, and various agents who are held responsible for causing them. In one legend or folk-tale it was the mischievous monkey. In another it was the tortoise, who sank in the waters and drowned the people who had their dwelling-place upon its back. In another it is caused by the killing of a sacred bird, which might be the vulture or cygnus. In a fourth the fountains of the great deep are opened by the taking out of the star, whereupon the deluge follows. A cause of the deluge is attributed to the star-gods, Sut in Egypt and Bel in Babylonia. It was caused by a failure in keeping time, and the failure is followed in a number of legends by the new heaven, in which the supreme time-keeper is the moon or the lunar divinity who is Taht in the Kamite representation.

Some most precious remains of the primitive wisdom now extant outside of Egypt are preserved by the oldest races of the world. Much of the matter is found amongst the people of the Polynesian islands, far more to the purpose than anything to be found in the Hindu or the Hebrew sacred books. The Samoans have what may, in a symbolical sense, be termed a deluge legend. Tangaloa, the originator of the heavens, was the builder. Of old the heavens were always falling down when they consisted of water without any bulwark or embankment. To put a limit, to build or make any firm enclosure, was to circumscribe the waters and secure a place of refuge from the dreaded deluge. In the time of Ptah, their great architect, the Egyptians were advanced enough in craftsmanship for the enclosure formed by him to keep out the waters of the deluge in Amenta to be made of either iron or steel, called the ba-metal. An ark was a primitive enclosure formed in the celestial water. This, as Egyptian, is the ark of Nnu, and Nnu is heaven, as water, also a name for the deity of the celestial water. In the Samoan legend, an ark is built before there was any water or water-flood, or before the firmament had been figured as water. " Tangaloa of the heavens and his son Lu = Shu built a canoe or vessel up in the heavens." When the vessel was finished there was no water to float it. Gaogao, the ancient mother, told her son Lu to have the vessel ready and she would make the water. She then gave birth to a lake, or the water of life, and also to the salt water, as it is said "there was no sea at that time." The lake we identify with "the lake of the thigh," or the meskhen of the water-cow. Sea and lake imply both salt and fresh water, the two waters of earth and heaven that were repeated in the two lakes of Amenta. The Samoan deluge lasted until the seventh day, like the Babylonian. As it is said of Lu, " He was not many days afloat, some say six, when (on the seventh) *his vessel rested on the top of a mountain called Malata*" (Turner, *Samoa*, p. 12). In a papyrus at Turin the god who claims to be self-existent says, " I make the waters and the Mehura comes into being." That is *heaven as the celestial water.* In a hymn to Ptah it is said, " The waters of the inundation cover the lofty trees of every region." These, however, are the waters of Nnu or the Nun (Renouf, *H. L.*, pp. 221–2), and not the overwhelming flood of water on the earth. When the mehura first came into existence it was a heaven imaged as the water that was undivided by the astronomers, the islands or other land-limits that were figured in the aërial vast ; and heaven as the celestial water was the Nnu or Nun. A "true explanation of the world-wide deluge myths " no longer need be sought for in the book of Genesis or in the tradition of a great flood that swept the plains of Mesopotamia ; nor in any vast cataclysm that might have been caused by the melting of the ice at the close of the glacial period (Huxley, *Nineteenth Century*, 1890, pp. 14–15). We find by the Egyptian wisdom that "the deluge," as it is commonly termed, belongs neither to geography, nor geology, nor history. Geology, the latest of the sciences, was comparatively unknown to the early world. Geology did not furnish the kind of fact with which the ancient science was concerned. Whatsoever the Egyptian "mystery-teachers of the depths" may have known of mines and metals, mythology was not geological in the least degree. Neither did the Kamite chronology include the computation of geological time.

It was confidently asserted by Bunsen that the deluge legend was unknown to the Egyptians. But they had all the deluges that ever were, as the Hir-Seshta informed Solon, including the "great deluge of all," whereas the Greeks could only muster two. But in no case were these geological catastrophes. M. Lenormant asserted that the story of the deluge was unknown to the black race, and that "while the tradition holds so considerable a place in the legendary memories of all branches of the Aryan people, the monuments and original texts of Egypt, with their many cosmogonic speculations, have not afforded one even distant allusion to this cataclysm." The statement sounds authoritative, but it is not true. Professor Sayce, following Lenormant, asserts that "no tradition of a deluge had been preserved by the Egyptians" (*Fresh Light from the Monuments*, p. 47). This comes of raking for human history, and for nothing else, in the Semitic *débris* of the Kamite astronomical mythology. Both are wrong, and both were equally misled through looking for the deluge with the Semitic versions for their determinatives. Bibliology has gone perilously near to ruining Assyriology and Egyptology for the first generations of students in this country. It is fortunate for genuine scholarship that there *are* livers out of Bible-burdened Britain.

To identify the deluge-legend in Egypt you *must* know *how* to look for it ; no use in *peering through the Semitic spectacles*. The legend of Atlantis re-told by Plato in Timæus was Egyptian, and no doubt with the legend came the name of lost Atlantis, transliterated through the Greek. As Egyptain, the word atr=atl has several meanings in relation to water. Atru is the water, the water-flood, the water-boundary, limit, measure, frontier, embankment. Egyptian in the early stages had no sign of *l*. But by substitution of the later letter *l* for *r* the word atr becomes atl, the root of such names as Atlantis and Atlantic. With this change of letter the Atarantes of Africa become the Atalantes. The word antu or anti signifies a division of land. Thus Atlanti, whence Atlantis, as a compound of two Egyptian words, denotes the land divided by the waters, or canals of water. Now the earliest *nuit* or nomes of Egypt were seven in number, and these were seven territories marked out, limited, and bounded by the atlu (atru) as river, canal, conduit, or water-boundaries. In the valley of the Nile, the land was bounded first by water as the natural boundary, and seven nomes would be enclosed by seven atlu, long before the land limit was marked out by the boundary-stones or stelæ. And atl-antu, we suggest, is the original for the names of Atlantis and the Atlantic Ocean. It is noticeable that in the Nahuatl vocabulary atl is also the water name, and that atlan denotes the border or boundary of the water (Baldwin, *Ancient America*, p. 179). Atlan thus becomes a name for the mound, island, or tesh that was placed as a limit to the water in Egypt. This would be the land of Atlan, as we find it both in Africa and America. There were seven such water limits to the land in Egypt when it was

divided into seven nomes.   And seven astronomes named after these
become the seven islands of the lost Atlantis, which sank in the
celestial waters, the heptanomis of the seven lands below having
been repeated in the mapping out of heaven in seven astronomes.
The heptanomis above, like the one below, was formed of seven lands
that were divided by the seven waters, canals, or atlu (atru), and both
together constituted the Atlantis of uranography, the only one that
could ever be lost by the celestial waters overflowing the celestial
lands.   The seven rulers of the astronomes attained the status of
divine princes in the celestial heptanomis.   And among the nomes of
Lower Egypt we find the nome of the Prince of Annu ; the nome of
the prince of Lower Egypt ; the nome of Supti (Sut) ; the nome of
Samhutit (Horus) ; the nome of Sebek ; the nome of Shu ; the nome
of Hapi.   Here then, if anywhere on earth, we find a geographical
prototype for the Atlantis that was lost in seven islands, according to
the records kept by the astronomers, which are preserved in the
mythography.   Among the many types of the heptanomis and its
septenary of powers and stations of the pole may be enumerated :—A
mount with seven caves ; seven islands in the sea ; the seven-
headed serpent whelmed beneath the waters ; a tree with seven
branches ; a fish with seven fins ; a pole with seven horns ; a cross
with seven arms ; the seven supporting giants ; the ark of seven
cubits ; the boat with seven kabiri on board ; the group of seven
cities.

It is not necessary to suppose that the Egyptians were the helpless victims of their own symbolism, who lived in mortal dread of the
celestial waters falling down and overwhelming them in a deluge
once for all.   But there can be no doubt that the water-flood on earth
against which the early race was powerless produced a profound and
permanent impression, so that the deluge idea became associated with
the firmamental water.   This can be proved by the mythical deluge
dramatically represented in the Ritual.   " I am the Father of the
Inundation," says Anup at the northern pole, whence the waters
issued in the deluge of the Milky Way, or White Nile of the Nun.
The Egyptian Ritual affords a study of the deluge mythos in the
phase of eschatology.   The passage for the soul in death has long
and universally been likened to a river or some dark water flowing
betwixt the two worlds of earth and heaven.   This in Egypt was the
Nun.   The way of the gods in their ascent and descent to earth was
by water.   The way of souls in their ascent to heaven is equally
by water, whether in the ark of the moon, the bark of Orion, or the
boat of the sun.   The manes on entering the other life thus addresses
the sailors of the solar bark, " O ye seamen of Ra, at the gloaming of
day let me live after death, day by day, as doth Ra."   That is by
means of the boat which keeps the sun or the soul of the deceased
afloat upon the drowning element (ch. 3).   In the chapter for
travelling on the road which is above the earth (ch. 4), the speaker
says, " It is I who voyage on the stream which divideth the divine
pair."   These are the two sisters Isis and Nephthys, whose stations in
the Osirian solar mythos were at the western and eastern sides of the
river which ran north and south in heaven as in Egypt. Some
prophetic tableaux show the deceased in his funeral bark, speeding

before the wind with all sail set, having started on his way to the next world the very day that he took possession of his new abode in death (Maspero, *Egypt. Arch.* p. 120). Amongst the words that are said on the day of burial to bring about " the resurrection and the glory," the deceased asks that he may see the ship of the holy Sahus traversing the sky ; that is, the ark of souls represented in the constellation of Orion. He also pleads, " Let the divine vessel Neshemet advance to meet me." The Osiris tells us that the name of his bark is " Collector of Souls." " The picture of it is the representation of his glorious journey upon the canal" (ch. 58). Safe in the ark, he crosses the waters in which the helpless souls are wrecked.

In the chapter by which the ship is sailed in the nether-world, the speaker not only sails across the water of Nnu, for he says, " I come from the lake of fire and flame, from the field of flame," and he stands erect and safe " in the bark which the god is piloting, at the head of Aarru," that is, on the summit of the mount, or final resting-place of the ark (Rit., ch. 98, Renouf), which the deceased had safely reached through fire and flood. On entering the solar bark the Osiris says, " I have come myself and delivered the deity from the pain and suffering that were in the trunk, in shoulder, and in leg. I have come and healed the trunk and fastened the shoulder and *made firm the leg.* And I embark for the voyage of Ra." The leg of Osiris, like the leg of Nut or the leg of Ptah, imaged the supporting power of the pole. The manes pleads, " Let not the Osiris Nu be ship-wrecked on the great voyage" (ch. 130). " Let not disasters reach him." " May the steering be kept clear from misadventure." " Let me come to see my father Osiris" (ch. 99). " O, thou ship of the garden of Aarru, let me be conveyed to that bread of thy canal as my father, the great one, who advanceth in the divine ship" (ch. 106, Renouf). " Lo, I sail the great bark on the stream of the god Hetep. I took it at the mansion of Shu "—the starry heaven (ch. 110, Renouf). " I sail upon its stream and range within the garden of Hetep " (ch. 110). When about to enter the bark of Ra, the speaker says, " O great one, let me be lifted into thy bark. Let me make head for thy staircase. Let me have charge of those who convey thee, who are attached to thee, and who are of the stars which never set " (Rit., ch. 102). These are the seven that pull at the rope, or as we should say, that keep the law of gravitation and equipoise ; the seven arms of the balance, or the seven bonds of the universe ; the seven tow-ers that became the later seven rowers, sailors, or Kabiri. These are sometimes called the seven spirits of Annu, that is at the pole, the mount of glory in the stellar mythos. Four of the seven can be identified as Amsta, Hapi, Tuamutef, and Kabhsenuf (Rit., ch. 97). "Said at the bark : Staff of Anup, may I propitiate those four glorified ones who follow after the master of all things ?" These are four of the seven that pulled the bark up to the landing-stage upon the summit with the primitive rope, who are afterwards stationed as the four oars at the four cardinal points, in a later heaven, and also as the children of Horus, who had previously been his brothers. There is a great bursting forth of the floods in Amenta, described in the Ritual as a vast and overwhelming inundation. This passage of the waters shows the deluge-legend in the Kamite eschatology. The Osiris calls upon the lord of the flood, "the great one who is shoreless," to save him. "Do thou save me!" "I who know the deep waters" is my name. But "I am not one who drowneth. Blessed are they who see the bourne. Beautiful is the god of the motionless heart who causeth the stay of the overflowing —or the flood. Behold! there cometh forth the lord of life, Osiris thy support, who abideth day by day." "The tunnels of the earth have given me birth." This overflow of the great waters called the flood also occurs in Sheol amongst the other trials and tribulations of the sufferer represented in the Hebrew book of Psalms. "The channels of waters appeared, and the foundations of the world were laid bare" (ch. 18). "He drew me out of great waters." As one means of salvation from the overwhelming waters the manes clings to the sycamore-tree which standeth in the lake of Akeb. He exclaims, "I embrace the sycamore, I am united to the sycamore-tree." That is, to Osiris in the tree, the tat or pole, the type of fixity to be clasped for safety amid the waters rising round the soul in death and in the darkness of the nether earth. Sufficient mythical matter for a legend of the deluge and the ark may be found in the 64th chapter of the Ritual. It is recorded in the rubrical directions appended to the chapter that it "was discovered on a plinth of the god of the Hennu-bark by a master-builder of the wall in the time of King Septi the victorious." Septi, or Seti, was a king in the first dynasty who lived and ruled in Egypt from 6,000 to 7,000 years ago. At that time the chapter was rediscovered as an ancient writing. We learn from this that the bursting forth of the waters in an overwhelming flood was based upon the natural fact of the inundation in Egypt. The imagery had been reproduced in heaven, and also in Amenta, the lower Egypt of the nether-world. A great catastrophe caused by the waters that have broken out of bounds is more than once referred to in the Ritual. The Osiris says to the powers, "Grant ye that I may have the command of the water, even as the mighty Sut had the command of his enemies on the day of disaster to the earth. May I prevail over the long-armed ones in their (four) corners, even as that glorious and ready god prevailed over them" (Renouf, ch. 60). The bursting forth of the waters is described as a great disaster. In this chapter there is an application of the deluge imagery to the sun in the mythos and the departed soul in the eschatology. With the Egyptians, the supreme type of helpfulness and charity, or of love to the neighbour, was an ark or boat that offered safety to the shipwrecked amidst the waters. Hence, when pleading in the Hall of Judgment the speaker claims to have "done the right thing in Tamerit" (Egypt), he clinches it by saying, "I have given bread to the hungry, water to the thirsty, clothes to the naked, and a boat to the shipwrecked" (ch. 125).

The subject-matter is very ancient. It belongs to that early time when Sut was a pre-Osirian form of the Good Being, in relation to the pole, the dog-star, and the inundation of the Nile. Here the deluge of the inundation is a deluge of destruction directed against the workers of evil. In short, it does what the inundation did for Egypt in washing away the results of drought, in cleansing from corruption and restoring a healthy new life to the land. Hence the deceased desires to have the same command over the waters in Amenta that Sut had when they burst forth in a drowning flood. Thus, 6,000 years ago the so-called "deluge legend" was ancient in Egypt, and it belonged to the time when Sut, in command of the waters, had not lost his place in glory ; and his deluge was employed to destroy the Sebau, the Sami, the Apap-dragon, the long-armed ones, and other evil enemies of God and man who were not human beings. In the same chapter Osiris has superseded Sut as lord of the flood. Further, the two divine sisters Isis and Nephthys were imaged as two birds. The ark of Nnu described in the Ritual is conducted over the Nun by two birds which represent the two sister-goddesses Isis and Nephthys. It is said to these in relation to the inundation, "Ye two divine hawks upon your gables, who are giving attentive heed to the matter, ye who *conduct the ship of Ra*, advancing onwards from the highest place of the ark in heaven." It is also said to Osiris, "Thy two sisters Isis and Nephthys come to thee, and they convey to thee the great extent (of the waters) in thy name of the great extender as lord of the flood (Teta, 274)." These allusions show that there was an ark to which the two birds were attached as conductors. They are represented as hawks, but as the birds of east and west, or the earlier south and north, are equivalent to the dove of day and the raven of night in Semitic tradition. Isis was the lady or bird of dawn, and Nephthys the lady of darkness. In this, the solar phase, the passage of the ark was from west to east, where it was conducted by the two birds or goddesses of the west and east. Heaven was flooded with a deluge of light at daybreak, and the nether earth was inundated with a deluge of darkness. The ark conducted through the waters by the two birds of light and darkness, or east and west, is described in a twofold character as the shrine of Osiris in the centre of the earth, and also as the ark of Ra that reaches the highest point in heaven (ch. 64, lines 5–8). It is the ark of the "lord of resurrections, he who cometh forth from the dusk and whose birth is from the house of death," or, from Amenta, as the re-arising solar god. The ark that rested on Mount Nizir in the Babylonian legend, or Mount Ararat in the Hebrew version, and on Mount Manu in the Hindu account, is described in the Ritual as the "ship of Ra" which attains "the highest place of the ark in heaven," with the mount of glory for anchorage and the pole for mooring-post. Deceased in the character of Nnu repulses the water of the deluge. "He is the image of Nnu, lord of the inundation and father of the gods" (Rit., ch. 136A). He manœuvres the ark or bark with which he voyages in heaven. "He turns back the deluge" that "devastates the leg of Nut," and "brings back strength to the fainting gods" by such means of dealing with the waters. In this chapter of the Ritual the devastating deluge is also alluded to (in line 1) as a mode of judgment. It is directed against the rebels. Those who are in the ark or the solar bark are saved from the great cataclysm which "devastates the leg of Nut" or sweeps away the support of the celestial waters, whilst the rebels are overthrown and reduced to non-existence. The rebels against Ra are identical with the "men" or the "race" that spoke and plotted evil against him in another version of the deluge myth. After the deluge of devastation there is a renewal, rejuvenescence, and rebirth. Seb and Nut (earth and heaven) are pleased at heart; they grow young again. The leg of Nut, which the deluge devastated, was a very early type of the celestial pole, as the bulwark, prop, or mainstay against the waters of the firmament. In one phase the ark of Nnu is the ark of the Nun as the celestial water. In the other it is the ark of Nnu as god of the celestial water. It is depicted in chapter 44 crossing the water of Putrata, the lake of darkness, and cutting its way through the coils of the Apap-dragon. The speaker is one of the manes in Amenta about to embark on board the boat of souls. He says, "O thou who sailest the ship of Nnu across that gulf which is void, let me sail the ship; let me fasten the tackle in peace, in peace. Let me fasten my tackle and come forth." "The place is empty into which the starry ones fall down headlong upon their faces and find nothing by which they can raise themselves up." The ship of Nnu is facing the west, where it has to cross the lake of darkness, or the great gulf of the waters, by night, the lurking-place of the devouring dragon, into which the setting stars go down, also the human souls that have not attained salvation on board the ark. We learn previously that the deluge is imminent. In other words, the waters of the Nun are traversed by the ark at night with the rescued souls on board. The shrine at the centre of the earth is one with the shrine in the ark of earth, and the ark of earth in one character is the ship of Nnu in the other; it is the ark of Osiris or Ptah in Amenta, and the ark of Ra in heaven, when "it comes forth in the east." But whether in the depth or height, the bark of inert Osiris or the living Ra would still be the bark of Nnu, the ark that swam the deluge of the celestial water. It is said that the bark of Ra is in danger of the whirlwind and storm, which affords a glimpse of the tempest commonly associated with the deluge in the legends and traditions of the great disaster. But the Osiris-Nu, or Nnu as god of the inundation, *turneth back the water-flood*, the deluge that has nearly overwhelmed the "leg of Nut" (or the pole) which supports the firmament; and he keeps the companions safe who are on board the bark until the resting-place is finally attained upon the summit of the mount. The land that is reached at last by the mariners in the ark of Nnu is called the "tip of heaven," at the place of "coming forth from the swathings in the garden of Aarru," and the "coming forth in exultation." These are the names of that celestial country for which the bark or ark of Nnu was sailed (ch. 99). It is also called the ship of the garden of Aarru (ch. 106). The speaker in chapter 98 says, "I stand erect in the bark which the god is piloting . . . at the head of Aarru." This is the Aarru of spirits perfected in the eschatology, the summit of which is in the region of the never-setting stars at the highest point of heaven. In the various deluge legends the ark was stranded on the top of the mount, as it was on Ararat and Nizir, Manu and Malata. Here the ark of Nnu becomes the bark of the blessed, whose landing-place in heaven is called Mount Hetep, at the summit of the pole. The pole is the mooring-post to which the cable of the vessel was made fast. The voyage cometh to an end, and praise is uttered to the gods who are in the garden of everlasting peace and plenty. When the passengers approach the landing-stage, Heaven opens its embracing arms; the lamps of heaven are lighted, the Khabsu gods rise up to offer acclamations. The "old ones" and those who have gone before are said to welcome the voyagers at their arrival on the mount of assembly and reunion. These are the two classes of spirits, superhuman and human, elemental and ancestral, otherwise called "the gods and the glorified." There was no need for an altar to be raised at this landing-stage upon the summit at the moment of debarkation to complete the parallel with the landing on Mount Ararat or Nizir in the Semitic versions.

The Ritual preserves the astral mythos in the form of drama. The voyagers who land upon Mount Hetep are souls of the departed, and not human beings. The rendering in the Ritual is not historical, not merely mythical, not simply astronomical. Sacrificial ceremonies are performed upon the altar and offerings made at the moment of debarkation. These are in two categories. In one Noah, Nnu, or the Osiris-Nu presents the oblation in propitiation to the gods upon the mount. In the second, those who have gone before as the ancestral spirits make offerings of the sacred cakes and other forms of food to the new-comers whom they welcome as their fellow-citizens to the eternal city (ch. 98, Renouf) on their landing from the ark of Nnu. *Thus far we trace the deluge-legend and the ark of Nnu in the phase of eschatology by means of the Ritual.*

We now turn to representations of the subject in the astronomical mythology which in earlier ages preceded those of the eschatology.

In several chapters of the Ritual a breaking forth of the celestial waters in a typical deluge is alluded to or described. In chapter 136A it is said of the god who has the mastery over the inundation, "He turneth back the water flood which is over the thigh of the goddess Nut at the staircase of Seb." The overwhelming water has here ascended to the summit of the mount or staircase, which, like the leg of Nut, was a figure of the pole. Thus the deluge is portrayed as submerging the pole when this was figured as the leg of Nut, and the water flood was then turned back by Nnu, the lord of the celestial water, whose ark of salvation from the deluge is the ship of heaven by name. Howsoever constellated, the bark of Nnu was the ark of heaven on the celestial water. Now when the change was made from a heaven of seven divisions to one of eight, as described in the very ancient papyrus containing the hymn to the god Shu, it is portrayed as superseding the ark of seven cubits with an ark of eight cubits, or the heptanomis by the octonary. This also indicates a change of pole, the pole that was imaged by the staff of Shu the giant. The hymn to Shu includes the legend of a deluge. It is called "a chapter of the excellent songs which dispel the immerged," that is, those who were drowned in the deluge as the evil creatures of darkness (Magic Papyrus, *Records of the Past*, vol. x. p. 137). It is said, "Those who are immerged do not pass along. Those who pass along do not plunge. They remain floating on the waves like the dead bodies on the inundation of the Nile, and they shut their mouths as the seven great dungeons are closed with an eternal seal." Now, there is reason to suppose that these seven great dungeons, sealed with an eternal seal, were a form of the superseded heaven in seven divisions answering to the seven caves in the Mexican mount, and to the book of seven seals in Revelation. In the same papyrus there is "a book of magical spells for remaining as dwellers in the country" where the great catastrophe occurs; it is said that "Horus has given the warning cry," "*subsidence of the country!*" This, as we interpret the text, is at the cataclysmal ending in time and space that was mythically dramatized as a deluge or inundation which overwhelmed the land above and effaced certain landmarks in the celestial waters. The cubit may stand for a general measure. Four measures or cubits typified an ark of the four quarters in space. Seven cubits were a fourth of twenty-eight measures in the circle of twenty-eight lunar signs. Thus seven cubits or measures in an ark, shrine, or tabernacle formed a figure of heaven in seven divisions. And when the heptanomis was followed by the heaven of Taht, the ark of eight cubits superseded the shrine of seven cubits, and the ape became the type of Taht in the octonary instead of in the heptanomis. The ark of seven cubits was continued as a sacred type in the religious ceremonies. For instance, it is commanded by the rubric to chapter 133, Papyrus of Nnu, that this chapter shall be recited over a boat four cubits in length on which the divine sovereign chiefs of the cities have been painted and a heaven with its stars portrayed. But in the Papyrus of Ani the boat is ordered to be made seven cubits in length. This, then, is a figure of the ark of seven cubits which preceded the ark of eight cubits and the heaven of four quarters that was imaged by the boat of four cubits. The heptanomis had been figured as an ark of seven measures in the waters of heaven, and this was followed by the ark of eight measures as the shrine of the kaf-ape, a zootype of Taht the lunar god, after there had been "a subsidence of the country" and the "secret abysses of the Nun" and the foundations of the deep had been laid open at the time of the deluge.

There had been no moon established in the stellar mythos. Other-wise stated, time was not yet computed by the lunar reckoning, or by Taht, the reckoner of time. In this sense the moon was not created until after the deluge. Thus, in some of the legends the moon becomes a resting-place or ark of safety riding on the waters. At Hawaii the typical deluge was called "the flood of the moon." Meru is likewise shown to be a form of the mythical mount that reached up to the moon. Also it is related in one of the Hebrew legends that paradise was exempt from the deluge or was preserved from the great disaster because it was planted on the summit of a mountain reaching to the moon.

In the Egyptian inscription called "the Destruction of Mankind" there is a rebellion against Ra, the sun-god, followed by a great destruction and a deluge. Atum-Ra had been established as the king of gods and men, the god by himself. There is a revolt against his supremacy. He calls the elder gods around him for consultation, and says to them, "You ancient gods, behold the beings who are born of myself; they utter words against me. Tell me what you would do in these circumstances. Behold, I have waited, and I have not destroyed them until I should hear what you have to say." The elder gods advise that they may go and smite the enemies who plot evil against Ra, and let none remain alive. The rebels are then destroyed "in three days of navigation." When the deluge of blood is over it is said by the majesty of Ra, "I shall now protect men on this account." "I raise my hand (in token) that I shall not again destroy men." The rebel powers, headed by the coiling and constricting Apap-reptile vomiting the deluge of the dark by night, were always in revolt against the lord of light, and this legend commemorates their overthrowal in a deluge of blood. The chief agent in the work of vengeance is Hathor, the lunar goddess, who is aided by the solar goddess, Sekhet, in executing the commands of Ra. The goddess started; she smote the enemies over all the land because they had plotted evil against the majesty of Ra. These enemies are drowned in the deluge then poured out; "the fields were entirely covered with water through the will of his majesty the god. And there came the goddess (Hathor) in the morning, and she found the fields covered with water; and she was pleased with it, and drank to her heart's content. She saw no more of the enemies, who were sunk in the waters that represented the flood of light which was now poured forth by Ra at dawn, and in which the creatures of the dark were drowned. It is said by his majesty, living and well, to his followers, "I call before my face Shu, Tefnut, Seb, Nut, and the fathers and mothers who were with me when I was yet in the Nun, and I prescribe to Nnu, who brings his companions with him"; these are the instructions given by the god to Nnu: "Bring a small number of them (his companions), that the beings may not see them"—these beings are the creatures about to be destroyed in the coming flood—"and that their heart may not be afraid, thou shalt go with them into the ark or sanctuary until I shall go with Nnu to the place where I stand," or to the summit of the mount on which the legendary ark at last was safely landed. The ark or sanctuary here indicated is the figure of a newly founded heaven which follows the deluge by which a previous world was wrecked. The inscription is very dilapidated, nevertheless it obviously contains a creation of "the men," as in the Assyrian revolt in heaven in the place of the creatures thus destroyed. When "his majesty arrived in the sanctuary," "the men" were going forth and bearing their bows and shooting their arrows against his enemies. These were not the enemies but the defenders of Ra. Hence it was said to Ra by "the men," "Let us smite the enemies, the rebels."

The celestial water was primarily assigned to the female Nu or Nut. Her heaven was imaged as the cow. At first it was the water-cow, and afterwards the milch-cow. And there was Nut (with) the "majesty of Ra on her back"; she was carrying the god in her form of the cow. This mode of locomotion on the cow's back or between the cow's horns (see the pictures) is now to be superseded by the building of the solar bark. "Said by the majesty of the god, I have resolved to be lifted up." "Who is it that Nut will trust with it?" i.e., with the new ark or sanctuary of the god. "Carry me, that I may see." Said by the majesty of the god, "Let a field of rest extend itself," and there arose a field of rest. "Let the plants grow there," and there arose the Sekhet-Hetep, or fields of the papyrus-reed. The beings who were destroyed were Sebau and Sami, representatives of the plagues of Egypt. The men who are created in their place are of the starry race. "The majesty of the god saw the inner part of the sanctuary in which he had been lifted up " (or the ark in which he made his voyage over the celestial waters), and he said, " I assemble and give possession of these multitudes of men, I establish as inhabitants all the beings which are suspended in the sky, the stars," and Nut began to tremble very strongly. " I assemble there the multitudes that they may celebrate thee," and there arose the multitudes. These are stars in one category, and in the other souls that were collected in the ark of salvation (Rit., ch. 58) or the ark of Nnu—that is, the ark of heaven and of the god of the celestial water. " Said by the majesty of Ra, My son Shu, take with thee my daughter Nut, and be the guardian of the multitudes which live in the nocturnal sky. Bear them on thy head, and be their fosterer." This is an allusion to his raising overhead the beautiful creation of the starry firmament which Shu sustains, whether in the form of the cow of Nut, the water of the Nun, or the ark of Nnu. After the destruction there is to be a new creation, and Ra is in need of support from Nnu and his companions. " Said by the majesty of the god (or his majesty) to the majesty of Nnu, My limbs have suffered long ; I cannot walk without support, or have others to support me." This will show that Nnu occupies the place of Noah in relation to the building of the ark or sanctuary, and in accordance with the instructions received from Ra. Ra informs Nnu that he needs some other means of supporting himself than the back of the cow. He calls upon Nnu and his three sons to assist him against his enemies the rebels. Thus the cow of Nut was to be superseded by the ark of Nnu when he became the representative of the heavenly water and master of the inundation. Nut says dutifully that she will act as it seems good to her father Nnu (l. 30). There had been various kinds and forms of the celestial or astronomical ark that was at first necessitated as the means of carriage for the gods, because the heavens had been imaged as the firmamental water. The great mother Apt, who was the image of all firstness both by name and nature in the likeness of the pregnant hippopotamus, was a kind of ark, and possibly the earliest that ever crossed the waters of the Nun. She carried her young ones in the cabin that was uterine. Child-Horus on his papyrus-reed was in the ark that saved him from from the waters, as the sign was constellated in the planisphere of Denderah. The Pleiades formed an ark as constellation for the Khuti ; the Lesser Bear for Anup and the seven voyagers round about the pole. Orion was the ark of the holy sahus, with Horus at the look-out. The ark of Taht was in the crescent moon that sailed the azure deep by night. Then Ra, the solar deity, resolved on being lifted up as god alone, the only one, who superseded all the elder powers. A new heaven was to be his tabernacle. This was the ark of Nnu. The change from one heaven to the other implied a great destruction of the rebels. A deluge was the *modus operandi*, and the ark the means of safety for the few just men and true, together with their *consorts*, who were saved from the catastrophe. As a symbol in sign-language the ark was built by Nnu, the master of the firmamental water, for the means of safety in the world all water against the coming flood and the subsidence of land, which was the land of Nnu.

In space it was the ark of the four quarters that was propelled by the four paddles of Hapi, Tuamutef, Kabhsenuf, and Amsta. Hence Seb (or the earth) "abideth stably" by means of the four rudders or oars (Rit., ch. 99). Hence also the four-square box that imaged the ark of Noë on the well-known Apamean coin. In Akar, or Amenta, it was the ark of Osiris; in earth the ark of Seb; in heaven the ark of Ra. Its mainmast was the pole. The nightlight on the masthead was the pole-star. In the myth it was the ark of Ra, "the bark of millions of years"; in the eschatology it is the ark of salvation, the refuge for eternity.

The sinking ones had looked for their deliverance from the waters to the bark of Anup, voyaging round the pole; also to the crescent-shaped ark of Taht seen in the new moon; then to the ark of Horus and the "holy sahus" constellated in Orion; and finally they sought salvation in the ark which Nnu and his three sons, Shu, Taht, and Seb, were now to build for Ra, the solar god.

The Egyptian ark or ship of Nnu is the ark of heaven, or, conversely stated, the ark of heaven is the ship of Nnu; and the ark of heaven was the revolving sphere configurated as a sailing vessel with two masts as we have found it figured by the mystery-teachers in their uranographic imagery of the celestial deluge. The ark is portrayed in the act of sailing over a vast, unfathomable, hollow void of formless space; as it is said, "the place is empty." Into this the helpless ones fall headlong unless they are saved on board the ark. In a vignette to the Papyrus of Anhai, it is Nnu that is seen uplifting the boat of the gods with seven persons on board, besides the beetle and the solar disk. The figure of Nnu in this drawing is both male and female, Nnu and Nut in one figure (Budge, *Papyrus of Anhai*, Pl. 8). Among the Assyrian fragments there is reference to a legend which has not come down to us. In this it is said that Ishtar counselled the destruction of mankind, whereas in the extant account of the deluge the goddess bewails their destruction and grieves bitterly over the loss of her children. Now Ishtar is an Akkado-Assyrian form of the goddess Hathor, who in the Egyptian mythos counsels the destruction of the beings, and executes the judgment passed upon them by the gods, with no wailing or weeping afterwards. This points back to the Egyptian original of another Akkado-Assyrian version.

According to the Hebrew reading of the legend, the deluge was provoked by the sins of men. "The Lord saw that the wickedness of man was great in the earth," and he determined to blot out and obliterate the race; . . . . "but Noah found grace in the eyes of the Lord" (Gen. vi. 5–8). The Chaldean and Hindu legends know nothing of *human* sin as a cause of the deluge. The sin against the gods, however, is described as the cause of a deluge in the so-called "destruction of men." Ra says to Nun and others of the elder pre-solar gods, "Behold the beings who are born of myself; they utter words against me." That is, they are in rebellion against the one true god. But these beings in this case were elemental, not mortal, and the sin was not human. When the deluge or destruction is over and past, Ra swears that he will not again destroy men. "Said by Ra: I now raise my hand that I shall no more destroy men." "I shall now protect men on account of this." So the Hebrew deity promises that he "will not again curse the ground any more for the sake of men : neither will I again smite any more any living thing," as in the "deluge of destruction."

This is the same thing, only written out large and told as if it were a human history, whereas the original is mythological. It relates to the superseding of the earlier gods, Nnu, Seb, Shu, and Taht, by Ra as the supreme being, or rather these old gods and elemental powers are to become the servants of his majesty Ra in the new heaven now established for the keeping of perfect time, with Ra as the head over all.

Ra had resolved to be lifted up in an ark or sanctuary. Nnu and his small number of companions who enter the ark or sanctuary are eight in number, four male, Nnu, Seb, Shu, and Taht, and four female, Sekhet, Nut, Hathor, and Tefnut, who can be paired thus :— (1) Nnu with Sekhet, (2) Shu with Tefnut, (3) Seb with Nut (4) Taht with Hathor. Nnu was the deity of the heavenly water, and Sekhet is in possession of the water on the night of the great disaster or the deluge (Rit., 57, 1, 2) ; Sekhet is also called the "very great one of the liquid domain" (149). These are certainly a pre-Semitic form of the eight in the ark, and as Nnu was *the first-born* of these gods, he may be called the father of the other three in the ark as represented in the biblical version. The whole world, however, that was divided between the three sons of Nnu, Shu, Seb, and Taht, was not on our earth ; was not in Africa, Asia, or Europe. Shu was to be the guardian of the multitudes in the nocturnal sky, Seb of the serpents in the cycles of time, and to Taht were assigned the nations of the north. *Taht had a double portion.* Ra says, "I shall give thee to raise thy hand in the presence of the gods. I shall give thee to embrace the *two parts* of the sky. I shall give thee to turn thyself towards the northern nations." This looks as if Taht were the prototype of Japheth. Shu, whose name signifies shade, and who was to be the guardian of those who are in the sky of night, agrees with Ham, the dark of colour or black. It was Shu who might have seen his father Nnu by night with his person exposed, as it was his work to lift up the nocturnal heaven or Nnu. This leaves Shem as the representative of Seb. Seb is the father of Horus on earth, and, as it was supposed, the Hebrew Messiah was to descend from Shem. Thus it is possible to identify the new point of departure for the threefold human race derived from Shem, Ham, and Japheth, considered to be the fathers of three different and diverse races of mankind. Ra describes the group of elder gods who preceded him as the fathers and the mothers. "Said by his majesty, I call before my face Shu, Tefnut, Seb, Nut, and the fathers and mothers who were with me when I was still in Nun," or previously to his issuing from the lotus in the bosom of the heavenly water. Here we have the "fathers and mothers" of the new race or races in the new world that followed the flood ready to the hand of the "sacred historian." These fathers and mothers are eight in number all told, who are mentioned by name : Nnu and Sekhet, Seb and Nut, Shu and Tefnut, Taht and Hathor. These are eight persons in four pairs of consorts, exactly the same as the eight consorts in the ark of Noah.

The moon-god Taht becomes the enlarger of the domains of Ra, as his lunar representative by night. Ra calls Taht before him : "Said by the majesty of the god (or his majesty) to Taht, Come, let us leave the sky and my abode, because I wish to make a luminary in the inferior sky and in the deep region where thou inscribest the inhabitants, and thou art the guardian of those who do evil . . . . . the followers whom my heart abhors. But thou art my abode, the god of my abode : behold, thou wilt be called Tehuti, the house of Ra. I shall give thee to send (lacuna) . . . . and there arose the ibis of Taht. I shall give thee to raise thy hand in presence of the gods, and there arose two wings of the ibis of Taht. I shall give thee to embrace the two parts of the sky with thy beauty and thy rays, and there arose the lunar crescent of Taht. I shall give thee to turn thyself towards the northern nations, and there arose the cynocephalus of Taht which is in his escort. Thou art under my dominion." This was written in the Book of Atum-Ra, who was also the god Huhi = Ihuh. Thus, in this new creation of Ra which was established after the old heaven had been overwhelmed by the deluge, the moon-god Taht was made *the enlarger of the domains of Ra*. As we read in the texts, "Ra created him a beautiful light to show the name of his evil enemy," the Apap-dragon of darkness. This enlargement turns on the moon-god becoming the ruler for Ra by night and establishing his sovereignty over the black race in the domain of Sut and in the inferior hemisphere. The "enlarging" in the Hebrew version is at the expense of Ham (= Kam, the black) : "A servant of servants shall he be unto his brethren," but "God enlarge Japheth." Ham is treated in the märchen as the "evil enemy" Apap, or the black Sut in the mythos, thus making the legend ethnical by this perversion of the meaning. Enlargement of the world denotes the formation of a heaven on a larger scale. Thus Taht, like Japheth, was the enlarger or the enlarged. Also one mode of the enlarging was by Taht becoming a luminary in the inferior sky and in the region of Amenta. And here we come upon the probable origin of the cursing of Canaan in the Semitic travesty. Ham = Kam represents the power and the people of darkness. Taht is to enlarge the borders of light at the expense of the domain of darkness. It is said to Taht by Ra, "In the deep region where thou inscribest the inhabitants, thou art the keeper of those who do evil, the followers whom my heart abhors." These were the darkies and the "black-heads" in the dark land of Amenta, who are to be subject to the rule of Taht by night, which has been converted in the Semitic perversion of the mythos into the servitude of Canaan and the children of Ham.

When it had been discovered that the moon derived its light and glory from the unseen sun there was a change of status for them both. The moon was previously a mother to the child of light whom she was unable to affiliate. And now, as it was mythically rendered, she learned that she was a wife (hemt) as well as a mother, and that her infant was begotten by the solar god. The transaction is portrayed as one of the mysteries of Amenta in the Ritual (ch. 80). The lady who gives light in darkness by night and

O O

overthrows the devouring monsters describes herself as a kind of ravisher to Hu the solar god. She retires with him to the vale of Abydos when she goes to rest. She seized upon the sun-god in the place where she found him. The result of this is that the twins Sut and Horus, the powers of darkness and light, that were previously born of the mother alone, are now attributed to the sun-god Hu or Ra as his children. Hathor had been the lunar lady, the slayer of the evil powers of darkness, and now the male god Taht is equipped in the house or ark of the moon as the teller of time for Ra. He is designated the "teller of decrees which Ra hath spoken in heaven" for Horus to execute on earth and in Amenta, with Taht and Anup as his two chief witnesses.

After the deluge in "the destruction of mankind" the god Ra establishes a covenant with those who have escaped from the flood. He says that what he commanded is well done, and that the destruction of his enemies removes destruction from themselves. "Said by the majesty of Ra, It is well done, all this. I shall now protect men on account of this. Said by Ra, I now raise my hand that I shall not destroy men," *i.e.* not again. The making of this covenant after the deluge is followed by the establishment of the New Year's festival under the direction of the young priestesses of Hathor. "Hence comes it that libations are made under the directions of priestesses at the festival of Hathor through all men since the days of old," (line 25). When the lunar orb has been converted into the abode of Ra by night it is said, "And there arose the crescent moon of Taht." Now the lunar crescent is the mythological bow (*Proc. Soc. Bib. Arch.* vol. vi. p. 131). The speaker in the character of the solar god issuing from the crescent moon exclaims, "I am the lion-god issuing from the bow, and therefore I shot forth" (Rit., ch. 132). When this was written it had been apprehended that the moon derived its light from the hidden sun, and shot the arrows forth with the growing, stretching crescent that was drawn bow-like to the full with all the force of the young lion-god. It was for this that Taht the lunar deity was wanted by Ra as his bowman by night to shoot the arrows of his light with the crescent of the monthly moon for his bow. For this the bow was set in the nocturnal heaven by Ra: "And there arose the crescent moon of Taht"=the bow. The crescent moon was figured as the bow in heaven for a sign that there should be no further deluge of destruction, because the keeping of time and season did not now depend upon the setting or non-setting stars. When time was reckoned by Tehuti the teller, by means of the dual lunation, a power was established that no flood which had submerged the pole or drowned the heptanomis, or the heaven in ten divisions, could in future overwhelm. Thus the deluge in the stellar mythos being over, and the powers of darkness being defeated and destroyed, chiefly through the direct agency of the lunar goddess Hathor, the bow of Taht was set in heaven with its promise that the waters of the wrath of Ra should not again cover the earth. This, like all that is Egyptian, was true mythos, not false explanation of natural fact. It does not mean that the moon was actually created there and then to give light for the first time.

That would not be mythology, but fictitious history. The Kamite account of this ancient wisdom is mythological; the biblical is pretended history.

It has now to be shown that the bow in the Kamite mythos, which we look upon as the original, was not the rainbow, which was afterwards substituted as more natural by those who knew no better. The lunar crescent was not only the bow of the deluge and sign of promise for all future time, it was also an ark of safety from the waters of the Nun, in which the young child of light was bosomed and reborn of the lunar virgin mother. In the Osirian cult Osiris was reborn in an ark of crescent shape which was a figure of the crescent moon. It is said to Osiris in the preparatory pangs of birth, "Taht is a protection for thee. He placeth thy soul in the lunar bark in that name which is thine of god Moon" or god An, another name of Osiris (*Records*, vol. ii. p. 119). The ark of the new moon was a means of resurrection for Osiris on the third night after his death, if we count the 17th Athyr as one. The priests brought out the sacred coffer containing a little golden ark. They also modelled a little image of the crescent moon.

The lunar mythos followed the stellar and preceded the solar, and in this the lunar crescent was an ark. In relation to which, the twin birds of light and darkness meet as it were in one when the black and white ibis is the typical bird of the dual lunation, because, as Plutarch says, its feathers resembled the halves of the moon as the bird of light in one half and in the other half the bird of darkness. Now the ibis or hebi in Egyptian is the messenger by name, and the crescent moon was the ark of the lord of light upon the waters of night. In the "Destruction of Mankind" Ra says to the moon-god, "Thou art my abode (his lunar ark), the god of my abode; behold, thou art called Taht, the abode of Ra. And there arose the ibis. I shall give thee to raise thy hand (Taht is also the hand of the gods) in presence of the gods. And there arose the two wings of the ibis of Taht. I shall give thee to embrace the two parts of the sky." The one white and black bird, as representative of the moon in the Egyptian rendering, was the white bird of the new moon and the black bird of the old moon, equivalent to the dove of light and the raven of darkness in the other legend. The moon was the ark on the waters as the abode of Ra by night or during the deluge of the dark. The bird that was given by Ra for Taht to send forth from the ark was the bird of light and the bird of darkness. In the latter half of the lunation, when the moon was renewed in its crescent shape, out flew the bird as messenger of light across the waters of the Nun, and in the dark half of the disk the bird was of raven hue. Such, we suggest, was the genesis of the two birds, or the double-feathered one, that issued from the lunar ark in the original mythos, which preserved the representation of the deluge and the ark and the two birds of day and night in the cult of Osiris or of Atum-Ra and Nnu. In the Chaldean account of the deluge the swallow is sent forth from the ark in addition to the raven and the dove. This also is a bird of the two sisters. In ch. 86 the manes makes his transformation into the swallow, when Horus is in command of the bark (line 5). But in the Vignette (Pap. of Ani) the bird called a swallow is a *martin*, another type of the white and black bird in one, like the ibis of the lunar ark. There is a chapter of the Ritual to be recited "when the moon renews itself on the first day of the month," the day, therefore, on which the lunar ark was launched upon the waters of the Nun and had to face the deluge. As it is said, "Osiris is enveloped in storm and rain; he is enveloped. But the beautiful Horus lendeth succour daily. He driveth off the storm from the face of Osiris in the moon. Behold him coming. He is Ra on his journey. He is the four gods who are over the upper region." The Osiris arriveth at his own time, and by means of his ropes is brought to the light of day (Renouf, ch. 135). The ark of Osiris on the waters is described as a kind of house-boat with gable ends, and the gable ends suggest that from this particular form of the house and boat in one may have descended the well-known children's toy of Noah's ark, as the ark of Noah in which eight souls, four males and four females, were saved from the deluge, and the ark of Nnu in the Kamite astronomy.

The new heaven was established on the four quarters that were founded upon the solstices and equinoxes by the great architect Ptah. Thus the teba or square box is a figure of the heaven that was based upon the four quarters which followed the ark of seven cubits, the ark of eight cubits, and other types of the ark that floated on the celestial Nun or is said to be carried on the back of the cow (Nut). The eight on board were not human beings, but four gods and four goddesses, or eight heavenly bodies. It is not the Hebrew Noah, as such, who will account for several other Noahs in different countries, but the Kamite Nnu, the "lord of the primordial water"—Nnu who is designated the father of the gods. By aid of the Kamite Nnu we can more fully identify the Hottentot Noh, who, as they told Kolben (in 1713), "had entered the world by a sort of window." The god Nnu of the Egyptian mythos will explain why the hero of Polynesian legend has the same name. The story is told by both Ellis and Fornander. The survivors from the deluge of Raiatea were saved on an island or mount called the tree reaching to the moon. In this version the mount and tree of the Ritual are identical, the island being named after the tree, whilst the tree that reaches up to the moon corresponds to the mount of Am-Khemen and the establishment of lunar time. In the Hawaian version, when Nnu had left his vessel, like Noah and Xisithrus, after the flood, to offer sacrifice to the god Kane, he looked up and saw the moon in the sky, and he thought this was the god, saying to himself, "You are Kane, no doubt, though you have transformed yourself to my sight!" so he made his offering and adored the moon. Then Kane descended on the bow and spoke reprovingly to Nnu, but, on account of it being a mistake, Nnu was forgiven by Kane, and the bow was left above in token of the god's forgiveness.

It was natural for those who knew nothing of the Egyptian wisdom to suppose that the deluge, the ark, and the character of

Nevid, Nav, or Nevion, in the British mythos, was derived from the Hebrew records. But the true and final explanation is that both were derived from the Egyptian on separate lines of descent. The Druids were teachers of the wisdom of Egypt in the British Isles ages before the Bible was heard of in Europe. The ark of Nnu, Noë, or Noah was the ark of the celestial waters. An ark with the Ali, or Ari, was an ark with the seven on board who were rulers in the heptanomis. This is extant as the ark of the seven Kabiri and the seven Hohgates, the seven who in Britain were the companions of Arthur in the ark. When we understand that the Hebrew ark of Noah (or נַח) was the ark of Nnu in Egypt, and is the ark of heaven by name in the astronomy, we are on the track for the first time to learn how certain later races of mankind could be said to issue from the ark of Noah after a particular form of the deluge in which the heaven in ten divisions was superseded by the heaven in twelve divisions, the birth-place as an ark being a geometrical figure of the contemporary heaven. The deluge legend in the book of Genesis can be directly traced to its Egyptian origin. Nnu was the master of the celestial water. Under the same name, and also as Num, lord of the inundation, he was master of the water in the Nile on earth. The deluge, all the deluges, and the whole of the arkite imagery, together with Noah himself in very person, are dependent on the beginning of creation with the water of the Nun or Nnu, and on heaven being the celestial Nnu by name in the Egyptian language. In the Adoration of the Nile it is Nnu the deity of the heavenly water that is invoked as mythical source of life and not simply the flowing river. The object of religious regard as element or place or person was the celestial Nnu or Nun, who when personified was the giver of the Nile and all its gifts. Nun or Nnu was the inundator of Egypt by means of the Nile. Moreover, the god Num who is lord of the earthly inundation was preceded by the ancient deity Nun (or Nnu), who had an ark or shrine, but was not worshipped in any temple hitherto discovered. It appears from inscriptions of Tahtmes III. at Thebes that Nnu the deity of the deluge and the ark had been continued in the character of *Num* as lord of the inundation of the Nile, with his ark or teba represented by the city of Thebes, that "heaven on earth," as it was designated by the Queen Hatshepsu. From these inscriptions we learn that Tahtmes rebuilt the sanctuary of Nnu, or rather that he built the temple of Amen-Ra at Thebes on the site of the ancient shrine. This, we are told, had a circuit wall of brick, and a canal which conducted the water of the inundation "to the shrine of the god Nun (Nnu) on the arrival of his season," which shows that Nnu was one with Num as the elder pre-solar god, and that Nun (Nnu) passed into the god Num as a solar god associated with the inundation. The temple built by Tahtmes was a shrine of Nnu and Amen, as in "No-Amen," the name of Thebes. In laying the foundation stone of the new temple Tahtmes records the fact that he had to remove the older shrine of the god Nun (or Nnu), and divert the course of the water that flowed to the shrine of the god Nnu, because it was in the way (inscription cited by Brugsch, *Egypt under the Pharaohs*, p. 178, Eng. Tr.). Brugsch calls this shrine of Nnu the temple of the god; other Egyptologists tell us that no temple was ever raised to Nnu or Num. But whether termed a temple or not, this ancient sanctuary was an ark-shrine and a type of protection from the waters. The ark of Num is called his lordly bark. It is said that with the inundation "he brings once more his lordly bark" (verse 5). Also, "Thou art the august ornament of the earth, letting thy bark advance before men and lifting up the heart of women in labour"; "All is changed by the inundation; it is a balm of healing for mankind" (verses 9 and 11). Thus Nnu as deity of the heavenly water was represented by the Nile as river and by Num as divinity when the sun-god was united with the water-god in Num or in Amen-Ra at Thebes. But the main point here is the ark of Nnu that comes again with the inundation once a year to Egypt. And if no temple of Nnu is known, he was expressly associated with a shrine which originated in an ark that was a means of safety to the ancient lake-dwellers of Africa. In the Papyrus of Nefer-uben-f (Budge) the god of the inundation is described as "the old man Nnu." Deceased is standing in the water and holding the sail of breath in his left hand. He prays that he may have power over the seven divine princes who dwell in the place of the god of the inundation—that is, of Nnu the lord of the celestial water as builder of the ark. He says, "I have power with my father, the old man Nnu. He hath granted that I may live." This is the father Nnu as Egyptian who became father Noah in the Hebrew version.

Noah was a just or righteous man, and perfect in his generations. This statement is put in the forefront of the Hebrew deluge legend. In the Ritual it is granted to the Osiris Nnu that he shall "carry maat at the head of the great bark and hold up maat among the associate gods." Maat stands for justice and rightfulness; and this is borne aloft upon the bark by the spirit of the just man made perfect, right up to the summit of the mount which is the landing-place for those who are in the ark. "And so it cometh that the Osiris-Nnu hath reached every one of his stations" in the ark that rests at last upon Mount Hetep, Mount Nizir, Mount Meru, or the Mount of Ararat. Nnu is identified with Noah by the Arab writer Murtadi (1584), who related that Num-Kufu, the builder of the Great Pyramid, dreamed of a coming deluge, and built the Pyramid as his ark of safety. He then "made his abode in the maritime pyramid along with Noah" (*Nat. Gen.* vol. ii. p. 226). That is along with Nnu, the god of the ark and the inundation, who was earlier than Num, and who had his teba in Thebes. This points to the pyramid of Num-Kufu being also a form of the ark, or rather to the ark of earth and heaven in several of its successive forms that were ultimately combined in one consummate figure of the heavens and earth as a stupendous monument and imperishable register of the astronomical mythology. And, if so, it becomes apparent that the sarcophagus at the centre was a co-type with the coffin, shrine or ark of Osiris in the midst of Amenta. This may help to show how fragments of the astronomical mythology have been put together in the book of Genesis without key or clue, and the old dark sayings of the ancient wisdom repeated minus the necessary knowledge for enlightening the world.

Earlier deluges than this of Noah are alluded to in one of the Jewish Haggadoth, which relates that in the time of Enos, as in that of Cain, a great tract of land was flooded by the sea. Which is but the end of a patriarchate described in terms of the deluge. (*En-cyclopædia Biblica*, col. 1297.) Items from several deluges are included in the Hebrew versions. For instance, the animals are said to enter the ark seven by seven, and also two by two. Here the numbers belong to two entirely different deluges, the one from which the seven (or eight), the other from which the pair, were saved. There is no such incongruous mixture in the Avesta. In this version Yima the shining is commanded by Zarathustra to "make a circle to all four corners as a dwelling-place for all mankind," and stock and store it against the deluge, which is the evil work of the destructive serpent of darkness. All forms of life that enter this enclosure do so in imperishable pairs. A lofty wall is to be made around it, and a window that gives light within. The one window we take to be the pole-star. The lofty wall answers to the high white wall of Ha-Ptah-Ka. It is lighted with self-created and eternal lights that shine above, and the created lights below (Farg. ii., l. 131). These correspond to the Kamite Urtu-Seku, the setting stars, and the Akhemu-Seku, or stars that never set, the everlasting self-created lights. The window of Yima's enclosure in heaven is repeated in the one light of Noah's ark (Gen. vi. 16). It is related in a Jewish legend that after the deluge two animals came out of the ark which were not among the twos or sevens that went into it. These two were the cat and the pig. And they belonged to the new creation of Atum-Ra. The cat, as solar type, is a symbol of Atum-Iu. It is said in the Ritual (ch. 17) the cat is Ra himself. It was in that form of the seer by night that the sun-god overcame the evil Apap in the darkness of Amenta. The pig or boar in the Osirian mythos is a type of the evil Sut, the opponent of the Good Being in Amenta. Amenta is the lower deck of an ark in which the pig of Sut was present. This is in an ark that could not be built until Amenta had been hollowed out by Ptah, the father of Atum-Ra, who was represented by the cat. Thus the addition of the cat and pig to the previous denizens will help to identify which ark it was they came out of after the deluge of Noah. As Egyptian, it was the ark in which Ra had resolved to be lifted up as "god alone," and the cat and pig were types belonging to the new creation that followed the "destruction of mankind." This was the ark of Nnu. The description of Noah's deluge is an agglomerate compounded from the mythical data and the actual inundation. The waters flowed in Egypt during a certain number of days. It is probable that the fullest flow was reckoned at forty days and nights (see Hor-Apollo). In a fragment of the Melchizedekian literature, found by Professor Sokolov, and appended to the Slavonic book of Enoch, the ark of Noah "floated forty days." And it is added, *altogether they were in the ark* 120 *days*. This is the exact length of the water season in the Egyptian year of 360 days, which was first divided into three tetramenes of 120 days each. It may also be noted that outside of Egypt rain took the place of the inundation, and the deluge of Noah consists of forty days and nights of rain. Fifteen cubits of fresh water constituted a good if not a perfect Nile, and this is the measure applied to the flood of rain-water in the book of Genesis. Fifteen cubits upward did the waters prevail, and the mountains were covered (ch. vii. 20). Fifteen cubits of water, however, could be no measure for a flood that covered all " the high mountains that were under the whole heaven " (ch. vii. 19). The waters: that prevailed on the earth for 150 days are also equal to an abundant inundation of the Nile, but these have been mixed up with the waters of the celestial Nun. Also the fifteen cubits of measure on the earth would be confused with the fifteen cubits, measures, or days in the half-circe of the luni-solar month of thirty days, in which the lunar crescent was the ark that is entered by Osiris, on the third day, to spread the actual water of life and light, not that deluge of destruction which was entirely mythical.

After the deluge, according to the euhemerizing of the mythos in the book of Genesis, Noah began to be a husbandman, and planted a vineyard; and he drank of the wine and was drunken; and he was uncovered within his tent, and Ham, the father of Canaan, saw the nakedness of his father, and told his two brethren without. And Shem and Japheth took a garment and covered the nakedness of their father (ch. ix. 20, 24). " And their faces were backward, and they saw not the nakedness of their father." Now in the mysteries of Amenta Osiris is covered by his son Horus to conceal his nakedness. " I am with Horus," says Taht, " on the day of covering Tesh-Tesh," one of the names of Osiris (Rit., ch. 1). It is also said to Horus, " O thou who coverest (or clothest) Osiris and hast seen Sut, O thou who turnest back " (ch. 28). Here the adversary of Osiris is present with Horus in this scene of concealing the father's nakedness, and the bad character of the black, evil-minded Sut appears to have been given to Ham as a son of Noah. In the Chaldean account of the deluge a sacrifice is offered at the coming forth from the ark. Hasisadra says, " I poured out a libation. I built an altar on the peak of a mountain. Seven jugs of wine I took. At the bottom of them I placed reeds, pines, and spices. The gods collected at its burning, the gods like Sumbe gathered over the sacrifice." (Deluge, Tab., col. 3, Smith.) The basis of the oblation in the Kamite sacrifice is the blood of the beings that have been destroyed. " Said by the majesty of the god, Let them begin with Elephantine, and bring to me the fruits in quantity. And when the fruits had been brought they were given . . lacuna." The sekti (miller) of Annu was grinding the fruits, while the priestesses poured the juice into the vases ; and those fruits were put into vessels with the blood of the beings, and there were *seven thousand pitchers of drink.* " And there came the majesty of the king of Upper and Lower Egypt, with the gods, to see the drink after he had ordered the goddess to destroy the beings in three days of navigation." Instead of the Assyrian seven jugs of wine the Egyptian has 7,000 pitchers of drink, and this is brewed from the blood of the massacred beings mingled with the juice of the fruits of the earth ; and here, as in the later version, the gods gather over the sacrifice "to see the drink." Shedding the blood of the wicked, in this great slaughter of the evil beings, was a mode of offering the oblation to the Good Being. Blood and the fruits of the earth were the two primitive forms of the offering, and these are blended together in a deluge of intoxicating drink.

A most primitive representation of this sacrifice which followed the deluge is made by the Ovaherero, an African tribe adjoining that of the Bushmen. They claim to have issued from the typical tree of the beginning, which is said by the missionary Reiderbecke to be a kind of Ygdrasil. The Ovaherero say that the sky was once let down in a deluge, by which the greater part of mankind were drowned. This they attribute to the Old Ones in heaven, whose wrath was appeased by the sacrifice of a black sheep (*South African Folk-Lore Journal*, vol. ii., pt. 5, p. 95). When the deluge of darkness had passed away at dawn, the black sheep was offered to placate and pacify the power of darkness, which exhibits the deluge and the deluge-legend in their most primitive forms. The sacrifice does not merely celebrate the return of light, as in a later phase, but is also a petitionary offering for future protection from the deluge of the dark. Before ever man appeared on earth, a feeling of joy and thankfulness had been expressed by the apes at the return of the light, whether lunar or solar; and when man came he followed on the track of the monkey in feeling thankful for the return of day. In the Egyptian hieroglyphics the word tua, to adore, is figured as a salutation to the dawn or morrow-day, and the typical adorer is the Kaf-ape, the saluter of the gods. Primitive worship signified salutation and sacrifice from the beginning. In various traditions, Babylonian, American, Hebrew, and others, the deluge is followed by a sacrifice, and this sacrifice after the flood has been configurated in the stars of heaven in a picture of the far-off past, with the offering laid upon the altar *at a point where the actual inundation in Egypt annually came to an end.* In the Hebrew account of the thanksgiving sacrifice it is said, "Noah built an altar unto Jehovah, and took of every clean beast and of every clean bird, and offered burnt-offerings upon the altar, and Ihuh smelled the sweet savour." The typical imagery derived from the actual seasons in Egypt, repeated in the planisphere, will also account for the Hebrew story concerning Noah's planting the vine and getting drunk immediately after the inundation. The vine that Noah is said to have planted may be seen in the decans of Virgo, where the star Vindemiatrix denotes the time of vintage in Egypt. It is a version of the mythos in which the water of the deluge was turned into wine by Horus, the ripening soul of the sun, that has been most pitifully vulgarised in the story of Noah's intoxication after the deluge. According to the planisphere Noah was on the water of the inundation, or he might have just landed when the grapes were ripe, and he got intoxicated apparently for the purpose of cursing Ham and consigning the dark race to the doom of never-ending slavery. Hebraists tell us that the name of Noah signifies rest, which leads to nothing in Hebrew. Whereas, in Egyptian, the same word Nnu is a name of the inundation, the deity of the celestial waters, and also for rest or repose. As natural fact this was the season of rest or of Nnu because of the deluge, during which the god was resting in his ark upon the waters, or, as might be, in his Teba of the Southern Apta at Thebes. The natural fact was formulated in a legend such as that of Nnu, Num, Noah, or Vishnu resting on the waters during a deluge in the course of a new creation; that is, during the Hindu period of Pralaya, when this was figured on the grand scale as described in the Puranas. For instance, Vishnu is said to repose in slumber *during four months of every year*, borne up by the seven-headed Naga-serpent Sesha (Kennedy, *Hindu Mythology*, p. 228; Moor's *Hindu Pantheon*). The four months of the inundation is historical in Egypt; the deluge in mythology is typical, and the type was variously applied to a natural phenomenon as a mode of measuring time. Nnu or Nu had become an Egyptian personal name. There is a papyrus of Nu in the British Museum containing various chapters of the Ritual. In these the speaker calls himself the Osiris-Nu, and, as the subject-matter shows, the manes here combines the two characters of Osiris and Nnu. Moreover, he is Nnu in the ark or bark, as lord of the inundation and victor over the deluge (Rit., ch. 36 A). The Osiris-Nnu is the speaker; not merely Nnu of the papyrus, but Nnu of the celestial water, or Nnu as THE Osiris. He says the Osiris-Nnu is strong to direct the ship of the gods, here called the boat of the sun, in which he comes forth from Amenta into heaven. Nnu saileth round about the heaven and "voyages along with Ra." Thus the mythos merges into the eschatology of the Ritual.

The water of the deluge in the Assyrian legend was not terrestrial. It is said in the opening lines :

> Then arose *the water of dawn at daylight;*
> It arose like a black cloud from the horizon of heaven.

It was a deluge feared by the gods themselves because the waters were celestial. Hence they sought refuge in the highest heaven. "They ascended to the heaven of Anu," the enclosure at the Pole. This was the heaven of the stars that never set; the heaven, the enclosure or ark of refuge, which is said to have rested on the mount when the flood subsided. It was Bel, the wise one, the counsellor of the gods, who caused the deluge, and he is a pole-star god, equivalent to Sut or Anup the judge, whose seat was above the summit at the north celestial pole. The deluge here was evidently the result of a change in the pole-stars; hence the tree re-planted in a circle by the gods. If Bel made the deluge when he represented the pole-star a change in the pole-star would be as the letting in of waters, otherwise called the flood. The ark was built against this contemplated change. The Greek tradition included two legends of the great deluge or cataclysm by which the race was destroyed. One of these was the flood from which Ogyges escaped with a few companions in a vessel. The other is known as the deluge of Deucalion, from which he escaped with Pyrrha his wife. Ogyges with his few companions are equivalent to Horus with the seven great spirits who were saved from the deluge in the ark of Orion. Deucalion and Pyrrha are equivalent to Atum and his consort Hathor-Iusāas. Among the Californian Indians they tell of a great flood (*i.e.*, heaven all water) from which only a coyote survived and a feather that was seen floating on the vast expanse of water. As the coyote looked at it the feather became an eagle which

joined the coyote on the "*Reed-Peak*," and these two were the creators
of men (Bancroft, vol. iii. pp. 87, 88). The reed-peak also answers
to the Kamite field of reeds upon the summit of Mount Hetep and
the Japanese "mid-land of the reed-expanse." The papyrus-reed or
lotus-flower is a cradle or ark in which the Child-Horus was uplifted
from the water of the Nun and saved from drowning. This becomes
the mythical reed in various legends, which is a co-type with the
tree as a means of emergence from the flood. The Navajo Indians
have piously preserved an account of the ascent from the waters of
the deluge, not by means of the tree or tower, but by building a huge
mound of earth to make a tall mountain in the north. Their
tradition is that the men of a world before our own, on being warned
of an approaching flood, resolved to build a place of refuge. "They
took soil from the four corner-mountains (quarters) of the world, and
placed it on the top of the mountain that stood in the north ; and
thither they all went, including the people of the mountains, the salt-
woman and such animals as then lived in the *third* world. When the
soil was laid on the mountain the latter grew higher and higher, but
the waters began to rise and the people climbed upwards to escape
from the flood. At length the mountain ceased to grow, and they
planted on the summit a great Reed, into the hollow of which they all
entered. . . . At the end of the fourth night from the time it was
planted the reed had grown up to the floor of the fourth world, and
here they found a hole through which they passed to the surface" and
were saved. The great reed evidently imaged the celestial pole. It
grew by night and did not grow in the daytime. The turkey was the
last to enter the reed, and the deluge rose and rose until the water wetted
the tip of his tail (W. Matthews, *American Antiquarian*, 1883, p. 208).
The tree had been an actual refuge for the human race. Hence it
became a typical refuge that was figured in the astronomy and eschatology. Salvation from the deluge by means of both the reed and the
tree is a mode of escape from the waters in the Ritual. The deceased
is one who knows the deep waters. But he is not to be drowned.
He exclaims, "I embrace the sycamore-tree. I am united to the
sycamore" (Rit., ch. lxiv). The sycamore is the tree of dawn,
and the speaker escapes from the waters just as the young sun-god
escaped from the deluge of darkness by climbing the tree or mounting
his papyrus-plant ; the one as solar in the mythology, the other as a
soul in the eschatology. This mode of ascent goes back to the time
when there was neither a bridge of heaven nor a boat upon the
waters of earth, nor a tower that was built to reach to heaven. In
the Norse mythos the ash-tree is called "the Refuge of Thor,"
because it caught and saved the young god when he was being swept
away by the overflowing waters of the river Vimur. This is the
same typical tree as in the Ritual, where it is the mainstay of the
Osiris, who is well-nigh drowned by the deluge of the inundation, but
who escapes by laying hold of the tree. We need to know in what
sense the reed or tree in heaven was a type of safety during the
deluge before we can interpret the Arawak version, in which it is
said the waters had been confined to the hollow bole of an
enormous tree by means of an inverted basket. The mischievous
monkey saw this basket, and thinking it covered something good

to eat he lifted it up, whereupon the deluge burst forth from the tree. The monkey is charged with being the culprit in several of the legends and märchen that we show to be survivals of the Kamite mythos, in which *Hapi was the ape that brought the deluge of the inundation*, and was also *in command of the celestial water in the mythology* (Rit., ch. 57). In a Red-Indian story of the deluge, Manabozho escaped from drowning by climbing to the top of the tallest pine-tree on the highest mountain in the world and waiting till the flood subsided. It is related in a Taoist legend that "one extraordinary antediluvian saved his life by climbing up a mountain, and there and then, in the manner of birds plaiting a nest, he passed his days on the trees, while all the country below him was one vast expanse of water. He afterwards lived to a very old age, and could testify to his late posterity that a whole race of human beings had then been swept away from the face of the earth" (*The Chinese Repository*, v. 8, p. 517). In this legend we have both the tree and the mountain used as means of escape in the same ascent. They were distinct as Egyptian types, but afterwards were sometimes fused in one, as the tree or reed upon the summit of the mount. The Indian tribes of Guiana say that when the great waters were about to be sent forth the chief Marérewána was informed of the coming flood, and he saved himself and his family in a large canoe. In order that he might not drift over the ocean far from the ancestral home he prepared a long cable of "bush-rope" and made his vessel fast to the trunk of an enormous tree, so that when the waters subsided he found himself at no great distance from his former abode. His canoe had been tied up to the pole, here represented by a tree. The reed-type also takes the form of the canoe as well as the tree. It is related in a Mexican tradition that the coyote, a co-type with the jackal and the dog, got wind of the coming deluge. To save himself from drowning he gnawed down a large cane that was growing on the bank of a river. This he entered, and then stopped up the end of it with a kind of gum to keep the waters out. Thus, at the time of the Chaldean deluge it is said that the great god Nera "tore up the Stake"—that is, the pole or mooring-post which is here represented by a stake, and a change of pole-star by the uprooting of the stake. Nera is a form of Nergal, the great Nera.

The legends of the deluge show that the primal paradise was an enclosure on the summit of the highest mountain, that of the pole, as a place of safety midst the celestial waters, which was typical of the refuge sought for on the hill-top when the floods were out on earth. The enclosure might be an ark, or palisade of wicker-work, a nest of reeds, or a city, walled and fortified, an island, a group of seven islands, or ten, or a zodiac, the idea of the deluge was ever present. And this had been the dominant idea in the burial of old Egypt's dead amidst the waters of the inundation. Every figure of the ark and every mode of arking or enclosing are extant somewhere or other in the astronomical mythology. Take the cave for example. In the Mexican version the seven who are saved from the deluge found safety in the seven caves of the celestial mount, the mount which toppled over at the summit with the changing of the pole. The cave was one of the natural types of the ark that preceded any form of refuge made by the hand of man. And there were seven of these altogether as a figure of the celestial heptanomis. The Welsh Barddas ascribe the building of an ark to Menwyd, who is called the dragon-chief of the world in the ancient British mythology. Menwyd is described as forming the ark by means of serpents joined together (*Nat. Gen.*, v. 2, p. 253). An ark is the means of safety amidst the waters whatsoever its formation may have been. Such an ark may be seen in the Sesha Naga-serpent with seven heads that bears up Vishnu during the deluge. This is a figure of the fore-world which preceded a great flood. Here the seven-headed serpent is likewise a figure of the heptanomis, or heaven in seven divisions, which sank in the celestial waters. The same great serpent in the waters with seven heads is also Akkadian.

A principle of arking, so to call it, was established when the great Bear, as the mother of the revolutions or time-cycles, and mistress of the waters, made the circle of the year in turning round "the Atlantean Pole." She, as the pregnant water-cow, was herself an ark of life that might be looked to as a divine type of safety by the sufferers from the water-floods on earth. The mother of time and station was the mistress of the firmamental waters; the mistress therefore of the enclosure in the waters which in the later rendering is a park, a garden, a paradise, or a harvest-field. In the Uganda legend it was a palisade of reeds around a spring of fresh water, the secret of which the woman knew, but failed to keep. When the circle of the bear was found to be untrue, and time was more correctly measured by the moon-god Taht, she, the mother of time and the mistress of the waters, was accused of being unfaithful to her trust, of letting in the deluge and losing the primeval home. As we have seen, she philandered with the moon-god Taht, who superseded Sut in her affections and in keeping time. The twins as Sut and Horus were re-born of her as lunar in the dark and light halves of the moon— the light eye of Horus and the dark eye of Sut. Apt had been the mistress of the waters in the stellar mythos from the first, and when it was found out that she was keeping time unfaithfully and incorrectly she was charged with betraying the secret to her lover, with overthrowing the bulwark and with letting in the deluge. This supplied the matter of sundry deluge-legends.

The Egyptians always kept on building closely in accordance with some primal type like this of the ark. In the beginning the earth itself was a mount or table-land that rose up out of the abyss as a kind of ark amidst the waters of space, an ark of one story. But when Amenta had been hollowed out by Ptah the opener of an under-world, there was an ark of two stories, fixed or floating. Whether called an ark or a house, it was two-storied. It was double-decked like a ship. It was also a house of two stories for Osiris in Abydos. With heaven added over all it becomes three-storied or triple-decked, with Amenta, earth and heaven answering to the three stories of the triple-deck. Now, it is commanded that the ark of Noah, or Nnu, shall be built "with lower, second and third stories," like the ship with three decks. This is a fragment of the genuine mythos which tends to show that it was the ark here identified as the figure of three worlds, viz., Amenta, middle-earth and heaven; a figure that agrees with the typical tree of the Akkado-Assyrian and the Norse mythology which had its roots in the nether-world, its stem in middle-earth and its branches high in heaven. But did the Egyptians ever launch this three-decker, and get it afloat in space? or did it remain a fixture in the mythical abyss?

It was argued in the *Natural Genesis* that the Kamite astronomers had measured the earth and knew it to be a globe rotating in space. It is now suggested that the ark of three stories was a compound image of the three regions built up deck by deck and completed by the arch-craftsman Ptah in a vessel that is called the ship of heaven in the Ritual. In the words of M. Lieblin, the Egyptians " knew that the earth circulated in the great ocean of heaven." And as the earth was the sekru-bark of Osiris in Amenta, it was the ark afloat upon the waters of the Nnu (*Nat. Gen.*, v. 2, pp. 60--61). In the time of Neb-Ka-Ra of the fourth dynasty the fact must have been a familiar one for a common peasant to call the king " the helm, or pilot of the earth which he navigates in space as the second brother of Taht," who was the navigator of the lunar bark. The ark of Nnu, which Ra commanded to be built for him when he was about to be lifted up upon the heavenly water, may be seen on the sarcophagus of Seti, in the Soane Museum. " The boat," says Lefébure, the translator of the text, " is supported by Nnu, whose bust and arms only are to be seen. The arms issue from the water and bear up the god. The entire scenes are surrounded by the waves of Nnu, which shows that the Egyptians looked upon the earth as a spherical body floating through the air. The boat is directed, as a passage made through the waves indicates, towards a spot where a disk is represented on a band. This band, studded with points, represents the earth as a landing-place for which the ark is bound " (*Book of Hades*, Records of the Past, vol. xii. p. 16). There is also a description of the ship of Nnu in the chapter of the Ritual by which one saileth a ship in the nether-world. In this the nature of the three decks as " lower, second and third stories " is described. The vessel is described in chapter 99 as the ship in which the abyss or void of Apap the devourer may be safely crossed. This is an empty space into which the starry ones fall down headlong to find nothing by which they can raise themselves up again. The manes supplicates the god : " Oh thou who sailest the ship of Nnu over the void, let me sail the ship. Let me be brought in as a distressed mariner, and go to the place which thou knowest." As previously shown, he has to know each part of the bark by name and to repeat the name of each before he is admitted on board. From this examination in the judgment-hall we learn the nature of the Ark and its three stories. The name of the lowest story is " akar," that is, *the lower earth.* The posts at stem and stern are " the *two columns of the nether-world.*" The ribs, also called the four paddles, image the gods of the four corners, Amsta, Hapi, Tuamutef and Kabhsenuf. These are the four who row the bark, and it is said that Seb, the earth, abideth stably by means of their rudders or oars. The " patrol who goeth round " is " he who piloteth the double earth." The " mooring-post," which represents the pole, is designated " the *lord of the double earth in the shrine,*" that is, Osiris as the power of the pole. The double earth is the earth of Amenta and the earth of Seb, or two of the three stories, the third of which is celestial. Hence Nut, or Heaven, is the name of the sail. Thus the three stories are identified with Amenta, earth and heaven, that were figured in the ark of Nnu which floated (earth and all) upon the waters of the firmament. This, when represented by the constellation *Argo Navis*, was an object-picture of the ark upon the great stream of the *Via Lactea*, by means of which the manes reached "the tip of heaven" at the pole, and after all the rowing and the voyaging attained the realm of rest upon the eternal shore. The Jewish Kabalists have a tradition that Noah's ark embodied an image of the world or was a figure of the whole universe. This IS the ark of Nnu in the astronomical mythology, the ark of Nnu that is described in the Egyptian Ritual as a subject of examination in the Mysteries of Amenta.

According to the Bhâgavata Purana (1, 3, 15), the ship of Manu was the earth itself. The "ship of the world" is a title given by the Barddas to the enclosure of Stonehenge, which points to its including an image of the earth as a form of the ark amidst the waters of heaven, like that of Seb which abideth stably in space by means of the four oars or paddles at the four cardinal points. An ark of the four quarters is described in the magic papyrus. It is said, "There are four mansions of life at Abydos," the mythical birthplace of Osiris in Amenta. In this we find another group of the four gods Nnu and Shu, Taht and Seb. The eternal city on the summit of the Mount of Glory was the final form of the ark in heaven. And after the Babylonian deluge when the ship touches the shore and its occupants have landed, as it is said, Gilgames "collected great stones," "he piled up the great stones." Instead of piling the mound of earth, or planting the typical tree, or launching the ark, the survivors now are the builders of a city with stones. They landed and "*left the ship by the shore*. They journeyed a stage of twenty kaspu. They made the stage ascent of thirty kaspu. They came to the midst of Erech Suburi." Then follows the building of Erech, the ark-city on the summit; or the new heaven that was divided into three parts; "one measure for the circuit of the city, one measure for the boundary of the temple of Nantur, the house of Ishtar; three measures together (for) the divisions of Erech" (*Records*, v. 7, 148—9). In Africa a conical hut like an ant-heap is the primeval type of a dwelling made by human hands. This was continued by the Egyptians in the cone of Hathor and the conical pyramid, or Ben-Ben of Sut-Anup as a figure of Polaris or Sothis surmounted by its star. This may be seen in the lake-dwellings of Africa, which are conical huts built on piles in the water of the divine land of Puanta as portrayed in the inscriptions of Hatshepsu's temple at Deir-el-Bahari. The reason given for such a type of house, says Sir John Kirk, is that the country at times is flooded (Lockyer's *Dawn of Astronomy*, p. 348, note 3), and thus the inhabitants escape the inundation. The conical hut is common in Africa both on land and water, and this is a figure of the primitive paradise and of the celestial pole, which was continued in Egypt as the round pyramidion, a co-type with the circular mound and conical cairn. Thus an ark on the firmamental water in the shape of a cone, a figure that represents the pole, crowned with its star, is identical with the pile-dwelling of the

African lakes, and images the same mode of escape from the waters, according to the mythos and eschatology of the Egyptians, as does the primitive lake-dwelling of the Inner Africans. The earliest ark of Nnu, or heaven, is an enclosure in the water of the Nun ; the latest is a paradise on piles ; we might say seven piles or poles which are co-types with the seven mountains or seven pyramids. But an ark, as a means of refuge in relation to a deluge of water, is not limited to the boat-type. The ark of Noë on the Apamean coin is figured as a box four-square. This, in Egyptian, is a Teba, Hebrew Thebah, the name of Noah's ark, and of Thebes as a form of the eternal city. There was an ark of the sphere which is described in the Thlinkeet legend as a vast floating building. At the time of the deluge it struck on the mount, or was driven on the rock and broken in two halves by its own weight. This agrees with the division of the heaven into north and south between Sut and Horus, as their two divine domains.

In several of the legends it is made known beforehand and announced that a deluge is coming, and with the warning instructions are given to build an ark or prepare some sort of refuge and means of escape for a favoured few. According to the Marquesan version, the lord ocean, or Fatu-Noana, who is like Nnu, lord of the celestial water, when about to send the devastating deluge, allows seven days for preparation. A tall building is to be erected which will tower above the reach of the waters. Cattle of all kinds are collected in pairs and marched into a vessel called the "Long Deep Wood." In this there is a family of four males and four females saved ; the same as in the ark of Noah, and of Nnu. The storm burst. The "sacred supporter" of the universe slumbered during the night of dissolution, as does Vishnu or Brahma in the Hindu version. A coffin on a sledge was a pre-Osirian type of the ark which was periodically drawn round the walls of the great sanctuary of Ptah the coffined one in the Mysteries of Memphis. The sledge or raft was naturally earlier than the boat, and the passage through Amenta, when this was imaged as solid earth, was represented by the sun-god Sekari in his coffin resting on a sledge. In the Ritual (ch. 100) the Osiris says, "I clear the path of the solar orb and tow along Sekari (a form of Ptah) upon his sledge." The Norsemen were accustomed to bury the bodies of their dead chiefs in boats on the hills, as a typical mode of crossing the celestial waters after death. The Garrows of Bengal, who cremated their dead, used to place the corpse in a dingy or small boat on the top of the funeral pile, for the typical crossing of the waters. The word ark in Egyptian signifies a circle, to encircle, bands, enclosings, encirclings, also number thirty, thence a month. Arkai is to appoint a limit, fix an end by decree. This was applied in measuring a cycle of time, which might be monthly, as in the Assyrian Arkhu. From this comes the arc, as part of a circle, which in Egyptian is to encircle or to make the circle. And thus the enclosure and ark are both forms of the circle. The enclosure made by Yima was an ark-circle but not an ark, or bark upon the waters. Still, the meaning is the same. It was the type of an enclosure and of safety from the deluge whether figured as stationary or afloat ;

and the heaven built upon four corners as a circular enclosure was an ark in space, we might say, the ark of space, when space was the celestial water. An ark of seven cubits was a figure of the celestial heptanomis, or heaven in seven divisions. An ark of eight cubits was a figure of heaven in eight divisions, either as Am-Khemen or the octonary of Taht. An ark of four cubits was a figure of heaven as the teba, or box of the four quarters. There was an ark of twenty-eight cubits reckoned as twice fourteen, based upon twenty-eight nights to the lunar month. This was the ark of the moon in which Osiris was reborn, or the child-Horus was preserved from the waters. The cubit was a measure in time for a day, as well as in space for a degree. Three hundred and sixty five cubits in circumference was the measure of a year of 365 days, on the tomb of Osymandyas (Diod. i. 49). Similarly, fourteen cubits were equivalent to fourteen days, or a half-moon, a *tenat* in the lunar month of twenty-eight days, and therefore equal to fourteen degrees. Thus the ark of the moon is not limited to the orb itself as a vessel that contained the new-born child of light. It is also the circle of a lunar zodiac, in which there were twenty-eight measures in time and space, = twenty-eight cubits that were divided into two fourteens, and four sevens. During fourteen days Osiris (or Horus) grew in glory, and during the other half of the lunation he was torn in fourteen pieces by Sut, the power of darkness. An ark of twice fourteen cubits is equal to a circle with twenty-eight stations, that is a lunar enclosure or zodiac. No dimensions of the ark are *directly* given in the Ritual, but there is an allusion which probably underlies the measurement of the lunar month or zodiacal circle of twenty-eight measures. One-half of the circle was marked out in fourteen divisions corresponding to one-half of the lunar houses. Also, the divine domain of Aarru was divided into fourteen sections (Rit. ch. 149), or, to put it in another way the mount of earth had fourteen steps to it : seven up and seven down. This would be the measure of one-half the circle, which was made out in twenty-eight lunar signs : fourteen in the lower and fourteen in the upper hemisphere. Sunset and sunrise were half-way round the circle, horizontally and perpendicularly, at the level called the summit of the mount. Now there is a scene at sunset described in the Ritual (ch. 108). Ra and the reptile of darkness watch each other, Ra from his ark, the monster from the mount. The depth of water underneath the solar bark at this, the level of sunset, is said to be seven cubits in its liquid part. This also serves to measure the lower half of the circle by seven cubits, or measures, downward and seven upward to the level of the mount, or the horizon. Seven steps down, applied either to the mount or to the lower half of the circle, would be identical with the course of the lunar goddess Ishtar, when she made her descent into the Assyrian Hades and was despoiled of all her ornaments and raiment as she passed through the seven gates downward, to be reclothed again in all her glory as she made the ascent through the seven upward gates. The object sought to be established here is the lunar circle divided into twenty-eight lengths of time, whether measured vertically by the mount of the earth or by the pathway of the moon. The seven measures answer to one-fourth

of the entire circle of twenty-eight cubits or measures of time;
fourteen below and fourteen above; fourteen from sunset to sunrise,
and fourteen from sunrise to sunset.

The lunar measurement and ark were earlier than the solar, and these
were afterwards applied to the luni-solar cycle of time.   In the luni-
solar month, the days, degrees, measures, or cubits, would be fifteen
instead of fourteen to the half-circle.   Thus, if the lower half of the
circle contains fifteen measures called cubits, instead of fourteen in
the lunar reckoning, there would be fifteen measures above the
mountain-summit on which the level of the equinox was marked, and
this may be the meaning of the Hebrew and Toltec statements that the
waters of the deluge prevailed fifteen cubits above the highest
mountains; the waters being celestial, the waters of Nnu or Noë.

We hear most of the ark as a teba or box, which is a figure of the
four corners, and as the measures of twenty-eight, fourteen, and seven
show, was a type of the lunar heaven that followed the stellar; the
ark of Taht which superseded the ark of Sut; the ark of eight
cubits, or the octonary, which took the place of the heptanomis.
The lunar nature of the Babylonian ark is also indicated by its
measures.   On the deluge tablet, as rendered by Smith, the builder
of the ark relates that, "in its circuit it was fourteen measures"; "its
frame fourteen measures it measured."   Now, as the cubit was the
typical measure, this was equivalent to fourteen cubits.   Boscawen
has it: "Two sides were raised.   In its enclosure fourteen ribs, also
fourteen they numbered above" (*The Bible and its Monuments*,
p. 117).   In this reckoning the ark of twenty-eight measures corresponds to the circle of twenty-eight lunar measures, or stations of
the moon.   Thus numerically the ark is identified as one with the
arc by the fourteen measures below and fourteen above, and the ark
of the moon was the ark of Osiris in the lunar mythos.   As the lunar
circle was divided in four quarters, and these four were each sub-
divided into seven, that may explain the statement of the builder,
who says he divided the interior seven times and (its passages or
parts) seven times (later version by Professors Haupt and Sayce).
This ark or abode is admittedly built "in a circuit" (col. 2), which
has fourteen measures above and fourteen below, sub-divided by seven
in the interior and by seven in its parts or passages.   There are two
fourteens sub-divided by the two sevens, equal to the lunar circle of
twenty-eight measures, the two lunations of fourteen days, and the
four quarters of seven days each.   And if the measure of fourteen
refers to one-half the lunar circle, it is possible that the measure of
fifteen cubits applied to the rising waters in the Hebrew version is a
measure taken from the soli-lunar month of thirty measures or days,
especially as the height of Noah's ark was to be thirty cubits.   The
ark of twenty-eight measures would be lunar only, the ark in which
Osiris rose again on the third day after his body had been torn into
fourteen parts and gathered together in the sekru (or ark) chest,
coffin (teba), for the revivication and resurrection in the ark of the
moon.   The ark of thirty measures (a measure in the hieroglyphics is
a cubit) would be soli-lunar in accordance with the thirty days to the
month; this, then, would be an ark of the sun and moon, which
followed the lunar ark of twenty-eight cubits.   The ark of seven

measures was the stellar heptanomis. The ark of eight measures is the octonary of Taht, the lunar god; a heaven of four quarters subdivided by eight semi-cardinal points into stations for the four wives, sisters or goddesses. Then followed an ark of the sun and moon and seven stars. Now, it is said in the Persian Rauzat-us-Safa that the Almighty fixed two luminous disks, one like the sun and the other like the moon, *on the wall of the ark*, and thus the hours of the day and night were ascertained (O'Neill, *The Night of the Gods*, p. 173). This is a mode of describing the additions made in the soli-lunar mythos to the ark of heaven, that was stellar at an earlier time, and is solar in its final phase. The arkite symbolism culminated as Egyptian in the ark of Nnu. This was the ark that was built "with lower, second, and third stories" (Gen. vi. 16), because it was a threefold figure of Amenta, earth and heaven in one, as it is represented in the Ritual. Once it is shown that Noah's ark is a geometrical figure of the heaven, there is no further difficulty respecting its size or content. The beasts of the earth, the birds of the air, the fish of the waters, and the human beings were all represented by the four types at the four corners, by Tuamutef, the jackal; Kabhsenuf, the hawk; Hapi, the ape: and Amsta, the man. These were accompanied in the enclosure by their consorts, Isis, the cow; Serkh, the scorpion; Nephthys, and Neith. Salvation from the deluge in the under-world is sought for by the Manes in the ark, whether called the ark of Osiris, or Ra, or Nnu. The experience attributed to Osiris as the god in Amenta, is also assigned to the soul of the deceased. In setting by night into the waters, the sun-god entered into the ark of earth, which is called his coffin or sarcophagus, in which he was enclosed by Sut, the power of darkness. In one form this was figured as the coffin-mountain, or neb-ankh, that was represented by the hill, Bakhu, the dimensions of which are given in the Ritual (ch. 109). The hill Bakhu was the place of sunrise where dawn broke on the coffin-lid; and the length of this coffin, or ark of earth, was 300 cubits. It is stated in the papyrus of Nebseni that the hill is 300 cubits in breadth. In other papyri it is said to be 300 cubits in length. This is connected with the measurement of the earth. Thus the ark of Osiris in the earth, and the ark of Noah are identical in length. The ark being also a figure of heaven, the 300 countries in Yima's kingdom are an astronomical measure equivalent to the 300 cubits of Noah's ark, and likewise to the area of 300 cubits of the Egyptian hollow hill, or ark of earth. It is possible to identify the constellation of Argo-Navis as the object-picture in the nightly heaven of the ark that Nnu constructed for the great god Ra, and thence the ark of Noah in the Hebrew version of the legend. In the pictures of the planisphere, which still remain on the celestial globe, it may be seen that the figure-head of the vessel is a ram. This was the type of the ram-headed Num, lord of the inundation, and Num was the later form of Nnu, the god of the celestial water, who was the builder of the ark for Ra. By day the solar orb was carried on the ark of Nnu, and by night the gods and glorified were seen in Argo-Navis on its voyage, as the "collector of souls" sailed *upward* for the circumpolar paradise along the river of the Milky Way. Now, Argo-Navis is the only constellation that is figured *hind-before* on the celestial globe. As

Aratos describes the vessel, "Argo by the great dog's tail is drawn; for hers is not a usual course, but backward turned she comes, as vessels do when sailors have transposed the crooked stern on entering harbour; all the ship reverse. And gliding backward on the beach it grounds sternforward, thus is Jason's Argo drawn" (Aratos, *Phainomena*, R. Brown, lines 342–348). But, what can be the meaning of an ark or ship that makes its voyage through the firmamental waters in this hindward way? We can but infer that it was an object-picture of the ark of Nnu, as "the bark of millions of years" receding in this backward fashion as it made the circuit of Precession.

The World's Great Year.

Once every six-and-twenty thousand years "the world's great age begins anew, the golden years return" (Shelley), but in no other than the astronomical sense of a re-beginning at the same point of departure as in the beginning. This will re-begin again and again in the great cycle of precession, but only as a matter of chronology. Nothing will be repeated except the cycle of time and the same phenomena belonging to the astronomical mythology. The divine fulfiller of the millennium in "the house of a thousand years," or in any other period, will no more come in person during the next 13,000 years than it was possible for him to manifest that way in the past half of the present cycle of 26,000 years. A knowledge of the facts constitutes the sole data of the truth, and such knowledge will ultimately put an end to the great delusion of the false faith that was founded in the uttermost ignorance of the astronomical facts.

In the great year of precession there are seven stations of the celestial pole, six of which are still identifiable in the constellations of Draconis, the Lesser Bear, Kepheus, Cygnus, Lyra, and Herakles. The pole changes, and its position is approximately determined by another central star about each 3,700 years. Seven times in the great year the station of the pole was raised aloft as land-mark amid the firmamental waters in the shape of an island, or a mound; a tree, a pillar, horn, or pyramid. Whichever the type this was repeated seven times in the circuit of precession, to form the compound and collective figure of the celestial heptanomis, so that the heaven rested, or was raised, at last upon the seven mountains or seven mounds; seven islands, seven giants, seven caves, seven trees, seven pillars, or other structures of support, as seven figures of the all-sustaining pole. Seven golden isles emerged from out the watery vast, or wisdom reared the seven pillars of her house; the heavens were borne upon the backs of seven giants, or the eternal city was built upon the seven hills.

It would take some six-and-twenty thousand years to build the heptanomis on the support of the seven poles. These were added one by one and figured collectively as seven sustaining powers of the heavens, such as seven hippopotami; seven crocodiles; seven bears; seven mountains; seven mounds of earth; seven trees or a tree with seven branches ; a serpent with seven heads ; a fish with seven fins ; seven horns of Sesheta the foundress ; seven pillars ; seven giants ; seven cyclops, with polaris for a single eye ; and lastly, there are the seven divinities called " the lords of eternity." Seven periods in precession correspond to seven stations of the pole. The length of time in each when measured by the changing pole-stars is about 3,700 years. Seven times the " Atalantean pole " sank in the waters of the deluge during the great year. This was figured as the seven sunken islands of the lost Atlantis. But there is another lost land of Atlantis, that passed away in ten islands, imaging a vanished heaven in ten divisions. The first was the heptanomis of the seven kings or rulers. The second is the heaven in ten divisions which ended with the deluge of the ten kings or patriarchs in the Semitic legends. These two vanished heavens will account for two great years, or two-and-fifty-thousand years of time.

The pole and equinox are travelling *pari passu*, one in the upper circle of the heavens, the other in the larger lower circle of the ecliptic, and the shifting of the equinox was correlated more or less exactly to the changing of the pole-star. The power that presided over the pole as Osiris was given rebirth as Horus in the vernal equinox. The pole-star symbolized the lord of eternity. Horus in the equinox (or the double equinox) was a traveller of eternity manifesting in the sphere of time ; in the Han-cycle of 120 years ; in the house of 1,000 years ; in the sothic cycle of 1,460 years ; or in the change from sign to sign, each 2,155 years. For two thousand years and more the pole-star in the Lesser Bear has coincided with the vernal equinox in the sign of Pisces. Previously the pole in Draconis coincided with the vernal equinox in the sign of the ram or the bull. A seventh of the ecliptic, not merely a third part, was assigned to one or other of the pole-star gods who became the seven lords of eternity. This will explain how the ram could be the special constellation of the god who was at the same time the ruler of the north pole-star. So, in the celestial drama portrayed in the book of Revelation, the fall of the dragon, or, astronomically, the change of pole-star, when a-Draconis was superseded, is followed by the exaltation of the lamb upon the solar mount of glory. The longer one dwells in presence of Egypt, the older grows the face of her unveiled antiquity. Not fifty merely, but more like a thousand centuries look down upon us from her summit of attainment, the pyramid of her glory, that she built for ever in the highest heaven of her heavens. It was asserted by Martianus Capella that the Egyptians had secretly cultivated the science of astronomy for 40,000 years before it was made known to the rest of the world (Lewis, *Astronomy of the Ancients*, p. 264). As time-keepers, the astronomers of Egypt had thought and wrought, observed and registered on the scale of the great year of the universe. The circuit of precession first outlined by the movement of the celestial pole was their circle of the eternal, or seven eternals, that was imaged by the Shennu-ring, and likewise by the serpent of eternity, when this was figured with tail in mouth and one eye always open at the centre of the coil. They not only laid great bases for eternity in this way, they built upon the basis of all time which culminated in the cycle of precession. When Herodotus was in Egypt, the "mystery teachers of the heavens" told him that during a certain length of time which had been reckoned by the Egyptian astronomers, "the sun had four times risen out of his usual quarter; that he had twice risen where he now sets, and twice set where he now rises. Yet, that no change in the things of Egypt had been occasioned by this, either in the productions of the earth 'or the river.'" And he adds, the Egyptians say, they know these things with accuracy because they always compute and register the years (B. 2, 142 and 145). Now there is no cycle in astronomy, save the circle of the precessional movement in which the phenomena thus unwittingly described by the faithful old chronicler could occur. One such cycle is certain, two are not improbable, and three are possible. After long study of the whole matter one sees perforce that the science of astronomy in Egypt, with its observed and registered cycle or cycles in precession, is actually older than any race of men on earth outside of Africa.

The Book of the Dead (chs. 114 and 123) not only proves the ancient Egyptians to have been acquainted with the precessional movement, it also gives us an account of the *actual changing of a pole-star*. The god Taht, the measurer of time, by means of the moon and the Great Bear, is to be seen in the midst of his mysteries, which are here described as those of keeping the chronology for the guidance of posterity. There is a change in the position of the Maat, or judgment-hall, which in the stellar mythos was at the station of the pole, and was shifted with the shifting pole. On account of this change, Taht comes as the messenger of Ra in the soli-lunar mythos to make fast that which was afloat upon the Urnas (Greek Ouranos) water; to re-adjust the reckoning and to "restore the eye" (Rit., ch. 114) by making it "firm and permanent" (ch. 116) once more for keeping time and period correctly on the scale of the great year. The backward motion of precession is described when Taht says to Atum Ra, "I have rescued the Atu from his backward course. I have done what thou hast prescribed for him." As Renouf remarks, "I do not think any astronomer would hesitate to say that precession is meant," by this "backward course" (Rit., ch. 123. Notes). The Atu is a mythical fish with some relation to the course of the solar bark; that is to its backward course, the course of Argo-Navis. Taht has "rescued the Atu from his *backward* course." He has allowed for this retrograde motion in precession, and has made the eye firm and fixed once more by means of his reckonings as a guide to posterity. Taht also says at the same time, "I have equally balanced the divine pair, (Sut and Horus) and put a stop to their strife." This changing of the pole occurs once every 3,714 years, or, in the round numbers of the outsiders, every 3,000 years. This is alluded to by Theopompus, who tells us that "according to the Magi," "one of the gods shall conquer, the other be conquered, alternately for 3,000 years; for another 3,000 years they shall fight, war, and undo one the works of the other; but in the end hades will fail, and men will be happy, neither requiring food, nor constructing shelter; whilst the god who hath contrived all this is quiet, and resting himself for a time" (Plutarch, *Of Isis and Osiris*, c. 47). The conflict is identical with the battle of Sut and Horus on the grand scale. Three thousand years in round numbers with a surplus known to the Urshi, point to a period in precession

(3,714) equivalent to a change from one pole-star to another, in the station of the pole, only the length of time is now applied to souls in the eschatology, passing through the astronomical cycle of the proverbial 3,000 years. The Chinese "peach-tree of the gods" is a magnificent image of the pole. It has seven branches that bear the fruit of immortality, the fruit which ripens once in 3,000 years. Three thousand, we repeat, being a round number for the cycle, where 4,000 would not have answered when the exact number is 3,714 years. The peaches from this tree of time or knowledge were seven in series, as is shown by the seven peaches which were brought by the mythical Wang-Mu when she visited the equally mythical Emperor Wa Ti. Also the seven peaches as total fruit of the tree tend to prove that the figure was employed as a round number in thousands, near enough for the non-initiated and the surplus allowed for in reckoning the total combination.

It is feasible to suppose that the hanging and suspending power of the firmament was an earlier source of wonderment than even the revolution of the heavenly bodies. There is a passage in the Argonauticon (2, 296) which appears to show that the notion of suspension preceded that of revolving. "And so it is that men call those isles, the isles of turning, though aforetime they called them the floating isles" (Pilotes). These were the islands figured in the firmamental sea. Thus under one image groups of the revolving stars were thought of as the golden isles afloat in the celestial waters of the firmament. A typical floating island called Chemmis was shown to Herodotus in the deep broad lake, near the precinct of the temple of Buto, where it represented the place of refuge in which the infant Horus (Apollo) was concealed and saved when sought for by the devouring Apap (Herodotus, B. 2, 156). This place of birth was first figured in the stellar mythos as a floating island of the pole. The islands of Atlantis, whether seven or ten in number, would not have become the sunken islands unless they had been floating isles at first; and they were floating as formations in the water of heaven. The earliest foothold in the infinite had been physically attained amongst the stars that do not set. This was a place of refuge and of safety from the deluge of the firmamental deep whenever the catastrophe occurred.

It may sound a paradoxical thing to say, but it is true that according to the mythical representation the earliest earth was a bit of ground solidified in the celestial waters for the planting of a stake, or tree, or building, raising a pile, or some kind of bulwark against the overwhelming water-flood. The Egyptian hieroglyphic-sign of land, locality, or station is the well-known cake, that looks like our Easter hot-cross bun, and is a figure of the land that was caked or coagulated amidst the waters. This first formation in the waters of the Nun was constellated at the place of equipoise and fixity, when this was at the pole. And in the Osirian mythos this first standing place remained as a throne of the Eternal on the mount amid the water of the upper deep. In what is termed the Japanese "Cosmology" there is a primitive rendering of this beginning. Two of the Kami-deities, Izanagi and Izanami, the brother and sister corresponding to the Egyptian Shu and Tefnut, who lifted up the paradise of Am-Khemen, are divinely deputed to make, consolidate, and give birth to the island of Japan. For this purpose they were provided with a heavenly spear made of a jewel; a dual figure of the pole and polaris. Thus equipped, the pair stood on the "floating bridge" of heaven, and churned the Isle of Onogoro from the waters. This is the earth or ground that was consolidated in an island called "the self-curdled." (Chamberlain (B. H.), *Kojiki*, 18, 19.) The matter that was condensed around the spear or pole with which they churned the waters formed the land of Nippon, or Japan. Onogoro, says Hatori Nakatsune, a native commentator, was originally at the north pole, but was afterwards shifted to its present position. (Satow (E.M.), *Pure Shinto*, p. 68.) That is when the island which was "self-curdled" in the celestial ocean gave its name to an earthly island in the Yellow Sea. To see that the jewelled spear was an emblem of the pole we have but to compare this legend with the Indian version called "the churning of the ocean," in which a mountain (the mount of the pole) takes the place of the spear as the typical churning-stick. (Moor's *Hindu Pantheon*.) But this was no cosmical creation of the earth itself amidst the waters of space. Such an interpretation is only an erroneous literalization of the legendary lore. When the primal pair of the Japanese Kami took possession of the island which had been coagulated from the deep, they stuck the spear into the ground or earth. This was a mode of planting the tree or establishing the pole as a primary foundation in the water of heaven, that was now repeated in the resting-place on earth as a likeness of the pole above. (Chamberlain (B. H.), *Kojiki*, pp. 18, 19.) Garcilasso de la Vega relates that the Inca told him how "Our Father" sent two of his children, a brother and sister, down from heaven. He gave them a golden rod, two fingers thick and half an ell long, and when they desired to rest anywhere they were to stick this into the ground, and wherever it entered the earth at one push, there they were to halt, establish themselves, encamp, and hold their court or build the city. Here the brother and sister are another form of Shu and Tefnut. In a Dog-rib Indian myth a planting of the pole occurs. It is said that the divine hero, Chapewee, stuck a piece of wood in the earth, which became a fir tree, that grew and grew and grew until it reached to heaven. Then Chapewee ascended the tree, and at the summit found a fine large plain and a beaten road to travel on.

The present writer contends that the deluge-legends of the world are based upon the astronomical mythology of Egypt, but that in the isolation of the primitive emigrants the ancient wisdom lapsed and the deluge as a mode of symbolism in astronomy was more or less lost sight of; and, from lack of knowledge, the mythical deluge was confused with the primitive concept of heaven as the water overhead. With the knowers the deluge was a typical figure; with the ignorant it was an actuality that might at any time recur, as did the water-flood on earth. The chief contribution made by the Semites to the astronomical mythology was in literalizing the legends which originated with the mythical mode of representation, and in putting forth an exoteric version of the ancient wisdom. Thus it was natural that in a country like Babylonia where the winter rains were held to be a curse the typical deluge of Nnu in the celestial waters should be confused with the flood of Bel or Noah *on the surface of the earth*. Pliny calls Belus the "inventor of sidereal science" (N. H. 6, 26), and Belus as the elder Bel was a form of the Egyptian Bar, a name of Sut. As Diodorus relates (1, 28, 29), the Egyptians claimed to have taught the science of astronomy to the Babylonians, and declared that Belus and his subjects were a colony from Egypt. Belus (the first Bel) being identified with Bar = Sut, this means that the colonising of Babylonia from Egypt was during the reign of Sut, or at least in the time of the primordial pole-star one great year ago, when the pole-star was previously in the Lesser Bear or the male hippopotamus. In astronomy the status of an arch-first depended on being foremost in time, and Sut was first as bull of the mother, or the male hippopotamus with the female. We hold the founder of astronomy to have been the establisher of the pole, whether as Sut, in the southern, or Sut-Anup in the northern heaven. And the most profoundly important of all the deluges was that which took place at the subsidence and submergence of the pole and changing of the pole-star, the star that fell from heaven, according to the astronomical mythology. The Book of Enoch says that, previously to the Noachian deluge, Noah saw that the earth became inclined and that destruction approached. Then he lifted up his feet and went to the ends of the earth, to the dwelling of his great grandfather Enoch (ch. 64). The "*Ends of the Earth*" was an expression for the two poles—the dwelling of Enoch being equivalent to that of Sut at the southern pole. The beginning, however, was not with boats or arks as a means of crossing the celestial waters of the Nun. Islands were figured earlier. Typical heaps of earth were raised by the mound-builders as ground to go upon, like stepping-stones in the celestial deep. These eventually were seven in number. The structure also ranged from seven mounds at first to seven cities finally. Naturally the mount or mound of earth, the tree, the papyrus-reed, or island was a type of emergence from or amid the waters earlier than the building of a boat or an ark in the celestial sea. The first ideas were those of suspension, fixity, and foothold in the liquid vast.

In various primitive legends the bulwark was raised against the waters but was overthrown because the faithless woman failed to keep the secret with which she had been entrusted. We have already cited one or two American and African instances. In a Muyscas myth, Huythaca was the old first mother who ruled when there was as yet no sun or moon. She is described as a very wicked woman who maliciously loved to spoil the work of her husband. It was she who caused a flood from which but a few persons escaped by seeking refuge on the mountain-tops. Bochica, the solar god, then put a stop to the deluge, and, being very wroth with Huythaca, drove her from the earth and changed her into the moon. The result of the flood, in this case, was the same as in the "Destruction of Mankind," *viz.*, the establishment of solar time. When the earth was dry again Bochica gave the year and the periodic sacrifices and the worship of the sun to the people who survived the flood. (Tylor, *Primitive Culture*, vol. i., pp. 318–319.)

Nut, the celestial wateress in the Ritual, was a keeper of the waters which the women of the legends failed to guard. Hence "the leg of

Nut " is a figure of the pole.   In one of the legends the children of Nut, that is the stars, have failed in keeping proper time, and been the cause of confusion and strife.   This is in an address to the moon-god Taht, who succeeded Sut the star-god as reckoner of time by means of the moon.   " Hail, Taht ! what is it that hath happened to the divine children of Nut ? They have done battle, they have made strife, they have wrought evil, they have created the fiends, they have made slaughter, they have caused trouble ; in all their doings the mighty have worked against the weak.   Grant, O might of Taht, that that which the god Tum hath decreed may be done.   Thou regardest not evil, nor art thou provoked to evil, nor art thou provoked to anger when they bring their years to confusion, and rush in and disturb their months ; for in all that they have done unto thee they have worked iniquity in secret " (Rit., ch. 175, Budge).   When the pole-star changed the bulwark would be overthrown, and the mistress of the waters would be charged with causing a catastrophe by which the " bulwarks " of her consort, who was Sut in the Egyptian astral mythos, were submerged.   The blame, of course, in after-times, was laid upon the woman, that is when the woman had taken the place of the primitive zootype, such as the water-cow or crocodile.   In Amenta Ptah is the builder of the bulwark that was raised against the waters, or to keep out the Apap-reptile.   But Sut-Anup, as a ruler at the pole, was an indefinitely earlier god who raised the bulwark to keep out the deluge.   In later ages, when Anup had become the son of Ra, one name for his dwelling-place upon the mountain, that was on the solar mount of glory, is called Ut, the " Town of the Embankment," which is equivalent to the pile of earth that was heaped up by the mythical mound-builders in seven mounds that formed the bulwarks or embankments at the seven stations of the pole in the circuit of precession.   When the deluge occurred at the celestial pole the type of stability and fixed foothold on land was whelmed beneath the firmamental waters.   If this was an island or a tree it sank and was lost sight of.   Hence the tree of the pole had to be replanted, or the embankment was to be raised anew when the deluge was over.   It is related by the Miztec tribe of Indians that " in the day of obscurity and darkness the gods built a palace which was a masterpiece of skill, and made their abode upon the summit of a mountain.   The rock was called ' the Place of Heaven.'   It was the primary dwelling of the gods.   The children of the gods planted a garden with fruit-trees.   But it is the old universal tale : there came a deluge ; the happy garden was submerged, and many sons and daughters of the gods were swept away " (Bancroft, *Native Races*, vol. iii., p. 71).   Inevitably, at times our earth gets substituted for the mound, the island, or the earth-heap piled as a fixture for foothold in the celestial waters.   The mound of earth was followed by the pyramidion of brick, wood, or stone, the earliest figure of the tower that was built to reach the sky.   Thus, when the flood of Noah came to an end, the tower of brick was raised by the survivors in the land of Shinar.   In this version we see the tower succeeding the mountain, and the mound as a typical figure of the station at the pole.   After the Assyrian deluge the tree was replanted in the circle or enclosure, and to replant the tree was to re-establish the pole in its new station ; the tree or wood that was said.

to be eternal. Noah likewise planted the tree which in his case was the vine. In the book of Enoch it is said *the portion of Noah* (in time) has ascended up to God, and now "the angels shall labour at the trees" (or tree) and "the seed of life shall arise from it." This may likewise be taken to denote a replanting of the tree as symbol of the pole. Xisuthrus, the Chaldean Noah, is called the King of Surippak, the ship-city, the city of refuge that was represented by or as an ark upon the waters. The building on land was earlier than the boat upon the waters, and when the gods decide to make a deluge it is said, upon the Chaldean tablet, "O man of Surippak, son of Ubarratutu, *destroy the house and build a ship.*" Here the ship or ark on the waters succeeds the dwelling-place on land. And both the ark and house were united in Surippak, the ark-city, or "City of the Ship." After the Babylonian deluge, Hasisadra says, "I built an altar on the peak of a mountain," and there he offered a sacrifice to the gods. The altar-mound, we repeat, is a figure of the pole. The structure overthrown by the deluge is rebuilt in several ways, the types ranging from the mound to the metropolis. Not only is the typical altar of the pole erected on the mountain-peak, but the structure was finally rebuilt on the scale of the eternal city. Thus, the ark-city of Surippak is succeeded by the city of Erech-Suburi. In raising this, "great stones" are dragged for a long distance to where the wall of the new enclosure is to be erected, on the summit of the ascent, in the midst of Erech-Suburi. Seven such structures were raised in the course of precession, at seven stages of the pole, and the journey from one stage to another is described in the legend of Gilgames (Deluge Tablet, column 6, George Smith, *Records*, vol. vii., p. 133). In the Noachian version the deluge is followed by the building of "an altar to the Lord" (ch. 8, 20). There is also a journey made to "a plain in the land of Shinar where the generations of Noah came to dwell. And they said one to another "Go to . . . Let us build us a city, and a tower whose top may reach to heaven, and let us make us a name lest we be scattered abroad upon the face of the whole earth." In this account we find three figures of the pole, the altar-mound, the tower, and the city; also the migration of the survivors to another station of the pole; which is a common feature in the astronomical mythos, particularly in the Aztec, Peruvian, and Mexican legends. So ancient was this erection and re-erection of the pole, which signified another station fixed in the celestial journeyings, that the erection of a pole in the earth became a sacred mode of marking the station and the camping-place for the wanderers over the surface of the earth, as with the two poles of the Australian Arunta, and the stave or rod of the Inca. The Tower of Babel was a symbol of the pole which had been overthrown or shifted by the waters of the deluge. To build the tower, then, was to replace the pole. The tower was the Babylonian Bab-illu, which the Hebrew writer has turned into the tower of "babble" and confusion. The story itself is found on an Assyrian tablet in the British Museum, with this difference: In the older legend the structure is a mound, whereas in the Hebrew version it is a tower built of brick. It is explained that Babylon corruptly turned to sin. "Great and small commingled on the mound." There was a revolt against the great god Anu, "king of the holy mound." The rebels are described as building a stronghold, but they were confounded in their work. What they did by day was all undone by night. The supreme god gave a command to make strange their speech. "For future time the mountain," or the mound, was overthrown by Nu-nam-nir, the god of lawnessness or no rule, and the destruction occurred, though not in the form of a deluge (*Records of the Past*, vol. vii., p. 131). In the Mexican pictures there is an earlier type of the pole as a point of departure than the tower of brick. It has been called the starting-point of the Aztecs after the deluge. In this the mount or mound of earth rises from the water, like an island from the ocean, with a tree upon its summit. The mount is thus identifiable with the pole by means of the typical tree. It is likewise identified with the pole as the mount that topples over, the crooked mount· Colhuacan, upon which the ark of Tezpi rested after the deluge. In one drawing the male and female pair are portrayed with the boat waiting for them on the water. In the other a man in the boat is paddling away from the point of departure. The pair are known to tradition as Cox-Cox and his consort. The picture is also said to illustrate the migration from a starting-point in Atlan, or Aztlan, the white mountain. Without recurring for the present to the beginning of astronomy in the equatorial regions, we look on Sut (or Sut-Anup), the first-born son of Apt (Kep or Kefa), the most ancient form of the Great Mother, as the founder of the celestial pole, or the eternal tree in the paradise, the garden or cultivated enclosure of the northern heaven. Sut and his mother became the primal pair in the Egyptian mythology.

Although the mother of all living things, one of whose names, Khefa, survived in Hebrew as Chavvah (Eve), the primal pair of beings were not constellated as the human parents of the human race, but as male and female hippopotami, or Behemoth and Leviathan, and later as the Greater and the Lesser Bears ; she as the maker of the circle, and he as the first to plant the tree, or erect the pole, the pillar, or the mound within the circle ; Job says of Behemoth, "he is the chief of the ways of God" (ch. 40, 19). Now, Behemoth is the Egyptian Bekhmut, the hippopotamus. This was female as the zootype of the Great Mother, and male as the image of Sut her son, who as the founders of the pole were "the chief of the ways" in heaven as establishers of a guiding-star at the pole. When the primal pair are represented in the book of Genesis by Adam and Eve they are the husband and wife in a later mythos that was solar. But in the primal legends the descent of the human race is traced to the primal pair when these were mother and son, or the brother and sister as represented in the Japanese creation of the pole.

The earliest flood, caused by the declination of the pole-star, set afloat a large number of legends. One of these relates that the new world which followed was peopled by a brother and sister. The Chins, on the Burma frontier, preserve the tradition of a universal deluge that was co-eval with the origin of their race. According to the Haka tradition all the hills were submerged, and every person was drowned except one brother and sister, who floated in a large earthen jar, and when the waters subsided settled on the Mun Ktlang mountain (*Pioneer*, Allahabad, October 22nd, 1897). The old earth-mother, who was represented as the bringer-forth of life from the waters in the shape of a pregnant hippopotamus, was imaged astronomically as the genetrix who brought forth her young from the firmamental water amidst the fields of papyrus-reed which formed the Sekhet-Aarru. The same in Apta at the northern pole as it was in Apta at the equator. This old mother of beginnings in the waters of earth and heaven was also repeated as the dragon-horse in the Chinese version of the astronomical uranography as well as in the Babylonian remains. It is recorded in the sacred books that a supernatural dragon-horse issued from the waters of heaven and made known the eight mystical diagrams to Tai-Hao, the first mythical or celestial ruler, who corresponds to Sut, the inventor of astronomy in Egypt, and Bel in Babylonia. The mother and son were the pair that preceded the individualising of the fatherhood ; and the son was mythically represented as both the child and consort, the adult or bull, of the mother.

According to the Indian tribes of Guiana, the primal pair were a male and female, saved from the Deluge in a canoe. This is a legend of the Tamanaks. It is the same representation in the ancient British tradition. The Welsh first parents, named Dwyvan and Dwyvach, are a male and female who found safety from the Deluge in an ark. Also on the Apamean coin the pair as Nu, or Noë, and his female consort are portrayed upon the waters floating in a box or teba, accompanied by a raven and a dove. There is also a primal pair connected with the tree in a legend of New Guinea who are called "the man and his mother." The man is so mighty that he thrusts a spear through the earth right into the heart of the rock, where the pair live in the condition of troglodytes. The spear evidently images the pole, which is mixed up, if not identified, with the tree, as is the spear of the male and female pair in the Japanese legend. The man and his mother climbed to the top of the tree, and there the strong man slew the giant, the Apap-monster slain by Horus, and the giant slain by Jack (Romily, H. H., *My Verandah* p. 118). The giant is a co-type with the Apap-serpent of drought and darkness ; and in another legend the monster is a serpent coiled about the tree. This may help us to understand the presence of the evil serpent with "the man and his mother" underneath the tree in the Assyrian garden of Edin. The mother is the old first genetrix, one of whose titles is "mistress of the mountains" as well as of the mount. The Samoans say that the first of the human race were a woman and her son. Turner tells us they have many tales about the doings of that woman and her son, from whom the race of men descended (*Samoa*, p. 330–1). Thus, man and woman originated as the mother and her son, or the sister and brother, who afterwards became the mythical mother and father in the solar legends, which reflect the later sociology. In one tradition of the Ainu it is related that the race originated with a primal pair of ancestors, who were a female bear and a dog. This is, of course, in accordance with the totemic symbolism, only the totemic symbols were not limited to the human groups. Totems of the nature-powers were also figured in the planisphere. In Africa the great first mother of all was constellated as the female hippopotamus, or as a crocodile. In

Greece she was imaged as the female bear. Sut, her son, was represented by a jackal which became the dog through change of fauna. These can now be traced to the Greater and Lesser Bears as two surviving constellations of the Great Mother and her dog, who constitute the primal pair of the Ainu, with the bear as the Great Mother and the dog (or jackal) as her son or consort when the pole was in the Lesser Bear, we might say one great year ago.

Sut, as ruler of the primal pole-star, was the Arch-First in heaven, as a male. This is the title of Tai-Yih, the Chinese great one. It is said that among all the shin, or spirits (the Japanese shintu gods), of the heavens, the highest one dwells in the star Tai-Yih of the constellation Draco (O'Neil, *Night of the Gods*, vol. i. pp. 513, 517). It is not enough, however, to identify the deity with the pole in general. There were seven of these gods, and everywhere the question is, which of the seven stations of the pole was the seat at the time? Draconis was the constellation of Horus-Sebek, the crocodile-dragon. Sut was the first-born child of the great mother Apt or Khep, and those two formed the primary duad that is sometimes called Sut-Typhon, the nearest approach to which name in Egyptian would be Sut-Tept, or Sut and his mother as the primal pair. According to one account of the origins in the Book of Genesis, Seth, Set, or Sut was the first-born child of Chavvah, as he had been of Kep or Kefa in the Kamite mythos. Sut was the primary ruler or over-lord, the earliest representative of power in heaven figured in an image of the male, or the lord, whose name was first called upon when Sut became the backbone of the universe, as establisher of the pole. He was the lord as male hippopotamus and consort to the lady who was his mother as the female. And here we may perceive that a fragment of the true tradition survived in the biblical statement that in the time of Seth "Men *began* to call upon the name of the Lord" (Gen. iv. 26). Sut, as male, was first of the seven brothers who in the Babylonian legend "came as begetters." This fact also is recognised in the text when it is said that "a son was born to Seth," or Sut, Egyptian, who was the first form of *the father as the elder brother* with whom the fatherhood began. It is said of Ialdabaoth that, being incensed with men because they did not worship or honour him as god and father, he being the oldest brother only, he sent forth a deluge upon them that he might at once destroy them all (*Irenaeus*, Book I. ch. xxx. 10). Sut acquired an evil character in later times, and became the original form of an anthropomorphic satan.. He was looked upon as the fallen leader of the angelic host because he had been first in glory as the ruling power at the primary station of the pole. This is the satan worshipped by the Izedis in Mesopotamia, for whom there is to be a restoration as well as a fall, which points to an astronomical origin in both aspects of the character. Sut, in the Ritual (ch. 175), is proclaimed as having been the first in glory. It is said "the power of Sut which hath departed was greater than that of all the gods." He was first as primary power of the pole, the first to sit upon "the mount of congregation" as the "most high" in "the uttermost parts of the north," or at the pole of heaven. Hence he was the reputed author of astronomy. Thus, when the pole-star of Sut in the jackal (or the hippopotamus) had fallen away from the true pole and lost its place as guide of ways in heaven, there was matter for the legend of a fall as a fable founded on a fact in the astronomical mythology. When so read, the fall of man from heaven is resolved into the fall of Sut, or Lucifer, the light-bringer, or the light that was uplifted at the primary station of the pole, the woman who was the foundress being charged by the Semites, the Chinese, and others with being his accomplice and instigator, a mode of unconsciously showing that she, the Great Mother, was the mover, which she was, but only as the *primum mobile*, not as the woman urging the man to his eternal misery. The following citation shows the primal pair as Ishtar and the elder Bel in relation to the mount of the pole and the mountains of its different stations. "O lady, mistress of the mountain, goodly stronghold of the mountains, mighty lock of the mountains, queen of the land of the four rivers. O lord, the mighty mountain, Bel!" (Tablet S. 954, B. M. Budge, Babylonian). In this imagery the Great Mother as Ishtar, is mistress of the mountain, and Bel is the lord, identical with the mount itself, which imaged the pole, when Bel was the star. In one of the Assyrian hymns this enclosure of the "lady of the eternal tree" and her comrade is spoken of as "the park of Ishtar." Nergal, the destroyer, is thus addressed, "O lord, the park of Ishtar thou establishest not" (Sayce, "Hymn to Nergal," Hib. Sect.), Nergal having been one of the overthrowers at the time of the Deluge. In the Assyrian hymns to the gods it is said that the lady of the eternal tree is the comrade of the bull, the great bull, the supreme bull. The tree is the pole; "the eternal wood" or Gis-Zida, which also seems to mean a mast, is the pole (Sayce). Now, it is a form of this pair of founders at the pole that we think may be dimly discerned on the Assyrian cylinder (see p. 453). The tree with seven branches represents the pole as a figure of the total heptanomis, and is consequently late. The pair beneath the tree are the mother and son, or male and female, of the legend as the primal pair who fell from heaven because they failed as keepers of the tree of knowledge at the pole. There is also a form of this primal pair to be seen in a drawing on one of the Greek vases which comes nearest to the Hebrew version of the woman tempting the man. The Great Mother is portrayed in noble nudity, Greek fashion, as divinely tall beside a youth to whom she is offering the fruit which she has plucked from the tree of knowledge, the tree that represented the pole when the knowledge was astronomical. The pair, like the female and male in the Assyrian garden, are underneath the tree, about the root of which the serpent coils.

As Kamite, or as Greek, the ancient genetrix was the teacher who in later legend is misrepresented as the tempter.

We now claim to have recovered the natural origin of the primeval paradise with the primal pair, the tree and serpent in the enclosure at the station first established at the fixed point of the celestial pole, of which so many versions and perversions are extant without one of them being scientifically correct or verifiable from lack of the long-lost data in astronomy. Egyptian mythology, the source and fountain-head of all the ancient wisdom and legendary lore, could not be understood apart from this, neither can the astronomy be explained apart from the mythology. To repeat. The garden is the enclosure at the pole that was first figured in the circle of the ancient genetrix.

The pole itself was represented by the tree. The evil serpent symbolizes the drought, the darkness, and the dearth in physical phenomena.   The reptile coils around the tree or is present in all the pictures, Egyptian, Babylonian, Hindu, Red Indian, Norse, and Greek, also as described in divers ancient legends.   The mother brought forth her child of life as the opponent of the evil serpent and protector of the tree, and the saviour in the Kamite mythology was converted into a saviour in the Semitic eschatology. The Chinese have a tradition in which original sin is attributed to a woman who overthrew her "husband's bulwarks through an ambitious desire for knowledge." As in the Book of Genesis and the legend of the wicked Huythaca, the sin is ascribed to the woman.   But we need to know what the bulwark was before we can see how it could ever have been overthrown. She was Primus, as builder of the bulwark or as planter of the pole, and, above all, as mistress of the waters which were under her control, or should have been, unless she had neglected them or entered into a league with the Apap-reptile, which was the primary evil power that overthrew the enclosure with the deluge of the dark or the waters of the firmament.

We meet with a form of the primal pair in Stanley's legend of Lake Tanganyika, one of the oldest in the world.   In this the woman had been trusted with the keeping of the waters.   But she betrayed the secret to her lover and the waters broke forth in a deluge of destruction, the proof of which catastrophe remains to this day in Lake Tanganyika.   The Khonds of Orissa have a divinized form of the primal pair in their ancient goddess, Tari Pennu, and her son, Buri Pennu, who answers to a pole-star god inasmuch as he was called "the light."   These can be identified with the prototypal pair, that is with Sut the establisher of the pole and his mother, because he is credited with creating a primal paradise, and she is charged with having maliciously caused its destruction, which is elsewhere rendered as a deluge of water or a fall from heaven.

Amongst the mummeries still religiously performed in Rome, and also by the English Ritualists, which are mystical at present from lack of meaning, there is a ceremony of "the seven stations of the cross," which is supposed to commemorate the seven resting-places of the cross on the way to Calvary.   But the same, or a similar procession, was celebrated at Abydos or Memphis when the tat-cross was carried round the seven resting-places that marked and memorized the seven stations of the pole.   In one of the ancient Chaldean oracles the seven stations of the pole are spoken of as the *seven poles*.   "The Chaldeans call the god (Dionysius or Bacchus) Iao in the Phœnician tongue (instead of the intelligible light), and he is often called Sabaoth, signifying that he is above *the seven poles*, that is the Demiurgus" (Taylor, "Collection of Chaldean Oracles," *Classical Journal*, No. 22). As Iamblichus says of the Chaldeans, "they not only preserved the memorials of seven-and-twenty myriads of years, as Hipparchus tells us they have, but likewise of the whole Apocatastes and periods of *the seven rulers of the world*" (Nat. Gen., vol. ii., p. 321).   It certainly was so with the Egyptians. These rulers were the seven born of the Great Mother as the seven powers of earth.   They were re-born of Nut, the mother-heaven, as the seven glorious ones, who were called the Khuti; the seven with Anup at the pole who were the executioners for the great judge; the seven wise masters of art and science in the lunar mythos with Tehuti; the seven sahus with Horus in Orion; the seven as moulders with Ptah in the making of Amenta; the seven as the souls of Atum-Ra who were the creators of man.

These are the seven that were uranographic figures in the astronomical mythology as the seven old, old ones; the seven patriarchs of enormous age; the seven giants of colossal stature; the seven rulers of the world; the seven lords or masters of eternity.

In later times the seven planets have been mistaken for the seven stars. But these ancient pole-stars we consider to be "the seven stars" of which it is related in the tradition reproduced by Plato that after many ages they would return and meet together again in their old places as in the beginning, and apparently at the time of the last deluge of all, or, as we read it, at the end of the great year.

It was these and not the seven planets that could ever return to an original station at the starting point. The planets were but five in number and not seven in the most ancient astronomy. The sun, moon, and seven stars were not the seven planets of modern science. The seven, called the first of the stars, which in the beginning were in heaven, are connected with the great year according to the book of Enoch, as is shown by their being cast out *until* the day of the "great consummation" in "the secret year," also called the "period of the great judgment."

The seven that were separate and single as rulers of the pole were also grouped together as a pictorial illustration in the planisphere. These are the seven in the constellation of the Lesser Bear who follow the bier or coffin of their lord, Osiris, in the Greater Bear. These are they of whom it is said, "Their places were fixed by Anup on the day of Come thou hither" (Rit., ch. 17), who became the seven lords of eternity, and who were looked up to as seven divine ancestors of Atum-Ra. The names of seven superseded watchers in heaven are given by Enoch as: Azazyel, Amazarak, Armers, Barkayel, Akebeel, Tamiel, and Asaradel. Here also is evidence that the seven rishis who meditated and forgot were the representatives of seven pole-stars. Dhruva was one of the rishis who was assigned a pole-star by Vishnu. He is said to have meditated himself into forgetfulness of his identity (or ceased to be a pole-star). The seven who slumbered and forgot are also represented by the seven sleepers in the cave at Ephesus with their dog, who answer to the seven with Anup and his jackal at the pole. The seven who slumbered and forgot likewise recur in the Norse mythology. These are the seven sons of Mimir who guard the land of Odainsakr, the land of the ever-living. They are represented as the smiths who forged the primitive weapons and who correspond to the seven Khnemmu or divine metallurgists of Ptah. Though sleeping till the dusk of the last day, they keep the enclosure safe until the final conflict comes betwixt the powers of good and evil. Then they are to wake and rise and help to establish the new heaven and rejuvenated earth. The seven under whatsoever name or type, watching or slumbering, are still the keepers of the world's great year and the enclosure of the seven never-setting stars that marked the seven stations of the shifting pole.

Before the building of the boat the seven had to keep their heads above water as the seven mythical, immeasurable giants, equivalent in the superhuman guise to seven great mountains imaging the seven starry summits. One of these giants is Ogg in Jewish legend, who is said to have waded through the deluge, clinging with one hand to the ark to keep afloat. The seven giants, as figures of seven colossal constellations, were tall enough to hold their heads, which are the seven pole-stars, above the waters that were deep enough to drown the other people of the heavens. But when the boat was built there was an ark of safety that could float upon the waters, and the primordial seven were mythically represented as being saved from the deluge in an ark as seven companions, Ali, Kabari, Hohgates, or other groups of the seven which had one origin in the astronomical mythology of Egypt. And when the boat was launched upon the water of earth the type could be applied to the water of heaven. Seven giants, in one rendering of the mythos, bore the world of the heptanomis upon their backs, each standing at his station as one of seven great props personified as giants. The unhuman hugeness of the giant was most naturally derived from the enormous pre-anthropomorphic types or zootypes of superhuman power. Sut, as the hippopotamus, is a giant. Sebek, as the crocodile, is a giant. Shu, as the lion, is a giant. An ape of seven cubits and also one of eight cubits is described as a giant. But the seven primal powers as Egyptian in *the earliest human form* are pigmies and not giants. Moreover, the giants were not human, whereas the pigmies are. In an Arthurian legend the Welsh Owein comes to a wide, open clearing with a great mound in it where there is a black giant, who stands upon one foot, and has only one eye in the middle of his forehead (Rhys, *Arth. Legend*). The mound, the giant with one foot and Cyclop's eye are perfect figures of the pole and pole-star, which have here been grouped together in a later legend. The Irish Crom, Cromm Cruiach, "the crooked or bent one of the mound," equates with the Mexican "crooked mountain" as the figure of a falling or deflected station of the pole. The Mexican tradition affirmed that it was in the first age of the world that the giants began to appear on the earth. These are the giants of the constellations who had been humanized as magnified non-natural men, and then transferred to our earth in the märchen that took the place of the gnosis, or science of the mythos. In the Aztec and Mexican versions of the deluge myths we find that when the great calamity occurred the land was peopled by giants. Seven of these who were brothers found safety by enclosing themselves in the seven caves of the mountain Tlaloc. The Indians of Cholula likewise relate that only seven inhabitants of this fore-world of the giants survived the deluge. In Southern California the Indians have a tradition of the beginning in which Quaor, the Lord, when he created the world, or the new order of things, placed it on the shoulders of seven sustaining giants (*Nat. Gen.* vol. ii. p. 220). This world of the giants was the celestial heptanomis beyond the deluge. In a tradition of the American Indians it is told that at the close of the deluge the last mammoth sprang across Lake Superior at a single bound and disappeared for ever in the wilds of Canada. Thus the last of the seven astronomes, or its mammoth-

The giants, who were seven in relation to the stations of the pole, are curiously identified with the mountains themselves as places of birth by Sanchoniathon. He says they were beings of vast bulk and stature, "*whose names were given to the mountains which they occupied.*" Of these, he tells us, children were begotten through intercourse with their mothers, "the women of those times without shame having intercourse with any man they might chance to meet." Here the giant and the mountain as human birthplace are identical as figures of the pole (Cory, *Ancient Fragments*, 1876, p. 6). These, then, are a form of those giants called the sons of God who "came in unto the daughters of men" (book of Genesis, also book of Enoch).

In the Hebrew märchen, the seven old ones who were the primordial powers, the seven wise masters, watchers, judges, rishis, manus, moulders, masi, Ali, Elohim, or Kabari are the seven patriarchs of Genesis who lived for such enormous lengths of time. They are the typical old ones in the Ritual, the fathers in the first and highest circle of the gods. The seven patriarchs were identified in the *Natural Genesis* (vol. ii., section 12) with the seven rishis in the lunar mythos of the Hindu astronomy. These, as measurers of the precessional movement of the pole by means of seven pole-stars, were also represented as making a revolution of the great year in the twenty-eight asterisms or mansions of the moon. The patriarchs had now been humanized. The Hindu patriarchate was a period of 71–2 years, or a mortal lifetime. Seven of these were the measure of a phœnix-cycle, a period of 500 years. Seven by seven the rishis or manus travel round the zodiac of 28 houses, in the circle of precession. Thus the time of their stay in each asterism would be a twenty-eighth part of the great year of 25,868 or, in round numbers, 26,000 years. This would give the patriarchs or manus something over 900 years in each of the 28 lunar stations, which is quite near enough as astronomical data to account for the age of the seven patriarchs in the book of Genesis. The age of Adam is 930 years. The age of Seth 912 years. The age of Enoch 905 years. The age of Kenan 910 years. The age of Jared 962 years. The age of Methuseleh 969 years. Thus, the age of six of the seven patriarchs is over 900 years each, and in the first list of two the patriarchs are seven in number. No reason has been adduced for rejecting this explanation. If the seven patriarchs, like the seven rishis, the seven taasu, or the seven masi, were astronomical characters, it is certain their ages are likewise astronomical. Noah, who is tenth in the second list of patriarchs, is the man of 500 years who never could be mortal. But it can be shown in what way he was an astronomical figure, like the rest of the seven, or the ten, according to the mode of measuring by the typical lifetime. The human lifetime was reckoned at 71–2 years; the age of a patriarch in human form. Seven of these periods in precession made a phœnix-cycle of 500 years, the age, therefore, of a divine or mythical man like Noah or the Buddha. A legend of the Jayas, in the Vayu Purana, relates, in after times, that the astronomical rulers were created by Brahma as his divine assistants, but that they got lost in meditation and forget to fulfil his ordinances. On this account they were doomed to be continually reincarnated and reborn in each manvantara or patriarchate up to the seventh, and thus they continued to be reborn in successive series of sevens all through the cycle of precession. The seventh was always reborn as a manu or a Buddha in the Puranas, and in the Hebrew version Noah is the man of 500 years as a typical measurer of time, and in this instance it is the particular period of time that is ended with a deluge (Gen. v. 32). Now among the Hebrew fragments of the ancient wisdom in the book of Genesis is the story of these patriarchs that was told according to the measuring by the lifetime. Previous to the deluge of Noah the lifetime of man or of the old, old ones was reckoned at something like 1,000 years. As we are told, "there were giants in the earth in those days." But after the deluge, time, or the age of man, was to be computed by shorter lengths. This is expressed in uranographic formulæ: "Yet shall his days be an hundred and twenty years," which period as Egyptian is the double Han-cycle. Thus the change from a lifetime of 1,000 years to a period of 120 years is obviously related to the double Han-period of the Sothiac-cycle. The double Han-cycle is a period of 120 years. Consequently the lifetime of man after the deluge is measurable by the length of this period, which was made use of in reckoning the cycle of Sothis. And whether the lifetime is reckoned at 120 years in the Sothiac cycle, or at 3,714 in the circle of precession, both are astronomical. The lifetime of the patriarch was a period in precession. Noah's lifetime was a phœnix-cycle of 500 years which ended with the Noachian deluge. After this the lifetime of man (who takes the place of the Bennu as an astronomical figure) was to be the Han-cycle of 120 years. Thus the heaven or zodiac in twelve divisions was probably based on the Sothiac-cycle. Twelve Han-cycles were twelve lifetimes in the year of Sothis, round numbers being employed, and the fractions gathered up to be quoted in the total combination, or filled in with the festivals, such as the Sut-Heb. This was a seven days' festival celebrated every thirty years. At the end of each Han-cycle it was seen that the legal year had gained a whole month on the actual year, and the 1st of Taht anticipated the heliacal rising of Sothis by thirty days. But this had been measured, allowed for, and ticked off by means of the four Sut-Heb festivals celebrated during the Hanti period of 120 years. By this intelligible change in the length of the lifetime the biblical text itself affords indubitable evidence that the lifetimes of the patriarchs were astronomical. If the Han-cycle of 120 years was a time-cycle, it is absolutely certain that the previous periods were so likewise, the one being reduced from the other by the Hebrew a-gnostic literalizers. The cutting up of time into smaller portions or shorter lengths is likewise indicated in the Chippewa legend, when the slayer of the giants is described as hacking their bodies into little bits, and saying to the fragments, "In the future let no man be larger than you are now" (*Nat. Gen.*, vol. ii. p. 240). This is equivalent to the lifetime being cut down to 120 years. Thus the lifetime of the patriarch, which in round numbers was 1,000 years in the old, was reduced to 120 years in the reckoning of the new cycle which followed the deluge of Noah.

The "seven rulers of the world" manifested one by one at great intervals of time, and were a means of keeping the reckonings on a colossal scale. The age of each, as representatives of the successive pole-stars, would be from three to four thousand years, or one-seventh part of 25,868 years. The seven, beginning as the Kamite Khuti, are well-nigh universal. The Japanese have *seven gods of fortune* and givers of good gifts, called the *Shichi Fukujin*, who sail each New Year's Eve as passengers on board the ship called *The Floating-Bridge of Heaven*, that carries the seven magical treasures, which include the lucky coat, the hat that makes invisible, the inexhaustible purse, and other possessions which are obviously the property of spirits promised conditionally to mortals on the earth. The two groups of Hebrew patriarchs which precede the deluge, seven and ten in number, correspond to the seven and the ten in Babylonian legend, who were rulers in the antediluvian world—that is, in the fore-world of the astronomical mythology. The seven fish-men, ascending one by one at vast intervals of time from the Nun or deep that was locally represented by the Persian Gulf at Eridu, we look upon as the seven rulers of the ancient pole-stars taking their stations successively in the circuit of precession, with the fish for their zootype. Unquestionably the seven fish-men are a form of the seven prediluvian kings, hence the appearance of the Annedoti at the same time with the king, the fish as zootype being earlier than the title of king. Thus the seven as fish-men, of whose "appearances Abydenus has made no mention," were followed by the three other rulers named Amompsimus, Otiartes, and Xisuthrus, and "so the sum total of all the kings is ten," seven of whom had been figured as Annedoti, or divine rulers in the celestial waters, who were afterwards completely humanized as kings. So in the book of Esdras, the Son of God is seen ascending from the sea to take his stand upon the mount, here called Mount Zion, as the man "whom God the highest hath kept a great season," and who was to regain the fish-type as ichthus "within four hundred years" (2 Esdras, vii. and xiii.). The seven Assyrian masi are known to have been stars in different constellations, as were the pole-stars. One was "the star of the eagle," one "the star of the wain," one "the star of the shepherd of the heavenly flocks," that might be compared with the "key of the crown" as first of the seven pole-stars in the heptanomis of Sut.

Tai Hao, the great celestial, was the first mythical or astronomical ruler in the Chinese divine dynasties. With him *commenced* the mystic diagrams called the Yi or changes, which were eight in number. These were revealed to him by the dragon-horse that issued from the Yellow river or the Milky Way (Mayers, *Manual*, 366, 44, 56). Tai Hao corresponds to Sut, the inventor of astronomy and ruler of the first pole-star; the dragon-horse answers to the water-horse that was combined with the crocodile in Apt, goddess of the Great Bear and mother of the seven rulers. According to M. Philastre in his version of the Yi king (p. 3), the name of the Chow dynasty and of the Chow Yi divining-book signifies circular movement, the revolution embracing the whole universe. This revolution, we think, does not merely mean that of the starry sphere, but the movement of the pole. Chow Yi would then mean the changes of the pole and pole-stars in the circle of precession. Thus the Chow dynasty of the sons of heaven would be the seven successive rulers of the pole, who reigned for six and twenty thousand years as scientific fact.

In the *Vision of Scipio* Cicero has preserved something of the ancient doctrine concerning the derivation of souls from above. The spirit of Africanus tells his son that souls or spirits were supplied to men from the eternal fires, which are constellations and stars. Now there are seven souls, because the elements were seven all told, and seven primary constellations, with seven stars for souls, otherwise called the seven great spirits or seven glorious ones. These became the seven begetters in the creation legend of Cutha—one to each of the seven representative constellations in which the elemental powers had acquired their souls and thus become the typical transmitters of souls to human beings. Sut, the soul of shade in the hippopotamus; Horus, the soul of light; Shu, the soul of breath; Hapi, the soul of water—such were the begetters of a soul in totemism. Thus the Ainu are the bears, the Arunta are the emus, the Zuni are the turtles. They have their totemic zootypes on earth, which also imaged the elemental spirits or souls in heaven that were represented by the constellation or the star for those who had preserved the primitive wisdom. Thus derivation from the tree and rock, which is mentioned by Hesiod and Homer, would, if astronomical, be derivation from the pole; whereas derivation from the hippopotamus, bear, vulture, ape, water-bird, jackal, tortoise, or other of the uranographic types would denote *the particular station of the pole*, and be a time-gauge to the beginnings according to the racial reckonings in the astronomical chronology. For instance, the Khatties of Central India trace their descent from a progenitor named Khat, who sprang from a staff that he had fashioned from the branch of a tree (Folkard). Descendants from a god whose hauling or towing force was represented by a rope would naturally be the ropemen. And the Spartans claimed to be the ropemen, from σπαρτογ = rope. As they sprang from the teeth of the dragon sown by Kadmos, it is possible that they dated from the ropeman who was ruler of the pole-star in the dragon from 4,000 B.C. to 1,000 B.C. in round numbers. When Ra calls on those who pull the rope of the solar boat in Amenta to tow him "towards the dwelling of stable things" and free themselves upon "the mysterious horizon," they say to Ra, "The rope is with Ak" = the pole-star. The upper end of the rope was fastened to the pole, whilst the bark was being towed round the ecliptic. The imagery here does but involve one rope and one pole-star at a time; but as the pole-stars in the course of precession were seven, there were seven ropes or bonds, all reckoned, and in one character the seven primal powers are called the seven Tesu or Tasu. These are the seven who hauled at the rope and who were the makers of the seven ties, bonds, knots, or fastenings of the cable to the pole when the rope was a primitive link of connection that preceded Newton's law of gravitation; the rope that is carried in the form of a noose by Shu-Anhur, who also carries the staff of the pole with which heaven was uplifted. The seven Egyptian Tesu are a kind of seven ropemen, who passed into the Babylonian mythology as the seven bonds by which the universe was bound and held together by the seven lords at the seven stations of the pole. In the Hindu representation the seven powers that hauled round the solar bark by means of the rope have been converted finally into the later seven horses which draw the chariot of the sun (Moor's *Hindu*

Pantheon). The seven became the first company of the gods in the Aarru fields as the rulers of the seven pole-stars, who were the formers or creators in the domains of space and time. These were the seven great in glory called the Khuti or spirits, represented by beautiful white water-birds, the prototype of Cygnus the swan. The seven Khuti still survive in the seven swans of legendary lore, more especially in India. The seven Khuti, as white birds on the celestial waters, represented souls or spirits, but as star-souls, not human souls, external to human beings, and so they became seven souls as seven swans in the folk-tales.

At every stage of development the tree of mythology has shed the leaves of legend that were blown about the world as the märchen of many lands. Before the boat was built the swimmers were water-birds, crocodiles, or hippopotami. The mode of thinking could not have been otherwise. When Anup as eighth was added as the power above the pole, and therefore the supreme one in the character of the great judge, the gods of the seven pole-stars were figured as "the seven arms of the balance" in the maat of eternal law and justice. When the boat was built and Anup became the master over the waters, the company of seven were placed pictorially on board the bark of the Lesser Bear as figures of the never-setting ones that were safe for ever from the waters of the deluge. The seven now were typical eternals in two categories of astronomical phenomena. They were stationary in the circle of the seven ancient pole-stars, and seven as rowers, boatmen, or kabari grouped in the bark revolving round the pivot of the pole. This was in the stellar mythos. When lunar time had been made out by Taht the measurer, the typical seven were advanced in status. These are his assistants as the seven Taasu, the sages or wise masters. They appear on board the bark in the shape of seven hawks called the offspring of heaven. The bird of air had then succeeded the water-bird as the type of the seven souls on board the bark in the lunar mythos. In the solar mythos the seven are pygmies or patakoi, the little sailors on board the bark with Ptah. Marcianus Capella tells us the Egyptians painted on their ships the seven pilots who were all alike and brothers, who are no doubt identical with the seven pygmy-patakoi or kabiri of Ptah. These were represented in the boat of Anup that voyaged round the pole as the seven rulers that were thus grouped together as a picture of the stars that never set. Sydik the just and the seven called his sons are the Phœnician form of Anup the judge and the seven khuti. The seven were not navigators as the seven hawks, jackals, apes, giants, planters of the tree, or builders of the mound. Navigation began with the boat or ark, and the seven in the boat, like the seven hohgates, were seen as the seven in the Lesser Bear, with Anup or Sydik, head over all, as an eighth to the seven. In one character the seven stars were regarded as watchers watching solemnly aloof. A non-setting star was imaged as a never-closing eye. In the Ainu legend of the god upon the summit, the watchers, who are the 6 + 1, are hares, and the hare was reputed to be so watchful that it slept with its eyes open. In Babylonia the deluge-makers are the seven with the ancient Genetrix, who is called "the mother of the seven gods," the seven that "heaped up the seat" or

built the mounds which were overthrown, as fabled, by the deluge.
Astronomically these were the gods of the seven pole-stars whose
seats were in the never-setting stars around the throne of Anu.
Thus, and in no other way, the seven powers caused the deluge, and
then ascended to their seats in the heaven of Anu and assumed their
thrones on high as rulers in the realm of eternity. The seven survivors are exactly the same in the astronomical mythos as if they had
made their escape from drowning in a boat, like the seven hohgates
or kabiri, or any other group of the seven companions. But the boat
or ship is here employed for the use of the human survivors who are
supposed to have been carried away on board the bark of Hasisadra
"to be like the gods"—that is, as manes and not as mortals. The
seven who are charged with causing the deluge in Babylonian legend
—Bel, Ea, Rimmon, Nebo, Marduk, Ninib, and Nerra—may be compared with the Egyptian seven—Sut, Sebek, Shu, Hapi, Tuamutef,
Kabbsenuf, and Amsta.

The tradition of the seven founders of the heaven that was based
upon the water went forth to the ends of the earth. They were seven
children of the old Great Mother, seven brothers or companions
when the social status was totemic and the fatherhood was not
yet individualised. In Egypt they are "the seven children of the
thigh"—the sign by which we can identify the ancient Genetrix with
the birthplace of beginning astronomically in the circle of the Bear
and the constellation called the Meskhen, or "the thigh." These are
the seven brethren called "seven kings," who appear as "begetters" in
the Cuthean legend. That is as begetters in group-marriage, who
were the totemic fathers that preceded the father as a known individual. They are the seven companions of Arthur in the ark; the
seven hohgates of the Californian Indians, who escaped from the deluge
in a boat and were fixed in heaven as stars that never set; the seven
dwarf-sons of the Polynesian Pinga, who correspond to the seven
pygmy boatmen and builders of Ptah; the seven mound builders on the
American continent, and various other sevens in the mythos that was
astronomical and became universal in the legendary form. They were
born as seven sons of the Great Mother, and were her boys when she
was "a mither but na wife."

No matter in what part of the world we discover this tradition of
the seven founders and seven stations of the pole, it involves at least
one bygone Great Year in the circle of precession independently of
where the astronomical mythology originated. In the later stage of
the eschatology, when Osiris was supreme as god over the pole, and
all other powers had become his powers (Rit., ch. 7), there are seven
arits or mansions in the great house of the eternal city. The seven
watchers, of the astral mythos, dwell in these; the seven who are
called the khus, the divine princes; the seven glorious ones who stand
behind Osiris, and who are called the makers of the seven mansions
for the god (chs. 17, 83–107, and 144). Before Osiris was, these were
the seven lords of law, of right, of truth, and justice: otherwise stated,
the seven lords of maat (judges), the seven arms of the balance
(executioners), the seven eyes (watchers), the seven pillars (supports);
and as they were also the makers of the seven arits, they are likewise
the seven mythical builders of the heptanomis; the seven powers that

can be followed as the seven with Anup, with Taht, with Ptah, with Horus, and with Ra, according to the series of phenomena.

It is now proposed to trace and tentatively localize the seven (or a seven) stations of the pole on which the heptanomis was founded in the circuit of precession. In the circle of precessional movement drawn by Pyazzi Smythe, he has filled in only six out of seven stations of the pole—one in the Dragon, one in the Lesser Bear, one in Kepheus,

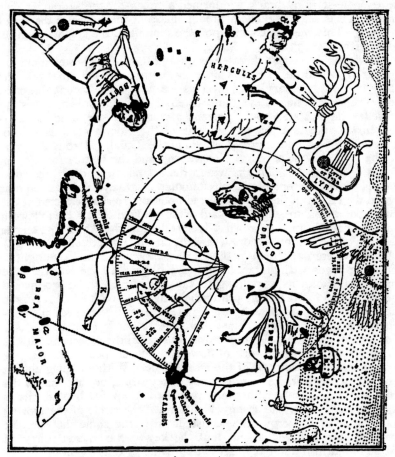

Star-map, representing the precessional movement
of the Celestial Pole of rotation and especially marking it
from the year 4000 B.C. to the year 2000 A.D.
Symbols adopted to represent the magnitudes or brightness of the stars, 1st ⊛, 2nd ⊕, 3rd ▲, 4th ■.

one in Cygnus, one in Lyra, and one in Herakles, or the Man. It is here we have to reconstitute and fill in a constellation *as a first one of the seven*. Various legends lead us to think that there was an ancient pole-star in "Corona Borealis," or the northern crown. A crown is a symbol of the highest, which at the pole would be the highest point. Then the star Alpha in this constellation is called "*Clava Corona*," the key of the crown; and a key-star at the crowning point is, to say the least, equivalent to the key-stone of an arch. Moreover, "the crown of heaven" was an Assyrian title of the pole-star, which tends to identify the pole-star with a constellation called the crown of the northern heaven. Apparently the pole and crown are also connected by an Akkadian expression concerning "the Bear making its crown-ship" in its revolution round the pole-star. The crown of heaven, however, was by no means limited to a single pole-star, although it may have originated as the crowning-point at the pivot of the pole. The seven pole-stars in their circle formed a crown for the supreme being, of whom it is said his diadem predominates at the zenith of the starry heaven. This was his crown upon the summit of the stellar mount of glory (Rit., ch. 133).

The seven pole-stars themselves did not form one constellation, but the crown would be figured typically as a group of stars that told the story in the customary way, even as we find it in Corona Borealis. Moreover, to the naked eye the constellation of the Crown, consisting of seven large stars, would present a picture of the other seven—the crown of stars upon the summit of the mount which is so prominent in the eschatology. It is said in the Ritual, "Here is the cycle of the gods (as the seven glorious ones), and the vulture (or kite) of Osiris" (ch. 136 B). This is where the balance was then erected at the place of judgment in the circumpolar maat, and also at the point where the crown of life was conferred upon the spirits perfected at the summit of the mount. It is also said of the glorified elect, "He followeth Shu and calleth for the crown. He arriveth at the Aged One on the confines of the mount of glory where the crown awaiteth him" (ch. 131). This is the eternal crown in the eschatology which had its origin in the seven never-setting stars of the mythology. In the Kabalah it is the crown of crowns pertaining to the Aged in which he had incised the forms and figures of the primordial kings who reigned aforetime in the land of Edom, but who could not preserve themselves and consequently passed away, "one after the other" (Ginsburg, *The Kabalah*, 21). The pole and crown are certainly associated in the May-pole with its framework of flowers always shaped in the likeness of a crown at the summit of the tree or pole. Without being able at present to prove it, we suggest that a key-stone, or key-star, to the arch or conical mount of heaven was first laid in the heptanomis as primary pole-star of the seven which formed the circle of the crown ; that a figure of the crown was constellated in the somewhat circular group of Corona Borealis, and that the key to the mystery may at last be found in the star represented by name as Clava Coronæ.

Now, if we take the island, for example, as the type of a station or place of landing, there was a subsidence of the land in the celestial waters, or, in sign-language, there was a deluge at each declination of the pole-star. Otherwise expressed, one of the seven mountains was submerged, one of the seven provinces or patalas was drowned, one of the seven pole-stars fell, or one of the seven rulers was dethroned in heaven. The earliest station of the pole may be assigned to Sut as the hippopotamus, or as builder of the mound ; *the crown would be a later figure of the highest position*. There was a constellation of the hippopotamus *as male*, to match the mother in the Greater Bear ; this was a zootype of Sut, her first-born son, however difficult it is at present to define the group of stars—that is, to distinguish the male hippopotamus from Draconis, which, by the bye, were two zootypes of Sut and Horus, the twin brothers. Though now unseen on the celestial globe, it is certain that there was a male hippopotamus among the circumpolar constellations, and this, as bull of the mother, represented Sut, the son of Apt, the water-cow (see "Calendar of Astrl. Observations," *Trans. Soc. of Bib. Arch.*, vol. iii. pp. 400–421). It is apparently portrayed in a miniature drawing which was copied by Lepsius (Lepsius, *Auswald*, 23). The hippo-potamus is figured in the tree, which here, as elsewhere, proves it to be the pole ; the tree and ladder, both of which are types of the ascent. The hawk that mounts the ladder is a soul ascending to the mount of glory in the country of the tree. Moreover, the hieroglyphic ▦

The Landing-place for Spirits, with the Tree of the Pole in the Constellation of the Hippopotamus.

is a sign of land amidst the waters ; the land for which the hawk is bound, which, as the eight disks show, was the paradise of Am-Khemen that was raised on high by Shu.

As Japanese Buddhist myth, the island of Japan might be localized astronomically by means of a legend in which it is related that an Apsaras appeared in the clouds over a spot that was inhabited by a dragon. An island suddenly rose up from the sea. The Apsaras descended on the island and was wedded to the dragon, which may be interpreted as a folk-tale of the time when the island of the pole was in the constellation Draco. (*Handbook*, Satow and Hawes.) The dragon that falls from heaven in the book of Revelation and goeth into perdition is said to be one of the seven who are imaged as seven kings, seven heads, seven horns, seven mountains, seven islands, seven lamp-stands, seven stars, seven eyes, or seven ruling powers.

The myth of lost Atlantis is Egyptian. This was told to Solon by Egyptian priests, and afterwards retold by Plato in Timaeus. It contains the story of two heavens that were sunken in the waters of the deluge. The first was in seven, the latest in ten divisions ; the heaven of the ten lost tribes, ten sons of Jacob, the ten patriarchs, and the ten Assyrian pre-diluvian kings. There is no deluge-legend of twelve islands that were lost or sunken in the sea, because the heaven in twelve divisions, based on the solar zodiac of twelve signs, was never sunk nor superseded. This has not passed away to leave the subject matter for the mythos. But there is a dragon with twelve heads to be met with in folk-lore who evidently images the solar god in the final heaven of twelve divisions which followed the heptanomis and the heaven in ten nomes. In the Hungarian folk-tale of Eisen Laezi, the hero is identical in character with Bata in the "Tale of the Two Brothers," and the wife of the twelve-headed dragon-king is one with the false accuser in the Egyptian story, and with Potiphar's wife in the Hebrew version. The only point at present is to establish the fact that there is a dragon with twelve heads who is the king and father of the youthful hero.

As the tree was planted anew or re-erected seven times over, it follows that there is a typical group of seven trees, as well as the one tree with seven branches, to be met with in the mythological legends. Also, as the law was given at the pole or the tree, there would be seven trees of the law established in the course of Precession. Finally the celestial trees were twelve in number when the zodiac of twelve signs had been established. (2 Esdras, ii. 18). The seven trees that stood around the mount of the pole are met with in a Chinese legend. Tradition says they grew upon the slopes of the Kun-Lin mountains; and one of them, which conferred the fruit of immortality, was a tree of jade, the imperishable stone that was a type of the eternal (*Babylonian and Oriental Record*, June, 1888). Seven would be the number in precession which were afterwards unified in the tree of seven branches. Other circles, other numbers. Seven trees would form the sacred grove or asherah-tree which is surmounted by the seven serpent hoods conventionalized on the Chaldean cylinders as co-type of the seven branches (D'Aviella, *Migration of Symbols*, figs. 63, 64, 79, etc.). It is probable that the tree of the pole-star was known in Egypt as the khabsu tree, or tree of the star, signifying the pole. Renouf says that khabsu is the name of a tree held sacred in various places in Egypt; and according to one reading (Rit., ch. 133), the trees of paradise that breathed the refreshing air of the north were khabsu trees. If so, these were seven in number, like all other types of the heptanomis, or the stations of the pole. There is a group of the khabsu gods who were a form of the seven great spirits, on the mount of glory, and who receive the ascending spirits of the just made perfect at the summit of the hill. They are identified by name as the gods of the lamp or the light, which were seven in number in the circumpolar heaven, equivalent to the seven lamp-stands or seven-branched candlestick upon the mountain in the book of Revelation.

The seven isles of the blessed were also known as seven forms of the oasis. The lords of Thinis and Abydos bore the title of masters of the oasis (Brugsch). Thus the ruler of the pole-star would be the lord of an oasis, or later paradise. The altar-mound was also an image of the pole. And periodically the Mexicans sacrificed seven batches of children on seven hills that served for altars. The Hebrews offered seven bulls and seven rams on seven altars. The Assyrian Lu-Masi were probably represented by seven rams of sacrifice. Blood was sprinkled seven times as an oblation. Wherefore seven times? We answer, because the powers or gods propitiated thus were seven in number, and there is a consensus of evidence to prove that the seven were represented as rulers, watchers, giants, masters, ali, elohim, or lords of eternity, in the seven pole-stars of the great period of precession. The seven altars are also identified by Homer with the pole when he calls the ark-city of Mycenæ "the altars of the cyclops." Cyclops were one with the giants, which are seven in number, and thus the altars of the cyclops are equivalent to the seven mountain-altars of the Phœnicians and the Mexicans, grouped in the seven-portioned city of the ark at Mycenæ. Erech is called the city of the seven stones (or zones); and seven stones were equivalent to the seven pole-stars (*W. A. I.*, ii. 50–55–57, Sayce.) Seven sacred black stones, possibly aërolites, were the images of the seven chief gods at Uruk, the great ones or the mighties (Conder, *Heth and Moab*, pp. 209, 210). Herodotus speaks of the seven stones which the Arabians smeared with blood in making a covenant (B. 3; 8.) Naturally, the stone, as the rock of eternity, remained a permanent figure of the pole, and doubtless seven precious stones were among the types. Hence we meet with the emerald mountain, the diamond mountain, the pearl mountain, the mountain of gold, the lotus mountain, with the jewel of the pole-star at the centre or "in the lotus."

The Mexicans also worshipped a class of gods who had been turned into stone. Three of these are mentioned by name as Tohil, Avilix, and Hacavitz. And it is said of these petrified powers that they could resume a movable shape when they pleased. These gods were three in the group of seven which is so often divided into two groups of three and four each, and which are the seven rulers of the pole. Becoming petrified as stones would denote the condition in which they stood as fixed figures of the pole, and if they were figures of the pole it was known to the astronomers that all in turn would again resume a movable shape as gods of the pole-stars. The seven stones set up at Stonehenge and elsewhere represent the giants that were also petrified and changed into enormous stones. These, too, stood for the seven stations of the pole in the circuit of precession, or the circle of Sidi. Under one title "Stonehenge" was called the circle of Sidi, or the circle of seven. These are a form of the seven giants that were turned into stone, those who were the builders of the heptanomis and the supporters of the universe, and whose megalithic monuments are found as witnesses in many lands. The seven stations sank with the heptanomis of Atlantis in the great deluge of all, but the stones remained as monuments called the "stones of the deluge," and four of the seven powers survived in the new heaven that was raised upon the four-fold foundation of the celestial tetrapolis which followed. The Roman palladium that fell from heaven has its origin, not simply as an aërolite, but as a copy of the stone that was a type of the divine abode established at the pal, or pole. Palladia in various other shapes are said by Phylarcos to have been flung down from heaven during the war of the giants. These constituted the typical foundations of the heptanomis that was built on high and repeated by the mound builders of many lands and copied by those who heaped the earth or raised the stone and shaped the pillar as the palladia of the dead. The capital of Maha-Bali or Great Baal, once famous on the coast of Malabar as Maha-Bali-puram, had a name which signified "the seven pagodas." These are another equivalent to the seven arits, churches, or other groups of seven sacred structures that imaged the heptanomis according to the period and the cult. The pole of heaven, as an image of sustaining power, was also figured in the constellation of Uarit, the leg. This at one time was the leg of Nut, the cow of heaven. At another it is the leg of Ptah, at another the leg of Osiris. As the leg of Nut, it is the leg of a cow, which may be seen in the drawing from the zodiac of Denderah (fig. on p. 311) in which the milch cow and leg are blended together in one figure. This supporting power of the pole was represented by King Hop, "lord of the heavenly hosts" in an annual ceremony of the Siamese during which the lord of the heavenly hosts, as the power of the pole, stood on one foot for three hours. If he let down his foot it betokened instability to the throne, but if he stood firm he was thought to gain a victory over the forces of evil (Frazer, *Golden Bough*, vol. i. p. 230). Many mysteries that were mythical or eschatological when first acted peter out finally in popular pastimes and provincial games. The writer has collected a volume of such, but will not be able to find room for them. The game of hop-scotch is a good example of the power that could stand upon one foot as that of the pole in the heaven of seven divisions. It has been suggested that the seven courts which are chalked out on the ground in this game represent the seven planetary heavens. But this explanation was put forward by a writer entirely ignorant of the celestial heptanomis and the seven heavens or astronomes that were preplanetary (paper read at the Anthropological Institute, Nov., 1885). The seven courts thus memorized we hold to be the seven courts which are identified with the seven divisions of heaven and seven stations of the pole. The question, if any, can be determined by the symbolical act of hopping on one foot. The seven foot-prints of Buddha also denote the seven steps in precession which are a co-type equivalent to the seven stations of the pole. The writer knows of no group of seven legs, or feet, but there is a giant who strides through space as the wearer of seven-league boots. Moreover, the Ritual positively *identifies the pole with the leg* by calling it the *leg of the seven* non-setting stars.

Now the pole-star being a star that did not set, in the course of the great year there would be seven of these that never set: the seven who are the lords of eternity. These were beyond the ken of ordinary knowledge, but an object-picture could be con-stellated, as in the seven stars of the Lesser Bear. Dhruva is the Hindu name of a pole-star; it is also the name of the power divinized in Dhruva, the god, who maintained himself upon one foot motionless as a stake=pole, until the earth inclined with his weight, or the station of the pole leaned over and sank down with the declination of the star that was Polaris at the time. Thus the sustainer at the pole as a power was able to stand on one foot for the period of 3,714 years on end (*Bhagavata-Purana*, ch. viii.). There are seven mountain peaks and seven footprints, and a foot-print on the peak is the symbol of a station in precession. Thus the footprint of Buddha upon Adam's Peak in Ceylon tends to show that this was one of the seven annular mountains in the seven-fold system of Mount Meru. Also, when the Buddhist footprint is represented by the sacred horseshoe it has in one form seven gems or nails, which still preserve a figure of the seven prints on one image. Seven footprints were assigned to Abraham. These are depicted on the south side of the Sakhrah rock at Jerusalem, and were shown to Nasir-i-Khusran in the year A.D. 1047. (Pal. Pilgrim's Text Society, p. 47, 1888).

The sun, moon, and *seven* stars are frequently grouped together on the Assyrian monuments. The Chinese call the sun, moon, and seven stars the nine lights of heaven. The same grouping is observable in the nine pyramids of the Mexicans—one for the sun, one for the moon, and seven small ones for the seven stars. The three pyramids of Gizeh answer to those of the sun, moon, and seven stars elsewhere. The Great Pyramid is in itself a sign of seven, comprising, as it does, the square and the triangle in one figure. There is a tradition that the Great Pyramid was designed by the Har-seshu, or servants of Horus. These were the seven Khuti in the stellar mythology who had been the rulers in the celestial heptanomis before they became the seven servants of the solar god. The seven periods of the pole-stars were also imaged by seven eyes, in consequence of an eye being a figure of the cycle. This type is presented to Joshua in the book of Zechariah in the shape of seven eyes upon one stone: "Behold, the stone that I have set before Joshua; upon one stone are seven eyes." These are the seven eyes of the Lord; also the seven lamps, the same as in the book of Revelation (Zech. iii. 9; iv. 1–12). As a mode of measuring time and period on the colossal scale of the great year, the eye came to the full, "as at first," seven times at seven stations of the pole in the cycle of precession. As a type, the eye might be full once a month, once a quarter, once a year, once in a thousand years, in 2,155 years, 3,714 years, or, as the great eye of all, the eye of the Eternal, once in 26,000 years (Rit., chs. 140 and 144). Hence the seven eyes of the Lord in the blue stone of the firmament. The submergence of seven pole-stars involved the same number of deluges in the cycle of precession, which culminated in "the great deluge of all." Apparently this was the deluge of Manu in the Hindu version, for the Manu, whose vessel was made fast to a stupendous horn, *i.e.*, the pole, was Vaivasvata, the seventh Manu, and the seventh Manu corresponds to the great deluge of all, as the latest of seven cataclysms in the world's great year. There were seven stations to the pole in measuring the circuit of precession; consequently each type or symbol of the pole may be repeated seven times, or is finally a figure of the number seven. Thus the pole, when elevated seven times as a tree, would be represented ultimately by the typical seven trees, or by a tree with seven branches; if by the mound, the mound would be erected seven times over; if by the horn, there would be seven horns—hence the dragon with seven horns; if by the fish, there would be seven fish or fish-men, finally symbolized by the fish with seven fins, or by the crocodile Sebek, whose name as Sevekh also signified the number seven. If by the star, as stella Polaris, this would be repeated seven times and grouped as the seven stars of a typical constellation at the pole, like that of Ursa Minor or Corona Borealis. If the eye be a figure of the pole-star as direct image or as emblem of the repeating cycle fulfilled in 3,700 years, there will be seven eyes = seven stars or seven lights in the circle of precession. Seven eyes become the seven watchers, jackals, judges, urshi, or rishis; and seven lights on one stand, or a candlestick with seven branches, forms an image of the seven single pole-stars in a cluster at the pole. If the figure is a cave, there would be seven caves to the mount; if it was a hall, there would be seven halls in the great house; if a church, there would be seven churches; if a city, there would be seven cities. Other types might be enumerated in relation to the mystery of the seven stars. The great deluge of all was that by which the total heptanomis was finally submerged; "every island fled away, and the (seven) mountains were not found" (Rev. xvi. 20, 21). In this the giants, the dogs, the apes, the birds, the tortoises or turtles, and the "men" were drowned, and lost Atlantis sank beneath the waters at first as the heptanomis, and later as the heaven in ten which was succeeded by the heaven in twelve divisions.

The seven stations of the pole were likewise marked as seven mounds or seven mountains, each of which in turn was a type of the birthplace on high and an image of the Great Mother who brought forth her child upon the mount as the hippopotamus, the crocodile, the serpent, the vulture, the water-bird, or other type that was astronomical in heaven and totemic on the earth. One title of the Great Mother was "mistress of the mountain" when the mountain was the pole, and this celestial mountain was repeated seven times in the circle of precession; hence there are seven summits in one form or other, as mountains, mounds, altars, stones, menhirs, pillars, or pyramids, answering to the seven stations of the pole. There is an allusion to the seven stellar summits or mountains in one of the Assyrian hymns. Ishtar exalts her glory in several phases of phenomena. Hers was the glory from the beginning. She was the goddess of the double horizon, imaged in the glory of the morning and evening stars. As queen of heaven in the moon, her glory is said to "glow in the clouds of heaven" and to "sweep away (or efface) the mountains altogether," as the flood of moonlight might put out the stars. These mountains, therefore, were celestial; only as such could mountains be obliterated by the glory of the goddess imaging the moon.

The Japanese have the group of seven mountains, which were the seats of the gods of seven pole-stars. These are Ma-Saka-Yama, Odo Yama, Oku Yama, Kura Yama, Ha Yama, Hara Yama, and To Yama (*Kojiki*, ii, 7, 8; O'Neil, *Night of the Gods*, vol. ii. p. 892). "These," says O'Neil, "seem to be alternative mythical names for the heaven's-vault mountain." But as a figure of the heptanomis the mount of heaven's vault was also seven-fold in seven stations of the shifting pole, determined by the seven successive stars, one for each of the seven mountain summits. At the back of Shan-ling, about sixty miles west of Canton, seven isolated limestone peaks abruptly rise up from the low green plain. These are called *The Seven Stars*. They were once a favourite resort for pious people, who went there to worship at the temples and the caves (Colquhoun, A. R., *Across Chrysê*, i., 37). These also we look upon as monuments of the seven ancient pole-stars, which are identified with seven mountains in the books of Enoch and of Revelation. There were seven mountains upon which the ark of safety rested as the place of landing from the waters during the vast cycle of precession; this may explain the Armenian tradition that Noah's ark was visible at various times, first upon one mountain peak, then upon another, including Mount Baris, Urdhu, Gudi, Nizir, and Ararat. Probably there were seven altogether identified, like the seven Alban Hills, with the seven rulers of the world in their watchtowers of the celestial heptanomis. The mount, or a mount of the pole, was known as the white mountain. The Alban Hills are the white mountains. They are seven in number; and equivalent to the seven stations of the pole which were imaged by the seven mountains of the heptanomis. The Chréais or Jaray race, who inhabit the high plateau which separates Cambodia from Annam, preserve a curious commemorative custom in relation to the seven mountains. They have two mysterious monarchs, whose functions are of that mystical order which we so often find to be astronomical. The two are known as the king of fire and the king of water. They inhabit successively seven towers built upon seven mountains, and every year they pass from one tower to another, never meeting each other and never seeing a human face. The kingship lasts for seven years, and the offices are hereditary in one or two families (Frazer, *Golden Bough*, vol. i. pp. 55–56, who cites *Le Royaume du Cambodge*, by J. Moura ; also Aymonier's *Notes*). Seven forts erected on seven mountains are equivalent to the seven altars raised on seven mountains by the Mexicans. The two kings of fire and water correspond to the two different cataclysms by fire and flood, described by Berosos as happening in the course of the Great Year.

According to the missionary Gill, the Mangaians hold that the seven inhabited islands of the Hervey group are the body or outward presentment of another seven in the spirit-world of Avaiki (*Myths and Songs of the Pacific*). These correspond to the seven sunken islands of the lost Atlantis, and both are a localized earthly form of the celestial heptanomis, which sank down in the course of one Great Year. The name of Mangaia signifies peace, and Mangaia in Avaiki was the paradise of peace, like the Egyptian Hetep. This, therefore, was a form of the paradise lost in the form of seven islands sunk in the Pacific Ocean as well as in the Atlantic Ocean and other waters, which were firmamental from the first. Egypt began in the form of seven Nui, a most ancient Egyptian name for the nomes or water boundaries. And in Polynesia Nui or Rapa-nui is the native name of Easter Island, where the colossal statues left by some mysterious race of primitive builders have been found. Nui is also the name of a group of the Nui as islands = nomes, which are found as seven in number in the seven islands or islets of Onoatoa. Each one of these has its own particular name, but Onoatoa embraces the whole seven. The seven Nui as islands in a group called Onoatoa offer a parallel to the seven islands of Avaiki, with the additional fact that they have the same name as the most ancient nomes of Egypt, which were seven in number.

After the septenary of pole-stars had been identified and established in the circle of precession, six of these were ever moving with the sphere, and there was always one remaining a fixture at the centre. If we take them as representatives of the seven Manus or Buddhas, it becomes evident that the condition of the motionless or sleeping Buddha was attainable by all the six, each in turn, that moved round the stationary one ; and in the seventh stage of precession the true Buddha, the prince, the Rishi or Manu, was re-born, and his birth was indicated by the stationary star that showed the new position of the changing pole. In his visions Enoch sees the " seven splendid mountains which were all different from each other." These are described as six, with " the seventh mountain in the midst of them." In furnishing the ark of testimony according to *the pattern seen in the mount*, instructions are given for the lamp-stand to be made with six branches going out of the candlestick. But it is added, " Thou shalt make the lamps thereof seven " (Ex. xxv. 37) ; this, then, was likewise a figure of six encircling the one that was a fixture in the centre. The six stars that kept revolving whilst the seventh stood or rested on one foot are to be met with in a legend of the Ainu. " Suddenly there was a large house on the top of a hill wherein were six persons beautifully arrayed, but constantly quarrelling (always in motion). Thereupon Okikurumi (a name connected with the wheel) seized a firebrand and beat each of the six with it in turn. Whereupon the six all ran away in the shape of hares " (Chamberlain, B. H., *Memoirs of Tôkyô University*, p. 32).

It is stated in the Chow Ritual that the Chinese rules for divining were contained in three books—the Lien-shan, the Kwei-Tsang, and the Kwei-chang. The name of the first signifies " United Mountains," a title that is said to have been derived from its first mystical and divining six-fold sign Kăn (O'Neil, *The Night of the Gods*, vol. ii. p. 892). These united mountains, determined, as stated, by the six-fold sign, appear to be a form of the six which, with the seventh at the centre, marked the seven stations of the pole in the circle of precession. The Zuni Indian system of the seven mountains is the same. These consist of six mountains which are stationed round the central one. When Remus saw the flight of the six vultures he was standing on the rock of the Aventine Hill—that is, the Bird-hill, which looks as if it represented the seventh to the six stars ; the one that was stationary on the pivot of the pole, whilst the other six were moving round it with the sphere. Thus there is a central mountain and a central land to the seven mountains. One of the seven united mountains is the tree-mountain. Elsewhere we meet with the stone-mountain, the mount of the papyrus reed, the ever-white mountain whence the Korean people came, the mount of the white wall, the pearl mountain. The mount of Saturn = Sebek, in the Dragon, was one of the seven hills in Rome. A " festival of the six " is made mention of in the Ritual (ch. 136, Pap. of Nu). This occurs in a chapter for making a spirit perfect, which memorizes the birth of a god who is called the newly-born, as the lamp in Annu at the pole. He is described as a god of the rope. It is said, " He is born, he of the strong cord. His cable is complete " (ch. 136, Renouf). This we understand to be a god of the rope that was made fast at one end to the solar boat and at the other to the star Ak at the pole. The luminaries in Annu are addressed. They are the seven Khus. One of these seven is newly-born, or his star is just lighted, as god of the lamp and likewise of the rope, and the event is celebrated at " the festival of the six "—not of the *sixth*. Moreover, he is called " the Prince of the inundation." There had been a deluge, and he has turned back the water-flood which had risen over the thigh of Nut at the staircase of Seb, god of the earth.

This figure of the one at the centre of the six will enable us to explain a mystery of the cyclops. These in one version of the mythos were seven in number, therefore they are a form of the seven giants or powers of the pole-stars—the seven that were 6+1. Now, it was fabled that all the seven could see with one single eye, and the single eye we take to have been the pole-star for the time being that was fixed at the centre as the eye of the group. The mythical unicorn was another figure of the horn-point at the pole. As such it was a type of Sut, the founder of the pole. Sut being first as founder, his was the single horn. It was as the symbol of sustaining power stationed at the pole that the unicorn became a supporter with the lion of the royal arms in British heraldry. The unicorn has but one eye, and thus it became a co-type with the cyclop as a figure of the one star of the pole. The unicorn is associated with the tree, because the tree also stands for the pole. Sometimes its single horn is stuck fast in the tree, which position intensifies the figure of stability at the pole. Futile attempts have been made to show that the unicorn was an emblem of the moon. But though the lunar orb might be imaged as a single eye, it would not, could not, be represented by *a single horn*. The ancients knew the moon was double-horned when it was figured as the celestial cow. The horn is another of those figures which, being single at first, became seven-fold as types of the heptanomis. Thus there is a group of seven horns to add to the rest. This group is portrayed above the head of Sesheta, a goddess of laying the foundations, which are seven in number, as figured by means of her seven horns upon a pole.

In the heaven of the heptanomis the ancient Genetrix had seven sons. The figure is repeated in the seven sons of Japheth (Gen. ch. x.), the seven sons of the divine lady of the holy mound in Babylonia, the seven sons of Quanwon in Japan, the seven sons of Albion, the white land in the north, and various other groups of the seven on board the ark, which was earlier than the foundations that were laid in the four quarters. The heptanomis came to an end with the great deluge of all ; and in the book of Genesis the deluge of Noah is followed by the new kingdom that was reared on a four-fold foundation, the seven cities on the other side of the flood being succeeded by the cities of the four quarters built on this. When Nimrod or Gilgames became "a mighty one in the earth" "the beginning of his kingdom was Babel and Ereck and Akkad and Kalneh, in the land of Shinar," and out of that land he went forth and built four other cities in Assyria. A heaven of the four quarters had then superseded the heptanomis or heaven founded on the seven stars or astronomes, and this was the figure followed in the building of the four cities on earth.

After the great deluge of all had taken place and the inhabitants of the heptanomis generally were drowned, it was seen that the seven pole-stars kept their places in the circumpolar heaven. And thus the seven gods sat in their circle round the tree of the pole, the fixed and never-setting stars for ever safe from all the deluges of time, as the seven lords of eternity. These are the seven that were saved when all the world was drowned. The Shenin in the Ritual are a group of spirits that surround the seat of the highest. The name denotes the circle of those ministers or officials that surround the throne of the god or the king. In one text this circle is called the shenin of fire. They are the spirits of fire = the saluting apes in the circle of the eternals. Their number is not directly given, but they are the princes who elsewhere are a form of the seven great spirits that surround the throne. Now, there is a stellar enclosure or circle of stars in the northern heaven which the Chinese recognize in the region of Draco and Ursa Major. These bear the names of ministers and officers who surround the sovereign, and therefore are identical with the Egyptian circle of the shenin. This is very probably the constellation of the Northern Crown, in which the seven were grouped as a numerical figure of the pole-star circle. The circle of the seven lords of eternity was first; the throne of the highest was erected in the centre. Thus the seven as servants (seshu), khuti, uræus-gods, saluting apes or angels, spirits, or lamps of fire, are depicted round the throne of God according to the mystery of the seven stars in Revelation.

As already said, the earliest form of an enclosure in heaven called the Aarru is depicted as a field of reeds, the habitat of the water-cow, who brought forth Sut, her first-born bull, upon the summit in a field of reeds that rose above the waters at the station of the pole when this was represented by the bed of reeds. Thus the ancestral pair that were saved from the deluge by climbing up the reed-mountain, like the Navajo Indians, would derive their origin from the reed. The main significance of the reed as a symbol of the pole depends upon its being a plant that grows up through the water and flowers above the surface to present the type of an ark or station or other means of escape from the mythical water that flowed betwixt this world and the other. We have now to suggest that the seven stars of the rulers were neither in the Great Bear nor the Pleiades, but that they were the past representatives of Polaris in the cycle of precession, and to show that the mystery of the seven stars in the drama of "revelation" was a mystery of the celestial heptanomis in the astronomical mythology. As we have seen, in various myths the land enclosed in the celestial sea was lost because the woman betrayed the secret of the waters, which then burst forth and overthrew the bulwarks that had been erected by the male, who in the Egyptian mythos was her son, the founder Sut. In other legends paradise was lost by the unwatchful dog. This, as the jackal, was the dog of Sut. Thus in one case the deluge was let in by the mother, and in another by the son, who were the primal pair as founders of the pole. Whilst in some parts of the world it was the dog (as typical guide) who let in the deluge, in Fiji it was the race of men that had tails like dogs who were destroyed by the deluge. In other legends mankind were changed into dogs after one of the several deluges. The Bonaks or root-diggers said the first Indians that ever lived were coyotes or prairie-dogs. The Chichimecs of South America are the dogs by name. In Africa these would have been totemic jackals. But without going back so far in time and space as the submergence of the southern pole and the declination and disappearance of its star below the horizon for those who travelled northward, there is another origin possible for the legend of the dog. The jackal or Egyptian dog was also constellated as the guide of ways in Sothis, and as

Stella Polaris at the northern pole. As the planisphere of Denderah shows, the dog's tail in which the pole-star Cynosura shines to-day was the tail of the jackal. Twenty-six thousand years ago the position was the same. The jackal of the mythos or dog of later legend was then the watcher in the circumpolar paradise or garden of the Tree. Now, whichever zootype represented the pole-star of the period —hippopotamus, jackal, ape, bird, tortoise, or dragon (crocodile)—it might be held responsible for the loss of paradise or enclosure through letting in the waters. This would be rendered according to the mythical mode, and afterwards related in a legend or a folk-tale.

In the precessional movement the celestial pole passed out of the jackal or dog into the group of stars now called Kepheus. There were seven stations in the circle of precession, though one, as we have said, is omitted or unidentified in the diagram drawn by Piazzi Smythe, betwixt Herakles and Draconis, which we have tried to fill in with the male hippopotamus of Sut as a group of stars that included Clavis Corona, but only *as a stop-gap*. We now pass on to the Lesser Bear. In the Egyptian eschatology (Rit., ch. 44, 2–3) the jackal Ap-uat represents a power of salvation from the drowning deep. In crossing the gulf of Putrata into which the helpless dead fall headlong and the sinking stars are swallowed by the dragon, the manes says, " Ap-uat lifteth me up." This power is shown to be localized in the region of the pole by the speaker saying (after being saved by Ap-uat), " I hide myself among you, O ye stars that never set "—that is, in the circumpolar paradise at the pole, where the jackal or the dog was the guide of ways. When the pole had passed from the constellation of Ursa Minor the power of salvation would have gone from the jackal to whatsoever type might represent Kepheus, and Ap-uat the guide as Cynosura would no longer be looked up to as a deliverer from the drowning waters of the deep. Commentators on the Korân repeat the ancient traditions concerning the Adite ancestors of the Arab race. These were the giants or kings of prodigious size and stature, like the monstrous figures of the primitive constellations in the heptanomis. After the deluge these were changed into monkeys. Now the Arabs claim descent from one Kahten or Kaften the Adite, and Kaften in Egyptian is a name of the great ape that was one of the seven giants of the pole-star constellations and a zootype of Shu, whom we identify with Kepheus. It is also said in the Codex Chimalpopoca that men were transformed into monkeys as the result of a deluge or great hurricane. As the pole was figured at seven successive stations in the heptanomis, it is possible that the Navajo Deluge myth contains a time-gauge. In this it is related that when " the men of a world before our own" were warned of an approaching flood they were living in " the third world" or station of the pole, and the place of refuge which they raised against the coming deluge was in " the fourth world" or station of the pole, which, according to the present reckoning, was in the constellation of Kepheus. The turkey just escaped, although the water was close enough after him to wet the tip of his tail. Now, it happens that the next position of the pole is in the constellation of the bird cygnus, also named the hen, the kite, and other forms of ornis. Moreover, the star Alpha was called Dzeneb in Arabic, or the tail. And this, according to the present reckoning, we consider to have been the fourth world or *fourth of the seven stations of the pole.* When the pole passed from the constellation Kepheus into Cygnus the swan it would give rise to a legend like that of the Gippsland blacks, who assert that the first lot of men were turned into ducks by the wicked moon. Cygnus the swan was known as Ornis the bird, the bird of Jupiter, and also as the kite. The kite is equivalent to the hawk in Egypt, and the " kite of Osiris " is mentioned in the Ritual by the speaker, who is in the region of the glorious ones, the circumpolar gods or seven great khus. He is at the place of the balance, " which is maat," the stellar point of equipoise, otherwise at the pole. He exclaims, " Here is the cycle of the gods and the kite of Osiris " (ch. 136 B). The name of Osiris may be a later insertion, but the kite remained, and this is a name for the constellation Cygnus or the Swan, the fifth of the seven pole-stars, beginning with Corona (or its equivalent) as the first. The pole-star was in the kite some seventeen thousand years ago. And here, says the speaker who has attained the summit of the mount, " here is the cycle of the gods and the kite (= cygnus) of Osiris."

Fourteen thousand years ago Polaris was the star Vega in the constellation now known as Lyra. Vega or Wega = Waki denotes the falling one. As *vultur cadens* it was the falling vulture. The Arabic name signifies the falling eagle, An-nasz-al-waki. Now, the vulture as Egyptian can be identified with the pole and possibly as a pole-star. The leg constellation was a figure of the pole. It is mentioned in the Ritual (ch. 149, 11th Aat, line 8) as the leg of the lake, and a co-type with the tree of the lake on which the glorified spirits alighted in the form of birds, and there is a chapter in the Ritual for assuming the form of a vulture and perching on the leg, a landing-place equivalent to the pole. " I am the divine vulture," says the speaker, " who is on the leg " or the pole. And a star known as the vulture stationed on the leg of the pole must be Polaris. We see that some fourteen thousand years ago the pole was in the constellation Lyra, and the pole-star was the " falling vulture " Vega. This may have a bearing on the legend of the vulture in the Mexican tradition of the deluge. It is related of the American Noah, named Coxcox or Tezpi, that he made a bark or, still more primitively, a raft, with which he saved himself, his wife, and children from the overwhelming waters of the deluge. When the god Tezcatlipoca decreed that the waters should retire, Tezpi sent forth a vulture from the bark. The bird did not return, but stayed to feed upon the bodies of the drowned. He sent out the humming-bird, which came back with a leafy branch in its beak. Then Tezpi, seeing that land was visible and growing verdant, left his ark upon the Mount of Colhuacan. This was the mountain of the seven caves in which the seven giants or great spirits dwelt. The name denotes the mountain that leans over at the summit, as it is depicted in the Aztec documents, a picture of the pivot toppling over with the change of pole-star. If we suppose the change to have been made and the deluge to have occurred when the pole-star was shifted from *a* Cygnus to the constellation Lyra the next pole-star would be the vulture, which afterwards became the falling one. Thus the vulture indicated the new land that was growing green across the water of the deluge, the mount on which another landing-place was found ; another altar was erected, and the sacrifice was offered up upon the summit of the mount by those who had escaped the great calamity, as it was mythically represented, whether the mount might be Colhuacan, Tulan, Annu, Ararat, Nizir, or Meru. And a pole-star known as the vulture would in the course of precession become the " vulture falling " whose " fall " is chronicled in the name of *vulture cadens.* If those who followed in the wake of the Egyptians, like the Euphrateans, Greeks, and Arabs, were not always masters of the gnosis, they could at least *transliterate the ancient names* and thus bring on part of the meaning. The Arabic name for the " falling vulture " was also the " falling eagle." And in some of the legends it is the eagle that foretells the coming deluge. A myth of the Pima Indians relates that a prophet was warned by the eagle of a vast cataclysm or deluge then at hand ; but the prophet took no heed, and the waters came that overwhelmed the world. This also we might call the deluge that occurred when the pole passed from its station in Cygnus into that of the eagle or vulture. The legend of the eagle is also extant amongst the Kamilaroi of Australia, who tell of a deluge from which two human beings only made their escape by climbing up a tree. And here the deluge is attributed to Pundjel, the eagle-hawk. The tree we understand to be a figure of the pole. Williams tells us that " the highest point of Koro Island has a name connected with the idea of a bird sitting there and lamenting over the submerged island." It is said in a chant, " The quiqui laments over Koro because it is lost" (*Nat. Gen.* vol. ii. p. 241). Thus the eagle is one of the seven constellations of the pole-stars, and in the ancient British mythology the eagle is one of *the seven Welsh old ones of the world,* called the eagle of Gwernabwy, who perched upon the rock he found there, pecking every evening at the stars. There he is said to have remained until the rock was worn down to the height of a man's palm. Such legends we suggest originated when the rock of the pole was in the constellation of the Eagle, which represented one of the old ones of the seven pole-stars or rulers of the pole. The earth is sometimes described as having been created on the back of a tortoise, and when the tortoise sank in the water there was an overwhelming deluge. A Mandan medicine-man told Catlin that the earth was a tortoise carrying dirt upon its back (*Nat. Gen.* vol. ii. p. 195). The mother of beginnings is portrayed in a legend of the Tuscarora Indians as an *enceinte* female in labour == Apt the pregnant hippopotamus goddess, who sank from an upper region and was received on the back of a tortoise which had a little earth upon its back, and this became an island upon which she bore twin sons, who correspond to the Egyptian Sut and Horus, and then passed away. The tortoise was a zootype of the earth itself amidst the waters of space, which was repeated as a figure of land or the landing-place in the heavens at the pole. It was once an Egyptian sign of the balance or scales in the zodiac at the point of equipoise where the land emerged from the deluge of the Nile. The tortoise was likewise a type of the constellation Lyra, in which the star Vega was the Stella Polaris fourteen thousand years ago (W. H. Higgins, *Stars and Constellations*, pp. 22, 23). In the signs of the North American Indians a landing after a voyage is typified by a tortoise. Those who found safety from the deluge on the turtle's back or on the tortoise would reckon their descent from the mountain of the pole when it was stationed in the constellation of the Tortoise or Lyra. Thus the Delaware Indians gave precedence to their turtle clan because it descended from the great *original tortoise*, not from any common turtle. The Iroquois turtle clan are likewise descended from a great fat turtle which threw off its shell and gradually developed into a man. This is exactly what did occur when the tortoise Lyra sank in the waters or the turtles were drowned, and the typical man was created at the next station of the pole. If we suppose the end of the period to have come for the pole to move out of Cygnus into the constellation Lyra or the Tortoise, the next landing-stage in the course of precession, the end was with the submergence of the pole-star or a deluge; and those who escaped from drowning when this station of the pole in Cygnus went under naturally sought a place of safety on the back of the tortoise or its co-type the turtle. Evidently this was what did occur when the deluge took place in the myth of Manabozho. The deluge was let in by the "black serpent monster," the representative of evil in physical phenomena. "At the island of the turtle or tortoise was Manabozho, the grandfather of men and beings." As he was born creeping, he is "ready to move and dwell in turtle land." Then "the men and beings" all go forth together "on the flood of waters, moving afloat everywhere seeking the back of the turtle." "All together on the back of the turtle then, the men were altogether. Much frightened, Manabozho prayed to the turtle that he would make all well again. Then the waters ran off: it was dry on mount and plain, and the great evil went elsewhere by the path of the cave." (*Nat. Gen.* vol. ii. pp. 180, 181.) According to the Mexican version, there were seven caves in the celestial mount, which answer to the seven stations of the pole. One of these was the cave of the turtle. In another account that was preserved in pictographs it is the turtles that declare war on Manabozho and produce the deluge. Manabozho first carried his grandmother to the summit of a lofty mountain. He himself climbed to the top of the tallest pine tree and waited until the waters had subsided. Then he created an island which supported him and became the new world. This was the new station of the pole, and the tallest pine was the tree of the pole that was planted or re-erected in heaven when the flood was over. One of the most striking survivals is that of the tortoise and its legend connected with the deluge in the religious ceremonies of the Indians. They say, "The world was once a great tortoise, borne on the waters and covered with earth. One day a tribe of white men had made holes in the earth to a great depth whilst digging for badgers; at length they pierced the shell of the tortoise, and it sank." The deluge followed, and drowned all the men but one, who saved himself in a boat, and when the earth re-emerged, he sent out a dove which returned to him with a branch of willow in its beak. The tortoise was a Mandan image of the ark in which people were preserved from the waters at the time of the deluge. That is, according to the ancient wisdom, when the pole was resting in the constellation of the Tortoise, after the deluge that drowned the land and submerged the mount in Cygnus or the Swan. There is no hint of the turtle in the planisphere, but the turtle and tortoise are equivalent and interchangeable types, and there is a tortoise in the heavens. The Arabic name of the constellation Lyra is the Tortoise, and but for the shell of the tortoise there would have been no Lyre. Some sixteen or seventeen thousand years ago the celestial pole passed out of the constellation Cygnus or bird, and a new guide-star was established as Vega in Lyra. In other words, when Cygnus sank the tortoise or the turtle offered its broad back for a landing place amid the waters of the deluge. Other of the American Indian tribes claim that their primeval home was in the old turtle land = the island of the tortoise. The Lenni-Lenape or Delaware Indians sing the song of the flood. In this it is related that the Being born creeping and the men all went forth from the deluge swimming afloat in the deep or crawling in the shallow water. Taking refuge on the back of the turtle or tortoise, when read astronomically according to the movement in precession, agrees with the passage of the pole out of Cygnus into the constellation of the Tortoise.

The Samoans tell a tale of the woman and child who were transformed, and afterwards came to the people of the village, when called for, in the shape of turtles (Turner, *Samoa*, p. 108). This is a cotype with the tortoise ; and when the pole passed from the sign of Cygnus, the new-born child would be brought forth by the old mother in the shape of a tortoise or a turtle, in accordance with the mythical mode of re-peopling the planisphere. Thus the primal pair would be said to have been changed into turtles, as the folk that dated from the period when the pole was in the tortoise or turtle and who were affiliated to the power above, the " big brother," the tortoise or turtle that never died, as the totemic tortoises. The "great original," whether of the turtles or hippopotami, crocodiles or jackals, apes or vultures, and finally of men, was configurated in the heavens on one or other of the mountains or islands that represented the seven stations, nomes, or seven heavens of the pole in the celestial heptanomis. The Hindu drawings (Moor's *Hindu Pantheon*, Pl. 49) show a form of the pole or central conical peak that rests upon the tortoise, which, as here interpreted, denotes the pole-star in the constellation Lyra, that was otherwise known as the Tortoise. The tortoise supporting the pole in the shape of a tree = mount or island standing in the water is also a Japanese figure of the sustaining power at the pole. In the temple of Meaco there is a Japanese representation of a tortoise in the water at the bottom of a tank or artificial well, with a tree springing up from the back of the tortoise. Thus the abyss of the waters, the earth at the bottom of the abyss, and the tree of the pole are uniquely imaged in one picture.

There was a tortoise-headed god in Egypt who has left his likeness in the tombs, but nothing else is known of him. The animal itself was a type of immobility, therefore of sloth or fixity, as a representative of the pole. In a Chinese myth the island of Pung-Lai was brought one day in all its mass by the tortoise. A tortoise or turtle appearing from the waters of earth was appropriate, as it was primitive to image the bit of land emerging from the waters of the firmament. This, however, was the mythical not cosmical earth that was supported by the tortoise amid the waters. ⸝The tortoise beneath the tree or the mound shows it was not our earth that is supposed to rest or to have been formed upon its back in the beginning. It is possible for the tortoise or turtle as a type of the earth itself to get mixed up in the irresponsible legends with the tortoise or turtle as an astronomical figure. Still the earth, as turtle, never was submerged by the mythical deluge, whereas the tortoise or turtle that was a type of station in the celestial water did sink down when that particular station of the pole was overwhelmed.

Some fourteen thousand years ago the pole in Lyra or the Tortoise corresponded to the vernal equinox in Leo. This is probably connoted in a plate of Lajard's *Mithra*, where the zodiacal lion is found with the star Radiatartakhu or Lammergeier = Vega as Polaris in Lyra (Pl. 56, 3).

An instructive example of the way in which the astronomical mythos may dislimn and lose its shape in later legend is apparent in the curious narrative found on a cuneiform tablet in the British Museum. This has been called "the revolt in heaven" which occurred at some time *before* the creation of man. The angelic host had previously existed in a state of perfect harmony. "The god of holy songs, lord of religion and worship, had seated a thousand singers and musicians, and established a choral band who to this hymn were to respond in multitude." "The divine being, god of the bright crown, spoke three times the commencement of a psalm. With a loud cry of contempt they broke up his holy song, spoiling, confounding his hymn of praise." Then the god of the bright crown "stopped their service, and sent them to the gods who were his enemies" and prohibited their return. "*In their room he created mankind.*" This is a legend of the angels so called who fell from heaven, and of whom it is said in the book of Jude, "They kept not their own habitations" (Jude vi). These in the book of Enoch are the seven stars which transgressed the commandment of God and came not in their proper season; and therefore they were bound and cast out until the time of the last judgment (Enoch, xviii. xxi. xxii). It is said in the cuneiform ,text, "May the god of divine speech expel from his five thousand those who in the midst of his heavenly song had shouted evil blasphemies," and the translator argues that there were but five thousand. But another reading is possible. There may have been six thousand altogether. For instance, in the Cuthean story of creation there is an allusion to another legend of the seven powers. It is said the progeny of Tiamat "grew up in the midst of the mountains and became heroes and increased in number." "Seven kings who were brethren appeared as begetters. *Six thousand in number were their armies*" (col. 1), and these we take to have included the five thousand loyal angels, "his five thousand" from whom the rebel thousand are to be excluded thenceforth and for ever as the sixth thousand. It is said of the god Ashur that he had seen the malice of those gods who deserted their allegiance to raise a rebellion, and "he refused to go forth with them." In one character Ashur is known to have been a representative of the pole; and according to the present interpretation he was the god of the coming pole-star, the seventh in our reckoning, the one that had not fallen away from the true pole. This would apply if Ashur at the time was a representative of the seventh polar power, the one that remained true whilst one thousand of the six thousand had risen in rebellion. As we interpret the mythos, the choral band who sang the hymn of praise, one thousand in number, are the sixth thousand of the six thousand corresponding to the sixth of the seven stars or stations in precession. At the time of the change from the sixth pole-star to the seventh the revolt of the thousand that was sixth in the series coincided with the falling away of the sixth star from the true eternal pole. Ashur as the seventh remained the god seven, who is re-born as the child considered to be the eighth; he refused to go forth with the one thousand of the past pole-star. And now follows the statement, "In their room, he, the god of the bright crown (*i.e.* the solar deity), created mankind." This, the seventh creation, we associate with the passage of the pole into the constellation Herakles, or *the Man*. The "lyre" imaged in the constellation Lyra had been fashioned from the muscles torn from Sut by Horus during the war in heaven. Thus the condition of harmony represented by the lyre, harp, or lute corresponds to the avocations of the thousand who are expelled from companionship with the other five thousand and who are described as "a thousand singers and musicians." These we now suggest were the denizens of "Lyra," whose lapse in allegiance is attributable to the falling away of the pole-star when the pole was passing out of that constellation into the sign of Herakles in which occurred *the creation of man.* It is a saying of Orpheus, reported by Plato, that "*in the sixth creation closes the order of song*" (Plato, *Philebus*, 66). That is, according to the present reckoning, when the pole passed out of the constellation Lyra into Herakles or the Man.

In the Bundahish, the deluge or *a* deluge takes place in heaven before the creation of man on earth. This saying can be read for the first time on the theory that man was the latest of seven creations, and that the man figured in heaven was the seventh in the series as a ruler of the pole and pole-star. Thus interpreted, there had been six deluges prior to the creation of man. Both in the book of Genesis and in the Bundahish the prototypal pair are created "man." Ahura-Mazda says to Mashya and Mashyoi, "You are man." "You are the ancestry of the world." They were now the ancestors with a human soul instead of the earlier elemental soul of life in water, air, earth, heat, plant, or animal; otherwise stated, the descent was now traced to the divine man or father in heaven instead of to Seb the god of earth, who was the representative of vegetation, and the gnosis was now applied on the scale of the Great Year. The Tlascatans say that after their deluge those who had been previously changed into monkeys were afterwards transformed into men. Now, if the hypothesis here put forth holds good, that the six zootypes and one human being were set in the circle of precession, it follows that at the time the pole passed into the constellation of Herakles or "the Man," the deluge took place when the tortoises, the apes, and other forms of the zootypes were transformed into human beings. This would correspond perfectly to the seventh creation in the later legends, which was the creation of mankind.

If we take the oldest record in the world, the Egyptian, we shall find that in the mythology the creation of man was the latest. Amongst the seven primordial powers one alone is human. In the constellation-figures man is scarcely to be found. Not until the time of Seb was the producing power of earth portrayed as male. Not until the time of Atum-Ra is the divinity impersonated in the form of a perfect man. Earth had been hugely imaged as a pregnant hippopotamus, a sow as the suckler, a goose that laid the egg for food, a sloughing serpent that was an image of self-renewal, but not by man as the measure of all things, including the elemental forces and powers of external nature. And not until the image of man had been adopted as a type of divinity in place of the totemic zootypes could men have traced their descent from man in the mythology. This occurs in Egypt when the hippopotamus of Sut, the crocodile of Sebek, the lion of Shu, the ibis of Taht, the beetle of Ptah were followed by the human likeness that was perfected and divinized in Tum or Atum, the original of Adam. In the Egyptian language the word tum signifies man, mankind, created man. The Egyptians also called themselves the Ruti, or the men ; the race *par excellence*, in contradistinction to the bulls, lions, crocodiles, serpents, apes, jackals, hawks, and other of the zootypes in totemism. They had attained this stage at the beginning of monumental times. Man, the human being, was pre-eminently the creation of Atum-Ra, the father-god. Various names of races signify man, or the men. The name of the Inoit, the Ainu, and other primitive folk means man, or the men. Descent from woman under the matriarchate had been represented by the zootypes, and when the fatherhood was individualized the human descent was from man. The birthland of man on high was figured astronomically as the island or nome or bit of earth, which was a station of the pole-star in the constellation of Herakles or the Man, from thirteen thousand to eleven thousand years ago, at the end of which time the great deluge caused the destruction of *mankind.* Instead of the races that were imaged by pre-human and totemic types, the tortoises, the apes, the birds, the dogs, it was now "*the men*" who were drowned in the last great deluge of all, when the pole-star in the Man or Herakles went under.

It is stated in the Chimalpopoca MS. that the creator produced his work in successive epochs, man being made from the dust of earth *on the seventh day.* Here again man is created or comes into existence in the last of seven periods, whatsoever the length of time or significance assigned to the cycle, which is one day in the book of Genesis and three thousand seven hundred and fourteen years in the astronomical mythology. In all the versions of the seven creations that of man was last. This is repeated when the mount or island of man is last of the celestial seven stations in the heptanomis. Now we can say the final word concerning "the destruction of mankind" in the great deluge of all, which put an end to the heaven in seven divisions that preceded the eight, the nine, the ten, and the twelve. At the ending in time when Vega in Lyra (the vulture or tortoise) ceased to be the pole-star, there was a deluge and subsidence of land at the pole and a change of star. The races drowned in this and previous deluges were totemic, therefore pre-human, therefore the predecessors of man in the astronomical mythology, the märchen, and legendary lore. Six races had been destroyed in half-a-dozen deluges before it came to the "destruction of mankind" that was memorized and mythically rendered in the Egyptian deluge when the pole-star was washed under in the constellation of the Man, the one of seven mighties, now for the first time in the human form. This is the one star group in all the heavens that was figured as "the man," the last of the seven rulers of the pole, corresponding at this point to the attainment of the human image in the last of seven so-called creations, which is that of Adam = Atum in the zodiac just where the Sekhet-Aarru or garden of Eden has been localized in the solar, which followed and completed the lunar and stellar mythos. Thus we can roughly trace the point at which the last of seven pole-stars coincided with the creation of man in heaven which was succeeded by the creation of Atum = Adam (or man) at the point of a new beginning in the zodiac. Such types of the pole-stars as the tortoise or vulture (in Lyra), the swan, the lesser bear (or jackal and the dragon), were figures of those creations which preceded that of the man who was mythical and astronomical. The Samoans relate that Tangaloa was the originator of men. He is their god in the height, or the eighth heaven. As a primitive way of saying how plucky he was and of showing how the eight powers, seven plus one, were all combined in him, he is called "eight-livered Tangaloa." A temple was built for him and termed the house of the gods, which was carefully shut up all round, and therefore is equivalent to Am-Khemen, the Egyptian enclosure of the eight great gods. These characteristics identify Tangaloa as deity of the pole and as eighth to the seven earlier powers. Now Tangaloa is said to have come over the ocean with a crew of seven others in a canoe, and to have taken up his abode in the bush inland of the settlement. Here the migration is the same as that of the $7 + 1$ Kami, the $7 + 1$ Kabari, the $7 + 1$ Toltecs, the $7 + 1$ with Arthur in the ark. The migration in each instance is purely mythical, and the data are simply astronomical. Lastly, *descent* from the mount or mound, the tree or the papyrus-reed, the enclosure or paradise of the pole, was followed in the Semitic versions of the deluge legends by a descent of the human race from the ark which was stranded on the mountain top of Nizir or Ararat. The ark of Nnu had then been built to float upon the waters of the firmament and to be figured in the ascending stars of Argo-Navis. This is the ark with eight on board, four females and four males, which was indefinitely later than the boat of the Mexican primal pair or the papyrus-reed of the four brothers in Egypt.

When the seventh station of the pole subsided, the seventh island of Atlantis sank, and all the seven were reckoned then to be over-thrown in the celestial waters. Under the other figure of the mount, the seven mountains now were totally submerged. This complete catastrophe is described by Enoch, who identifies the seven mountains with the seven stars and the seven great spirits. He likewise gives the reason for their overthrowal. "I beheld seven stars, like great blazing mountains, and like spirits (the Khamite khus are spirits), entreating me." The stars are those which "came not in their proper season" (ch. 18). Again, "I beheld seven stars of heaven bound together like great mountains" (ch. 21, 3). Their crime is that they "transgressed the commandment of the most high." Therefore they are bound until the time of the great judgment and the consummation or end of all things, which we shall find particularly recorded in the book of Revelation. From thirteen thousand to eleven thousand years ago the vernal equinox was passing through the Lion sign. *Pari passu* in the movement of precession, the north celestial pole was leaving its station in Lyra, or the tortoise, and passing into the sign of Herakles or the Man. Thus the creation of man or Atum in the zodiac can be partially paralleled in the cycle of precession at a certain station of the pole in the constellation of the heavenly man, who is Atum or Adam in the astronomical mythology. All the conjunctions, the mythical characters, the scenery of this beginning—the Great Bear, sun, moon, and seven stars, together with the inundation—met in that sign and were constituted a fixture for two thousand one hundred and fifty-five years.

Ten thousand seven hundred and seventy-five years ago the equinox began to move out of the Lion sign into that of the Crab, and then and there a legendary catastrophe occurred. This was the conclusion of an astronomical period which, like the year in Egypt, ended with a deluge. It occurred eight thousand two hundred and seventy-five years before the date of the conversation in Egypt betwixt Solon and the Hir-Seshta, and seven hundred and thirty-five years short of the nine thousand, but near enough when we are dealing with round numbers. The astronomical facts were so well known that in speaking of the inundation at the end of the cycle it was foretold that the "deluge would take place when the heart of the Lion entered the first minute of the Crab's head at the declination of the star"—that is, the star Regulus, the law-giver, in the Lion sign. At this point of readjustment the great deluge of all was marked by the submergence of the last of the seven pole-stars in "the Man" just when the shifting of the pole coincided with a deluge as a typical ending in the solar zodiac. For when the heaven of Atum-Ra was established on the four corners, the typical ending previously marked by the changing pole-stars was duplicated in the zodiac by the precession of the equinoxes, and both went on together in two modes of measuring the movement. As the type of an ending in time, a mythical deluge occurred when a pole-star was submerged in the celestial waters, and the great deluge of all took place at the end of the cycle in precession called the Great Year of the World. It was mythic-ally rendered as the sinking of Atlantis in seven islands which represented the seven astronomes in the celestial heptanomis. The last " great deluge of all " is the subject of the story told to Solon by the priests of Sais. Of this, and the conflagration that was caused by the fall of Phaethon, they sagely said, " This takes the form of a myth, but in reality it signifies a declination of the bodies moving round the earth in the heavens." The astronomers knew that the deluge was mythical and the myth was astronomical, whether the end of the particular period was represented by fire or by flood. Moreover, this greatest deluge can be approximately dated. Plato's account of what the priests of Egypt said to Solon identifies the "*great deluge of all*" as having occurred *about* nine thousand years before that time—*i.e.* about 9600 B.C., or eleven thousand five hundred years ago. That date was given by the Egyptian priests with particular precision. They said the city of Sais had been founded eight thousand years before the time when Solon was in Egypt. After carefully examining their sacred registers, they told him that the city of Sais was eight thousand years old, and that it was founded a thousand years after the cataclysm called the "great deluge of all." In their account we get to the bottom of the " lost Atlantis." According to the present diagnosis, then, the primary pole-star in the northern heaven may be *Clava Coronae*, the key of the crown, when this was in the enormous constellation of *the male hippopotamus*—that is, of Sut, the first-born of the female hippopotamus. Polaris in its second form was the star Alpha in the Dragon. The third station was in the Lesser Bear, the fourth in Kepheus, the fifth in Cygnus the Swan, the sixth in Lyra or the Tortoise, the seventh in Herakles or Man. Each of these in turn had been a station of the pole, a landing-place for foothold in the firmamental waters ; each had been the sufferer from a deluge at the declination of the pole and consequent change of pole-star. Hence the number of deluge legends in the astronomical mythology, including " the great deluge of all " as the last of the seven. If we take the length of the Great Year in round numbers at twenty-six thousand years, and divide the total into seven equal parts, this gives some three thousand seven hundred and fourteen years as the time for the pole to rest in each of the seven signs. Six thousand years ago the pole-star was in Draconis. Three thousand seven hundred and fourteen years earlier the pole had entered the Hippopotamus (or Crown), and three thousand seven hundred and fourteen years earlier still it was in the constellation of Herakles or the Man. Thus, eleven thousand four hundred and

4,000
3,714
3,714
———
11,428

twenty-eight years B.C. the pole was represented by the last of the seven pole-stars in the constellation of the Man. The end of the Great Year determined by the great deluge of all then occurred in that sign, according to the Egyptian account, about 9600 B.C., or nine thousand in round numbers, with various surpluses to be added in the total reckoning. Naturally, the deluge that destroyed mankind instead of the totemic tortoises, jackals and dogs, vultures and swans, apes, crocodiles and hippopotami, occurred when the pole was in or was passing from the isle of the Man. Thenceforth the deluge would be looked on as a literal destruction of *the human race*, and was so construed in the Semitic legends, as it still is by the Christian clergy. This is but the rough sketch of a pioneering pen. Greater exactitude in dates must be left to the scientific astronomer who may have mastered the mythology. My suggestion is that one Great Year in the circle of precession was reckoned to have been ended with the passing of the pole from the constellation of Herakles eleven thousand years ago, which is near as need be, for the present purpose, to the time assigned by the Egyptian priests for the sinking of the lost Atlantis in the last great deluge of all.

Now, the human birthplace had been localized according to the different stations of the pole, which were seven in number altogether. There were seven countries, nomes, or cities, determined by the pole-stars. Each race claims a particular place for a starting point in the migration from the mount, or the tree, or the back of the tortoise, and various races have preserved some fragments of the stories told about the wanderings and migrations from one land to another, as in the legends of the North American Indians, the Aztecs, and the Arunta of Central Australia. The so-called "primitive cradle of the human race in Ararat or Urdhu, the district of the mountain of the world" (*Trans. Society Bib. Archaeology*, vol. vi. p. 535), had its prototype in the planisphere and the birthplace at the pole. Ararat is but one form of the mythical mount. We derive the name from the Egyptian root "rat," which signifies the ascent, the steps of ascent, the footstool, the figure of ascent. In the developed form, Arrut or Ararat also denotes the staircase or steps of ascent, which is the mount of seven steps, or the staircase = the mount. In one form the ark of Ararat was the circumpolar paradise ; in another it is the eternal city, like Thebes, which is called the "august staircase of the beginning of time, the utat of the universal lord" which led up to the particular region where the Eye was then at full as the figure of a period in precession. When the pole had passed into the sign of Herakles the Man, the typical mount which had been figured in the Hippopotamus, in Draconis, in the Lesser Bear, in Kepheus, in Cygnus, and in the Tortoise naturally became "*the mountain of mankind*" by name. This was the birthplace of the human race who descended from Atum, Admu, or Adam as the man, and eventually the men who descended from "the mountain of mankind."

The giant with his staff who figures in the popular pastimes is probably a survival of Herakles with his club, as one of those old giants that imaged the sustaining power of the pole, the last of whom was in the likeness of a mighty man.

The mount, as a point of emergence from the waters, is looked up to and addressed by the manes in the Ritual (ch. 42) at the coming forth from Amenta. It is called "*the pedestal of the gods,*" "*the land of the white crown,*" and "*the land of the rod or staff*" = pole. That this is the land (Rit., ch. 42) of the celestial pole, the mount, or the tree is proved by the vignette in which the deceased is drawing a cord around the tat emblem of stability, which is another figure of the pole to which he clings for safety in the waters.

The mount of migration from which the various races claim to have descended, like the Aztecs from the island-mountain Colhuacan, is finally the pole which had seven starting-points and stations in the circuit of precession. According to a Norse legend, the land of the immortals was to the north· of Finland, in the neighbourhood of the White Sea. That, however, does not signify the original home and birthplace of an Aryan race in Europe. It is but a local representation of the paradise in the northern heaven and the white water of the Milky Way or sea of solar light. The mythical birthplace on the mount of heaven for the people of the pole will explain how it was that the ancient Britons could claim that they were emigrants from Troy. In the true tradition this would mean the celestial, not the mundane Troy—the Troy that is still figured by seven circles cut in the sod by children in Wales. Troy was one of the forms of the enclosure on the summit, in the astronomical mythology which was Terui in Egyptian as a name of Sesennu. It is a common tradition that the human birthplace was in paradise, and the descent from thence has been misrepresented as the fall from heaven. This in the astronomical mythology was the enclosure of the circumpolar Aarru around the tree upon the summit of the stellar mount, descent from which was from the mountain, or one of the seven mountains, of the pole. One most fertile source of confusion has been the result of the mythical legends having been converted into ethnical traditions. This birthplace above belonged to the astronomical mythology, and it has been converted into the human birthplace on the mountain and high places of our earth by the human child being laid in the cradle of the beginnings that were not human. That is, by the astronomical tradition being made ethnical, the polar paradise being made geographical. Thus, the descent from the circumpolar paradise in the astronomical mythology has been the cause of a wild-goose chase in search of man's lost heaven at the North Pole of the earth, by the usual literalizing of the legend in its Hebrew guise. The mount from which the different races claim descent has been sufficiently identified as the astronomical mountain of the north, the mount of paradise, the one fixed point for landing at, or launching from, the summit of the pole. This also is the Babylonian "mountain of the nations." The Babylonians at first were mound-builders. The mount of heaven was imitated in the mound, the holy mound called the mound of Anu and Nebo and Ishtar. Afterwards they built the tower of Babilu, and the temple called Kharsag-Kalama, the "mount of the nations." This shows that the name of the astronomical mount was given to the building that was afterwards reared above the mound. The "mount of the nations" was the mount of a starting-point, and of the divisions or ways in the heavens which we now trace to the station of Polaris in Herakles. The starting-point of the Aztec migration is from the mythical one-tree-hill of the pole. According to the picture-writing, both mount and tree are combined in one figure. In the Boturini and Gamelli Careri copies the mount of earth is portrayed with the tree upon the summit. The tree on the mount (a teocallis) is very rudely represented in the Aztec picture-writing as the starting-point of the migration by water from the mount in the beginning. From this point also the seven Toltecs commenced their wanderings in a boat, like the seven Hohgates, the seven Ali, Ari or Kabari, the seven

S S

dwarf sons of Pinga, and other forms of the seven in the celestial heptanomis.

The point of departure for the mythical migration is made ethnical in the märchen. The Navajo Indians derive their origin from the top of the divine mountain in the north, where the pole is represented in their mythology by the great reed which saved their progenitors from the waters of the deluge in the region of the stars which never set (Matthews, "The Navajo Mythology," *American Antiquarian,* 1883, p. 208). The Ainus descended from the region of the bears, which was at the summit of the very lofty mountains in the north—that is, at the pole. They likewise claim to derive their origin from the bear as their mother and the dog as their father, which can be read astronomically. The she-bear took the place of the female hippopotamus, the original great mother of the Egyptians, whose constellation was the Great Bear. The dog represents the earlier jackal, the zootype of Sut or Anup, as Apuat the guide of ways. The jackal = the dog in the planisphere of Denderah still remains a figure of the pole. One of the mythical Chinese emperors, Hwang-ti, was born in the bear-country and inherited the bear, the original type of which, as male, was the hippopotamus of Sut, the first deity of a pole-star. Hwang-ti was the first celestial builder, the first to construct an astronomical instrument. He is said to have been the inventor of wheeled carts; hence his name of Hien Yuan. Now Sut, in the male hippopotamus, as already explained, was the primal power of the pole-star; he was the inventor of astronomy, and first of the seven who heaped the mound and made his seat upon it. He was the first of all the star-gods, and was the fixed one at the centre of the revolution or hub of the wheel, and therefore the inventor of the wheel. The Dyak chief whose name denoted "the bear of heaven" may be claimed to have been a descendant from the celestial bear, whose title was consequently astronomical and not simply totemic (Brooke, C., *Ten Years in Sarawak*, vol. i. 189). The bear and wolf clans of the Iroquois descend from the primal pair who were represented by the great bear as mother and the jackal = wolf or prairie-dog as her son and consort. The types of totemism had attained to a celestial setting in the astronomical mythology. They were no longer merely of the earth, but also represented the "big brothers" in the sky, from whom descent was claimed by the totemic groups. These were the bear that lived again in future food, the serpent that renewed itself, the panes bird that never died, the turtle of eternity, and other types of superhuman powers that were constellated round the pole of heaven. Thence came the races that descended from their stations in the mount, or from the circumpolar paradise, as the bears (or hippopotami) and crocodiles, the jackals (or dogs) and apes, the swans and tortoises, each from the mount according to the period. In Greece the Meropes were the people of the thigh, and the thigh or leg of heaven was a figure of the pole: thus the birthplace of a stellar race was figured in the meshken of the "thigh," the group of stars now represented in the northern heaven by the lady of the seat or chair in the constellation Cassiopeia. One title of the pole was the Mount of the Khuti, or Mount Khuti. Thence the Khuti or Guti would supply a race-name of lofty lineage for those who dated their descent from Mount Khuti. The Egyptian Khuti came to be looked upon as seven divine ancestors who did not originate as spirits of human beings, but were the ancestors of Ra. Now there is a Mount Gudi = Khuti in the north-east of Babylonia, and an ancient widely-spread tradition affirms that when the deluge was over the ark of Noah rested on this mount. The name is obviously one with that of the Guti or Khuti of the tablets; whence the gutim and the Hebrew goim as a name for mankind, and also for the mountain of mankind. Again, Mount Shennu is another title of the pole as the mount of the Shennin, who were spirits or gods of the highest order, and who might be called the upper seven, from whom we should derive the Japanese and Chinese Shin and Shintu gods, which were originally seven, as were the Shennin round the pole or mount of the Most High in Egypt. Various difficulties that have been felt regarding the other world of Homer can be met and vanquished when we know from whence the system of Greek mythology was derived. The double paradise, one in the subterranean Amenta and one in the celestial garden of the gods, will explain the duality of the Homeric other world. Hades proper, like Amenta is beneath the earth; the happy other world of the dead is across the " divine sea " or okeanos, the celestial water of the Kamite Nun. Hesiod in the Theogony describes the Greek Tartarus as being " in a recess of earth having broad ways," which can be identified with the dark parts of Amenta. The mount of the immortals called Olympus is one with Mount Hetep in the Egyptian representation. Hence the Kimmerians of Homer may be derived from the Egyptian Khemi or Akhemu, the dwellers in the northern heaven, whether as never-setting stars or spirits of the glorified—that is, the Khuti. The city of the Kimmerians in the north is described as being covered with shadow and vapour. The sun does not behold them when he goes toward the starry heaven, nor when he turns back again from heaven to earth. It is always night in the land of the Kimmeroi. It was after sunset that the vessel reached the extreme boundary where stood the city of the Kimmerians (*Odyssey*, books 11 and 12). The Akhemu are the souls of the dead, or the never-setting stars that circle round about the northern pole of heaven, but not in the arctic regions of the earth nor on the horizon of the north. The dead were those who voyaged in the bark of heaven for the city of the Akhemu at the summit of the pole. When the Osiris deceased has attained the summit at the head of Aarru, he exclaims, " I stand erect in the bark which the god is piloting . . . and the Akhemu (stars or spirits) open to me, and my fellow-citizens present to me the sacred cakes with flesh " (Rit., ch. 98). In another chapter the speaker says, " I arrive at my own city." This was the city of the glorious ones who had risen to the region of the Akhemu-Seku or never-setting stars. And this, it has now to be suggested, was the city of the mythical Kimmeroi. The voyage was the same in the Greek, the Irish, or Assyrian legends as in the Egyptian astro-mythos. And as the Khemi or Akhemu were the northerners in this polar sense, the same origin may well account for the people of the north, in Chaldea, Japan, or Britain, being named the Kami, the Gimmeroi, or the Kymry, who derived their northern name on earth from that celestial birthplace in the northern heaven. Lastly, the dragon-mound was known to the Druids as a type in the astronomical mythology. Thence came the Dracontiae and the serpent-mounds of Britain, which, it may be feasibly inferred, were heaped up as images of the pole and its station when *a* Draconis became the pole-star about 4,000 years B.C.

THE EXODUS FROM EGYPT AND THE DESERT OF AMENTA

Book X

WHEN roughly classified, the myths and legends generally show two points of departure for the migrations of the human race, as these were rendered in the stellar and solar mythology. One is from the summit of the celestial mount, the other from the hollow under-world beneath the mount or inside the earth. The races that descended from the mount were people of the pole whose starting-point in reckoning time was from one or other station of the pole-star, determinable by its type, whether as the tree, the rock, or other image of a first point of departure. Those who ascended from the nether-world were of the solar race who came into existence with the sun as it is represented in the legendary lore, that is, when the solar mythos was established. The tradition of the pole-star people found in various countries is that they were born when no sun or moon as yet had come into existence. That is, they were pre-solar and pre-lunar in their reckoning of time. These are they, as was said by the Egyptians, who issued from the eye of Sut, or Darkness, the earliest type of which we reckon to have been Polaris, whether as the pole-star in the southern or the northern heaven. These were the Nahsi and the Blackheads of the dim beginnings in the stellar mythology. Following them, come the people born from the eye of Horus, which was a symbol of the moon. These were held to be the lunar race. Lastly came the children of the sun. Thus, the eye as symbol of a repeating period was *stellar as the eye of Sut*; it was *lunar as the eye of Horus*; it was *solar as the eye of Ra*. In the stellar mythos men descended from the summit of the mount, which was an image of the pole. And still in legendary lore they try to tell us from which of the seven stations they descended as a time-gauge in the pre-historic reckoning of their beginnings. But in the solar mythos they *ascended* from the under-world which had been hollowed out beneath the mount of earth for the passage of the sun. Thus there are two points of departure in the astronomical mythography, one from above and one from below. The oldest races that have kept the reckonings are descended from one or other of the seven stations in the mountain of the north, and in the later mythos men ascended from the earth below, or from below the earth; the human ascent being figured in the upward pathway of the sun. These were the solar race who followed the lunar and stellar people of the past. These, when born in Egypt, were the children of the sun-god Atum, who became the Hebrew Adam as the father of the human race.

Before Amenta was created by the excavator Ptah within the nether earth there was no typical *ascent* of man. Indeed there were no men until the time of Tum, since which time the race has been considered human. When the sun-god Ra arose up from the earth, or from the Lotus, as the father of created man, or man the mortal, the legend of the human *ascent* was established. In the "creation" of Atum, instead of being reckoned as the offspring of the old First Mother or the group of the seven pre-solar gods, men became the children of Ra, who are said to have come into existence as tears from his eye, or as germs of an elemental soul proceeding from the solar god. Stars were the children of Ra the sun-god in the solar mythos. Souls were the offspring of Ra the holy spirit in the eschatology; and here we may possibly delve down to one of the tap-roots of the legendary "Exodus." The stars were looked on as a race of beings having souls of light that emanated from the sun. To these the solar race, as human beings, were affiliated by means of the totemic types, which included the crocodile of Sebek, the beast of Bes, the hawk of Horus, the scarabeus of Kheper. Hence it is said by the god Ra to the righteous in Amenta, "You yourselves are tears of mine eye in your person of superior men. I have shed abroad my seed for you" (*Book of Hades*, 5th division, D). These were the seed of Ra, who, as figured, were born like a tear from his eye, as a mode of effluence, and being solar they were the superior race of men, the Ruti, or men *par excellence*. Under the name of Khabsu in Egyptian the stars are synonymous with souls. These in their nightly rising from Amenta were the images of souls becoming glorified. They came forth in their thousands and tens of thousands from the lower Egypt of the astronomical mythos, the earliest exodus being stellar. Thus we can realise the leader Shu, who stands upon the height of heaven, rod in hand, and who was imaged in the constellation Kepheus as the Regulus or law-giver at the pole.

In the "Destruction of Mankind" the stars are said to be "the multitudes which live in the nocturnal sky." In this under-world Taht, the moon-god, is called the luminary of Ra "in the inferior heaven," and in the deep region where he "inscribes the inhabitants"; and it is said to him, "Thou art the keeper of those who do evil, whom my heart abhors" (Pl. C., lines 65–70). Taht was the reckoner of the stars here called the inhabitants of the nocturnal heaven, or sky of Amenta, whose names or numbers were inscribed by him, possibly as six hundred stars, which number was extended by the Jewish Kabalists to their six hundred thousand souls in Guph. Be this as it may, here are the souls in Amenta represented by stars as inhabitants of the under-world. And in the new creation by Atum-Ra, god of the nocturnal sun, they are spoken of as "these multitudes of men." Ra orders that his heaven shall be depicted as a field of rest, and there arose the elysian fields or paradise of plenty on Mount Hetep. In this new heaven, says Ra, "I establish as inhabitants all the beings which are suspended in the sky, the stars! said by the majesty of Ra (to Nut), I assemble there the multitudes that they may celebrate thee, and there arose the multitudes." These multitudes as stars had been the inhabitants in the deep region of the inferior sky. Ra having been "lifted up" as god alone in this new heaven of the astronomical mythos, the stars that were in the lower are to be assembled and grouped together in the upper heaven. This is followed by the stellar exodus from "lower Egypt and the desert of Amenta" under the leadership of Shu-Anhur, the uplifter of the sky together with its inhabitants, the stars, called the children of Nut, or heaven. It is said by Ra "my own son Shu, take with thee my daughter Nut, and be the guardian of the multitudes which live in the nocturnal sky," or the sky in the lower Egypt of Amenta; "put them on thy head and be their fosterer," or sustainer. (Pl. B, line 42.) Then, as said in the hymn to the god Shu, "Uplifted is the sky which he maintains with his two arms" as "king of Upper and Lower Egypt" in his new character of Shu-si-Ra, who, in the solar mythos, had become the son of Ra. In the Ritual, ch. 110, heaven is described as the mansion of Shu, "the mansion of his stars," which was nightly renewed as "the beautiful creation which he raiseth up."

We have now delved down to *an origin for the Egyptian exodus in the stellar mythos*. Shu was the uplifter of the sky under his name of Anhur with his rod. As raiser of the firmament he uplifts the starry host or multitude of beings known as the offspring of Nut, or later, the seed of Ra, or later still, the children of Ra. These were previously the dwellers in the lower Egypt of the mythos who are to be set free from this realm of darkness and gathered together in the land of light, the starry heaven of Nut on high. Their deliverer was Shu-Anhur, the leader up to Heaven, with his rod, as "repeller of the dragon coming out of the abyss." (p. 2, lines 5 and 6.) This exodus belongs to the rendering in the mythology, and underlies the *Peri-em-hru* or coming forth to day according to the *Book of the Dead*, in which the mythos has become the mould of the eschatology. The resurrection of souls has taken the place of the stars in the stellar, and of the sun in the solar mythos. The exodus was now the coming forth of the Manes from "Egypt and the desert" as localities in the mysteries of Amenta. This was then made geographical and practical by literalization in that exodus of the Israelites from the land of the Pharaohs which has hitherto passed as biblical history.

In reviewing M. Renan's work on Israel, a recent writer asks, what then is the origin and significance of the exodus and its attendant plagues and prodigies? "Whence did they come, where or when were they invented? The monuments are never likely to tell us." No, not if we are looking for the Palestinian Jews in Egypt as an ethnological entity, or for the ancient Egyptian fables as biblical facts. But when we get clear of that cloud of iridescent dust which the Jewish writings have interposed betwixt us and the monuments, we shall find they do tell us more or less what was the origin of the wonderful tale by which the world has been beguiled so blindly through mistaking verifiable myth for God's own historic word. The sufferings of the Chosen People in Egypt and their miraculous exodus out of it belong to the celestial allegory of the solar drama that was performed in the mysteries of the divine nether-world, and had been performed as a mythical representation ages before it was converted into a history of the Jews by the literalizers of the ancient legends. The tale of the ten plagues of Egypt contains an esoteric version of the tortures inflicted on the guilty in the ten hells of the under-world. We have seen somewhat of the descent of mankind from a celestial birthplace that was constellated as an enclosure on the mountain of the pole. We have now to trace the *ascent* from the regions of the nether-earth, which, as Egyptian, is an exodus from Lower Egypt and the "desert" of Amenta. We shall have to make the journey through this nether-earth once more in following the exodus of the Israelites from Egypt in the character of the manes issuing from Amenta. The legend of the exodus or coming forth to-day, like those of the creation, the deluge, and the lost paradise in the book of Genesis, belongs to that mythology which underlies and is the source of all the märchen and the folk-lore of the world. The clue, as will be shown, has been preserved in what is commonly termed the wisdom of the ancients, which we hold to be Egyptian in its origin and derivative on all the other lines of its descent. We find the mythos, the legends, and the folk-tales of the world are all involved in the Egyptian wisdom, and the Hebrew traditions are demonstrably the *débris* of Egyptian myth and eschatology. But, of all the various versions of the coming forth or exodus from out the under-world, not one has caused such deep perplexity as this of Israel issuing from Egypt, in which the mythos has been misappropriated and converted into an ethnical history. As Egyptian, it was not pretended that the children of Ra were ethnical, or that the mysteries of Amenta were transactions in the earth of time.

The way up from Amenta was variously portrayed as an ascent by means of steps; by scaling a mount, or by climbing a tree, a grape-vine, a reed, a bean-stalk, or a papyrus reed. In the legends of many races we find the tradition of a deliverance from some subterranean dwelling-place which was their primeval home. This exodus from the under-world is common in the märchen of the red men. With the Lenni Lenape Indians, the beginning was in a subterranean abode up out of which they were led by the wolf as their chief totemic zootype. Now, the wolf is an equivalent for the jackal. In Egyptian the wolf and jackal (Seb) are synonymous; and the jackal was the guide of roads in Amenta who led the people through its wilderness, and showed a way for them to ascend into the world of light. All the myths and legends of an under-world depend upon there being an under-world, or nether-earth, and this again depends on there being a double-earth which was hollowed out by the God who represented the nocturnal sun for the passage through the mount of earth by night, and who as Egyptian was Ptah, the founder of Amenta.

In the Mandan tradition of their origin, it is related that the whole nation once resided in one large village underground beside a subterraneous lake. A grape-vine extended its roots down to their habitation, and gave them an upward view of the light. Some of the more adventurous spirits climbed up the vine, and found themselves in a lovely region full of buffaloes, and rich with every kind of fruit. From this they returned with the grapes they had gathered, like the men who had gone forth to spy out the land in another version of the mythos. Their fellow-countrymen were so delighted with the taste of their newly-found fruit that men, women, and children determined to leave their lower earth and ascend to the upper by means of the grape-vine. But when the people were about half-way, a corpulent woman who was clambering up the vine broke it with her weight. This closed the aperture upon herself and the rest of the nation, and shut out the light of the sun. But when the Mandans die, they expect to return to this, the original country of their forefathers, the good reaching the ancient village of the vine by means of the lake which the wicked will not be able to cross by reason of the burden of their sins (Lewis and Clarke). This land of the forefathers was that of the ancestral spirits, the country of the tree of life, here identified with the vine. The subterranean lake is one with the lake in Tattu. The corpulent woman is the Great Mother, who was the *enceinte* Apt or Hathor in Egypt, whose tree is the sycamore-fig. The double-earth is the same as in the Ritual. Consequently the vine is the tree of dawn up which the sun and souls ascended from the Tuat by means of the tree. The exodus from the nether-earth, or Lower Egypt, is the same as in the Hebrew and other versions of the mythos, the original of which is provably Egyptian. The Quiché "Popul Vuh" portrays the ancestors of the race as wanderers in the wilderness upon their way to the place where the sun was to rise. They also crossed the water, which divided whilst they passed, and which they went through just as if there had been no sea. They passed on the scattered rocks rolled on the sands, that served for stepping-stones. This is why the place was called "ranged stones and torn-up sands," the name that was given to it on their passage through the waters that divided as they went. "At last they came to a mountain where, as they had been told, they were to see the sun rise for the first time" (Bancroft, vol. iii. p. 51). This was the mount of glory in the solar mythos, and the waters which were crossed were those of the celestial Nun. The "ranged stones" in the waters correspond to the twelve stones that were set up by Joshua to mark the spot where the waters were held up for the Israelites to pass dry-footed through the river Jordan. In the Hawaiian tradition the king of the country, named Honua-i-lalo, was the oppressor of the Menehune people. Their god Kane sent Kane-Apua and Kanaloa the elder brother to bring away the oppressed people, and take them to a land which Kane their god had given them. The legend further tells how they came to the Red Sea of Kane, Kai-ula-a-Kane, and were pursued by Ke-Alii Wahanui. Thereupon Kane-Apua and Kanaloa prayed to Lono, and then they waded safely through the sea, and wandered in the desolate wilderness until at last they reached the promised land of Kane, called "Aina-Lauena-a-Kane." This, says Fornander, is an ancient legend, which also contains the story of water being made to gush forth from a rock (Fornander, *An Account of the Polynesian Race*).

The passage of the Red Sea and the destruction of those who follow the fugitives are also found in a Hottentot fable. Heitsi-Eibib was once travelling with a great number of his people, when they were pursued by the enemy. On arriving at the water which had to be crossed as the only way of escape, the leader said, " My grandfather's father! open thyself that I may pass through, and close thyself afterwards." So it took place as he had said, and they crossed the water safely. Then the pursuing enemy tried to pass through the opening likewise, but when they were in the midst of the divided water it closed upon them and they perished. (Bleek, *Hottentot Fables*, p. 75.) In this the personification of the water as the first father, God the grandfather, is in accordance with the Egyptian Nnu or celestial water, who is represented as the primordial male divinity, the father of the fathers, including Ra the solar god. The Nnu or Nun identifies the water as celestial, and it is this that divides to let the sun-god and his followers pass through dryshod. These in the Ritual are pursued by the Apap and the Sebau to the edge of the horizon. Then the water of day overwhelms the powers of darkness, and Apap the dragon with all his evil host are overthrown, submerged, and drowned in the waters of the lower Nun (Rit., ch. 39). They are described in the " Magic Papyrus " as the " immerged," who do not " pass," or go along, but remain floating on the waters like dead bodies drifting on the inundation ; with their mouths for ever shut and sealed (*Records*, vol. x. 151). In another version of the Hottentot legend a Nama woman and her brothers are pursued by an elephant. " Stone of my ancestors," cry the fleeing ones, " divide for us." The stone opens and they pass. The pursuer used the same words, and the rock opened for him also, but it closed on the elephant and crushed it to death (Bleek, *Hottentot Fables*, pp. 64, 65). The fable can be read by means of the Egyptian wisdom. It belongs to the war that was waged for ever betwixt the powers of darkness and light. In the Egyptian mythos the pursuing monster as the Apap-dragon of the deep, in place of the elephant, pursues the children of light who are escaping from the under-world. They reach the rock of the horizon or the Tser-hill, which opens for the " coming forth " and closes again when the pursued ones have passed through in safety. Shu = Moses stands upon the rock to smite it with his rod, with the result that the waters of day gush forth in light. This is the water of heaven set flowing from the rock of the horizon for those who are followed by the Apap-reptile of darkness and consuming drought. The sun-god in the Ritual staggers forth upon the mount with many wounds, but Apap is caught and crushed and cut up piecemeal in the place appointed for the dragon to be drowned in the red lake of the mythos (Rit., ch. 39). Through this Red Sea the followers of Ra, of Heitsi-Eibib, or Jehovah, pass in triumph on their way to the land of promise on the mount of glory. But the hosts of evil are continually overthrown.

The starting-point of the Mangaian migration was from Savaiki in the shades. The natives of the Penrhyns speak of going down to Savaiki in death, and they say their first ancestors came up as heaven-bursters from the same country. All such origins are mythical, not historical or geographical, although the mythical land gets localised on the surface of the earth as it is in the heptanomis of the Hervey Isles. Savaiki was known as the home of the ancestors, but the only ancestors first known were the ancestral spirits, and it was these as manes that sought deliverance from the under-world. In one of the traditions the Egyptians were reputed to come from the land of Puanta, the Ta-neter or country of the gods, the land of glory, or the golden land. When it is said to the sun-god, " Adoration to thee who arisest out of the golden," it means out of Puanta, the nether-land of dawn (Rit., ch. 15, hymn 1). This land of the gods as a mythical locality was *in the under-world*, not on the surface of our earth; it is not the Puanta that was geographical in the south. The people from Puanta, the land of the gods, are those who had a solar origin. They issue from the land of glory with the sun. The gods and the glorified came up from this divine land when they emerged from Puanta in the Orient.

One title of the first chapter in the Ritual is " The chapter of introducing the mummy into the *Tuat* on the day of burial." This applies to the mummy interred on earth, and also to the Osiris or manes in Amenta, who was figured in the mummy-form. The Tuat is a place of entrance to and egress from *the under-world*. And in the Pyramid Texts (Pepi, i. 185) those who are in the Tuat are called *the Tuata*. Now, as the Tuat was in Tanen, the land (ta) beneath the waters of the Nen, they are the *Tuata-Tanen*, in whom we propose to identify the Irish mythical heroes or divine ancestors called the Tuatha de Danan. In the oldest account of the Tuatha it is said they came from heaven. Therefore their origin was not human. In issuing from the Tuat of Amenta they came from the lower paradise of two from which they brought the wisdom and the symbols of the Egyptians as their sacred treasures, including the four precious things belonging to the Tuatha de Danan. The Tuatha are described as *the gods and the not-gods*, a title that exactly corresponds to the Egyptian two classes of spirits called the gods and glorified. According to Giraldus in his *Topographia Hibernia*, it was a guess of the learned that the Tuatha " were of the number of the exiles driven out of heaven," and if they were of those who came from the land of promise and issued from the Tuat, they would come from the subterranean Aarru or earthly paradise. The hills and mounds of Erin are the places of entrance to and exit from the invisible world of elfin-land, which answers to the hidden earth of the manes in Amenta. When euhemerised by tradition, the Tuatha de Danan are said to have retired into the hills and mounds after they were utterly defeated in battle. In other legends Dagda and his sons were once the rulers over this nether-land, and they are said to lie buried there with " the síd or fairy-mound of the brugh as covering for their resting-place " (Rhys). The brugh was originally the place of burial. He who sleeps at Philae is he who sleeps in the brugh, the burgh, or bury. The name written in hieroglyphics is Piruk = brugh, and there the mummy slept in the burgh of Amenta, or with the Tuata in the Tuat of the nether-world. The divine mother of the Tuatha is known by the name of Danan. The Tuatha are the tribe or people of the goddess Danan, who is also the deëss of death. Now, there is an Egyptian goddess Tanan who is a form of Hathor = the amorous queen in the earth of Tanen, the land of the nocturnal sun and the domain of the dead. The god Tanen is lord of that land, and the goddess is identified with Hathor by her head-dress. The name of Tanan may also be written Tann. This agrees with the naming of the Welsh and Irish goddess Danu or Danan. Her name takes the form of Don in Welsh, and the deities who descend from her, like Gwydion and Arianrhod, are called the children of Don. The Tuatha de Danan are also termed the Fir Déa, or men of the goddess. Hence we propose to identify the goddess Tanen with Danan or Danu, the Great Mother of the Tuatha de Danan, who were the people of the goddess as the souls of the dead in the divine Neter-Kar, *i.e.* in Tanen, and who issued from the Tuat with the sun or solar god as the men of the Goddess, who was Tanan in Egypt, Danan in Ireland, and Don in Britain. The men of the goddess, as we suggest, were the Tuata of the Pyramid Texts, who as divine ancestors became the Irish Tuatha de Danan. The same word is represented by the Irish Tuath for the tribe; Breton Tud, Gothic Thiuda, Saxon Theod, for a people; the Oscan Tauta for a community; it is also extant in the name of the Teutons. One of the chief attributes of the Tuatha de Danan is the power they have of assuming any form at will, and this is a supreme trait of those who come forth when the Tuat is opened (Rit., ch. 2). Chapter 64 is the one by which the Tuata take all forms that each desireth, whether on entering or coming forth from this the womb of Amenta. The transformation of the manes has come to be called shape-shifting, but there is no beginning with it as a faculty of the wizards in Ireland. There are various hints in the Irish fairy-lore of the Tuatha de Danan being one with the spirits of the dead. Their relation to the prehistoric mounds is the same as that of the Tuata with the mount of Amenta. There is also a still prevailing confusion in the Irish mind betwixt the fairies and the ghosts, which is very natural when we know that the fairies originated in the spirits of the elements which have got mixed up with the manes of the dead. According to Cæsar, the Druids taught the Gauls that they were all descended from *Dis Pater*, the Demiurge— that is, from the god of Hades or Amenta, who is Tanan as consort of the goddess, and whose name was taken by Ptah-Tanan, the better known *Dis Pater*, who was earlier than Osiris in the Egyptian cult, and from whom the solar race *ascended*, whether from Puanta or from the Tuat. Thus interpreted, the Tuatha or tribes who brought the ancient wisdom out of Lower Egypt or the Tuat may have been genuine Egyptians after all, as the much-derided traditions of the Keltæ and the Kymry yet allege and strenuously maintain. "The oasis of Tuaut" is another bit of ancient Egypt still surviving in the country of Morocco, where it testifies, like some strange boulder on the surface, to the buried past.

The birthplace of the stellar races was in the celestial north. The solar race were they who came forth from the East. In going down to Amenta, as manes, they were the westerners; in coming forth they are the easterners. Thus, when we are told that Abraham came from Ur of the Kasdim, or the Magi, which was his birthplace, that goes far to identify him as a solar god, just as Laban, the white one, was a lunar deity, and Ur a mythical locality. Ur is an Egyptian name for that which is eldest, first, great, principal. The course of the sun-god by day is reckoned to run from *Ta-Ur to Am-Ur*, *i.e.* from east to west. Ta-Ur then is Egyptian for the land of the east, and the migration thence is solar, that is—mythical,—and would be astronomical when the birthplace is designated "Ur of the Kasdim" or Chaldees. Ur of the Kasdim is self-identified by name with the Magi, astrologers or astronomers. Moreover, the frequent coupling of Ur and Martu in the astrological tablets points to Ur as a name for the east being juxtaposed to Martu for the west, "Ur and Martu" meaning east and west, and not Ur a city on earth and Martu a quarter in the heavens.

It has been pointed out by translators that various place-names in the Egyptian Book of the Dead denote celestial localities, and are not geographical. They are names in the astronomical mythology which had been first derived from Egypt on earth, that were afterwards applied to Upper Egypt in heaven and Lower Egypt in Amenta. The heaven above and Amenta below were divided into Upper and Lower Egypt. The Egyptian cities of Thinis, Hermopolis, Memphis, Thebes, Annu, and others were repeated in the planisphere as mythical localities which furnish place-names for the eschatology in the Ritual. When Osiris triumphs, and "joy goeth its round in Thinis," that is the celestial, not the earthly city (Rit., ch. 18). When the deceased in Amenta exclaims, "May Sekhet the Divine One lift me up so that I may arise in heaven and issue my behest in Memphis" (Rit., ch. 26), it is the heavenly Memphis, the celestial Ha-ka-Ptah, or spirit house of Ptah, the enclosure of the white wall on high, that is meant. When the priest says in the first chapter of the Ritual, "I baptize with water in Tattu, and anoint with oil in Abydos," the scene of the baptism is in Amenta, not on earth. Rekhet, the place where the two divine sisters waited and wept for the lost Osiris, was a locality in the earth of eternity, but Rekhet was also geographical in Egypt.

At first the localities, as Egyptian, were topographical, next they were constellated as uranographical, and finally they constituted a double Egypt of the other world in the earth and heaven of eternity.

The Egyptian Exodus is a mystery of Amenta. It is described in the Ritual as the Peri-em-heru or "coming forth to day" from "the Hades of Egypt and the desert" (*Records*, vol. x. p. 109). Thus when Horus comes forth in his resurrection it is said that "Egypt and the desert are at peace" (Rit., ch. 183). Egypt and the desert were the two parts in the double-earth that was divided between Sut and Horus, betwixt whom was internecine war that only ended temporarily at the coming of the prince of peace who came to set the prisoners free from the land of bondage, of drought and darkness, of Apap and the plagues of Egypt in the underworld.

The sufferers depicted in the mythos were at first the stars that fell down headlong into the abyss to be swallowed by the dragon, of whom it is said, "Eternal Devourer is his name" (Rit., ch. 17). This was in the astronomical mythology. In the eschatology the prisoners are the manes or body-souls of the dead who passed into Amenta, the earth of eternity, as it were by way of the grave. Both were the children of light, mythical or eschatological, otherwise the children of Ra, at war for ever with the creatures of darkness in the nether-earth. The exodus or coming forth from this nether Egypt is represented astronomically on the great Mendes Stele. On one side Horus Behutet, the great god, lord of heaven and giver of life, is described as coming "*out of the horizon on the side of Upper Egypt*," and on the other side of the Stele "*the coming out of Lower Egypt*" is spoken of instead. That is the exodus from Kheb or Lower Egypt, which is Amenta in the eschatology (*Records*, vol. viii. 91). This is the exodus from Egypt of the lower earth according to the representation in the solar mythos that preceded the version in the eschatology by which it was followed and enforced. In the making of Amenta the Egyptians mapped out Egypt in the nether-world in accordance with Egypt on earth, only on a vaster scale. They had their Lower and Upper Egypts in the other life as they had in this. But Khebt, the Egyptian original of the Greek Eguptos, is more expressly the Lower Egypt, hence the lower of the two Egypts in the mythical representation. This was the Egypt below, through which the nocturnal sun and the souls of the deceased passed on their way up to the land of liberty and light. This was the Egypt where the Lord (as Osiris, or the elder Horus) was crucified in the Tat (Rev. xl. 8), or where the solar god suffered his mortal agony, his death and burial; the Egypt from which he rose again. Here was the wilderness of the wanderings during the forty days of the Egyptian Lent, which represented the forty days of the seed that was buried in the earth to attain the new life in the regermination of Osiris, which forty days were disguised as forty years in the historic version of the Jewish exodus. It is unfortunate and humiliating to us as a nation that Egyptology and Assyriology in England should have first fallen into the hands of devout believers in the biblical "history." Archæology had to call itself "biblical" in order that a society might be founded for the study of Egyptology and Assyriology, and Egyptian exploration was for a long time limited to looking for "biblical sites" in Egypt, which are only to be met with as mythical localities in Amenta. Nor is this mania of the historic-minded yet entirely extinct! Jewish or Gentile commentators who know nothing of the astronomical mythology, or the Egyptian origin of the Hebrew legends, have never been able to apply the comparative method to these writings. There is but one Egypt for them. But there was another Lower Egypt, another Red Sea, another dragon, another deliverance from Rahab and the Apap-monster, and another exodus, which have not hitherto been taken into account by the Hebraists. It was not to Egypt topographically that the ransomed of the Lord were to return singing the songs of Zion. There is another and a truer version of these mystical matters possible, even as there was of old.

The creation of Amenta in the Egyptian mythos has been already explained as the work of Ptah and the seven Knemmu or navvies who were his assistants in opening up the under-world, and who in the Hebrew rendering become the seven princes that digged the well, referred to in one of the fragments of ancient lore (Num. xxi. 18), which seven princes in the Semitic legends are identified with the chariot of the Lesser Bear. Amenta was a second *terra firma* for the souls of the departed, a mental fulcrum to the eye of faith laid on the physical foundation of the solar mythology for those who travelled the eternal road. Thus the *origin* of the exodus, as Egyptian, was in the coming forth of the heavenly bodies from below the horizon in the mythical representation. This was followed by the coming forth of the manes from dark to day, from death to life, from bondage to liberty, from Lower to Upper Egypt in the eschatology. In the coming forth of the Israelites from "the Hades of Egypt and the desert," it is said the Lord went before them by day in a pillar of cloud, to lead them the way; and by night in a pillar of fire to give them light: that they might go by day and by night: the pillar of cloud by day, and the pillar of fire by night departed not from before the people" (Ex. xiii. 21, 22). It is possible that the zodiacal light supplied a natural image for the pillar of cloud and the pillar of fire described in the book of Exodus. The zodiacal light is a phenomenon visible in Egypt at certain seasons of the year. It is seen as a conical pillar of cloud towards the east in the morning, just before sunrise, and towards the west at sunset. In the pale light of dawn it is a pillar of cloud, and in the ruddy glow of sundown it becomes a veritable pillar of fire. It is said of the Great One God, "the living one, who liveth everlastingly," and who was Atum-Huhi in his temple at On, "He traverseth the heavens, and compasseth the nether-world each day; he travels *in the cloud to separate heaven and earth, and again to unite them*"—that is, at morn and evening in making the passage of Amenta. The "Lord of the Cloud" is also addressed as the guide of navigation. The flame of the sun is the protection of those who cross the double-earth. He who "commands heaven causes his disk to appear in the desert" (Rit., 99). "He who purifies the water" "appears on the liquid abyss" (101). "He marches for the dead; for those who are overturned" (l.). The opening chapters of the Book of the Dead are called the Peri-em-hru or coming forth to day. In other words, this was the Kamite exodus of the manes from Amenta in the eschatological phase of the mythos, which has been converted by literalization into the "history" found in the book of Exodus. The Hebrew märchen are the legendary remains of the Egyptian mythos, whether in the book of Genesis or the book of Exodus. The "coming forth to day" with which the Ritual opens is the Egyptian exodus, and the Hebrew exodus is likewise the coming forth to day.

An entrance to the mythical Amenta, previously shown, was localized at Abydos as the cleft or the mouth of the rock, a narrow gorge in the Libyan range of hills. Opposite this entrance stood the temple of Osiris Khent-Amenta, a name which denotes the opening to the interior of Amenta. Through this gorge the solar bark passed into the mountain of the west, and bore the image of the dying solar god on board. Once a year also there was a feast of the dead, or, as we have it in survival, of All Souls, and there came a funeral flotilla to the mouth of the cleft on one of the first nights of the year. This answers in the mythos to the starting-point in time of the Jewish exodus as history, in the first month of the year.

Two ways of entering the other world are represented in two different categories of the ancient legend, both of which are derived from the same fundamental origin. One is by means of the dividing waters, the other by means of the passage that opens and closes in the earth at evening or in the equinox. In the Egyptian mythos the entrance to Amenta is both by land and water. The god on board the solar bark, or the children of Ra = Israel on board the bark of souls, passed through the cloven rock by water. Previously the water had to be divided for the travellers to pass. But the waters thus divided were celestial, being mythical. They are the waters divided by Shu-Anhur with his rod as leader of the manes from Amenta up to heaven. It is not written in the Old Testament what the Lord did for Israel in the vale of Arnon, but the Targum of Jerusalem tells us that when the Beni-Israel were passing through the gorge or defile, the Moabites were hidden in the caverns of the valley, intending to rush out and slay them. But the Lord signed to the mountains, and they literally laid their heads together to prevent it; they closed upon the enemy with a clap, and crushed the chiefs of the mighty ones, so that the valleys were overflowed with the blood of the slain. Meanwhile Israel walked over the tops of the hills, and knew not the miracle and the mighty act which the Lord was doing in the valley of the Arnon. Thus the miracle of the Red Sea was reversed. In the one case the waters stood up in heaps and were turned into hills; in the other the solid hills flowed down and were fused, whilst Israel passed over them as if they were a level plain. In the one miracle the Red Sea was turned into dry ground; in the other the dry ground was turned into a red sea of blood. The hills that rushed together to make a level plain are a familiar figure of the equinox, to be found in varied forms of legendary lore (Book of Beginnings, vol. ii. pp. 356–357). This account therefore is as good as the biblical one, and it tends to prove that both belong to the astronomical mythos, and that the crossing here was in the equinox.

In the mythos of Amenta the promised land of plenty, the land of corn and wine and oil, was the Aarru-field of divine harvest that awaited the righteous who had been wanderers in the wilderness and who fought their way to it through all the obstacles of the underworld. These obstacles can still be traced in the Jewish narrative compared with the books of Amenta and the mysteries of Taht. All through the journey of this Egypt underground, the objects besought and fervently prayed for are a good passage through the waters and all other hindrances, and a safe way out upon the eastern side, where lay the promised land. One great object of the manes in knowing the words of great magical power in Amenta is to obtain command over the waters. The deceased prays that he may have command over the waters which he has to pass through, even as Sut had command of force on the "night of the great disaster" (Rit., chs. 57 and 62). These waters are the Red Sea of the Jewish exodus, in which the Apap-dragon lurks and lies in wait. The later scholiasts tell us that the habitation of this monster was the Red Sea. Thus the Red Sea is identifiable with the lake of Putrata in which the dragon lurked that lived upon the drowned, the dragon that was turned into the cruel Pharaoh in the Hebrew version of the exodus.

It is evident that the Jews were in possession of an esoteric rendering of the same mystical matter as is presented exoterically in the books ascribed to Moses. There were two versions of the dark sayings and the hidden wisdom, the esoteric and the exoteric, amongst them, as there were amongst the Egyptians, and these have doubled the confusion. The Christian world has based its structure of belief simply and solely on the exoteric version ; thus the door of the past just now being opened anew in Egypt was closed to them and locked ; they were left outside without the key, and in the darkness of the grossest, crassest ignorance the Christian faith was founded. We have now to recover such " history " as is possible from the Pentateuch by eliminating the mythos and the eschatology. Fragments of the original mythos crop up in the Haggadoth, the Kabalah, the Talmud, and other Hebrew writings, which tend to show that in the earlier time and lowermost strata *the same matter had been known to the Jews themselves as non-historical.* Thus it is provable and will be proved that " biblical history " has been mainly derived from misappropriated and misinterpreted mythology, and that the mythology is demonstrably Egyptian which can only be explained in accordance with the Egyptian wisdom. This is not to say that the books of Genesis, Exodus, and Joshua are intentional forgeries, but that the data were already more or less extant as subject-matter of the mysteries, and that an exoteric version of the ancient wisdom has been rendered in the form of historic narrative and ethnically applied to the Palestinian Jews. The most learned of the Rabbis have most truthfully and persistently maintained that the books attributed to Moses do but contain an exoteric explanation of the secret wisdom, though they may not trace the gnosis to its Egyptian source. The chief teachers have always insisted on the allegorical nature of the Pentateuch. Two laws, they tell us, were delivered to Moses on Mount Sinai. One was committed to writing, as in the Pentateuch ; the other was transmitted orally from generation to generation, as is acknowledged by the Psalmist when he says, " I will open my mouth in a parable ; I will utter dark sayings of old, which we have heard and known and our fathers have told us." Parables and dark sayings of old are the allegories of mythology and enigmas of the ancient wisdom uttered after the manner of the mysteries. Now the subject of this psalm is the story of Israel in Egypt and the exodus from the old dark land. The plagues of Egypt are described. " He set his sign in Egypt ; he turned their rivers into blood." " He sent them swarms of flies which devoured them, and frogs which destroyed them." He also gave their increase to the caterpillar and their labour to the locust. He killed their vines with hail and their sycamore-trees with frost, and " smote all the first-born in Egypt." The coming forth is also described. The Psalmist tells of the marvellous things that were done " in the land of Egypt." How the Lord " clove the sea " and " caused them to pass through " whilst the waters were made " to stand as an heap." How he led them forth with a pillar of cloud by day and of fire by night. How he clove the rock in the wilderness " and gave them drink abundantly as out of the depths," and " opened the doors of heaven " and " rained down manna upon them to eat." This was heard and known orally as a tale that is told in dark sayings of old which did not originate in the biblical history of the exodus. They are " tried as silver is tried " in the refineries of the nether-earth. They go " through fire and through water," and are " brought out into

T T

a place of abundance" in the pleasant Aarru fields. This journey is described in various psalms. "Working salvation *in the midst of the earth*, thou didst divide (or break up) the sea by thy strength; thou breakest the heads of the dragons in the waters. Thou breakest the heads of Leviathan in pieces" (Ps. lxxiv. 12–14). In the Hebrew Song of Moses we are in the same nether-earth, where the matter is eschatological. The adversaries are the same opponents of the chosen people—the same, that is, in the book of Deuteronomy as in the Book of the Dead. Ezekiel (xx. 36) makes an allusion to "*the wilderness of the land of Egypt*," which points to the lower Egypt of the mythos in Amenta. Egypt itself, as the land of the living, the cultivable land, was the very opposite of the wilderness.

Amenta in the Book of Hades, and also in the Ritual, is described as consisting of two parts, called "Egypt and the desert land or wilderness." This latter was the domain of Sut in the Osirian mysteries. One part of the domain, named Anrutef, is self-described as the place where nothing grows. It was a desert of fruitless, leafless, rootless sand, in which "there was no water for the people to drink" or, if any, the water was made bitter or salt by the adversary Sut or the Apap-dragon. The struggle of Sut and Horus (or Osiris) in the desert lasted forty days, as these were commemorated in the forty days of the Egyptian Lent, during which time Sut as the power of drought and sterility made war on Horus in the water and the buried germinating grain. Meantime "the flocks of Ra" were famishing for lack of pasture and for want of water in the wilderness. These forty days spent in the desert of the mythos have confessedly been extended into the forty years of the history. They were the forty days of suffering in the wilderness of the under-world which lay betwixt the autumn and the vernal equinox. And when it is threatened by Ihuh that only the children shall go forth with Joshua, it is said, "Your children shall be wanderers in the wilderness *even forty days*, for every day a year" (Num. xiv. 33, 34).

The lower Egypt of Amenta was a land of dearth and darkness to the manes. It was the domain of Sut at the entrance in the west. Here was the typical wilderness founded on the sands that environed Egypt. Aarru or the garden far to the eastward was an oasis in the desert ready for the manes who were fortunate enough to reach that land of promise. The domain of Sut was a place of plagues; all the terrors of nature were congregated there, including drought and famine, fiery flying serpents and unimaginable monsters. There were the hells of heat in which the waters were on fire; there were the slime-pits, the blazing bitumen, and brimstone flames of Sodom and Gomorrah. The desert of engulfing sands, the lakes of fire, and the deluge of overwhelming waters had to be crossed, and all the powers of death and hell opposed the passage of the glorified elect, the chosen people of the Lord, who were bound for bliss in the land where their redemption dawned upon the summit of the mount. This then was the land of bondage where the manes were in direst need of a deliverer. The typical tyrant and taskmaster in the Hebrew "history" has never been identified on earth, and it may be somewhat difficult to identify him in Amenta, but it is not impossible. The devourer of the people in that land takes several forms. The Apap-monster lies in wait and has to be encountered at the entrance to the valley of the shadow of death. But there is one typical devourer. The Red Sea is his dwelling-place, and "eternal devourer is his name." Another of his names is Mates, the hard, cruel, flinty-hearted. He is described as having the skin of a man and the face of a hound. His dwelling is in the red lake of fire, where he lives upon the shades of the damned and eats the livers of princes. As he comes from the Red Sea, his overthrowal is in the Red Sea, like the overwhelming of Pharaoh and his host. The same typical devourer has another figure in the judgment hall, where it is named Amemit. Here it has the head of a crocodile. Where we might speak of the jaws of death, hell, or destruction, the Egyptians said or showed the jaws of the crocodile. Those who are condemned to be devoured pass into the jaws of the devourer. Thus the crocodile is the devourer, the typical tyrant, the cruel, hard-hearted monster who bars the gate of exit and will not let the suffering people go up from the land of bondage. When the manes seeks his place of refuge in Amenta or in the Ammah (Rit., ch. 72), he prays for deliverance from the crocodile in the land of bondage. He also says, "Let not the powers of darkness (the Sebau) have the mastery over me," and he prays that he may reach the divine dwelling which has been prepared for him in the Aarru-fields of peace and plenty, where there is corn of untold quantity in that land toward which his face is set. This is the chapter "by which one cometh forth to day and passeth through Ammah or the Ammah," in seeking deliverance from the crocodile or dragon in the land of bondage. Protection is sought in Ammah because the god who dwells there in everlasting light is the overthrower of the crocodile. The crocodile is the dragon of Egypt to the Hebrew scribes, who use it as an image of the Pharaoh. When Ezekiel writes, "Thus saith the Lord God: Behold, I am against thee, Pharaoh, King of Egypt, the great dragon that lieth in the midst of his rivers," the imagery is derived from the Egypt of Amenta, however it may be afterwards applied. The great dragon, as typical devourer in the land of bondage, is here identified with the Pharaoh of Egypt, as it also has been in the book of Exodus.

Amenta is spoken of at least once in the Ritual as the place wherein the living are destroyed. It is also described as the Kâsu or burial-place. One of the twelve divisions of this under-world was known as "the sandy realm of Sekari," the place of interment. The dead were buried underneath their mounds in this domain of Sekari, which was a wilderness of sand. This is the probable origin of the wilderness full of buried corpses in the book of Numbers. For, after all the promises made to the children of Israel, they are suddenly turned upon by the Lord and told that their carcases shall fall in this wilderness. "Your little ones will I bring in, but as for you, your carcases shall fall in this wilderness" (Num. xiv. 31, 32). Now, the carcases that were to rot in the wilderness are equivalent to the mummies buried in the sandy realm of Osiris-Sekari, god of the coffin and the desert sand. In the Kamite eschatology those who made the exodus from Amenta to the world of day are those who rise from the dead in the desert called "the sandy realm of Sekari" = the wilderness. Moreover, they rise again as children who are called "the younglings of Shu." And Shu was the leader and forerunner of this new generation of divine beings, called his "younglings," from the "sandy realm of Sekari," when their redemption from that land of bondage dawned (Rit., ch. 55). The wilderness of the nether-earth being a land of graves, this gives an added significance to the question asked of Moses, "Because there were no graves in Egypt, hast thou taken us away to die in the wilderness?" (Ex. xiv. 11), which as the domain of Osiris-Sekari was depicted as a cemetery of sand, where the dead awaited the coming of Horus, Shu, Ap-uat (or Anup), the guide, and Taht, the lunar light, as servants of Ra, the supreme one god, to wake them in their coffins and lead them from this land of darkness to the land of day. Amenta, as the place of graves, is frequently indicated in the Hebrew scriptures, as in the description of the great typical burial-place in the valley of Hamon-Gog. This was in the Egypt described in the book of Revelation as the city of dead carcases, where also their lord was crucified as Ptah-Sekari or Osiris-Tat. Amenta had been converted into a cemetery by the death and burial of the solar god, who was represented as the mummy in the lower Egypt of the nether-earth. The manes were likewise imaged as mummies in their coffins or beneath their mounds of sand. They also rose again in the mummy-likeness of their lord, and went up out of Egypt in the constellation of the Mummy (Sahu-Orion), or in the coffin of Osiris that was imaged in the Greater Bear.

In the Ritual the power of darkness called "the devourer of the ass," which was a solar zootype, is Am-ā-ā, the great, great devourer by name. Am signifies the devourer, of whom it is said eternal devourer is his name (Rit., ch. 17). This Am-ā-ā, the great, great devourer, is apparently the Amalek of the biblical legend: Melek, the lord of rule, being suffixed to the name of Am, to describe the character. "Then came Amalek and fought with Israel in Rephidim," in the region of the Rephaim, Sheol or Amenta (Ex. xvii. 8). "The Lord hath sworn he will have war with Amalek from generation to generation." These are the two great opponents, who were Apap, the devourer of the ass, and Ra in the wars of Amenta. The wars of the lord, as Egyptian, were waged against the adversaries of Ra or Osiris in Amenta. These adversaries were the powers of evil, the Apap-dragon of drought, the serpent of darkness, the Sebau, the Sami, together with Sut and his co-conspirators in the later rendering of the mythos. The adversaries of the Good Being are annihilated in the tank of flame (ch. i.). Osiris is thus addressed: "Hail to thee, the great, the mighty, whose enemies are laid prostrate at their blocks! Hail to thee, who slaughterest the Sebau and annihilatest Apap! Thou hast utterly destroyed all the enemies of Osiris" (Rit., ch. 15). Chapter 18 is in celebration of the triumph of Osiris over all his adversaries, who are slaughtered and destroyed. The great slaughter of the adversaries is carried out in the nether-world (ch. 41) or secret earth of Amenta, at a place called Suten-Khen. Also the plagues of Egypt had previously been let loose by the Lord on Abram's account. "And the Lord plagued Pharaoh with great plagues" before "Abram went up out of Egypt" (Gen. xii. 17; xiii. 1). This is a bit of the same myth of Amenta, which was earlier than the

Mosaic exodus. The scenery of Sodom and the pits of bitumen may be found in the Ritual, together with the night of reckoning, which is the "night of fire against the overthrown, the night of chaining the wicked in their hells, the night on which their vital principles are destroyed" (Rit., 17). In the Hebrew version this "reckoning" on the fatal night when the Typhonians (or Sodomites) were destroyed in the hells of fire and sulphur takes the shape of "reckoning," whether there are fifty, forty-five, forty, thirty, twenty, or ten righteous persons to save the doomed city from destruction (Gen. xviii. 24–32). In the legend of the monkey, the god who reposes in Amenta and traverses the darkness and the shadows, when he rises gives up the pig to the plague (Book of Hades). Now the pig was a type of the evil typhon. In one of the pictures a pig called the devourer of the arm (of Osiris) is being driven by the monkey, which was a lunar zootype. Thus the pig which is here given to the plagues shows that in the true mythos the plagues of Egypt were let loose *on the Typhonians* or powers of evil, the Sebau, the Sami, the conspirators of Sut, the children of darkness, whether from a physical or moral point of view, and that this was in the lower Egypt of Amenta. These in the Hebrew version have been transformed into ethnical Egyptians who so cruelly oppressed and preyed upon the suffering Israelites. Thus the plagues of Egypt occurred twice over in a land which was not the Egypt of the Pharaohs, and the people who suffered from them were not Egyptians. This agrees with the hidden gnosis in the Wisdom of Solomon, and also in the book of Revelation, where the plagues are of the same mystical nature, but are only *seven* instead of *ten* in number. The "wilderness" was obviously a place or state in which the shoes and clothes of the people did not wear out. This was only possible to the manes in the desert of Amenta. The two regions of the clothed and unclothed are named in relation to the judgment hall of Mati. The clothed and unclothed are well-known terms for the elect and the rejected manes; the children of light and the offspring of darkness. In the trial scenes the spirits who are judged to be sound and pure are told that they may pass on as the clothed, whilst the condemned are designated the unclothed. Thus the clothed ones pass safely and freely through the desert region of the unclothed. In the Hebrew version we read, " I have led you forty years in the wilderness, (and) your clothes are not waxen old upon you, and your shoe is not waxen old upon your feet" (Deut. xxix. 5). There can be no doubt about these being the divinely clothed and fed, as described in the Ritual, where they eat of the tahen and drink of the water made sweet by the tree of life, and pass, as the clothed, through the wilderness which is called the region of the naked. To say that the clothes and shoes of God's own people did not wear out during a period of forty years is a mode of showing they were divinely made for everlasting wear, but not on earth, where nowadays they wear out all too fast for Gentile as for Jew. Apparently the Hebrew manna represents the Egyptian tahen which was given to the manes for food in the wilderness of Amenta. In passing through the desert or the region of the unclothed, the manes tells of the tahen that was given for sustenance (ch. 124). So far as the tahen is known, it agrees well enough with the Hebrew manna. "When the dew that lay (on the ground) was gone up, behold, upon the face of the wilderness a small round thing, small as the hoar-frost on the ground," which was "like unto wafers *made* with honey." Wafers made of tahen were also eaten sacramentally as food of heaven in the Osirian eucharist. In the mystery of opening the mouth and of giving breath to the breathless ones in Amenta, the Egyptians made use of an instrument called the ur-heka, or great magical power. It is sometimes a sinuous, serpent-like rod without the serpent's head. At others it has the head of the serpent on it, united with the head of a ram. Both ram and serpent were types of the deity Khnef, who represented the breath of life or the spirit, Nef, Hebrew Nephesh, which was assumed to enter the Osiris when the mummy's mouth was typically opened to inhale the breath of future existence. Here then is a magical rod that turned into a serpent, which may be seen figured in the Vignettes to the Ritual as a form of the magical rod with which the mouth of the deceased was opened in the mysteries of Amenta. It is held by the tail in the hand of the magician or priest who performs the ceremony of apru, *i.e.*, opening the mouth, in illustration of the chapters by which the mouth is opened in the nether-world (Vignettes to chs. 21, 22, 23). The rod is changed into a serpent at the time when the Lord is desirous for Moses to become his mouthpiece. Moses objects, whereupon the Lord asks, "Who hath made man's mouth? Now therefore go, and I will be with thy mouth and teach thee what thou shalt speak." The contest ends in Moses having his own way, and in Aaron becoming a mouth to Moses. Moses is to take in his hand the rod wherewith he is to "do the signs" (Ex. iv. 1–17).

Here then we identify the serpent-rod of the Egyptian priests that was known by name as the great magical power, and it was sometimes a rod, at others a serpent. This we take to be the original of that rod with which the tricks are played in the Hebrew märchen by the Lord God of Israel for the purpose of frightening Pharaoh. "And the Lord said unto him (Moses), What is that in thine hand? And he said, A rod. And he said, Cast it on the ground. And he cast it on the ground, and it became a serpent: and Moses fled from before it. And the Lord said unto Moses, Put forth thine hand and take it by the tail. And he put forth his hand and laid hold of it, and it became a rod in his hand" (Ex. iv. 2–5). The type of great magical power is thus turned to account in astonishing the natives and in giving lessons to the magicians of Egypt. In both scenes we have the opening of the mouth. In both we have the serpent-rod with which the signs and wonders are wrought. And it is admitted that Pharaoh had wise men, sorcerers, "magicians of Egypt," who had rods which became serpents as types of transformation. These rods are to be seen in the hands of the wise men portrayed in the Ritual, but not for any such fool's play as is described in the book of Exodus.

There are two serpents in Egyptian symbolism—one is a type of evil, the other is the good serpent. One is the Apap of drought, darkness, and death or negation; the other is the Uræus-serpent of life, that was worn on the frontlets of the gods and the glorified manes as a sign of protection and salvation or safety (ch. 34). In the chapter by which a person is not devoured or bitten to death by the eater of the head, which is a snake, an appeal is addressed to the solar Uræus as the source of life, the flame which shineth on the forehead of the glorified. In the seventh abode there is a serpent named Retuk (the cartouche in my copy reads Ruruk or Rerek), that lives on the manes and is said to "annihilate their magical virtue" (149). The speaker says, "I am the master of enchantments" (149). He is the magician, the prototype of Pharaoh's, who worked by enchantment (Ex. vii. 11). The "fiery serpent" of the wilderness may be traced in this great serpent of Amenta, whose name is "dweller in his flame." However rendered, the hieroglyphics identify the mythical serpent of fire as the fiery serpent of the Hebrew märchen. The lifting up of the serpent can also be paralleled in the text when the speaker exclaims, "I am raised up to (or as) the serpent of the sun"—that is, the Uræus, the good serpent when compared with Apap. The serpent Aker is joined to the nocturnal sun as he traverses the Amenta (or the wilderness) by night. Thus Aker, the serpent of fire, is the good serpent that is raised up as the fiery serpent in the exodus. The evil serpent Apap is then told that he must retreat before this uplifted solar serpent (which accompanies the orb in the Egyptian triad) and in presence of the revivifying sun. And in this way the mythos furnished matter for the märchen and the folk-tales about the evil serpents that bit the wandering Israelites, and how they were saved and healed by an image of the good serpent, which always had been lifted up in Egypt as a solar symbol of healing and of life. In playing off the serpent of fire against the serpent of darkness, the deceased anticipates Moses with Nehushtan the brazen. He exclaims triumphantly, "I understand *the mystical representations of things*, and by that means I repulse Apap" (108). Also in the zodiac of Esné fiery flying serpents are to be seen on the wing in the decans of Cancer as the sign of heat and drought (Drummond, *Œd. Jud.*, Pl. 8). The children of Israel, as followers of the solar god, are the children of Ra, or Atum-Ra, under whatsoever racial name; and these are to be met with even by name, making the passage through the lower Egypt of Amenta on their way to the promised land. People named the Aaiu, an Egyptian plural equivalent to our word Jews, are described in the under-world. Their god is the ass-headed Aiu, or Iu, who was one of the gods of Israel that led the people up out of Egypt—that is, the ass was one of the zootypes of the god Aiu, as the calf, bullock, or ox was another. We had to dredge this nether-earth for much of the sunken treasure of Egyptian wisdom that has long been lost in its authentic shape. And in Amenta we find the ass-headed god of the Jews, respecting whom they have been so ignorantly derided and maligned. His name, we repeat, is Aiu, Au, Aai, or Iu, both as god and as the ass in old Egyptian; and this name survived in the forms of Iao, Iau, Iahu, Ieou, and others. The god was Atum-Ra in Egypt, and Aiu the ass-headed is one of the types of the solar god. Aiu appears ass-headed in Amenta as a god stretched out upon the ground who has the solar disk upon his head, with the ears of an ass projecting beside the disk. He is holding the rope by which the solar boat was towed up from the nether-world (Lefébure, *Records*, vol. x.

p. 130). The figure lying on the ground denotes the god who was Atum-Aiu, the sun by night in the earth of eternity. The people who are with Aiu in this scene are amongst those "who guard the rope of Aiu, and do not allow the serpent Apap to mount towards the boat of the great god." These are the Aiu as the people of Iu. It is said of them, "Those who are in this scene walk before Ra (Atum-Iu). They charm (or catalepse) Apap for him. They rise with him towards the heavens."

The Book of Amenta, called the Book of Hades by Lefébure, shows this god in his mummied form as one with Osiris in the body and with Ra in soul ; otherwise it is Atum in the body, or mummy, and Iu in soul. And just as Ra the holy spirit descends in Tattu on the mummy Osiris, and as Horus places his hands behind Osiris in the resurrection, so Iu comes to his body, the mummy in Amenta. Those who tow Ra along say, "The god comes to his body ; the god is towed along towards his mummy" (*Records*, vol. x. p. 132). The sun-god, whether as Atum-Iu (Aiu or Aai) or Osiris-Ra, is a mummy in Amenta and a soul in heaven. The imagery is quite natural : the nocturnal sun became a mummy as a figure of the dead, and a soul or spirit in its resurrection as a figure of the living. Atum, or Osiris, as the sun in Amenta, is the mummy buried down in Khebt or lower Egypt, and Iu in the one rendering, or Horus in the other, raises the mummy-god. This is the meaning of the ass-eared Aiu when he is portrayed in the act of hauling at the rope of the sun or raising the mummy in Amenta. The god Aiu is represented mummified upon the tomb of Rameses the Sixth—that is, in the character of Atum the father, buried as the mummy in lower Egypt. Thus we identify the ass-god Aiu or Iu (an ancient Egyptian name of the ass) in lower Egypt, and his followers, who are the Aiu by name. The followers of Iu = Aiu then are the Aiu, Ius, or the later Jews. They fight the battle of the sun-god in the nether-earth, where the dragon Apap was the cruel impious oppressor ; and when they do escape from this, the land of bondage for the manes, they are the Aaiu or the Jews, who "rise behind this god to heaven," and their exodus is from Khebt, the lower Egypt of Amenta. The whole story of the faithful Israelites who would not bow down to the gods of Egypt is told in a few words relating to the Aiu (or Jews) in Amenta. As it is said, "These are they who spoke the truth on earth and did not rise to (prohibited) adorations" or heresies (Lefébure, Book of Hades, *Records of the Past*).

The legends of the exodus, like those in the book of Genesis, originated in the astronomical mythology, in which the making of Amenta is followed by the Peri-em-hru or coming forth to day from the lower Egypt of the under-world and the wilderness or desert. The story of this exodus is inscribed in hieroglyphics on the sarcophagus of Seti, now in the Soane Museum. The Book of Hades, or Amenta, and the Book of the Dead suffice of themselves to prove that "the Egypt and the desert" of the exodus were in Amenta, and not in the land of the pyramids. This was "the Egypt and the desert" in which the flocks of Ra were shepherded and fed. "Horus says to Ra's flocks, Protection for you, flocks of Ra, born of the great one who is in the heavens. Breath to your nostrils, *overthrowal to your coffins*" (Book of Hades, 5th division.

legend D). These are the manes in Amenta called the flocks of Ra, who are shepherded by Horus as Har-Khuti, lord of spirits. The overthrowal of the coffins shows that this was the deliverance of the dead, and that the exodus or coming forth to day was synonymous with the resurrection from the dead.

Amenta had been mapped out in twelve domains, according to the twelve astronomical divisions and the twelve gates which the sun passed through by night. "As it is said, the great god travels by the roads of Hades, to *make the divisions* which take place in the earth" (Book of Hades). There are various groups of *the twelve* as divine personages or children of Ra in this lower Egypt of Amenta.

As characters in the mythos, Jacob and the ten tribes, sons, or children correspond to Ra the solar-god, with his ten cycles in the heaven of ten divisions (Rit., ch. 18), whilst Israel—the same personage—with the twelve sons, answers to the same god, Ra, in the heaven of twelve divisions or twelve signs of the zodiac.

It has now to be admitted that the twelve sons of Jacob are not historic, and the historical exodus must follow them, for that is founded on the twelve sons going down into Egypt as historic characters, and the people of Israel coming out of it as their direct descendants hugely multiplied. The twelve, as sons of Jacob, go down to Egypt in search of corn, and in the Book of Amenta we get a glimpse of the twelve or *their mythical prototypes* who make the journey as characters in the astronomical mythology. Twelve *gods of the earth* are to be seen marching towards a mountain, which shows they are on their way to the nether-world, as it is depicted upside down. Twelve gods *in the earth of Amenta* are marching towards another mountain, and these two mountains form a sort of gorge toward which the divine boat voyages. This is the entrance to Amenta, and these are the twelve as sons of Ra, who are on their way down to the lower Egypt of the mythos, the prototypal twelve who are the sons of Israel in the Hebrew version. These are said to be "those who are born of Ra, born of his substance, and which proceed from his eye." Thus Ra is the father of the twelve. Ra has prepared for them "a hidden dwelling" in this Egypt of the lower earth or desert of Amenta. Twelve persons called the blessed are portrayed as worshippers of Ra. Twelve others are the righteous who are in Amenta. Twelve mummies standing upright, each in a chapel with open doors, are "the holy gods who are in Amenta." Twelve men walking represent "the human souls which are in Amenta." Twelve bearers of the cord with which the allotments are measured for the glorified elect are represented by twelve persons carrying the long serpent Nenuti. These bearers of the cord in the Amenta are those who prepare the fields for the elect. Ra says, "Take the cord; draw, measure the fields of the manes, who are the elect in your dwellings, gods in your residences, deified elect, in order to rejoin the country, proved elect, in order to be within the cord." Ra says to them of the enclosure, "It is the cord of justice." Ra is satisfied with the measurement. "Your own possessions, gods, and your own domains, elect, are yours. Now eat. Ra creates your fields and appoints you your food." "The gods are content with their possessions, the glorified are satisfied with their dwellings." The followers of Har-Khuti, lord of spirits, are the twelve, who take the place in the solar mythos of the earlier seven Khuti in the stellar mythos, five more being added to the seven. These are the twelve as the children of Ra, who cultivate the fields of divine harvest in the plains of Amenta, where they reap for Ra as followers of Horus the beloved son : " They labour at the harvest, they collect the corn. Their seeds are favoured in the land by the light of Ra at his appearance." Thus the twelve are the cultivators of corn in Egypt. They give food to the gods and to the souls of the elect in Amenta. As the bearers of food they are twelve in number. In one scene the twelve are portrayed in two groups of seven and five persons. The seven are the reapers. The five are seen *bending towards an enormous ear of corn*. These are described as the twelve who labour at the harvest in the land of corn which is in the earth of eternity. The scene with the twelve in a posture of adoration suggests the sheaf of corn in Joseph's dream. " Behold, we were binding sheaves in the field, and lo, my sheaf arose, and also stood upright ; and behold, your sheaves came round about, and made obeisance to my sheaf " (Gen. xxxvii. 7). In one form the Aarru enclosure was portrayed as the field of divine harvest, and the twelve were the typical reapers of the corn that grew there seven cubits high (Book of Hades, *Records of the Past*, vols. x. and xii). This is sufficiently suggestive of the twelve enormous sheaves in Joseph's dream, and of the reapers being a form of the twelve harvesters. The twelve as gods were also rulers in the twelve signs which formed the final circle of the Aarru paradise. And in Joseph's second dream his star is greeted with obeisance like his sheaf. " Behold, the sun and the moon and the eleven (other) stars made obeisance to me," he who was represented by the twelfth star as well as by the twelfth sheaf (Gen. xxxvii. 6–9). Horus in the harvest-field of lower Egypt has two characters, one pertaining to the mythos, one to the eschatology. In the first he is one of the twelve as harvesters : the twelve who row the solar boat, the twelve to whom the stations were assigned or thrones were given in the zodiac. In the other character he is Har-Khuti, lord of spirits, and in this phase he is the supreme one at the head of the twelve, who are now his servants.

The pictures show the children of Ra both as the group of twelve and also as the twelve *with* Horus. In one scene Horus is depicted leaning on a staff, and eleven gods are walking towards Osiris. These are the twelve altogether, of whom Horus is one in presence of the father. But on the tomb of Rameses the Sixth the twelve appear, *preceded by Horus*, the master of joy, leaning on his staff. These are the harvesters : seven of them are the reapers, the other five are collectors of the corn (Book of Hades). Thus the fields of divine harvest are twelve in number ; the cultivators are twelve in number ; the reapers and bearers of food are twelve in number ; the children of Ra = Jacob-El or Isiri-El are twelve in number. So it was not left for the historic Israelites to map out the land of promise in twelve allotments betwixt the twelve tribes and twelve children of Ihuh. Amenta in twelve sections with twelve gates represented the heaven in twelve divisions, and the chart was as old as the solar zodiac of twelve signs that was already in existence, as we reckon, in the heaven of Atum-Ra some 13,000 years ago. Not only was the promised land mapped out in twelve divisions in accordance with the twelve signs of the solar zodiac or the twelve pillars raised by Moses round the mount—not only did the chosen race, as children of the one god Atum, take possession of the land allotted to them, or the land appointed them by lot, as Joshua renders it ; title-deeds were also issued to the glorified elect.

This lower Egypt, the land of corn, in the Book of Hades is not geographical. Like Annu, Thebes, and Memphis in the Ritual, it is a mythical locality in the earth of eternity. It is the lower domain of the double earth, the country of the manes called Amenta that was hollowed out by Ptah the opener. It is the lower Egypt named Kheb, to which Isis was warned to flee by night as the place of refuge for the infant Horus when his life was threatened by the Apap-monster. Lower Egypt is the land of death or darkness, leading to the world of life and light. It is here that " Horus says to the flocks of Ra, which are in the Hades of Egypt and the desert," " Protection for you, flocks of Ra, born of the great one who is in the heavens " as Atum-Ra. These flocks " in the Hades of Egypt and the desert " are the chosen people, the deified elect, as the children of Ra. Amenta was a land of darkness until it was lighted by the nocturnal sun. This was the origin of the typical " Egyptian darkness." But in the Egypt of this lower hemisphere the god prepared a secret and mysterious dwelling for his children where *the glorified elect were hidden in the light.* " Ra says to the earth, Let the earth be bright. My benefits are for you who are *in the light.* To you be a dwelling." " I have hidden you." (Book of Hades, 1st division.) Food is given them because of the light, in which they are enveloped. This divine dwelling created by Ra for the elect is entitled " the Retreat." As it is said, " The earth is open to Ra, the earth is closed against Apap. Those who are in the Retreat worship Ra." This Retreat is equivalent to the biblical land of Goshen, where the chosen people dwelt in light. In the book of Exodus there is a three days' solid darkness over the land of Egypt, " but all the children of Israel had light in their dwellings " (ch. x. 22, 23). The land of Goshen in the Hebrew version represents the Retreat of Ammah in the Ritual. Ammah is a locality that is traversed in knowing the spirits of Annu or of attaining the garden eastward. Those who belong to the state of the elect are hidden in Ammah. They are described as being concealed in light by Ra. Ammah is a region reserved for the gods and the glorified spirits who are the children of light bound for the land where there is no more night. It is a place impenetrable to the creatures of darkness and to those who are twice dead—dead in their sins as well as in the mortal body. These are they who do not rise again from lower Egypt. There is no deliverance or exodus for them ; they do not enter Ammah, or follow Shu, the lion of strength, who leads up the elect into the land of light. Ammah is the sixth one of fourteen abodes in the 149th chapter of the Ritual. It is an abode of peace reserved for the blessed, where the evil dead cannot enter. It is a mystery to the manes. The god who is there is called the overthrower of the crocodile or dragon. The deceased in saluting Ammah asks that he may take possession of its *stuffs in peace.* " O Ammah ! Reservation of the gods ; mystery for the manes where the dead may not enter. Hail to thee, O Ammah the august. I come to see the gods who are there. Open to me, that I may take possession of your stuffs." (Cf. the spoils.) Ammah is the Goshen of the Ritual, reserved and set apart for the glorified as a place impenetrable to the powers of evil or the dead who do not rise again, and for whom there is no exodus or coming forth to day (149). It is the work of the worshippers in Amenta to destroy the enemies of Ra and defend the great one against the evil Apap. They "live on the food of Ra, and the meats belong to the inhabitants of Amenta. Holy is that which they carry unto the dwelling where they are concealed." This divine food is apparently repeated in the quails and manna that were sent from heaven, according to the biblical account.

Dreadful massacres are perpetrated in taking possession of this promised land mapped out in twelve divisions. Ra says, "I have commanded that they should massacre, and they have massacred the beings." He orders his followers to destroy the impious ones in a suppression of blood. But these beings are not the human inhabitants of Canaan or any other land on earth. The wars of the lord in these battles of Amenta are fought by his true and faithful followers on behalf of Un-Nefer the good being. The enemies who are doomed to be slaughtered by the invaders are the Sebau and Sami, the creators of dearth and darkness, who were in possession of the land, and who are for ever rising in rebellion against the supreme god Ra. It was these dwellers in the ways of darkness who were to be annihilated by the children of light, the glorified elect, the chosen people, who are then to take possession of the land. Ra says to them, "Your offerings (made on earth) are yours. Take your refreshments. Your souls shall not be massacred, your meats shall not putrefy, faithful ones who have destroyed Apap for me."

Thus the massacres by which the Israelites were enabled to clear out the inhabitants of Canaan and take possession of their lands had been previously committed by the followers of Ra. Ra says to those who are born of him, and for whom he had created the dwelling-place in the beautiful Amenta, "Breath to you who are in the light, and dwellings for you. My benefits are for you." But the beings there massacred were not human. In the biblical version it is said of a mythical event, "It came to pass, when Pharaoh would hardly let them go, that the Lord slew all the first-born in the land of Egypt, both the first-born of man and the first-born of beast" (Ex. xiii. 15). This insane proceeding on the part of the Lord may be explained by reference to the original. From this we learn that amongst the beings massacred or sacrificed were "*quadrupeds and reptiles*" (Book of Hades, 1st division, legend E). The Hebrew historian has discreetly omitted the first-born of the reptile, unless it is included as a beast. Again, one name of the keeper of the 17th gate is "*lord of the massacre and of sacrificing the enemy at midnight!*" (Rit., 145). With this we may compare the passage, "And it came to pass at midnight that the Lord smote all the first-born in the land of Egypt . . . and there was a great cry in Egypt: for there was not a house where there was not one dead" (Ex. xii. 30).

Now, amongst the glorified elect or chosen people who are the children of Ra, the ass-god, Aai, or Iu, there is a group of his defenders and followers who accompany him, and who are said to rise with Ra towards the heavens to be "for him *in the two sanctuaries*," and to "make him rise in Nu" (heaven). These are among the worshippers of the ass-headed god Iu, who are called the Aaiu (the Ius or Jews) by name. Apap is threatened thus, "O impious cruel one, Apap, who spreadest thy wickedness. Thy face shall be destroyed, Apap! Approach thy place of torment. The Nemu are against thee: thou shalt be struck down. The *Aaiu are against thee*: thou shalt be destroyed." It is these Aaiu as worshippers of the god Iu that we claim to be the Ius or later Jews of the mythical legends so long supposed to have been historical. Thus the glorified elect, the blessed, the righteous, who are in Amenta, that is in the lower Egypt of the mythos, are the chosen people of the most high god, who was Ra in his first sovereignty as the ass-headed Iu = Iao, Aiu, or Iahu; Atum-Huhi as god the father, Atum-Iu as god the ever-coming son. The Aaiu or Jews, then, are amongst those who "rise for Ra." "They beat down Apap in his bonds." Apap is stricken with swords. He is sacrificed. Ra rises at the finishing hour; "he ascends when the chain is fixed." Those who are in this scene drag the chains of this evil-doer (Apap). They say to Ra, "Come Ra; advance Khuti! The chain is fixed on evil-face (Neha-her), and Apap is in bonds" (Book of Hades, 10th division). This is the scene of making fast the dragon in the pit which is preparatory to the rising of Ra. These Aiu or Jews accompany the sun-god when he makes the journey through the valley of darkness, the lake of Putrata, and the desert in "the Amenta of Egypt," where they are protected as the "flocks of Ra." Amidst the people that dwell in darkness and black night they are the glorified elect, enveloped and concealed in light, and fed mysteriously in the wilderness with food supplied from heaven. *Earth opens* to let them pass when they are pursued by their old enemy, and closes to protect them against the devouring dragon. Hence it is said by those who render the great serpent impotent by their magic, "Earth opens to Ra! Earth closes to Apap!" The monuments of Egypt are as truly and honestly historical as the geological record. Both have their breaks and their missing links, yet are perfectly trustworthy on the whole. And these monuments, from beginning to end, have no word of witness that the Jews or Hebrews ever were in Egypt as a foreign ethnical entity. They know nothing of Abraham as a Semite who went down into Egypt to teach the Egyptians astronomy. They know nothing of Jacob except as a Hiksos Pharaoh, *or a divinity*, Jacob-El, whose name is found on one of the scarabei. They know nothing of Joseph and his viziership, nor of the ten plagues, nor of the going forth in triumph from the house of bondage to attain the promised land. These and many other wonderful things related in the Word of God are known to the Egyptian records, but not as history. There is another Egypt not yet explored by the bibliolaters: the Egypt of mythology and the Kamite eschatology.

Unless we take into account the mound of the Jew in the neighbourhood of On and the temple of Atum-Iu (W. M. F. Petrie, *Hyksos and Israelite Cities*), the only way of identifying the Jews in Egypt is by the name of the Iu or Aiu in the lower Egypt of the mythical Amenta, where we find the twelve sons or children of Israel, under the name of the Ius or Aiu, as worshippers of the god who was known in Egypt as the ass-headed Iu, Aiu = Iao, Ieou, or Iahu, and who, as we see from the scarabei, may also have been known in Egypt as Jacob-El, the father of the twelve who were reapers of the corn in the harvest of Amenta.

The writer has previously suggested, in *A Book of the Beginnings*, that Jacob represents the god Ra as Iu in Kheb, the lower Egypt of Amenta. Jacob was known as a divinity in Northern Syria by the name of Jacob-El, and Joseph by the name of Joseph-El. The El is a Semitic suffix to the names, denoting the divinity of both, versus the ethnical origin of Jacob and Joseph. These, according to the present showing, were among the gods of Egypt as Huhi the father and Iu the son, or sif in Egyptian, Iu-sif being = Joseph in Hebrew. Thus we propose to identify the mummy of Jacob in Egypt with the mummy of Atum or Osiris as a form of the mummy-sun that was portrayed as being carried up from Amenta. Jacob, as we read, was embalmed in Egypt, and the mummy in its coffin was taken up by Joseph and carried to the land of Canaan. This was the land of promise, which is the Aarru-paradise, the field of the tree of life up which the sun-god climbs in his resurrection from the coffin. The "burying-place" of Jacob is "before Mamre," where the tree of Atum in the garden or meadow, the Sekhet-Hetep, is represented by the oak or terebinth under which Abraham dwelt. Joseph the son (Iusif) is the same character in carrying up the mummy of Jacob that Horus the beloved son is to the dead Osiris in his coffin. Horus acts as the raiser-up of the mummy. This is expressed when the speaker says, "I am he who raises the hand which is motionless" (Rit., ch. 5). Elsewhere Horus comes to raise the mummy of Osiris. Thus the carrying up of Jacob out of Egypt by the son may be parallelled by the resurrection of Osiris, coffin and all. One name of the burial-place for the mummy-Osiris in the Ritual is Sekhem. The deceased is enveloped as a mummy in Sekhem. He rises again and goes, as pure spirit, out of Sekhem. Also the well of Jacob near Shechem answers to the water of Osiris, and the oak or terebinth in Shechem to the tree of life in the pool of the persea or the water of life. The fields of Shechem correspond to the Sekhet-Hetep or fields of peace and plenty, the oasis of fertility which prefigured the celestial paradise. "The parcel of ground that Jacob gave to his son Joseph" was in Shechem, also called Sichem. This is a parallel to Sekhem as place of burial given by Osiris the father to Amsu-Horus the son, who rose again as the living mummy or sahu after the burial, and went up from the lower Egypt of Amenta and the sandy wilderness of Sekari as the god in the coffin or sekeru-bark. The Egyptian Sekhem was no doubt localized as a sanctuary when Judea and Palestine were sown over with the old Egyptian names. Osiris was the reputed holder of property in Sekhem, unless we understand that his mummy, the body of the lord, constituted the property that was held in that sanctuary (Hymn to Osiris, lines 1 and 2).

The lower Egypt of Amenta is a land of bondage to the manes who were doomed to labour in the harvest-field. Chapter 5 is called the chapter by which work is not imposed upon a person in the nether-world. But provision is made for the work being done by proxy. Chapter 6 is the chapter by which the funeral statuettes may be made to do work for a person in the nether-world. "Be thou counted for me," says the speaker, "at every moment, for planting the fields, for watering the soil, and for removing the sands." Thus there was a system of *enforced labour* in the lower Egypt of Amenta. The land of bondage is likewise alluded to as the land of rule in the Book of the Dead. In the chapter by means of which the manes come forth to day and pass through Ammah or the Ammehit it is said, "Hail to you, ye lords of rule (or ruling powers), living for ever, whose secular period is eternity. Let me not be stopped at the Meskat (or place of punishment); let not the Sebau have the mastery over me; let not your doors be closed upon me." And amongst other pleas in this invocation it is said, "Deliver me from the crocodile of this land of rule," or, as it got interpreted, this land of bondage in the lower Egypt of Amenta. In this chapter the crocodile has an evil character, and the evil crocodile is the mythical dragon, the dragon of Egypt, a figure of the Pharaoh who kept the people in bondage and would not let them go from out their prison-house in the Meskat where the evil Sebau had the mastery over the manes, who plead, "Let not the powers of darkness obtain the mastery over me. . . . . I faint before the teeth of those whose mouth raveneth in the nether-world" (Rit., chs. 72 and 74, Renouf).

The Apap-dragon of Amenta is the real Pharaoh who held the people in bondage, but in certain of the Semitic legends Atum-Ra, the great judge and punisher of the wicked, has been mixed up with the cruel Pharaoh who would not let the people go. According to the Arab traditions, the name of the Pharaoh who detained the chosen people, the elect children of light, was known as "Tamuzi." Castell gives this as the Arabic name of the Pharaoh who hindered the exodus of the Israelites, which name goes to the root of the matter, for Tamuzi appears in the Ritual as Atum-Ra, commonly called Tum. The name of this Ra or Pharaoh is derived from "tumu" to shut up, to close. Tum as the setting sun was the closer in the western gate. As shutter up of day or of autumn he wears the closing lotus on his head, the antithesis to Horus rising out of the opening flower of dawn. Atum was the closer as well as the opener of Amenta by name. Those who were captives in his keeping down in the Amenta were hindered from making their exodus until the plagues were passed or the conditions of freedom had been all fulfilled.

The entrance to Amenta figured in the Egyptian itinerary was "the mouth of the cleft," as it was termed at Abydos. This is apparently represented in the Hebrew legend by the mouth of the gorge at Pi-ha-hiroth, "which is before Baal-Zephon." Thus the opening in the mount of the swallowing earth is at the same point as the passage of the Red Sea which also opened for the Israelites to pass when pursued by Pharaoh and his host. There are, however, two starting-points in the biblical exodus of the Israelites. No sooner had they set out on the old road that ran from Rameses to Succoth (or Thuku) and Etham or Khetam, the border-fortress in the land of Thuku, than they were commanded to turn back for a fresh departure from Pi-ha-hiroth, the pass or gorge which was entered by the mouth of the cleft. At this point of divergence the local topography is brought to confusion and serves no further use for localizing the journey. We have to go back and start from the entrance to Amenta by the mouth of the cleft in the rock that was figured at Abydos as the beautiful gate of entrance to Khent-Amenta. This two-fold starting-point at least coincides with the two modes of entrance, one by land and the other by water. At Pi-ha-hiroth we enter the Red Sea of the mythos, the water of the west that was red at sunset, but not the geographical Red Sea. This was entered by the boat of the sun and the boat of souls which passed through the cleft by water as depicted in the vignettes (Maspero, *Dawn of Civ.* Eng. Tr. p. 197). We are now upon the track of the exodus from the lower Egypt of the nether-earth, which was mythical in the lesser mysteries and mystical in the greater, and able to show where and how and why the children of Israel pursue the same route through Amenta as do the children of Ra in the Book of Hades (*Records of the Past*, vols. x. and xii.). At Pi-ha-hiroth the Israelites come to the mouth of the cleft and enter on the passage of the Red Sea, pursued by Pharaoh the dragon and his evil host. In the book of Exodus the Israelites, of course, are treated as the glorified and the Egyptians as the powers of darkness, the conspirators against the elect, the chosen, the children of light. Or, according to the Ritual, by the Apap-dragon and the Sebau, whose habitat is in the Red Sea of the mythos and therefore was not geographical. The Egyptians made the passage by water, but by substituting the miracle for the mythos, "the children of Israel walked on dry land in the midst of the sea." After crossing the waters they enter the wilderness, which is true to its character in the Egyptian books of the nether earth.

When the land that flowed with milk and honey is promised to the children of Israel, it is said by Ihuh, "I will send my terror before thee—I will send the hornet before thee, which shall drive out the Hivite, the Canaanite, and the Hittite from before thee" (Ex. xxiii. 27, 28). Now the hornet, wasp, or bee was a type of Ra the solar god, and thence of the Egyptian Pharaoh. Hor-Apollo says, "They depict a bee to denote a people obedient to their king" (B. i. 62), the force of the creature's sting being emblematic of the supreme power. Also the abait or bird-fly, a bee, wasp, or hornet, was their guide to the Aarru-garden in the Ritual. "I have made my way into the royal palace," says the Osiris" (ch. 76), "and it was the bird-fly (abait) that led me hither"—that is, to the land flowing with milk and honey. Apparently this symbolic abait or bee as guide to the Aarru-paradise has been turned into the hornet that drove the people out of the land in the Hebrew rendering of the story. When Moses sends the explorers ahead to spy out the land of Canaan, and they come back afraid because it is inhabited by the Anakim or giants, "Caleb stilled the people before Moses, and said, Let us go up at once and possess it, for we are well able to overcome it" (Num. xiii. 30). Caleb the explorer who had been sent forward by Moses to spy out the land of promise is another of these converted divinities. In the Semitic languages Caleb is the dog, and the dog as Egyptian was the jackal, apuat, the guide of ways, the zootype which was the guide of ways in the solar mythos, and the guide of souls to the garden of Amenta, wherein grew the grapes of paradise in brobdingnagian clusters which are to be seen in vignettes to the Ritual. Shu as son of Ra is the great leader of the people to the promised land ; Anup the jackal = dog was the guide ; and these two are represented in the book of Numbers by Joshua (or Hoshea) the son of Nun, and Caleb the son of Jephunneh. Those two, the leader and the guide, both in the astronomy and the eschatology, are the only two in the Hebrew version that are to go forth in the exodus from the wilderness and burial-place of the dead. "And they came unto the valley of Eschol, and cut down from thence a branch with one cluster of grapes, and they bare it upon a staff between two " (carriers). "And they returned from spying out the land at the end of forty days." They showed the fruit of the land to Moses and the Israelites, and said, "We came unto the land whither thou sentest us, and surely it floweth with milk and honey, and this is the fruit of it" (Num. xiii. 23–28). The colossal cluster of grapes seen in Eschol by those who were sent to spy out the promised land is of itself almost sufficient to prove the mythical nature and Egyptian origin of the land that flowed with milk and honey and bore the grapes that took two men to carry one cluster. Not only was the circumpolar paradise the land of the seven cows, called the providers of plenty ; as Egyptian it was also the garden of the grape-vine by name. Not as Eden, but as Aarru the garden of the vine or the grapes. In one of the Hebrew märchen it is said that when the explorers of the promised land returned they related, " We have seen the land which we are to conquer with the sword, and it is good and fruitful. The strongest camel is scarcely able to carry one bunch of grapes ; one ear of corn yields enough to feed a whole family ; and one pomegranate shell would contain five armed men. But the inhabitants of the land and their cities are in keeping with the productions of the soil. We saw men the smallest of whom was six hundred cubits high. They were astonished at us, on account of our diminutive stature, and laughed at us. Their houses were also in proportion, walled up to heaven, so that an eagle could hardly soar above them " (Baring Gould's *Legends of the Old Testament Characters* vol. ii. p. 118 ; Weil, p. 175). These are based upon the gigantic inhabitants of Amenta in the Ritual, who have been vastly exaggerated in the märchen. This grand domain was constructed for the manes who as the glorified ones have joined the powers of the east at the point of coming forth where Shu uplifts the sky for Ra and blows off the divine barge with favouring gales. The great or glorified ones are said to be each nine cubits (about 18 feet) in height, and therefore this is the land of the giants to which the Israelites were bound under the leadership of Joshua and the guidance of Caleb the dog. This region of things gigantic may be found in the mystical abodes of the Ritual through which the manes have to pass on their way to the world of light and blessedness. The second abode is called the "greatest of possessions in the fields of the Aarru. The height of its corn is seven cubits ; the ears are two, its stalks are three cubits." The spirits also are said to be seven cubits in stature (ch. 149). Of the fifth abode it is said, "Hail, abode of the spirits, through which there is no passage. The spirits belonging to it are seven cubits long in

U U

their thighs. They live as wretched shades." " Oh, this abode of the spirits." In chapter 109 the inhabitants are nine cubits in height. The passage through the Hades in the eleventh abode is described as the belly of hell. "There is neither coming out of nor going into it, on account of the greatness of the terror of passing him who is in it." That is, the devouring demon, the Am-Moloch. The same fear is reflected in the faces of the spies from the land of giants ; they had seen the same sight. The Moabites called the giants who dwelt there in times past the Emim (Deut. ii. 11), and the Am-am in Egyptian are the devourers. Am is the male devourer, Am-t the female devourer in the Ritual. As said in chapter 109, " It is the glorified ones, each of whom is nine cubits in height, who reap the Aarru fields (in the divine domain of the promised land) in presence of the powers of the east " (Renouf). The giants as Rephaim are also Egyptian (Rit., ch. 149, 5th Abode). These giants of Amenta and the religious mysteries still survive in the grotesque masks of the Christmas pantomime, which represent the huge inhabitants of an under-world that is the lowermost of three, the highest of which is on the mount of glory. Emim, Anakim, Rephaim, and Zamzummim are all giants— hence the Anakim under different names, nine cubits high ; and this land of the giants as Egyptian was in the nether-earth, the original of the Hebrew Sheol, in which the giants are identifiable as non-human inhabitants of a foreworld that had passed away. It is to that fore-world and its people, the children of darkness, that the writer of Deuteronomy refers, and as its inhabitants were altogether mythical (or eschatological), the children of Israel, and of Lot, who drove them out and destroyed them utterly, could not be human nor the trans-action humanly historical. The land of the mythical giants can be localized in Amenta, but not elsewhere.

The lower or sub-terrestrial paradise, otherwise called the garden of Aarru, was the garden eastward, the garden of the mount in Amenta, which was in prospect throughout the journey. This was the paradise to which Shu-Anhur was the leader from the western mountain and Anup-Ap-Uat was the guide as dog or jackal. It was the paradise of all good things, including the gigantic grapes and grain, the milk and honey, as types of food and drink in ever-lasting plenty.

The point of emergence from Amenta was at the double gate of glory on the summit of the eastern mount ; otherwise expressed, this was the place of exit from the lower to the upper Egypt of the mythos as celestial localities. Anhur was the uplifter and supporter of the heaven and its inhabitants by night. Shu was the deliverer by day who brought the solar orb to the horizon. In the Hebrew rendering Moses sustains the *rôle* of Anhur, and Joshua that of Shu, the halves of the whole round being extended to the circle of the year. The earthly paradise was planted as the Allu or elysian fields to the eastward of the nether-earth where stood the tree of life, and where the mountain of the double earth was climbed to get a glimpse of the land of promise that was visible over-sea. Upon this moun-tain " Moses stood, to view the landscape o'er," or rather the sky-scape. The lower paradise was but a picture and a promise for the wanderers in the wilderness of Amenta. The upper was the paradise of all the ancient and pre-solar legends. Thus far the deliverer as Anhur or as Moses was the conductor of the children of Ra or Israel. High on Mount Hetep, in the heaven of eternity, was the paradise of spirits perfected. This was the land of promise and final fruition both in one, the land overflowing with milk and honey. The milk, called "the white liquor which the glorified ones love," was supplied by the seven cows, providers of plenty in the meadows of the upper Aarru. Here also was the land of corn in limitless abundance. No words could say how much. Lower Egypt was a land of corn, but the legendary promised land of corn, honey, and oil was in the Aarru fields of the mythos. These were the fields where the corn grew seven cubits high, with ears three cubits long and in eternal plenty for all comers. The landing-place upon Mount Hetep at the summit of attainment is called "the divine nome of corn and barley" (Rit., ch. 110).

The Egyptians were already tillers of the ground when Ptah laid out and planted the lower Aarru-paradise, as their other field of work, in an earth that was ruled or tyrannized over by the powers of evil, headed by the Apap-dragon. This was the earth of the abyss, the primeval desert which had to be reclaimed by the pioneers and planters of that under-world. It was laid out strictly on the allotment system. Each one of the manes had a portion in which to plough and sow and reap. The seed grown in the harvest-field of life on earth was garnered up to sow and bring forth a hundredfold in this, the field of divine harvest, which was so magnified by tradition because its bounty had been divinized. The Egyptian authorship of a paradise of peace and plenty is pre-eminently shown by their converting the "earth of eternity" into a world of work, the harvest-field that was cultivated by the manes, who dug and hoed and sowed in it, and reaped the corn according to their labours (Rit., ch. 6). Amenta was made from sand converted into fertile soil well watered by the all-enriching Nile. It was like lower Egypt, the land of honey, the land of the sycamore fig-tree, which was a veritable tree of life to the Egyptians. It was the land of the grapes that grew in clusters of prodigious size. It was the country of abundant corn. Not that the Egyptians thought the other world a replica of this, but such was the natural plan on which they wrought in making out the unknown by the known. They dramatized another inter-mediate state, and acted the eschatological drama in accordance with conditions familiar to them in this world. The Aarru-paradise in Amenta is copied from Egypt in the upper earth. The fulfilment of all blessedness was in its being a likeness of the dear old land made permanent and perfect in the spirit-world. It was the promised land for those who were prepared to take possession of it and to drink of the sacred Nile *at its celestial source*. Its tree of life was the same sycamore fig-tree that had always been the tree of life and food in season.

The journey from the lower Egypt of the mythos through the deserts of Amenta was from west to east, from the place of sunset to the point of sunrise which was called the solar mount of glory. At sunset Anhur-Shu upraised his mansion of the starry firmament which he uplifted nightly, standing on the steps of Am-Khemen. This presented a stellar picture of the upper Egypt or the upper paradise for which the wanderers in the wilderness were bound. At dawn the mount of sunrise in the garden eastward was attained. This was the mountain of Amenta, also called Shennu or Shenni= Sinai. Shena in Egyptian signifies the point of turning in the orbit of the solar course. This point was figured on the mountain where the lions rested as supporters of the solar disk at dawn, or Shu uplifted Ra from out the darkness of Amenta and held the orb aloft with his two hands. At this point Anhur's place as leader of the chosen people was taken by his *alter ego* Shu. The Magic Papyrus describes the warrior-god as "king of upper and lower Egypt" in his two characters of Anhur and Shu-si-Ra. By night Shu-Anhur was the uplifter of the firmament for the Egyptian exodus or coming forth to day from out the darkness of Amenta or of "Egypt and the desert" (Rit., ch. 110). (See the figure of Shu as the uplifter, p. 315.) Under the name of Anhur he is the leader of the upper heaven, rod in hand. His starry image probably was seen as Regulus in the constellation of Kepheus, the ruler there, arrested with the rod or staff still lifted in his hand. He repels the crocodile or dragon coming out of the abyss, the crocodile that is the dragon of Egypt and the Pharaoh of the Hebrew writers. This repelling of the crocodiles that issue from the abyss corresponds to the overthrowal of Pharaoh or the dragon and his host in the Red Sea. Anhur is the lord of the scimitar. He is designated "smiting double horns"; "the god provided with two horns," like Moses. "Uplifted is the sky which he maintains with his two arms," like Moses. This two-fold character of Anhur is indicated when he is described as "the king of upper and lower Egypt, Shu-si-Ra." This was the Egypt of Amenta. Thus, as the king of lower Egypt he was Anhur the uplifter of the firmament for the chosen people to come forth. At daybreak he assumed the character of Shu, the son of Ra, who lifted up the solar disk at dawn on the horizon, otherwise upon the mount of sunrise. As Regulus on the horizon in the zodiac the leader of the manes changed to Shu, who is then called "the double abode of Ra." The Magic Papyrus, which contains "the hymn of the god Shu," is called "the chapter of the excellent songs which dispel the submerged." It is the celebration of the great victory over the Apap-reptile and all dangerous animals lurking in the depths of the mythical Red Sea. It is said to Shu in the hymn, "Thou leadest to the upper heaven with thy rod in that name which is thine of Anhur. Thou repellest the crocodile coming out of the abyss in that name which is thine of repeller of crocodiles." The crocodile, of course, is the dragon of Egypt. The wicked are overthrown by Anhur the valiant as the lord of events. His sister Tefnut accompanies him. She is a form of Sekhet, "the goddess in her fury," the "chastiser of the wicked." "She gives her fire against his enemies, and reduces them to non-existence." She is the Kamite prototype of Miriam, the sister of Moses. Tefnut accompanies her brother in his battles with the Sebau and the submerged. Elsewhere she changes her shape into a weapon of war. She shouts her defiance against "the wicked conspirators," exclaiming, "I am Tefnut thundering against those who are annihilated for ever!" and against those that "remain floating on the waves, like dead bodies on the inundation," just as it was on that day when "Israel saw the Egyptians dead upon. the sea-shore" (Ex. xiv. 30). Tefnut, the prototype of Miriam, "gives her fire" against her brother's enemies to reduce them to non-existence by their being submerged in the waters, where "Miriam the prophetess, the sister of Aaron, took a timbrel in her hand, and all the women went out after her with timbrels and with dances. And Miriam answered them, Sing ye to the Lord, for he hath triumphed gloriously; the horse and his rider hath he thrown into the sea" (Ex. xv. 20-21). Moses corresponds to Anhur. He is the leader of the children of Israel during the first part of the journey towards the promised land. He conducts them through the Red Sea where Israel saw the Egyptians dead upon the sea-shore; through the sandy wilderness, the waterless wastes, and the ways of darkness. "Then came Amalek, and fought with Israel in Rephidim." This, as we reckon, was the great battle of the autumn equinox. It was not a battle fought by human beings once for all on mundane ground, but a war betwixt the Lord and Amalek, that went on for ever, from generation to generation, because it was periodic in the phenomena of external nature, and not a duel betwixt the Lord of heaven and an earthly potentate or people. The description of holding up the hands of Moses to maintain the equilibrium shows the equinoctial nature of the conflict. The going forth at the equinox is further identified by the month of the year. The Jewish new year still begins about the time of the autumn equinox, a little belated in consequence of its not having been carefully readjusted. "And the Lord spake unto Moses and Aaron in the land of Egypt, saying, This month shall be unto you the beginning of months: it shall be the first month of the year to you" (Ex. xii. 1, 2). This was the year that opened with and was determined by the full moon nearest to the autumn equinox. For six months thenceforth the moon was ruler of the year as the great light in the darkness of the double earth. Again, at the time of the vernal equinox there is another poising of the scales, if not a standing still of sun and moon, and another great battle in which the sun-god finally overcomes the dragon of darkness and all the evil powers that war against the light of life and welfare of the world; also against the children of Ra on their journey as souls or manes from the lower Egypt of the mythical Amenta to the upper heaven on the mount of glory.

The present writer has previously suggested that the name of Moyses, or as some Hebrews pronounce it, Mouishé, was derived from the dual name of Shu, one of whose names was Ma, the other Shu, and Ma-Shu denotes Anhur, who manifests in the two characters of Ma and Shu. In the address to the god it is said, " Thou blowest the divine barge off with a favourable wind in that name which is thine of the goddess Ma." Thus Ma, the goddess of truth, law, and justice, is here identified with Shu in a feminine character. The feather of Anhur also reads both Ma and Shu—Ma as light and Shu as shade. But, after all, the origin of the name is of little importance compared with the traits of character. This female character of Ma-Shu has also been assigned to Moses. There is a tradition, reported by Suidas, that the Hebrew lawgiver and author of the Jewish laws was a Hebrew woman named Musu, which is equivalent to Ma-Shu in Egyptian. Shu is the very personification of light and shade. The name reads both light and shade. This dual character of the god is to be read in the face of Moses, who wears the glory on it when in presence of the Lord upon the mount, and who covers or shades his face when he turns to speak with the people in the valley. He likewise is the personification of light and shade : Moses under the veil is Shu in the shade ; Moses wearing the glory of God upon his face is Shu who "sits in his father's eye," the eye of the sun ; *Shu-ari-hems-nefer*—who keeps his residence radiant—which is a title of Shu at Philae. (Pierret, *Le Panthéon Egyptien*, pp. 22–3.) "When Moses had done speaking with the people, he put a veil on his face. But when Moses went in before the Lord to speak with him, he took the veil off until he came out." And when he came out and spake unto them that which he was commanded, they saw the skin of Moses' face. "And Moses put the veil upon his face again until he went in to speak with him" (Ex. ch. xxxiv–35). The glory on the face of Moses is described as sending forth horns, which is a way of portraying the god provided with "two horns," that is a title of Anhur. Moses performs the same act as Shu the supporter of the firmament, but in the heaven with twelve supports instead of the earlier four erected by Shu-Anhur, which followed a readjustment that was made by the Hir-seshti of On in the heaven of Atum-Ra. Anhur was the elevator and supporter of the heavens, and Shu-si-Ra is the upholder of the solar disk. Moses with his arms uplifted on the mount, or with the "rod of God" in his hand, is the Hebrew version of Anhur the sustainer of heaven standing on the mount. Joshua, who becomes the supporter of Iah the solar god, is identical with Shu when he is the son and supporter of Ra upon the horizon east and west. Shu was at first the son of Nun, the deity of the celestial water, who was also called the father of the gods. He afterwards became the son of Ra as the supporter of the solar disk on the horizon "with his two hands." Joshua also had a double character, like Shu. In the first he is called Hoshea, the son of Nun. In his later *rôle* Joshua becomes the upholder of Ihuh and his change of name is connected with the change in character. The name of Joshua or יהושוע contains the name of Ihuh united to a word signifying assistance or help. In the form ישוא it denotes a lifting up, an upholding, as in the Egyptian name of Shu, to uphold, which describes him in the character of the uplifter to Ra the solar god. This should suffice to demonstrate the identity of Joshua, the son of Nun and the supporter of Ihuh, with Shu, who became Shu-si-Ra as the uplifter of the solar disk. Thus Shu, the son of Nun and supporter of the firmament as an elemental power, was afterwards personalized as the supporter of the sun-god Ra. Ra is Ihuh. The name of Shu denotes the supporter, and the deity whom he supported on the mount was Atum-Huhi ; and in this character Shu became the leader of the children of Ra (or of Israel) as Io-Shua, who proclaims himself to be the supporter of Ihuh in the book of Joshua (xxiv. 15, 16). The firmament is the Nun by name, and Shu the uplifter of the firmament is called the son of Nun. Thus Shu in his uplifting of the firmament is the uplifter of his father. Now, to show once more how widely fragments of the Egyptian wisdom were scattered to become the later legends of many lands, let us glance for a moment at "the exploits of Maui," a Polynesian form of Shu. Shu was the son of Nnu (Nun), and in Mangaia the name of Nnu is rendered by Ru. Ru is the father of Maui, and one of the exploits of Maui is to hurl his father Ru aloft, sky and all, to a tremendous height, so high indeed that the sky could never get back to earth again. Now for the conversion of the Kamite myth into the Mangaian märchen. Nnu or Nun was also the firmament upraised by Shu. Nnu as firmament was personalized in Nnu the father of Shu; and where Shu uplifts the sky, now personalized, Maui is humorously described as assuming gigantic proportions, and exerting prodigious strength to toss his father so far aloft that he was for ever entangled and suspended among the stars of heaven, and never could come down again (Gill, *Myths and Songs*, p. 58).

Various legends derived from the Egyptian mythology were compounded in the Hebrew book of Exodus.

One of the most remarkable of all the parallels to be adduced is to be seen in the fact that in one particular type there is a blending of Shu with Horus in Horus-Shuti, and that this is repeated in the story of Moses, who represents the deliverer as Horus in the ark of papyrus, and Anhur in other aspects of the character. Moses is the water-born. Josephus explains the name as signifying one who was taken out of the water. Pharaoh's daughter called the name of the child Mosheh, and said, "because I drew him out of the water" (Ex. ii. 10). Shu-Anhur likewise is the water-born. He is addressed in the Magic Papyrus as "the unique lord issuing from the Nun," which is the firmamental water, and from which Shu as the breathing-force was born as the son of Nun.

The growth of a legend from its source in the primitive representation or *mythicizing* of natural phenomena down to its becoming humanized at last as biblical and historical may be exemplified by the story of the child who was saved from the waters in a little ark of bulrush or papyrus-reed. It is told of Sargon in Assyria, of Maui in New Zealand, and various other children who were drawn forth from the water at the time of their birth. It is the myth of the child-Horus, first and far away the oldest in the world. The story has to be read backward in Hebrew a very long way before its primal meaning can be comprehended. In going back we meet at first with the child-Horus floating in an ark upon the waters. The speaker in the Ritual at the time of his re-birth says, "I am coffined in an ark like Horus, to whom his cradle is brought." This cradle is often represented as a nest of papyrus-reed=the ark of bulrushes in the biblical version (Rit., ch. 130). This in its most primitive Egyptian form was the flower of the papyrus-plant, or later lotus. On this child-Horus is upborne from out the waters, which led to the Egyptian ark or boat that was made of papyrus-reeds. When the legend of child-Horus on his papyrus, or in his nest of reeds, took its Hebrew form, the little ark in which the child was saved is made of bulrushes, or some other form of rush called גֹּמֶא, which probably represents the Egyptian kama, a reed, the reed of Egypt, therefore the papyrus-reed. According to the legendary lore, repeated with a wise word of caution by Josephus, the young child Moses, saved from the river in the ark, was adopted and named by Thermutis. This name is a title of the Great Mother Mut in Egyptian, the consort of Amen-Ra. But the genesis of the name from Mut the mother and Ta-Ur, which signifies the first and oldest, she who was personalized in Ta-Urt, shows that the Mut or mother, Thermutis, in her primordial form was Ta-Ur-Mut = Thermutis. Again, we learn from the same source that the black or Ethiopian woman who became the second wife of Moses was named Tharuis or Tharvis. In the Greek rendering of the Egyptian Ta-Ur (or Ta-Urt) this name becomes Thoueris, and in Ta-Ur (t) we can identify the prototype of Thermutis and the original of Thoueris or Tharuis (*Antiq.* B. 2, 10, 2). Both the foster-mother and the wife of Moses are here traced back to the old First Mother as Taurt and Thermutis, who are one and the same, in the Egyptian goddess that first brought forth the divine child from the waters or from the marshes and the bulrushes, as Uati or as Apt, the water-cow, the most ancient form of the Great Mother in Egyptian mythology. In the Hebrew legends the same old mother, under two names which are resolved into one, supplies two characters as the foster-mother and the consort of Moses. Now, the old First Mother Ta-Ur-Mut, who saved the young child from the waters in her primitive ark, is designated "the mother of him who is married to his mother." In like manner the mother (or foster-mother) and wife of Moses are one and the same in Taurt, who was both mother and spouse of Sebek, the youthful solar god. Moses is saved from the water by Thermutis (Ta-Ur, as Mut, the mother), and he was married to Thaueris, who is the same by name and nature as Thermutis. Thus Moses also was both the child and the consort of his mother, which had been the status of the young sun-god from the time when the human fatherhood had not been individualized. Lastly, the two characters of the old First Mother were represented by the two mothers in the Osirian mythos. These are the two divine sisters, Isis and Nephthys, into which the old First Genetrix was divided as the water-mother and the mother-earth. Isis is the wateress. Hes, her name, signifies the liquid of life. Nephthys is an earth-mother who carries the basket of seed on her head. As it is said in the Ritual, Horus the child is produced by Isis (from the water) and nourished by Nephthys (on the earth) (Rit. 17). And these two forms of the divine mother can be detected even in their biblical guise as the mother and the foster-mother of the young child Moses, one of whom saves him from the waters in the ark of bulrushes, just as Isis mothers Horus in the element of water and Nephthys nourishes and mothers him on land.

There is nothing human or historical about the young child saved from the waters under any name whatsoever, in any kind of ark, no matter in what language the legend may be told or in what waters the little ark may float. The same legend is related of the mythical Sargon in the cuneiform tablets. He says, "My mother the Princess conceived me; in a secret place she brought me forth. She placed me in a basket of reeds; with bitumen my exit she closed; she gave me to the river, which drowned me not." When Sargon says, "My mother knew not my father" (*Records of the Past*, vol. v. p. 3, First Series), he is claiming to be that divine child whose only parent was the divine virgin mother, like Neith, the bringer-forth of Horus (or Helios) without the male progenitorship.

The hidden birth of the Child-Horus is also repeated for the Hebrew infant, of whom it is said that when his mother saw that he was a goodly child "she hid him three months" (Ex. ii. 2, 3), to preserve him from the death decreed by the cruel Pharaoh. The time may not be given in any known hieroglyphic text, but the length is correct according to the astronomical data. Child-Horus at a later time was born in the winter solstice and the concealment in the nether earth came to an end in the vernal equinox. Therefore his mother hid him in the marshes and the rushes of Amenta for three months. When the babe was placed in the ark of bulrushes and laid in the flags by the river's brink his sister was in charge of him. "And his sister stood far off to know what would be done to him" (ii. 4, 5). And in the Hymn to Osiris it is said of the Child-Horus, "His sister took care of him by dissipating his enemies and repelling bad luck. She is wise of tongue, and beneficent of will and words" (*Records*, vol. iv. p. 101), as was the sister of Moses in her suggestion to the daughter of Pharaoh. Horus on his papyrus is the youthful god uplifted from the dark waters and saved from the coils of the Apap-reptile—a salvation that is effected by the two divine sisters Isis and Nephthys, one of whom was the conceiver of the child, the other being the nurse. Here as elsewhere it is the same in the mythos as in the "history." In the biblical version the daughter of Pharaoh and the sister of Moses take the place of Isis and Nephthys. Here the cruel Pharaoh in the book of Exodus plays the same part as Herod and other tyrants who massacre the innocents, inasmuch as he commands the two midwives to kill all the male children at the time of their birth by drowning (Ex. i. 22). The human innocents were to be murdered *en masse* so as to include the divine child in the massacre. Only two midwives were appointed to deliver all the parturient women of Israel in Egypt. The mythos will also answer for this limited number. In the Osirian system the divine child was brought forth by the two sisters Isis and Nephthys. In an earlier rendering these were Sekhet and Neith. Josephus states that the two midwives given to the Jewish women by the Pharaoh were Egyptians (Ant. ii. 9. 2). And as *the midwives were but two for all the multitude of the children of Israel*, they are evidently a form of the two mythical bringers-forth, who were Isis and Nephthys in the Osirian religion and Iusāas and Neb-hetep in the cult of Atum-Ra.

In certain of the extra-biblical features of the Mosaic mythos the lower Egypt of Amenta is plainly indicated as the real land of the exodus. For example, when Moses went into India, he and his army enjoyed the light of the sun *during the night-time*, and this could only occur in the lower earth which the sun illuminated by night—that is, the land of Amenta. India, Sindhu and Hendu each represent the Egyptian Khentu, which is a name for the interior. Thus, we identify the mythical India with Khentu, and Khentu is the interior within the earth where the sun shone at night for Moses and his warriors in the Osirian Khentu-Amenta. Also when Moses is identified with Shu-Anhur this may account for his legendary reputation outside the Bible history as a mighty warrior. Anhur in Egypt is Har-Tesh, the red god Mars, or Arês, who passed into the Greek mythology by name as the great warrior Onouris = Anhur. Shu-Anhur is addressed under various names connected with his deeds. "Thou wieldest thy spear to pierce the head of the serpent Nekau, in that name which is thine of the god provided with horns." "Thou seizest thy spear and overthrowest the wicked (the Sebau), in that name which is thine of Horus the striker!" "Thou destroyest the An of Tokhenti in that name which is thine of Double abode of Ra." "Thou strikest the Menti and the Sati in that name which is thine of Young-elder!" "Thou strikest upon the heads of the wicked in that name which is thine of Lord of Wounds!" (Mag. Pap. pp. 2 and 3).

In one of the Rabbinical legends it is related that when Moses was condemned to lose his head for killing an Egyptian, the Lord permitted that his neck should become as hard as a pillar of marble, which caused the sword of the executioner to rebound and kill the wielder of the weapon. This in the mythos is the state of the justified manes in Amenta, who prays that his neck may be invulnerable at the block of execution. In the Hebrew märchen the Manes becomes a man called Moses.

Fragments of the ancient wisdom survive in many foolish-looking legends. The Rabbins relate that Moses was born circumcised. So the kaf-ape is said to have been born in the same condition. "It is born circumcised, which circumcision the priests adopt." (Hor-Apollo, B. i. 14.) Now Shu in one of his divers characters is said to have taken the form of a kaf-ape (Magic Papyrus, p. 8. *Records*, vol. x. p. 152). Thus Shu, or Ma-Shu, as the ape in the mythos becomes the man Moses or Mosheh, who is said in the märchen to have been born circumcised, when the anthropomorphic type had taken the place of the zootype. In another legend Shu the giant is portrayed as acting the part of a crazy man. The two characters are coupled together when it is said, "Though didst take the form of a kaf-ape, and afterwards of a crazy man" (Magic Papyrus, pp. 8, 9). This may possibly supply a gloss to the action of Moses when he waxed angry and smashed the tables of the law (Ex. xxxii. 19). For this reason: Shu in this character is called "the giant of seven cubits" (or he represents a shrine of seven cubits), and he is then commanded to make a shrine of eight cubits. And Moses, after breaking the tables of the law and acting uncommonly like a crazy man, is commanded by the Lord to hew two other tables of stone like unto the first, so that the Lord might write upon the second tables the words that were on the first set which the crazy man had broken.

Shu-Anhur is described as he "who putteth a stop to them whose hand is violent against those who are weaker than themselves" (Rit., ch. 110). This is the character in which Moses begins his personal history. The first thing he does is to slay an Egyptian whom he saw oppressing a Hebrew (and bury his body in the sand). On the "second day" "behold two men of the Hebrews strove together, and he said to him that did the wrong, Wherefore smitest thou thy fellow?" (Ex. ii. 11-13). This contention in the Ritual is betwixt the twin-brothers Sut and Horus when Shu-Anhur reconciles the two warrior gods where Moses tries to reconcile two fighting men who were fellow-Hebrews.

Moses is said to have built an altar, and to have called it "Jehovah-Nissi, the Lord is my banner." This, to say the least, is suggestive of a title of Anhur, to whom it is said, "Thou comest here upon thy stately stand in that name which is thine of being in thy stately stand," or on the standard (Am aat). Here there is the same dual rendering possible as in the Hebrew, the stately stand and standard being equivalent to the banner. Moses carries the "rod of God" in his hand. With this rod he divides the Red Sea for the people to go over on dry ground. With this he smites the rock in Horeb, and causes the water to spring forth abundantly. The plagues descend on Egypt at the stretching forth of Moses's wonder-working rod. Shu-Anhur is likewise the bearer of the rod. He is represented with the rod in his hands, and is designated "Lord of the rod." In the Hymn to Shu it is said, "Thou leadest the upper heaven with thy rod in that name which is thine of Anhur," the uplifter of heaven (Magic Papyrus, 2, 5). The origin of smiting the rock to make the water come forth is connected with the rock of the Tser Hill, the mount of sunrise. The first waters that issued out of this rock were the springs of dawn and the floods of day. In the Ritual we meet with the hero who causes the water to gush forth. He says, in the character of the great one, who has been developed into a chief, "I make the water to issue forth," or "I make water to come" (117). The striker of the rock with his rod or staff was Shu-Anhur, the impersonator of the force that burst up out of the rock at sunrise when the waters of day were once more set free. The water of dawn is called the "water of Tefnut," she who is the twin-sister of Shu, and of which water the children of light "drink abundantly." As one of these—who are the prototypes of the children of Israel—says, "I drink abundantly of the waters of Tefnut." The waters of dawn (or the tree) were ascribed to the female source, whether as Tefnut or as Hathor. And it is noticeable that in the Hebrew version the first to make the water come forth by miracle for the people to drink is Miriam, whose relation to Moses is identical with that of Tefnut to Shu. The legend of the one god who reveals himself upon a summit of a rock, whether to Shu or Moses, is a matter of mythology, not a subject of human history, and as such the mythos is Egyptian. "And God spake unto Moses and said unto him, I am Iahu, and I appeared unto Abraham, unto Israel, and unto Jacob as El Shaddai, but by the name of Iahu I was not made known to them" (Ex. vi. 3). In the original rendering of the mythos Ra reveals himself to Shu and the elders as the deity in spirit, living in truth. He has become greater than the god who created him. He tells them that although later in point of time, he is the one primeval source who has been giving them light all the while, and in this new character he assumes his sovereignty as god over all, the one beside whom there is none other. This is the deity in the Ritual who says, "I am the self-orginating force. Behold me, how I am raised upon my throne" (ch. 85). He is no longer merely solar, or one of the seven elemental powers. He is the god in spirit—the spirit that is divine, and a type of that which lives for ever. This accounts for the change of name or title which follows the change in status. Ra was known by other titles in the mythos, but as Huhi the eternal he was previously unknown. In this character the god reveals his secret self as the supreme one, whose name is then expressed by the titles of Huhi the eternal and Ra the holy spirit. The Hebrew deity Ihuh was not simply the one god in a single form of personality; he is the Egyptian one god in his various attributes. He is the one god both as the father and the son, who in the words of Isaiah (ix. 6) is the everlasting father and the prince of peace, who as Egyptian was Atum-Huhi the eternal father, and Iusa the ever-coming son; Atum-Ra as closer on the horizon west, and Atum-Horus as opener on the horizon east. He is the Egyptian god of Sinai as the lord of Shenni; the god who was " lifted up" in his ark-shrine of the sanctuary on the mount. He is the god of the Urim and Thummim, or lights and perfections; the Urai or Urur, of the winged disk and other figures of the Egyptian symbolism; the one god who was solar in the mythos and the holy spirit in the eschatology. In the book of Exodus the one god Ihuh supersedes all other gods, El-Shadai and the Elohim; and, like the Egyptian Ra, he assumes the sovereignty as Ihuh the eternal. It was in this new character Ra issued his commands for an ark, shrine, or sanctuary to be made, in which he was to be lifted up by Shu, the supporter of Ra.

Ages before the Hebrew Pentateuch was written and ascribed to Moses, the one god had been worshipped at On or Annu as Egyptian under the title of Atum-Ra, and if he was made known to Anhur by revelation, whatsoever that may imply, the revelation was Egyptian. This is the god who was one by nature and dual in manifestation; one in the solar mythos as the closer and opener of the nether-world; one in the eschatology as Huhi the everlasting father, and Iu the ever-coming son as prince of peace; the one god, called the holy spirit, who was founded typically on the human ghost. This is the living (Ankhu), self-originating, and eternal god. This is he who was to be lifted up as god alone in his ark or tabernacle on the mount of glory—that is, as Ra-Harmakhu on the double horizon or in the dual equinox; the deity who gave the law upon Mount Shenni through the intermediation of Anhur or Ma-Shu, the son of Ra.

In the so-called " destruction of mankind " the solar god resolves to be lifted up in an ark or sanctuary by himself alone. This sanctuary is carried on the back of Nut, the celestial cow. "There was Nut. The majesty of Ra was on her back. His majesty arrived in the sanctuary. And his majesty saw the inner part of the sanctuary." This creation of the sanctuary for the one god Ra upon the mount is followed in the Hebrew book. Ihuh says to Moses, "Let them (the children of Israel) make me a sanctuary, that I may dwell among them. According to all that I show thee, the pattern of the dwelling and the pattern of all the furniture thereof, even so ye shall make it." "And they shall make an ark of acacia-wood." The two together, the sanctuary and the ark, constituted an ark-shrine of the true Egyptian pattern. As Egyptian, the ark of Ra-Harmakhu represented the double equinox in the two horizons. This was the "double abode of Ra" in the dual domain of light and shade, the model of the Jewish arks or tabernacles that were to be erected equally in sun and shade. The part open to the rays of light was exactly to balance the shade or veil of the covering, and not to have more sun than shade (Mishna, Treatise Succah, ch. 1). This was in accordance with the plan of the Great Pyramid in relation to the luminous hemisphere and the hemisphere of shade at the two equinoxes. The sanctuary of Ra was a figure of the heavens. The Hebrew ark was a portable copy, a tabernacle fitted for an itinerating deity. It was the Kamite custom to represent the heaven in miniature as an ark of so many cubits. There is an ark of seven cubits, one of eight cubits, another of four cubits, in which the god was "lifted up" or exalted. Inside the ark there was a shrine for the deity, with a figure of the god within the sanctuary. As water was the primary element of life, the nature-powers were held to have come into being by water. Hence their images were placed within the shrine that was carried on board the papyrus bark and borne upon the shoulders of the priests. These tabernacles, consisting of a boat and shrine, were the sacred ark-shrines of Egypt. Thus the beginnings were for ever kept in view. The ark-shrine on the water represented by the boat became a type of heaven as dwelling-place of the Eternal. Thus an ark of Nnu was constellated in the stars and pictured on the waters of the inundation. The ark of Atum-Ra was depicted with the solar orb on board, which was always red. In the religious mysteries, as already shown, an ark of four cubits imaged the heaven of four quarters or, as the Egyptians phrased it, of four sides. As we have seen, there was an ark of seven cubits for the heptanomis, and one of eight cubits for the octonary. This ark-shrine of eight cubits is to be built for the god to float in after there has been a great subsidence of land in the celestial waters. So likewise in the "destruction of mankind," when Ra becomes the supreme one god, he orders an ark or tabernacle to be made for his voyage over the heavens. The inscription was engraved in the chamber of the cow that was herself a form of the ark as the goddess Nut.

William Simpson in 1877 called attention to the Japanese ark-shrines or mikoshi, "which have many points of likeness to the Jewish ark of the covenant, and which are carried on men's shoulders by means of staves. Mikoshi signifies the high or honourable seat. Temo-sama may be translated 'heaven's lord'" (*Trans. Soc. of Bib. Arch.* vol. v. p. ii. 550). Now, the first type of heaven's lord that is known to astronomical mythology was the ruler of a pole-star, whose high or honourable seat was at the pole, like that of Anup on his mountain. In some of these arks, we are told, there is the small figure of a deity, which is no doubt the "heaven's lord" intended by the name. There were seven of these lords of heaven altogether, who, as here suggested, had been rulers of the seven pole-stars in succession. Now, Simpson tells us that there are seven of these arks preserved in the temple of Hachiman at Kamakura, Japan. "They are said by some to be state-norimans, but as these shrines are connected with the deified Mikado, they are most probably temo-samas or mikoshis as well as norimans." This is confirmed by a statement of Kaempfer's. He says, "The mikoshi themselves being eight," the eight seats or ark-shrines answer to the Kami when the eighth one had been added to the seven as over-lord, but seven was the primary number of the Kami as of the Egyptian Akhemu or never-setting ones. We infer that seven ark-shrines or seats were typical of the seven rulers, in addition to all the other forms of the septenary, mounds, mountains, islands, menhirs, towers, temples, or cities that were raised on high to symbolize the seven stations marked by pole-stars in the circuit of precession. Now, Israel is charged by Amos with having borne an ark-shrine that was obviously the tabernacle of a star-god or gods who were once the Elohim after which she went a-whoring (Amos, v. 26). The passage in the revised version runs thus, "Yea, ye have borne siccuth your king and chiun your images, the star of your god, which ye made to yourselves." The most probable rendering depends on siccuth being a tabernacle or ark of the god, corresponding to the Egyptian sekhet, for an ark, shrine, or cabin, and on chiun, from chun, denoting the pillar or pedestal of the star. Kûn signifies to found, set up, erect, heap up, and establish; it denotes the highest point, at the centre, and is applied to the founding of the world. The name was assigned to Saturn as god in the highest. But Sut was the earlier founder of a world as god of the pole, in conjunction with his mother, who first represented the mount. The siccuth as tabernacle, ark, or female abode is equivalent to the ben-ben or beth of the child, the god or king who as Sut was figured at times within the cone. The chun as pedestal would be the pillar of the star, and the images would signify the ark of the pole and its star—in short, the Great Mother and her child, who were the primeval female and male as Apt (or the Egypto-Semitic naked goddess Kûn) and Sut, later Sut-Anup. The so-called tabernacle was a "hut," which agrees with the conical pillar or ben-ben as a figure of the pole. The god of the pillar originated as god of the pole; Sut was primarily and pre-eminently god of the pillar, and El-Shaddai we hold to have been a form of Sut-Anup on his mountain of the pole.

In the solar mythos the mount was figured on or as the horizon at the point of equinox, the point of turning and returning from Amenta in the circuit of the year, or from the lower Egypt of the mythos. Hence it was named Mount Shenni = the Hebrew Sinai. This was the place of crossing or passing over the line in the exodus or coming forth from the land of bondage when commemorated as an historical passover. The first day of the first month was the day of the equinox. The Hebrew dual year, sacred and civil, was based upon the double equinox. Hence the ark-shrine of Ihuh (Jehovah) is identifiable with that of Atum-Huhi, whose title of Ra-Harmachis shows that he was the deity of the double horizon, the double abode, or double sanctuary, first as Horus, next as Ra. This may be gathered from the statement, "And the Lord spake unto Moses, saying, On the first day of the first month thou shalt rear up the tabernacle of the tent of meeting. And thou shalt put therein the ark of the testimony" (Ex. xl. 1)—that is, on the mount which was the equinoctial meeting-point upon the summit, the point at which the rescued spirits went on board the bark of Ra, as represented in the Ritual. "The tabernacle of the tent of meeting" is the full title of the portable dwelling-place that was built for Ihuh on Sinai, according to the imagery shown to Moses in the mount. "Moreover, thou shalt make the tabernacle with ten curtains. The length of each curtain shall be eight-and-twenty cubits, and the breadth of each curtain four cubits." These numbers correspond to the ark of heaven in ten divisions, with the four corners and the twenty-eight measures of a lunar zodiac. Ten cubits also was to be the length of each board of acacia-wood. The seven-fold candlestick we look on as a figure of the celestial heptanomis and its mystery of the seven stars. It was thus the symbolism was compounded and continued in the later rendering of the imagery.

The mount of the horizon in the equinox was the place of the two lions called the Sheniu, which also tend to identify the mount with Sinai. These two lions, the two kherufu or kherubs that support the sun upon the horizon, are repeated in the two cherubim that were portrayed upon the ark of testimony. One symbol of Mount Hetep is a table piled with food. This is reproduced in the table of shew-bread that was to be always set as the oblation in the presence of the Lord. Ihuh was to commune with Moses from between the two cherubim. The position is that of Atum-Ra-Har-Makhu in the equinox when he rises as the sun-god from betwixt the two kherufu or lions on the mount (Rit., Vig. to ch. 18). Atum-Ra-Har-Makhu was the lion-god of the double force, or the power and glory of the sun upon the mount of the horizon. He rose up betwixt two lions which imaged the double solar force, and was also represented by the fore-part and the back-part of the lion.

The lion in sign-language was an Egyptian type of the terrible (Hor-Apollo, 1, 20). This was applied to the sun or solar god as an image of his double force, and represented by Anhur and Tefnut. The hinder part of the lion that is carried on the head of Anhur is a sign of force. But the fore-part, the face and front of the lion, which reads *peh-peh*, denotes the glory of the double force. The fore-part of the lion or lion-god being the symbol of his glory, this was not to be seen by Moses, who is told to stand in the cleft of the rock whilst the glory of the Lord, or fore-part of the lion, passes by, and he is only to see the deity's hinder part. As Egyptian, the cleft in the rock was the place of entrance to and egress from Amenta. The solar god who rose again as lord of terror was the lion of the double force, the power and the glory of the god being figured and differentiated by the hind-part and the fore-part of the lion. In strict accordance with Egyptian symbolism, the dual nature of Ihuh was made known to Moses—that is, if the promise was kept and the Lord revealed his hinder part (Ex. xxxiii. 18, 23). Moreover, it was made known by means of the lion or the man-lion as zootype. Moses asks to see the glory, and the Lord replies, "Thou canst not see my face" and live, so terrible was the glory imaged by the lion's face. The glory being in front, the power was behind, and this alone could be seen by the mortal who desired to live. The unbearable glory obviously depended on the Lord as solar lion because he had first shown his face to Moses "*as a man.*" "And the Lord spake unto Moses face to face as a man speaketh unto his friend" (Ex. xxxiii. 11). On one occasion, when Anhur comes into the presence of the solar god, it is said, "Turn thou back, O Rehu; turn thou back from before his mightiness = the glory, or, as otherwise said, "from him who keepeth watch and is himself unseen," or is not to be seen, which is equivalent to the Hebrew "Man shall not see me and live." Now, according to the astronomical mythology—with the twin lions stationed east and west—the lion of the hinder part was to the west, the lion with the face of glory to the east, the place of sunrise. The entrance to the nether earth was in the west. This was the side of the Amenta through which the first of the two leaders was Moses; he was to see the back part only, whether of the double horizon, or the god in person, or the lion of Atum-Ra. Thus, the statement that Moses was not to see the glory or fore-part is equivalent to his not being allowed to enter the promised land upon the other side of the water, which was visible from the mountain of Amenta that reached up to the sky.

As shown by the Vignettes, there is an Egyptian origin likewise for "the burning bush" in which the one god was manifested to Moses in Mount Horeb. The Lord as Iahu-Elohim was previously revealed to Moses in his solar character. As it is said, "Moses was keeping the flock of Jethro," and he "came to the mountain of god unto Horeb." "And the angel of the Lord appeared unto him in a flame of fire out of the midst of a bush: and he looked, and behold, the bush burned with fire, and the bush was not consumed. And Moses said, I will turn aside now, and see this great sight, why the bush is not burned" (Ex. iii. 1, 3). Now, this "burning bush" is to be seen full blaze in pictures to the Ritual. There is a vignette to chapter 64 in which the burning bush is saluted (figure, Papyrus du Louvre, 111, 93; Renouf, Book of the Dead, Pl. 17). In the texts the golden unbu is a symbol of the solar god. It is a figure of the radiating disk which is depicted raying all aflame at the summit of a sycamore-fig tree which thus appears to burn with fire, and the tree is not consumed. It images the lord of the resurrection going forth from the state of the disk to give light (Rit., 64). The manes, without shoes on his feet, saluting the tree with the flaming disk in or upon it, from which there issue tongues of flame, addresses the god concealed in the solar fire, who is going forth from the state of the disk, saying, "Shine on me, O unknown soul!". "I draw near to the god whose words were heard by me in the lower earth" (64). This was the burning bush in which the sun-god manifested as Tum, whose other name is Iu or Unbu, the burning bush being the solar unbu. There are two corollaries following this identification: the one is that the god of the burning bush is the same as the god of the flaming thornbush named the "unbu," and the god being the same, the person addressed by the god is the same in both versions, and the lion-god who is Shu-Anhur in the Ritual is the prototype of Moses in the book of Exodus. Further, in the manifestation of the burning bush *duality of person is implied*. First it is "an angel of the Lord" that appears "in a flame of fire out of the midst of a bush." Then the Lord or Elohim speaks in person and calls on Moses by name (Ex. iii. 4). These two correspond to the divine duality of Ra and Unbu in the original representation, when Unbu (Horus or Iu) as the ever-coming son of god the eternal father (Huhi), is the manifestor for Ra in the flowering thorn. The burning bush, then, is identical with the "golden unbu" of the Egyptian Book of the Dead, and the "golden unbu" of the Pyramid Texts is literally the "golden bough" of later legends—as in the English work of that name.

Here we may say in passing, that *The Golden Bough* contains a learned, large, and serviceable collection of data, but the theories of interpretation derived from the writings of Mannhardt are futile. Besides which, mythology is not to be fathomed in or by a folk-tale, and *The Golden Bough* is but a twig of the great tree of mythology and sign-language—a twig without its root. The reception of the work in England served to show how prevalent and profound is the current ignorance of the subject-matter. It was hailed as if it had plumbed the depths instead of merely extending the superficies. The writer never once touches bottom ; never traces the comparison home either in the Assyrian or the Egyptian version. In the former, for example, Gilgames goes to the other world in quest of the tree of life and the fountain of youth. His desire is to learn how to become immortal. In that other world across the water, not in the nether-earth of Arali, there grows the tree of renewal. Like the Kamite Unbu, it is described as similar to the bush of hawthorn in flower, and its thorns are said to " prick like the viper." When Gilgames touches the shore of that upper paradise, he is told of this tree, shrub or plant, and it is said that if he can lay hold of it without his hand being torn, gather a branch and bear it away, it will secure for him eternal youth. The tree is identical with that which grew in the sacred grove at Nemi, from which no branch was to be broken. And beyond the Babylonian legend lies the Egyptian myth in which the tree is rooted. The Egyptian golden bough is a bush of flowering thorn. It is a symbol of the young solar god who says, " I am Unbu, who proceedeth from Nu (heaven), and my, mother is Nut " (Rit., ch. 42 ; Pyramid Texts, Teta 39). " I am Unbu of An-ar-ef, the flower in the abode of occultation " (Rit., ch. 71). This identifies the golden bough with Horus in the dark and the bush that flowered at Christmas like our Glastonbury Thorn. The golden bough or burning bush is a solar symbol of Atum-Huhi, who says to Anhur, " O lion-god, I am Unbu," and who thus identifies himself with Ihuh in the burning bush. " I am Unbu," says the Egyptian deity in the flowering thorn, where the Hebrew god announces that he is Ihuh from the midst of the burning bush.

The golden calf in Israel had also been the gilded heifer in Egypt. Hes, the sacred heifer, was adored under the name of Isis in the time of the old empire. This was also a type of the golden Hathor, the habitation of Horus, her calf. The setting up of the golden calf for worship is likewise evident in " The destruction of mankind." It is " said by the majesty of Ra (to the calf-headed Hathor), Come in peace, thou goddess, and there arose the young priestess of Amu." " Said by the majesty of Ra to the goddess : I order that libations be made to her at every festival of the new year under the direction of my priestesses. Hence it comes that libations are made under the direction of the priestesses at the festival of Hathor, through all men, since the days of old " (Pl. B., lines 24–6). This was the worship of the golden calf, thus instituted as Egyptian. There was a special form of the cow-headed goddess called the golden Hathor, and a particular type of her child or calf known as the golden Horus. Both were imaged in one by the virgin heifer, or, as in the Exodus, by the golden calf, the image of the goddess of Amu. A dual type of deity originated with the child that was potentially of either sex, or both. Hence the boy like Bacchus with the female mammæ, and the lad in Revelation with the feminine paps and girdle, or Horus with the female breasts. Also the lock of childhood, or the long hair

X X

of the Egypto-gnostic Christ, represented this dual type of deity, as well as "the long garment in which was the whole world," because it had been the clothing of both sexes for the child.   Hathor in Egypt was the goddess of the golden calf, or heifer with the golden neck. One of her titles was Nub the golden (Wilk., vol. iii., p. 115), and the goddess Iusāas, consort of Atum-Ra and mother of Iusa in the cult of On, was *a form of the golden Hathor*, as is shown by the ears of the heifer in her headdress.   Hathor was the Egyptian Venus, also the goddess of music and dancing, and of female ornaments, including precious stones, particularly the turquoise.   The calf or heifer of gold was a befitting figure for the cult whose gods were Iu the calf, Iusāas the cow, and Atum-Iu the bull—the gods which they, the Jews or Ius, brought out of Egypt in the Hebrew exodus.   So soon as the metal was fused, the image fashioned, and the calf set up, the festival of Hathor-Iusāas followed.   "And Aaron made proclamation, and said, To-morrow shall be a feast to Ihuh.   And they rose up early on the morrow and offered burnt offerings, and brought peace offerings; and the people sat down to eat and drink, and (then) rose up to play" (Ex. xxxii. 5–6).   The festival was phallic, for the people remembered Iusāas, the consort of Ihuh and the divine mother of the non-ethnical Jews, who were born Egyptian.   In connection with peace offerings, one might mention that Iusāas was also called Neb-hetep, the lady of peace, and her son, Iu-em-hetep, was the prince who comes with peace.   But the libation to the cow-headed or calf-headed goddess was turned into waters of bitterness when Moses, according to the story, "took the calf and burnt it with fire, ground it into powder and strewed it upon the water, and made the children of Israel drink of it" (xxxii. 20).

There is but one calf mentioned in the book of Exodus, but in the first book of Kings we see the type is dual.   "The king took counsel, and made *two calves of gold;* and he said . . . Behold *thy gods*, O Israel, which brought thee up out of the land of Egypt" (1 Kings, xii. 28).   These in Egypt were the heifer that imaged the mother as the goddess Iusāas, and the calf of Iu, her sa or su—that is, her son— Iusāas being a form of the golden Hathor, who was the goddess of Mount Sinai.   Also it was pardonable, if not pleasing in the sight of Ihuh, that Jehu *did not forsake* the golden calves of Jeroboam (2 Kings, x. 29, 31).   The golden calf was the great symbol of sin in the eyes of the monolaters, because it was a figure of both sexes and pre-eminently sacred to the divine mother, Neith, Hathor, or Iusāas.   Although the one god as the god in Spirit was evolved in the Egyptian cult of Ptah and Atum-Ra as Huhi the eternal, he was compounded with the child and mother of an earlier religion.   His consort Iusāas was a form of Hathor, the mother of fair love, who was the Egyptian Venus, and the child was Iu (em-hetep), the wise youth who became the Hebrew prince of peace.   These were the gods which brought the Hebrews up or were brought up by them out of Egypt.   The later monotheists sought to exclude the child and mother from the nature of the deity, which was a holy family in itself, consisting of the father, mother, and child.   The mother was cast out, for the god to be imaged by a figure of the father alone.   But the goddess was continued in her types of the birthplace.   Hers were the ark, the tabernacle, the sanctuary, the temple, the meskhen, the holy of holies, as the abode of the divine child or reborn god. Hence the Hebrew tabernacle or ark-shrine is the mishken, which as Egyptian is the meskhen, the chamber of birth, that was imaged in the constellation of the "thigh" or haunch of Nut in the astronomical mythology. This change had been made in the theology of Annu, as witnessed by the legend of the cow in the tomb of Seti I., in which the god is "lifted up" in his sanctuary as male alone. Nevertheless, there was a continual recrudescence of the old Egyptian cult, and a return to the worship of the mother, as is shown in Israel by the setting up of the golden calf, and the denunciation of it by the later writers.

This worship of Hathor in the mount had already extended from Sinai to Jerusalem as an Egyptian cult. Eusebius relates that when Constantine was about to build the Basilica, he discovered a "mound of Venus" already raised above the Saviour's tomb (*Life of Constantine*). This was a mount of the mother, who was Hathor-Iusāas in Egypt; and no one was buried in or born from the typical mount of Venus except child-Horus, or his other self, Iu-em-hetep, whose mother was a form of the Egyptian Venus. The primitive mound had been perpetuated, as it was in the Tel-el-Jehudieh (near On). The mount which typified the means of ascent from the valley of Amenta to the summit where the glorified elect were taken on board the bark of Ra is variously represented in the Hebrew version of the exodus. As in the astronomical mythos, it is the one mountain with several names, and, being celestial, it may be localized in numerous sacred sites on earth as the place of worship. The mount upon which Moses stood in conversation with Ihuh is identified with the celestial height, when it is said to the children of Israel, "Ye yourselves have seen that I have talked with you from heaven." This, again, is celestial as the mount on which the pattern of the divine dwelling, or ark and tabernacle of the Lord, was shown to Moses. In the Ritual it is the mountain of Amenta that touches the sky. It is said almost in the opening of the book of Exodus, when the call is made to Moses by Ihuh, "When thou hast brought forth the people out of Egypt, ye shall serve God upon this mountain" (Ex. iii. 12), which is here called Mount Horeb, the mountain of God. It is also said of the chosen people, in this ancient fragment of the mythos, "Thou shalt bring them in, and plant them in the mountain of their inheritance, the place, O Lord, which thou hast made for them to dwell in, the sanctuary, O Lord, which thy hands have established," where "the Lord shall reign for ever and ever." This was in the mount of Jerusalem on high, the celestial mount of the gathering and congregating together in the Aarru-Salem = Aarru-Hetep in Jerusalem below by those who built the city as outcasts or colonists from Egypt. The mountains are several. Elsewhere it is Mount Zion or Sinai. But the mountain of God, the holy mountain, is one, because it was astronomical; therefore in the eschatology it is the mount for which they were bound as spirits, and not as leprous and abominated mortals fleeing from the land of the Pharaohs. In making the passage from Amenta, the supreme object of attainment is the mount of peace and plenty, called Mount Hetep in Egyptian. Hetep is a word of various meanings besides peace and plenty. It is the mount of the oblations, one sign of which is a table piled with provender. The mount itself presents the oblations to the gods and the glorified upon the summit, on a scale that is worthy of the eternal feast. And this, we would suggest, is the prototype of the Oblation described by Ezekiel (xlviii.), which is colossal in its magnitude. It is commanded that a huge oblation shall be offered to the Lord, with the sanctuary in the midst thereof. It is to be "an oblation from the oblation of the land," just as Hetep was the oblation to the heaven from the offerings made by the worshippers on earth as contributions to the table of the Lord. The mound-builders raised their mount or mound of oblation in Britain the size of Silbury Hill. Here it is to be a city the size of paradise, or the New Jerusalem, the eternal city built upon the square, and therefore a heaven of the four quarters, raised upon twelve pillars erected round the mount. The difficulty of identifying Sinai as a geographical mount, according to the book of Exodus, may be explained when we know that the beginnings were not geographical, and that the mount on which Shu-Anhur shared the throne of Ra his father was the mountain in Amenta, not on earth. It was the stellar mount of glory in the eschatology which had been the mount of sunrise in the mythology.

After the passage of the Red Sea, in the exodus, the children of Israel arrive at "the wilderness of Sin, which is between Elim and Sinai" (Ex. xvi. 1). This wilderness can be identified in the Ritual with Anrutef, the region of sterility. After passing the red pool, lake, or sea, we come to the desert of Anrutef, which is said to be near *Sheni*. Here there is some evidence to show that the Hebrew Sinai is derived from the Egyptian Sheni. Ra, the solar god, is designated lord of Sheni in the Ritual. The speaker in chapter 36 says, "I am Khnum, the lord of Sheni," or Shennu, equivalent to Sinai in Hebrew. When Osiris becomes the supreme lord of the mountain in Amenta he is also described as the "commander in *the region of Sheni.*" He is a form of that lord over all who gave the Commandments on Mount Sinai. Horus also issues from the region of Sheni with the other divine chiefs who repulse the enemies of Osiris in these battles against his enemies. He also is the lord who came from Sinai. The word Shennu or Sheni in Egyptian also denotes an orbit, the circuit or circle, to turn and return. Hence the solar god was designated lord of Sheni. Mount Sheni, as the place of turning and returning, is the mount of the equinox. This was the mount of the two lions, and these also are the Sheni by name. Ra may be Khnum or Amen or Atum, according to the cult. The Ra of Annu was Atum, otherwise Huhi, whom we also identify as the Hebrew god Ihuh. In the vignettes to the Ritual, Atum-Ra, the one god living in truth, is portrayed upon the summit of the mount of glory, with the seven spirits praising him upon the mount (Naville, *Todtenbuch*, Kap. 16, A.) the mount of the circle of turning and returning and of the lions, therefore Mount Sheni = Sinai. The mount of glory in the Ritual is represented in the book of Exodus as a mount of fire or the mount on fire—that is, with the solar glory. The circuit of fire about the mount is the "sheniu of fire." This occurs as the title of a chapter in the Ritual. Thus the sun-god Ra or Atum-Huhi = Ihuh was the lord of Sheni. His throne was on the mount of glory where he sat surrounded by the Sheniu who form the divine circle of the celestial court. "The Sheniu of this chapter," says Renouf, "are living personages who attend upon the Osiris and greet him (on the mount of glcry) with their acclamations. The word is often translated 'princes,' 'officers,' but it signifies those *who are in the circle* of a king or god, hence 'ministrants,' 'courtiers,' as in the rubric to ch. cxxv." (Renouf, Book of the Dead, xxx. note I). These Sheniu constitute the upper circle round the throne of God upon Mount Sheni in Egyptian, or Sinai in Hebrew. Here it may be noted that the Japanese call their divine Kami, the 7+1 primeval powers, the Shin, whence came the Shintu gods, which as stellar correspond to the Egyptian Sheniu, who are a group of gods in the upper celestial circle, and of whom it is said "the Sheniu marshal the Osiris" on his way to the "mount of glory" (Rit., ch. 130).

The descriptions of Mount Sinai in the book of Exodus show that it was the mount of glory in the solar mythos—that is, the mount of sunrise in the daily course, and the mount of the equinox as the horizon of the annual sun. Various meanings of the word Sheni coincide in showing that the typical Mount Sinai, Sin, or Ba-Shen was the Mount Sheni in the Egyptian astronomical mythology. We have to remember that as far back as the time of the first dynasty Egypt included the mount and surrounding region of Sinai as a part of the double kingdom. Thus the Sarabit el Khadem was considered very holy ground by the Egyptians seven thousand years ago. It was the seat of Hathor there, whose sanctuary of the mother was a primitive cavern in the rock. The turquoise mines of the Sinaitic peninsula were also worked by the Egyptians for the gems of the goddess to whom they were consecrated. In fact, Mount Sinai was Egyptian at any time from seven thousand to thirteen thousand years ago, both as a geographical locality and as a sacred site. The deities who were worshipped on it were likewise Egyptian. It was the seat of Hathor, of Atum-Ra, and Horus the calf. There is a vignette to the Ritual in which this dynasty of divinities from On or Heliopolis may be seen grouped together on the mount. The scene portrayed is on Mount Sheni, which became the Hebrew Sinai. In this, as in the Osirian dynasty of deities, Atum the father was the bull, Iusãas the mother was the cow or heifer; and the calf as a type of renewal for either sex was an image of all three, as was the child-Horus in the anthropomorphic representation. The calf is again represented in another vignette in presence of the god with the worshipper (Naville, *Todt.*, Kap. 108 and 109) in the attitude of adoration behind the calf. This is literally the worship of the golden calf, which was a dual image of both Hathor the Egyptian Venus and of Horus as her calf (ch. 108). So ancient is it, when measured by the mythos, that Horus is the crocodile-headed Sebek as the son of Hathor, who was represented at Annu by the heifer-headed Iusãas. These three are designated the powers of the east. Horus of the solar mount is represented by the calf in presence of the great god Atum-Ra and the star of dawn, or of Hathor as the morning-star. Professor Petrie's explorations show us that a transformation of this old Egyptian religion into a Semitic or Syrian cult took place at

Sinai amongst the miners, many of whom were no doubt slaves who were sent to work the mines, according to the Egyptian practice of devoting captives to the service of the gods. But the goddess Hathor and her child Horus, who were the objects of worship at Sarabit el Khadem in the Sinaitic peninsula, did not originate as Syrian or Semitic deities. They were Egyptian from the first, and were continued wheresoever the Egyptian miners went, whether as the diggers for the turquoise gems of Sinai, the tin of Cornwall, or the gold of the Zimbabwe in Mashonaland.

The summit of Amenta at the head of the valley was attained upon the horizon in the east. It was the mount of glory in the solar mythos, which is Sinai, the mount of the glory of god and the seat of judgment in the book of Exodus. ("Now these are the judgments which thou shalt set before them," Ex. 21, i.) This is the height on which the kneeling Anhur, in the character of Shu-si-Ra, uplifts the solar orb upon the horizon, called the mount, from the summit of which the hosts of darkness were hurled down the steps and for the time being annihilated. Also from this Pisgah-height the promised land was visible as the paradise across the firmamental waters, which are represented by the river Jordan in the Hebrew exodus. A peak of Mount Sinai in Arabia Petrea is known by the name of Djebel Mousa, the mount of Moses, which is traditionally identified as the scene of the events and occurrences on the mount described in the book of Exodus. Taking Mousa or Mouishé to be the Hebrew equivalent for Ma-Shu, the lion-god Shu, Mount Sinai is a localized form of the typical mount on which the lion-god stood to uplift the heaven or sustain the solar disk with his two hands. This in the annual course was at the equinox, and therefore on the mount at the point of turning and returning, or on Mount Sheni = Sinai.

From the peak of Pisgah Moses is shown the land here called Canaan as the land flowing with milk and honey, oil, corn, and wine, which was one and the same in all the legends of this paradise of peace and plenty at the summit of the mount. Those who went up from the valley to the top of the mountain neither died there nor were buried there. They were the glorified spirits of the dead, or the leaders of the starry host, like Shu upon the mount of Am-Khemen. Upon the solar mount of glory or Mount Sheni, the mount of the Sheniu, was the Egyptian maat in which the law was given on the mount. This is the hall of justice. The maat was a double law court, first erected for Anup at the pole; but in the solar myth the place of equipoise was changed, and the maat was represented where the annual or periodical assize was held. This was at the point of equinox, which was at one time imaged in the sign of the Scales. Maat or mati in Egyptian is the law. The maat was the hall of justice or of law. The tablets of mati in the maat were the books of the law. Ages before Osiris was enthroned as the great judge in the maat, Atum-Iu the son of Ptah was the divine law-giver in the great hall of justice which was figured on the mount, with Anhur as the intermediary. A divine law-giver was worshipped in Egypt as Atum-Iu, the original giver of the law which was given first by him to Egypt, not to Israel. But when Atum-Huhi had become the Hebrew Ihuh, the law was repeated at second-hand in Israel. The tables of the law are identical by name with the tablets of mati, and the comparative process will show that the matter is the same so far as the Hebrew records go ; and if the law were divinely revealed and had any superhuman authority, it would be as the law of mati, which was first inscribed in the papyrus of Ma-Shu or Anhur, and not as the law of the Hebrew Moses, written in the later letters of the Penta-teuch. Several meanings are connoted by the word maat or mati in Egyptian, such as law and justice, truth and right. The equilibrium of the universe was expressed by maat, which represented the natural immutable and eternal law. The balance is a symbol of maat and its oneness in duality. It was erected as a figure of the equinox, or the two halves of night and day at equal poise. Makha is a name for the scales and to weigh. The scales were erected at the place of poise and weighing in the equinox. Har-Makhu was the deity of the double equinox, who represented the duality of mati in the oneness of the equinox. The Sphinx was a figure of this duality in oneness at the equinox. The feather of Shu (or Ma) was another type of the same duality, in this case the duality of light and shade which meet and mingle in one at twilight. The Hebrew "two tables of the testimony, the tables of stone, written by the finger of God" (Ex. xxxi. 18), are the equivalent of the laws, or truths and commandments that were "consigned, performed, engraved in script, and placed beneath the feet of Ra-Har-Makhu in the great temple at On to last for ever. The tables of the law and commandments represent the tablets in the hall of maati. The tablets in the Ritual (ch. 28) are expressly assigned to the god Atum-Ra. "This whole heart of mine is laid upon the tablets of Tum, who guideth me to the caverns of Sut" or through the dark passages of Amenta. The tablets of Tum are records of the law or maat. They are kept by Taht the divine scribe in the hall of judgment. We learn from the Ritual (ch. 28) that the Egyptian tables of the law are the tablets or kanu of Atum-Iu ; the same word denotes carving in ivory and engraving on stone, and Atum-Huhi is the Kamite original of the Semitic Ihuh. The tables of Moses were the tables of the law, and the law in Egyptian is ma (mati in the plural). The tables or tablets of the law were pro-duced in the judgment hall, and we know from the pleadings of the deceased in what is called the negative confession that these tables of the law contained the commandments or prohibitions concerning the things which the manes says he has not done because of the "thou shalt not" in which the law originated. The speaker, addressing Taht-mati, the recorder in the great hall, says : "O thou bearer of peace offerings, who openest thy mouth for the presentation of the tables (or tablets), for the acceptation of the offerings and for the establishment of mati (law or justice) upon her throne ; let the *tables* be brought forward and let the truth be firmly established" (Rit., ch. 41). These tablets, we repeat, were the tables of the law (ma, maat, or mati) ; they are produced at the trial before the judges when the heart (character) of the deceased is weighed in the balance of Mati and the goddess (of law or justice) is established on her throne. Otherwise stated, when the law was given in the judgment hall upon Mount Sheni or the mountain of Amenta. The religion of Egypt was based on maat, that is, on law, or more abstractly on truth and justice. And the law was impersonated in the goddess Mati, the Kamite original of the Greek Themis. It is said in the Ritual, "The gods and their symbols come into existence by virtue of law" (ch. 50). This in one sense was by means of Ma or Ma-Shu, the intermediary betwixt the great god and the people; who is represented in Israel by Moses. It is said that the Ten Commandments were given by Ihuh, the Egyptian Huhi, to Moses on Mount Sinai. The Jewish Commandments, however, are not limited to ten in number. The ten are followed by a series of judgments or laws (Ex. xxi., xxii., and xxiii.). And here it may be observed that the laws and judgments are identical in Hebrew, as in the duality of maati for law and justice in Egyptian. Also in the book of Deuteronomy (xxvii.) twelve statutes are enacted under the form of commandments, enforced with twelve curses. And in the Papyrus of Ani there is a company of twelve gods sitting on twelve thrones as judges in the maat or judgment hall upon the mount—a picture that suggests "the House of the Lord" in the celestial Jerusalem, of which it is said, "there are set thrones for judgments, the thrones of the House of David" (Ps. cxxii. 5). These, as described in Revelation, were likewise twelve in number. The maat is identified with the mount of God by Zechariah when he says, "Jerusalem shall be called the city of truth (maat) and the mountain of the Lord of Hosts the holy mountain" (viii. 3, 4). The law was given to Israel on Mount Sinai, where the sanctuary or divine dwelling answers to the maat. Also when Ihuh comes "to judge the world with righteousness, and the peoples with his truth" (Ps. xcvi. 13), that is according to maati in the maat. "Thou shalt have no other god but Ihuh," in the book assigned to Moses, was preceded ages earlier in the books of Ma-Shu and Taht at On by "Thou shalt have no other god but Huhi the eternal one," besides whom there was none other in the cult of Atum-Ra. Thus the god Ihuh is one with Atum-Huhi the eternal. Mount Sinai is one with Mount Sheni, whether as the mount of the lions or of turning in the solar orbit ; and Moses is one with Anhur. The tabernacle or sanctuary of Ihuh is one with that of Atum-Huhi. The tables of the law that were given to Moses are identical with the tablets of the law in the hall of mati. This taps once more the sealed-up source of "God's Word," which was derived from the Egyptian wisdom written in the books of Taht and Shu that were preserved in the great library of On (Annu), where Atum-Huhi was god the father, and Iu was the ever-coming son, the prince of peace in person, the Egyptian Jesus, Iusa, or Iu-em-hetep.

Most of the Hebrew commandments are acknowledged and fulfilled by the speaker, who protests in the judgment hall that he has neither said nor done any evil thing against the gods, but the following quotations will show that the Hebrew commandments were compiled directly from the Egyptian. The pleadings are in reply to the commandments which the deceased declares he has kept. The following parallel will briefly indicate how directly the Mosaic commandments were borrowed from the wisdom of Egypt :—

Egyptian.	*Hebrew.*
" I have not blasphemed a god."	" Thou shalt not take the name of the Lord thy God in vain."
" I have not committed adultery."	" Thou shalt not commit adultery."
" I have not committed theft."	" Thou shalt not steal."
" I have not borne false witness (or told lies) in the tribunal of truth."	" Thou shalt not bear false witness against thy neighbour."
" I am not a murderer."	" Thou shalt do no murder."
Rit. of the Resurrection, ch. 125.	Exodus, ch. xx..

Shu-Anhur, the prototype of Moses as giver of the law, has been somewhat overlooked as a god of the writings in which the revelation of Ra was made known by him to men. When he is mentioned in the Ritual as the author of writings called " his rules (or laws) and his papyrus," Renouf considers this to be an error of the scribes, and moots the opinion that the god Taht is meant (Book of the Dead, ch. 110). Nevertheless, Renouf is wrong. Shu is said to work in the abode of the books of Seb, that is, of earth (Rit., ch. 17). This we can identify with the great library at On or Annu. (See *Records*, x. 138.) " The papyrus or writing, mahit, of Shu " are mentioned in the Ritual when the speaker says, " I am in unison with his successive changes, and his laws (or rules) and his writings " (Rit., ch. 110). The book of the laws is the book of ma or mati, which was presented by the duality of Shu-Anhur and represented in that of Moses and Joshua. Shu is called " truth " (Magic Papyrus, p. 1, line 9). And as is shown by " the hymn to the god Shu," among the records that were kept in the great temple library or, as it is called, " the royal palace at On," there were writings ascribed to Shu-Anhur, the lord of truth or mati. It is said of him, " He made hereditary titles " for Ra, " which are in the writings of the lord of Sesennu "—that is, in the collection of Taht, here called " the scribe of the king Ra-Har-Makhu " ; and these titles were " consigned, performed, engraved in script under the feet of Ra-Har-Makhu," or beneath the feet of the statue of the god. Moses likewise is the writer of " hereditary titles " for Ihuh. He also fulfils the same *rôle* as transmitter of titles in the book of Exodus. When he asks for the name of the new divinity " God said to Moses, I am that I am." And he added, " Thus thou shalt say unto the children of Israel : I am (Eyeh) hath sent me unto you. This is my name for ever, and this is my memorial for all generations " (Ex. iii. 13–16). The writings of Shu-Anhur were preserved at On among the 36,000 books that were traditionally ascribed to Taht. He wrote them as the mouthpiece of Ra, or Atum-Huhi the father of Iu, who was carried into Judea as Ihuh the god of the Ius, Aaiu, or Jews, who brought on the sacred writings that had been " consigned, performed, engraved in script," and memorized for ever in " the royal palace of On," or Heliopolis Magna. Now the priest named Osarsiph by Manetho, who was afterwards called Moses, is reputed to have been born at On (Annu), and to have been a priest of the great temple there, the temple of Atum-Ra-Har-Makhu, where the writings were kept, including those in which Ma-Shu had made hereditary titles for Ra-Har-Makhu to be transmitted from generation to generation for time and eternity. The most perfect rendering of the name "I am" would be "the self-existent," and in the hymn to the god Shu Atum-Ra is designated "the self-existent" (p. 1, l. 9). Also his other title of Kheper signified "he who is" in the Egyptian tongue. Amongst the subject-matter of the exodus is the revelation of the one god that was made to Moses on the mount, which revelation had previously been made to Anhur. It is to Anhur that the one god Ra who is to supersede all other gods and elemental powers is revealed as Huhi the eternal. Anhur is represented as being the medium of communication betwixt the god and mortals. "His substance is blended with the substance of Ra" as intermediate power. He makes divine law known to men (Magic Papyrus). As it is said, the people present their offerings to the god with Anhur's own hands. Moses is represented as being the same to Ihuh that Anhur was to Atum-Ra—his medium for communication with the people, the medium that was the human mouth-piece for the god. So the ancestral spirit that inspires the Zulu Inyanga says to the medium, "You will not speak with the people; they will be told by us everything they come to inquire about" (Callaway).

We learn from the very ancient magical texts that amongst the 36,000 books ascribed to Taht by tradition there was a particular collection known as "The Four Books." These had the titles of (1) The Old Book, (2) The Book to Destroy Men, (3) The Great Book, (4) The Book to be as God. There was also a group of four books that were astronomical and astrological. Whether these were the same or not, the "Four Books" were in the temple of the sun at Annu or On, where Osarsiph is said to have been a priest. The number does not coincide with that of the Pentateuch. But then the books originally assigned to Moses were *only four in number, not five*. The wisdom of Egypt, in which Osarsiph was so profoundly learned, would naturally be written upon rolls of papyrus in the library at On, from which it was carried forth in one of the exodes from Egypt. The original nucleus of the Hebrew collection consisted of "the precepts of the Pentateuch" (by which the law was given), "together with their traditional implications" (Montefiore, C. G., *Hib. Lect.*, p. 469). This, in a limited or possibly primitive sense, was the Jewish torah. In Egyptian the Teruu is a roll of papyrus, and the torah has the form of the papyrus-roll. Also torah, תורה, denotes the whole law, and in Egyptian teruu signifies all, entire, the whole.

There is a tradition of the assumption of Moses in the so-called apocryphal "Assumptio Moysis" (*Apocryphal Literature*, vol. ii., p. 177). Such a mode of translation bodily does not apply to any human being, under whatsoever name. But it was the way in which Anhur made his exit from the mount or from the mouth of Ra. Anhur is an entirely mythical character, and if he be the prototype of Moses, it would seem to follow that this is the origin of the legend concerning his disappearance on the mount. The present writer does not attempt to fathom the meaning of the mythos *in the form of märchen* to which the tradition belongs, but the disappearance of Moses from the mount may be taken as identical with that of the god who represented wind and in the solar mythos was the breathing force of the rising sun personified. With the cessation of the breeze, or, if very fierce, the tornado, Shu-Anhur might be said to pass away, as a current saying has it, " like the devil in a high wind." It is recorded (Deut. xxxiv. 5) that Moses died עַל פִּי יְהוָה, literally " upon the mouth of the Lord " (Ihuh). And Shu-Anhur was the breath of the Lord. He was the spirit of Ra as the breathing solar force emaned from the very mouth of the god, or, as might be, he was represented by the panting lion on the mount of dawn. At sunrise on the mount the all-embracing, all-absorbing fires of Ra did veritably swallow up the force of Anhur, who passed away as breath from the mouth of the solar god. The personality of Shu-Anhur is united with that of Ra, the supreme lord. His very substance is blended with the substance of Ra (Magic Papyrus, i. 6), and is absorbed into it as nutriment when he passes away upon the mount or makes his change in character. Also there is a legend of Anhur's final disappearance from the mount, an occurrence that took place during a nine days' tempest, and of which Maspero says, " We may here note the most ancient known reference to the tempest whose tumult hid from men the disappearance or apotheosis of kings, who ascended alive into heaven " (Maspero, *Dawn of Civilisation*, Eng. tr. p. 178). Thus Shu-Anhur as an elemental power had represented breathing force with lion-like capacity, the equinoctial wind, the breeze of dawn, but in the solar myth the increase of the twilight current was attributed to the sun ; it was considered to be breath of Ra, the lord of all, which died upon the mount of sunrise. This becomes the vanishing of Moses on Mount Pisgah, *Alphi-Jehovah*, in the Hebrew märchen. In rendering the fact, which was scientific in relation to Ra and Shu at sunrise, without due knowledge, the Hebrew writer has apparently made Jehovah swallow Moses bodily as a human being, although the statement is somewhat reticently made, in causing him to die like breath upon the mouth of the lord. This was the " burial of Moses," and there need be no wonder that " no man knoweth of his sepulchre to this day."

When Moses passed away or was dislimned upon that mountain of the Abarim, his *rôle* as army leader of the Israelites was taken over by the young man Joshua, who answers perfectly to Shu when the part of Shu is carefully discriminated from that of Anhur. Anhur was the uplifter of the stellar heaven in various forms—his "upliftings" are mentioned in the texts—whereas Shu was the supporter of the sun-god in the solar mythos. In the first character he pushes up the heaven with his rod, as prototype of Moses with his rod. In the second he uplifts the solar disk upon the horizon as the servant and supporter of the great god Ra. Shu had been all that Joshua is going to be when he tells the children of Israel to " put away the gods which your fathers served beyond the river and in Egypt. But as for me and my house, we will serve the Lord "—the Lord being Ihuh, one with the Egyptian Huhi, the new god Atum-Ra. When Shu becomes the leader in his name of Shu-si-Ra there is a river to be crossed. " I am Shu," he says, " the image of Ra," " sitting in the inside of his father's sacred eye," or the solar disk.

"I am the chosen of millions coming out of the lower heaven. When my name is spelt on the bank of the river, then it is dried up." This in the Hebrew account is Joshua coming to the river Jordan. After the death of Moses "Ihuh spake unto Joshua the son of Nun, Moses's minister," saying, "Arise; go over this Jordan, thou and all this people, unto the land which I do give them, even to the children of Israel" (Joshua, i. 2). The white bull was the bull of Shu, who was called the bull, the master of strength. And according to one of the Jewish märchen, at the conquest of Canaan *Joshua rode upon a bull.* When they came to the river "all Israel passed over on dry ground." It is the same with Joshua at the river as with Shu, at whose name "spelt on the bank" the waters dried up for the passage. Shu is the opener of the gates for egress from Amenta on behalf of Ra and the glorified elect who made their exodus from the lower Egypt of Amenta pursued by the Apap-dragon and all the host of darkness. The Osiris thus addresses Shu: "O thou who leapest forth, conductor of the manes and glorified ones from the earth, let the fair path to the tuat (point of egress) be granted to me which is made on behalf of those who are in pain" (Rit., ch. lxiv.)—that is, on behalf of the sufferers in the Egypt of the lower world. The earth here mentioned is Amenta, from which the manes and the glorified were conducted first by Anhur to the presence of the solar god upon the mount of glory, and afterwards by Shu on board the solar bark.

Shu became the harbinger of Ra and leader in the coming forth from lower Egypt considered as an astronomical locality that was afterwards represented to be geographical in the Hebrew exodus. Thus, in the round of night and day Shu-Anhur enters the Amenta at evening to conduct the children of Ra up from the lower Egypt of the mythos. His *alter ego*, Shu, takes up the leadership upon the horizon east at dawn, to end the journey in the promised land or upper paradise of plenty and perpetual peace.

The land of promise on the other side of Jordan is that paradise across the water which was on the summit of Mount Hetep at the pole, hence the circumpolar paradise of the heptanomis, or heaven in seven astronomes. Thus in the book of Joshua the promised land is mapped out and measured in accordance with the astronomical mythology of the heptanomis. When the racial names are added in place of the divine, the seven divisions are called the seven lands of "the Canaanite, the Hittite, and the Hivite, and the Perizzite, and the Girgashite, and the Amorite, and the Jebusite" (Joshua, iii. 10). The final heaven attributed to Atum-Ra, as an astronomical formation, was in twelve divisions. This formation had been repeated in the making of Amenta. The previous heaven, considered to be antediluvian, was in ten divisions. These were represented by the ten circles of Ra in the Ritual (ch. 18) and by the ten divine domains of the blessed in the paradise upon the summit of Mount Hetep (Rit., ch. 110). This celestial formation was also represented by the ten tribes that were lost upon the other side of the waters, and by the ten sons of Jacob who preceded the twelve sons of Israel. But the later formation was repeated when Moses set a boundary to the mount and erected twelve pillars, "according to the twelve tribes of Israel" (Ex. xxiv. 4). The same figure of formation is again repeated when Joshua is commanded to set up twelve stones in the midst of the waters, and also in the Gilgal-circle which became the lodging place (Joshua, iv. 20) of the Israelites, who were continually on tramp in making the journey of the manes through the subterranean world, which was in twelve sections of space, with the twelve gates through which Ra passes with the blessed on his right hand and the damned upon his left, in accordance with the Egyptian rule of perspective (Book of Hades). In one form of the mythos, then, the Israelites divide the promised land into twelve lots among the twelve tribes. This is in accordance with the ground-plan of Amenta, in which twelve sections of space are shown to be successively enclosed as the possessions of the glorified elect, the chosen people who originate as the children of the sons of Ra, headed by the twelve who reap the harvest-field with Horus in the lower Egypt of Amenta. The gods of this nether earth in twelve divisions are twelve in number. The fields of divine harvest are twelve, the harvesters are twelve. The bearers of the measuring cord are twelve. The lots are also twelve. All being in accordance with the heaven that was mapped out in twelve domains. Thus the land of promise in the solar mythos was the *terrestrial paradise* of legendary lore. This was the land mapped out in twelve divisions where the type of plenty is the harvest-field of Amenta, and the cultivators are the twelve with Horus as the children of Ra. They formed the twelve colonies altogether under the suzerainty of local gods, and were the prototypes of the twelve tribes called the children of Israel. In the second stage the promised land is that more ancient circumpolar paradise upon Mount Hetep first mapped out in seven divisions, where the water-plants (aarru) supplied a primeval natural type of plenty. Both forms of the double paradise have been reproduced as Hebrew, one in the book of Exodus, the other in the book of Joshua. The land that was to be inherited by the children of Israel is also described as a form of the celestial heptanomis which preceded the heaven in twelve divisions. Mount Pisgah represents the mountain of Amenta, the summit of which reached up to the sky (Rit., ch. cxlix.). This was the top of attainment for Moses, whose journey here comes to an end midway. But from this point the second upper land of promise might be seen. This is the circumpolar paradise or the celestial city in seven divisions, and in attaining this upon the stellar mount of glory Joshua brings the mythical exodus to its own proper ending.

Hence the men who were prospecting on behalf of Joshua "went and passed through the land, and described it by cities *into seven portions* in a book" (Joshua xviii. 9).

The promise made to Moses (Ex. iii. 17) was that the Lord would lead the children of Israel "up out of the affliction of Egypt unto the land of the Canaanite, and the Hittite, and the Amorite, and the Perizzite, and the Hivite and the Jebusite; unto a land flowing with milk and honey." The Girgashite is omitted from this list of names. But when Joshua had crossed the Jordan "he came unto Jericho," and the men of Jericho who fought against Israel are said to be the

Amorite, the Perizzite, the Canaanite, the Hittite, the Girgashite, the Hivite, and the Jebusite. Thus Jericho in itself becomes a form of the heptanomis in which the tribes and totems are but seven in number, corresponding to "the seven portions in a book." This may account for seven priests encompassing the city seven times upon the seventh day, blowing seven times on seven trumpets of ram's-horns in order that the city walls might fall down flat. Here let it be remembered that in the astronomical mythology the localities are primarily celestial (Joshua, xxiv. 11). The descriptions point to the heaven thus taken by storm as being a form of the celestial heptanomis or upper Egypt of the seven astronomes—the upper paradise that was indefinitely more ancient than the twelve divisions of the solar heaven established by Ra in his first sovereignty, who is Atum-Huhi, the Hebrew Ihuh. In short, the siege of Jericho as a subject of the astronomical mythology is identical with the siege of seven-circled Troy.

In various survivals of the self-same mythos there is a Delilah who betrays the city when it is besieged, and who becomes the consort or the ally of the captor. This in the Greek version is Helen of Troy. We learn from Plutarch that in the wars of Sut and Horus, Ta-Urt (Greek Thauris), the concubine of Sut, deserted and came over to the side of Horus, and was pursued by a serpent (of Isis and Osiris 19). Ta-Urt was the Great Mother in the constellation of the Great Bear, the old harlot of the heptanomis who deserted Sut and joined herself to the solar Sebek-Horus as "the great mother of him who was married to his mother." Rahab the harlot, who dwelt on the top of the wall in Jericho, the city of the seven tribes, is another survival of the pre-monogamous Great Mother, the whore of later language. Rahab in the Psalms and the book of Job is the crocodile, a symbol, a nickname for Egypt. In Assyrian, rahàbu is a monster of the waters = the crocodile. The crocodile was a type of the old Great Mother Apt or Ta-Urt, not only in lower Egypt (Kheb), but in the upper Egypt where the waters were celestial; and Apt the goddess passes into Hathor as the amorous queen (Ps. lxxxvii. 4, lxxxix. 10; Job, xxvi. 12). The scarlet signal placed in the window by Rahab is of the true typhonian colour, the proper hue of the red dragon or hippopotamus—that is, of the old harlot sitting on the waters of heaven (Rev. xvii. 15).

In conclusion, the children of Israel, under Moses, travel through Amenta. They take possession of a land divided into twelve domains, which the Egyptian manes had already cultivated in the nether earth as a map of heaven in twelve divisions. Under Joshua they cross the water to take possession of the ancient heptanomis which had been configurated by the Egyptians as the upper circum-polar paradise. They are led to this land flowing with milk and honey by the hornet = the Kamite wasp or bee. This was the heaven mapped out of old by the Egyptians as the pastures of the seven cows who provided milky abundance in the Sekhet-Hetep, or the evergreen meadows of divine Aarru. And it is the Great Mother, whether in her stellar or lunar character as Apt or Hathor in the mount, who plays the part of traitress and surrenders the city to the solar god.

The paradise looked up to by the most primitive races was a heaven of perpetual plenty. That type was preserved by the Egyptians in the fields of celestial food upon Mount Hetep, but, as before said, there was no unearned increment to be derived from these elysian fields. "I am master there," says the beatified spirit who has attained his allotment and built his homestead. "I am in glory there; I eat there; I plant and I reap there; I plough there; I take my fill of love." "I net the ducks and I eat the dainties." "I am united there to the god Hetep," the good Osiris, as the deity of plenty and of peace (ch. 110, Renouf). The Aarru was their oasis in the desert, well watered, with the sand turned into soil for seed by ceaseless human labour, and transferred into the nether earth or into the upper paradise. But in transmogrifying Kamite mythology into the Semite history, a remarkable omission has been made by the inspired writers of God's Word. In the Egyptian original the elect people are chosen as the *cultivators* of the Aarru fields, which are measured out and the allotments made for the express purpose of cultivation. "Holiness to you, cultivators," says the god Ra. The Egyptians in their lower paradise of plenty reaped the produce of their labours, but they had to earn it individually first. In the Jewish version of the Aarru it is a land flowing with milk and honey, corn, oil, and wine. But *there is no demand for work*, no thought of cultivation, or of earning an eternal living. On attaining this land of promise they were to enter into an inheritance prepared by the labours of others, with no need to become the cultivators on their own account; and this position of the chosen people as non-cultivators of the soil has been religiously preserved by the non-agricultural Jews for this world and by the Christians for the world to come. Also the Jews have been and are to-day the victims of their misappropriated mythos. The mount was a stone of stumbling in their path, the rock on which they split. Their racial and religious origins are still at war in every meeting of the Zionists. The Zion of the visionaries is based on a celestial foundation. It is Jerusalem the golden; Jerusalem above, not to be confounded with a sacred site in Palestine. In the remotest parts of Africa the Jews would be much nearer "home" than in the Zion localized in Palestine which represented the eternal city on high, according to the Egyptian eschatology. The ideal of the racial Jews is a paradise on earth, whereas the religious ideal was the city in the heavens figured ages earlier on the summit of the mount, which was Hetep, the mount of peace, in Egyptian, and in Hebrew it was Mount Salem, or the later Jerusalem.

THE SEED OF YSIRAAL.

Only one mention of the people of Israel occurs by name on all the monuments of Egypt. This was discovered a few years since by Professor Petrie on a stele erected by the King Merenptah II. Not that there is any possibility of identifying these with the Israelites of the biblical exodus. The "people of Ysiraal" on the monument belong to those who were amongst the confederated Nine Bows, the marauders, North Africans, the Kheta, the Canaanites, the Northern Syrians, and others with whom they are classed. "Every one that was a marauder hath been subdued by the King Merenptah, who gives life like the sun-god every day." This inscription gives an account of the Libyan campaign, and concludes with the following description of the triumph of King Merenptah: "Chiefs bend down,

saying, Peace to thee ; not one of the Nine Bows raises his head.   Vanquished are
the Tahennu (North Africans) ; the Khita (Hittites) are quieted ; ravaged is
Pa-kanana (Kanun) with all violence ; taken is Askadni (Askelon ?) ; seized is
Kazmel ; Yenu (Yanoh) of the Syrians is made as though it had not existed ; *the
people of Ysiraal is spoiled—it hath no seed* (left) ; Syria has become as widows of
Egypt ; all lands together are in peace (Petrie, *Contemp. Review*, May, 1896).   The
people of Ysiraal (Israel) are here included, together with the Syrians, and amongst
the confederated "Nine Bows" who made continual incursions into Egypt as
invaders and marauders, and who are spoken of as having been exterminated.
Hence it is said, "The people of Ysiraal is spoiled ; it hath no seed."   But there is
nothing whatever in the inscription of King Merenptah corresponding to or
-corroborative of the biblical story of the Israelites in the land of Egypt or their
exodus into the land of Canaan.   The campaign against the Libyan confederacy had
been undertaken by Merenptah, who, according to the inscription, was born as the
destined means of revenging the invasion of Egypt by the Nine Bow barbarians.
In proclaiming the triumph of the monarch the inscription says, "Every one that
was a marauder hath been subdued by the King Merenptah."   The people of
Ysiraal in this inscription are identified by the Pharaoh with the nomads of the
Edomite Shasu or shepherds, and are classed by him with the confederate
marauders who invaded Egypt with the Libu, and were defeated with huge
-slaughter at the battle of Procepis (Pa-ar-shep, which is also recorded on the
monuments.   They were a tribe or totemic community of cattle-keepers, one of
·"the tribes of the Shasu from the land of Aduma" who went down into Egypt in
. search of grazing ground to find sustenance for their herds in the eastern region of
the Delta.   At this very time, when the people of Ysiraal and their seed were being
·"wiped out" or annihilated as the Israelites in Syria, there was an exodus of the
Edomite Shasu which has been pressed into the service of false theory on behalf of
·biblical "history."   These tribes had considered the eastern region of the Delta,
as far as Zoan, to be their own possession, until they were driven out by Seti I.
Now they bestirred themselves anew, under Meneptah II. (Merenptah), but "in a
manner alike peaceful and loyal."   "As faithful subjects of Egypt, they asked for
. a passage through the border fortress of Khetam in the land of Thuku (Heb.
Succoth), in order that they might find sustenance for themselves and their herds
in the rich pasture-lands of the lake districts about the city of Pa-Tum (Pithom)"
·(Brugsch, *Egypt under the Pharaohs*, Eng. tr. one vol. p. 317).   An Egyptian
· official makes the following report on the subject.   He says : "Another matter for
the satisfaction of my master's heart : we have carried into effect the passage of the
. tribes of the Shasu from the land of Aduma (Edom) from the fortress (Khetam) of
Merenptah-Hetephima, which is situated in Thuku (Succoth), to the lakes of the
· city Pa-Tum, of Merenptah-Hetephima, which are situated in the land of Thuku, in
· order to feed themselves and to feed their herds on the possessions of Pharaoh, who
is there a beneficent sun for all peoples.   In the year 8 . . . Sut, I caused them to be
conducted (according to the list of the days on which the fortress was opened for their
:passage)." (Brugsch, citing Pap. Anastasi, 6).   Merenptah also had his royal seat in the
city of Ramses.   Here we meet with the field of Zoan and the store-cities of Pithom
and Ramses which have been imported into the second book of Moses, and futile
.efforts have been made to show that this record corroborated the biblical version
·of the exodus.   But in this exodus we find the Shasu or shepherds are peaceful and
loyal people, faithful subjects of the Pharaoh, who are politely conducted from the
land of Edom through the fortress (Khetam) to the lake-country of Succoth (or
Thuku), the first encampment assigned to the Israelites, where they would find
abundance of food and fodder for themselves and their flocks and herds instead of
wandering in the wilderness for forty years, according to the other story.   At the
:same time, or thereabouts, the people of Ysiraal in Syria were cut up root and
branch by Merenptah.   The passage through the land of Thuku, Hebrew Succoth,
here described is apparently the route adopted by those who converted the
·"coming forth" from Amenta into the biblical exodus from Egypt, and it tends to
affiliate the cattle-keepers in the land of Goshen to the nomadic tribes of the
Edomite Shasu (Gen. xlvi. 32).   But we shall not overtake the children of Israel
as an ethnological entity on this line of route, nor as the people who perish by
the million in the wilderness of sand that formed the land of graves in the desert
domain of Sekari.   For that we shall have to "turn back" and encamp before
Pi-ha-hiroth, and pass through the mouth of the cleft into the wilderness of
. Amenta.   But it is useless trying any further to confuse the Jewish exodus with the

mythical "coming forth" from the lower Egypt of Amenta, with intent to re-establish a falsely-bottomed history. The eruption of the Libyans and their confederated invaders in the time of Merenptah is a matter of historic fact. That they were vanquished and driven back by Merenptah is equally historical. They at least made no triumphant exodus from Egypt as 600,000 fighting men, for they never got there, but were fatally defeated on the borders of the land. The only people, then, known by the name of Israel to the Egyptian monuments are the people of Ysiraal who had their very seed destroyed, as claimed by the Pharaoh beloved of Ptah. These can be identified as a North Syrian contingent of fighting men who had joined the Libyans, or the old confederation of the Nine Bows, in their attacks on Egypt, and were hunted back in wreck and ruin, if not entirely destroyed, by Merenptah, the so-called "Pharaoh of the exodus." Thus, if these were the same people as those of the Hebrew exodus, the deliverance of the Israelites from Egypt would be turned into the deliverance of Egypt itself from the Libyan confederacy of raiding barbarians amongst whom the Israelites were a hardly distinguishable unit. What then was "the seed of Israel" as an ethnological entity in the eyes of Merenptah, or the writer of his inscription? They fought as mercenaries and marauders for the Libyan king, who had made war on Egypt collectively, and were driven backward all together in one common, overwhelming rout. They came and went, and left no record of their past. Israel in Syria was not Israel in Egypt. Israel in Egypt is not an ethnical entity, but the children of Ra in the lower Egypt of Amenta, who are entirely mythical.

THE TITLE OF PHARAOH

By the bye, so far as hitherto known, the name of "Pharaoh" is only found in Hebrew. Some Egyptologists derive it from Par-ao, the great house. The present writer is of opinion that this title of the Ra was more probably derived from Paru the lion than from Para the house. The Pharaoh personated the lion, or the lion-god, and sometimes wore the lion's tail as the emblem of royalty. Then he was Paru as the lion and the hak as ruler. Thus the king as lion-ruler would be the Paruhak = Pharaoh. Moreover, and this seems conclusive, the lion-god is addressed as the god Paru (Rit., ch. 162), and the full spelling of the name (Paruhak) is extant in the Ritual. In an address to Sekhet (ch. 164) the goddess is called the divine mother of Parhakasa, who is the royal wife of Paruhak-Khepera, the king as lion-ruler or Pharaoh. Probably the Paruhak originated with Kheper-Ptah and his consort Sekhet, who were the parents of the lion-god Atum-Ra, and therefore of Ihuh in Israel. The chapter in which the lion-ruler appears as the Paruhak is one of the most ancient in the Ritual. It is said to have been written partly if not entirely in the language of the blacks (the Nahsi) and the Antiu of Nubia (ch. 164), which takes us beyond Egypt as now known to the country of Sut-Nahsi, whence the Egyptians came in their course of descent from the equatorial regions where they had dwelt in a land of equal day and night, the prototype of their double earth and of time in Amenta. We find from chapter 162 that this lion of the double force, the Paruhak, is invoked as the protector of his people. His whip is used against their enemies. He is saluted as the lion of the double power who answers prayer and comes to those that call upon him and invoke him as the "protector of the wretched against the oppressor" (Rit., 162). These were the manes in Amenta. A corroboration of this origin of the Pharaonic name may be found in Ezekiel (xxxii. 2): "Son of man, take up a lamentation for Pharaoh king of Egypt, and say unto him, Thou wast likened unto a young lion of the nations." Which he was as the lion-ruler Paruhak.

Y Y

EGYPTIAN WISDOM IN THE REVELATION OF JOHN THE DIVINE

Book XI

THE process of making Scripture history from the Egypto-gnostic remains, without the gnosis or science of the ancient wisdom, may be seen approaching its climax in the Book of Revelation attributed to John the divine.

It has been commonly assumed that this book constituted an historic link between the Old Testament and the New; but the Sarkolatræ, or worshippers of the word made flesh in *one* historic form of personality, the carnalizers of the Egypto-gnostic Christ, have never yet discovered what the revelation was intended to reveal. It has been taken as a supplement to the Gospels as if the history of Jesus had been continued into the wedded life after the marriage of the bride with the lamb, and that they dwelt together ever after in that new Jerusalem which came " down out of heaven " " as a bride adorned for her husband," when the tabernacle of God which was to dwell with man took the place of the old Jerusalem that was destroyed by the Romans. The present contention is that the book is and always has been inexplicable because it was based upon the symbolism of the Egyptian astronomical mythology without the gnosis, or " meaning which hath wisdom," that is absolutely necessary for an explanation of its subject-matter; and because the débris of the ancient wisdom has been turned to account as data for pre-Christian prophecy that was supposed to have had its fulfilment in Christian history.

For example, the lamb alone has power to open the book of seven seals. His power comprised the powers of the " seven spirits of God," the primordial seven. And, as represented astronomically, when the vernal equinox passed from the sign of Taurus into the sign of Aries the son of God was imaged as a lamb, instead of the earlier calf or still earlier lion ; thenceforth his was the power and the glory and the majesty, and his the book of life then newly-opened, in the cycle of precession for another 2,155 years. But in the Book of Revelation the drama of the mysteries has been mistaken for human history, and a mythical catastrophe for the actual ending of the world. The book as it stands has no intrinsic value and very little meaning until the fragments of ancient lore have been collated, correlated, and compared with the original mythos and eschatology of Egypt.

To some extent we are now able to identify the wisdom of Egypt in the Book of Revelation and to "make sense" of the apocalyptic visions, so long and so erroneously assumed to have been unveiled to a Christian named John in the isle of Patmos, for the first time since the ancient astronomy was made nonsense of in the futile and fatuous attempt to turn the hidden wisdom into prophecy intended to prove the truth of a spurious history.

The apocalypse of John might be described as "scenes and characters from the mysteries of Taht-Aan," who was literally Aan = John, the divine penman. This was the sacred scribe to whom the 36,000 books or papyrus-rolls were attributed by tradition. In short, *Taht-Aan was the pre-Christian John the divine.* His typical bird, the ibis, is still known in Egypt by the name of John. His other zootype, the kaf-ape, is *Aan* by name. The name of Aani signifies the saluter. This is the character personalized in John. Speaking of the angel, he says: "And when I saw him I fell at his feet as one dead." "And when I heard and saw, I fell down to worship before the feet of the angel." To salute was a primitive mode of worshipping; hence the ape, Aan, was an ideographic figure of the saluter. The object of the present section, then, is to show that the matter of "revelation" was derived from the Egyptian astronomical mythology and eschatology, and that the Jesus of this book is one with Iu, the su or son of Atum-Ra, who was portrayed as the divine man and bringer of peace to earth a many thousand years ago. The prototype of Patmos is to be seen in the Ritual (ch. 175). John is in the isle of Patmos, "for the Word of God and the testimony of Jesus." He writes of the god who died and is alive again, saying, "Behold he cometh with clouds; and every eye shall see him" "and they which pierced him" are to mourn (ch. i. 7). To see how ancient this is, let us turn to the 175th chapter of the Ritual of the Resurrection. It is "the chapter of not dying a second death." The divine sufferer is thus addressed: "Decree this, O Tum, that *if I behold thy face I shall not be pained by thy sufferings.*" This Tum decrees. The great gods have given him the supremacy, and he will reign "*on his throne in the isle of flame* for eternities of eternities" (Naville, Rit., ch. 175).

The mission of Taht-Aan, the saluter of Horus, could not be better stated than in the words of John the divine concerning the Christ of the gnosis called the Word. "That which was from the beginning, that which we have heard, that which we beheld, and our hands handled, concerning the Word of life (and the life was manifested, and we have seen, and bear witness, and declare unto you the life eternal which was with the Father, and was manifested unto us); yea, and our fellowship is with the Father, and with his Son Jesus Christ: and these things we write that our joy may be fulfilled" (1st Ep. John, i. 1–4). Taht-Aan had indeed beheld and heard and handled "the Word of eternal life" manifested in Horus or Jesus, the ever-coming son, for, as bearer of the symbolic Utat, he carried Horus in his hands and held him aloft as the true light of the world, and the symbolic likeness of a soul in human nature that was begotten by Ra, the holy spirit and the father in heaven. Such was the revelation of Tehuti-Aan or Taht-Hermes. The position of Aan, the divine scribe, in relation to Horus, the only-begotten son of God, is repeated on behalf of John in the Gospel. It is in the character of Taht-Aan that "there came a man, sent from

God, whose name was John." The same came for witness of the light. He was not the light, but came that he might bear witness of the light (ch. i.), as did Taht-Aan, who carries the Eye of Horus in his hands and testifies that Horus is the true light of the world, as son of Ra the solar god, and of the holy spirit in the eschatology. John likewise gives his personal testimony, not without hard swearing, regarding "that which was from the beginning, that which we have heard, that which we have seen with our eyes, and our hands handled, concerning the Word." But the testimony of Taht-Aan concerning the Word or logos as Horus was far anterior and just as personal. Moreover, he handled it by carrying in his hands the eye of light, the talismanic maatkheru, and the papyrus-roll or book of life.

The Ritual is the book which contains the divine words that bring about the resurrection to the glory of eternal life. It is a book of the mysteries in which the revelation was dramatically enacted. As before said, the chief revelation made by Aan, as we have it in the now recovered Book of the Dead, is made by the father in heaven on behalf of Horus, the divine son on earth and in Amenta. Horus as the Word gives voice to the decrees which Ra hath spoken in heaven. In his form of the divine son Horus executes those decrees, and Taht-Aan, the giver of the written words (Rit., ch. 151A), is the recorder of the decrees for human use. It is announced in the opening chapter of the Ritual that Ra, the holy spirit, "issued the mandate which Taht-Aan hath executed" (ch. 1, Renouf). This was the revelation made by the father in heaven as testifier to Horus the son who is the "word made truth" in the books of Aan. It is the same opening in the Book of Revelation. The mandate is divinely given to John that he shall write "the revelation of Jesus Christ, which God gave him to show unto his servants," and John, like Aan, bears "witness of the word of God," which was primarily personalized in Iu as the son of Ptah at Memphis.

The revelation of Taht-Aan in the Ritual begins with the resurrection or *coming forth in Amenta from the life on earth.* The opening chapters contain the words which bring about the resurrection and the glory, the recorder of which is Taht-Aan. It is Aan, as writer, who effects the triumph of Osiris over his adversaries on the day of weighing words, or on the judgment day. "Ra issued the command to Aan that he should effect the triumph of Osiris against his adversaries, and the command is what Aan hath executed" in writing the Ritual (ch. 1). The Revelation of John is termed "the Revelation of Jesus Christ, which God gave him to show unto his servants; and he sent and signified it by his angel unto his servant John, who bore witness of the Word of God and the testimony of Jesus Christ, of all things that he saw" (Rev. i. 1, 2). Jesus is accompanied by the seven great spirits whose place is before the throne of God. As Egyptian these were the seven servants or seshu of Horus. Thus "the Revelation of Jesus Christ" was given to John by God the Father "to show unto his servants," the first of whom are the seven spirits which are before his throne. This is the same as the revelation of Horus that was given him by Ra to be written down by Taht-Aan, the scribe of the gods. Therefore we hold that John the divine, as seer in the isle of Patmos, is a form of Aan (or Taht) upon the Mount of Glory in the

Isle of Flame. Not only are the seven seshus of Horus given to Jesus as his servants in Revelation ; they are also grouped around him in their various characters by name, as (1) the seven spirits of God ; (2) the seven as spirits of fire ; (3) the seven as stars ; (4) the seven as eyes ; (5) the seven as golden lampstands ; (6) the seven ruling powers, as heads of the dragon ; (7) the seven as angels of the seven churches.

Thus the book ascribed to John the divine purports to contain "the Revelation of Jesus Christ" = Horus, that was given him by God the Father to show unto his "bond-servants," and these bond-servants answer to the seshu or servants of Horus in the original scripture. The subject-matter of this revelation is sent by Jesus to "his servant John, who bore witness of the Word of God and of the testimony of Jesus Christ" to be set forth as a prophecy of things about to happen that were seen by him in vision ; but which had been unfolded by the mystery-teachers of the heavens in an indefinitely earlier time, and in accordance with the gnosis by means of which alone it could be understood.

For the Hebrew versions of the astronomical mythology in Revelation and in the Book of Enoch could not have been comprehended while the world lasts without the restitution of the Egyptian original as gloss and guide. Enoch, like John, was in the spirit. His internal sight was opened, and he beheld a vision which was in the heavens. But *his* vision was admittedly astronomical. In it he "beheld the secrets of the heavens and of paradise according to its divisions" (ch. 41). The record of his visions is called "the book of the revolutions of the luminaries of heaven"; and is said to contain "the entire account of the world for ever, until a new work shall be effected, which will be eternal" (ch. 71). Enoch says, "I beheld the ancient of days, whose head was like white wool, and with him another whose countenance resembled that of man," and who is called the "Son of Man" in contradistinction to the "son of the woman" (ch. 46). "I beheld the ancient of days, while he sat upon the throne of his glory, and the book of the living was opened in his presence, and while all the powers which were above the heavens stood armed and before him" (ch. 47, 3). Enoch was "elevated aloft to heaven." He saw the new Jerusalem. It was a spacious habitation built with stones of crystal, with walls and pavement all of crystal. He saw that the new heaven contained an exalted throne, the appearance of which was like that of frost. To look upon it was impossible. One great in glory sat upon it, whose robe was brighter than the sun, and whiter than the snow. No mortal could behold him. "Then the Lord with his mouth called me, saying, Approach hither, Enoch, at my holy word" (ch. 14). He sees the giants who had been the watchers in heaven as rulers of the seven colossal constellations of the heptanomis in "their beginning and primary foundation" (ch. 15). Seven watchers are called up for judgment, and when tried are found to have been unfaithful to their trust because they came not in their proper season. They are judged, found guilty, and cast down into the flaming abyss like the seven mountains overthrown in Revelation.

There is also another great judgment day commemorated in the

Book of Enoch. This is the judgment of the seventy. Enoch says, "I saw the throne erected in a delectable land. Upon this sat the Lord of the sheep, who received all the sealed books, which were opened before Him. Then the Lord called the first seven white ones, saying, Take those seventy shepherds; and behold, I saw them all bound, and all standing before Him. First came on the trial of the stars. Then the seventy shepherds were judged, and, being found guilty, were thrust into the flaming abyss into which the primary seven had been previously plunged" (Enoch, ch. 89). The seventy were rulers, angels, princes, watchers, timekeepers, here called shepherds in a heaven of ten divisions, which preceded the twelve and the seventy-two. This is the heaven of the Ritual, attained by spirits perfected upon the mount of glory; the paradise of peace upon the summit of Mount Hetep at the "Atlantean pole" consisting of ten divine domains which answer in the eschatology to the ten islands or celestial nomes in the Astronomy. Thus, it is apparent that a great judgment of Maat upon the mount, as represented in the Ritual, was uttered in or at the end of the heaven in ten divisions. And this had previously taken place when the seven rulers were overthrown, and the heaven in seven divisions passed away.

The day, or a day of judgment, was periodic, like the deluge. It was the ending of a time, an age or æon, sometimes called "the ending of the world" by those who were ignorant of the sign-language. It was but an ending of the world, according to the astronomical mythology, when the time had come for "the dead to be judged" and for "them that destroy the earth" to be exterminated like the Sebau in the Ritual. This ending was also announced by "a great earthquake, when a tenth part of the city fell" (ch. 11, 13). There was a judgment annually in the solar mythos. This is still celebrated yearly by the Jews: the same assizes that were held each year or periodically in the Egyptian great hall of dual justice. But the drama appears so tremendous in the Book of Revelation because the period ending is on the scale of a great year. It is not the ending of the world, but of a great year of the world. It is the day of doom, the "time for the dead to be judged," upon the hugest scale (11, 18). The last great day of judgment is known to all the genuine books of wisdom commonly called apocryphal, but the nature and mode of judgment were only made known to the initiated in the mysteries. The great judgment of all, like the great "deluge of all," was held at the end of the great year of all, in the cycle of precession. At the termination of this vast period it was the Judgment Day. Then followed the conflagration by fire or the catastrophe by water, or the subsidence of the mountains, islands, nomes, provinces and other types of the Heptanomis; or the overwhelming deluge of the pole. The Revelation of John and of Enoch both preserved a fragmentary version of the drama ascribed to Taht-Aan as the mysteries of Amenta, such as: the mystery of the Great Mother who sat on the celestial waters; the mystery of the dragon, with seven heads and ten horns, upon which the woman rode; the mystery of the seven stars; the mystery of the first-born from the dead who rose again as the faithful and true witness on behalf of God the Father.

In the first place, the subject of Revelation was not derived from the canonical gospels. The fundamental matter existed ages on ages earlier. The cult of the lamb and the bride is at least as old in the astronomical mythology as the time when the vernal equinox entered the sign of Aries, and the lamb of Sebek succeeded the calf of Horus on the mount as the type of sacrifice in the cult of the Sebek-heteps in Egypt (*Nat. Genesis*). The doctrinal teaching of the mysteries is also partially apparent in Revelation and in the other writings ascribed to "John." A fragment of the genuine pre-Christian gnosis previously cited is retained almost intact in the First Epistle of John, who says of Jesus the Christ, "This is He that came by water and blood, not in the water only, but with the water and with the blood. And it is the Spirit that beareth witness, because the Spirit is the Truth, for there are Three who bear witness, the Spirit, and the Water and the Blood: and the three agree in one" (1 John, 5, 6, 7, 8). After the poor pitiful apologetics of the Patristic obfuscators in this, as in a myriad instances, it is a comfort to touch the truth upon Egyptian ground. Horus came by water, as the child of the mother and bringer of food, when he was represented by the papyrus-shoot, or by Ichthus, the fish of the inundation. He also came by blood as the incarnate mortal child of Isis. Lastly, in his second advent, Horus or Iusa came in the spirit as the only-begotten son of Atum-Ra, the holy spirit, who was the father of spirits in the Egyptian eschatology.

In Revelation it is said, "Be thou faithful unto death and I will give thee a crown of life" (Rev. ii. 10). The crown of Horus was the crown of life that was the gift of his father Tum. Horus was lord of the diadem. Through him the deceased is made master of the double crown. The Son of Man has on his head a golden crown (Rev. xiv. 14). The double crown worn by Horus of the kingly countenance is magnified into many crowns upon the head of the Logos or "word of God" in Revelation (xix. 12). It was Atum who conferred the crown of triumph on the faithful followers of that example which was set before them by his son. "Thy father Tum hath prepared for thee this beautiful crown of triumph, the living diadem which the gods love, that thou mayst *live for ever*" (ch. 19, Renouf). Deceased, in presence of the great cycle of the gods, is the "great one who seeketh the crown" (ch. 133). "He followeth Shu and calleth for the crown" (ch. 131). "He arriveth at the Aged one, at the confines of the mount of glory, and the crown awaiteth him. The Osiris raiseth it up" (ch. 131). This crown of life was always in view, not only to the mind's eye; it was also figured as an object-picture to the climbers up the mount of glory. Probably our *Corona Borealis* is an extant representative of the ancient constellation that was imaged as the crown, which, when figured in the stars that never set, was a likeness of the eternal diadem that was conferred on those who had attained the mount of glory. It was an Egyptian practice to place a floral crown upon the mummy in the sheta or coffin. The mummy of Aahmes I, the first king of the eighteenth dynasty, was found to have been garlanded with roses for its burial. The "chapter of the crown of triumph" (Rit, ch. 19) shows the continuity of the custom in the nether-world, where the garland of earth becomes the crown of triumph for eternal wear. In the Ritual the judgment is designated that of the clothed and the naked. The righteous are clothed in the white robe of the worthy by the hands of Taht, and the wicked are synonymous with the naked in antithesis to those who are the clothed. There is a comment on this in Revelation, "Blessed is he who watcheth and keepeth his garments lest he walk naked and they see his shame" (Rev. xvi. 15). The ransomed spirits in the Ritual who are redeemed from the mummy condition and all the ills of the corruptible flesh put on the pure white robe of righteousness, called the vesture of truth, which is given to them by Taht for their entrance into and coming forth from the boat of the sun. And being assimilated to Horus, who fought his battle against Sut with a branch of palm, the symbol of victorious renewal of life, the righteous also have the branch of palm given to them as typical of their conquest over death and Hades. The crown of triumph and eternal life, which is called the crown of Makheru as an emblem of the word made truth, is placed by Atum on the brows of those who are justified because they were faithful unto death and thus have won the crown of life, to live for ever with their God in heaven since they lived for God, for truth, for right, for justice, and humanity, on earth (Rit., ch. 19, 1–3). In one chapter of the Ritual it is said of the deceased, "The mouth of N has been thirsty; but he will never hunger nor thirst any more; for Osiris-Châs delivers him and does away with hunger." In Revelation it is said "they shall hunger no more, neither thirst any more, for the lamb which is in the midst of the throne shall be their shepherd, and shall guide them unto fountains of the waters of life" (Rev. vii. 17). These take the place of the water-spring and the vases in the Ritual (ch. 178). A second death is spoken of several times, called the "Extinction of the Adversaries of the Inviolate God," "on the night when judgment was passed on those who are no more" (ch. 18). Those who suffer the second death are also spoken of as those who are buried for ever. That is, they have no part in the resurrection from Amenta. The deceased says in ch. 42 "I am he who dieth not a second time." In the rubric to ch. 135 it is said of the defunct "he dieth not a second time *in the nether-world*." In Revelation (ch. xx.) it is proclaimed that the part of the condemned guilty shall be in the lake that burneth with fire and brimstone; which is the second death. This, in the Ritual, is the lake or tank of flame in which the evil Sebau and the enemies of the good being are annihilated or extinguished for ever.

On the judgment day, in the Ritual, those that overcame are those who passed in triumph through the searching examination of the judgment-hall. As we read in Revelation, "he that hath an ear, let him hear what the spirit saith. To him that overcometh, to him will I give of the hidden manna, and I will give him a white stone, and upon the stone a new name written, which no one knoweth but he that receiveth it" (ch. 2, 17). This was given to the initiate both in the totemic ceremonies and religious mysteries. In the mysteries of Amenta a white stone, or "a pillar of crystal" is given to the initiate. As he comes forth in triumph from the examination he is asked what the judges have awarded him, and he replies "a flame of fire and a pillar of crystal" (ch. 125). It is said of the Lord and his servants "his name shall be upon their foreheads." In the Ritual "the name of Ra is upon the Osiris (ch. 130), and his token of honour is on his mouth." This is said in the book of life, which is here called "the book by which the soul is made to live for ever." It is also said that the Osiris has been initiated in the mysteries, but he "hath not repeated what he hath heard in the house of the God who hideth his face" (Rit., ch. 133). He keeps the secret sacredly. But the original book of life was no mere volume in which a name might be written. The words of power in the Ritual were derived from the Holy Spirit itself by Horus, and inscribed by Taht for human use. These divine words were to be made truth in the life lived on earth, so that the spirit, when it entered the hall of judgment, was, as it were, its own book of life, written for the all-seeing eye. It did not live because Osiris died, but because the divine words or immortal seed had quickened and taken root, and been fulfilled = made truth in the individual human life (Rit., ch. 94) as the gnosis of Salvation. In Revelation we read of the voice which was heard from heaven, "I heard it again speaking with me, and saying, 'Go! take the book which is open in the hand of the angel that standeth upon the sea and upon the earth.' And I went unto the angel, saying unto him that he should give me the little book. And he saith unto me, 'Take it, and eat it up; and it shall make thy belly bitter, but in thy mouth it shall be sweet as honey.' And I took the little book out of the angel's hand, and ate it up; and it was in my mouth sweet as honey; and when I had eaten it, my belly was made bitter" (Rev. x. 8–11). A mode of obtaining knowledge by swallowing the book was also employed by Ptah-Nefer-Ka in the Egyptian "Tale of Setnau." "He placed a new piece of papyrus before him. He copied each word which was on the roll. He had it dissolved in water. When he saw it dissolved he drank it. He (then) knew all that it contained" (Records, vol. iv. p. 138). In the original rendering the book of life was figuratively the food of soul. In the Hebrew version the book of life is turned into an edible and eaten actually as a result of literalising the ancient gnosis. It was not a man named Jesus who was crucified in Egypt as the Lord (Rev. xi. 8). These are the mysteries of Amenta, and the Egypt signified is the Egypt of that netherworld. It is the place of burial in the sandy realm of Sekari that will account for the streets that were choked with dead bodies. The lord who was crucified in that Egypt was Ptah-Sekari, in the cult of Memphis, Osiris in the religion of Abydos and Iu at Annu. The "crucified" belongs to a later terminology. The cross as Christian was preceded by the Tat; the cross of Ptah or of Osiris-Tat—the god who was immanent in the wood or tree of the cross, and who gave up his life periodically in or on the cross as the sustainer of the universe. In the mysteries of Amenta, the Tat-cross was annually overthrown and re-erected as the symbol of salvation; and it was there the Lord was crucified in Egypt. A brief synopsis will suffice to show that the Book of Revelation contains a version of the astronomical mythology which was derived from the Egyptian wisdom. The vanishing heaven is the celestial heptanomis that was formed in seven astronomes, on seven hills, or seven islands, which sank and passed away like the lost Atlantis in the last great deluge of all. The most ancient genetrix is reproduced as the great harlot. She is the beast that sat upon the waters as a pregnant hippopotamus. Her seven "sons of the thigh" are here as the seven kings who were made drunken with the cup of her fornication or promiscuous sexual intercourse. These, as powers, are the seven heads of the scarlet-coloured beast or solar dragon upon which the woman rode. By a change of type, the scarlet-coloured beast becomes the "Scarlet Lady" of later theology; the woman in red being substituted for the red water-cow. The Great Mother is now denounced as the great whore living in adultery with her own children who originated in the seven elemental powers, to pass through several phases of phenomena as the seven with Anup, with Ptah, with Horus, or with Jesus and with Ra. In Revelation the mother of mystery is called "Babylon the Great, the mother of harlots and of abominations of the earth," who has the name of mystery written on her forehead (ch. xvii. 5). But there was an earlier Babylon in Egypt, known to the secret wisdom, which is traditionally identified with the locality of Coptos, nominally the seat of Kep, the Kamite mother of the mysteries. The mother of mystery did not originate with the scarlet woman of Babylon (nor as the red rag of the Protestants), although the title of the Great Harlot was applied to her also, who was the mother of harlots and to whom the maiden-tributes were religiously furnished in that city. Hers is a figure of unknown antiquity in the astronomical mythology, which was constellated as the red hippopotamus that preceded the Great Bear. The red hippopotamus (Apt) had already become the scarlet lady in the Ritual. Hence the Great Mother, as Sekhet-Bast, who is higher than all the gods, and is the only one who stands above her father, is called *the lady of the scarlet-coloured garment* (Rit., ch. 164, Naville). The Kamite Constellation of the "birthplace" may also serve to show cause why the "great harlot" should have been abused so badly in the Book of Revelation. The creatory of the Great Mother was depicted in the sign of the meshhen to indicate the place of bringing forth by the cow of heaven whose "thigh" is the emblem of great magical power in the hieroglyphics. The mother of mystery also carries "in her hand a golden cup full of abominations, even the unclean things of her fornication" (ch. 17, 4), such as *the mystery of fecundation by water*, which was the primitive mystery of Kep. This was symbolised in Egypt by the water-vase, and constellated in the sign of Krater, the urn of the inundation. It has been shown that the gods of the Egyptian mythology originated in seven elemental forces that were born of earth, the mother of life, and who were then continued in a variety of characters as the primordial seven powers. These are reproduced as the progeny of the mother-earth, where they are called "the kings of the earth" over whom "the first-born of the dead" is to become the ruler (ch. 1, 5) as Jesus in the Book of Revelation, the same as Horus (or Iu) in the Ritual, the god "who giveth light by means of his own body" (ch. 83). The astronomical mythology was taught in mysteries by the mystery teachers of the heavens. One of the chief of these was "the mystery of the seven stars"; the seven that are described in the Ritual as "the seven glorious ones," "the seven spirits of fire," "the seven great spirits," who are also termed "the lords of eternity." As never-setting stars the seven were beyond the bounds of time ; hence they became the witnesses for eternal continuity. Thus seven stars that never set were made a group of witnesses for the eternal in the eschatology. These in the Book of Revelation are the seven spirits of God, the seven spirits of fire, the seven eyes, the seven golden lamps, or lampstands ; as variously typified "before the throne" on the celestial summit.

Certain deities in the Ritual are called the Khabsu gods of light, or of the lamp. When the risen Osiris passes over heaven unto the west, it is said the Khabsu gods of the lamp rise up to greet him with their acclamations. "Acclamation cometh from the mount of glory, and greeting from the lines of measurement" (Rit., ch. 130 and 133). This is when the light arises in Kher-Aba and the child, "he of the strong cord," *is re-born upon the mount of resurrection* (ch. 136A). The number is not directly given in the "Book of the Dead." But the gods of the lamp are obviously reproduced in "Revelation" as the spirits of the golden *lampstands*, whether as the group of seven or as the "two witnesses," which are "the two olive trees and the *two lampstands* standing before the lord of the earth" (Rev. xi. 4). The word Khabsu is the name for a lamp, but, in the present instance, the determinative shows that a heavenly body is meant. Also, if a plausible correction, made by Renouf, be allowed, there were Khabsu trees upon the mount of glory as well as deities of the lamp. Khabsu is the well-known name of a sacred tree (Renouf, Rit., ch. 133, Note 4). This may be compared with the two olive trees in Revelation, which were also two lampstands, as the two witnesses whom we shall identify with Anup the stellar god upon his mountain, and Taht-Aan as the lunar lamp of Ra. Moreover, the word Khabsu signifies the soul or spirit as well as the star. Hence it is probable that the seven stars called spirits, the spirits of God, and spirits of fire, were represented by the seven Khabsu stars, or lamps, which were held in the hand of the young solar god as head of the seven, whether as Jesus or as Horus. No matter how these things were shown, or are said to have been shown, to John in Patmos, what we are concerned to know is their fundamental significance and to identify them with the lesser or greater mysteries, which are the mysteries of Taht-Aan in the Egyptian Book of the Dead..

The writer John, who follows afar off in the wake of Taht-Aan, makes an attempt at showing some of the mysteries in his Book of Revelation. Amongst the more prominent are (1) the mystery of the seven stars ; (2) the mystery of the woman, and the beast with seven heads ; (3) the mystery of the two "witnesses" and the four "living creatures" ; (4) the mystery of the war in heaven ; (5) the mystery of God (ch. 10, 7) ; (6) the mystery of renewal in the ancient heavens when every isle and mountain vanished and the heptanomis passed away. In the mysteries of Amenta there is a resurrection of the body-soul, or manes, and a transformation into spirit. This was on the day upon which the god in spirit, Ra, calls from heaven to the mummy-Osiris in Amenta. This summons to the transformation of the mummy into spirit, "Come thou hither !" or "Come thou to me !" (in "Pistis Sophia" it is "Come thou to us !"), that was uttered in the mystery of Tattu, is repeated and applied to John in Revelation as the mode of resurrection into the spirit. John says: "I saw and beheld a door opened in heaven, and the first voice which I heard, a voice as of a trumpet, speaking with me, one saying, '*Come up hither*, and I will show thee the things that must come to pass hereafter.'" Obviously this was the transformation into spirit that was represented in the mysteries. Hence the saying of John, "Straightway I was in the spirit" (Rev. iv. 1, 2), as was the Osiris at the call of Ra (Rit., ch. 17). This cry of "Come" is repeated by each of the four "living creatures," who are the same in the mount that the divine powers, Amsta, Hapi, Tuamutef, and Kabhsenuf, were in the resurrection from Amenta (Rit., ch. 1).

John says "there came one of seven angels that had the seven bowls and spake with me saying: 'Come hither, I will show thee the judgment of the great harlot that sitteth upon many waters; with whom the kings of the earth committed fornication'" (ch. 17). The kings of the earth were the seven spirits of earth who were at once the children and the consorts of the mother in accordance with the primitive polyandry. "I will tell thee the mystery of the woman, and of the beast that carried her, which hath the seven heads and the ten horns. The beast that thou sawest was and is not; and is about to come up out of the abyss, and to go into perdition." That is following the final judgment. It is explained that "the woman whom thou sawest is the great city, which reigneth over the kings of the earth." This was the kingdom of the seven (Rit., ch. 17), who ruled with the great mother in the celestial heptanomis. Some light may be shed on the mystery of the four-and-twenty elders, seated on their four-and-twenty thrones, by the Egypto-gnostic gospel, "Pistis Sophia." In this cryptic work the "mysteries" are said to be four-and-twenty in number. The mystery of God the Father is the first, the mystery of God the Son is last. These two are the first and the last in Revelation, the closer and opener of Amenta in the Ritual. And all the twenty-four are included in the one great, unique, ineffable mystery of the Father, manifested by the Son, as the dove, or the calf, or the lamb, upon the mount of sunrise in the mythos, and on the stellar mount of glory in the eschatology.

In Revelation the heaven in seven divisions comes to an end when the seven thunders have uttered their voices and the seventh angel has sounded the trumpet of doom. Then was "finished the mystery of God, according to the good tidings which he declared to his servants the prophets" (ch. x., 7), which shows the interpretation of the Kamite astronomical mythology by means of biblical prophecy concerning the coming Messiah. The heaven that "was removed as a scroll when it is rolled up, and every mountain and island were moved out of their places" (ch. vi., 14, 15), is also imaged as a book which had been closed and sealed with seven seals. This was the book of doomsday; the record possibly kept for six-and-twenty-thousand years. The book is seen in the right hand of him that sits upon the throne, "a book written within, and on the back close-sealed with seven seals" (ch. v., 1, 2). We may not have all the necessary details for perfecting the parallel and proving the prototype to have been Egyptian, but we observe that in the end of the world or the "subsidence of a country," described in the "magic papyrus" (*Records*, vol. x., 151–2) as an overwhelming deluge, there is mention made of "the seven great dungeons that were sealed at the time with an eternal seal." It is also evident that these seven dungeons were sealed singly one after the other, as it is said of the evil beings who are at the time submerged : "What is immersed, do not let it pass out! Seal the mouths, choke up the mouths, as the shrine is sealed up for centuries." There is an echo of this in Revelation (ch. x.). "And when the seven thunders uttered (their voices) I was about to write: And I heard a voice from heaven saying, 'Seal up the things which the seven thunders uttered, and *write them not.*'" The record is to be sealed not only for centuries, but with the seal of eternal silence, or, as it is imaged, with the sevenfold seal.

Seven times over in the great year the typical catastrophe occurred. The station of the pole was changed. The island was submerged, the mountain was dislimned. Then was the day of judgment when one of the seven dungeons of eternal doom was sealed, and this was repeated until there were seven altogether. It is in this papyrus that the ark or shrine of seven cubits is superseded by the ark of eight cubits, and the heptanomis of Sut is to make way for the octonary of Taht. In Revelation the heptanomis of seven astronomes is symboled by the book of judgment sealed with seven seals. Seven seals are broken for the opening of the book. Seven angels sound upon seven trumpets. Seven thunders utter their voices. Seven plagues are loosed by the seven angels from the seven bowls of the wrath of God. Seven kings are overthrown, and seven mountains pass away, at this the final judgment of the great harlot and her seven children of the thigh ; her meskhen, or other "unclean things of her fornication" that were set in heaven as primitive uranographic signs, by those whose learning came to be unintelligibly interpreted and unintelligently abused by the ignorant fanatics of a later religious cult.

At the end of each three thousand seven hundred years in the cycle of precession the pole-star changed, or, as represented, *a star fell from heaven.* Thus, when the second angel sounded, a mountain (one of the seven) sank down flaming to be quenched in the celestial sea. This was one of the seven mountains upon which the ancient harlot sat. At the same time a great star fell from heaven, which was one of the seven pole-stars. When the fifth angel sounded another pole-star fell. The fall of the total seven has not been followed out one by one in stars. But the fall or wreck of the heptanomis piecemeal has been otherwise described ; Enoch saw it as seven blazing mountains overthrown. Seven types of the over-toppling mount or station of the pole may be assigned approximately : (1) to the mount of the hippopotamus (or northern crown) ; (2) to the mount of the dragon ; (3) the mount of the ape ; (4) the mount of the jackal (or dog) ; (5) the mount of the bird (cygnus) ; (6) the mount of the tortoise (or lyra) ; and (7) the mountain of mankind.

To revert for a moment to the beginning of the Book, the drama opens in Revelation the same as in "the Book of the Dead," with "*the resurrection and the glory*" of the coming Son. "Behold He cometh with the clouds, and every eye shall see Him." It is the risen

Lord of Resurrection who says: "I was dead, and behold I am alive for evermore, and I have the keys of death and of hades" (ch. i. 18). This is Horus of the resurrection risen from Amenta in his triumph over death and hell or Sut and Akar. He proclaims himself to be the all-one, Har-Sam-taui-Neb-Uâ. Jesus, like Horus, is the "faithful witness" for the Father, the first-born of the dead and the ruler of the kings of the earth who were the seven elemental powers that were born of the ancient mother, and afterwards elevated in another character to the sphere, as spirits in glory, and lastly, as the seven lords of eternity. Risen Horus comes as the anointed only-begotten son of God; *His* revelation is to make known the Father which is in heaven as the God in Spirit. We learn from Irenæus that the Egypto-gnostic Christ (or Horus) came to teach the seven powers who preceded him and who had no knowledge of the Father, and to create in them the desire to investigate the divine nature and to make that nature known. This was the revelation through the Christ who is the "faithful witness, the first-born of the dead, and the ruler of the kings of the earth," who taught it as a mystery of revelation. The secret of the mysteries was with Aan. The mysteries of Amenta in the Ritual are chiefly eschatological. But some of them are plainly astronomical. In one of the texts it is said of Taht-Aan, "And now behold Taht in the secret of his mysteries. He is the maker of endless reckonings" (ch. 130).

As Egyptian, the day of judgment was the day of reckoning, and the books were kept by Taht-Aan, who was called the reckoner of all things in earth and heaven. An item in precession is likewise recognisable in Revelation in the statement concerning the seven rulers of the heptanomis. "They are seven kings: the five are fallen, one is, the other is not yet come" (ch. xvii. 10). There is a date in the statement as it stands. The time indicated is that of the sixth pole-star, which as here reckoned out was the pole-star Vega in the constellation of the lyre or tortoise some fourteen thousand years ago.

The "mount of glory" has been well preserved in the "Revelation of John." It is described as a throne set in heaven with "one sitting on the throne, and round about the throne were four-and-twenty thrones, and upon the thrones were four-and-twenty elders sitting arrayed in white garments; on their heads were crowns of gold" (ch. iv. 4). And in the midst of the elders was the lamb "standing on the mount Zion," which shows the identity of the throne and mount and astronomically with the zodiacal sign of Aries. The mount in Revelation has been turned into the throne of the Father and the Son, but it is the same throne as that of Osiris, from beneath which the water of life wells up, with the four genii standing before the shrine. These become "the four living creatures full of eyes," around the throne, in the four corners of the mount. The probability is that the four-and-twenty elders had been objectified in the astronomy by four-and-twenty stars, which represented twenty-four divine judges who appear in the Babylonian calendar. These were twenty-four zodiacal stars, twelve to the north and twelve to the south (Diodorus, ii. 30; Sayce, *Hibbert Lectures*, p. 72). As characters in the Egyptian wisdom, the earliest pre-solar powers were called the old ones or the elders. As Egyptian, they are traceable to the two different groups of the twelve described in " Pistis Sophia " as the subject of four-and-twenty mysteries. These were the twelve who had their thrones as rulers (or æons) in the zodiac and the twelve as spirits with Horus-Khuti, lord of spirits, in the harvest-field or heaven of eternity.

The Mount is indeed the place of congregation, not only for the spirits of the just made perfect, but also as the final gathering-place for all the principal personages in the Pantheon of the Kamite mythography. The old great mother and her seven sons are there ; the seven great spirits or the glorious ones, the Khus with Horus-Khuti ; the four who kept the quarters as Egyptian gods or powers ages before they were christened "angels" ; the twelve as rulers in the zodiac ; the dragon, the woman with child, and others, which are identifiably Egyptian, are all included in the astronomical imagery of the Celestial Mount. The seven Halls, Arits or watch-towers assigned to the seven spirits in the Great House of Osiris, are utilised as the seven churches which are assigned to the seven angels in the Book of Revelation. The seat of justice in the solar mythos was shifted to the point of equinox, and the balance was erected on the later mount of glory in the zodiac. This is the mountain of Amenta in the eschatology. It is described in the Ritual (ch. 149) as the exceeding high mountain of the nether-world, the top of which touches the sky. Whether stellar or solar, this was the mount as judgment-seat. " And I saw a great white throne, and him that sat upon it. And I saw the dead standing before the throne, and the books were opened ; and the dead were judged out of the things which were written in the books, every man according to their works" (Rev. xx. 11–14). In the Ritual, it is said, the gods "fashion anew the heart of a person (in spirit) according to what he hath done," i.e., according to his works, in the body (ch. 27 and 75). There is also a call to judgment in the Ritual (ch. 136B). "Come! come! for the Father is uttering the judgment of Maat," says the speaker, who is Horus in the Osirian myth and Iu in the cult of Atum-Ra.

There is a description of the books being brought into the judgment-hall upon the Mount. "Oh, thou who callest out at thine evening hours, grant that I may come and bring to him (the Father) the two jaws of Rusta, and that I may *bring to him the books which are in the celestial Annu, and add up for him his hosts.*" Bringing away the jaws of Rusta is equivalent to carrying off "the broken bonds of Death and of Hades " by him who was dead and is alive for evermore (Rev. i. 18). He who has conquered death and hell and carried away the gates of the prison-house has also vanquished the evil dragon. He exclaims, " I have repulsed Apap and healed the wounds he made." There was a great Egyptian library at On or Annu, the Greek Heliopolis. Hence in heaven itself, or the Celestial City, the books of Taht were kept in Annu. Thus, speaking of the judgment, the Osiris says : "Grant that I may bring to him, the Judge, the books which are in Annu, and add up for him his heavenly hosts." The deceased says : " I am come to thee, O my Lord, that I may look upon thy glory. I know thee, and I know the names of *the forty-two gods who make their appearance with thee in the hall of righteousness.*" But in the papyri of Ani and of Nunefer, the judges or assessors in the Maat appear as Twelve in number sitting on twelve thrones instead of the forty-two, or the twenty-four, which offers a prototype for the twelve judges on the twelve thrones in Revelation and in the canonical gospels. In one of the pictures to the Ritual Horus stands upon the Mount in presence of his father as the calf, which was a type of sacrifice in the Osirian religion earlier than the lamb (Naville, Todt, Kap. 108). " I come," says the speaker, " so that I may see the process of Maat, and the lion-forms." These are the Kherefu = Cherubs (ch. 136B) stationed at the seat of judgment on the Mount. " Let the fathers and their apes (the spirits of fire) make way for me, that I may enter the Mount of Glory and pass through where the great ones are." " Here is the cycle of the gods." " I poise for him," the Judge, " the balance, which is Maat." " Come! come! for the Father is uttering the judgment of Maat." This was the final judgment on the Mount, where the spirits of the just were passed as perfected. The invitation to " Come, come," and hear the judgments delivered on the day of doom, is equivalent to the words in Revelation, " Come up hither, and I will show thee the things which must come to pass hereafter. Straightway I was in the Spirit: and behold, there was a throne set in heaven, and one sitting upon the throne." " And I saw in the right hand of him that sat on the throne a book written within and on the back, close-sealed with seven seals " (Rev. iv. 1, and v. 1). It is said in the Ritual (ch. 133), " Rā maketh his appearance at the Mount of Glory with the cycle of his gods about him. The strong one issueth from his hidden dwelling." " Be thou lift up, O Rā, who art in thy shrine, on the day when thou discernest the land of Maat"; that is, where the hall of judgment stands upon the Mount of Glory. The ancient of days in the Semitic version is Ra, the solar god, who typifies the eternal in the Ritual. He is called " the aged one at the confines of the Mount of Glory" (ch. 131). He is the aged one upon his throne, as in the books of Enoch, Daniel, and John the Divine. The ancient of days together with the Son of Man preparing for the judgment is described by Enoch. " At that time I beheld the ancient of days, while he sat upon the throne of his glory, while the book of the living was opened in his presence, and while all the powers which were above the heavens stood around and before him " (ch. 47, 3). Another was present whose countenance " resembled that of man," and who accompanied the ancient of days. This is the Son of Man to whom Righteousness (or Maati) belongs. It is said of this great judgment in the Ritual, " The glorious ones are rightly judged, and the evil dead are parted off" (ch. 18). In the mysteries of the Ritual, " He that sitteth upon the throne," as the great judge in Amenta is Osiris, with Horus as the beloved only-begotten Son. But in the earlier cult at Annu, Atum-Ra was the judge, as God the Father, with Iu-em-hetep as God the Son, that is, as Iu the Su = Jesus the ever-coming Son. At the opening of the book for the Judgment Day in Revelation we read, " I saw a strong angel proclaiming with a great voice, 'Who is worthy to open the book, and to loose the seals thereof?'" " And one of the elders said unto me, 'Behold, the lion that is of the tribe of Judah, the root of David, hath overcome to open the book and the seven seals thereof'" (Rev. v. 2, 5). This was the book containing "the things which the seven thunders uttered" (Rev. x. 4). The book therefore of Seven Great Mysteries. Now, among the other writings ascribed to Taht there was a book of the seven mysteries of Amenta, or of the seven festivals with which the seven mysteries were celebrated. (1) The day of the Monthly festival of the sixth-seventh; (2) The festival of the fifteenth; (3) The festival of Uaka; (4) The festival of Taht; (5) The festival of the birth of Osiris; (6) The festival of Amsu; and (7) The festival of "Come thou hither." Thus there were seven great mysteries corresponding to the seven festivals for which the record was written. It is a book by which is revealed all that has happened from the beginning, consequently it was a book of Revelation that was written by Aan, the divine scribe. By means of this book the Manes for whom it was written can enter what John calls "the spirit" by becoming a Spirit, so that the gods are able to come near him and touch him, "for he has become as one of them." It is this book of Revelation concerning the seven mysteries and their celebration of which Aan is speaking when he declares it is to be copied in its entireness and is not to be added to by commentaries. This we cannot but associate with the book of the Seven Great Mysteries that is sealed with seven seals in Revelation. The book that was sealed with seven seals is a record of all time, or of the seven ages in the cycle of precession, that was kept by Taht the measurer, reckoner and divine recorder; the god who "rescued the Atu from his backward course," and who "repeated the ancient ordinances and words for the guidance of posterity" as teller of time by means of the moon (Rit., ch. 128).

Seven stars in a group were witnesses to the power that was permanent at the pole, the power of stability, of equilibrium, and of the scales of justice which they served as "the seven arms of the balance" on the day of judgment. But there are "two witnesses" particularly specialised in Revelation. These are said to be "the two olive-trees and the two lampstands standing before the Lord of the earth" (ch. xi. 4). These two witnesses are to be met with in the Egyptian judgment scenes. In the second tale of Khamuas, a scene of the Osirian judgment is portrayed. The seven halls or mansions of Osiris and the lords of eternity are here described as the seven "arits" or watch-towers, the same as in the Ritual (ch. 144). The seven are represented as a series, the seventh being the last. It is said that, "They entered the seventh Hall, and behold! Setme saw the figure of Osiris the great god seated upon his throne of fine gold, and crowned with his atef-crown"; "*Anup the great god being on his left, and the great god Taht on his right, with the gods of the council standing in their places: standing and making proclamation.*" The Balance was set in the midst before them, and they were weighing the evil deeds against the good deeds, the great god Taht (Aan) recording, with Anup giving the word to his colleague (Griffith, *Second Tale of Khamuas*, pp. 46, 48). These are the prototypal "*two witnesses*" stellar and lunar for the Father and Son in the solar mythos. Taht-Aan was the witness for Horus, the only-begotten son of the father. In the mythos, which preceded the eschatology, Taht-Aan was the light of the world as the god whose luminary was the moon. Read doctrinally, he was not the true light, but he came that he

z z

might bear witness to the true light. The lunar god was one of the powers in nature that was born of the motherhood; whereas Horus, of the resurrection, was begotten by the father, and Taht bore witness that Horus, not Aan, was the true light of the world, and the one direct representative of the father-god, who was Ra the holy spirit in the eschatology. Horus (or Iu) is the Word that was with God the Father in the beginning. He is the only Son who issued from the Father; the Son who converses with the Father; the Son who was instructed of the Father to reflect and reveal the nature of the God in Spirit as the One Eternal Power. Anup may be traced in Amenta as the witness for Horus the child, who was the Word; Aan is the witness for Horus the adult who is the word made truth. Hence, he is the giver of the talismanic makheru; also the divine scribe who avouches the truth of the Word in the writings. These, as Egyptian, are the "two witnesses" who were present in the hall of judgment.

In the astronomical mythology the earth was the coffin of Osiris; the coffin of Amenta which Sut, the power of darkness, closed upon his brother when he betrayed him to his death. Then the four "living creatures" or "four glorified ones" who rose again with Horus from the dead were stationed at the four corners of the coffin of the earth, in which Osiris as the elemental god was buried. In the Egyptian drawings, the earth is represented by the lotus or papyrus-plant on which the four attendant spirits stand. This is equivalent to the four corners on which a new heaven had been based in the creation of Atum-Ra. These were four of the primordial powers which had been the brothers of Horus in the earlier mythos who are now called his children, when Horus is said to have "come to light in his own children." This is in the resurrection as it was rendered in the Osirian eschatology (Rit., ch. 112). Thus, when Horus rose again upon the mount of resurrection in Amenta he was accompanied by the spirits of the four corners with whom his fold was founded (Rit., ch. 97). The scene of the mystery on the mount is reproduced in the Gospels. According to Matthew, when Jesus "opened his mouth" to deliver the Sermon on the Mount, only four of the disciples accompanied him. These were Simon-Peter, Andrew, and the two brothers John and James (chs. iv., v. and x.). The Kamite four are also reproduced in Revelation as the four living creatures. "The first creature like a lion, the second creature like a calf, and the third had the face of a man, and the fourth creature like a flying eagle" (ch. iv., vii.). As Egyptian, they are also four great spirits at the four corners of the mount; and in Revelation they are the "four angels standing at the four corners of the earth, holding the four winds of the earth" (vii., 1). Also, their names under each form of the four are the same. In their primary form they are the "four living creatures" with the eyes, which, as Egyptian, are ape-headed, jackal-headed, bird-headed and human-headed. In a secondary phase they were given the human figure; and both forms of the four are repeated in the Revelation of John. According to Revelation, the four living creatures are full of eyes, round about and within, and they have no rest day and night, as they were moving round for ever with the sphere. Being astronomical figures, the eyes of these were stars. And in the Ritual, the four are eyes or stars to the four quarters. The vignettes to ch. 148 show them as the four eyes, or guiding-stars, one to each quarter: north, south, east and west.

When the heptanomis, or heaven in seven divisions, passed away, as rendered in the mysteries of the astronomical mythology, the seven ruling powers were fabled to have fallen, as described by Enoch in his book of the heavens. But in another representation the powers of the seven were unified in one great sovereign power. This was assigned to Horus, the primordial solar god who was born of the Old Mother as one of the seven that were unified in him, and re-born as Horus of the resurrection. Horus, in his earliest image, was the crocodile-headed Sebek, as the fish of the inundation, and the crocodile was the Kamite prototype of the solar dragon. The seven powers were variously portrayed as seven stars, seven eyes, seven spirits, seven islands or mountains on which the "woman" sat; seven uræus-deities, seven fins of a fish. According to the ancient wisdom, or the gnosis, says the writer, the seven heads of the beast on which the woman sitteth are seven mountains, and they are also seven kings, elsewhere called the kings of the earth, the kings who committed fornication with the woman, and were made drunken with her wine. "I will tell thee the mystery of the woman and of the beast that carried her, which hath the seven heads and the ten horns. The beast that thou sawest was, and is not, and is about to come up out of the abyss, and go into perdition. And they that dwell on the earth shall wonder, when they behold the beast, how that he was, and is not, and shall come!" The seven heads of the beast "are seven kings," that were rulers in the celestial heptanomis. "Five of these are fallen, the one is, the other is not yet come. And when he cometh he must continue a little while."

There would have been no dragon with seven heads but for Sebek the crocodile-headed deity, whom we look upon as the oldest type of the solar Horus in the Egyptian mythology. The seven powers born of the Old Mother as the spirits of earth or gods of the elements, here called the kings of earth, were compounded into one great power as the sun-god Horus who preceded Ra. This was the crocodile-headed Sebek in relation to the ancient Mother, and thus the crocodile became the solar dragon, upon which the woman rode; the seven powers being at the same time seven kings and also seven mountains "on which the woman sitteth," each type being a representative of the celestial pole. The goddess Apt, who is the female dragon, inasmuch as the crocodile was one of her zootypes, is called "the Great Mother of him who is married to his mother," that is, to Sebek-Horus, the crocodile or dragon as male. He, as child of the Great Mother, was made her consort in the mythos of the mother and child. He became the husband of the mother as the divinised adult, and seven powers are equal to the seven heads of the male dragon or crocodile. By the bye, there is an Egyptian talisman or fetish in the Berlin Museum composed of a sevenfold figure of the crocodile. The crocodile was an image of the god Sebek, being the prototypal dragon; and seven crocodiles are equivalent to the beast with seven heads, on which the woman rode, in the Book of Revelation, as the great harlot of primitive promiscuous intercourse (Erman's *Egypt*, p. 149). During the changes that occurred in heaven, the seven-headed beast on which the woman rode is represented as losing one of its seven heads. Thus, the change of type from an image of the beast to that of the human figure which occurred when the crocodile-head of Sebek was replaced or added to by the head of the human Horus is plainly indicated. It was given to the second beast, or to the first beast in a second character, that an image should be made to the beast who had the stroke of the sword, and lived. "And it was given unto him to give breath to it, even to the image of the beast, that the image of the beast should both speak and cause that as many as should not worship the beast should be killed." Naturally, the image that could speak was of *the human type*, as is Horus An-ar-ef when portrayed as the seventh of the group who were represented in the image of the beast before the human figure was adopted for "the first beast whose death-stroke was healed." Thus the beast that came up out of the waters, called the sea, as a crocodile, or dragon, having ten horns and seven heads, and upon his horns ten diadems, was smitten unto death, as it seemed, in one of its heads: "And I saw one of its heads, as though it had been smitten unto death; and his death-stroke was healed; and *there was given to him a mouth speaking great things*" (ch. xiii. 5). The beast that came up out of the sea is the solar dragon under two different types, but in both characters it is the dragon or crocodile. In the first, it has seven heads and ten horns, and is like unto a leopard, and his feet are as the feet of a bear, and his mouth as the mouth of a lion. In the second shape he had two horns like unto a lamb, but he spake as a dragon (ch. xiii. 11). This was Sebek, who, under one type, was the crocodile, and under the other, a lamb. The dragons are somewhat mixed in Revelation. There are five altogether: (1) the Apap-dragon (ch. xii. 9); (2) the dragon that gave power and dominion to the beast (ch. xiii. 2); (3) the dragon on which the woman rode; (4) the lamb that spake as a dragon; (5) the dragon constellated in Draconis as a uranographic sign in heaven. There was at first no human type in the septenary of powers. They were figured as seven serpents, seven hawks, seven apes, seven crocodiles, or other forms of the typical seven, but with no human head amongst them; when there was as yet no Horus as the human child, or Atum as the divine man, all seven had been imaged by zootypes. But in the later mythos the human type was introduced, as that of Horus, the child of the Virgin Mother. The seven-headed beast then lost one of its pre-human heads. Sebek-Horus, the crocodile or dragon-headed, was changed into the human Horus. As crocodile, he was the child of Apt. As Har-si Hesi, he became the child of Isis in a human guise. Thenceforth the human type was one amongst the seven, and the beast, *qua* beast, lost one of its original heads, which, as Egyptian, was seen to be replaced by the human type when the wound was healed.

The acclaiming of Horus or Jesus above the seven previous powers is a subject of the first chapter in Revelation. He is exalted as "the first-born of the dead." This is "the faithful One," who is the True Witness for the Father in Heaven as Horus or Iu in his resurrection. The other seven did but represent a soul in matter. The soul that rose up from the dead was an immortal spirit, and *as an eighth one it was added to the seven*. This was as the sun that rose again from the underworld in the mythology, and as the Divine Enduring Spirit in the eschatology. In one cult, it was the crocodile-headed Sebek-Horus who is the seven-headed dragon in Revelation. As it is stated clearly enough, "the beast that was and is not, is himself *also an eighth*, and is one of the seven" (Rev., ch. xvii. 11). This, as Egyptian, became "the ruler of the kings of the earth," as did Horus in his resurrection from the dead at his second coming, which was from the Father in Heaven. Time was when the eighth one was the highest power. Sut-Anup was the highest as an eighth one to the seven great spirits in the stellar mythos. Taht—following Sut—was an eighth one to the seven in the lunar mythos. Lastly, Horus was the highest in the solar mythos as the lord of resurrections, and as eighth one to the seven, he whose symbol was the eight-rayed star of the Egypto-gnostic Pleroma, which was first made historical when it was called the star of Bethlehem. As the Egypto-gnostics said, "Seven powers glorify the Word." These powers were the contributions of the seven spirits which out of gratitude to the Propator had contributed whatsoever each one had attained in himself of the greatest beauty and preciousness; they skilfully blended the whole in producing a most perfect being, and the very star of the Pleroma (namely, the gnostic Jesus, the Christ, the Saviour, Logos—*everything*), because he was formed from the contributions of all the powers that preceded him who was the Horus or Jesus of the Resurrection, the outcome and first fruit of all (Iren., bk. 1, ch. 2, 6).

The faithful and true witness, as Egyptian, is Horus-Maat-Kheru, the word made truth; he who made the word truth by his resurrection, in the likeness of the Living God. The first Horus, or Horus in his first advent, was the Word; and the promise made by him as founder was fulfilled by Horus at his second coming as the "faithful witness," the first-born from the dead. In Revelation, this "faithful and true witness" is called "the beginning of the creation of God" (ch. iii. 14). That is as a creation of the god in spirit, who, as Atum-Ra at Annu, was the Holy Spirit. Har-Ur, the elder Horus, was the child of the virgin goddess; Horus in spirit was "the beginning of the creation of God," the lord of resurrections who had wrested "the keys of death and hades" from the grasp of their grim keepers for the deliverance of the Manes from Amenta (Rit., ch. 64). The scales or balance was erected in the Maat or Hall of Twofold Justice for the weighing of hearts and also of words, and in Revelation one of the four living creatures is portrayed with the scales in his hand. "I saw, and behold, a black horse, and he that sat thereon had a balance in his hand" (ch. vi. 5). The balance, as Egyptian, was the scales of justice. In Revelation, the scales are turned to commercial account for the weighing out of grain by the pennyworth. "And I saw the heaven opened, and behold, a white horse, and he that sat thereon called Faithful and True; and in righteousness he doth judge and make war. And his eyes are a flame of fire, and upon his head are many diadems; and he hath a name written, which no one knoweth but he himself. And he is arrayed in a garment sprinkled with blood; and his name is called the Word of God. And the armies which are in heaven followed him upon white horses, clothed in fine linen, white and pure. And out of his mouth proceedeth a sharp sword, that with it he should smite the nations; and he shall rule them with a rod of iron; and he treadeth a winepress of the fierceness of the wrath of Almighty God. And he hath on his garment and on his thigh a name written, King of Kings and Lord of Lords" (ch. xix. 11, 16). The sign-language of Egypt will tell us why the name of the King of Kings and Lord of Lords was written on his Thigh. The thigh or khepsh was a type of power. In one shape it is called the Ur-heka, or great magical power, which was feminine at first. It is a thigh-shaped instrument made use of to open the mouth of the dead in the resurrection (Rit., ch. 23). At the time of his re-arising the Osiris exclaims: " Let me seize the khepsh which is under the place of Osiris, with which I may open the mouth of the gods " (ch. 69). In another *rôle* Horus is the divine husbandman, the sower and the reaper, as the power of germination; of harvest and of vintage. In this character he is known as the god Amsu, who is portrayed in the human form like him who is described in Revelation as the Son of man. " I saw, and behold, a white cloud, and on the cloud one sitting like unto the Son of man, and wearing on his head a golden crown, and *in his hand a sharp sickle*, and another angel came out from the temple crying with a great voice to him that sat on the cloud, ' Send forth thy sickle and reap, for the hour to reap is come, for the harvest of the earth is over ripe.' And he that sat on the cloud cast his sickle on the earth, and the earth was reapt. And another angel came out from the temple which is in heaven, he also having a sharp sickle," and it was said to him, " Send forth thy sharp sickle and gather the clusters of the vine of the earth, for her grapes are fully ripe " (ch. xiv. 19). Horus usually carries the fan or flail as husbandman, but he is also the reaper and the vintager; hence the fig-leaf was his emblem. Horus the reaper in Amenta has twelve followers in two groups of seven and five. These are the reapers in the Aarru-fields, where the corn grows seven cubits high and the harvest is reapt for eternity. The twelve are called the "blessed," who reap with Horus for his father Ra, and therefore are the blessed of his father. The harvest-field is in the earth of eternity, where Horus appears in human form with the fan in his hand as the master of joy and lord of the twelve, who are likewise portrayed in human form as the Manes. In the gospels Jesus is depicted in this character of the reaper. As such he comes like Horus with the fan in his hand that shows him to be the thresher and winnower of the corn. As lord of the harvest-field he calls to him the twelve and constitutes them reapers of the harvest on earth which was reapt in Amenta, the other earth, by Horus and the twelve. It is made doubly certain by the context that the twelve in the gospels were astronomical characters. Their names were written in heaven like those of the twelve gods, the twelve kings, or the twelve apostles that are coeval with the founding of the zodiac. The twelve in the gospels were followed by the seventy and the seventy-two (*cf.* the two versions), which represent the two different divisions of the planisphere into its ancient seventy, and later seventy-two parts that were assigned to those whose names were written in heaven and had been read there for ages on ages of time by the astronomers and the men who knew. So ancient was the matter as mythical representation in the Egyptian wisdom that the reaper of the harvest in Amenta, who has twelve followers there, had been set aloft in the planisphere as Horus the reaper in the fields of food, who is extant to-day as the husbandman and reaper on the stellar map; but as Boötes, and not as the " historic " reaper of the harvest.

Horus appears in the various characters of Har-Tema, the revealer of justice; Har-Makheru, the word made truth; Har, the red god who orders the block of execution. These are phases of Har-Makhu, the god of both horizons, all of which are reproduced in Revelation. Michael, the warrior angel who overthrows " the dragon and his angels," is the Hebrew form of Har-Makhu, who is Atum-Huhi in the person of his own son. This is Har-Tema, he who makes justice visible, in the cult of Osiris. He is the avenger of the wrongs inflicted on his father by the Apap-dragon and his dark host of the Sebau or fiends by the evil Sut, and also by the criminals who on account of their own deeds are self-condemned to die the second death upon " the highway of the damned " (Rit., ch. 18).

The mythology of Egypt has preserved the prototypal uncorrupted version of what has been termed the "awful tradition of a war in heaven." This was made out magnificently at last in Milton's epic poem, but the original war in heaven was simply elemental and had no more awfulness or terror in it than a thunderstorm. We can trace this warfare of the elements from the beginning in chaos; the terrors were evoked from the mind of man. A battle was fought each four-and-twenty hours betwixt Har-Makhu, the sun-god of both horizons, and the dragon of darkness, who is hurled down from the horizon of the east into the pit with all his angels or fiends called the Sebau or Sami. This great battle, fought in the Ritual during the last hours of the night, becomes a typical last great battle in a contention that is fought out on the scale of the great year in the Book of Revelation called " the war of the great day of God the Almighty," when " the kings of the whole world," or the seven kings who ruled in the celestial heptanomis, are to be " gathered together into the place which is called in Hebrew Har-Magedon " (ch. xvi. 14, 16). Now it is feasible to infer that the name of this battle-ground was derived from that of Har-Makhu as the place where the Makha, or scales of justice, was erected for the judgment on the night of the great battle when the Sebau were defeated and the day when the adversaries of the good being were finally annihilated. This was at the point of equinox (Rit., ch. 18). The battle of Har-Magedon is preceded by the pouring out of the seventh bowl and the sound of the great voice from the throne that said: " It is done!" " And every island fled away, and the mountains were no longer found," for this was the end of the heptanomis and the substitution of the heaven in twelve divisions, which was the heaven of Atum-Ra or Atum-Iu, who says: " I am he who closeth and he who openeth, and I am but one. I am Ra at his first appearance. I am the great god self-produced," and who became the Hebrew deity Ihuh (Rit, ch. 17, Renouf). The war in heaven, or in external nature, was first. Next it was made astronomical. Lastly, it was eschatological or theological, as in Milton's version of the *Paradise Lost*. In the Ritual the evil Apap is bound in chains each morning. " Chains are flung upon thee

by the scorpion goddess, and slaughter is dealt out to thee by Maati.
Apap is fallen and is in bonds" (ch. 39). The same drama was
represented yearly in relation to the annual sun and the autumn
gathering of All Souls. In Revelation the drama represents a larger
period of time. A thousand years intervene betwixt the first and
second resurrection. "I saw thrones, and they that sat upon them,
and judgment was given unto them." Those who rise again are
said to "reign with Christ a thousand years," or with Horus in the
house of a thousand years, and the rest of the dead lived not until
the thousand years should be finished. This is the first resurrection.
Then follows the last judgment, the second death, and the new
Jerusalem built for the children of Israel, whose thrones are twelve in
number as foundations of the final heaven.

We read in Revelation that the great dragon is that "old serpent"
who is called the devil and Satan (ch. xii. 9). And again, it is said:
"I saw an angel coming down out of heaven, having the key of the
abyss and a great chain in his hand. And he laid hold on the dragon,
the old serpent which is the devil and Satan, and bound him for a
thousand years, and cast him into the abyss, and shut it and sealed
it over him" (ch. xx. 2, 3). These are the two types of the Egyptian
devil. The Apap-reptile was that old serpent, the devil in pre-
anthropomorphic guise. Sut was the anthropomorphic Satan or evil
adversary in the later theology. Also the dragon and Sut are
treated as if identical in the Ritual (ch. 108). In the chapter of
chaining the evil one, this is the Apap in one aspect and Sut in the
other. It is said : "Then Sut is made to flee with a chain of steel
upon him. Then Sut is put into his prison." The evil one is said to
be "pierced with hooks, as was decreed against him of old." Horus
makes war upon the powers of evil on account of what they have
done against his father Osiris in Amenta. But especially on Sut the
power of drought and darkness now represented as the adversary
Satan in an anthropomorphic shape, which brings us to the latest
stage of the war in heaven, earth, and Amenta. "Horus says to
these gods, 'Strike the enemies of my father, punish them in your pits
(in the bottom of hell) for the evil they have done to the great one,
my father. Your particular duties in Amenta are to keep the pits of
fire in accordance with Ra's command, which I make known to you.'"
To the condemned, he says : "You are bound for ever, you are tied
by strong cords. I have ordered your detention. My father prevails
against you, your curses are judged against you before Ra. Your
contempt for justice comes back to you. Bad for you is the
judgment of my father. O Ra ! praise be to Ra ! thy enemies are in
the place of destruction !" (*Book of Hades*, Second Division, Legends.)

The battle of Har-Magedon was not a mortal conflict to be fought
at some far-off indefinite future time. It had been fought already in
the Ritual, and was periodically repeated in the mysteries as the final
struggle betwixt light and darkness, or the solar god and apap-reptile.
The great battle depicted in the Ritual is fought by Har-Makhu
(Gr. Har-Machis) and the evil dragon. Har-Makhu was the solar
god of the double horizon or equinox, and the nightly battle was
ended on the horizon east. In the Ritual the dragon of darkness is
shown at night and morn in relation to the double horizon on two

sides of the mount.   At the close of day, when the sun-god sinks into
the water of the west as Ra or Horus, he is confronted by his natural
enemy, the evil serpent Apap, the destroyer or devourer that rises up
gigantic from the bottomless abyss.   Daylight is described as coming
to a stand (Hâu) like a tidal wave at the poise.   With sunset the
Apap "turneth down his eyes to Ra ; for there cometh a standing still
in the bark and a deep slumber within the ship.   And now he (the
dragon) swalloweth seven cubits (in some texts three) of the great
water" (Rit., ch. 108).   This is the monster that drank up all the
water in the world, whether as dragon, toad, snake or other reptile,
here caught, as Kamite, in the act, and the water that it drinks is daylight ; the great water flowing round the mount of earth by day.   The
war of light and darkness goes on through the night down in Amenta,
the lurking-place of the dragon who seeks to destroy the tree of life
at its roots, but is for ever foiled by the god who represents the
nocturnal sun in the shape of a great cat, as seer in the dark, and
protector of the persea or ash, which is the Kamite Tree of Life by
name.   All night the war goes on betwixt the solar god and his
old adversary.   At dawn the host of darkness is repulsed and beaten
for another day.   The last great overwhelming wrecking, ruining
charge is described in the Ritual (ch. 38).   It is the prototype of
the war in heaven described in Revelation, when Michael and his
angels went "forth to war with the dragon ; and the dragon warred,
and his angels ; and they prevailed not.   And the great dragon was
cast down, the old serpent, he that is called the devil and satan, the
deceiver of the whole world.   He was cast down to the earth" (Rev.
xii. 7, 9), which in the Ritual is the Nether Earth of Amenta.   "The
stormy voice of bellowings" is heard from the dying monster, and Ra
the conqueror staggers forth upon the horizon, fainting with his many
bleeding wounds.   But Apap has fallen, and the song of triumph is
raised, "Apap is fallen ! fallen ! fallen !"   Apap, the enemy of Ra,
goeth down to be cut up piecemeal and drowned in the lake of
heaven.   The "gods who are on the roads" overthrow him.   There
are ten groups of the Tata-gods of a heaven in ten divisions (Rit.,
ch. 18).   The gods of the four quarters bind him.   The avenging
goddesses fall on him furiously.   Chains are flung upon him by
Isis-Serkh.   Death is dealt out to him by Maftit, the lynx-goddess.
Ra is satisfied ; he makes his progress peacefully.   The monster has
relinquished his hold on the Tree of Life and also disgorged the waters
of light, and the solar bark is once more sailing joyfully across the
heaven of day.   The Apap-dragon with the chains upon him is to be
seen in pictures to the Ritual, also on the sarcophagus of Seti
(Bonomi, Pls. 10 and 11).   In Pl. 11 the scorpion-goddess Serkh
is putting the chain upon the Apap-reptile in presence of the executioners, who include the four children of Horus.   The angel who
comes down out of heaven, having the key of the abyss and a great
chain in his hand, who lays hold of the dragon and binds him for a
thousand years (Rev. xx. 1, 2, 3) is "Akar" in the Ritual, the chief
of the gate of the abyss, who has overthrown and bound the dragon
of the deep, so that Ra can navigate in peace.   Such was the
Egyptian battle of Har-Magedon as fought by Har-Makhu against
his old enemy, the Apap-dragon.

We find the breaking loose from the pit, the recapturing and chaining down of the dragon or serpent of evil in the abyss, is described in the magic papyrus as well as in the Ritual. It is Amen-Ra, who is addressed as the Egyptian Apollo, piercing the python of the abyss when he rises in revolt. "Thou disposest of the Abut-Unti. Nubi shoots his arrows against him. Akar springs forward and watches over him, and restores him to his prison, devouring the two huge eyes by which he prevailed. A fierce devouring flame consumes him, commencing from his head and wasting all his members with its fire." From this text we learn that one Egyptian name of the huge typhonian reptile in the abyss is Abut-Unti, from which we may suppose the name of the Abaddon in Hebrew was derived ; Abut or Abtu being a form of the Apap which typifies non-existence or Unti (Rit., 93). The beast that was taken and cast alive into the lake of fire that burneth with brimstone is to be found, lake and all, in the seventeenth chapter of the Ritual (lines 67–68) in Baba, the eternal devourer, whose dwelling is in the lake of fire, the red lake, the pool of the damned, in the fiery pit of the "recess" in Amenta. The banquet of Baba, lord of gore, who extracts the heart and other viscera from the corpses doomed to be consumed at his feast, and who eats the livers of princes, becomes the "great supper of God" in Revelation, at which is eaten the flesh of kings and captains, and all kinds of men, great or small (xix. 17, 18).

It is the same war in the Book of Revelation betwixt the serpent and the seed of the woman that it was in the Book of Genesis, without having any significance in the fulfilment of supposititious prophecy as human history. After the great dragon the old serpent was cast down to the earth ; he continued the battle. "The dragon waxed wroth with the woman (the great mother in a later character) and went away to make war with the rest of her seed" (Rev., xii. 17). The application to the seed has been extended, but the woman and her child remain the same as when she was Isis and he was Horus, and both were pursued by the dragon, or crocodile, in the marshes of lower Egypt, and the mother made her escape with her infant upon the two wings of the Vulture or the Hawk. This war made by the evil dragon on the great mother is reproduced directly from the Egyptian Mythos. When mortal Horus was brought forth among the reeds or bushes of the marshes he and his mother were pursued by the Apap-dragon. Isis tells Osiris that a very great crocodile was following after his son, and that she hid herself among the bushes for the purpose of concealing the young child born to be a king or to become the Royal Horus, whatsoever the opposition. In this text he is said to be born for repulsing Tebha, a form of the devourer who seeks to destroy the divine heir, for answering on behalf of his father Osiris. (Budge, "The Book of Overthrowing Apap," *Proc. Soc. Bib. Archy.*, 1886, p. 17.)

In Revelation a great sign is described in heaven; " a woman arrayed with the sun and the moon under her feet, and upon her head a crown of twelve stars ; and she was with child ; and she cried out, travailing in birth, and in pain to be delivered. . . . And the dragon stood before the woman which was about to be delivered, that when she was delivered he might devour her child ; and she was delivered of a son, a man-child who is to rule all nations with a rod of iron ; and her child was caught unto God and unto his throne, and the woman fled into the wilderness, where she hath a place prepared of God." (ch. xii.). This marks the course of development and the change from the Great Mother in the stellar to the bringer forth of the child in the lunar mythos. As Egyptian, the first Great Mother Apt was imaged in the likeness of the water-cow, the cow of earth. In her later lunar character as Hathor, she was imaged in the likeness of the milch-cow. And in the vignette to the last chapter of the Ritual this Great Mother is portrayed in these two of her forms, as Apt the water-cow and Hathor the milch-cow, in which two forms she receives the Manes in the mountain of Amenta as the mother in earth and in heaven, the mother in the Great Bear and the mother in the Moon. Hathor has now the upper and Apt the lowermost place of two, as it was when the stellar was succeeded and to some extent superseded by the soli-lunar Mythos. But Apt was never cast out of heaven in the genuine version as the drama is represented in the Book of Revelation, although the matriarchate was superseded by the fatherhood of Atum-Ra. Thus it is demonstrated little by little, item by item, that the main subject-matter of the Book of Revelation is the drama of the last judgment, of which we get great glimpses in the mysteries of Amenta. The judgment seat is set upon the highest hill in heaven called " the mount of the resurrection and the glory " (Rit., ch. 1). The one eternal judge is seated on the throne. He also appears in the two characters of God the Father and God the Son ; the lion and the lamb ; the first and the last ; he that was dead and is alive again for evermore. The lords of eternity are round about him on their thrones ; the shennin or officials of the celestial court are present as the seven spirits of fire ; the two witnesses, who are Taht-Aan and Anup in the Egyptian judgment scenes ; the keepers of the four corners of the mount ; the old, old ones, or four-and-twenty elders, with various other Kamite prototypes, are all there. The old Great Mother and her seven earth-born spirits are judged, rejected and cast out of heaven. Apt, so to say, is now succeeded by Hathor as the Great Mother in the later mythos, and Sebek the dragon by Horus as the lamb of the goddess. In this new heaven it is Horus, or Jesus, of the resurrection who was raised to the supremacy as lord over all. And in such ways did the Egyptian wisdom supply the original data for the Christian Revelation. The heaven in seven divisions is not the only celestial formation that declines and passes away as a mystery in Revelation. When the seventh bowl was poured out and the heptanomis came to an end with a mighty earthquake the celestial city " was divided into three parts," or, as we read it, into the triangular heaven of Sut, Horus, and Shu as gods of the south, north, and equinox. Also the ten horns or powers of the solar dragon indicate a heaven in ten domains, ten islands, or ten circles of Ra, in the Ritual, which preceded the ultimate heaven in twelve divisions. This is intimated when "the tenth part of the city fell" as one of the ten divisions passing away in the course of precession.

The ancient heaven passed away " as a scroll," or as the book of the eternal sealed for the great judgment with the seven seals. There is a new heaven built on twelve foundations in place of the earlier seven or ten. "He that sitteth on the throne said, 'Behold I make all things new!'" (ch. xxi. 5). This, in the Ritual, is the son of God who is reborn upon the mount of glory as the lamb, or the child that was the connecting link with the eternal parent in the sphere of time. The new heaven in the Book of Revelation is based upon the twelve zodiacal signs for its twelve foundations. This was as old as the heaven of Atum-Ra, in which the twelve kings rowed the solar bark around the ecliptic thirteen thousand years ago. Following the making of Amenta by Ptah, the creation of a new heaven and earth was ascribed to Atum-Ra, the highest deity developed in the Egyptian theology previous to Osiris Neb-er-ter. Hence the creation, or a creation was proclaimed to be the work of Atum by the priests of Heliopolis. In the eschatology it is said of the house on high, "Tum buildeth thy dwelling, the Lion-faced God (Tum or Atum) layeth the foundation of thy house, as he goeth his round" in fulfilling the solar circle, which was completed with the twelve thrones, twelve stars, twelve gates, or twelve foundations of the final zodiac. This foundation, as the imagery shows, was extant at the time when the solar lion-god first rose up in the strength of the double lions, and the mount of the vernal equinox was in the sign of Leo. In Revelation the equinox has travelled to the sign of Aries, which will account for the lamb upon the mount in place of Horus the calf. In this new rendering the earth was thought of as the lotus of the nun from which the sun of dawn arose. This is shown by the four keepers of the cardinal points or corners of the earth that stand on the papyrus-plant in the presence of the Lord of all things, who was Atum in the earlier and Osiris in the later cult. These, in Revelation, are "the four living creatures full of eyes" that were "in the midst of and around about the throne." The throne was now upon the mount of glory in the equinox, with the four corner keepers "round about the throne"; the solar heaven being founded on the four quarters previously established by Kheper-Ptah. The opening day of this new creation in the cult of Atum-Ra, at Annu, was called the day of "come thou to me," or "come thou hither." It is described in the Ritual (ch. 17) as the day on which their places were fixed by Anup for the seven glorious ones who follow the coffined one in the Osirian mystery of the resurrection, as previously set forth. These are the seven great spirits who are represented by the seven never-setting stars in the right hand of him who moves in the midst of the seven golden lampstands or khabsu lamps as the Supreme One, the only God-begotten Son, in whom the seven powers in the mythology were unified to image an eighth one in the eschatology. As the elder Horus and child of the Mother he had been one of the seven, and in Horus of the resurrection he is now the Son of the Father, divinised in spirit as eighth one to the seven. This is the twofold figure seen upon the mount in Patmos as "the Son of man."

In one phase, Horus or Iu-em-hetep was the type of an eternal child, the *raison d'être* of which was in the human child being an image of both sexes, or, as the Ritual expresses it, both souls of the god and goddess in one figure. As it is said in the Ritual (ch. 115), Horus assumed the form of a female with the sidelock of childhood. Horus was also portrayed as a male child with feminine mammæ. It is said in the pyramid texts, "Hail, Unas, the nipples of the bosom of Horus have been given to thee, and thou hast taken in thy mouth the breast of thy sister Isis." This was the mystical divine male-female of the gnosis; the youth with female paps like Bacchus, or Serapis; Horus with the cteis; Venus with the beard; the Christ as Charis or Jesus as Saint Sophia (Didron, fig. 50). The Son of man portrayed in Revelation is the Egypto-gnostic Jesus. The garment worn by him is that "long garment in which rests the whole world"; the garment that was worn by Iu-em-hetep, in the temple at Annu, as the son of Atum-Ra. This long garment was the sign of both sexes, like the sidelock of the child in Egypt; and it is worn by a figure that is both male and female as shown by the feminine paps and golden girdle, and was worn originally on account of the female nature of the type.

This is the very effigy of child-Horus or Iu-em-hetep, the son of Ptah, who was the dual representative of the biune parent. But in no case could such a dual figure have become "historical" or been "made flesh" except in some hermaphrodital shape of monstrous personality, whether in Egypt, Nazareth, or Rome.

It is now proposed to show that God the Father in Revelation was Atum-Huhi, the Eternal Being in the religion of On, who had become the Jewish god Ihuh, and that the Jesus of this book was Iusa, the coming Son of god and demonstrator of eternal life upon the mount of resurrection in the Ritual and in the Book of Revelation. Atum-Huhi (Atum-Iu or Atum-Ra) was the only deity in all Egypt who was expressly worshipped by the title of the "Ankhu," or the ever-living one eternal god. This is he who is reproduced by name in Revelation, saying: "I am the first and the last, and the *living one*" (Rev. i. 17). In the coming forth to day from out the dark of death which is the resurrection in the Ritual, Atum-Iu, the closer and the opener of Amenta, carries in his hands the keys that close and open the underworld. These are the Ankh-key of life, and the Un-sceptre, with which Amenta is closed and opened. These are repeated in the Book of Revelation as the keys of death and hell. The god in spirit was the highest type of deity attained as the "holy spirit" in the cult of Atum-Ra. Now, there is a typical character in Revelation called "*the spirit*," but which is not otherwise identified. "Hear what the spirit saith: 'To him that overcometh, to him will I give to eat of the tree of life, which is in the paradise of God'" (Rev. ii. 7). It is this god in spirit who proclaims the blessedness of the dead "which die in the Lord" to "rest from their labours" (xiv. 13). And calls on those who are athirst to come and take of the waters of life freely (ch. xxii. 17). He is also the spirit with the bride, but distinguished from the lamb. "The spirit and the bride say 'Come'" (xxii. 17). As Egyptian, then, "the spirit" in the eschatology was Atum-Ra the holy spirit, in the cult of Annu; Iusāas, a form of Hathor, was the bride, and Iu-em-hetep, he who comes with peace, was their son, whom we identify as the Egyptian Jesus in the Book of Revelation, in Pistis Sophia, in the Apochrypha, and in the Book of Taht-Aan.

The "entire god" was a mystical title of Amen-Ra as the child and husband of the mother. According to the gnosis, there was a triune being, distinct from the male trinity, consisting of the mother, child, and adult male, in one person. The figure-head of this triad might be either the mother, the father, or the child, according to the cult; and whereas the knowers worshipped the "entire god" who was three in one, one sect would exalt the mother; on the other hand, the Jews became monotheists by eliminating both the mother and the son from the godhead, and setting up the father by himself alone as the "entire god," the Kamite Neb-er-ter. Irenæus cachinnates in a ghastly fashion at the gnostics who assigned but one consort to both the father and son. But, it is the same with the spirit (father) and the lamb (son) in connection with the bride in Revelation, as it was in Egypt and as it still remains in Rome. Fortunately, the mystical bride had two characters not to be easily taken away by the Bishop of Lyons. She was the virgin in one, the gestator in the other. As virgin she was the bride of Horus, the lamb of god. As gestator she was the consort of the lion-faced man or man-faced lion who was Atum as god the father. According to the Kabalists these two were the macrocosm and microcosm. The two figures are said to comprehend three persons—namely, the father, the son, and the mother, who was the bride of both. The lesser man or microcosm was a figure of double sex, the feminine half being conjoined to his back as the hinder female part. This is equivalent to the Horus of both sexes, and to Jesus as Saint Sophia. This was he whom the gnostics called Pan and Totum, the all-one, who became the manifestor as the evercoming son. This all-oneness of the son is described in the Ritual and proclaimed by Atum the father, when it is said that "Horus is the father! Horus is the mother! Horus is the brother! Horus is the kinsman! Horus is seated upon the throne, and all that lives is subject to him. All the gods are in his service. So saith Atum, the sole force of the gods, whose word is not to be altered" (Rit., ch. 78). Horus was now the *all-one* as manifestor in physical and spiritual phenomena for all the powers which had been summed up in Atum as the one god in spirit and in truth. This same triad of the mother, father, and son was known to the Sethians. With them the father of all is styled the first man = Atum or Adam. "His Ennua, going forth from him, produced a son, and this is the son of man—the second man," or second Adam. "The father and son both had intercourse with the woman, whom they call the mother of the living," and the triad constituted the "entire god," in accordance with the Egyptian doctrine (Irenæus, *Against Heresies*, Bk. I., ch. 30). Atum, who was god the father in spirit, had assumed the sovereignty of Ra, the creator as god almighty, the one true god, the only one, because he was the god in spirit, not merely in physical phenomena, but in that new heaven which was opened on the day of "Come thou to me." This is the position acknowledged by the worshippers in the new temple of god (Rev. xi. 17). "We give thee thanks, O Lord God, the Almighty, which art and which wast, because thou hast taken thy great power and didst reign." That is he who had assumed the sovereignty as sole ruler in the luni-solar heaven that followed the passing away of the heptanomis and the heaven in ten divisions.

Atum Ra is not only to be identified as the closer and opener of Amenta; the first and the last, and the "living one"; the spirit with the bride; the god who sat upon the throne was also of a red complexion. He was like unto "a sardius" to look upon, which is the especial colour of Atum in the vignettes to the Ritual. In Revelation, when the "throne is set in heaven, and one sitting upon the throne," there was a rainbow round about the throne like emerald to look upon (ch. iv. 3). Also in the original mythos the throne "like emerald to look upon" was a figure of the Egyptian dawn that was imaged as a great emerald sycamore tree, a lake of emerald, green fields, and other evergreen things upon the mount of glory. Ra, in the Ritual, is said to be "encircled with emerald light," which was the emerald dawn surrounding him on the solar mount. As it is said, "thy body is of gold, thy head of azure, and emerald light encircleth thee" (ch. 15). The gods who are in the green light of dawn are also called "the emerald ones" (Rit., ch. 110).

When Horus at his second coming rises from the dead it is as the son of God to whom was given the throne of the eternal with power to share the sonship with his followers. He is received with "a cry of adoration to him in Suten-Khen." There is exultation in the place of Horus in his darkness, previously described as a world "without water and without air; all abyss, utter darkness, sheer bewilderment" (ch. 175), as the condition of the soul in matter that was imaged by the mortal Horus without sight. "He of the strong cord is born (ch. 136), his cable is completed," and the ark of earth made fast to heaven once more for another period in precession, or the shennu-circle of eternity. "Glory is given to the inviolate one," "by generations yet unborn." "Ra exalteth him." The gods of the lamps "rise up to greet him with their exclamations of great joy"; he who comes was the re-establisher of time "for millions of years" (ch. 130). He comes in raiment like the dawn as the true light of the world newly kindled for the night of death. "He putteth an end to the opposition of Sut," the power of darkness (ch. 137 B, 2, 3). This, then, is Horus the son of God in the Osirian cult or Jesus in the religion of Atum-Ra, with God the father in the great judgment scenes upon the mount. He comes "to witness the process of Maat (or the judgment) and *the lion-forms which belong to it.*" He comes to erect the scales of justice for his father, who is "uttering the judgment of Maat." He now appears as Horus triumphant who has torn out the jaws of Rusta, conquered the evil Apap, and brought the books which are kept in Annu to his father in the hall of judgment called the Maat. Here, says the speaker, "here is the cycle of the gods, and the kite of Osiris," which represents his son Horus. "Grant ye that his father may judge in his behalf; and so I poise for him the balance, which is Maat (that of law and justice) and I raise it that he may live. Come! come! for the father is uttering the judgment of Maat. O thou who callest out at thine evening hours, grant that I may come and bring to him the two jaws of Rusta, and that I may bring to him the books which are in Annu, and add up for him his heavenly hosts" (ch. 136 B, Renouf). These are the books of Taht-Aan that were examined on the great day of reckoning called the judgment day (Rev. iv.). In the parallel scene, the father sits, Osiris-like, upon his throne, with the four-and-twenty elders, the seven great spirits, and the four living creatures round about.

A striking picture of the god in his characters of the closer and the opener is presented by John in the Book of Revelation. The father-god, he who closes, is seated on the throne. In his right hand he holds the book that is closed with seven seals; the book which "no one in the heaven or earth, or under the earth" is able to open. In his other character, that of the son, represented by the lamb, "he taketh it out of the right hand of him that sat on the throne." This is the opener of the book and the breaker of the seven seals thereof. "And when he had taken the book, the four living creatures and the four-and-twenty elders fell down before the lamb," who alone has power to break the seals and open the book. His taking of the seven-sealed book from the right hand of him that sat upon the throne is followed by the "adding up for him his hosts." In this reckoning it is declared that the number of angels round the throne "was ten thousand times ten thousand, and thousands of thousands" (ch. v. 11). These in the astronomical mythology would signify the souls that had attained eternal setting as the hosts of heaven, represented by the Akhemu-Seku or stars which never set. The spirits in glory, called the Khus, are numbered in the Ritual as in Revelation. In the Papyrus of Nebseni, the number of the Khus or spirits is reckoned as "four millions, six hundred thousand, and two hundred" (Rit., ch. 64, *Papyrus of Nebseni*). It is not said on what grounds the computation was made. In Revelation the number of the saved and sealed is computed at one hundred and forty-four thousand.

The mysteries of Osiris, Isis, and Horus, though the latest in evolution, have been given the foremost place in the Ritual and have somewhat obscured the pre-Osirian mythology. But Atum was the great judge upon the mount of Amenta at a far earlier period than Osiris. And one of the judgments in the Ritual is described as that of Atum-Ra. This takes place "when the eye is full on the last day of the month Mechir"; on the night wherein the eye is full and fixed for the judgment (Rit., ch. 71). "Ra makes his appearance on the mount of glory with his cycle of gods about him." "Atum rises pouring out his dew." "His majesty gives orders to the cycle of his followers." "They fall down before Atum-Harmachis," or Atum-Horus. "His majesty orders them to praise the eye." "His glorious eye rests in its place on his majesty in this hour of the night." At the fourth hour of the night, on the last day of Mechir, "the majesty of the eye is in the presence of the cycle of the gods, and his majesty rises, as in the beginning, with the eye upon his head as Atum-Ra." The Khabsu-gods lift up their lamps by night. When Ra passes over heaven unto the west upon his daily round, these gods of the lamp rise up with exclamations of delight to show the way. They are stars upon the summit of the mount which are said "to receive the cable of Ra from his rowers." Twelve rowers rowed the bark by day around the zodiac. At night the seven starry powers at the pole took the rope in hand to haul the vessel through the underworld. Thus a mystery of the seven stars, as servants of the solar god, was interpreted in the astronomical mythos before the law of gravitation could be known (Rit., ch. 130). As it is said, "Oh Ra, who smileth cheerfully, as thou comest forth in the east, the ancients, and those who are gone before acclaim thee" (ch. 64). These "ancients," who came from the "primeval womb" as earlier powers than Ra (ch. 133), appear in Revelation as "the elders." They are also called "the fathers." The

Osiris in the character of Horus risen on the mount, says " Let the fathers and their apes make way for me, that I may enter the mount of glory, where the great ones are " (ch. 136 B). Naturally enough, " the apes " do not appear as apes in Revelation. But we may discern them in " the seven spirits of fire," or the seven lamps of fire, burning before the throne, which are *the seven spirits of God* (ch. iv. 5). As Egyptian, the apes are spirits of fire. In sign-language the hot-natured or fiery-tempered Kaf-Ape was made the image of a spirit of fire. Thus seven apes are equivalent to seven spirits of fire. They could " make way " for the Osiris in the mount, as they were keepers of the way and openers of the gates of dawn for Ra in his rising. The numbers vary. But there is a picture to the Ritual in which *the seven spirits of fire around the throne of Ra are seven apes around the mount of glory* (Naville, *Todt. Kap.* 16 A). In Revelation, the son of God promises to give the morning star to him that overcometh. " As I also have received of my father ; I will give him the morning star " (Rev. ii. 28). The morning star was equally identified with Horus. " I know the powers of the east : Horus of the mount of glory, the calf in presence of the god, and the star of dawn " (Rit., ch. 109). The powers represented in the vignette are Atum-Ra, the father, with Horus (or Jesus) the son, as a calf, the later lamb. This is Horus of the morning star. In the vignette to the previous chapter (108) the powers are Atum, the father, Horus (as Sebek), the son, and Hathor as the bride (Naville *Todt. Kap.* 108, 109). Here is an application of the imagery to the deceased which is as old as the Pyramids. The morning star was given by Horus to his followers who were reborn in Sothis. The rebirth of Pepi was in or as the morning star. And " his guide the morning star leadeth him to paradise, where he seateth himself upon his throne " (Budge, *Book of the Dead*, Introd., pp. 141, 143). When Pepi goeth forth into heaven he is led by Septet, the female Sothis, and his guide is the morning star. She is the bride whom he calls his sister. He seats himself upon his throne of ba-metal. This throne has lions' heads, and feet in the form of hoofs called the hoofs of the bull, Sema-Ur. Thus the lion and the bull, or bullock, meet in the throne of Pepi, which is the throne of god upon the mount of glory (*Pyramid Texts*, 304), and the types are equivalent to Atum the man-faced lion and Iu the son, as calf, later lamb, together with the bride in Sothis.

As Egyptian, then, Atum-Huhi was the God in Spirit, who was adored at On, as God the Holy Spirit, with Hathor-Iusāas, the bride, and Horus as the calf. And in one of the vignettes to the Ritual (Naville, *Todt. Kap.* 109) these three are grouped together *on the mount*, the same as in the Book of Revelation (Naville, *Todt. Kap.* 108).

About the year 2410 B.C. the vernal equinox was moving out of Taurus into the sign of Aries, and the type of Horus changed from the calf upon the horizon to the lamb upon the mount. Horus is called " the Lamb, Son of a Sheep." As a fact in the astronomical mythology the lamb was then exalted to the highest place, and Hathor-Sothis became " the bride, as the wife of the lamb." In the Book of Esdras we come very near to the fulfilment of a Sothiac cycle. " These tokens shall come to pass, and the bride shall appear, and she coming forth shall be seen that now is withdrawn from the earth," and "my Son Jesus shall be revealed with those that be with him, and they that remain shall rejoice within four hundred years. *And the world shall be turned into the old silence seven days, like as in the former Judgment: so that no man shall remain. And after seven days the world, that yet awaketh not, shall be raised up, and that shall die that is corrupt. And the earth shall restore those that are asleep in her, and so shall the dust those that dwell in silence; and the secret places shall deliver those souls that were committed unto them. And the Most High shall appear upon the seat of Judgment."* In this reckoning "my son Jesus" is no more historical or ethnical than the bride. The bride, who was now withdrawn from the world in fulfilling her period, identifies Sothis and her cycle, which is to be completed in four hundred years, when the Coming One will be reborn as the Bennu or Phœnix, the Messu or Messiah, whose rebirth was reckoned and redated by that cycle. The bride or Shtar, the betrothed, as Egyptian, was Hathor-Sothis, who was "withdrawn" from the world in completing the Sothiac cycle; and Iusāas-Neb-hetep, the mother of Iusa, was a form of Hathor in the cult of Atum-Ra. Thus, Atum was the God in Spirit, Hathor-Iusāas is the bride, and Iusa is the son who was imaged by the calf or lamb according to the time and position on the ecliptic. As Egyptian, the mystical bride and child were astronomical. The prophecy of their return to earth and reappearance within four hundred years, in the secret wisdom of Esdras, is astronomical. Consequently, the fulfilment with the marriage of the bride and the lamb or Virgin Mother and Child in Revelation was likewise astronomical, and Jesus was that character in the astronomical mythology which was and is, and is to come for ever as the Son who is the manifester for the Father under whatsoever type or name, whether as the lamb, calf, the crocodile, the beetle, the dove, the hawk, the fish, the green corn, the grapes, the shoot of the papyrus-plant, or as Horus in the human image of the eternal Child.

To all appearance "John" has reproduced the astronomy in "Revelation" so as to agree with the entrance of the vernal equinox into the sign of the Ram which occurred about the year 2410 B.C., when the starry dragon as Draconis ceased to be the station of the polestar and so was fabled to have fallen from heaven; and the lamb became the typical victim that suffered death and rose again in the sign of the ram at Easter, as Horus in one cult, Sebek in the other, and as Jesus the "Lamb of God" in the Book of John.

The drama comes to an end with the marriage of the bride and the lamb. This is the same in the astronomical reckoning as shifting the birthplace of the child in the circle of precession from the sign of the bull to the sign of the ram, as it actually took place four thousand three hundred years ago. The natural result of this change was that the lamb from that time became the type of Horus instead of the calf. And the great change was marked in Egypt by the crocodile-headed Sebek being portrayed by the Sebek-heteps with the head of the lamb now added to the form of the dragon (*Book of Beginnings*, also *Nat. Genesis*).

The biblical writings abound in phrases too indefinite for anything but the faith that can supply its own fulcrum. One of these is the "foundation of the world." Can any Christian explain this "foundation of the world"? For them, this had to be historically laid or relaid some nineteen centuries ago. But, according to the Book of Revelation, the sacrificial lamb was slain from the "foundation of the world." In the Gospel of Matthew, Jesus is made to say, "Come ye blessed of my Father, inherit the kingdom prepared for you from the foundation of the world" (Matt. xxv. 34). Here the kingdom of the elect was already prepared and in no wise dependent upon any slaying of the historic lamb. On the other hand, the lamb (or calf, or other animal) had been slain for ages annually, as the type of the foundation laid in blood-sacrifice; and Sebek or Jesus in Egypt had been the lamb that was slain as the foundation of the world. He is addressed as the lamb, son of a sheep, and as such was the Lamb of God who did not take away the sins of the world, and did not profess to have the power. It is in totemism that we find a first foundation laid in sacrifice which is afterwards religiously described as the foundation of the world. The lamb was one of the sacrificial types; Osiris, in the human form of his son Horus, is another; and from the Osirian mysteries we may learn the meaning of this "foundation of the world" which, like so many other mysteries, has been imported into the Christian scheme, to be continued as one of the mysteries of ignorance and wondering faith, and to be accepted on the condition that it was never to be explained. In the Book of Revelation Jesus is " *the lamb that hath been slain from the foundation of the world*" (xiii. 8). But in the Epistle to the Hebrews (ix. 26) this foundation is shifted. Here the lamb has *not* " suffered since the foundation of the world," but " now *once* at the end of the ages hath he been manifested to put away sin by the sacrifice of himself." In that way the astronomical was turned into the supposed historical Lamb of God. In the new heaven that is finally established the mother and child are re-enthroned in glory as the lamb and the bride who is the wife of the lamb, together with " the Lord God, the Almighty " (Rev., ch. xxi., xxii.; *cf.* ch. i. 8). And these were the three persons who previously composed the " entire god " in Amen, the hidden Ra, who was a form of Atum-Ra, or Huhi the Eternal.

The prevalence and persistence of the lamb in the gnostic-Christian iconography point to a starting-point when the vernal equinox occurred in the sign of Aries. In the early ages of what is termed Christianity the lamb, not the man, upon the cross was the sacrificial type of the divine victim, as it had been of Sebek-Horus in Egypt at the time of the Sebek-hetep dynasty. "And I saw in the midst of the throne and of the four living creatures, and in the midst of the elders, a lamb standing as though it had been slain, having seven horns and seven eyes which are the seven spirits of God, sent forth into all the earth." The lamb is but a type that is here employed at its current value in symbolism, like the calf, as a sign of sacrifice, which like other types in Revelation has to be read by means of the mythology. As Egyptian, the lamb, " son of a sheep," had been a type of Horus who was called the child. This was Har-Ur, the first or elder Horus, who was " born but not begotten " of the virgin

3 A 2

mother. The seven powers, or spirits, that were unified in Horus who became the all-one as " an eighth to the seven," are now represented by the seven horns and seven eyes of the lamb, which are correctly described as the seven powers or " seven spirits of God."

The new Jerusalem was built upon the square. " The city lieth four-square, and the length thereof is as great as the breadth ; the length and the breadth and the height thereof are equal." This was the heaven of Atum based upon the four quarters of the solstices and the equinoxes which followed the making of Amenta (Rev. xxi. 16).

At first the form impressed upon the universe, in the Kamite mythology, had been feminine. It was the womb, the meskhen, or creatory of the great mother, as bringer-forth of life and the elements of life. Finally, this was superseded by the image of the man ; the divine man described by Plato, who bicussated and was stamped upon the universe *in the likeness of a cross*. Now the new heaven in the Book of Revelation was formed according to " *the measure of a man* " (Rev. xxi. 17). This was the heaven founded on the four cardinal points, which were represented by the cross of the four quarters. The cross of the four quarters, or the earlier Tat-pillar was a figure of the power that sustained the universe as the Osiris-Tat or as the later man upon the cross. Thus the divine man, as the cruciform support of all in Ptah-Sekeri or Osiris, was the prototype of the Crucified. This god of the four quarters is portrayed as Atum-Ra in the Ritual (ch. 82). It is he who says (by proxy) " My head is that of Ra and I am summed up as Atum, four times the arm's length of Ra, four times the width of the world." Thus Atum, the divine man, was a quadrangular figure of the four quarters in the heaven founded according to "the measure of a man" which is reproduced in Revelation. We learn from the Ritual that man became the measure of the universe in consequence of the god being divinised in the human form, who in his coming to earth as the heir of Seb says, " I come before you and make my appearance as the god in the form of a man " (ch. 79) ; he who is identified in the same chapter as Atum-Ra. As Atum was the first god who assumed the form of man, that may account for the new heaven being designed according to " *the measure of a man*," as described in Revelation (xxi. 17, and Rit., ch. 82). This was what took place at Annu when Iu, the son of Atum-Ra, designed the " temple," as the new heaven was called. Moreover, as Atum-Ra was the divine man, this tends to prove that " the son of man " who is Jesus in Revelation was one with Iu, the Su or son of Atum-Ra. And here it is possible that we come upon the origin of the Swastika cross as a typical figure of the heaven that was founded on the four corners according to the measure of a man. From the most primitive forms of the Swastika known we learn that in its origin it was derived from the human figure. The Swastika found in Egypt proves it to have been derived from the form of a man. The four limbs, which eventually became four feet or four legs, were at first the two arms and two legs of the human figure (*Pro. Bib. Arch.*, Nov. 1900). This, then, is the divine man whose image was extended crosswise on the universe as a type of creation, and who, as Atum in the character of Iu the son, was the Egyptian Jesus. A portrait of the Good Shepherd has been discovered in an underground

Roman cemetery with the Swastika figured twice upon his tunic. He carries the pan-pipes in his right hand and comes in the attitude of dancing (Lanciani, Rodolfo, *New Tales of Old Rome*, p. 117). This in the mythos was the youthful solar god, and Horus of the resurrection in the eschatology. "The tabernacle of God" is now "with men, and he shall dwell with them." As it had been ever since the child, as Horus, was incarnated in the blood of Isis, to assume the human figure when "the Word was made flesh" in the beginning.

The mystery of Messiahship, which had been rendered in the Kamite wisdom thousands · of years before, was now repeated as Hebrew prophecy in the Book of Revelation. In the sign of the bull, the bride had been represented by the sacred heifer, and Horus the child was imaged as the calf upon the horizon. "The calf in presence of the god" is as we have seen with Horus of the solar mount, in a vignette to ch. 109 (Naville, *Todt. Kap.*). The victim as the sacrificial calf is also spoken of in the Ritual (ch. 84) when the speaker says, "I am the calf painted· red on the tablets." Again he speaks of being the calf or the bull of the sacrificial herd with the mortuary gifts upon him (ch. 105). One sign later in precession, there was a change of type. The vernal equinox now entered Aries and the lamb upon the mount was substituted for the calf as the sacrificial victim, just as the fish was substituted 2,155 years later for the lamb.   ·

The new heaven of Revelation is the "heaven of eternity" in the Ritual, at the summit of Mount Hetep ; the mould of the mythos being continued in the eschatology. For this reason there was no night there, and no more sea, and "death shall be no more." "Neither shall there be mourning, nor crying, nor pain any more ; the first things are passed away." And this is the vision of a spirit-life in the heaven of eternity that is no longer simply astronomical.

The astronomical enclosure of the non-setting stars ; the tree of life, the water of life, the sacrificial lamb, remain as types of salvation and eternal sustenance in what the "Revelation" terms "the paradise of God" (ii. 7), which is identical by name with the garden of the beginning in the Book of Genesis.

In some of the Papyri, the dwelling-place upon the summit of eternal attainment, described in the *Book of the Dead* (ch. 110), is called the City of the Two Eyes, or Merti the Double Eye, the two eyes that we hold to have been the stars of the two poles seen in Equatoria. Merti was also a place-name in Egypt. Thus, the stellar paradise upon the mount that was established in the region of the pole before the time of moon or sun remained the type of a future heaven described in Revelation which had "no need of the sun, neither of the moon to shine upon it : for the glory of God did lighten it," and the light of it, or the luminary, "was like a stone most precious"—otherwise it was the star Polaris. The light of the pole-star in the primal paradise is likewise referred to in the Talmudic Legends of the future heaven. It is said, "There is a light which is never eclipsed or obscured, derived from that upper light by which *the first men could view the world from one end to the other*" (*Avodath Hakodesh*, f. xlvi. c. 1, 2 ; Stehelin, vol. ii., pp. 20–24). Only one polestar is reproduced in Revelation, but in the elder legend, as we see, the first

men could *view the world from one end to the other*, which included
both poles (or polestars) that were seen at first upon the level of the
equatorial plain and are repeated in the latest eschatology. Finally,
the injunctions at the end of the book should be compared with the
Rubrical Instructions of the Ritual. The writer of Revelation says,
" Blessed is he that keepeth the words of the prophecy in this book.
I testify unto every man that heareth the words of prophecy of this
book. If any man shall add unto them, God shall add unto him the
plagues which are written in this book ; and if any man shall take
away from the words of the book of this prophecy, God shall take
away his part from the tree of life, and out of the holy city, which are
written in this book" (xxii., 7, 18, 19). In the Ritual, at the end of
the book by which the soul of the Osiris is perfected in the bosom of
Ra, it is said, " Let not this be seen by anyone except the minister of
the funeral and the king. By this book (or according to it) the soul
of the deceased shall make its exodus with the living and prevail
amongst, or as, the gods. By this book he shall know the secrets of
that which happened in the beginning. No one else has ever known
this mystical book or any part of it. It has not been spoken by men.
No eye hath deciphered it, no ear hath heard it. It must only be
seen by thee and the man who unfolded its secrets to thee. Do not
add to its chapters or make commentaries on it from imagination or
from memory. Carry it out (or execute it) in the judgment hall.
This is a true Mystery, unknown anywhere to those who are
uninitiated" (Rubrical Directions to Rit., ch. 149, Birch ; 148, Pierret).

THE JESUS-LEGEND TRACED IN EGYPT FOR TEN THOUSAND YEARS.

BOOK XII

THE Messianic mystery which has caused unparalleled mental trouble to the world did not originate with, nor was the solution to be found in, the biblical collection of the Hebrew writings. The Egyptian "mesu," to anoint, and as a name for the Anointed, is earlier than the Jewish Messiah. Nor would there have been any typical Christ the anointed but for the making of the Karest-mummy. We have to look a long way beyond these books to learn how salvation came into the world by water, or a saviour could be represented by the fish. It was thus salvation came to Egypt periodically in the new life of the Nile, and thence the saviour, who was imaged in the likeness of a fish. According to the mythical rendering Horus-Iu-em-hetep was a saviour because he came with plenty of food and water in the inundation, as the shoot of, or as the child on the papyrus. In the eschatology he represented the saviour who showed the way by which the Manes might attain eternal life, when immortality was held to be conditional and dependent upon right conduct and true character. A doctrine of messiahship was founded on the ever-coming Messu, or child of the inundation in the pre-anthropomorphic phase of symbolism, in which the type might be the fish, the papyrus-shoot, the beetle, hawk or calf, each one of which bears witness that when the infant-likeness was adopted as a figure of the ever-coming saviour or messiah *the human type was just as non-historical as any of its predecessors*. The advent of the Messu (the Hebrew Messiah) was periodic in accordance with the natural phenomena : not once for all. Once for all could have no meaning in relation to that which was ever-coming from age to age, from generation to generation, or for ever and ever. Eternity itself to the Egyptians of the Ritual was æonian, and synonymous with millions of repetitions, therefore ever-coming in the likeness of perennial renewal, whether in the water-spring of earth or the day-spring on high, the papyrus-shoot, the green branch, or as Horus the child in whom a saviour was at length embodied as a figure of eternal source. At the foundation of all sacrifice we find the great Earth-mother, following the human mother, giving herself for food and drink. Next the type of sacrifice was that of the ever-coming child. Ten thousand years ago a divine ideal of matchless excellence had been portrayed in elder Horus as a voluntary sacrifice of self, not for the sins of the world, but for human sustenance. This voluntary victim took the parent's place, and suffered in the mother's stead. Thenceforth the papyrus-plant was represented by the shoot ; the tree by the branch ; the sheep by the lamb ; the saviour by the infant as an image of perpetual renewal in life by means of his own death and transformation in furnishing the elements of life. Next Horus, as the foremost of the seven elemental powers, passed into the solar mythos, where the typical virgin and child were reproduced and constellated as repeaters of periodic time and season in the Zodiac.

The Jesus-legend is Egyptian, but it was at first without the dogma of historic personality. We have now to follow it in the circuit of precession, where it might be traced back to a beginning with the sign of Virgo. But for the present purpose, the birthplace of the virgin's child was in the sign of Leo when the vernal equinox was resting in the lion constellation.

The Messu, or the Messianic prince of peace, was born into the world at Memphis in the cult of Ptah as the Egyptian Jesus, with the title of Iu-em-hetep, he who comes with peace or plenty and good fortune as the type of an eternal youth. Here we may note in passing that this divine Child, Iu-em-hetep, as the image of immortal youth, the little Hero of all later legend, the Kamite Herakles, had been one of the eight great gods of Egypt who were in existence *twenty thousand years ago* (Herodotus, 2, 43). This wondrous child, who is the figure of ever-coming and of perennial renewal in the elements of life, was also known by name as Kheper, Horus, Aten, Tum or Nefer-Atum according to the cult. He was continued at On or Annu. The title likewise was repeated in the new religion, when Iu-em-hetep became the representative of Atum-Ra. His mother's name at On was Iusāas, she who was great (as) with Iusa or Iusu, the ever-coming child, the Messiah of the inundation.

Such doctrine, however, did not originate as uterine or come the human way, although it might be expressed in human terminology.

We have now to track the ever-coming child Iusa, Iusu or Jesus in the sphere of time as the son of Iusāas and of Atum, who was Ra in his first sovereignty ; not merely in the round of the lesser year, but in the movement of precession as determined by the changing equinox or by the shifting position of the pole. As we have shown, the Zodiacal signs were set in heaven according to the seasons of the Egyptian year and in the annual circuit of the sun. The birthplace of the Inundation and the Grapes was figured in or near the sign of Virgo or the Virgin, the mother of the child who brought the new life to the land in water as Ichthus the fish and in food as Horus on his papyrus. But Horus the traveller of eternity has to be tracked and followed in the movement of Precession. And thus the new beginning for the present quest is in the sign of Leo.

The priests of On attributed a new creation of the world, or the heavens, to Atum-Ra. This was the cultivated enclosure or garden of a new beginning. And this garden of a new beginning or creation was visibly featured in the southern heaven. There ran the river Nile as the one water from its hidden source, as it flowed in the starry stream Eridanus, and meandered through the Aarru-garden that was made for Atum, in the likeness of which the future paradise was represented in Amenta (Rit., ch. 150, Vignette). According to the Osirian rendering, the later Aarru-field is the garden of the grape (Rit., Vignettes). The typical tree of life in an Egypto-Greek plani-sphere is the grape-vine. This is the tree still represented by the female vine-dresser and the male grape-gatherer in the Decans of Virgo (Higgins, W. H., *Arabic Names of the Stars*). Orion rose up when the grapes were ripe to represent the Deliverer, who was coming "full of wine." The goblet or "mixing-bowl" in which the drink was brewed to hugely celebrate the Uaka-festival of the Inundation is constellated in the sign of "Krater." The ancient enemy of man, the evil dragon of Drought, is imaged in the form of "Hydra," waiting to devour the Virgin's child the moment it is born.

At one time the birthplace in the stellar mythos was where Sothis rose as opener of the year and herald of the Inundation. This was the star of Hathor and her Messu or Messianic babe who came to make war on the dragon and to bruise the serpent's head. And Iusāas was a form of Hathor. The fulfilment of the primitive promises of the coming child as bringer of all good things was annual in the astronomical mythology. The babe, the birth, the birthplace and the bringer to birth, were all continued in the solar cult, from this, the starting-point, with Sothis now as the announcer of the Inundation, and the life of vegetation figured as the young deliverer Horus on his papyrus, or the later Atum-Horus issuing from the lotus on the day of "come thou to me," the first day of the Egyptian year or new creation.

Time in the old year of the Great Bear and the Inundation had not been subject to the changes in Precession. In this year there was but one birthplace for the typical child who originated in Horus of the Inundation as the figure of food and bringer of the water, and there-fore of salvation. Also there was but one date for the birthday of the child, namely, the first of the month Tekki (or Thoth) which we equate with July 25, when the five *dies non* are also counted in the reckoning of the year. If Ra had not discovered the co-partnery of the Great Mother and Sebek-Horus the Fish of the Inundation, and substituted the time of the sun, the birthplace of the babe might have remained for ever fixed in heaven. Time in the ordinary year was always kept and reckoned by the recurring seasons; firstly by the Inundation. In the greater year this time was rectified by the retrocession of the equinoxes and the changing position of the pole. Thus time was kept by double entry. And when the birthplace of the Messianic child was made zodiacal it travelled round the backward circuit of precession to fulfil a course of six-and-twenty thousand years. The great year might have gone its way unrecognized but for this change of polestars or the backward lapsing of the equinoxes being observed and registered by the astronomers. It was solar time, which had to be continually revised and readjusted by means of the stars. The Inundation was a fixture in relation to the earth, and a primary factor in the year of the Great Bear, the end and re-beginning of which were memorized by means of the "Sut-Heb" or "festival of the tail"—that is, the tail of the Great Bear as pointer at its southernmost longitude, which was dependent on the revolution of the sphere. The Great Bear, hippopotamus or crocodile, was then the Stellar bringer-forth to Horus of the Inundation. But with Horus, born of Virgo in the Zodiac, the birthplace of the babe was figured in the vernal equinox, and thus became subject to the changes in precession. It parted company with the lesser year of the Inundation to travel from sign to sign around the circuit of the world's great year.

Fourteen thousand years ago the vernal equinox coincided with the sign of Virgo and the autumn equinox with the sign of Pisces. And here the learned writer Eratosthenes has a word to say upon this point. He is a most unimpeachable witness for the Egyptians ; a better could not be subpœnaed. He was born in the year 276 B.C. He was keeper of the great Alexandrian library and the most learned Greek in Egypt at the time. Amongst other subjects he wrote on was astronomy, and he testifies to the fact that the festival of Isis, which *was celebrated in his time at the autumn equinox, had been celebrated when the Easter equinox was in Virgo*. This perfectly agrees with the position of Isis, the Virgin Mother in the Zodiac. During those six months in the great year = six signs, the child as periodic fulfiller of time and season in the Zodiac, together with the birth and birthplace, was receding through the six signs in precession, from Virgo to Pisces. Thirteen thousand years later the autumn equinox coincided once more with the sign of Virgo. Now there is no meeting-point of the mythology with the astronomy more obvious than in these two signs of the Zodiac. But it is impossible that this imagery should have been constellated in the planisphere the *last* time the equinoxes entered them, which was about the year 255 B.C., where they still linger at the present moment. And the time before that, in round numbers, was 26,000 years previously.

It is a fixed fundamental fact that the death and rebirth of the year were commemorated at this time from the 20th to the 25th of July, when the birth of Horus was announced by the star Sothis or the Bennu = Phœnix. It is equally a fact that when the solar Horus had entered the Zodiac the birthplace was shifted from sign to sign, *according to the movement in precession*, from Virgo to Leo, from Cancer to the Gemini, from Taurus to Aries, from Aries to Pisces. The pathway of eternity was now depicted in the circle of precession. In this the sonship of Horus was continued after the fatherhood of God had been established, and Horus became the manifester for the eternal in the sphere of solar time. Hence the sayings of Horus in the Ritual. "I am Horus, the prince of eternity." "Witness of Eternity is my name" (ch. 42). He calls himself "the persistent traveller on the highways of heaven," which he surveys as "the everlasting one." "I am Horus," he says, "who steppeth onwards through eternity"— without stopping or ever standing still. This was Horus, otherwise the Egyptian Jesus, as the ever-coming son (Iu-sa) in all the years of time that culminated in the all-inclusive cycle of precession. Horus as the shoot, or the later wheat-ear (spica), had been brought forth when the birthplace was in Virgo. If we look on this as a sign in precession, the next birthplace *in the backward course* is in the sign of Leo, in which Horus was the lion of the solar power that was doubled in the vernal equinox. When the Osiris comes to witness the judgment on the mount of glory (Rit., ch. 136 B), he sees "the lion forms" called the Kherufu, which are three in number. Two of these are figures of the Double Force, as shown in the vignette to ch. 18, and the one in the centre is the lion of the double lions = the double force, as the lion or as the solar disk. Now Atum is this solar lion on the mount which is in the equinox, and which can be thus identified with the lion-sign or sign of the lions in the Zodiac. Atum is the god with the lion's face, who is also called the man-faced lion. He is said to lay the foundations of the eternal house (Rit., ch. 17). That is, in building the new heaven which was based upon the equinoxes in the circuit of precession, at a certain starting-point, including all the previous foundations laid by Ptah and Taht, Shu and Sut, and by the first great Mother in the Heptanomis.

It is a tradition common to the Quichés, the Aztecs, the Bushmen, the Australian aborigines and other ancient races that their ancestors existed before the creation of the sun. The Bushmen say that the sun did not shine on their country in the beginning. It was only when the children of the first Bushmen had been *sent up to the summit of the Mount* that the sun was launched to give light to the South African world (Bleek, *Bushman Folk-Lore*, p. 9). So in Egypt it might be said there was no sun before the creation of Ra, when Atum issued from the lotus on the day of "Come thou to me." It is stated in the texts that light began with this new creation, when the sun-god rose up from the lotus; that is, the solar light which followed the lunar and the starlight which preceded day in accordance with the mythical representation. Atum-Horus sinks at evening in the waters as the closer of day, with the lotus on his head. At dawn he rises from the lotus, the opening flower of dawn. But, instead of commencing with the sign of Virgo, the present writer traces this *new beginning* in the solar mythos to the time when the vernal equinox was in the sign of Leo, now some 13,000 to 15,000 years ago, according to the reckoning in the greater year. By this, however, it is not meant that equal day and night were then coincident with the birth of the Inundation or the heliacal rising of the dog-star on the 25th of July. The position of the equinox has to be made out according to the precessional year, not by the lesser year. This difference constitutes the difficulty of the reckoning. The time of equinox was determined in the lesser year by the recurrence of equal day and night, but the *position* of the equinoxes in the *annus magnus* was determined by the risings of the herald stars. Amongst other figures of the god Atum, he is portrayed standing on a lion, in others he is accompanied by his mother the lioness, Sekhet or Bast. The annual resurrection of the solar god was always in the Easter equinox, and when the funeral couch is figured in the lion-form, and the rising of the dead is from the lion-bier, the fact is registered in the eschatological phase of the astronomical mythology. It is said in the Ritual (ch. 64), "He who lulleth me to rest is the god in lion-form." Another note of this zodiacal beginning with the birthplace in the sign of the lion is recognizable in the arrangement of the twelve signs as double houses for the seven planets. In ancient astrology five of the planets had each one a house on either side of the Zodiac excepting the sun and moon; these had but one house between the two—that is, in the lion-sign; or rather, the lion-sign was the only double house of the Zodiac, and this was of necessity founded at the place of the equinox. The double house of the astrologers is identical with the great hall of Mati, the place where the balance was always set up in whichever sign the equinox occurred for the time being. The place of the equinox *was* the hall of Mati, or rather the double equinoxes formed the double house of Mati.

The Egyptian founders of astronomical science did not begin with mathematical calculations. They had to verify everything by observation through all the range of periodic time, and this was the only method that was fundamental or practical at first. It was by direct observation, not by calculation, that the wise men of Egypt and Meroë attained their knowledge of precession. By ages on ages of watching and registering they perceived that the backward movement of the equinox, as immense in time as it is slow in motion, had to be reckoned with as a factor of vast magnitude; and that this long hand on the face of the eternal horologe was a determinative of the hugest cycle of all, so far as they could measure periodic time. By imperceptible degrees the movement itself had become apparent, and the point of equal day and night was observed to be passing out of one group of stars upon the ecliptic into another; which sometimes coincided with a change of polestars.

We have now to trace the vernal equinox in precession, from the sign of the lion through the signs of the crab, the twins, the bull, the ram, until it entered the sign of the fishes, about 255 B.C. For 2,155 years Atum-Horus manifested, as Iu-sa, the coming son in the vernal equinox, or as the lion of the double force, when this was in the constellation Leo. The next sign in precession is the crab, the Kamite original of which was the beetle, and the beetle was an emblem of Ptah and Atum as a type of the God who came into being as his own son, that is Iu-sa, the child of Iusāas. When the equinox had receded from the lion-sign to the house of the beetle—our crab—the young Jesus of the Zodiac was there brought forth as Kheper the beetle, the "good scarabæus," which type and title he retained until the Christian era. In this sign of the beetle we find the crib or manger of the infant figured in an early form. The star called "El Nethra" by the Arabs, and "Prœsepe" by the Greeks, which is in the eighth lunar mansion, is the crib or manger by name. In Cancer, then, the Horus of the Zodiac was reborn in his solar character as the beetle of the Nile, the reproducer of himself by transformation. Thus Horus had been born in his solar character as a young lion in the sign of Leo, in the month of the lions; and reborn 2,155 years later as a beetle in the sign of and in the month of the beetles (for the lunar beetle, see *Hor-Apollo*, 1, 10). Also the ass, another zootype of Iu, is figured in this sign of the beetle or crab. Here, then, we find the crib, or manger, of Iu, the ass, in the sign which was the birthplace in the vernal equinox from 12,000 to 10,000 years ago, and therefore the original birthplace of the divine infant that was born in a manger or a stable, and was attended by the ass of Atum and the bullock of Iu.

When the equinox entered the sign of the Twins, it no longer coincided by a month in the great year with the birthplace in the crab; and there was now a difference of two months betwixt the day of the equinox in the twins and the opening day of the sacred year, on the 25th of July, at the time when the equinox was in the sign of the lion. And two months in the great year are equivalent to 4,310 lesser years. Next Iusa, the coming son, the second Atum, was born of Hathor-Iusâas, the cow-headed goddess, in the sign of the bull, where the equinox rested from the year 6,465 to the year 4,310 B.C. In this sign the divine child was brought forth in the stable as a calf or a bullock. The lunar cow was in the stable of the solar bull, where the young babe was born and laid in a manger now as Horus or Iu, the calf. Mother and child might be and were portrayed in human form, but it is the cow that gives the name of " Meri," and but for the cow-headed Hathor-Meri there would have been no human Mary as a virgin-mother in the Jesus-legend. Hathor-Meri was the mother of Horus, the Su in the "house of a thousand years," born in the stable or the manger of the bull. He had been brought forth as a young lion in the house of the lions, as a scarabæus in the sign of the beetles, and now was manifested as the calf in the sign of the bull. And it was as the lunar cow in the "house of a thousand years" that the mother brought forth her child as a calf in the stable which was rebuilt for the oxen, that is, for the bull, the cow and calf, when the birthplace passed into the zodiacal house, stable, or byre of Taurus. In re-erecting the house of heaven on earth when it was going to ruin, or, at the end of the period, King Har-si-Atef says he has *built the stable for oxen in the temple.* (Stele of King Har-si-Atef, left side.—*Records*, v. 6, p. 90.) In this stable of the temple the mystery of the birthplace was sacredly performed, and the child born in a manger (the Apt) was exhibited to the worshippers every year. The ox and the ass that were present at the birth of the Divine child in the stable at Bethlehem were extant in this sign. The ass had been present without the ox when the birthplace was in the sign of the lion ; and again when the birthplace was in the sign of the crab. The manger in which the little Jesus lay is figured in the sign of cancer, and the birth of the babe in that sign with the manger for his cradle had occurred 8,875 years B.C. Also the ass on which the child Iusa rode is standing by the manger in the stable. The ass in the birthplace is a representative of the sun-god Atum-Iu, and when the ass and ox are found together in the stable the birthplace is in the sign of the bull.

Horus or Iusa in the "house of a thousand years" was the bringer of the millennium, which was renewed in the following cycle. Sut or Satan was loosed for a little while, seven days at most, during the Saturnalia ; then he was bound in chains for another cycle of time, whilst Horus took possession of the house once more on a lease of a thousand years to establish his reign of peace, plenty and good luck in the domain of time and law, justice and right by the inauguration of another millennium. The Divine mother and child had been humanized in the Egyptian religion when the stone monuments begin for us, at least ten thousand years ago, but the zootypes were still continued as data in sign-language. This was the knowledge that was in possession of the Wise Men, the Magi, the Zoroastrians, Jews, Gnostics, Essenes and others who kept the reckoning, read the signs, and knew the time at which the advent was to occur, once every fourteen lifetimes ($14 \times 71 - 2$ years), in the "house of a thousand years," or once every 2,155 years, when the prince of peace was to be reborn as the lamb in the sign of the ram, or as Ichthus the fish in the sign of Pisces. He had been born as a calf in the sign of the bull ; as the beetle in cancer; as the lion in Leo ; as the red shoot of the vine in Virgo ; as lord of the balance in the Scales. And when the Easter equinox had moved round slowly into the sign of the ràm, the coming fulfiller of the cycle was Jesus or Horus, that " Lamb of God," who is supposed to have become historical 2,410 years later to take away the sins of the Christian world.

Before passing on to follow the vernal equinox into the sign of the fishes (we may add the corn, of which this also was the sign on account of the harvest in Egypt), we must glance back for a moment to the birthplace and the beginning with the Inundation, which was the source of so much astronomical mythology that necessitated continued readjustment of the reckoning in precession. The fish, a figure of plenty brought by the Inundation, was continued as a symbol of Atum-Horus. The type might be changed from the crocodile of Sebek to the silurus or electric eel of Atum, but the fish remained as an emblem of Ichthus, or of Ichthon, that saviour of the world who came to it first in Africa by water as the fish. We have already seen that the mystical emblem called the " Vesica Pisces," as a frame and aureole for the virgin and her child, is a living witness to the birth of Jesus from the fish's mouth, as it was in the beginning for Iusa or Horus of the Inundation. This will also explain why Ichthus, the fish, is a title of Jesus in Rome ; why the Christian religion was founded on the fish ; why the primitive Christians were called Pisciculi, and why the fish is still eaten as the sacrificial food on Friday and at Easter. There is evidence to show the impossibility of this sign having been founded in the year 255 B.C. as the sign of the vernal equinox, either in relation to Horus the fish or Horus the bread of life, or Iu the Su (son) of Atum-Ra. For instance, the wheat-harvest in Egypt coincides with the Easter equinox, and always has done so since wheat was grown *and time correctly kept.* In the Alexandrian year the month Parmuti, the month of the mother of corn, begins on the 27th of March, or about the time of the equinox when this had entered the sign of Pisces. According to the table of the months at Edfu and the Ramesseum, Parmuti was the very ancient goddess of vegetation, Rannut. Rannut was the goddess of harvest and also of the eighth month in the year, which opened with the month Tekki or Thoth. From Thoth, the first month, to Rannut-Parmuti, the eighth month, is eight months of the Egyptian year, equivalent to two tetramenes in the year of three seasons.

When Horus had fulfilled the period of 2,155 years with the Easter equinox in the sign of Aries, the birthplace passed into the sign of Pisces, where the ever-coming one, the Renewer as the eternal child who had been brought forth as a lion in Leo, a beetle in cancer, as one of the twins in the sign of the Gemini, as a calf in the sign of the bull, and as a lamb in the sign of the ram, was destined to manifest as the fish, born of a fish-mother, in the zodiacal sign of the fishes. The rebirth of Atum-Horus or Jesus as the fish of Iusāas and the bread of Nephthys was astronomically dated to occur and appointed to take place in Bethlehem of the Zodiac about the year 255 B.C., at the time

when the Easter equinox entered the sign of Pisces, the house of corn
and bread; the corn that was brought forth by the gestator Rannut in
the eighth month of the Egyptian year, and was reaped in the month
named from Parmuti the Corn-Mother; and the bread that was
kneaded by Nephthys in the house of bread.

Horus, or Jesus, the fulfiller of time and law, the saviour who
came by water, by blood and in the spirit, Horus the fish and the
bread of life, was due according to precession in the sign of the fishes
about the year 255 B.C. A new point of departure for the religion of
Ichthus in Rome is indicated astronomically when Jesus or Horus was
portrayed with the sign of the fish upon his head, and the crocodile
beneath his feet (fig. p. 343). This would be about the year
255 B.C. (so-called). But the perverters of the Jesus-legend, in con-
cocting the Christian "history," had falsified the time in heaven that
the Egyptians kept so sacredly on earth during the ages on ages
through which they zealously sought to discern the true way to the
infinite through every avenue of the finite, and to track the Eternal by
following the footprints of the typical fulfiller through all the cycles
and epicycles of renewing time.

The type of sacrifice once eaten in the totemic or mortuary meal, as
the fish, is still partaken of on Good Friday as the image of Ichthus;
the same in Rome at present as in Heliopolis or Annu in the past.
The type was changed from sign to sign, from age to age in the
course of precession. The commemorative customs light us back as
far at least as the sign of the Gemini, when twin turtle-doves, two
goats, or twin children were sacrificed. Indeed, there is some evidence
extant to show that the ass, a figure of Atum-Iu, which may be found
constellated in the decans of cancer, was at one time the type of
sacrifice, and which, to judge from its position, was of course anterior
to the "twins." (Petrie, *Egyptian Tales*, p. 90.) The ass has been
obscured by the lion and other sacred animals, but it was at one time
great in glory, particularly in the cult of Atum-Iu, the ass-headed or
ass-eared divinity. The ass has been badly abused and evilly treated
as a type of Sut-Typhon, whereas it was expressly a figure of the
solar-god, the swift goer who was Iu the Sa of Atum; and Iu-Sa is
the coming son or the Egyptian Jesus on the ass. Mythically
rendered, he made his advent as a lion, or it might be said that he
came riding on an ass. Horus, the sacrificial victim, as the calf, was
an especial type in the Osirian cult. The lamb is heard of as
expressly Jewish; the lamb that was roasted on the cruciform spit to
image the Crucified upon the cross at Easter, when the lamb was yet
the typical victim. When the equinox passed into the ram-sign
Horus or Iusa became the lamb "son of a sheep," who as son of the
father was the son of God, an especial type with the Sebek-heteps.
When the vernal equinox entered once more into the sign of the
"fishes" the time had come for the type to change back again to the
fish which had been eaten as a typical sacrifice thousands of years
before when the crocodile was eaten once a year as the zootype of
Sebek-Horus, "the almighty fish in Kamurit" (Rit., ch. 88), the
bringer of plenty in the inundation of the Nile.

The advent of a Jewish Jesus, as the fish Ichthus, was dependent on
the Messu or Messiah-son being incarnated when the vernal equinox

was entering Pisces in the circuit of precession, where the female bringer-forth was figured as the mother-fish, instead of the sheep, the cow or the lioness.

The astronomers knew and foretold that the Divine babe was to be born in the sign of the fishes, the sign of the Messiah Dag, of An, of Oan or Jonah. It is probable that the name of Rome was derived from an Egyptian name for the fish, and that Roma was the fish-goddess. Rem, Rum, or Rome signifies the fish in Egyptian. Be this as it may, the fish-man (or woman?) rules in Rome. The ring with which the Pope is invested, his seal-ring, has on it the sign of the fish, and Ichthon the Saviour was brought on in Rome as Ichthus the fish, or otherwise personified as the "historical Jesus." This is illustrated in the Catacombs, where the fish emaning Jonah from its mouth has been supposed by Christians to represent the resurrection of an historical Jew. The name of the Piscina given to the baptismal font likewise shows the cult of the fish. Those who were baptized in the Piscina as primitive Christians were known by name as the *Pisciculi.* "Ichthus" also was the secret password and sign of salutation betwixt the Christian Pisciculi.

Bryant copied from an ancient Maltese coin the figure of Horus, who carries the crook and fan in his hands and wears a fish-mitre on his head. This was Horus of the Inundation, who was emaned from the water as a fish and by the fish, but who is here portrayed in a human form with the fish's mouth for a mitre on his head. (Bryant, v. 5, p. 384.) The wearer of the *os tincæ* on his head is not only the fish-man in survival, the petticoated Pope is likewise a figure of the ancient fishwoman; she who sat upon the waters and on the seven hills of the celestial Heptanomis as a water-cow, who brought forth from the mystical mouth of the fish. The Pope is dressed in the likeness of both sexes. The "*os tincæ*" of the papal mitre, equally with the star Fomalhaut in Piscis Australis of the planisphere, and the mouthpiece of the divine Word, is still the same antique as when the ancient Wisdom was first figured as the female fish, the crocodile, and the male fish was a likeness of the Saviour who came by water in the Inundation before Horus could come by boat, or float on the papyrus-plant in human form; so long has the fish been a zootype of emaning source in the Egyptian eschatology. The Pope impersonates the mouthpiece, the fish's mouthpiece of the Word, and, as the imagery shows, the Word, or Logos, is the same that was uttered of old as a fish by the ancient mother-fish with the *os tincæ* or mouth of utterance from which a child is born; so that the mother-church in Rome, as represented by the Pope, is still the living likeness of the fish-mother, who brought forth Horus of the Inundation as her fish in the Zodiac, at least some 12,000 or 13,000 years ago, and had never ceased to do so annually up to the time of rebirth in the sign of the fishes, when Papal Rome took up the parable but suppressed or omitted the explanation concerning the Christ now apotheosized as Ichthus the fish. Thus, as previously demonstrated, the proper date for the commencement of Christianity or equinoctial Christolatry is some-where about 255 B.C.

One of the most perfect illustrations of fulfilment attained by the mythos may be studied in a scene that was copied from the Roman

Catacombs by De Rossi (*Rom. Sott.*, 2, pl. 16). In this the seven great spirits appear in human guise, who are elsewhere represented by the seven fishers or the seven lambs with Horus, ignorantly supposed to be an historic personage. These seven are with the fish in the sign of the two fishes, who are figured as the two fishes laid out on two dishes. Moreover, lest there might be any mistake in reading the picture it is placed between two other illustrations. In one of these the lamb is portrayed as the victim of sacrifice ; in the other a fish is lying with the bread upon the altar. So that *the central picture shows the result of the transference from the sign of the ram to the sign of the fishes.* In another scene the seven who were followers of Horus are portrayed together with seven baskets of bread (Bosio, pp. 216, 217). In relation to the group of seven spirits in the Roman Catacombs it must be noted that the company of twelve, as followers of Horus, or disciples of Iusa, was not a primary formation. It was preceded by the group of seven, the seven who were with Horus, the leader of that " glorious company," from the beginning ; the same in the eschatology as in the astronomical mythology. They are the seven with Horus in the bark of souls or Sahus that was constellated in Orion. In the creation attributed to Atum-Ra, which opened on the day of "come thou hither," otherwise upon the resurrection day, the seven great spirits are assigned their place in this new heaven ; they are called the seven glorious ones " who are in the train of Horus " ; and who follow after the coffined one, that is Osiris-Sekari, whose bier or coffin was configurated in the greater bear. They who followed their lord as his attendants in the resurrection were also grouped as seven khuti in the lesser bear.

In his various advents Horus was attended by the seven great spirits termed his seshu, or his servants. So Jesus, according to Hebrew prophecy, was to be attended by the seven spirits called (1) the spirit of the Lord ; (2) the spirit of wisdom ; (3) the spirit of understanding ; (4) the spirit of counsel ; (5) the spirit of might ; (6) the spirit of knowledge ; (7) the spirit of the fear of the Lord (Is. xi. 1, 2). These, as Egyptian, were they who had originated as the seven elemental powers and who afterwards became the Khuti as the seven great spirits. But in their Hebrew guise they are evaporized and attenuated past all recognition except as a septenary of spirits. The seven with Jesus as a group of attendant powers or followers may be seen in the seven doves that hover round the child *in utero ;* the seven solar rays about his head ; the seven lambs or rams with Jesus on the mount ; the seven as stars with Jesus in the midst ; the seven as fishers in the boat ; and lastly, the seven as communicants who solemnize the Eucharist with the loaves and fishes in the mortuary meal of the Roman Catacombs. There are various pictures in the Catacombs which can only be explained by the pre-Christian gnosis. This alone can tell us why the divine infant should be imaged as a little mummy with the solar halo round his head, or why the so-called "Star of Bethlehem" should be figured with eight rays. Such things are Egypto-gnostic remains belonging to the Church in Rome that was not founded on the Canonical Gospels, but was pre-extant as gnostic ; the Church of Marcion and of Marcelina. Several of these pictures contain the group of the seven great spirits who were with

3 B

Horus of the Resurrection at his advent in the sign of Pisces, as they had been with him in the previous signs when he was the lamb, the calf, the beetle or the lion. Two pictures are copied by Lundy, one from De Rossi's *Roma Sotteranea Christiana* (vol. i.) and one from Bosio (*Rom. Sot.*). In the one scene seven persons are seated at a semicircular table with two fishes and eight baskets of bread before them. In the other scene, seven persons are kneeling with two fishes, seven cakes and seven baskets of bread in front of them (Lundy, *Monumental Christianity*, figs. 169 and 171).

Now, there is nothing whatsoever in the canonical Gospels to account for or suggest the eight baskets-full of cakes which are somewhat common in the Catacombs. These we claim to be a direct survival from the Egyptian; the eight loaves or cakes which are a sacred regulation number in the Ritual. According to the Rubrical directions appended to chapter 144 it is commanded that *eight* Persen loaves, *eight* Shenen loaves, *eight* Khenfer loaves, and *eight* Hebennu loaves are to be offered at each gate of the seven arits or mansions of the celestial Heptanomis. These offerings were made for the feast of illumining the earth, or elsewhere (ch. 18), the coffin of Osiris, and therefore for the festival of the Resurrection and solemnizing of the Eucharist. The seven persons present with the Lord are identifiable with the typical seven followers of Horus as the seven khuti or glorious ones. The speaker, who personates the lord of the seven, says " I am the divine leader of the seven. I am a khu, the lord of the khus." The Osiris Nu thus celebrates the monthly festival by offering eight loaves or cakes at each of the seven halls. The khus were seven in number or eight with Horus their lord, in whom Osiris rose again from the condition of the dead. The chapter is to be repeated over a picture of the seven sovereign chiefs, which we now claim to be the original of the seven personages that keep the sacramental ceremony in the Catacombs when the eight cakes are figured on the table of the seven personages who have been termed the " *Septem Pii Sacerdotes* " (Northcote and Brownlow, *Rom. Sott.*, vol. 2, pl. 17, p. 68). But to return, our starting-point for tracking the movement in precession was with the vernal equinox in the sign of Leo, on the birthday of the year that was determined at the time by the heliacal rising of the star which announced the birthplace of Horus, now figured in the solar zodiac, nigh where the evil dragon Hydra lay in wait to devour the babe as soon as it was born. This was about 11,000 years B.C., or 13,000 years ago. During these eleven thousand years, by the changes in precession and the continual rectification of the calendar from old style to new, July 25th at starting had receded to December 25th in the end. That is, the birthday of the coming child Iusa or Horus in the Lion sign, celebrated on the 25th of July, came to be commemorated on the 25th of December at the end of this period, by those who kept the reckoning, and this, as will be shown, is precisely what did occur in the evolution of the Jesus-legend.

Two birthdays had been assigned to Horus of the double horizon, one to child-Horus in the autumn, the other to Horus the adult in the vernal equinox. These were the two times or *teriu* of the year. But when the solstices were added to the equinoxes in the new creation of the four quarters established by Ptah for his son Atum-Ra, there was a further change. The place of birth for the elder, the mortal Horus who was born child of the Virgin Mother, now occurred in the winter solstice and the place of rebirth for Horus the eternal Son was celebrated in the vernal equinox, with three months between the two positions instead of six. If the birth occurred at Christmas with the winter solstice in the sign of the Archer, the Resurrection at Easter would occur in the sign of the fishes as at present. The equinoxes, of course, remained upon the double horizon, whereas the winter solstice took place in the depths of Amenta, and this became the place of rebirth for the child-Horus as Iu-sa, the coming son in the astronomical mythology. Horus in the autumnal equinox was now succeeded by Horus who suffered in the winter solstice. The Jews still celebrate their mysteries annually *as* mysteries. And it is instructive to note that with them the *two times* remain equinoctial, and have never been changed to the winter solstice and Easter equinox. The Jews have subterranean reasons for not accepting the Messiah born at Christmas. Theirs are the mysteries of the double horizon ; or of Ra-Harmachis. The double birth of Horus at the two times, or the birth of the babe in the winter solstice and the rebirth as the adult in the Easter equinox is acknowledged in the Egyptian Book of the Divine Birth. The celebration of the Nativity at the solstice is referred to in the calendar of Edfu, and it is said that "everything is performed which is ordained" in the "Book of the Divine Birth." Also, it was commanded in the calendar of Esné that the precepts of the Book on the Second Divine Birth of the child Kahi "were to be performed on the first of the month Epiphi" (cited by Lockyer, *Dawn of Astronomy*, pp. 284–6). The child Kahi is a pseudonym for the child-Horus. He is the revealer, the logos or word, and the "Revelation of Kahi" is associated with New Year's day, when this occurred on the 26th of the month Payni. Now the first and second "divine births" (or the birth and rebirth) of Horus were celebrated at the festivals of the winter solstice and the Easter equinox, and these are the two times of the two Horuses identified by Plutarch, the first as manifester for Isis, the Virgin Mother, the second as Horus, the Son of God the Father, when he tells us that "Harpocrates (Har the Khart, or child) is born about the winter solstice, immature and infant-like in the plants that flower and spring up early, for which reason they offer to him the first-fruits of growing lentils ; and they celebrate her (Isis) being brought to bed after the vernal equinox" (of Is. and Os., ch. 65). Here are the three months between the two birthdays which were celebrated at the two festivals now known as Christmas and Easter. Two different birthdays were likewise assigned to the Greek Apollo. One of these was commemorated by the Delians at the time of the winter solstice ; the other by the Delphians in the vernal equinox.

According to the decree of Canopus (B.C. 238) the date of Osiris's entry into the moon at the annual resurrection had then receded to the 29th of Choiak, equivalent to December 26th, *in the Alexandrian year*, which was established in the reign of Augustus, B.C. 25. "The entry of Osiris into the sacred bark takes place here annually at the defined time on the 29th day of the month Choiak." In this way the Christmas festival, by which the " Birth of Christ " is now celebrated, can be identified with the yearly celebration of the rebirth of Osiris (or Horus) in the moon. Moreover, we can thus trace it, following the course of precession, from the 17th of Athor (October 5th in the sacred year ; November 14th in the Alexandrian year), mentioned by Plutarch, to the 29th of Choiak, our December 26th. The next day, December 27th, was the first of Tybi, and this was the day on which the child-Horus was crowned, and the festival of his coronation celebrated. If we reckon the 25th of December (28th Choiak) to be the day of birth, the day of resurrection and of the crowning *in Amenta* is on the third day. In the month-list of the Ramesseum, Tybi is the month dedicated to Amsu, the Horus who arose from the dead in Amenta, and who was crowned as conquerer *on the third day*—that is, on December 27th = Tybi 1st. There are several symbols of this resurrection on the third day. First, Osiris rises on that day in the new moon. Next, Amsu figures as the Sahu-mummy risen to his feet, with right arm free, as ruler in Amenta, the earth of eternity. Thirdly, Horus the child is crowned in the seat of Osiris for another year. Fourthly, the Tat was erected as a figure of the god re-risen, and a type of eternal stability in the depths of the winter solstice. Thus the resurrection on the third day was in Amenta and not upon this earth.

The Egyptians celebrated their festival of the resurrection every year, called the feast of Ptah-Sekari-Osiris, in the month Choiak (November 27th, December 26th, Alexandrian year). The rite is otherwise known as "the erection of the Tat-pillar." Erman recovered a description of the festival from a Theban tomb. Of this he says : " The special festival was of all the greater importance because it was solemnized on the morning of the royal jubilee. The festivities began with a sacrifice offered by the king to Osiris, the 'LORD of Eternity,' a mummied figure, wearing the Tat-pillar on his head." It lasted for ten days, from the 20th to the 30th of the month Choiak, the 26th being the great day of feasting. The royal endowment of the temple at Medinet Habu for the sixth day of the festival included 3,694 loaves of bread, 600 cakes, 905 jugs of beer and 33 jars of wine. This was the great day of eating and drinking, corresponding to our Christmas gorging and guzzling, but on the 22nd December, instead of the 25th, of a somewhat later period. The festival was devoted to the god Osiris-Ptah-Sekari, who had been dead and was alive again ; cut in pieces and reconstituted with his vertebræ sound and not a bone of his body found to be broken or missing. The festival of the sixth day is clearly the Ha-k-er-a feast that was celebrated on the sixth night of the Ten Mysteries. Moreover, the ten days of the festival that was sacred to the god Osiris-Sekari are also in agreement with the ten nights of the mysteries (Rit., ch. 18). In the scene copied from the Theban tomb the " Noble Pillar" of the Tat-cross is to be seen lying pronely on the ground where it had been overthrown by Sut and the Sebau. The object of the festival was to celebrate the re-erection of the Tat and turn the Cross of death once more into the Cross of life as the symbol of resurrection. The king, as representative of Horus who reconstitutes, his father, with the aid of the royal relatives and a priest, pulls the pillar upright. Four priests bring in the usual table of offerings and place them in front of the Tat. So far, says Erman, we can understand the festival. But the further ceremonies refer to mythological events unknown to us. Four priests with their fists raised rush upon four others, who appear to give way; two more strike each other, and one standing by says of them, "I seize Horus shining in truth." Then follows a great flogging scene, in which fifteen persons beat each other mercilessly with their sticks and fists; they are divided into several groups, two of which, according to the inscription, represent the people of the town Pa and of the town Tepu. This is evidently the representation of a great mythological fight, in which were engaged the inhabitants of Pa and Tepu, *i.e.*, of the ancient city of Buto, in the north of the delta. "The ceremonies which close the sacred rite are also quite problematic; four herds of *oxen and asses* are seen driven by their herdsmen, and we are told in the accompanying text four times they circle round the walls on that day when the noble Tat-pillar is re-erected."

Raising the Tat-pillar was typical of Horus in his second advent raising the dead Osiris from his sepulchre and calling the mummy to come forth alive. The gods in Tattu on the night of the resurrection, symbolized by this re-erection of the Tat, are Osiris, Isis, Nephthys, and Horus the avenger of his father. Thus in re-erecting the Tat, Amenhetep III. with his queen Ti and one of the royal princesses were personating Horus the avenger and the two divine sisters in the resurrection of Osiris. (Rit., ch. 18.)

The Christians celebrate the birth of the divine babe at Christmas and the death and resurrection at Easter; whereas the birth and death were commemorated at the same season in the Egyptian mysteries of Ptah, and later of Osiris—as it was in the beginning, when the death was that of the old year and the rebirth that of the new year; otherwise, the death of Osiris and the birth of Horus, or the death of Atum and the rebirth of Iusa. The new year came to be reckoned from the shortest day when the sun had reached its lowest point and the shadow of darkness or the dragon its utmost length. The sufferings of the Sun-god were naturally accredited to him at that time, and the death and resurrection in Amenta were both timed to the solstice. The sun was lord of light as ruler of the lesser year. The Apap-monster was the reptile power of darkness, and of desert drought. This dreaded adversary of the sun was now the uppermost, Osiris in Amenta was the victim in the winter solstice. The suffering and death of Osiris were the cause of the long period of mourning, of fasting and supplication that was memorized in the mysteries. In the winter solstice the birth took place below, in Amenta, the earth of Sut, and habitat of the Apap-reptile. In the equinox at Easter, Horus the fulfiller was transformed from the human child to the divine hawk-headed Horus, who rose from the underworld as the spirit of life and light and food, and who was then re-fleshed or re-incorporated anew on earth, conceived of the Virgin, incarnated in her blood once more, to be brought forth in human shape again at Christmas; and by the gestator in the divine form, as Horus of the resurrection now reborn at Easter.

The last night of the old year (July 24th), "the night of the child in the cradle," had been named from the new birth as the Mesiu ; also the evening meal of the next day, the first of the new year, was called the " Mesiu." These were the exact equivalent of our Christmas Eve and Christmas Day on December 24th and 25th, after a lapse of 11,000 years in time according to the movement in precession. The sacred old Egyptian year, which opened on the first of Tekki (or Thoth) as the year of the great Bear and the inundation, began upon the 25th of July in the year of 365 days. Therefore July 24th was the last night of the old year and the 25th (or the 20th in the year of 360 days) was New Year's Day, the birthday of Horus the child, or fish of the inundation. Time was sacredly kept by means of the festivals, and these were redated age after age from old style to new. The decree of Canopus is both explicit and emphatic on the necessity of correctly readjusting the calendar to the lapse of time, whether in the Sothiac cycle or the movement in precession so that " the case shall not occur that the Egyptian festivals by which time was kept—now celebrated in winter—should be celebrated some time or other in summer, as has occasionally occurred " in times past, in consequence of the calendar being incorrectly kept (*Records*, vol. 8, p. 87).

For example, a new year was introduced by the Egyptian priests B.C. 25, in the name of the Roman Emperor Augustus, which is known as the Alexandrian year. When this new year was established a readjustment was made to allow for the lapse in precession and to correct the calendar. At this time the so-called " sacred year " was for the *last time* readjusted. This was that year of 360 days which was based on the twelve moons or months of thirty days each and on the reckoning permanently figured in the 360 degrees of the ecliptic that was to be kept in endless sanctity howsoever supplemented by other reckonings in the total combination to be united in the great precessional year of $360 \times 71 - 2 = 26,000$ years. In this corrected calendar *the first of Choiak, which fell on October 18th in the sacred year is shifted to November 27th in the Alexandrian year, and there is a rectification of time to the extent of forty days.* These forty days in the lesser year represent nearly 3,000 years in the cycle of precession. In other words stellar time was corrected by the time of the sun and determined on the grand scale by the position of the vernal equinox. This had now receded to the sign of Pisces, when Horus or Jesus, who had been the " Lamb of God " in the previous sign, and the calf in the sign of the bull, was figured as the fish by the Egypto-gnostic artists (fig. on p. 343). Thus the cult was continued without a break in Rome. Augustus personally posed himself in the character of the expected one, the Prince of Peace, the Messiah of the astronomical mythology and thence in the eschatology.

At the time when the change of equinox from Aries to Pisces occurred in the great year, or in connection with this event, the birthplace was rebuilt as the crib or cradle, meskhen, or holy of holies in the temple for the new-born babe. Now the temple of Hathor at Denderah was last rebuilt in the time of the Ptolemies, a century or so B.C. The inscriptions show that this rebuilding of the temple was attributed to Augustus. He never was at Denderah in person, but the ruler in Rome was assigned the place of the king or Pharaoh in Egypt as rebuilder of the temple for Hathor and her babe, and the king on earth was the royal representative, first as the Repa, then as the Ra, of the king, who was divine or astronomical. Augustus was invested with this divinity, and thus the Egyptian doctrine was continued in the person of the Emperor in Rome. Augustus proclaimed himself to be not merely a human likeness, but the very God himself on earth. "The reverence due to the gods," says Tacitus (*Annals*, i. 10), "was no longer peculiar; *Augustus claimed equal worship. A mortal man was directly adored, and priests and pontiffs were appointed to pay him impious homage.*" Thus the apotheosis of a mortal had begun and a kind of papacy was already established as a bridge betwixt Alexandria and Rome. The vernal equinox was now in Pisces, and Horus, as type, was the fish instead of the lamb or ram. "Ichthus the fish" had been a title self-conferred by Alexander in his apotheosis 300 years earlier. So Augustus, in relation to the same fulfilment in astronomical time was Ichthus the fish in Rome before the title was conferred upon a supposed historical Jesus of Nazareth. Thus the festival now dated Choiak 29th in the Alexandrian year had been celebrated 3,000 years earlier in the sacred year, and we behold it being readjusted according to the reckoning in precession as it had been aforetime.

It has often been a matter of wonderment why the birthday of the Son of God on earth should be celebrated as a festival of unlimited gorging and guzzling. The explanation is that the feast of Christmas Day is a survival of the ancient Uaka festival, with which the rebirth of the Nilotic year was celebrated with uproarious revellings and rejoicings, as the festival of returning food and drink. It was at once the natal-day of the Nile, and of the Messu or Messianic child under his various names. It is called the birthday of Osiris in the Ritual (ch. 130). Osiris, or the young god Horus, came to earth as lord of wine, and is said to be "full of wine" at the fair Uaka festival. The rubric to chapter 130 states that "bread, beer, wine, and all good things" are to be offered to the manes upon the birthday of Osiris, which, in the course of time, became equivalent to our New Year's festival, or Christmas Day. The grapes were ripe in Egypt at the time the imagery was given its starry setting. This offers a datum as determinative of time and season. The times might change in heaven's "enormous year"; other doctrines be developed under other names; the grapes be turned to raisins. But the old Festival of Intoxication still lived on when celebrated in the name of Christ. The babe that is born on Christmas Day in the morning is Horus of the inundation still.

The mythical ideal of a saviour-child was Egyptian. But this ideal did not originate in the human child. The child was preceded by other types of eternal, ever-coming youth. Each year salvation came to Egypt with the waters just in time to save the land from drought and famine, and the power that saved it was represented by the shoot of the papyrus, or the fish as the bringer of food and drink on which the salvation of the people depended ; and the bringer of these was Horus the saviour, as the Messu of the inundation. Horus the jocund who rose up as Orion "full of wine," with Krater for his constellated "cup" that held 7,000 gallons of intoxicating drink ; Horus who brought the grapes to make the wine ; who drowned the fiery dragon Hydra, was 'he who came to Egypt as a veritable saviour once a year. The same mythical character passed into Greece and is also repeated in the Canonical Gospels as the wine-bibber who comes eating and drinking.

In this way the birth of the child at Christmas and the rebirth at Easter came to represent the keeping of time in the great year, which can be calculated by a twofold process of reckoning, from the original starting-point. On the one hand, the lapse of time in the course of precession is five months = the equinox passing through the five signs, that is, from July 25th (the first of Taht) to December 25th. On the other hand, the time taken for the equinox to travel through the five signs is *the exact equivalent in the great year* to the five months' lapse in the solar year of 365 days. The reckoning has to be made one way by the lesser year, from July 25th to December 25th in accordance with the natural fact. The other way it has to be computed on the scale of the great year in the cycle of precession. The total result of this twofold and verifiable computation is that on the one side we are ultimately landed with a birthday of Iusa in the solstice at Christmas, and on the other hand we are landed with the birthday or day of rebirth for Iusa at Easter, when the equinox was entering the sign of the fishes, about 255 years before the time that has been falsely dated " B.C."

One knows well enough that Christian credulity is quite capable of still assuming that this Jesus who manifested during 10,000 years in the astronomical mythology, and who was accreting the typical character of the unique person all that time, is but the fore-shadow *cast back-wards* by the historical figure in whom they believe as the one reality of all realities. Nevertheless, the fact remains that, such being the character pre-extant, there was nothing left to have any historical human origin at the wrong end of 10,000 years.

This is a strictly scientific and not-to-be-controverted demonstration of the indubitable truth that the birthday of the Messiah now cele-brated on the 25th of December had been celebrated for at least 10,000 years on the corresponding day as the birth of the Egyptian Messu at the feast of the Messiu on the first day of the Egyptian year, which was the 25th of July, from the time when the Easter equinox was in the sign of the lion. There is evidence also that the lapse of time was religiously rectified in the readjusted calendar according to the course of precession from July 25th down to December 25th, when the winter solstice coincided with the sign of Sagittarius and the vernal equinox first entered the sign of Pisces, in the year that was erroneously dated. Through all the ten or eleven millenniums in-tervening the Messu had periodically manifested in the annual inun-dation and as the fulfiller of time in the house of a thousand years, whilst the Easter equinox kept travelling and the birthplace shifting, from virgo to the lion, from the lion to the crab, from the twins to the bull, from the ram to the fishes. All that went to the making of the latest legendary saviour, barring the false belief, was pre-extant on entirely other grounds in the Egyptian mythology and eschatology; and when the Easter equinox entered the sign of the fishes, about 255 B.C., the Jesus who is the one verifiable founder of so-called Christianity was at least 10,000 years of age and had been travelling hither as the Ever Coming One through all this period of time. During that vast length of years the young Fulfiller was periodically mothered as mortal by the Virgin with Seb for his reputed earthly father and with Anup the baptizer as his precursor and announcer in the wilderness. All that time he had fought the battle with Satan in the desert during forty days and nights each year in every one of those 10,000 years as a matter of fact in the natural phenomena of time and season in Egypt. During those 10,000 years that ideal of the divine incarnated in Iusa the Coming Son had gone on growing in the mind of Egypt preparatory to its being rendered historically as the divine man of a later cult by those deluded idiotai who dreamt the astronomical forecast had been fulfilled in Hebrew prophecy and in veritable human fact, through their ignorance of sign-language and the wisdom of the past.

The two birthdays at Christmas and Easter which were assigned to Iusa in his two characters of child-Horus and Horus the adult, Horus the Earth-born and Horus the Heaven-born in the Osirian mythos, were brought on as the two birthdays of Jesus. But there was a diversity of opinion amongst the Christian Fathers as to whether Jesus the Christ was born in the winter solstice or in the vernal equinox. It was held by some that the 25th of March was the natal day. Others maintained that this was the day of the incarnation. According to Clement Alexander, the birth of Jesus took place upon the 25th of March. But in Rome *the festival of Lady-day* was celebrated on the 25th of March in commemoration of the miraculous conception in the womb of a virgin, which virgin gives birth to the child at Christmas, nine months afterwards. According to the Gospel of James (ch. 18) it was in the equinox, and consequently not at Christmas, that the virgin birth took place. At the moment of Mary's delivery on what is designated "the day of the Lord" the birth of the Babe in the cave is described. It occurs at Bethlehem. Joseph went out and sought a midwife in the country of Bethlehem. "*And I, Joseph, walked, and I walked not: and I looked up into the sky, and saw the air violently agitated; and I looked up at the pole of heaven, and saw it stationary, and the fowls of heaven were still; and I looked at the earth and saw a vessel lying, and workmen reclining by it, with their hands in the vessel, and those who handled did not handle it, and those who took hold did not lift, and those who presented it to their mouth did not present, but the faces of all were looking up; and I saw the sheep scattered, and the sheep stood, and the shepherd lifted up his hand to strike them, and his hand remained up; and I looked at the stream of the river, and I saw that the mouths of the kids were down, and not drinking; and everything which was being impelled forward was intercepted in its course.*" There can be no doubt of this description being equinoctial. It is a picture of the perfect counterpoise between night and day which only occurs at the level of the equinox when the Lord of the balance is reborn in the house of a thousand years, or at some other fresh stage in the circuit of precession : and the Messiah Dag was now in the house of the fish and of bread, with the prophecy fulfilled according to the astronomical reckoning.

This duality of the divine birth at Christmas and Easter has been the cause of inextricable confusion to the Christians, who never could adjust the falsehood to the fact ; and now at last we recover the fact itself that will be fatal to the falsehood.

It will be elaborately demonstrated that the concocters of Christianity and its spurious records had a second-hand acquaintanceship with the Egyptian Ritual, and that they wrought into their counterfeit Gospels all that could be made to look more or less historical-like as a sacerdotal mode of obtaining mastery over the minds of the utterly ignorant, who were held to be the "better believers." But they never could determine whether the divine child was born at Christmas or at Easter, which was naturally impossible to the one-man scheme of supposed historic fulfilment. Again, in the Christian version the crucifixion = the death of Osiris, has been postponed until Easter. This makes the period of mourning wrong. In Egypt there was a time of fasting for forty days during the Egyptian Lent. The mourning and the fasting naturally *followed* the suffering and the death of Osiris, which supplied the *raison d'être*. But when the death was shifted to Easter, to be *celebrated in accordance with the Jewish Passover*, to which it was hitched on, the long time of fasting remained as in Egypt, and for the first time in this world the death was preceded by the mourning with which the murder is supposed to have been commiserated and solemnized. The fourth Sunday in Lent is commonly observed in Europe by the name of "Dead Sunday." But the death then celebrated or "carried out" has no relation to a personal crucifixion that is assumed to have occurred once upon a time at Easter. Such customs followed Christmas or the death in winter with a prehistoric significance varying in accordance with the old style and new in the keeping of the festivals ; whereas there is no death at Christmas in the Christian scheme to be celebrated before Easter or to account for the mourning-festival during Lent. The death and rebirth at Christmas, or New Year, and the resurrection at Easter can only be explained by the Osirian mysteries, and these are still celebrated throughout Europe, precisely the same as in Asia and in Africa. The Ritual also has a word to say concerning the Jewish Sabbath of Saturday, and the Christian Sabbath sacred to the sun. The ancient Egyptians celebrated festivals on the first, the sixth, the seventh, and the fifteenth of the month. The feast of the first and the fifteenth was a festival of Ra and the day was dedicated to Horus, who represented the earlier sun, and whose Sabbath was the seventh day, or Saturday in the earlier cult. It is said in the Ritual, "I am with Horus on the day when the *Festivals* of Osiris are celebrated, and when offerings are made on *the sixth day of the month*, and on the Feast of the Tenait in Heliopolis" (Rit., ch. 1). This Tenait was a feast associated with *the seventh day of the month*. Here then is a feast of *the sixth and seventh*, or night and day, corresponding to the Jewish Sabbath. Osiris entered the moon on the sixth day of the month. The seventh was the feast-day, when "couplings and conceptions did abound." This was celebrated in Annu, the city of the sun, and thus far the day was a sun-day. The word *tenait* denotes a measure of time, a division, a week *or* a fortnight. A feast-day on the seventh, dedicated to the solar god, would be the sun's day, or *Sunday once a month.* Now, two great festivals were dedicated to Ra, the solar god, upon the seventh and fifteenth of the month. Here, then, is a fifteen-day fortnight, or solar half-month (fifteen days), which was correlated with the half-month, or *tenait*, of fourteen days in the lunar reckoning. The sixth of the month was a moon-day, on the night of which the love-feast or Agapæ began with the entrance of Osiris, earlier Horus, into the moon, or the conjunction, say, of Horus or Hu with Hathor. This was on Friday night. The next day was a phallic festival in celebration of the celestial conjunction; it was the day assigned to Sebek = Saturn in conjunction with his mother. The festival was luni-solar; hence it was celebrated on the *sixth and seventh of the month*, like the Sabbath of the Jews, which is *repeated later on the sixth and seventh days of the week.* Now, if we start with Sunday as the first of the month, the tenait festival fell on Saturday as a Sabbath of the seventh day. The second festival of Ra, that of Sunday, was on the fifteenth of the month, which would be eight days after the Tenait-feast upon the seventh of the month. The tenait on the Saturday and a feast of the 15th on a Sunday show the existence of a Sabbath celebrated on Saturday, the 7th, and another, *eight days later*, on Sunday, the 15th *of the month.* These, however, were monthly at first, as the festivals of Osiris or Ra, and not weekly, as they afterwards became with the Jews and the Christians. The festival of Saturday as the seventh day of the month is Jewish. The Sabbath of Sunday, the day of Ra, is a survival of the festival celebrated on the 15th of the month in ancient Egypt as the sun's day, or Sunday, once a month.

It was the custom at one time in Rome for the mummy, or corpse of the dead Christ, to be exhibited in the churches on Holy Thursday, the day before the Crucifixion, and if the symbolical corpse is not now exposed to the public gaze, the Holy Sepulchre is still exhibited. This has the appearance of commemorating two different deaths, the only explanation of which is to be found in the Egyptian mythos. Osiris was the *Corpus Christi* at Christmas or in the solstice. He died to be reborn again as Horus in various phenomena on the third day in the moon; also from the water in his baptism; after forty days in the buried grain; and at the end of three months, in the Easter equinox. In the Kamite original the night of the Last Supper, and of the death of Osiris, and the laying out of his body on the table of offerings are identical. It is the "night of provisioning the altar" and the provender was the mummy of the god provided for the mortuary meal. That was the dead Christ, or *Corpus Christi* (Rit., ch. 18).

Holy Thursday is especially consecrated by the Roman Catholic Church as a commemoration of the Last Supper and the institution of the eucharistic meal, at which the corpus of the Christ already dead was laid out to be eaten sacramentally. It is similar in the Gospels.

The Last Supper is there celebrated, and the body and blood of the Christ are there partaken of *before the Crucifixion has occurred*. This, in the Egyptian original, would be the corpse of Osiris, the karest-mummy of him who died in the winter solstice three months before the resurrection in the equinox occurred at Easter. Seven days of mourning for the burial of Osiris were also celebrated at the end of the month Choiak. This was known as the "*fêtes des ténèbres*," which, according to Brugsch, commemorated the "*sept jours qu'il a passé dans le ventre de sa mère, Nût*"—equivalent to Jonah being in the belly of the fish, only the days of darkness in this phase are seven instead of three. These seven days of mourning are the prototype of Passion week in the rubrical usage of the Roman Church, during which the pictures of the cross (and Crucifixion) are all covered up and veiled in darkness. Here the funeral ceremony followed the burial of Osiris, whereas in the Christian version the *fêtes des ténèbres* precede the death and burial of the supposed historic victim.

According to the synoptics, it was on the 15th of the month Nisan that the Crucifixion occurred. But according to John, it was on the 14th. These two different reckonings are solar and lunar. When time was reckoned by the lunar month of twenty-eight days, the 14th was the day of mid-month, or full moon, the day of the equinox and of the Easter Pasch. In the luni-solar reckoning of thirty days to the month, the 15th was the day of full moon in the equinox. The two dates for the Crucifixion are identical with these two possible dates for the equinox. There was a fortnight, or half-moon of fourteen days, and a half-month of fifteen days. The French fortnight is *quinze jours*, or fifteen days, and this is the fifteen-day fortnight of the Christian festivals, the Passion and the Resurrection. The 14th Nisan was true to the lunar calculation of time, but the 15th was also needed for the solar reckoning, and, as usual, the Christian founders have brought on both in aiming at the one supposed event. It has lately become known, from a lexicographical tablet belonging to the library of Assurbanipal, that the Assyrians also kept a Sabbath (Shapatu) of the 15th day of the month, or full moon in the luni-solar reckoning.

Thus the crucifixion assigned by the synoptics to the 15th Nisan was according to the solar month, and the 14th assigned by John was lunar, both being astronomical, and both impossible as dates in human history. The festival of the seventh day is Jewish, and a festival of the eighth day was continued by the Christians. Barnabas (Ep. 15) says, "We observe the eighth day with gladness, in which Jesus rose from the dead." This identifies the eighth day as a Sunday, and only in the Egyptian way of celebrating the 15th following the Tenait on the seventh can the eighth day be a Sabbath. The seventh day was Saturday, the day of Sebek. The eighth day was Sunday, *once a month*, the day of Ra, and thus the eighth day became the Lord's day in the pre-Christian religion; and the origin of both festivals or Sabbaths of the seventh day and of the 15th, eight days afterwards, can be traced to the sun-god as Horus and the sun-god as Ra (Rit., ch. 113, 7). "The ancients speak of the Passion and Resurrection Pasch as a fifteen days' solemnity. Fifteen days (the length of time) was enforced by law of the empire and commanded to the universal Church" (Bingham, 9, p. 95; Gieseler, *Catholic Church*, sect. 53, p. 178). Fifteen days include the week of seven days and the period of eight days. Both days—Saturday the day of Horus and Sunday the day of Ra, as the seventh-day feast and the eighth-day Sabbath—were being celebrated as their two feast-days by the Christians in the middle of the fifth century, and these were known as the feasts of Saturday and of the Lord's day, or Sunday (Socrates, *Hist. Eccles.* lib. v. cap. 22, p. 234). When Dionysius the Areopagite arranged the dates for the Christian celebration of the festivals he had only the pre-Christian data to go upon. Both the dates and data were Egyptian, and these had been continued with the calendar and the festivals more or less correctly. But the early Christians never really knew which was the true Sabbath, the seventh day or the eighth, so they celebrated both. As now demonstrated, according to the record of the mystery-teachers in the astronomical mythology of Egypt the legend of a child that was born of a mother who was a virgin at the time is at least as old as the constellation in the zodiac when the birth-place (in precession) coincided with the sign of Virgo some 15,000 years ago. The virgin, in this category, was the goddess Neith. The child was Horus-Sebek, the great fish of the inundation that typified the deliverer from drought and hunger, and was, in other words, the saviour of the world. Thus, by aid of equinoctial precession, the origin and development of the Christian legend and its festivals can be scientifically traced in the pre-Christian past from the time when the virgin birth of the divine child and the house of birth were in the sign of Virgo, or in Leo for the present purpose, reckoned by the movement in precession.

We shall find the virgin motherhood of Jesus, the divine sonship of Jesus, the miracles of Jesus, the self-sacrifice of Jesus, the humanity of Jesus, the compassion of Jesus, the Sayings of Jesus, the resurrection of Jesus had all been ascribed in earlier ages to Iusa, or Iusu, the son of Iusāas and of Atum-Ra. Thus Egypt was indeed the cradle of Christianity, but not of the current delusion called "historic Christianity." The saying attributed to the Hebrew deity "out of Egypt did I call my son" was true, but in a sense undreamt of by the Christian world. Such was the foundation of the Jesus-legend in the astronomical mythology with Horus of the inundation on his papyrus, or Iusa = Atum-Horus in the zodiac. As we shall see, nothing was added to the Egypto-gnostic "wisdom" by the carnalizers of the Christ in Jerusalem or Rome except the literalization of the mythos and perversion of the eschatology in a fictitious human history.

A religion of the cross was first of all established in the mysteries of Memphis as the cult of Ptah and his son Iu-em-hetep, otherwise Atum-Horus, who passed at Annu into Atum-Ra, the father in spirit, with Iusa, son of Iusāas, as the ever-coming Messianic son.

We have evidence from the pyramid of Medum that from 6,000 to 7,000 years ago the dead in Egypt were buried in a faith which was founded on the mystery of the cross, and rationally founded too, because that cross was a figure of the fourfold foundation on which heaven itself was built. The Tat-cross is a type of the eternal in Tattu. But whether as a fourfold, a fivefold, or a twelvefold support it was a figure of an all-sustaining, all-renewing, all-revivifying power that was re-erected and religiously besought for hope, encouragement, and succour, when the day was at the darkest and things were at the worst in physical nature. The sun apparently was going out. The life of Egypt in the Nile was running low and lower toward the desert drought. The spirit of vegetation died within itself. The rebel powers of evil gathered from all quarters for the annual conflict, led by Apap and the Sebau in one domain, and by Sut and his seventy-two conspirators in another. At this point began the ten mysteries grouped together in the Ritual (ch. 18). The Tat for the time being was overthrown. The deity suffered, as was represented, unto death. The heart of life that bled in every wound was no longer felt to pulsate. The god in matter was inert and breathless. Make ye the word of Osiris truth against his enemies! Raise up the Tat, which portrayed the resurrection of the god; let the mummy-type of the eternal be once more erected as the mainstay and divine support of all. It was thus that the power of salvation through Osiris-Tat was represented in the mysteries. Fundamentally the cross was astronomical. It is a figure of time, as much so in its way as is the clock. It is a measure of time made visible upon the scale and in the circle of the year instead of the hour. A cross with equal arms + denotes the time of equal day and night. Hence it is a figure of the equinox. Another cross † is a figure of time in the winter solstice. It is a modified form of the Tat of Ptah ⊤ on which the four quarters are more obviously portrayed in the four arms of the pedestal. This was re-erected annually in the depths of the solstice where the darkness lasts some sixteen hours and the daylight only eight—the measure of time that is imaged by this Tat-figure of the cross. These two are now known as the Greek and Roman crosses, and under those two names the fact has been lost sight of that the first is a type of time in the equinox, the other a symbol of the winter solstice. The two crosses are scientific figures in the astronomical mythology. They were symbols of mystical significance in the Egyptian eschatology: and they formed the ground plan of the Ka-chambers of King Rahetep and his wife Nefermat in the pyramid of Medum (Petrie, *Medum*).

The tree was first of all a sign of sustenance when the sustainer was the Great Earth Mother; Apt in the Dom Palm, Uati in the papyrus plant, Hathor in the sycamore, or Isis in the persea-tree. On this the type of Ptah was based as the Tat-image of a power that sustained the universe. Osiris-Tat then typified the power that sustained the human soul in death. This was buried with the mummy as a fetish in the coffin, where the dead were seen to lie at rest in the eternal arms. And thus a cultus of the cross was founded many thousand years ago. The Christian doctrine of the crucifixion, with the human victim raised aloft as the sin-offering for all the world, is but a ghastly simulacrum of the primitive meaning: a shadowy phantom of the original substance. The doctrine had its beginning with an idea of *up-bearing*, but not in the moral domain. When the sky was suspended by

Ptah in Amenta the act was symbolized by raising up the Tat-type of stability and support.   This not only sustained the sky of the nether-world, it also imaged the divine backbone of the universe.   The Tat, was a figure of the pole and the four corners, which united in one the "five supports" or fivefold tree of the Egypto-gnostic mystery (*Pistis Sophia*, B. 1, 1–3).   Otherwise stated, it was a symbol of the power that sustained the heavens with the supporting pole and the arms of the four quarters.   This power was personified in Ptah as well as figured in the Tat.   Hence the god is seen *within the type* as Ptah-Sekari or the later Asar-Tat.   Then the type of the eternal is the eternal's own self : the power that sustains the universe in very person who is Ptah in one cult, Osiris in the other.   The superincumbent weight and pressure on the sustaining power is probably indicated by the squelched face and compressed features of the Osiris-Tat (Wilkinson, *Ancient Egyptians*, vol 3, pl. 25).   The sustaining power within the Tat would make the god and the cross to be one as they are in the Osiris Tat.   Deceased arises from the tomb *as the Tat*.   He says "I am Tat, the son of Tat" (Rit., ch. 1), or of the eternal who establishes the soul for eternity in the mystery of Tattu (Rit., ch. 17).   Hence the figure of a god extended crosswise as the sus-tainer of the universe could be equivalent to the cross.   The Hindu figure of Witoba, for example, is portrayed in space as the Crucified without the cross (Moor's *Hindu Pantheon*).   On the other hand, the Swastika is a form of the cross without the crucified.   In the Christian Iconography, as Didron shows, *Christ and the cross are identical*, as were Horus and the Tat.   The cross takes the place of the Tat as symbol of supporting power, and the god as the sustaining force within the Tat may account for the legend of the gospel Jesus being the bearer of the cross on which he was to suffer death.   A resurrec-tion of Osiris from death in the month Choiak is mentioned in several texts (as in the *Pap. Biling. Rhind.*, ii. 4, line 8, ed. Birch, plate 8) without giving the day of the month, but of course rebirth and resurrection in Amenta were identical, and the resurrection is also signified there by the raising of the Tat-pillar or cross.   When the Tat was annually overthrown it was raised again by the uplifting power of the god represented by the Son as the sign of resurrection. Thus the genesis of the legend of the cross, like to that of the Christ, can be traced in Egypt to the cult of Ptah at Memphis, where the religion of the cross originated ; and to Annu or On, where it was continued in the cult of Atum-Ra with Iu-em-hetep as the Egyptian Jesus.   This, as we show, was Iusa the Jew-God brought out of Egypt by the Ius or Aius, or when the name is spelt with the letter J, by the *Jews*.   For 13,000 years has Iu the Egyptian Jew been coming astrono-mically as Iu the Su or Iu-sa, the son of Atum, or rather as Atum mani-festing in the person of the son.   For 13,000 years he has been the bringer of good-will and peace and plenty to the world in accordance with the meanings of his title, Iu-em-hetep.   And as this Jesus is the ever-coming-one who is always figured one foot before the other and best foot foremost in the act of coming, never-hasting never-halting, and as Iu is the Jew we see in this wanderer of eternity with no rest for the sole of his foot through all the cycles of time, the original per-sonification of him who lives in later legend as the "Wandering Jew."

How often has it been confidently declared that the idea of a divine fatherhood was introduced into the world some time after A.D. by an historical Jesus ; whereas it is a matter of scientific demonstration that the doctrine was established in the cult of Ptah, and perfected in the religion of Atum-Ra ; in both of which Iusa or Jesus was the ever-coming son as demonstrator for the eternal in the sphere of time.

The doctrine of a future life, or in modern phrase, the immortality of the soul, was also taught at Memphis many thousand years ago under at least four different figures of the re-arising human spirit. One of these was the Apis called "the second life of Ptah" ; one the Scarabæus termed "the old one who becomes young" ; a third was the Hawk of soul emerging from the mortal mummy ; and a fourth Iu-em-hetep, as the type of an eternal child.

Until the time of Ptah, the Totemic types prevailed in the Egyptian astronomical mythology. There was only the Great Mother, in several characters, with her children, the same as in Totemism. But when the fatherhood was founded in Ptah his predecessors were designated his children. We learn from a hieroglyphic inscription on the temple of Iu-em-hetep at Philæ that he was called "the great one, son of Ptah, the creative god, made by Tanen (a title of Ptah), begotten by him, the god of divine forms, who giveth life to all men." On one line of development he became the father-god as Atum-Ra at Heliopolis ; on the other he was God the son as Atum-Horus or Iu-em-hetep, he who comes with peace or rest.

Christian ignorance notwithstanding, the Gnostic Jesus is the Egyptian Horus who was continued by the various sects of gnostics under both the names of Horus and of Jesus. In the gnostic iconography of the Roman Catacombs child-Horus reappears as the mummy-babe who wears the solar disc. The royal Horus is represented in the cloak of royalty, and the phallic emblem found there witnesses to Jesus being Horus of the resurrection. The resurrection of Osiris, the mummy-god, is reproduced in the Roman Catacombs as the raising of Lazarus. Amongst the numerous types of Horus repeated in Rome as symbols of the alleged "historic" Jesus are "Horus on his papyrus" as the Messianic shoot or natzer ; Horus the branch of endless ages as the vine ; Horus as Ichthus, the fish ; Horus as the bennu or phœnix ; Horus as the dove ; Horus as the eight-rayed star of the Pleroma ; Horus the Scarabæus ; Horus as the child-mummy with the head of Ra ; Horus as the black child, or

Bambino ; Horus, of the triangle (reversed) 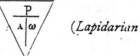 (*Lapidarian*

Gallery of the Vatican, Lundy, p. 92). Horus in his resurrection betwixt the two trees ; Horus attended by the two divine sisters, or two women ; Horus as the lion of the double force ; Horus as Serapis ; these and others were reproduced as Egypto-gnostic by gnostic artists in illustration of Egypto-gnostic tenets, doctrines, and dogmas. The Catacombs of Rome are crowded with the Egypto-gnostic types which had served to Roman, Persian, Greek, and Jew *as evidence for the non-historic* origins of Christianity. To Marcion of Pontus, for example, the epicene Serapis would represent the soul of both sexes which was the non-historical Egypto-gnostic Christ. Horus of the inundation brings the fish and grapes for the Uaka festival ("Called Christ as a Fisherman," Lundy, fig. 54). Horus still issues from the mummy as the young sun-god with the head of Ra, the same as in the Ritual. The soul of Ra still issues from the sepulchre as the phœnix=bennu; and Osiris comes forth at the call of Horus from the tomb. Amsu still rises from betwixt the trees of Nut and Hathor as the good shepherd with the lamb upon his shoulder, wearing the cloak of royalty, and carrying the panpipes in his hand as a figure of the All-one, that is, as Horus of the resurrection. Double Horus, as the child of the virgin and the son of God the Father, is portrayed in both his characters as the heir of Seb, god of earth, and the heir of Ra, the father in heaven. As the heir of Seb he is seated on a throne that is supported on the head of an aged man, who represents the god of earth ("Sarcophagus of Junius Bassus," Lundy, fig. 41). As the heir of Ra he is enthroned in heaven, or on a figure of heaven (Nut), as Horus divinized (Lundy, fig. 42; Didron, figs. 18 and 66). The ox and the ass which appear in the Roman Catacombs with the worshippers of the new-born infant are witnesses for Iusa, and not for an historical Jesus. Iusa in Egypt had been represented by both the ass and the ox, or the short-horned bullock, in the cult of Atum-Ra at On. In a sculptured sarcophagus of the fourth century, the three Magi are offering gifts to the divine infant, or mummy-child. These, according to their caps, are Zoroastrians. They are worshippers, however, of the risen Christ. Only the risen one in this case is Mithra, son of the sun, and not the Jewish Jesus. The story of Jesus riding on two asses, or on an ass and the foal of an ass, in the triumphal procession to Jerusalem also shows that he was one with Iusa, the Egyptian Jesus. It has been suggested that the Gospel narrative was derived from the Greek tradition of Dionysius riding on two asses. But it is of incomparably greater likelihood that it was derived from the Hebrew prophecy being converted into an historical event. Either way, there was one origin for both in the Egyptian mythical representation. As already shown, Iu, the ass in ancient Egypt, was a type of Atum-Ra, and his son Iusa in the Kamite mythos. It was a zootype of the swift-goer where there was no horse, and bearer of the solar god who was Atum in the two characters of the father and the son, the old one and the young one, or, in sign-language, the ass and the foal of the ass, upon which the Messu, or Messiah rode, in coming up to day from Amenta. Iusa is portrayed with asses' ears. Iu is both the ass and the god under one name, and if not portrayed as riding on an ass, or, according to the Märchen, on two asses, he is represented by the ass with the solar disc upon his head, at the sides of which are the two ears of an ass. According to Lefébure "he seems to raise himself by means of a rope" ("Book of Hades," *Records of the Past*, v. 10, 130). Thus, and in no other way, the youthful sun-god rode upon the ass as Iusa or as "Horus with the royal countenance," considered as the son of Ra (*ib.*, p. 131). The twin-lions form another tell-tale type. Ciampini says two lions used to be stationed at the doors of ancient churches and basilicas in Italy, not as mere ornaments, but for some mystical signification (*Vet. Mon. I. C.* 3, p.35). As Egyptian, the type is as old as the Kerefu, which were stationed in the sign of Leo at our point of beginning in the Jesus-legend where Iusa was born as Atum-Horus, the lion-faced, supported by the two lions on the ecliptic, which imaged the double force of the young sun-god coming in the strength and glory of the father, Atum-Ra, whether supported by the two lions or riding on the ass. Thus the two lions supposed to be guarding the doors of the church in Rome were at that time guarding the double-doors of the horizon, through which the solar god came forth at Easter in the equinox.

Naturally it was for mythical not for historical reasons that the child-Christ remained a starrily-bejewelled blackamoor as the typical healer in Rome. Jesus, the divine healer, does not retain the black complexion of Iu-em-hetep in the canonical Gospels, but he does in the Church of Rome when represented by the little black bambino. A jewelled image of the child-Christ as a blackamoor is sacredly preserved at the headquarters of the Franciscan order, and true to its typical character as a symbolical likeness of Iusa the healer, the little black figure is still taken out in state, with its regalia on, to visit the sick, and demonstrate the supposed healing power of this Egyptian Æsculapius thus Christianized. The virgin mother, who was also black, survived in Italy as in Egypt. At Oropa, near Bietta, the Madonna and her child-Christ are not white but black, as they so often were in Italy of old, and as the child is yet conditioned in the little black Jesus of the eternal city. According to local tradition the image of the black bambino was carved at Jerusalem out of the root of a tree from the mount of Olives. This supplies another illustration of Egyptian origin. In the solar mythos the divine babe rises from the emerald tree of dawn. In the Ritual he issues from the Asru-tree (ch. 42). But under one Egyptian type the tree of dawn is the bakhu or olive-tree, the "son of oil," from which the solar light was born. Hence mount Bakhu, the solar birthplace, is the mount of Olives, and the infant born from the tree of dawn was represented by the image carved out of the tree upon mount Olivet. In this, as in unnumbered other instances, the mythos lives obscurely in the legend which is still capable of reconversion. The cult of the child who was black is further illustrated at the festivals of the Bambino in Rome, when sermons are preached from the pulpit by " the mouths of babes and sucklings." There is a little black doll in the hieroglyphics which is a determinative of the word "men" to be concealed. This appears alongside of Atum as variant to the Ankh-symbol of life, and is very suggestive of the little black bambino as a figure of child-Horus in his darkness, or Iu-em-hetep in Amenta. From this stand-point it is possible to see how it came to pass that the Jew-God could have a son born to him with a black complexion, and thus account for the black Jesus that is worshipped in the cult of papal Rome. Surely the profoundest sigh of an ever-warring world went up to heaven in the cult of Iu-em-hetep, who was worshipped as the giver of rest, the Kamite prince of peace. The bringer of peace was the giver of rest to the weary ; the word hetep having both meanings. From the time of the fifth dynasty the Egyptian dead were buried "em-hetep" or "*In pace*" in the great resting-place of Amenta. This giver of rest was the leader of his followers into the kingdom of rest, where they reigned with him in the glory of the father. In one of the sayings of Jesus, or Iu-em-hetep, "Jesus saith" of him who seeks, "Astonished he (the seeker) shall reach the kingdom, and having reached the kingdom he shall rest" ("New Sayings of Jesus"). It is also said in the Gospel according to the Hebrews, "He that wonders shall reach the kingdom, and having reached the kingdom he shall rest." "The promise of Christ (or Jesus) is great and wonderful and rest in the kingdom to come and life eternal" (Clement II., Epis. v. 5). And in the Acts of Thomas it is said that "they who worthily partake of the goods of this world have rest, and in rest shall they reign."

Iu-em-hetep is portrayed as the youthful sage and precocious teacher. He is the "heir of the temple," depicted as the teacher in the temple; the boy of twelve years who wears the skull-cap of wisdom, and sits in the seat of learning. He holds a papyrus on his knee and is in the act of unrolling it for his discourse. This is he who personated the divine Word in human form as the wise and wondrous child of whom the tales of the infancy were told. Hence he was the mythical teacher, and reputed author of the "Sayings" and writer of the Books of Wisdom. But it cannot even be pretended that any historic personage named Jesus, alleged to have been born into the world in the year one, or four, of the present era, could have been the author of "the wisdom of Jesus" in the Apocrypha. But there is the book, and there is the name to be accounted for. In the "New Sayings of Jesus," found at Oxyrhynchus, it is said in the opening paragraph "These are the words (or logoi) which Jesus *the living* spake to . . . and Thomas, and he said unto (them) 'Every one that hearkens to these words shall never taste of death.'" And this is a common formula in the rubrical directions of the Ritual. For example, the 64th chapter is to be recited in order that "the soul of the person may not die a second time" or may not suffer the second death. It is also said of ch. 20, "Let the person say this chapter and he will come forth by day after death, and escape from the fire." These are the words of life that deliver the soul from second death in Amenta. Of chapter 70 it is said, "If this scripture is known upon earth he will come forth by day (from the dead) and walk among the living. His name will be uninjured for ever." Ch. 130 is entitled "a book by which the soul is made to live for ever." By means of ch. 180 the manes takes the form of a *living* soul. In truth one half of the Ritual consists of the magical words of power that save a soul from the dreaded second death; the rest describe the way of salvation together with the transformations and trials which have to be undergone in the course of working it out. Iu-em-hetep was pre-eminently the divine healer, the medicine-man amongst the Egyptian gods. He was the good physician of souls as well as the healer of bodily disease. He was the caster-out of evil demons, the giver of sleep and rest to sufferers in pain. Æsculapius was a Greek version of Iu-em-hetep, "the great son of Ptah." The Greeks called his temple near the city of Memphis "The Æsculapion." "Under the Ptolemies a small temple was built in honour of Iu-em-hetep on the island of Philæ"; and a Greek version of the hieroglyphic inscription was placed over the door by the command of Ptolemy V. (Budge, *Gods of Eg.*, vol. i., p. 23). Iu-em-hetep is not mentioned by name in the " Book of the Dead," but it is said to the deceased in "the Ritual of Embalmment " " thy soul uniteth itself to Iu-em-hetep, whilst thou art in the funeral valley," where he takes the name of Horus as lord of the resurrection.

The cult of Iu-em-hetep was eclipsed or much obscured by the Osirian religion. In fact Iu-em-hetep was but a title of him who was the bringer of peace and good luck, and who was Atum-Horus as the son of Ptah ; hence Iu-em-hetep is far better known as Horus the son of Osiris. Nevertheless, this cult of Iusa the child, the little hero sayer and healer, had a remarkable recrudescence and a considerable increase in Saitic and Greek times. We find that a temple was erected for his worship at Sakkara between the Serapeum and the village of Abusir. This is near enough in time to help in establishing a link betwixt the Egyptian Iusa and the Jesus of the Gospels, who was brought on from Memphis as Iu the Sa or son of Ptah, to Annu as Iu the ever-coming sa or son of Atum-Ra, thence to Alexandria as Iu-em-hetep, and to Greece as Imuthes, or Æsculapius, the god of healing there as he had been in Egypt, and to Rome as Jesus the Egypto-gnostic Christ.

In the transition from the old Egyptian religion to the new cult of Christianity there was no factor of profounder importance than the worship of Serapis. As the Emperor Hadrian relates, in his well-known letter to Servianus, " *those who worship Serapis are likewise Christians ; even those who style themselves the Bishops of Christ are devoted to Serapis.*" The very Patriarch himself (Tiberias, head of the Jewish religion), when he comes to Egypt, is forced by some to adore Serapis, by others to worship Christ. " *There is but one God for them all.*" Clearly this was but a difference in type and title. According to inscriptions at the Serapeum of Memphis, the ancient Egyptian Serapis was born of the Virgin Mother, when she was represented by the sacred heifer—a far earlier type than the mystical *human* Virgin. Serapis was " *the second life of Ptah.*" Hence, as Diodorus says (I. 25), Serapis was a name given to all persons after their death or in their resurrection.

Prehistoric Christianity was founded, as Egyptian, on the resurrection of the human soul from the deaf and dumb, the blind and impotent inertia imaged in death, and its coming forth to day as demonstrated by the reappearance of the eidolon or double of the dead. The Egypto-gnostic Christ only existed in the spirit as a spirit or a god. Their Christ was represented by the superhuman types of the risen mummy ; the eight-rayed star of the pleroma ; the divine hawk ; the mystical dove ; the sacred beetle ; the lion, fish or lamb ; not by the man in an individual form of historic personality. That is why there is no portrait of the man Christ-Jesus. There is no human portrait for the reason that there was no man.

THE JESUS-LEGEND IN ROME.

Before it could be for the first time understood, the story outlined so elusively in the canonical Gospels had to be retold in accordance with the astronomical mythology, and more especially in terms of the Osirian eschatology. The legend was so ancient in Egypt that in the time of Amen-hetep, a Pharaoh of the 18th dynasty, it was humanly applied to his child and to his consort Mut-em-Ua in the character of the divine woman, the mother who, like Neith, was ever-virgin. A passage and a picture from the " Natural Genesis " (vol. ii., p. 398) may be repeated here. The story of the Annunciation, the miraculous conception (or incarnation), the birth and the adoration of the Messianic infant had already been engraved in stone and represented in four consecutive scenes upon the innermost walls of the holy of holies (the Meskhen) in the temple of Luxor (which was built by Amen-hetep III. about 1700 B.C., or some seventeen centuries before the events depicted are commonly supposed to have taken place. In these scenes the maiden queen Mut-em-Ua, the mother of Amen-hetep, her future child, impersonates the virgin-mother, who conceived and brought forth without the fatherhood. The first scene on the left hand shows the god Taht, as divine word or logos, in the act of hailing the virgin queen and announcing to her that she is to give birth to the coming son. (That is, to bring forth the royal Repa in the character of Horus or Aten, the divine heir.) In the second scene the ram-headed god Kneph, in conjunction with Hathor, gives life to her. This is the Holy Ghost or spirit that causes conception, Neph being the spirit by nature and by name. Impregnation and conception are apparent in the virgin's fuller form. Next, the mother is seated on the midwife's stool, and the child is supported in the hands of one of the nurses. The fourth scene is that of the Adoration. Here the infant is enthroned,

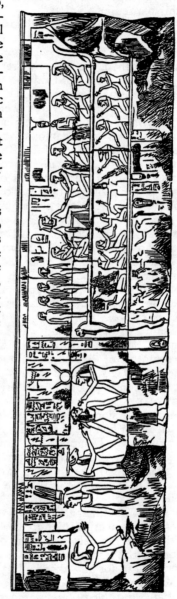

The Annunciation, Conception, Birth, and Adoration of the Child.

receiving homage from the gods and gifts from men. Behind the deity, who represents the holy spirit, on the right three men are kneeling offering gifts with the right hand, and life with the left. The child thus announced, incarnated, born and worshipped was the

Pharaonic representative of the Aten-sun or child-Christ of the Aten-cult, the miraculous conception of the ever-virgin mother imaged by Mut-em-Ua. (The scenes were copied by Sharpe from the temple at Luxor.) Thus the divine drama was represented humanly by the royal lady who personated the mother of God, with her child in this particular religion.

And here a dogma of "historic personality" may be seen in the germ. Indeed, when the Pharaoh first assumed the vesture of divinity and a doctrine of historic personality for the Messiah could be and was established, Ra was the representative of God the Father and the Repa was a type of God the Son, as heir-apparent for the eternal. The father was the ever-living and the son the ever-coming one. These, in the cult of Annu, were Atum-Ra the father, and Iusa, the Egyptian Jesus, the coming son. The eternal existence of the father was thus demonstrated by the ever-coming of the son. These divine characters of the Ra and Repa, so to say, had become historical in Usertsen First according to a record of the twelfth dynasty. In this the king says of his God, the double Har-makhu, "I am a king of his own making, a monarch long-living, *not by the Father*. He exalted me as lord of both parts ; as an infant not yet gone forth ; as a youth not yet come from my mother's womb." This was in the character of the unbegotten Horus, the Virgin's child, who had no father (*Records*, vol. 12, pp. 53-4), and who as Har-makhu was earlier than God the Father, Ra. We learn from a still older document that the Son of God may be said to have become historical in Egypt early in the fifth dynasty ; that is, as the *Son of Ra*. The earlier Pharaohs were not the sons of Ra, they were Horus-kings. The "Son of Ra" then gave historic personality to the god who was first imaged in the human form of Atum-Iu. Thenceforth the Repa, or heir-apparent, was the representative of that ever-coming son who was the child of Iusāas in the cult of Annu, and who was, in fact, the Egyptian Jesus or Iusa, the coming son in historic personality as the royal representative of Ra.

Another version of the ancient legend that was at length converted into Christian history has recently been discovered in Egypt. This was written in Demotic, but however late the copy, the internal evidence shows that it is an Egyptian folk-tale containing matter of the indefinitely more ancient mythos. That is the all-important point. The story is told of one Si-Osiris, the son of Khamuas, a famous high priest of Ptah at Memphis who was head of the hierarchy of his time, about 1250 B.C. The tale of Khamuas, so far as it goes, is a perfect parallel to the story of the marvellous child that is told in the Gospels, canonical or apocryphal, which contain some portions of the mythos reduced to the status of the Märchen. There was one origin for all—that is, Egyptian. The mythos is the parent of the Märchen, and the unity of the Märchen is traceable to the Egyptian mythology and eschatology—there, and nowhere else. It is the story that had been dramatized and narrated by the Egyptians during many thousand years in the cult of Ptah-Sekari at Memphis ; of Aten and of Atum-Iu at Annu, and of Osiris in Egypt generally. Only minds completely crazed or fatally confused by the current Christomania would suppose that the details of the story, which is as old at least as the cult of Ptah in Memphis, were derived from the "historic" version that was canonized at last as Christian. The Ritual is a permanent reply to all such false assumptions. At least the "Book of the Dead" is not a forgery of post-Christian gnostics.

The folk-tale here is told of Si-Osiris, son of Setme-Khamuas, who was incarnated as the human representative of Horus the divine. It is said of Horus, son of Pa-neshe, "*he being in the shape of Si-Osiris* made an effort of written magic against the man of Ethiopia." Moreover, this Horus comes up from Amenta on purpose to contend against the black art of Hor, son of the negress, and in doing this assumes the shape of the human Si-Osiris. As the translator remarks, "the end of the story shows that Si-Osiris is really Horus, son of Pa-neshe, who had obtained leave from Osiris to revisit the earth."

Setme-Khamuas, the son of Pharaoh Mer-ma-ra (King Rameses II.), took to wife his sister Meh-wesekht, whom he loved devoutly, but they had no child, and their hearts were grieved because of it. The childless wife is spoken with one night, by superhuman visitants, in a dream. They tell her (or words are spoken to the effect) that she shall conceive and bear a child. Khamuas, her husband, is also informed in a dream that his consort, who is called his sister, just as Isis is the sister of Osiris, has conceived and will bear a son. "The child that will be born, he (shall be named) Si-Osiris (Osiris' son); many are the marvels that he shall do in the land of Egypt" (Griffith, *Stories*, p. 43). Meh-wesekht is told that she will find a melon-vine, which shall be to her for medicine, and she is to give of it to Khamuas. Then "she lay down by her husband and she conceived seed of him" (*Stories*, p. 43).

In this account of conception the melon-plant, its gourd or its flower, takes the place of the papyrus, lotus or lily presented to Isis the virgin and to Mary. This is referred to after his birth by the child Si-Horus, who, in speaking of his coming forth, says, "I grew as that melon-vine, with the intent of returning to the body again that I might be born into the world" for a purpose variously described in the different texts. In this he becomes incarnate to combat the power and influence of evil in the form of black magic (*Stories*, pp. 43–65). Si-Osiris is really Horus, the son of Osiris in Amenta. This he leaves to visit earth and become the son of Meh-wesekht, the sister and consort of Khamuas. He says, "I prayed before Osiris in Amenta to let me come forth to the world again. It was commanded before to let me forth into the world. I awoke; I flew right up, to find Setme, the son of Pharaoh, upon the Gebel of On and the Gebel of Memphis, the place of burial in the desert." Si-Osiris, like Jesus in the "history," has the power of suddenly becoming invisible; as it is said, "Si-Osiris passed away as a shade or spirit out from the land of Pharaoh and Setme, his father, nor did they see him" (*Stories*, p. 65). Like the young Jesus in the Gospel (Luke ii. 40), the child grew and waxed strong. The exact words are, "The child grew big; he waxed strong; he was sent to the school. He rivalled the scribe that had been appointed to teach him." "The child, son of Osiris, began to speak with the scribes of the House of Life (in the temple of Ptah); all who heard him were lost in wonder at him" (*Stories*, p. 44). "Now when the royal Si-Osiris had attained the age of twelve years it came to pass that there was no good scribe (or learned man) that rivalled him in Memphis in reading or in writing that compels"; that is, in uttering the Ur-hekau or mystical words of great magical power. As the translator remarks, it is curious to find that linguistically the tale is somewhat closely related to the new Egyptian of the twelfth century B.C.; that is, to the time of Khamuas, one of the chief characters, as the date of the original document.

But not only in Egypt was the divine hero, the Prince of Eternity, represented by the royal child born heir-apparent to the throne. It was the same in Rome. For instance, the birthday of Augustus Cæsar was hailed in Rome as that of the Messianic Prince of Peace. In a well-preserved Greek inscription of eighty-four lines, in which an ancient account is given of the introduction of the Julian calendar on the birthday of the Emperor Cæsar Augustus, September 23rd, it is written :—

"On this day [*i.e.*, the birthday of Augustus] *the world has been given a different aspect*. It *would have been doomed to destruction* if a great good fortune common to all men had not appeared *in him who was born on this day*. He judges aright who sees in this birthday the beginning of life and of all living powers for himself. Now at last the times are passed when man must regret that he has been born. From no other day does the individual and all humanity receive so much good as from this day, which has brought happiness to all. It is impossible to find words of thanksgiving sufficient for the great blessings which this day has brought. *That Providence which presides over the destinies of all living creatures has fitted this man for the salvation of humanity with such gifts that he has been sent to us and to coming generations as a saviour. He will put an end to all strife and will restore all things gloriously.* In his appearance, all the hopes of the ancestors have been fulfilled. He has not only surpassed all former benefactors of mankind, but *it is impossible that a greater than he should ever come. The birthday of this god* [*i.e.*, *Augustus*] *has brought out the good news of great joy based upon him. From his birth a new era must begin.*"

The Egyptian Repa or the Roman Cæsar was enacting on this earth, approximately, the character assigned to the son of God in the Egypto-gnostic mysteries. The world would have been doomed to destruction but for the rebirth in time of the Messu or Messiah, the Repa or divine heir, who represented the eternal as the child, the ever-coming prince of peace, who is also imaged as the living link which connects and unites the past and future in the present, by means of him who became the representative of the deity on earth, whether in Egypt or in Rome, in India or Japan (Rit., ch. 42, 4, 5). But the man whose coming changed the world, and saved it by renewal, was mythical, and his advent was æonian from age to age, under whatsoever name. Thus, in Rome the Emperor Augustus personalized the coming prince of peace in an historical character.

The repetition of this as Christian legend in the Gospels is no mere replica of "heathen" sentiments, images, types, and phrases. It is a reproduction of the Egyptian astronomical mythology and eschatology in the disguise of a pretended history.

In Egypt the Pharaoh and his son for ages had represented Ra and the Repa, the divine heir-apparent or the prince. As Egyptian the fatherhood and sonship of the one god were founded on the Pharaoh and the heir-apparent, the Ra and Repa, who constituted the King that never died. The son of God was born as manifester for the eternal, and the ruler as Pharaoh, emperor or king, was the earthly representative of the God with whose divinity the new historical ruler was invested as the Anointed, the Repa, the Prince, the Cæsar, the Mikado, the Cyrus, or the Christ. This birth of the eternal in time was astronomical. But it was humanized for the birthday of Amen-hetep in Egypt, for Alexander in Greece, and for Cæsar-Augustus in Rome before the era that was designated Christian. The virgin-mother in mythology, and there never was any other, is she who made her proclamation in the Temple of Neith at Sais that she proceeded from herself and bore the child without her peplum being lifted by the male. The myth reflects the matriarchate from a time when the fatherhood was not yet individualized. The mother with child, the great or *enceinte* mother, is at the head of the Kamite Pantheon as the mother of life and a figure of fecundity. This type of the mother and child retains its position in the Christian iconography when the child Jesus, like Kheper, is exhibited in the Virgin's womb surrounded by the seven spirits as doves (Didron). The mother with her child *in utero* or in her arms was indefinitely earlier than the typical father and son whose worshippers were opposed to the more primitive representation of nature. Horus, at first, is the child of Isis only, with Seb as putative or foster-father, who was not the begetter.

Thus the mother might remain a virgin. Horus, the child, was an image of the god, made flesh in human guise. He is the mortal Horus, very imperfect, sometimes sightless, at others a cripple, but divine ; the divine victim in a human shape, which was now the manifesting mask of the deity or superhuman power, instead of the totemic zootype. And naturally the divine child thus humanly featured involved the mother of the god in a human effigy. The child assigned to the earth-father Seb = Joseph is Horus up to twelve years of age, and then he passes from the mortal sphere.

A virgin mother in the ancient wisdom is she who was fecundated by her own child as bull of the mother in the moon, in the earth, or in other phenomena that were at first entirely non-human. But the doctrine survived when the divinized mother and her child were rendered anthropomorphically. Thus the gnostic Jesus in the *Pistis Sophia* says, " I found Mary, who is called my mother, after the material body ; I implanted in her the first power which I had received from the hands of Barbêlô, and I planted in her the power which I had received from the hands of the great, the good Sabaoth " (Mead, B. I., 13). That is in the character of the mythical child who fecundates his own mother. And here the overshadowing of Mary by " the power of the Most High " (Luke i. 35) is suggestive of another overshadowing of the Virgin who conceives. This is described in the magic papyrus (*Records of the Past*, vol. 10, p. 141) as a " concealment " of the mother in the process of generation.

" On Horror's head horrors accumulate " in manufacturing history from the mythos. Horus, the fatherless, was the fecundator of his own virgin mother, but neither as the human Horus nor the divine

Horus was it pretended that he was other than the typical figure in a mystery, or that the doctrine came the human way. Jesus in the same character, called the Mamzer ממזר by the Jews, is the same fatherless fecundator of the virgin mother when the two are Jew and Jewess. To the truly religious sense this is a most profane parody of the sacred Osirian drama. Thus the fragments of a great complex in dogma and doctrine were collected together in relation to the conception of the Messianic child. First, the virgin mother was the insufflator of a soul. Secondly, there is a begettal in which the offspring fecundates the mother—this of course is in the mythical representation. Thirdly, according to Matthew, the divine child was *either* conceived or begotten of the Holy Ghost.

It is the type that tells so many secrets of the non-historical beginnings : and nothing has been bottomed, nothing could be fundamentally explained with the Egypto-gnostic wisdom still unknown. The dove that laid the egg is pre-eminent as a type in the conception and the birth of Jesus. At first the insufflating spirit of life, whether called holy or not, was female. This was demonstrated by the Mother-nature. In the Gospels the Holy Spirit as female suffices for the miraculous conception of the child-Jesus who is generated without a father. But *Pistis Sophia* witnesses that the gnostic Jesus proceeded from the father in the likeness of a dove. And that the mystery of all mysteries, the first and final mystery, was this of the dove, considered to be the bird of God the Father. By this means the Holy Spirit is portrayed as male, whereas according to the secret wisdom the dove had been a female type of spirit from the first. The gnosis was so ancient as Egyptian that the dove had been succeeded by the hawk as the bird of Ra, the Holy Spirit as male. The hawk was now the symbol of the father and the son, that is, of Ra and Horus. Whereas the dove as mother-bird was primary. The female nature of the mystic dove is also shown by its co-type the pigeon, still employed in modern slang as a survival of sign-language. Thus the earliest human soul was insufflated by the mother, and the mother divinized was represented by the Dove, the bird of soul when soul was first attributed to female source. Lastly, the same bird was given to the Holy Spirit as God the Father, and as a type of the Trinity consisting of Father, Son and Holy Spirit, with the mother veiled and hidden by the dove. It may be noted in passing that the dove was not necessarily a type of sensual desire although it became associated with Venus in Greece. There was nothing licentious in Hathor or Iusāas. The earliest Venus was a personification of the *enceinte* mother, not a goddess Lubricity provocative of lust, but in all simplicity and seriousness a type of tenderest maternity. The dove had been the bird of Hathor as the insufflator of a soul of breath. In this character it is portrayed with brooding wings extended on the bosom of the mummy as quickener of the spirit for a future life. On the tomb of Rameses IX. the dove appears in place of the hawk as a co-type of Horus at the prow of the solar boat. Also, in a statuette of the 19th dynasty there is a human-headed dove which takes the place of the hawk as a zootype of the soul. It is seen hovering over the bosom of a mummy. The divine Horus rises again in the form of a dove, as well as in the shape of a hawk. " *I am the*

Dove: I am the Dove," exclaims the risen spirit as he soars up from Amenta, where the egg of his future being was hatched by the divine incubator (Rit., 86, 1). Here the bird of Hathor is also the bird of Ra, and thus the dove became the bird of the Holy Spirit, female in the mother, and male in the divine child Horus, and finally in the Father. In the Councils of Nice and Constantinople, the fathers condemned Xenora, who derided the imaging of the Holy Spirit by the dove. And to show how the type will persist, in *The Catholic Layman* for July 17th, 1856, there is a Papal picture of the Christian Godhead that was extant in that same year, as the trinity of the Father, Son and Holy Spirit. In this, God the Father and God the Son are represented as a man with two heads, one body and two arms. One of the heads is like the ordinary pictures of Jesus, or Serapis, the other is the head of an *old man* surmounted by a triangle. Out of the middle of this figure is proceeding the Holy Ghost in the form of a dove (*Catholic Layman*, July 17th, 1856).

The dove, then, as an emblem of the Holy Spirit, also shows the gnostic nature of the beginnings in the Gospels termed Canonical. " Now the birth of the Christ was on this wise. When his Mother Mary had been betrothed to Joseph, before they came together she was found with child of the Holy Ghost," or, as rendered in sign-language, with the dove as emblem of the Holy Spirit. Hence, in the Iconography, child-Jesus is represented in the Virgin's arms or womb, surrounded by the seven doves as symbols of the Holy Spirit (Didron, fig. 124).

We might say that the dove of Hathor-Iusāas came to Rome on board the papyrus-boat, in which the mother Isis crossed the swamps to save her little one from the pursuing dragon (Plutarch, *Of Isis and Osiris*, 18). For the papyrus-boat is obviously the bark of Peter in the Roman Catacombs (Lundy, *Mont., Christ*, fig. 139). Iusāas, the mother of Iusa = Iusu, the Egyptian Jesus, was a form of Hathor-Meri, and was brought on in the cult of Rome as Mary, the mystical dove and mother of Iusu, now believed to have become historical. A dovecote was the dwelling where she brought him forth in Rome. As Cyprien Robert says, " The first basilicas, placed generally upon eminences, were called *domus columbæ*, dwellings of the dove, that is, the Holy Ghost" (Didron, 1, 439, Eng. tr.).

Now Atum was the holy spirit in the eschatology of Annu; the first who ever did attain that status in theology. His consort was Iusāas, who, in the character of Hathor, was the female holy spirit, as the dove. Their child was Iusa, the Egyptian Jesus. This was he who says, on rising from Amenta as a spirit, " I am the dove, I am the dove" (The " Menat." Rit., ch. 86). Thus, the gnostic mystery of the dove is traceable to Atum as the holy spirit, and to Iusāas-Hathor as the Mother of the Coming Son (Iusa), he who emanated from them as the dove. This mode of incarnation is followed by a second descent of the holy spirit in the baptism of Jesus. " Lo, the heavens were opened unto him, and he saw the Spirit of God descending as a dove, and coming upon him; and lo, a voice out of the heavens saying, This is my beloved son in whom I am well pleased." Thus, the child that was conceived of the virgin in the first descent of the spirit is authenticated as son of the father at the time of the second descent of the holy spirit as the dove. And this, as Egyptian, is the doctrine of the dual Horus, who was born of Isis, the virgin, and afterwards begotten in spirit as the beloved son of Ra, the holy spirit. Jesus when *mothered* by the virgin-dove, whether at On or Bethlehem, is Iusa the coming child of Hathor-Iusāas; and Jesus when authenticated by the bird from heaven is Iusa as the son of Atum-Ra, the holy spirit who is *fathered* by the dove. This fatherhood of Jesus in his baptism is vouched for by the writers of the canonical Gospels. And in "the Gospel according to the Hebrews," Jesus speaks of His "Mother, the Holy Ghost." He says, "the Holy Spirit, my mother, took me and bore me away to the great mountain, called Thabor." Which can be understood as a saying of Iusa, the Egyptian Jesus.

Iusa of Annu went to Rome as Ichthon of Annu. Jesus went to Rome as Ichthus, the fish. The black Iusa went to Rome as the Bambino. He went to Rome as the ass-headed Iu, and also is the dove as bird of resurrection in the Catacombs. He is found there in the several characters of Horus, Serapis, Mithras, and under various types. But nowhere is the "historic" personage discoverable, living or dead, in subterranean Rome.

According to the Osirian eschatology in the Ritual, Horus, the son of God, was with his father in heaven before he descended to our earth as the bringer of peace and goodwill (hetep) to men. In coming forth from heaven, he is said to reveal himself by disrobing himself to present himself to the earth. He issues forth as Horus, the son of Isis, the child of the Virgin Mother, saying, "I am Unbu." That is, "I am the Branch." He also describes himself as the mortal Horus who was born blind and dumb in "the abode of occultation," En-arar-ef (Rit., ch. 71). Jesus is born at Bethlehem, in the house of bread. Horus comes forth in Annu, the place of bread. The vesture of Horus is girt on him by Tait, the goddess of food. This answers to the swaddling-clothes in which the child was wrapped when the mother laid him in a manger. Offerings are made to the child who is received by the worshippers with "bendings of the head in Annu" (Rit., ch. 82). The reason why the divine child should be born in a manger is not because there was lack of room in the inn, but because the child had been previously born as a lamb or a calf before the type was humanized, and when the crib, or manger, was the earliest cradle of the little one. The birth of the babe in a manger was anciently exhibited in Egypt, and the origin is traceable to-day. The mother can be identified with the cattle-shed and the manger. For instance, Hathor was the hat or hut; Nephthys is the house; Isis, the seat; the old first mother Apt was the crib; and Apt the crib is also the manger which was a type of the cattle-shed when her offspring was a calf. The Apt was the birthplace when this was the womb of Apt, the water-cow. The name was then applied to the manger, the crib, the hold of a vessel, and to the city of Apt, or Thebes, in Egypt, which is the city of the manger by name. The child born in a manger or Apt=crib is the wise way of showing a continuity of type which survived in Egypt down to Ptolemaic times. The child was incarnated to live and eat the bread of Seb=Joseph beneath the tree of Hathor—one of whose names is Meri. In various legends, the child was brought forth beneath the tree, and in our ancient carols the tree, as a cherry-tree, bows down for Mary to eat of its fruit at the command of the child, who is yet in the mother's womb. The oblations offered in Tattu and the adorations made in Annu are the same as in the story of the Magi, who bring their presents and bow down before the babe in Bethlehem. This rebirth is referred to in the tale of Sanehat: "Thou shalt see thyself come to the blessed state, they shall give thee the bandages from the hand of Tait, the night of applying the oil of embalming" (*Egyptian Tales*, p. 114, Petrie); where the making of the Karast-mummy is a type of the birth of the Christ or Anointed. Horus comes to record the words of God the father with his mouth; the same mouth that draws to it the spouse of Seb as wet-nurse for the child. Like Jesus in the Christology of John, he is the Word made flesh; and the spouse of Seb is the prototype of Mary, the spouse of Joseph, who is portrayed as the suckler of Jesus in the Christian version of the legend. At his coming there are cries of adoration in Suten-Khen, the royal birthplace, and of exultation in An-arar-ef, the city of the blind. The whole cycle of the gods is filled with satisfaction at seeing Horus inherit his throne to rule over the earth. There are bendings in Annu where the different generations of the Rekhet, the Pait, and the Hamemmat bow down before him. The evil Sut is filled with consternation at what has taken place. This reception of the child in Annu, the house of bread, as a celestial locality, is the prototype of the jubilation heard in Bethlehem. When "Suddenly there was with the angel a multitude of the heavenly host praising God" (Luke ii. 13). These are the acclamations uttered in Annu, on the divine babe making his appearance there (Rit., ch. 125), and being declared the heir of Seb, the god of earth, from whom he issued in the character of Iusa, the child of Iusāas. At his advent Horus says the gods come to him with their acclamation, and the female deities with jubilation, when they see him. Horus, in the litany of Ra, is called the son of Ra, proceeding from Tum. "He has placed your offerings before you; he accords you the favour of receiving your portion as his father Ra commanded. He is his darling. He is his descendant upon the earth." "Show the way to his spirit. Show him his dwelling in the midst of the earth." What we may term the human history of Horus is passed in the earth of Seb, his foster-father on earth, whose bread he eats, and in whose house he dwells with Isis, the virgin mother. There is neither date nor history of Horus betwixt the age of twelve and thirty years. The child-Horus quits the house of Seb and the virgin to reappear in the house of his father Osiris in the earth of eternity. This will explain why the youthful Jesus leaves his mother and his earthly father Joseph to be about his heavenly father's business when he is twelve years of age. Also, this fact in the mythical representation will account for there being no further mention of Joseph in the Gospels after the journey to Jerusalem (Luke ii. 43, 50). Seb ceases to be the foster-father and protector of Horus, who disappears from the earth of time (or Seb) to reappear in the earth of eternity.

The infant Horus was suckled by Isis in solitude. She is said to have nursed him in secret. No one knew the hiding-place, but it was somewhere in the marshes of Amenta, the lower Egypt of the mythos. As an earthly locality, the place where Isis hid herself to suckle her child was identified in the marshes of the Delta. This part of the programme is fulfilled in the Gospel according to Matthew, and there only, by the flight into Egypt. So soon as the babe was born, " an angel of the Lord appeared to Joseph in a dream, saying, Arise and take the young child and his mother, and flee into Egypt." And the child was there until the death of Herod, "that it might be fulfilled which was spoken by the Lord, through the prophet, saying, Out of Egypt did I call my son" (Matt. ii. 13, 16). The child of the mother had to be taken down into Egypt in order that the Son of God might be brought up out of it, and for the mythos to be fulfilled as biblical history.

At the birth of Horus the life of the young child was sought by the evil Sut. The mother was warned of the danger by Taht, the lunar god, called the great one. He says to her, " Come, thou goddess Isis, hide thyself with thy child"; and he tells her it is well to be obedient. She is to take the child down into the marshes of lower Egypt, called Kheb, or Khebt. There, says Taht, "these things will happen : his limbs will grow ; he will wax entirely strong ; he will attain the dignity of prince of the double earth, and sit (or rest) upon the throne of his father." Then the child and mother make their way to the papyrus-swamps. It is said that the plants were so secret that no enemy could enter there. " Sut could not penetrate this region, or go about in Kheb." Nevertheless the child was bitten by the reptile, as the story is rendered in the sorrows of Isis, the pre-Christian *mater dolorosa* (Budge, *The Gods of the Egyptians*, vol. ii., ch. 14). " Horus in Kheb" (Egypt) was a title of the divine child. Kheb was in the north of Egypt, and it was there that Horus passed his early days, and was reared in secret by his mother Isis. Horus lands upon the earth of Seb at eventide. He sits upon the seat of Ra, which is on the western horizon, and receives the offerings upon the altars. He says, " I drink the sacred liquor each evening, in the form of the lord of all creatures" (Rit., ch. 79). The descent of Horus, as a child, to earth was daily or yearly according to the mythos. Every night the sinking sun was received by the mother in the breeding-place, or Meskhen, of the western mount, where she prepared him (or he her) for his new birth daily in the East. The point at which the god descends to earth at evening is well portrayed in the oblong zodiac of Denderah. In this the child-Horus is seated *on the mount* of the western equinox in the sign of the Scales. The sign of the Scales, Makhu, was once the sign of the autumn equinox, and at that point child-Horus touches earth for his descent from heaven. In this sign the child is portrayed sitting on the mount in the disc of the full moon. As seen by night, the mount of earth, or the horizon, is the mount of the ecliptic, the meeting-point of earth and heaven. The full moon is the mother who is Virgo in the previous sign, and in the sign of the Scales she has brought forth the child.

In the Gospel of pseudo-James (ch. 22) it is John, the child of Elizabeth, who is sought for by Herod. " And Elizabeth groaned and said with a loud voice, Mount of God, receive a mother with her child. And suddenly the mountain was divided, and received them. And light shone through to them." It is *the same story* of the mother and child when applied to the infant John instead of Jesus.

The opening of the mount is in the equinox, and it is there the pursued ones attain safety by entering the earth to escape from Apap, the devouring dragon. Seb is the Egyptian Joseph, as consort of Isis, the earth-mother and foster-father of the child; and at this point in the western equinox where Horus enters the earth or the earth-life, Seb, as god of earth, takes charge of the child and mother to convoy them on the way to the lower Egypt of Amenta.

Going down into Kheb or lower Egypt, as rendered in the Ritual, is descending to the secret earth of Amenta, where the mother hid her infant in the marshes, when they were pursued by Sut, otherwise the crocodile. Now it is related in the Gospel of pseudo-Matthew (ch. 18), that when Joseph and Mary were on their way to Egypt with the child-Jesus they came to a certain cave, and " Behold there suddenly came out of the cave many dragons, seeing which the youths cried out with excessive fear. Then Jesus descending from the mother's lap stood on his feet before the dragons, and they adored Jesus." In this scene, Jesus saves his father and mother from the dragons, which obey him; and the dragons we may consider to be crocodiles in accordance with Hebrew use and wont. In the Ritual, there is a chapter on repulsing the crocodiles in which Horus saves his father from the four crocodiles (these are eight in the Turin text of the Ritual). " I am the one," he says, " who saves the great one from the four crocodiles. I am the one who delivers his father from them." " I am the one who cannot be overthrown by the principles and powers of evil " (Rit., ch. 32), or, as it is otherwise rendered by Renouf: " O son who conversest with thy father, do thou protect this great one from these four crocodiles. I know them by their names and their way of living, and it is I who protect his own father from them." He orders the crocodiles to go back, one by one, to their quarters, and they obey him with docility. Ra has given him possession of lower Egypt, in which the living are destroyed, and the crocodiles or dragons of the waters do not triumph over him (ch. 32, 9). Coming, as Horus, to make ready the horizon, he repulses the crocodiles of darkness (ch. 136, 8, 9). The dragons of a " certain cave " that is found upon the way to Egypt are an Egypto-gnostic version of the crocodiles of Amenta in the Ritual. Thus, the animals in attendance on the child-Jesus in the apocryphal Gospels are witnesses for the child-Horus. Horus, as the youthful sun-god on the horizon, is accompanied by the two lions, Shu and Tefnut. He is attended by the two lions. He is lighted in their recesses by the two lions (ch. 3, 1, 2). The power of two lions is represented by the head-dress of Horus. He is strengthened by the double force of the two lions. He arrives each day in the dwelling of the two lions (ch. 78, 20–22), with the two lions who are his protectors. It is also said of the Osiris, " He is furnished with two lions " (ch. 144).

The lions are likewise in attendance upon Jesus in the Gospels of the Infancy. The lions adored him, and kept him company in the desert. They walked along with the child; bowed their heads before him, and showed subjection by wagging their tails (Gospel of pseudo-Matthew, chs. 19 and 35).

The "apocryphal" Gospels are not a mere collection of "foolish traditions" or fables forged or invented to supply an account of that

period in "our Lord's" history, respecting which the accepted
Gospels are almost silent. They are *disjecta membra* of the original
matter; the mythos reduced to the state of Märchen; the story of
the miraculous child told as a folk-tale which was at last repeated as
a history in the Gospels with matter like the above omitted because
it was too naturally incredible, and could not be utilized by the most
desperate expedient of miracle.

When, or where, the mythos was no longer interpreted astronomically, from lapse of the necessary knowledge, the folk-tales and
legendary lore began to take the place of the ancient wisdom that
was scientifically verifiable. Celestial localities were made geographical. The descent of the little sun in the lower hemisphere is
described as the journey of the child-Horus into lower Egypt, accompanied by the Virgin Mother and Seb, or Joseph, the earthly father.
It is observable that in an Egyptian planisphere, according to Kircher,
the god Seb is figured, on a large scale, in the Decans of Scorpio,
with the symbolic goose of earth upon his head. This, at one time,
marked the western equinox; the point at which the earth of Seb, or
the mountain, opened to protect the mother and child, when they
sought refuge from the dragon, the scorpion, or serpent that stung
the infant on the way to Egypt in the nether earth, and where " earth
helped the woman " (Rev. xii. 16) in her flight.

The origin of the " Holy Family " can be traced to this initial point
of the journey down to Egypt. The moon at full was the mother
with the child who rode upon the ass attended by the old man Seb.
This was the " woman clothed with the sun and the moon under her
feet, and upon her head a crown of twelve stars," who was persecuted
by the crocodile of darkness. At the autumn equinox the Apap-
reptile reared its loathly form from out the abyss to pursue the
mother and destroy her Babe. But the earth opened and helped the
woman, or Seb protected her as foster-father to the child of light.
According to the astronomical mythos, the Pool of Putrata, or lake
of darkness, lay upon the western side of the mount. This was the
habitat and lair of the dragon, " eternal devourer is its name " (ch. 17,
40, 44). Here the reptile lurks and watches the ' " bight of Amenta "
for its prey. With wide-open jaws of the crocodile it swallows the
sinking stars (in the mythos), and the souls that fall into darkness
(in the eschatology). Above all, the dragon of darkness lies in wait
for the virgin mother and her forthcoming child, who is the saviour
of vegetation and preserver of the light. The journey into Egypt
can be followed a little further in the Gospels of the Infancy. The
Arabic Gospel says the mother and child remained three years in
Egypt, and the Lord Jesus wrought very many miracles in Egypt,
which are not found written either in the Gospel of the Infancy or
in the perfect Gospel (Cowper, H. B., *The Apocryphal Gospels*,
p. 191). The child-Jesus in Egypt is the child-Horus in Egypt,
and the traditions of Horus have been assigned to an "historic"
Jesus. "These," as Wiedeman puts the cart before the horse, "have
affected a series of Coptic texts which, in making use of the well-
known apocryphal account of Christ's journey through Egypt as a
child, describe the triumphal march of the Saviour along the valley
of the Nile, and relate how he drove his foes from place to place,

destroying them as he went" (*Religion of the Ancient Egyptians*, p. 77, Eng. tr.).

According to the Gospel of pseudo-Matthew, the Holy family, fleeing from the murderer Herod, came into the borders of Hermopolis and "entered into a certain city of Egypt which is called Sotinen." Nothing has been made of this statement geographically. But Sotinen evidently represents the Sutenhen (earlier Suten-Khen) of the " Book of the Dead" (ch. 17). This is a celestial locality of great importance to the legend of Horus in Kheb. In "the childhood of Jesus, according to Thomas," one year is thus accounted for. "Now when they had come into Egypt they found a lodging in the house of a certain widow, and they lodged one year in the same place" (ch. i.). It may be remembered that in one of her characters Isis is the widow of the dead Osiris. In a small papyrus now at the Louvre there is an incantation against the evil serpent that stung the infant, in which the goddess Isis is the speaker. She says, "I am Isis the widow, broken with sorrow" (Deveria, *Catalogue des Manuscrits Eg. du Louvre*). Isis is the original widow who has an only son, and it is she who seeks the lost Osiris, and brings him to rebirth as Horus, her child, in the house of the widow. In the Kamite version of the journey into Egypt the *Herrut*-reptile takes the place of Herod, and the child-Horus is bitten by the serpent, though not stung to death. This event occurred when Isis was about to go down into Egypt for the safety of her child. M. Revillout (in 1881) described a Demotic papyrus at Leyden, which gives an account of the attack made on Horus by the serpent. This text corroborates the statement of Plutarch and Aristides (*Apology*, par. 12) that the scene of the serpent's attack was in Syria. It occurred when Isis was about to go down into Egypt, for Horus, the divine heir, to take possession of his father's kingdom. When Isis and the child were setting out, Horus began to weep and cry because the serpent had stung him (*Proceedings of the Society of Biblical Archy.*, May, 1892, p. 372). Isis protects her child and heals his wound. This is the journey of the virgin mother from Syria down into Egypt, as represented in the mythos. The massacre of the Innocents is a common legend. In the Jewish traditions there is a massacre of the little ones at the time of Moses' birth, in which the Pharaoh plays the part of the monster Herod. So universal was this murder that no distinction was made betwixt the children of the Egyptians and the Jews. On the day that Moses was born the astrologers told Pharaoh they had seen in the stars that the deliverer of the Jews had been born that day, but they could not tell whether his parents were Egyptian or Jewish. Therefore Pharaoh kills not only all the Jewish boys born that day, but also all the Egyptians (for authorities see *Proceedings of the Society of Biblical Archæology*, December 4, 1888). It is the old, old story of the child that was born to be king in defiance of all obstacles.

The origin of the innocents that were massacred by the monster Herod can be traced in accordance with the ancient wisdom. A primitive soul of life was derived from the elements; the soul of Shu from wind or air; the soul of Seb from the earth; the soul of Horus, son of Ra, from the sun, which became the supreme source of the

3 D

elemental souls that preceded a human soul. When the solar force
was looked upon as the highest soul of life in nature, the souls of
future beings were considered to be emanations from the sun as a
source of life in external nature that was superhuman. This gave
rise to the class of beings known as the Hamemmat, which originated
as germs of soul that issued from the sun. They are described as
circling round the solar orb in glory. The word hamemmat signifies
that which is unembodied or not yet incorporated. We might say the
hamemmat were pre-existing souls when souls were derived from the
elemental forces in the germ, and the highest of these was solar.
They are the germ-souls of future beings which originate as children
of the sun portrayed in a human form. As offspring of the sun,
they are called the children of Horus, who, as the child-Horus, is one
with them; and if they can be destroyed in the germ, or, as the
Ritual has it, in the egg, the devourer of souls may succeed in slaying the divine heir himself, who is destined to bruise the serpent's
head and win the victory over all the powers of evil as the lord
of light and link of continuity in life. Being at enmity with the
sun, the reptile of darkness seeks to devour the new-born child
of light. For that purpose he lies in wait till the woman clothed with
the sun shall bring forth. He seeks the life of the young child-
Horus, and other lives are involved in taking this. For Horus is the
head of the solar race, the hamemmat or future beings that issue
from the Eye of the sun. These future souls are called the "issue
of Horus." They are the Innocents of the legend that are supposed
to suffer, whereas the child of light, the divine offspring of the solar
god, is sure to escape from the coils of the monster who has been
rendered anthropomorphically as the ruling tyrant—the monster
Herod in a mortal guise. Thus, if any little children were murdered
by the Apap-monster, the dragon of darkness, these would be the
offspring and issue of the solar disk in the domain of physical
phenomena—little ones that were neither human nor spiritual beings,
but the seed or germs of souls about to be. The parallel to the
slaughter of the innocents can be traced in what is termed "the
slaughter which is wrought in Suten-Khen"; that is, in the khen or
birthplace where the young child-Horus was reborn as the royal
Horus. Each one of the manes or the "younglings of Shu" had to
pass through this place of rebirth where the Herrut-reptile lay in
wait. Chapter 42 is the one "by which one *hindereth the slaughter
which is wrought in Suten-Khen.*" Here the manes speaks in the
character of Horus the babe. "I am the babe" is said four times.
As human manes, he is one of those who may be destroyed, but is
safe so far as he has become assimilated to Horus. He tells the reptile, the herrut = Herod, that he is not to be seized or grasped by
him, and that neither men nor gods, neither the glorified nor the
damned can inflict any injury on him who is Horus the divine child,
born and bound to fulfil his course as the ever-coming One, who
"steppeth onward through eternity" (ch. 42). Sotinen, "a certain
city on the borders of Hermopolis," is the dreaded place in Amenta,
where the slaughter of the innocents was periodically wrought. The
would be destroyer of the child is addressed in one of his reptile-
forms, "O serpent Abur!" (the name rendered "great thirst" is

equivalent to that of the dragon of drought), thou sayest this day
"the block of execution is furnished (Rit. ch. 42), and thou art come
to contaminate the Mighty One." In another chapter Horus exults
that in making his descent to the earth of Seb for putting a stop to
evil *his nest is safe.* "Not to be seen is my nest. Not to be broken
is my egg. I have made my nest on the confines of Heaven" (Rit.,
ch. 85). He rejoices on account of his escape from the slaughter
of the innocents which followed his descent into the earth of Seb.
Thus in the Osirian mythos the child-Horus was with the widow in
Suten-Khen, and in the Gospel of the Infancy it is the child-Jesus
with the widow in Sotinen.

THE EGYPTO-GNOSTIC JESUS.

On one line of its descent the Jesus-legend was brought on to
Rome from Egypt by the mystery-teachers whom we term Egypto-
gnostics, and whose Jesus was no Word-made-flesh in one historic
form of personality, either at Nazareth or at Bethlehem, but was
absolutely non-historical. One of the most important of all the
written gnostic remains is the *Pistis Sophia.* And whether we
look on this as the work of Valentinus or another, it continues the
Jesus-legend from the Egyptian source, and constitutes a further link
betwixt the genuine mythos and the spurious history.

These books of Ieou are the books of Jesus, like the "Wisdom
of Jesus" in the Apocrypha and the lately discovered "Sayings of
Jesus," that is, when the only real Jesus has been discovered in Iusa
the son of Iusāas, he whose Jewish name is Ieou, Iao or Iah, as
derivatives from Iu, in Egyptian. The two books of Ieou are said to
contain the Mysteries, the first being the lesser, the second the
greater mysteries, as the *Pistis Sophia* carefully explains. Here we
reach the Egyptian rootage of the Jewish Ieou, whom the *Pistis
Sophia* calls "Ieou the first man, the legate of the first order"
(p. 333). Now as Atum was the first man, the created man, who
under one of his names was Iu, the Egyptian Jesus, this also
tends to identify the Egypto-gnostic Ieou with Iu-em-hetep, the
author of the Sayings and the books of wisdom which included
these books of Ieou. One of the two books had the general title of
The Book of the Great Logos, according to the Mystery, an equivalent
for the Logoi or Sayings of Jesus, which were Christianized as
the *Logia Kuriaka* or Sayings of the Lord, and on which the
canonical Gospels were eventually founded.

Pistis Sophia, like the Ritual, is mainly *post-resurrectional,* with the
briefest allusion to the earth-life. It begins with the after-life
in which Jesus has risen from the dead, like Amsu the good
shepherd. It opens with the resurrection on the Mount of Glory, the
same as the Ritual. The localities, like those in the Egyptian book,
are not of this world. They are in the earth of eternity, not in
the earth of time. *Pistis Sophia* begins where the Gospel story comes
to an end. Jesus rises in the Mount of Olives, but not on the mount

that was localized to the east of Jerusalem.   The Mount of Olives, as
Egyptian, was the mountain of Amenta.   It is termed Mount Bakhu,
the Mount of the Olive-tree, when the green dawn was represented by
this tree instead of by the sycamore.   Mount Bakhu, the Mount of
the Olive-tree, was the way of ascent to the risen Saviour as he
issued forth from Amenta to the land of spirits in heaven (Rit.,
ch. 17).   So when the Egypto-gnostic Jesus takes his seat upon the
Mount of Olives or the Olive-tree, he is said to have "ascended into
the heavens" (*Pistis Sophia*, Mead, G. R. S., whose version is the
only one in English: London, 1896).   Jesus "descended into hell,"
according to the Christian creed.   This forms no part of the Gospel-
legend, but we find it in the Book of the Dead ; also in *Pistis Sophia*.
Hell or Hades in Greek is the Amenta, as Egyptian.   Horus
descends into Amenta, or rather *rises* there from the tomb, as the
teacher of the mysteries concerning the father, who is Ra the
father in spirit and in truth.   This descent into the under-world is
spoken of by Horus in the Ritual (ch. 38).   He goes to visit the
spirits in prison or in their cells and sepulchres.   Those "who are in
their cells," the manes, "accompany him as his guides."   His
object in making this descent is to utter the words of the father in
heaven to the breathless ones, or the spirits in prison.   The passage
shows the speaker as the divine teacher in two characters on earth and
in Amenta.   Speaking of Ra, his father in the spirit, Horus says, " I
utter his words to the Men of the present generation," or to the
living.   He also utters them to those who have been deprived of
breath, or the dead in Amenta.   So in the *Pistis Sophia* the gnostic
Jesus passes into Amenta as the teacher of the greater mysteries.
As it is said of his teaching in this spirit-world, "*Jesus spake these
words unto his disciples in the midst of Amenta*" (p. 394, Mead).
Moreover, a special title is assigned to Jesus in Amenta.   He is
called Aber-Amentho.   "Jesus, that is to say Aber-Amentho," is a
formula several times repeated in *Pistis Sophia*.

According to the Ritual, a glorious "vesture" is put on in the
place where the human soul becomes eternized or is made immortal.
This is represented in the mystery of Tattu, where the body-soul
in matter (Osiris) is blended with the holy spirit Ra ; the female
with the male (Tefnut with Shu), or Horus the child of twelve years
with Horus the adult of thirty years.   The transaction occurs on the
day that was termed "Come thou to me" (Rit., ch. 17).   This call
is reproduced in the *Pistis Sophia* as "Come unto us" on the day
of Investiture, when Jesus puts on the divine vesture in his character
of Aber-Amentho, or Lord over Amenta, a title which identifies the
Egypto-gnostic Jesus with Horus in Amenta.   The call is made
to him by the attendant spirits, "Come unto us, who are thy fellow-
members " ; " Come unto us, for we all stand near to clothe thee with
the first mystery (that of the father) in all his glory " ; " Come therefore quickly, that thou mayst receive the full glory, the glory of the
first mystery," the mystery of God the father (*P. S.* 16–19).

The *Pistis Sophia* is a book of those Egypto-gnostics with
whom the Father-God is Ieou = Ihuh, and God the son is Iao = Iah
(*P. S.*, B. 2, 192, 193, Mead).   It contains an Egypto-gnostic version of
the mysteries, astronomical and eschatological.

Relics of the ancient wisdom have been piously preserved in this, the most important of all the gnostic remains, *i.e.*, for the purpose of establishing a link betwixt the Egyptian origins and the canonical Gospels, and for showing how the "History" was concocted. The Jesus who is teacher of the twelve in *Pistis Sophia* is the Egypto-gnostic Jesus who had been from of old the ever-coming son of the eternal father, whom we trace by nature and by name as far back as the time of Ptah in Memphis. This is the Jesus, or the Horus, of the Egyptian mysteries, and not of any Judean biography. In the religion of Atum-Ra the names of Horus and of Iu or Jesus were employed to denote the same character, and both names were continued for the one type by the Egypto-gnostics. The gnostic Jesus is the son of God who had been with the father from eternity. Hence it is he alone who knows the father and is able to expound the mystery of his nature to the Twelve. This is the first, great and only ineffable mystery, which is before all others and embraces all the rest. Jesus proceeding from the father as a spirit, divine in origin, impersonates the soul that became incarnate in the human form. The great primordial and ineffable mystery, from which the others radiate, and in which the total twenty-four revolve as the central source of an eternal evolution and involution, is the mystery of God the father becoming God the son. God the father is the holy spirit represented by a bird. This bird in the Egyptian symbolism was the hawk, or dove. In the gnostic version it is the dove. One chief difference between the two birds is in the dove being a type of the mother and child, whereas the hawk was the bird of the father, Ra, and the son; the holy Spirit, and Horus the son of the father. In the *Pistis Sophia* the son proceeds from the father in the likeness of the dove where Horus proceeded from the hawk-headed Ra in the likeness of a hawk. Under whichever type the duality of the father and son was indicated by one bird as symbol of the God in spirit, who was over all the powers which had been (elemental or astronomical) rulers in the realms of matter from the beginning.

The gnostic Jesus utters the Sayings or *Logia Kuriaka* on the mount, and is also the revealer of the greater mysteries of Amenta. According to the *Pistis Sophia*, when Jesus expounded the greater mysteries to the twelve it is said "Jesus spake these words to his disciples *in Amenta*" (Books of the Saviour, P. S. 394, Mead). He had previously taught the lesser mysteries to the twelve disciples in the life on earth. It is the same with Jesus as with Horus in Amenta. When Horus passes from the life on earth he rises from the tomb wearing the double feather and wielding the whip as his sign of sovereignty. He is Amsu-Horus, Lord of Amenta. This is the title of the gnostic Jesus, who is designated "Jesus, that is to say Aber-Amentho"—which we take to be Jewish-gnostic for Jesus, the mighty or great one, who in his resurrection is the Lord or Master over Amenta (Books of the Saviour, *Pistis Sophia*, 358, Mead). And Jesus "Aber-Amentho" is an Egypto-gnostic equivalent for Osiris "Khent Amenta."

The mysteries of Amenta, as in the Book of Revelation, are more or less repeated in the mysteries of *Pistis Sophia* which contains sufficient data to identity a gnostic version with the Kamite original.

There are twelve divisions in Amenta corresponding to the twelve hours of darkness. Twelve gates or doors successively enclose twelve sections of space, and the doors are guarded by twelve serpents, one serpent "to each door." These twelve divisions of the nether regions are repeated in *Pistis Sophia* as twelve dungeons of infernal torment. The surrounding gloom is represented by the Apap-dragon of darkness. As it is said, "the outer darkness is a huge dragon with its tail in its mouth" (B. 2, 320). There are twelve rulers or guardians to the twelve dungeons who take the place of the Egyptian twelve serpents (*Book of Hades, Records*, vol. 10). They have the faces of serpents, dragons, basilisks, crocodiles, cats, vultures, bears and other beasts; for, as it is said of the rulers of "these twelve dungeons which are inside the dragon of outer darkness," "each hath a name for every hour, and each one of them changeth its face every hour" (B. 2, 322). A dog-faced demon, called the eternal devourer, who lives upon the damned, is described in the Ritual (ch. 17). The deceased prays to the great Osiris, "Deliver me from that God who liveth upon the damned, whose face is that of a hound, but whose skin is that of a man, at the angle of the pool of fire." This "dog-faced one" and his rivers of fire reappear in the *Pistis Sophia*. Certain sins are to be renounced in order that the manes may escape from "the judgment of that dog-faced one" and from the "judgments of Amenta," "from the fires of Amenta," and "from the torments which are in Amenta" (B. 2, 255–256). Knowing the magical names in Amenta has the same power, according to the *Pistis Sophia*, as with the Book of the Dead. For instance, the dragon of outer darkness has twelve names written on the doors of its dungeons, and, as it is said, whosoever shall understand the mystery of one of the names, if he is abandoned in the outer darkness and he pronounceth the name of the dragon, he shall be saved and receive the treasure of light (B. 2, 335, Mead). To know the name was to obtain possession of the magical word of power which meant salvation.

In the Egyptian hall of judgment there are forty-two assessors, and the deceased has to plead in their presence that he has not broken any of the forty-two commandments (Rit., ch. 125). A version of these is retained in the *Pistis Sophia* in the shape of forty-four renunciations, two having been added to the Egyptian forty-two. By renouncing these forty-four sins the deceased is saved from the dog-faced devourer of souls, from the dragon of outer darkness, from Ialdabaoth = Sut, prince of the powers of darkness, and from the torments of the twelve dungeons of the outer darkness, all of which are Egyptian. The lesser mysteries were astronomical; the greater mysteries are spiritual. The astronomical nature of the "lesser mysteries" is convincingly shown in the *Pistis Sophia*; also the astronomical origin of the Twelve who were taught those mysteries by the Egypto-gnostic Jesus *sitting on the mount*. The mystery of the five supporters, the mystery of the seven amens or seven voices (in the heptanomis), the mystery of the nine guardians of the three gates of the treasures of light (= the Put-circle of the nine gods who were in three threes), the mystery of the great forefather, the mystery of the triple powers or of the trinity, and lastly the mystery of the twelve saviours who preserve the treasure of light in heaven and on earth, are all identifiable as primary types in the astronomical mythology of Egypt.

The teacher of the mysteries is an Egyptian type. He was the Her-Seshta. Brugsch enumerates seven classes of such teachers: (1) the mystery-teachers of heaven; (2) the mystery-teachers of all the lands, which were first of all celestial; (3) the mystery-teachers of the depth (Amenta); (4) the mystery-teachers of the secret word; (5) the mystery-teachers of the sacred language; (6) the mystery-teachers of Pharaoh; (7) the mystery-teachers who examine words. The divine child manifests to men as expounder of the mysteries or revealer of the hidden wisdom of which he is the word, the sayer, or the teacher. The teacher of the lesser mysteries was child-Horus or Iusa, the youth of twelve years. These were the mysteries of matter and of mythology revealed by the child of the mother at his first advent. The teacher of the greater mysteries was Horus the adult, who expounded the nature of the fatherhood, the begettal or duplication of the divine soul, and all the other mysteries of the resurrection in and from Amenta, as the son of God the father in heaven. But the Egypto-gnostic Jesus is the fulfiller of both the first and the second advent; the first as the child of twelve years, the second as the Horus of thirty years; the first in the life on earth, the second in Amenta; the first as solar in the astronomical mythology, the second as spiritual in the eschatology; the first as the utterer of parables, the second as the expounder of the greater mysteries.

In vain do we try to make out the doctrinal mysteries of the eschatology, whether it is called Egyptian, Hebrew, Coptic, Gnostic, or Christian, until we have mastered the mythology. Without this foundation there is no foothold. Neither is there any help in an exoteric version of the esoteric wisdom. The group of powers was seven or eight, nine or ten, before it included the twelve. And the character is the same in the mythos when the group is twelve as when it was ten or nine, eight or seven or four—that is, it was astronomical.

Pistis Sophia commences formally after the manner of an historic document, whilst being, from beginning to end, entirely non-historical. It opens with a date that is astronomical, and also with what the Ritual terms "the manifestation to light" at the time of full moon—that is, when the eye was full or the circle complete in Annu, where the divine heir was born. "It came to pass, when Jesus had risen from the dead in the first advent, that he passed eleven (should be twelve) years speaking with his disciples and instructing them up to the regions of the first statutes only and up to the regions of the first mystery—the mystery within the veil—the veil that was rent in death, which is before all mysteries, because it is the mystery of the One Eternal God and the son who issues from the father in the likeness of a dove, just as Horus issued from the father in the likeness of the hawk or dove, or the canonical Christ as the dove. "It came to pass, therefore, that the disciples were sitting together on the Mount of Olives, speaking of these things, rejoicing with great joy, and being exceedingly glad, and saying one to another, 'Blessed are we before all men who are on earth, for the Saviour hath revealed this unto us, and we have received all fulness and all perfection'"—

as these were received upon Mount Bakhu, the Mount of the Olive-tree, in the ascent of Horus from Amenta. "And while they were saying these things the one to the other Jesus sat a little apart from them." "It came to pass, therefore, on the fifteenth day of the month, Tybi (or Tobe), the day of the full moon, on that day when the sun had risen in its going, that there came forth a great stream of light shining exceedingly. It came forth from the light of lights. And this stream of light poured over Jesus and surrounded him. He was seated apart from his disciples and was shining exceedingly. But the disciples saw not Jesus because of the great light in which he sat, for their eyes were blinded by the great light" on this, the Egypto-gnostic mount of the transfiguration (pp. 4, 5, Mead). (By the bye, the fifteenth of the month Tybi in the esoteric Gospel sounds somewhat suggestive of "the fifteenth year of the reign of Tiberius" in the exoteric Gospel according to Luke.) "And Jesus said to his disciples, I am come from that first mystery which is also the last mystery" of the four-and-twenty mysteries which he had now come to expound, because "his disciples did not know that mystery."

In the Egyptian tale of Khamuas, Si-Osiris, *i.e.* Horus the son of Osiris, comes forth from Amenta to spend twelve years on the earth. This has an important bearing on the statement in the first part of *Pistis Sophia*. The time spent by Horus the elder in the great hall of Seb, or on earth, in mortal form, was *twelve years* in the original mythos, this being the Egyptian limit of child-life. *It is twelve years in the tale of Khamuas.* But in the *Pistis Sophia* the time is given as eleven years, which has the vagueness of the märchen. This tends to show the origin of the tradition reported by Irenæus, that the ministry and teaching of Jesus extended over a vague period of ten or more years, and that the Lord lived on to be an old man, the old man being a literalized version of the old child, Har-Ur, the elder Horus (Iren., B. 2, ch. 22. 5). During those twelve years he was the child of the mother only, as in the Gospels of the Infancy. He is her Word or logos, and the teacher of those lesser mysteries that led up to the one great ineffable mystery which was now held to be the source of all the rest.

We hear little of the wonderful child as divine teacher in the canonical Gospels, but some of the excluded matter appears in the apocryphal Gospels. In the canonical Gospels the child-Jesus is the teacher at twelve years of age. This corresponds to Horus as wearer of the lock, and to Iu-em-hetep, the youthful sage, each of whom had been portrayed as the typical teacher twelve years old. It was during those years that the child-Horus or child-Jesus taught. Something of this may be read in the so-called "apocryphal Gospels," ignorantly supposed to contain the lying inventions concocted by the gnostic heretics to discredit and destroy a veritable human history. There is a very *naïve* confession in the "Arabic Gospel" that, during the first three years of the infancy, the child-Jesus "wrought very many miracles in Egypt which are not found written either in the Gospel of the Infancy or in the Perfect Gospel" (ch. 25). Such stories had been told for ages of the child-Horus, who was a miracle-worker in and from the womb; and also of the child as Iusa, son of Atum-Ra, and earlier still of Iu-em-hetep, the son of Ptah. The miracles were a mode of demonstrating the divinity of the ever-coming little one, Iu-Su. At three years of age he performs the miracle of making a dead fish live (Latin Gospel of Thomas, B. 3, ch. 1). At five years of age he takes clay and models twelve sparrows, which he commanded to fly, whereupon they lived and flew aloft (Latin Gospel of Thomas, B. 2, ch. 2). Horus or Jesus, Egyptian, Jewish, or Gnostic, the little hero of the mythos, is one and the same divine son of the Virgin in mortal guise.

Horus, at his coming-forth from Amenta, as the Word or Teacher, says: "I make my appearance on *the seat of Ra*, and *I sit upon my seat which is upon the horizon*" (Rit., ch. 79). The horizon and the mount are identical in Egyptian, and this seat of Ra, the father in heaven, assumed by Horus in his ascent from Amenta, is the mount of earth according to the solar mythos—that is, the mount of sunrise, which is Mount Bakhu in Egyptian, the Mount of the Olive-tree, the prototypal Mount of Olives. In the *Pistis Sophia* Jesus takes his seat upon the Mount of Olives as the divine teacher, word or logos, who utters the Sayings to his disciples. This is the advent of Jesus which is dated the fifteenth day of the Egyptian month Tybi, the day of full moon, by which the resurrection or new birth was always reckoned. This month in the Alexandrian year (B.C. 25) began December 27th, which is near enough as a date for the nativity at Christmas, when measured in the circle of precession. The "coming-forth to day" is illustrated by the great flood of light that emanated from the light of lights and "enveloped him entirely." "The multitude of the heavenly host praising God" (Luke ii. 13) is described. "And all the angels with their archangels, and all the powers of the height, all sang from the interior of the interiors, so that the whole world heard their voice." "But the disciples sat together and were in the greatest possible distress" (B. 1, p. 6, Mead). In the Ritual when Horus stands or is seated (on the Mount of the Olive-tree) "in the (human) form of that god who is raised aloft upon his pedestal" or his papyrus, it is said "the gods come to him with acclamation, and the female deities with jubilation." "They rejoice at his beautiful coming-forth from the womb of Nut," or, as it might be rendered, the womb of Meri, for Meri=Mary is another name for Nut the mother-heaven (Book of the Dead).

The gnostic Jesus, on emerging from Amenta, takes his seat as teacher of the twelve disciples on the Mount of Olives. The way up from Amenta for the sun-god in the solar mythos was on the eastern side of the four-faced mount of earth which on that side was known as Bakhu, the Mount of the Olive-tree. The way of ascent, worked out in the mythos, served for the manes in the eschatology. Thus Jesus in the ancient character of sun-god, or as the divine child who taught, or who was the word in mortal guise, attains the landing-stage upon the Mount of Olives or the olive-tree of dawn, when he issues in or from Amenta, like Horus in the tamarisk, as Jesus of the resurrection. The divine child is not merely born in human guise, but also as the youthful solar god. Hence in the beginning of the narrative the disciples are sitting round him on the Mount of Olives with Jesus shining like the sun in glory (*P. S.*, B. 1, 4). The scene had been already set in the astronomical mythos. He images the sun-god on the mount; the twelve are round him in the zodiac. And, as it is noted, although Jesus is in their midst, he is "a little apart from his disciples."

Thus *Pistis Sophia* shows the physical foundation of the mysteries. Astronomical science was taught as matter of the mysteries, but the science being physical these were classified as the lesser mysteries, whereas the greater mysteries were eschatological. The twelve on earth, or in matter, were the companions of elder Horus, the son of Isis, the suffering saviour. The twelve in Amenta are the associates of Horus, the triumphant saviour, the beloved only-begotten son of God the father. The twelve with Horus or Jesus risen from Amenta are freed from the environment, the darkness, the stains of matter, as pure spirits to be wholly perfected. They have attained the beatific vision, as the children of light. They have passed through death and the purgation of matter to become clear spirit when risen to the status of Horus the immortal. With Horus or Jesus, in the character of the young sun-god, the twelve were astronomical powers, rulers, or saviours of the treasure (light) in the physical domain. With Horus or Jesus, the saviour as son of God the father, they are the twelve glorious ones or gods of Amenta, the twelve who as spirits are the children of Ra the holy spirit; in short, they are the twelve in the eschatology who were the chosen twelve with Horus on earth as sowers of the seed, and the twelve with Horus as reapers of the harvest in Amenta.

Our starting-point, then, is that Jesus or Horus in coming to earth and assuming the vesture of mortality issues forth in Amenta; not the Greek Hades, nor the Hebrew Sheol, but the Egyptian Amenta, that other world in which the dead as sleepers wake to life in spirit, and where the mortal Horus makes his transformation and arises as the first-fruits of them that slept—a resurrection of Horus that was celebrated in Egypt when the "first-fruits of the earth" were the shoots of the papyrus-plant or sprouts of the lentils, as described by Plutarch. When Jesus, in his second advent, issues *from* Amenta to become the teacher of the twelve upon the Mount of Olives, the disciples are already seated on the mount. Jesus suddenly appears to them, a little apart from them, in such a dazzle of glory as to be at first invisible to them. This glory of light was composed of various lights. "The light was of every kind, and of every type, from the lower to the higher" (*P. S.* 1, 5). It was the glory of the youthful solar god upon the mount of sunrise, with the lesser lights surrounding him. So in the Ritual it is said of the sun-god, who was Horus in his beautiful coming-forth, "Ra maketh his appearance at the mount of glory, with the cycle of gods about him" (Rit., ch. 133, Renouf). This was upon the Mount Bakhu or the olive-tree of dawn, and the cycle of gods about the "golden form" of Horus are the astronomical originals of the disciples with the Egypto-gnostic Jesus on the mount of sunrise called the mount of glory. The twelve disciples of the Lord are no more human than was their teacher. But when the word was made flesh and Jesus assumed the human guise, his followers likewise conformed to the anthropomorphic type of Horus the mortal in the life that was lived, as mythically represented, for twelve years as the child of Seb on earth. The twelve with Horus in the harvest-field are reapers, and reapers, mariners, fishers, or teachers demanded the anthropomorphic type. The human type, however, does not necessarily imply the human personage, either in the teacher or as the taught, any more than the zootypes imply that the god was a crocodile, a hawk, a lion, or that the goddess was a water-cow, a serpent, a tree, or a cleft in the rock.

As the gnostics truly declared, in reply to the pretended " History," the twelve apostles were a type of the twelve æons, who were set in the zodiac as timekeepers and preservers of the light. (Irenæus, Bk. 2, ch. 21, 1.) That is, they who knew vouched for the apostles being the same as the æons who were the twelve powers of the twelve saviours of the twelve treasures of light with the gnostic Jesus on the mount, whose twelve stations were figured in the zodiac ; and who were the twelve powers in matter, in physics, or in the astronomical mythology which preceded the twelve as great spirits with Jesus or Horus in the eschatology. Even if there had been twelve men as a group of teachers, fishers, or harvesters, in every city, town, or village of the earth who called themselves the disciples, or apostles, of Jesus, Horus, or the Lord, it could not change one jot or tittle of the fact that the twelve were teachers of astronomy, whose names were written in heaven as attendants on the youthful solar god ; and who in the second phase became the twelve great spirit sin Amenta as reapers of the harvest for Har-khuti, the Egyptian lord of spirits. The god at the head of a group or cycle of powers was a teacher from the first. Sut, Anup, Taht and Ptah were typical teachers of astronomy in the stellar, lunar and solar mythos, when the group was seven, eight, or nine in number. Jesus (or Horus) is the only teacher in the heaven of twelve astronomes. He was the only-begotten son in spirit who was made flesh in his incarnation to enter the human sphere as child of the mother, that is of matter as the matrix of spirit. He became the greatest of all the teachers in the astronomical mythos, and "the twelve" who had been pre-solar teachers and preservers of the treasures of light were now his servants (Seshu), his followers, his apostles. And being the Only Son of God it was Jesus alone who knew the nature of the Father, which knowledge he now expounded to the twelve in the higher mysteries of Amenta. Jesus describes the twelve in the two different categories, astronomical and spiritual, and says, " When I first came into the world I brought with me twelve powers. I took them from the hands of the twelve saviours of the treasure of light " : that is, from the twelve who are called the æons in the astronomy ; the twelve who had been the powers in physical phenomena. These were unified in him ; he gathers their powers to himself in passing through the twelve signs of the zodiac as the youthful solar god. At an earlier stage of the mythos the powers that were gathered up in the one supreme power were but seven in number, called the seven souls of Ra ; in the final zodiac they are twelve. Jesus also describes the founding of the twelve as his ministers on earth in matter, or in the lower range of the mysteries. The first Horus imaged a soul in matter ; the second was the likeness of an immortal spirit. Jesus brought the primary soul to the twelve who are his associates in the life on earth. But that was before he was invested as a Sahu or spiritual mummy to become the lord of the resurrection as *Jesus* Aber-Amentho.

The typical twelve, who latterly became the teachers of, and for, the Word, were as ancient as the signs of the zodiac, or the twelve great gods of Egypt, which according to Herodotus were extant some 20,000 years ago. They were the twelve as kings, who rowed the solar-bark for Ra, with Horus on the look-out at the prow. They were the twelve in various characters and in several countries into which the gnosis of the mysteries passed from out the birthplace of the ancient wisdom; although the twelve have no such universal radius as the seven, or the four, because of their comparative lateness in Egypt. They were the twelve princes of Israel (Num. i. 44), the twelve sons of Israel; the twelve judges on twelve thrones with the Son of man sitting on the throne of his glory (Matt. xix. 28); also the twelve that sit at the table with the son in the new kingdom founded by him for the father (Luke xxii. 14). They are the twelve knights that gathered round the table of Arthur; the twelve gods with Odin in their midst, with others that need not be enumerated now. At his second advent, which is in the spirit, the Egypto-gnostic Jesus says to the disciples, " I am come now, and not (as) formerly before they had crucified me." That is when he was represented as the afflicted mortal suffering in the flesh. (*P. S.* 1, 10.) He has now come in the spirit which was imaged by the dove, and not as formerly or aforetime when he was incarnated in matter, for the twelve years on earth, as the lifetime of the child was reckoned. Becoming a spirit is described as putting on the vesture of everlasting light. And the coming forth of Jesus as a spirit, or the Christ, is described as his investiture, the same as with Horus in Amenta. He says, " The times are fulfilled for me to put on my vesture. Lo, I have put on my vesture, and all power hath been given to me by the first mystery "—or God as the one eternal source. He issues from this source as the light of all the lights; a light that is infinitely beyond the star-fires, the moon-light, and the splendours of the sun, in the mythical representation. All the previous powers of light had contributed to fulfil the glory of this vesture. These powers belong mainly to the astronomical mythology as the lights that were revealed and set forth in the lesser mysteries of the physical domain, which, according to gnostic terminology, were designated the rulers in matter. Amongst these are " the seven amens which are the seven voices "; the five supports, the nine guardians, the three powers, the twelve saviours of light, all of whom are recognizably astronomical. (*P. S.*, B. 1, 14, 18, 19.) He wears the glory now, " as of an only-begotten from the father." In making this transformation Jesus presents an outer view of God the father as the first ineffable mystery of all the mysteries. When he came previously, in his first advent, it was from the mother as the mortal, or the mould of soul in matter. Now he issues from the father in spirit as revealer of the mystery of which he alone has ever had an inner view. He is now invested with the glory of the father. This investiture of Jesus in spirit might be claimed as pre-eminently

Egyptian if all the rest were not pre-eminently so. As a mystery of Amenta this investiture took place when the deceased became a Sahu and put on the divine vesture of a spiritual body, or the soul of Horus. The Sahu signifies the invested, and it is identical with the Karest or the Christ.

There is one datum which by itself alone might dispel any doubt respecting the Egyptian origin of the *Pistis Sophia*. It is this: the day of investiture is the day of "Come thou to us," or "Come unto us." (B. 1, 17-19.) This, in the Kamite eschatology, was the day of "Come thou hither," on which Ra called to Osiris in Amenta, "Come thou hither," or "Come thou to me." (Rit., ch. 17.) In the *Pistis Sophia* this is the call, not only of Ra but of all the powers of light who raise the cry of "Come unto us" that Jesus may receive the glory of the Father as his vesture for the resurrection. In the so-called earth-life "Jesus had not told his disciples the whole distribution of all the regions of the great invisible, and of the three triple powers, and of the four-and-twenty invisibles." "Nor had he told them of their saviours, according to the orders of each (of the twelve) as they are; nor had he told them of the region of the saviour of the twins; nor the region of the three amens; nor those of the seven amens, which are also the seven voices. Nor had Jesus told his disciples of what type are the five supporters, or from what region they had been brought forth. Nor had he told them how the great light had emanated, nor from what region it had been brought forth." (B. 1, 2, 3, Mead.) In brief, as the data when identified will show, he had not instructed them in the spiritual nature of the mysteries, which is the object of the second coming. But now the teacher in Amenta says to the twelve, "Rejoice and be glad from this hour. From this day will I speak with you freely, from the beginning of the truth unto the completion thereof; and I will speak to you face to face without parable. From this hour will I hide nothing from you of the things which pertain to the height." (B. 1, 3, 1, 8, 9, Mead.) This is said by Jesus Aber-Amentho, or Jesus in the spirit-world of Amenta, who had "Come forth to day" at his second advent. When he is expounding the profounder mysteries, Jesus says to the disciples, "As for the rest of the lower mysteries, we have no need thereof, but ye shall find them in the Two Books of Ieou, which Enoch wrote when I spoke with him from the tree of knowledge, and from the tree of life, which were in the paradise of Adam." (B. 2, 246, Mead.) In this passage Jesus identifies himself with Iao the son of Ieou = Ihuh—and also in the character of the solar god who spoke with Moses from the midst of the burning bush.

It was shown in the mysteries why and how the Twelve Immovables, or Unspeakables, "rent themselves asunder," to move, to manifest, to reveal, to find utterance by means of God the Son as teacher of the mysteries in Amenta (B. 2, 219-226). *Pistis Sophia* marks the change of the twelve rulers from one category to the other. These things, said Jesus, speaking of the change which he had come on earth, or entered the lower domain of matter, to effect, "these things shall come to pass at the time of the completion of the æon (or cycle), and of the accession of the Pleroma. The twelve saviours of the treasure, and the twelve orders of each of them, which are the emanations of the seven voices and of the five trees (or supports) shall be with me in my kingdom," which was in the heaven of eternity. Jesus speaks of those "who receive the mystery of light when they shall have quitted the body of the matter of the rulers" (B. 2, 201), who were the rulers in matter versus the life in spirit, or in Horus as the lord of light who was the witness to the light of life eternal.

Jesus is described in *Pistis Sophia* as passing through the twelve signs of the zodiac. The ram, bull, twins, crab, lion, balance, scorpion, bowman, goat, and waterer are all mentioned by name. (*B. of the S. in Pistis Sophia*, 366-372, Mead.) He passes through the twelve signs in his character of solar god. He takes a portion of their light from the twelve æons who were the Kronian rulers. "And the twelve powers of the twelve saviours of the treasure of light, which I had received from the twelve ministers of the midst, I cast into the sphere of the rulers . . . and I bound them into the bodies of your mothers." The rulers of the Decans thought that these twelve were "the souls of the rulers." But, when in the fulness of time they were brought forth into the world, there was no soul of the rulers in them ; they were recognized as beings of a superior nature. Jesus is to reign as king over these twelve saviours, the twin-saviour, the nine guardians, the three amens, the five supporters, and the seven amens and all the other characters, which had been "light-emanations," and which would have no meaning if Jesus had not likewise had an astronomical character. (B. 2, 230, 231.) For these names connote the seven rulers of the Heptanomis ; the five supports of a heaven that was based upon a figure of the pole and the arms of the four quarters ; the solar trinity ; the nine gods of the put-cycle, the Twin-Horus, and the heaven that was perfected at last as the heaven of the twelve tribes, twelve sons, twelve brothers, twelve kings, twelve reapers, twelve rowers, twelve fishermen, twelve voices of the word, twelve teachers, who began as saviours of the treasure of light in physical phenomena ; and who were assigned a spiritual status with Jesus in that kingdom of the Father which they had assisted in establishing for ever ; and finally in the heaven of eternity. These, however, are mysteries that never could be understood whilst a fictitious history of Jesus barred the way. Horus or Jesus in Amenta is the founder of a kingdom for his Father in heaven, and for his followers in spirit-world, at the head of whom are the typical twelve who now become the children of Horus. This heaven for spirits made perfect is built upon foundations that were laid in the mythology. The Ritual shows us how the four foundations of this new heaven were laid by Horus in establishing the kingdom of God. First, he himself united the "double earth," or the two worlds in one, by his death, burial and resurrection. Then he prays to his Father in heaven that the "four brothers" of "his own body" or flesh and blood may be given to him as protectors of his own person "in dutiful service." (Rit., ch. 112, 11, 12 ; and 13, 8.) These four who were his brothers previously are the first of the twelve with Horus "on his papyrus," or monolith, or on the mount. The four brothers of Horus who were first chosen to become his children had been astronomical as the ancient gods or. divine supports of the four quarters, Amsta, Hapi, Tuamutef and Kabhsenuf. With these four as supports the foundations of the kingdom of

heaven were laid, and "the fold" of the good shepherd established
in Amenta, the earth of eternity.   The explanation here is that
Horus was born one of the twelve like Joseph, but as the young
solar god, and beloved son of the father Ra, he obtained his supremacy
as the head over all the rest of the brethren.   Then the twelve became
his founders, reapers, fishers, his disciples, pupil-teachers or his
children.   As it is said in the Ritual (ch. 112, 9, 10), these are
"the circle of gods who were with him when Horus came to light in
his own children"; that is, when the twelve powers were assimilated
to the son of God, who was in them as they were in him at the
second coming.

The gnostic Jesus, the mystery-teacher of heaven, issues from the
father in Amenta in the likeness of the dove as the expounder of the
greater mysteries to the twelve disciples.   He now says to the disciples,
"*I will tell unto you the mystery of the one and only ineffable, and all
its types, all its configurations, all its regulations . . . for this mystery
is the support of them all*" (B. 2, 226, Mead).   This first ineffable mystery
—looking within, as *Pistis Sophia* phrases it—is the mystery of God
the Father.   The first ineffable mystery—looking without—is the
mystery of God the Son.   It is the mystery of the one God in the
two aspects of the Father and Son; hence the mystery of the one
and only ineffable, "looking within," is also the mystery of the
one and only word or logos "looking without" (B. 2).   Jesus
says, "I am come from the first mystery which is also the last"
(B. 1, 1).   The power now given by the first mystery, within the veil,
to him who personates the mystery to men, looking without, is
received by the Son from the Father, from whom he emanated in the
likeness of the dove, or the hawk.   And not as previously in the likeness of a puny mortal, the human Horus—born of the virgin mother
as her blind and deaf, her dumb and impubescent child.

Pistis Sophia shows the twofold character of the teaching on the
earth and in Amenta.   The "wisdom of Jesus" in the Apocrypha
was taught in parables.   Jesus in the canonical Gospels speaks to
the multitude in parables, and "without a parable spake he nothing
unto them" (Matt. xiii. 34).   But he says, "The hour cometh when I
shall no more speak unto you in parables, but shall tell you plainly
of the Father" (John xvi. 25).   This promise is fulfilled by the
Egypto-gnostic Jesus after his return to the regions from whence he
came into the earth-life.   He says to the disciples, "I have gone to
the regions whence I came forth.   From this day I will speak to you
face to face without parable" (B. 1, 8, 9).   *Henceforth* he speaks to
them plainly of the Father, and, as it is frequently said, "*without
parable.*"   This is after that second advent which the Jesus in the
Gospels is not permitted to fulfil, but which is still expected by the
millennarians.

Various sayings that were uttered aforetime in the earth-life are
now expounded by Jesus in Amenta "without parable."   He says to
the disciples, "When I shall be king over the seven amens, the five
supports (or trees), the three amens, and the nine guardians; king
over the child of the child, that is to say, over the twin-saviours (or
the double Horus); king over the twelve saviours and the whole
number of perfect souls—then all those men who shall have received

the mystery in (or of) that ineffable, shall be fellow-kings with me. They shall sit on my right hand and on my left in my kingdom ; therefore I said unto you *aforetime*, ' Ye shall sit on my right hand and on my left in my kingdom, and ye shall reign with me '" (B. 2, 230). Speaking of the greater mysteries, which are spiritual, Jesus says, " *I have brought the mysteries which* break all the bonds of the counterfeit of the spirit (*i.e.*, the bonds of matter) and all the seals which are attached to the soul, the mysteries of which make the soul free, and ransom it from the hands of its parents, the rulers, and transform it into the kingdom of the true Father, the first Father, the first One, ineffable and everlasting mystery." " For this cause have I said unto you *aforetime*, ' He who shall not leave father and mother to follow after me is not worthy of me.' What I said then was, ye shall leave your parents the rulers, that ye may all be children of the first, everlasting mystery" (B. 2, 341). This is the esoteric true interpretation of a saying that has been used exoterically (Matt. xix. 29 ; Mark x. 29). The *parents* signified were not human, but those rulers in matter who preceded the one God, the Holy Spirit, whom the Son made known in the mysteries of Amenta under his title of Jesus Aber-Amentho. Again, he exclaims, " I said unto you *aforetime*, ' Seek that ye may find.' " When he said that it signified " Ye shall seek out the mysteries of light, which purify the body of matter. I say unto you, the race of human kind is material. I tore myself asunder, I brought unto them the mysteries of light to purify them . . . otherwise, no soul in the whole of human kind would have been saved " (B. 2, 249, Mead). Salvation here is brought by means of the Son of God the Father becoming incarnate to redeem the human race from matter by inculcating the virtues of purification which were taught by Horus or Jesus in the mysteries of Amenta.

The gnostic Jesus also gives an esoteric rendering of the Resurrection when he says that " All men who shall achieve the mystery of the resurrection of the dead which healeth from demoniac possessions, and sufferings, and every disease, which also healeth the blind, the lame, the halt, the dumb, and the deaf, (the mystery) which I gave you aforetime—whosoever shall receive of these mysteries and achieve (or master) when if he ask for anything whatsoever . . . it shall at once be granted unto him " (B. 2, 279). In the resurrection the deceased transforms into a spirit, and it was in the mysteries of Amenta, and in the spirit-life, that these miracles were achieved, not in the life on earth. In the Ritual the deceased goes where he pleases, does as he pleases, and assumes whatsoever form he pleases as he masters mystery after mystery according to the gnosis. In the canonical Gospels we find an exoteric rendering of these mysteries of Amenta, which the lie-enchanted Christian world believe in as historical miracles performed on earth by an historical Saviour named Jesus. There were seven preservers of the treasures of light in the celestial heptanomis, whether as rulers of constellations or as lords of pole-stars, who first upraised the starry firesticks which were kindled on the seven hills of heaven. The *Pistis Sophia* shows the way in which an additional five were added to the seven in completing the first twelve saviours of the treasure of light. This is indicated when it is said (B. 2, 189), " The twelve saviours of the treasure, and *the twelve orders of each of them*, which are the emanations of the seven voices and of the five supports, shall be with me in the region of the inheritance of light; they shall be kings with me in my kingdom." Which shows that the first twelve were combined as the 7+5 that were pre-zodiacal, and that they are to become kings in the kingdom of eternal light; which twelve were stationed in the solar zodiac, or round the mount of glory. There is frequent reference in *Pistis Sophia* to the mystery of the five supports. These are also figured as five trees, one of which is said to be "*in the midst*" (B. 1, 3 and 18, B. 2, 191, 196). These five tree-supports, with the great one in their midst, are equivalent to the tree-type of eternal stability imaged as the Tat of Ptah (or as Ptah himself), which is a figure of support at the four corners with the pole as the central great pillar of support. It is also equivalent, as a symbol, to the group of Horus and his four children in the Osirian mysteries. The Kamite twelve, as reapers in the harvest-field with Horus in Amenta, were also put together from two earlier groups of seven and five, the same as in the gnostic mysteries of the twelve supports or the pole-tree of heaven with twelve branches in the zodiac. A sketch, however tentative, may be drawn of the original characters in the astronomical mythology, that were given the twelve thrones under one name or another in the final zodiac. (1) Sut, (2) Horus, (3) Shu, (4) Hapi, (5) Ap-Uat, (6) Kabhsenuf, (7) Amsta, (8) Anup, (9) Ptah, (10) Atum, (11) Sau, (12) Hu, as the Kamite originals of the twelve who rowed the solar bark for Ra.

We claim, then, to show that the typical Twelve, who are called apostles or disciples in later language, originated in twelve characters which had represented twelve stellar powers in the astronomical mythology, and that these were afterwards given thrones or seats as rulers in the twelve signs of the zodiac or in heaven. These, in the *Pistis Sophia*, are designated twelve preservers or saviours of the treasure of light: They form the cycle of twelve lesser gods around the sun-god on the summit of the mount, and are the same in signification, whether called gods in the Ritual or disciples of the Egypto-gnostic Jesus in the *Pistis Sophia*. These are at first the twelve with Horus the mortal, Horus in matter, Horus in the mythos, Horus the youthful solar god. But when he makes his transformation and becomes the Son of God the Father, in the spirit life, they are his companions in Amenta; the twelve great spirits to whom he expounds the mysteries of the fatherhood; in short, they become the typical twelve as characters in the Kamite eschatology.

According to *Pistis Sophia* the localities of the teachings, whether in the midst of Amenta, or on the Mount of Olives, were celestial, and not mundane. As it is said, "Jesus and his disciples remained in the midst of an aerial region, in the paths of the ways of the midst which is below the sphere." This is the starting-point from which the twelve accompany him, through the regions that are mapped out by the zodiacal signs (*Books of the Saviour in Pistis Sophia*, 359–371), when they "go forth three by three to the four quarters of heaven to preach the gospel of the kingdom" (390). It is also said that "Jesus stood at the altar, and cried aloud, turning towards the four angles of the world" (358). Here the "altar" is urano-

3 E

graphic. It was figured in the constellation *Ara* as a co-type with the summit called the Mount of Hetep, or of Heaven, in the astronomical mythology.

DOUBLE HORUS, OR JESUS AND THE CHRIST.

It was a saying of Philo's that "the logos is double." This it is as the double Horus, or as Jesus and the Christ, who was dual as manifester for the Virgin Mother and afterwards for God the Father: double by nature, human and divine ; double in matter and in spirit ; double as child and as adult, double as the soul of both sexes. But when the word "logos" comes to be used for the divine Reason we are in the midst of Greek metaphysic and doctrinal mystification. These two, blended in one person, constituted the double Horus who was that double logos spoken of by Philo, the figure of which was founded, as Egyptian, on the two halves of the soul, or pair of gods in the mystery of Tattu (Rit., ch. 17). Horus in these two characters was Horus with the tress of infancy, and Horus who becomes bird-headed at the transformation in his baptism. In his first advent Horus is the sower in the seed-field of time ; in his second he is the lord of the reapers in the harvest of eternity. In the astronomical mythos Horus was the king of one year. Naturally that was as ruler of the seasons in the annual circuit of the sun. As the prince of eternity he was the typical adult of thirty years, and lord of the Sut-Heb festival, who is called "the living Horus, the powerful bull, lord of the festivals of thirty years," which are termed "the years of Horus as King" (*Rec. of the Past*, vol. 10, 34). This was the royal Horus in whom the child that was destined to be a king attained his manhood and assumed his perfect sovereignty.

As already shown, the genesis of the double Horus is portrayed in the Ritual (ch. 115). In this description "two brethren come into being." One of these was the wearer of the female lock, as the child-Horus. His birth was mystical. He was both male and female in person, or, as it is said, "he assumed the form of a female with a lock," the sign of pre-pubescence in either sex, and hence a type of both. He is also called "the Afflicted One," which denotes the mystery of the Virgin's child. The second is "the active one of Heliopolis." He is "the heir of the temple." The first is also called the heir, and the second the heir of the heir. He has the divine might of "the son whom the father hath begotten." This was "the only-begotten of the father." Thus the "two brethren" were Horus the child who wears the long tress that is the sign of either sex, and Horus the adult who images the power and glory of the father as the god in spirit.

Iusa, the Jesus of On, like Horus in the Osirian cult, was born bi-mater. His two mothers were Iusāas and Neb-hetep, the two consorts of Atum-Ra. These two mothers were at first two sisters in the mythos. One of them was the mother in the western mountain, or later in the winter solstice ; the other gave birth to Horus on the horizon in the eastern equinox. It follows inevitably that the Gospel-Jesus has two mothers who were sisters, and two places of birth and rebirth. When the mythology was merged in the eschatology, and Ra became the father in heaven, he is described as having two companions who are with him in the solar bark. In this text the two sister-mothers with whom Ra consorts in the "divine ship" are Isis and Nut, who are the bringers-forth of Iusa or Jesus in his twofold character: child-Horus at his first advent being the son of Isis (Har-si-Hesi) the earth-mother, and in his second advent, or rebirth in spirit, the son of Nut, the heavenly mother. Such is the origin of the two mothers who were two sisters, and two consorts in two places of birth and rebirth represented in the "historic" narrative by Nazareth and Bethlehem as the birthplace of the shoot or natzer in Virgo, and the house of bread in Pisces, which two places of birth corresponded to the two seasons of seedtime and of harvest in the old Egyptian year.

Not only had Horus two mothers, Isis the virgin who conceived him, and Nephthys who nursed him. He was brought forth singly, and also as one of five brothers. Jesus has two mothers, Mary the Virgin who conceived him, and Mary the wife of Cleopas, who brought him forth as one of her children. He, likewise, was brought forth singly, and as one of five brethren. Horus was the son of Seb, his father on earth. Jesus is the son of Joseph, the father on earth. Horus was with his mother the Virgin until twelve years old, when he transformed into the beloved son of God as the only-begotten of the father in heaven. Jesus remained with his mother the Virgin up to the age of twelve years, when he left her to be about his father's business. From twelve to thirty years of age there is no record in the life of Horus. From twelve to thirty years of age there is no record in the life of Jesus. Horus at thirty years of age became adult in his baptism by Anup. Jesus at thirty years of age was made a man of in his baptism by John the Baptist. Horus in his baptism made his transformation into the beloved son and only-begotten of the father, the holy spirit, represented by a bird. Jesus in his baptism is hailed from heaven as the beloved son and only-begotten of the father God, the holy spirit that is represented by a dove, which denotes the mystery of all mysteries concerning the origin of the Egypto-gnostic Christ.

The elder Horus came to earth in the body of his humility. The younger came from heaven to wear the vesture of his father's glory. The first was the child of a baptism by water. The second is Horus the anointed or Christified; the oil upon whose face reflected the glory of the Father. This was the double baptism of the mysteries which is referred to in the Ritual by the priest who says, "I lustrate with water in Tattu and with oil in Abydos" (ch. 1). The duality manifested in Horus is shown when he is said to come into being as two brethren, the same that *Pistis Sophia* describes as "the Saviour-twins"; also when the transformer Kheper takes the form of two children—the elder and the younger (Litany of Ra, 61). Again, in the seventy-first chapter of the Ritual, Horus divinized is called "the owner of twin souls, who lives in two twin souls," now united in the eternal one. It is the potential duality of sex in the child-Horus that will account for Queen Hatshepsu being designated Mat-Ka-Ra, the true likeness of the solar god, called the golden Horus. She assumed the habiliments of both sexes in token that the divinity was

3 E 2

dual, and that this duality was reproduced in the golden Horus whose various phases of twinship included the two souls of sex. The golden Horus was a supreme type because of the twofold nature of the soul. It was this duality of Horus that is referred to by Hatshepsu when she says "the *two Horus-gods* have united the two divisions (south and north) for me." "I rule over this land like the son of Isis"; "I am victorious like the son of Nut"; which two likewise constitute the double Horus (Inscription: *Records*, vol. 12, 134). It is said of the Osirian Horus in his twofold genesis from matter and spirit, "Horus proceedeth from the essence of his father and the corruption which befell him" (Rit., ch. 78). That is in the incarnation or immergence in matter as the opposite of spirit, according to the later theology. Matter was at this time considered to be corrupt, and matter was maternal, but spirit was paternal and held to be divine. This will also explain the language of the Ritual applied to Osiris when he is spoken of as suffering decay and corruption, although inherently inviolate and incorruptible. The Osiris is embalmed in the divine type of him that never saw corruption. Yet Horus the child is born of Isis, into the corruption of matter in his incorporation, and all the evil that was derived from matter or the mother-nature has to be purged away in becoming pure spirit like Horus at the second advent, when he has become the glorified, anointed, only-begotten son. These were the two halves of a soul that was perfected in oneness, when Horus the child was blended with Horus the adult in the marriage-mystery of Tattu, but not till then, and not otherwise. "The two Horus-gods" is a title of the dual Horus in the Pyramid-texts of Teta. The Olive is there said to be "the tree of the two Horus-gods who are in the temples." Horus proclaims himself to be the issue of Seb (or Earth) whose spouse is Isis, and affirms that his mother is Nut (ch. 42). That is as the double Horus. Horus the human soul on earth, and Horus as a spirit in Amenta; Horus born of two mothers who were two sisters, and who in the different theologies may be Neith and Sekhet; Iusāas and Nebhetep; Isis and Nut; or two Marys, the two Meris who were at first the cow of earth and the cow of heaven. The child of Isis, the virgin heifer, was imaged as the calf, the red calf of sacrifice, also by the golden calf. After his death he rose again as the bull in the likeness of his father, Osiris, the bull of eternity. In the solar mythos he was born as a calf in the autumn equinox that became a bull in the Easter equinox when this occurred in Taurus. The type was repeated in the eschatology, when the manes is baptized to become the anointed in the character of Horus, who says, "I am the divine bull, son of the ancestress of Osiris" (Rit., ch. 147).

The story of Jesus in the canonical Gospels follows the totemic and mythical representation. Like Heitsi-Eibib and the human Horus he is the child of a virgin mother, the child of Mary only up to twelve years of age. Then the same change occurs with him as with the totemic youth at puberty. He waxes in force and stature, and is immediately "about thirty years of age." This is the age of Amsu-Horus when he has made his transformation from childhood into manhood as the khemt or typical adult of thirty years, at which time he rises in Amenta as a sahu in the glorified body. The transformation of Horus who was a child of the mother alone, the immaculate virgin Neith, she who came from herself, is reproduced by Luke. When Horus the child transforms he is only twelve years of age. As a child with Mary Jesus "waxed strong and was filled with wisdom, and the grace of God was upon him" (Luke ii. 40). The "grace of God" in Egyptian is termed "khemt" for grace and favour, and it is as Amsu-Horus that the child waxes strong and is in favour with, or endowed by, God the Father. The way in which he "waxed in stature" can be seen in the effigy of Amsu-Horus, the divinized adult who is the fulfiller at puberty, mythical in the vernal equinox, human in the harvest-field, and in the resurrection eschatological. But there had been no fecundator of a human mother by her own child since the days of utter and incestuous promiscuity until the time when the mythical Horus (or Jesus) was made human in a personal and historical character as the fertilizer of a Hebrew virgin.

The titles given to two Egyptian priests who, in succession, present the deceased person to the gods are the An-mut-ef and Si-meri-ef. These are two titles of Horus in his two characters, first as the support of his mother, and secondly as the beloved son of his father. According to Egyptian doctrine, the incarnation of the elder Horus was no isolated individual event. Nor was a soul made flesh in any single form of personality. It was the soul of the totem, family, stock or tribe, and lastly of the individual that was represented in the typical figure of Horus or Jesus, child of the virgin mother. The soul of flesh that was born of the mother's blood and made a type of in mythology could no more be limited to a single person than the soul that was previously derived from air, earth, water or other element of life. It was in keeping with natural law that, when the pubescent virgin had conceived, the incarnation of a human soul commenced. The mother, as the insufflator of that soul, was the mode and means of the incarnation which was effected in her blood, the flow of which was diverted to that end. The earliest embodiment then of a soul that was derived from a *human* source, and not simply from the elements of external nature, was by incarnation in the blood of the female who was mythically represented as the virgin mother. Thus the embodiment of the human soul, when descent was traced from the mother only, was by incarnation, and not by begettal. As it is said of the elder Horus, Har-si-Hesi, he was born but *not begotten*. The second Horus is begotten of the father with a second mother Nut, who is added as the bringer-forth above. It was comparatively late before the begettal of a human soul was ascribed to the individual progenitor. As shown by Egypt in the mirror of the mythos, this was not earlier than the time of Ptah when the double primitive essence was first recognized. A pair of souls were then derived, the one from matter, the other from spirit; one from the motherhood, the other from the fatherhood, both of which were blended in Ptah, the epicene parent. Child-Horus literally embodies the first half of a soul that was human primarily and in a latter stage divine. In its first phase this soul was derived from the mother's blood and quickening breath as a body-soul. In its second, the source is spiritual, a causative source from the father in heaven. For example, the Ka, or highest soul of seven, is thought of in the Ritual as food or sustenance for the body and the means of duration. It is also looked upon as a typical sacrifice to that end. Hence the speaker says, "Am I not the bull of the sacrificial herd: are not the mortuary gifts upon me, and the powers above Nu" (ch. 105). Horus in the second phase says, "I am a soul and my soul is divine. I am he who produceth food. I am the food which perisheth not—in my name of self-originating force, together with Nu," the mother heaven. (Rit., ch. 85.) This is he who possessed the "powers above Nu" as bringer of the bread of life from heaven. "The bread of God which cometh down out of heaven and giveth life to the world" was this imperishable food of soul that gave eternal life to men: and which when personified in Horus imaged a saviour from death in matter. When the Osiris deceased attains the type of the sacred hawk he speaks of being invested with the soul of Horus. "Horus has invested (him) with his own soul for the seizing of his inheritance from Osiris at the Tuat." "It is I, even I, who am Horus in glory" (ch. 78). Horus had come again in glory from the father as revealer of the bliss towards which his followers were bound (ch. 30 B). When Horus was invested with the soul that is to be eternal, he becomes hawk-headed, in the likeness of the father, as Jesus was invested with that other bird of soul, the gnostic dove, when he was proclaimed to be the beloved son of God the father in his baptism.

Paul's doctrine of the resurrection is founded on this mystery of the double Horus. As taught by the Egyptian wisdom, continuity was conditional, and the power of resurrection was personally secured by living the life of human Horus in fellowship with his sufferings as the bearer of his cross by which the power of his resurrection in the after-life was attained through becoming Horus the divinized adult. Paul's resurrection is obtainable on the same conditions of becoming. As a struggling mortal he hopes "by any means" to attain "unto the resurrection from the dead," and says, "Not that I have already attained or am already made perfect; but I press on." In Paul's Epistles, Christ takes the place of Horus the anointed by whom the power of the resurrection was made manifest in the mysteries, and the doctrine is the same as in the Ritual. In his own body and sufferings Paul was living the life and trying to emulate the character of Horus the mortal, whilst looking forward to the future fulfilment as it was portrayed in Horus glorified, whose second coming in Tattu as representative of Ra the holy spirit and the power of resurrection is perfectly described by Paul. The manes in the Ritual says, "My enclosure is in Heaven," as it was imaged on the mountain summit in the eternal city. Paul writes, "Our own citizenship is in heaven: from whence also we wait for a Saviour, the Lord Jesus Christ, who shall fashion anew the body of our humiliation (which was one with the maimed, deformed and suffering human Horus, changed and glorified in the resurrection) that it may be conformed to the body of his glory" as it had been set forth scene by scene in the mysteries of Amenta by the divine scribe Taht, and preserved sufficiently intact to make it out as pre-historical and non-historical in the once-more living Egyptian Book of the Dead (Phil. iii. 20–21).

The reason why the Virgin's child should make his change and pass away when twelve years old, and why the divinized adult should not take up the story until thirty years of age, to leave no record during eighteen years, is to be explicated by the Egyptian wisdom. It is because the two as double Horus, or as the dual Jesus Christ, are no more than types, and have no relation to an individual human history, Kamite, Hebrew, Persian, Gnostic, or Christian ; and in this unity, as before said, the different versions all agree.

The *Pistis Sophia* tells us more about the double Horus, the two-fold Messiah, or twin Saviour, than all the records outside the Ritual put together ; more particularly in the astronomical phase of the mythos, only in this work the double Horus is the Egypto-gnostic Jesus, who does fulfil the second advent in accordance with the map of mythology. In one representation of his nature Horus is portrayed as the ruler, both in time and eternity. In time he is the foster-child of Seb, god of earth, brought forth by the mother-moon or Virgin in the zodiac as the king of one year. This is Horus in the circle of the lesser year. At his second advent, as fulfiller on the vastest scale, he is said to travel the everlasting road as the ever-coming prince of eternity. It was thus the first Horus, or Jesus, represented the solar god that made the circuit of the signs in the forward motion through the zodiac, whereas the second Horus, or Jesus, was the " traveller of the heavenly road," the backward way in the hugest all-embracing circle of precession.

The gnostic Jesus represents the double Horus, human and divine, more fully and definitely than does the Jesus of the canonical Gospels and independently of any personal history. The first and second advents are both fulfilled by the Jesus of *Pistis Sophia*. As the youth of twelve years who was Horus the word, he instructs the disciples " up to the regions of the first statutes only" and is the teacher by means of parables. In his second advent he says, " I will speak with you face to face without parable." He then unveils and expounds the greater mysteries from centre to circumference ; from the first to the last. In the same gnostic scripture Mary, the mother of Jesus, describes her son in accordance with the Egyptian gnosis of the double Horus, which was not derived from the canonical Gospels. She thus addresses him : " When thou wert a child *before the spirit had descended upon thee*, when thou wert in the vineyard with Joseph, the spirit descended from the height and came unto me in the house (so) like unto thee I knew him not, but thought that it was thou. And he said unto me, 'Where is Jesus, my brother, that I may go to meet him ?' And when he had said this unto me I was in doubt and thought it was a phantom tempting me. I seized him and bound him to the foot of the bed which was in my house." Jesus, the mortal, is in the vineyard with Joseph. He hears Mary tell her *naïf* story to Joseph, and exclaims, " Where is he that I may see him? I am expecting him in this place." Mary continues : " We went together ; we entered into the house, we found the spirit bound to the bed, and we gazed upon thee and him and found that thou wert like unto him. And he that was bound to the bed was unloosed. He embraced thee and kissed thee, and thou also didst kiss him ; ye became one and the same being " (*P. S.*, B. 1, 120, Mead).

The two Jesuses, one in matter and one in spirit, or Jesus and the Christ, are identical with Horus, the prince in the city of the blind, and Horus who reconstitutes his father. The meeting and the blending of the two into one being is a gnostic version of the mystery enacted in Tattu, where Horus in spirit meets with Horus the mortal, or Ra, the holy spirit, embraces Osiris, the god in matter, and the pair are united in the one double divine soul, which dwelleth in the place of establishing a soul that is to live for ever (Rit., ch. 17, 16–18).

In the opening chapter of Matthew's Gospel the birth or generation of Jesus is called "the birth of Jesus Christ" (ch. i., 18), a twofold character equivalent to that of the double Horus, who was Horus in the flesh until twelve years of age, and Horus in the spirit from the age of thirty years. In other versions it is designated "the birth of the Christ." But in accordance with the genuine doctrine these are two births entirely distinct from each other, one for Jesus the Virgin's child and one for the Christ as an effluence of the Holy Spirit emanating from the father in the form of a dove. Horus the Virgin's child was born but not begotten. At his second advent he became the divinized adult as the only son begotten of the father. This was the anointed son, and the anointed is the Christ, or Christified. The Christ was constituted by a begettal in spirit, when the spirit of God descended from heaven as the dove, or the hawk of soul, and the youth of twelve years was transformed into the man of thirty years. There was no Christ until this change of state and type took place, and could be none without the necessary transformation by which it was accomplished. This was represented in the transformation and transubstantiation of the mummy; in the baptism, circumcision, regeneration, resurrection, and other modes of the mystery, in which the body-soul was converted into a likeness of the eternal spirit; child-Horus into Horus the adult, or Jesus into the Christ. But, to compare as we proceed, the Word in the Kamite original was the first, or elder Horus, the child-Horus born of the Virgin Mother, he who issued out of silence as the inarticulate Logos (Rit., ch. 24). He is called the Kheru in Egyptian, which not only signifies the Word, but also denotes a victim doomed to be sacrificed, whether as the sufferer in the Tat, on the cross, or as the victim bound for slaughter. The second Horus, Horus in spirit, was the demonstrator of eternal life in his resurrection from the sepulchre who is thus the word-made-truth that was personalized in Har-Ma-Kheru. This second Horus, who is the fulfiller that follows the founder, is referred to in the Gospel, parenthetically, in a way that blends or confuses the two in one as the word. "And the Word became flesh, and dwelt among us (and we beheld his glory, glory as of the only-begotten from the father) full of grace and truth." This is the merest passing allusion to the second Horus who was the anointed, only-begotten Son of God the Father; that is, to Horus, glorified, who followed human Horus in the flesh, but could not be so easily made to look historical.

The difference betwixt "the Son of Man" and "the Son of the woman" may also be explicated by the doctrine of the double Horus. The "Son of Man" is a title of Jesus in the Gospels, which has been supposed to denote the Son of God in the body of his humanity. But there was a " Son of Man " with an esoteric and mystical significance, who was known to the gnostic teachers as Anthropos the son of Anthropos ; also as Monogenes. Horus the Saviour in his first advent was the child of Isis ; that is, the son of woman when the woman is divine. In his second advent he is Iu, the Su or Son of God the Father, who became the Son of Man by title thus : Atum-Ra, son of Ptah, was the earliest god in the likeness of the perfect man. He was the first man in the same sense that the Jew-god Ieou in the *Pistis Sophia* is called the " First Man " (333) as the divine begetter in the human likeness. Ieou is the first man, and Iao is his son. Thus Iao, or Jesus, is "the Son of Man." He comes to earth as the one God in the form of man. This, in the Ritual, is the Egyptian Jesus, Iu-em-hetep, the Son as Revealer of the Father Atum-Ra. The Father gives authority to the Son " to execute judgment, because he is the Son of Man " (John v. 27). That is at the second coming, when he is to appear in the power and the glory of the Father, as did the second Horus with the oil upon his face which expressed the glory of his divinity. This is " the Son of Man " who was in heaven whilst on the earth (John iii. 13), and who was to "come in his glory, and all the angels with him " (Matt. xxv. 31) ; and who did so come to judgment periodically as Horus in the mysteries of Amenta (Rit., ch. 125). But the title is applied to Jesus indiscriminately in the Gospels, where the two Horuses are continually confused together by the concoctors of the human history, which was limited in locality as much as possible to this earth, to make it the more convincing in its appeal.

In the Ritual Horus says : " I am the heir, the primary power of motion and of rest." He was the heir in several characters. In the first he is the heir of Seb, the earth-father. In the second he is the heir of Osiris. When Osiris and Ra are blended in one Horus becomes the heir of Ra, the father in heaven, as the inheritor and the giver of eternal life to his followers. " The two earths have been decreed to Horus absolutely and without condition " (ch. 19). Because it was he who joined the two Horuses together, and as Paul phrases it, "made both one, and brake down the middle-wall of partition, that he might create in himself of the twain *one new man* " (Eph. ii. 14, 15). As son of Seb he is the Virgin's child on earth, or in matter. As son of Osiris he is Amsu the Divine Manes in Amenta, and as Har-Sam-Taui he is the uniter of the two earths in one, the conqueror who makes the word of Osiris truth against his enemies, and thus becomes the founder of the future kingdom of heaven for his father in the spirit as the double Horus, he who wins and wears the double diadem.

The dual Horus—Horus as mortal and Horus in spirit, Horus as child of the Virgin and Horus begotten of the Father, Horus twelve years of age and Horus the adult of thirty years—is reproduced in the Gospels, however briefly, although the object of the writers was not to distinguish between the two natures, human and divine, whilst both were limited to the one life on this earth. Still, there is a dual Jesus, or Jesus and the Christ, corresponding to the double Horus. Child-Horus is portrayed as the child-Jesus up to twelve years of age. In his baptism by water it is prognosticated by John that Jesus is to come as the Baptizer with the Holy Spirit and with fire. This is he "whose fan is in his hand," and this is the transformation that was made by Horus the mortal when he became Horus rising in spirit with the fan, or khu, in his hand. Jesus in the same circumstances is the same character. The Spirit of God the Father descends upon him in the likeness of a dove, which indicates that he is now the Christ in Spirit. The Virgin's child has changed into the Son of God the Father, and the change is authenticated by the " Voice out of the heavens, saying, this is my beloved Son" (Matt. iii. 16, 17). The transaction is one of many that could only take place in the Earth of Amenta, but which are represented perforce in the earth of time, because the matter of the pre-existent mythos was rendered as a human history in the exoteric Gospels.

It has to be repeated again and again that the primitive mysteries of totemism were continued and developed as spiritual in the Egyptian eschatology. Child-Horus at twelve years of age represents the typical youth that passed into the ranks of the adults at puberty, who was circumcised and regenerated in the rite of Baptism, blood, water or oil being used for the purpose of lustration. This is repeated in the transformation of child-Horus into Horus the adult, the child of twelve years into the sherau of thirty years ; otherwise the child of the mother into the son of the father. Thus, the child-Horus becomes the beloved son of the father in his baptism, as did Jesus. In the Ritual (chapter of the baptisms) the speaker at the fourth portal says : " I have been baptized in the water with which the Good Being was washed at the time when he had his contention with Sut (Satan), and when the victory was given to him." In the baptism at the fifth portal, he says he has washed himself, or has been baptized in the water that *Horus was washed in when he became the beloved son of his father, Osiris.* " Su-meri-f" is the son whom the father loves, hence the beloved son, the anointed, or the Christ when Christified. In one of these baptisms (eighth portal) the baptizer is mentioned by name as Anup. He was the typical baptizer, the embalmer and anointer of the dead from of old, before the time of the solar Horus, or Osiris. " I have been washed in the water wherein the God Anup baptized when he performed the office of embalmer and binder-up of the Mummy." Or, as it is otherwise said, when he became the chief minister to Osiris in the later cult. Here we find (1) that Anup was the baptizer in preparing Osiris (or the mortal Horus) to become the Horus in spirit, the anointed and beloved son of the father in the rite of embalmment, or baptism ; that Osiris, or Horus, was baptized preparatory to or at the time of his contest with Sut (Satan) ; and that the baptism of Horus took place when he became chief minister, the beloved son *Su-meri-f* of his father, he who had previously been the pillar of support (An-mut-f) to his mother. (Naville, *Texts* ; Budge, *Book of the Dead*, ch. 145.) There is a baptism in the Ritual which takes place at the time when Horus makes his transformation into the menat, the bird of soul as a swallow, dove or pigeon. That is when mortal Horus has become a spirit (ch. 85, 1), with the head of a bird, whether as the Divine hawk or the dove, and the same transformation takes place in the baptism of Jesus, when the dove from heaven descended and abode upon him as the sign to show that he was now the Son of the Father in Spirit.

There was a double baptism in the ancient mysteries: the baptism by water and the baptism by spirit. This may be traced to the two lakes of heaven at the head of the celestial river in the region of the northern pole, which were also repeated as the two lakes of purification in Amenta. The manes says, "I purify me in the southern tank, and I rest me at the northern lake" (ch. 125). They will account for the two forms of baptism mentioned in the Gospels. John baptizes with water, Jesus with the Holy Spirit and with fire. This twofold baptism had been represented by the two celestial lakes or pools that were configurated in the northern heaven which are to be read of in the Ritual (ch. 97) as the baptistry of Anup. One of these was the lake of purification by water; the other by spirit. This latter was the lake of Sa by name, in which the gods themselves were wont to be vitalized in their baptism. Sa signifies spirit; the Sa was a divine or magical fluid which made immortal; and the baptism in this sacred lake of Sa was literally a baptism of the holy spirit. The scene of the baptism by John can be paralleled in the Ritual (ch. 97). Horus claims to be the master of all things, including the water of the Inundation. When he comes to be baptized, it is "*said at the boat*," called "the staff of Anup," "Look upon me, oh ye great and mighty Gods, who are foremost among the spirits of Annu; let me be exalted in your presence." The plea for baptism is very express. "Lo, I come, that I may *purify this soul of mine in the most high degree*: let not that impediment which cometh from your mouth be issued against me, *let me be purified in the lake of propitiation and of equipoise*: let me plunge into the divine pool *beneath the two divine sycamores of* heaven and earth." After the baptism, he says, "*Now let my Fold be fitted for me as one victorious against all adversaries who would not that right should be done to me. I am the only one just and true upon the earth*" (Rit., ch. 97, Renouf). In the Gospel, when Jesus cometh "unto John" = Anup the baptizer, "John would have hindered him." "But Jesus answering said unto him, suffer me now for thus it becometh us to fulfil all *righteousness*" (Matt. iii. 14, 15)—a probable rendering of the Egyptian word Maat! In the Egyptian baptism three elements are involved: the elements of water, fire and spirit. Osiris represented water, Horus the solar fire, and Ra the holy spirit. These elements agree with the three persons in the trinity that were Osiris the father, Horus the son, Ra the holy spirit, in whose names as father, son and holy ghost the rite of baptism still continues to be practised. The second character was fulfilled by Horus when he became bird-headed as a spirit in the resurrection. This fulfilment is obvious if not perfectly accomplished on behalf of Jesus after his baptism. "And Jesus, *full of the holy spirit*, returned from the Jordan, and was led *in the Spirit*" (Luke iv. 1, 2). He also returns "in the power of the Spirit" (iv. 14). The same change has occurred with him as with Horus in the same circumstances. It is now that he makes the announcement. "The *Spirit of the Lord is upon me*, because he hath anointed me to preach good tidings to the poor: he hath sent me to proclaim release to the captives and recovery of sight to the blind, to set at liberty them that are bruised, to proclaim the acceptable year of the Lord. To-day hath the scripture been fulfilled in your ears." This was the fulfilment, according to Jewish prophecy, of that second advent which took place, and could only take place in spirit-world, and not in the life on earth, except as a performance in the religious mysteries.

Another episode in the canonical account of Jesus will serve to illustrate the transformation from the child of twelve into the adult of thirty years. When Jesus was twelve years old, says Luke, his parents went up to Jerusalem at the feast of the Passover. When they were returning to Nazareth they found the boy had tarried behind in Jerusalem. After three days they discovered him in the temple sitting in the midst of the doctors, both hearing them and asking them questions. They were astonished ; and his mother said unto him, " Son, why hast thou thus dealt with us? Behold, thy father and I sought thee sorrowing." And he said unto them, " How is it ye sought me? Wist ye not that I must be on my father's business? "—or must be about the things of my father. This, in the original, is a legend of the infancy and of the time when the child-Horus made his transformation into Horus the adult, to become the fulfiller for his father, " and," as he says, " to take the *lead.*" Osiris in his maimed and mutilated state was represented by the child of Isis, the Horus of twelve years, or the moon in the fourteen days of waning light, or the sun in the winter solstice. Thus Isis in search of the scattered limbs and members of Osiris was in search of her child (Rit., ch. 157). As it is said in the " Hymn to Osiris," " she went round the world lamenting him. She stopped not till she found him. . . . She raised the remains of the god of the motionless heart. She extracted his essence. She bore a child. She suckled her babe in secrecy. No one knew where it happened " (*Records*, vol. 4, pp. 101–2). In the text quoted from the Ritual the child of the papyrus-marshes has changed and come forth as the ruler, he who fights the great battle against Sut. Horus was then about his father's business. He had now transformed from the child of Isis only, or Horus in the secret place, into Horus the begotten of the father, the Horus of thirty years. This is the original of the story told by Luke of the child-Christ when he was twelve years of age. Mary, like Isis, searches the districts for her missing child, who is found after three days, which is the length of time assigned to the transformation of Osiris for renewal in the moon. Meantime he, too, has " made a great battle," asserted his supremacy, and " ordered what was to be done," although the nature and mode of the contest have been changed. He has also given terror and caused his mother to fear. When reproached by his mother, who had sought him sorrowing, he asks his mother and father if they did not know that he must be about his father's business, or attending to the things of his father.

There is a chapter of Isis seeking for child-Horus at his going forth from the marshes in which the papyrus grew ; that is, when Horus is the child of twelve years who transforms into the living likeness of the father as the man of thirty years. A vulture with outspread wings is the emblem of the seeking mother, who goes about searching the " mysterious retreats " of Horus in which he hides himself after leaving the marshes. Her son goes forth to face misfortune, to command the chiefs of the district. He fights a great battle. He calls to remembrance what he has done, imposes fear on them, establishes his terror, his mother Isis having made charms for the protection of her child (Rit., ch. 157; Naville and Renouf). Horus in his two characters of the child and the adult is called the lad in the country, and the youth in the city or in the town (Rit., ch. 85). As the lad in the country he is the child with Isis the virgin mother, and Seb the earth-god, who was his foster-father during his childhood. As the youth in town he is in his father's house, and is "the heir of the temple" in Heliopolis (ch. 115). When Horus the child passes into Horus the adult he becomes the heir to the "things of his father." The Egyptian word "khetu" for "things" is most idiomatic, and "the things of my father" in the Greek is uniquely perfect as a rendering of the Egyptian "khetu."

It is as the youth in town or in Heliopolis = Jerusalem, that Horus says "I am a soul, and my soul is divine"; this was derived from Ra, his father in heaven: "I take the lead. I put an end to darkness. I put a stop to evil." And when Horus goes to Abydos to see his father Osiris, all the great gods, together with the groups of the gods, come forth to meet and greet him with their acclamations. He is hailed by them as "the king of hosts" who cometh to unite and take possession of the two worlds. His *father's house* is seized (in the juridical sense of *seizin* or feudal possession) "in virtue of the writs," which have been issued on behalf of the divine heir, "the heir of the temple" (ch. 138), the "son whom the father hath begotten" (ch. 115). Abydos is the mythical rebirth-place of Osiris, and it was there that Horus took possession of his father's house. In the Gospel it is Jerusalem. Twice over in one brief chapter of the Ritual (115th) Horus is called "the heir of the temple." He says, "It is with reference to me that the gods say, Lo, the afflicted one is the heir of Annu." This was as Horus the wise and wonderful child. And again it is said of Horus the divine adult, "active and powerful is the heir of the temple; the active one of Annu, the son whom the father hath begotten." In the Ritual the temple is in Annu; it is otherwise termed the hat-saru, or house of the prince. Horus enters this as the child of the mother, and he comes forth as the son of the father, and the wielder of the whip as the symbol of his sovereignty. Here is the parallel to the child-Jesus sitting in the temple as a teacher of the teachers, laying down the law to the masters of the law. As the Word of truth, Horus "assembles the chiefs of truth" or law. These are the acolytes who sit with Osiris in the great hall of Maat. The lords of truth (or the law) collected there to watch over iniquity, as they sit in "Seb's great dwelling," recognize the lad as the lord of justice, and delegate authority to him as their chief. The original of a scene in the temple is traceable in the "Hymn to Osiris." Horus has grown strong in the dwelling of Seb. "The divine company rejoices when the son of Osiris comes, even Horus steadfast of heart, with (or as) the word made truth: the son of Isis, the flesh of Osiris." Horus in the hall of Mati was in the house of his father Osiris seated on the judgment-seat surrounded by the chiefs of truth as the lad who is acknowledged now to be the universal master, and the lord of law and of very truth itself. The father's house in the Gospels becomes the temple at Jerusalem, the "chiefs of truth" collected there are the doctors or Tannaim, and the divine child Horus, the royal Horus, wearer of the double crown, has been converted into the child of Joseph the carpenter.

According to John, the first thing that Jesus did after his baptism was to prove his power by turning water into wine. This is immediately followed by his foray in the temple at Jerusalem. He makes a scourge of cords, where Horus, as "heir of the temple," wields the whip or flagellum on the enemies of his father. Jesus lays on lustily with his flagellum and drives out those who have made the Father's house a house of merchandise or den of thieves. He thus proves himself to be, like Horus, "active and powerful," "the heir of the temple" who hath the might divine as the only son, whom "the Father hath begotten," in the one instance by vanquishing Sut on the pinnacle, and in the other by driving out the evil-doers = the Sut-Typhonians from the temple (John ii. 14–17), both of which events are stated in two different Gospels to have followed immediately after the baptism, in which occurred the transformation of Jesus into the dove-headed Son of God the Father.

In the Ritual the subject of chapter 138 is the "Entry into Abydos," and it describes a scene of triumph for Horus analogous to the entry of Jesus into Jerusalem. He is the lord of life in Abydos. He exclaims, "O gods of Abydos. Let us be joyful. Do not hinder me from seeing my father. I am the Horus of Khem-Ka, the red shoot (or branch = natzer) which nothing can injure, whose hand is strong against his enemies : avenger of his father, striking his enemies, repelling violence : governor of multitudes, chief of the earth, who *takes possession of his father's dwelling with his arms."* The object of this triumphant entry is for the divine heir to take possession of his father's dwelling. This he effects by force of arms. "And Jesus entered into the temple of God, and cast out all that bought and sold in the temple and overthrew the tables of the money-changers." And he saith unto them, "It is written my house shall be called a house of prayer : but ye have made it a den of robbers" (Matt. xxi. ; Rit. 138).

Amsu-Horus rises in Amenta with the signs of government upon his shoulder in the shape of the crook and the whip (or khu). As bearer of the crook he is a form of the Good Shepherd who comes in that character to look after his father's flock or herd. As wielder of the whip he came to drive out and scourge the enemies of his father. The Christ who is portrayed as the Good Shepherd in one character is also described as making his advent with the fan in his hand, which in the hand of Amsu is the flail or whip. This, in another scene, becomes the whip or scourge with which Jesus drives out the illegal occupants of the temple. The passover of the Jews being at hand, Jesus went up to Jerusalem, and "he found in the temple those that sold oxen and sheep and doves, and the changers of money sitting" together in this compound of menagerie and mart, which is as if the Stock Exchange and Smithfield Market met together in St. Paul's Cathedral. "And he made a scourge of cords, and cast all out of the temple, both the sheep and the oxen : and he poured out the changers' money and overthrew the tables, and to them that sold the doves he said, take these things hence ; make not my father's house a house of merchandise" (John ii. 13–17). This portrait of the wielder of the whip driving out the sheep and oxen is the reverse to that of the good shepherd with the crook, and this historic fulfilment of the mythos is a very puerile parody of Amsu-Har-Tema, the doer of justice, scourging the foes of his father out of the temple in his consuming fury of resentment, so soon as ever he had taken in hand the whip of his divine authority. Horus is not mentioned as riding into Abydos on an ass, but in the cult of Atum-Ra the solar disk was hauled up from Amenta by the ass-eared god Iusa, and Iusa was the original rider on the ass or the foal of the ass.

Immediately following this clearing out of the temple it is said that Jesus hungered—and seeing a fig-tree by the wayside he came to it and found nothing thereon. He is described as coming to the fig-tree hungry, when figs were not in season, and because there was no fruit upon it he sterilized it for ever, "and immediately the fig-tree withered away" (Matt. xxi. 19). This is in the character of Horus the avenger, who comes to the fig-tree in the Aarru-garden and says, "*I am Amsu-Horus, the avenger of his father the Good Being. I carry out for my father the overthrowal of all his enemies,*" including the fig-tree, as it is rendered in the Gospels. In the Ritual the cedar is quoted in the place of the sycamore-fig. The speaker, in addressing the keeper of the twenty-first gate, says, "Thou keepest the secrets of the Avenging God (Har-Tema) *who causes the Shennu-tree to bear no fruit*" (Rit., ch. 145).

The earth-life ceases for Horus at the age of twelve. Partly because he typified an impotent or impubescent body-soul in matter, mere soul of the mother-blood, and the difference between child-Horus and Horus divinized was expressed by the difference betwixt the child of twelve and the perfect man of thirty years. It ceased by the transformation into that which was typical of another life. Child-Horus passed away from earth to make his change or to be made "a man of" in the mysteries of Amenta. He rose again as Amsu in ithyphallic form to show the potency of soul or spirit in the after-life by means of the natural figure. Thus, according to the genuine mythos, at the time of the baptism in the Jordan, when Jesus had attained the age of twelve, the earthly life came to an end, the mother's child had for the first time found his father. But that was not in this world. The second Horus was begotten in Amenta, not on earth. Also the baptism of regeneration, and other of the spiritual mysteries, occurred in that earth of eternity and not upon the earth where mortal beings dwell. In the totemic mysteries circumcision was a rite of puberty which marked the transformation of the youth into the man, and this, like other typical customs, was continued in the religious mysteries. When Horus makes his change and rises in Amenta as Horus the adult, *it is in a figure that has suffered the rite of circumcision, as the portraits of the risen Amsu prove.* Thus circumcision, like baptism, was a rite of regeneration and resurrection or re-erection from the dead; that is, from the state of the inert Osiris, the impubescent Horus, or, doctrinally, from the status of the uncircumcised, the unbaptized, who were "unhouselled, unanointed, unannealed," and who might thus remain in mummied immobility. The first Horus is impubescent; the second is circumcised to show that he has risen in the likeness of the father, "full of grace and truth," "the image of the invisible god, the first-born of all creation." Amsu-Horus, the risen Sahu, is identical doctrinally with the gnostic Christ of Paul, who tells his hearers that they have been circumcised in him who includes the pleroma of the godhead bodily, "with a circumcision not made with hands, in the putting off the body of the flesh, in the circumcision of Christ; having been buried with him in baptism, wherein ye were also raised with him through faith in the working of God, who raised him from the dead" (Col. ii. 10–12). When Horus rises from the dead he wields the weapons and he bears the symbols of his sovereignty. He has been baptized and circumcised, or lustrated with water, with oil, with the Holy Spirit, and crowned with the double feather. The doctrine is the same whether the risen one be Horus or the Christ; and there was nothing historical in the death, the baptism, the circumcision, the resurrection of Amsu-Horus, either as the Karast mummy or the Christ.

A difficulty all through with the concocters of the Gospel history was this dual character of Horus in two lives and two worlds. They had only the one lifetime to go upon in one world. Jesus had to become bird-headed in the human lifetime and on earth. Whereas the human Horus made his change into the "second-born, the golden hawk," *after* he had passed into Amenta. It was as a spirit in the earth of eternity that he became bird-headed in the likeness of his father Ra, not on the earth of Seb, where he was imaged in the likeness of mortality, as the human Horus. Still, the risen Jesus acts the part of Horus in issuing from the sepulchre as a spirit. After his death and burial, he appears to the disciples in the *rôle* of the second Horus who represents the Father after the resurrection in spirit. He tells them that the Father hath sent him. "And when he had said this, he breathed on them, and saith unto them, Receive ye the Holy Spirit" (John xx. 21, 22). This is in the character of the hawk-headed Horus who, as the son of Ra, is given power from the Father to breathe the Holy Spirit. It is a mystery of Amenta, with no meaning elsewhere. In this the Horus who had conquered death and risen again in triumph as the Beloved Son of God the Father, became the representative of the Holy Spirit with power to impart it to the breathless ones, and raise them from the dead; he who, as Horus or Jesus, in this character was "the resurrection and the life." But, in the gospels of the Sarkolatræ it had to be demonstrated that the risen Christ was not a spirit or anything superhuman, if the history was to be accepted as simply human and limited to the life on earth.

Horus, in his first advent, was the word-made-flesh in mortal guise, according to the Kamite doctrine of the incarnation. In his second advent, he is the word-made-truth as Horus the fulfiller in the spirit, according to the Kamite doctrine of the resurrection. In his baptism, Horus the word-made-flesh transformed into the word-made-truth, according to the Kamite doctrine of baptismal regeneration, each of which doctrines was of necessity perverted in the exoteric rendering. The scene of this rebirth in Amenta was underneath the tree of dawn—the tamarisk, persea, olive, or sycamore-fig-tree. The desire of the manes is literally to be with Horus under the fig-tree at the time of his resurrection from Amenta, a figure that was derived from the

Horus-sun arising from under the tree of dawn in the mythology. Horus reborn as the sun of morning, says, " I am the babe. I am the god within the tamarisk-tree " (ch. 42). The olive was another tree of dawn. The transformation of Osiris into Horus, or of Amsu into Horus the bird-headed, was effected underneath this tree. One of the seven khus, or great spirits who are the companions of Horus in his resurrection is named Kheri-bakhu-f or " he who is under the olive-tree," which is equated by the fig-tree in the Gospel of John for the green tree of dawn. On a papyrus at Dublin the Osiris prays that he may be under the sycamore (fig-tree) of Hathor at the rising of Horus (*Trans. Soci. Bib.*, vol. viii., p. 218). This, according to John, was the place where Nathaniel had been with Jesus before the two had ever met on earth (John i. 48, 49). " Now," says Andrew, " we have found the Christ." He calls upon Nathaniel to " come and see." Jesus recognizes him. Nathaniel says, " whence knowest thou me ? " " Jesus answered and said unto him, before Philip called thee, when thou wast under the fig-tree, I saw thee " (John i. 41–49).

The two characters of the double Horus, commonly ascribed to Jesus, are also portrayed upon the gnostic monuments in the Roman catacombs. In one character he is the little old and ugly Jesus. In the other he corresponds to Horus of the beautiful face. The first is the suffering Messiah, the despised and afflicted one, who was considered to be of an ignoble origin compared with that of Horus the younger. He was the child of the Mother only ; the soul in matter ; the heir of Seb, and therefore of the earth earthy. Horus the younger is the man from heaven ; the immortal Son of the Divine Man who is in heaven, Horus in his glory and his majesty. These often occur together on the same monuments in their irreconcilable contradiction of each other (Bosio, *Rom. Sott.*). But the " elder Horus " did not mean the aged Horus, for he was at the same time the child-Horus. The title has been misinterpreted by the artists of the catacombs who have represented " the afflicted one," the Man of sorrows, as diminutive, and pensive, old and ugly, whereas, according to the true type, he was never more than twelve years of age, and always wore the lock of childhood. " Old Child " was his name.

Horus in his childhood was the sower of the seed in the fields of his father. This Mystery follows that of the great battle in which Osiris is avenged and the associates of Sut are slain in the shape of goats, and the fields are prepared for the seed by being manured with their blood. The vignette is given by Naville from the tracing taken by Lepsius of the now lost papyrus Busca. The picture represents the great hoeing in Tattu. The long text at Denderah (Mariette, tom. 4, pl. 39) contains directions to be observed on the festival commemorative of the ancient custom. Two black cows are put under a yoke of am-wood, the plough is of tamarisk-wood, and the share of black bronze. The ploughman goes behind, with a cow led in a halter. A little child with the side-lock attached to its head is to scatter the seed in the field of Osiris. Barley is sown at one end, spelt at the other, and flax between the two. The Kher-heb in chief recites the office for the sowing of the field (Renouf, *Book of the Dead*, ch. 18, note 9). The child with the side-lock represents the Horus of twelve years who leaves his mother at that age and goes forth to be

3 F

"about his father's business." That business, as here shown, was the sowing of seed for Osiris, the divine husbandman. Jesus at twelve years of age is said to leave the Virgin on his father's business for the purpose of sowing the seed of the word ; the word that was to be made truth in the fields of divine harvest. Osiris is the husbandman as God the father, and child-Horus the seed-sower as the son, in human form. Sut, the anthropomorphic Satan, is the opponent of Horus in the harvest-field ; he undoes what Horus does. As the prince and power of drought and darkness, he is busy in the night. He sows the tares, the thorns and thistles, the weeds or "devil's-dung" amongst the good seed of Osiris sown by Horus. Horus has his assistants in the seed-sowing and the reaping of the harvest. These are grouped as the two, the four, the seven, and finally the typical twelve who are the reapers in the Aarru-fields, which are in the earth of eternity. There is no exact parallel scene in the canonical gospels to this of the seed-sowing in the Ritual, but the child that sows the seed in his father's field, survives in the Gospels of the Infancy. As we read in the Gospel of Thomas (ch. 12) at the time for sowing the child went out with his father to sow corn in their field, and when his father sowed, the child Jesus also sowed one grain of corn. And having reaped and threshed it, he made "a hundred quarters of it," and bestowed the corn upon the poor. "Now Jesus was eight years old when he wrought this miracle," during his first advent. At his second coming, Horus is the reaper in the fields of harvest. This is he "whose fan (or flail) is in his hand" when he rises from the sepulchre. The harvest at the end of the world was reaped by the followers of Horus at the end of the age or cycle of time. It was periodic in the mythology, like the harvests of the earth, and therefore periodic in the eschatology. He that sowed the good seed in the Egyptian mysteries was Horus the son of Isis, or the human Horus, who reappears as Amsu the husbandman in the fields of divine harvest, otherwise as Horus-Khuti the master of joy with his twelve followers who are the reapers of the harvest in Amenta. This is portrayed both in the nether-world and in the upper paradise of Hetep on the summit of the mount. The object of the beatified deceased is to attain the harvest-field in Hetep, that he may take possession of his allotment there, and be in glory there, and plough and sow and reap the harvest there for ever, "doing whatsoever things were done on earth," but changed and glorified. This was to be attained, not at the end of the world, but at the end of all the trials, the purifications and purgatorial pains, the strenuous efforts made in climbing up the ascent to reach at last the paradise of rest upon the summit ; the place of re-union and reconciliation ; the land of the tree of life and the water of life, of perennial plenty and of everlasting peace. Here the reapers, called the "angels" in the Gospel, show the harvest-field is not upon the earth of time. They are the twelve with Horus in the fields of divine harvest. Horus tells Osiris at the harvest-home that he has cultivated his corn for him in the Aarru-fields of peace ; and in the person of Har-khuti with the twelve as lord of spirits gathered in the harvests of eternity.

Two opposite characters are assigned to Jesus in the Gospels, in one of which he comes with peace, in the other he is the bringer of the sword. He is the bringer of peace on earth (Luke ii. 14; John xvi. 27), who says he has not come to bring peace on earth (Luke xii. 51). "I came not to send peace but a sword" (Matt. x. 34). Horus had appeared previously in these two *rôles*. He is "Horus the peaceful." As Iu-em-hetep he comes to bring peace and good fortune on earth and make wars to cease. Horus also comes with the sword as the avenger of his father when he pierces Sut to the heart, and annihilates the rebel powers. Har-tema is a title of the second Horus. The word Ma for justice also signifies the law. And he who reveals and makes justice visible is the Horus who not only fulfils the word by making it truth, but who also comes to *fulfil the law*, or maat. This is the character assigned to the Jesus of the Gospels, who says, "Think not I came to destroy the law. I came not to destroy but to fulfil. Verily I say unto you, till heaven and earth pass away, one jot or one tittle shall in no wise pass away from the law till all things be accomplished" (Matt. v. 17, 18). This law is the maat of the Ritual. And in the Gospel the speaker assumes the position of Har-tema, who was the fulfiller of justice or the law. In the earth-life Jesus is the word or speaker in parables. In that way the "Inarticulate Discourse" of Horus is assigned to Jesus, with the usual misrendering of the hidden meaning, as the matter of parables which no one but the duly initiated could possibly understand. Indeed they were prepensely intended to be non-intelligible to all others. As it is said to the disciples, "Unto you it is given to know the mysteries of the Kingdom of God, but to the rest in parables, that seeing they may see not and hearing they may not understand" (Luke viii. 10). Child-Horus opened his mouth in Sign-language only. Jesus only opens his in parables. At his second coming he is to speak no more in parables but to tell the disciples plainly of the father. That is how the twofold character of Horus was to be fulfilled by Jesus, and as it had been already fulfilled by the Egypto-gnostic Jesus in "Pistis Sophia." Also, however indirectly, Jesus is identified with the child-Horus as the teacher who was a babe and suckling and who exclaims "I am the babe" (repeated four times) in the Ritual (ch. 42). Jesus says, at the time when "he rejoiced in the holy spirit" (Luke x. 21), "I thank thee, O Father, Lord of heaven and earth, that thou didst hide these things (the things which had been given him to teach) from the wise and understanding and didst reveal them unto babes. (Such babes as Horus with the side-lock.) All things have been delivered unto me of my father and no one knoweth who the son is save the father." But in the course of making out a human history from the mythos and the eschatology in the Ritual, Jesus has been forced to remain on the earth not only after he was twelve years of age but after he was thirty years, when he ought to have been a manes in Amenta. The "Pistis Sophia" retains the true version of Horus, or Jesus, in Amenta, when it says "Jesus spake these words unto his disciples *in the midst of Amenta*" (390) and describes him in the character of Aber-Amentho, the lord of Amenta, in which he rose again triumphant over death.

That which was taught by Horus, or Jesus, the Word in the sayings and parables, was made truth by Horus-Makheru, the fulfiller indeed. And this fulfilment at the second coming is imitated by Jesus when he says "These things have I spoken unto you in parables (or in proverbial sayings). The hour cometh when I shall no more speak unto you in parables but shall tell you plainly of the father" (John xvi. 25). The teaching of child-Horus did not contain a revelation of the father in spirit. This was the mission of Har-Makheru, the fulfiller of the word in truth, as it was acted in the mysteries to be repeated in the mortal life, for human use. This second part is promised in the Gospels but remained a matter of prophecy that never was fulfilled. Albeit the doctrine survives in the Christian " Word-of-truth " with no foundation in the historical life of Jesus. The Christian advent of Horus-Makheru, the word-made-truth, the beloved son who represents the father, from beginning to end of the Ritual, still awaits the ending of the world or that last day which was annually solemnized in the Egyptian mysteries. As Paul the Christian Gnostic puts it, " the kingdom of God is not in word, but in power." That is in fulfilment as the word-made-truth (1 Cor. iv. 20). The first Horus was the word, the second is the power : the heir of glory who hath the might-divine of the only-begotten Son of God the Father (Rit., ch. 115). This, wherever met with, is Egyptian first of all as Horus, who was the word or logos in one phase of character, and in the other of two he was the power. As the word he represented the virgin mother. As the power he imaged the glory of the father. Horus was the word in the earth of Seb, and he is the power in the earth of Sut. In the canonical and apocryphal Gospels both the word and power have been continued and fused into one, as there was but one life to be represented, that on earth, in the "history." It is said of the child-Jesus in the Gospel of Thomas (chap. 4), "Every word of his becometh at once a deed." "Every word of his is at once a deed " (ch. 17). "Every word he speaketh forthwith becometh a deed " (4). The sum and substance of the doctrine of Maati is to make the word of Osiris truth against his enemies. Elder Horus was that word in person. The word was also uttered in dark sayings which constituted the ancient wisdom. Then it became the written word of Taht Aan, the scribe of the gods, and Horus at his second coming was the divine ensample of the son who made the word of Osiris truth against all opposition as the fulfiller of the word and the doer in truth. The word of the Christ, according to Paul, is identical with the Makheru, or word-made-truth by Horus the fulfiller. He likewise speaks of "the word of the truth of the gospels " (Col. i. 6). The power of his Christ is that of the risen Horus ; it is the power of the resurrection to eternal life ; and both are the same, because both represented one meaning, namely the soul of man that rose again from death, and was personalized in Horus or in Iusa.

Although the second character of Horus is realized by Jesus in his baptism; in his becoming the beloved and anointed son of God; in his contests with Satan as a spirit ; in proving himself to be the " heir of the temple " ; in his breathing the Holy Spirit into the breathless, raising of the dead, and in various other ways, such fulfilment had to be repudiated on account of the alleged Judean history. Hence he promises that if he goes away from the disciples he will send them the Comforter, the Paraclete, or advocate, " even the Spirit of Truth *which proceedeth from the father."* " A little while, and ye behold me no more ; and again a little while and ye shall see me." This was the short time betwixt the first and second coming of the Lord, which was about three nights in the mysteries. " If I go not away the comforter will not come unto you." Whereas in the Egyptian judgment scenes the comforter has come already. Horus in his second character is the paraclete or advocate with the father. One by one he introduces the faithful to Osiris (in the vignettes to the Ritual), and is the intercessor and the mediator with the father on behalf of his children. In the papyrus of Ani, for example, Horus the intercessor or advocate introduces Ani to his father, saying " I have come to thee, O Un-nefer, and I have brought unto thee the Osiris-Ani. His heart is right ; it hath come forth guiltless from the scales. It hath not sinned against any god or goddess. Taht hath weighed it according to the decree pronounced unto him by the company of the gods ; it is most right and true. Grant that he may appear in the presence of Osiris ; and let him be like unto the followers of Horus for ever and ever."

The process of converting parts of the Osirian drama into Gospel narratives and of making the wisdom of the mystery-teachers portable for ordinary use, is obvious still in various of the parables of the double-Horus. For instance, in his first estate child-Horus was the sower of the seed, and in his second character at the second coming he is the reaper of the harvest. Thence comes the parable of the sower. In the pictures to the Ritual Horus is the sower who goes forth to sow the seed in the field of his father. And when he sows the wheat the enemy, that is Sut the power of darkness, comes by night and sows the field with tares and thorns and thistles, it being his work to undo all the good that Horus does. This is represented in a parable by means of which " the kingdom of heaven is likened unto a man that sowed good seed in his field ; but while men slept his enemy came and sowed tares also among the wheat and went away." The disciples ask for an explanation and the answer is " he that soweth the good seed is the son of man ; and the field is the world, and the good seed, these are the sons of the kingdom ; and the tares are the sons of the evil one ; and the enemy that sowed them is the devil ; and the harvest is the end of the world ; and the reapers are the angels " (Matt. xiii.). Thus the matter of the drama was reproduced piecemeal in religious märchen and exoteric narratives.

THE MYSTERIES AND THE MIRACLES.

The Mysteries were a dramatic mode of representing the gnosis or science of the Egyptian mythology and eschatology. They are the mysteries of Amenta. It was in these the dead were raised, the blind were made to see, the dumb to speak, the deaf to hear, the lame to walk, the manes to become bird-headed. Hence the scenes of their occurrence were in spirit-world, where the manes made their transformation visibly, and the mortal put on immortality. The greater mysteries were founded on the resurrection from the dead with the Ka or the bird-headed Horus as the representative of a survival in spirit. As we have seen in the " Pistis Sophia," Jesus tells the disciples that " *the mystery of the resurrection of the dead healeth from demonial possessions, from sufferings and all diseases. It also healeth the blind, the dumb, the maimed, the halt* " ; and he promises that whosoever shall achieve the gnosis of this wisdom shall have the power of performing these mysteries of the resurrection which only become miracles when exoterically rendered in the canonical Gospels (*P. S.*, B. 2, 279). Amenta in the mythos was the secret earth of the nocturnal sun. In the eschatology it is the spirit-world in which the dead became once more the living, and attained their continuity by being proved and passed as true for all eternity. If they failed, it was here they died the second death, and never rose again. Amenta was the world of the blind, the deaf and dumb, the maimed, the halt, and impotent *because it was the world of the dead.*

Thus the miracles of the canonical Gospels repeat the mysteries of the Ritual, and the scene of these was in the earth of the manes, not in the earth of mortals. It was there the deliverer wrought his " miracles " in the eschatological representation, whether as Horus, the son of Osiris, or as Iusa, the son of Atum-Ra. The Egyptian religion had no need of miracles. It did not postulate the supernatural. The superhuman and ideally divine were a part of and not apart from nature. The nether-earth was the other half of this and the Gospel history has been based upon that other earth of the manes being mistaken for the earth of mortals. In the Ritual, and in the gnostic writings, we find the mystery, the events, the characters, the Christ, the Virgin-Mother, the miracles, replaced upon their own proper footing and on the only ground of their existence which is eschatological and was a means of working out the drama in Amenta by means of the mythology that was previously extant. The so-called miracles of Jesus were not only impossible on human grounds ; they are historically impossible because they were pre-extant *as mythical representations* which were made on grounds that were entirely non-human in the drama of the mysteries that was as non-historical as the Christmas pantomime. The miracles ascribed to Jesus on earth had been previously assigned to Iusa the divine healer who was non-historical in the pre-Christian religion. Horus, whose other name is Jesus, is the performer of " miracles " which are repeated in the Gospels, and which were first performed as mysteries in the divine nether-world. But if Horus or Iusa be made human on earth, as a Jew in Judea, we are suddenly hemmed in by the miraculous, at the centre of a maze with nothing antecedent for a clue ; no path that leads to the heart of the mystery, and no visible means of exit therefrom. With the introduction of the human personage on mundane ground, the mythical inevitably becomes the miraculous ; you cannot have the history without it ; thus the history was founded on the miracles which are perversions of the mythology that was provably pre-extant.

Not only is it represented in the Gospels that Jesus raised the dead but that he also conferred power on the disciples to do likewise. They are to preach and proclaim that the kingdom of heaven is at hand, to "heal the sick and raise the dead" (Matt. x. 5–8). So the followers, called the "Children of Horus," had the power given them previously by their Lord to *raise the dead*. In the Pyramid texts of Teta (line 270) it is said, "Horus hath given his children power that they may raise thee up"; that is, from the funeral couch. But this resurrection was in Amenta, the earth of eternity, not in the earth of time, and those who were raised up for the second life are the manes, not mortal beings in the human world. It was not pretended that they were Egyptians in the time of Teta, the first king of the sixth dynasty. The Christians babble about the mysteries of revealed religion, which mysteries never were revealed except to those who had been duly initiated. These were mysteries to the Christians simply because they had not been revealed to them. They are the mysteries of ancient knowledge reproduced as miracles of modern ignorance. Such mysteries of the Christian faith, as the Trinity, the Incarnation, and the Virgin Birth, the Transfiguration on the Mount, the Passion, Death, Burial, Resurrection and Ascension, Transsubstantiation and Baptismal Regeneration, were all extant in the mysteries of Amenta with Horus or Iu-em-hetep as the central figure of the pre-Christian Jesus.

This mode of making miracles from the mysteries can be traced in the canonical Gospels. For instance, according to John, when Jesus reappears to the seven fishers on board the boat to cause the miraculous draught of fishes it is *after his resurrection from the dead*. Consequently, the transaction is in *a region beyond the tomb*, therefore in spirit-world, not in the life on earth. Whereas in Luke's version, his reappearance was in the earth-life and is not a reappearance after death. Yet the miraculous draught of fishes is the same in both books; and either the transaction is historical in Luke and has been relegated to the after-life in another world by John, or else the mythical version was first and has been converted into an historical event by Luke. But here, as in other cases, there is no corroboration of the history to be adduced, whereas the priority of John's version is attested by the Ritual where the fisher, the seven fishers, the fishing and the fish belong not to this earth but to that other world beyond the tomb and to the mysteries of Amenta.

When Sebek in the Ritual (ch. 113) catches the fish in his marvellous net this is proclaimed by Ra to be "a mystery." But when Simon Peter in the Gospel catches the great draught of fishes the mystery becomes a miracle.

Mythology knows nothing of miracle, nor the need of it. Miracle has no place in the Egyptian Ritual. But the Ritual shows us how the necessity for it arose as a *modus operandi* when the gnosis had to be accounted for by ignorance and the mythos was converted into human history. For example, the sun or the sun-god Atum is described in the Ritual as going over the surface of the lake of Mati, in Abydos, the place of rebirth, or of sunrise. That which is done mythically by the god is performed by the manes on the eschatological plane, and as he is in the human likeness, it follows that he must walk the water in the sun-god's track. He says, "the great God who is there is Ra himself. *I walk on his road;* I know the surface of the lake of Mati. The water of Mati is the road by which Atum-Ra goes to traverse the field of divine harvest" (Rit., 17). In the first phase the sun (or solar god) traverses the celestial water at dawn. In the eschatological continuation the human soul in Amenta does the same because assimilated to the character of the god. It is but a mode of representing phenomena in the two worlds of the double earth, the imagery of upper earth being repeated in spirit-world. But if we substitute a human being for the solar god or the manes in Amenta, and make him walk the water in our world on the surface of the sea or lake of Galilee, instead of the lake of Mati in Amenta, the water-walking can only be done by miracle. Such is the genesis of the Biblical miracles in both the Old Testament and the New. This we are now able to prove twice over by means of the original matter and mode of the mythos in the Egyptian eschatology that was humanized or literalized in legends and at last converted into Christian history.

You cannot rationalize the Bible miracles by reducing them to what may be thought reasonable dimensions. As Matthew Arnold said, "this is as if we were startled by the extravagance of supposing Cinderella's fairy godmother to have actually changed the pumpkin into a coach-and-six, but should suggest that she did really change it into a one-horse-cab." It is not a matter of degree or proportion, but of a radical difference in the fundamental nature of things. It is not the kind of transformation that was applied to the primary facts, nor is this transformation the result of imagination. It was not a result of the faculty of imagining that a man should be supposed to walk the water and not sink. Such an imagining was controverted by all the past of human experience. When the Egyptians portrayed a human impossibility—a miracle—they depicted a pair of feet walking on the water. This was a mode of superhuman force first made manifest by the elemental powers such as light and darkness, the wind, or the spirit of the storm. The water-walker was an old type of deity. The Christian miracles are false modes of explaining that which was ignorantly misappropriated. The gnostic interpretation of the Kamite mysteries had no need of miracles, no reversal or violation of natural law. The process by which miracles, or total violations of natural law, arose, was through perversion of ancient knowledge by later ignorance—not in the false or exaggerated reports of eye-witnesses. Nor could anything be settled by a conflict of opinions in the domain of ideas. We must have some foothold and ground of fact to go upon even to fight the battle. As it is in physical science, we have to ascertain the knowable. It avails nothing to take refuge in the unknown or to enshroud ourselves in mystery. The legends of mythology were not ideal, nor based upon abstract ideas. They were not first evolved from the inner consciousness, but from facts in outward nature that are for ever verifiable. The mysteries that "historic Christianity" took over without understanding, and preserved as food for faith, or as problems for metaphysical speculation, are fathomable and even simple when truly interpreted, but they have and can have no solution *on the supposed historic ground*. And with its bogus miracles surreptitiously derived from the ancient mysteries by falsification of the myths, it has destroyed or tended to destroy all standing-ground of common sense in natural reality. With its "historical" virgin mother of a God who was her "historical" child, it has made a double mockery of nature, human and divine. With its risen corpse for an anointed Christ the only Son of God, it has deified an image of death itself and made a mortuary of the human mind.

When it is conclusively proved that the Christian miracles are nothing more than a pagan mode of symbolical representation literalized, there is no longer any question of contravening, or breaking, or even challenging any well-known laws of nature. The discussion as to the probability or possibility of miracle on the old grounds of belief and doubt is closed for ever. A glance at the Egyptian pictures will show that the Horus or Christ is the young sun-god who walks the waters in Amenta not on the upper earth, and that the evil spirits who enter the swine and are driven down into the lake are the souls of those who were condemned in the great judgment as typhonian, the black pig being a type of Sut the evil being. A study of these miracles as they were originally rendered will lead to an understanding of their true significance, and here as everywhere else the truth of the matter once attained must ultimately put an end to the false belief:

Falsehood hath nothing in the world to do,
But lie to live and die to prove the true !

With what facility the miracle could be manufactured for the exoteric Gospels, canonical or apocryphal, may be seen from the legends in *The Arabic Gospel of the Infancy* (ch. 37). In one character the youthful sun-god, Horus or Jesus, was represented as a sort of divine dyer. He is called the great one who produces colours. In a passage of the Ritual (ch. 153), as rendered by Birch, it is said that "the great one journeys to the production of colours." These are the colours which are produced when the sun, or the child-Horus, or Jesus, rises from the lotus to dye the blue heaven with the hues of dawn. This is shown by a reference in the same passage to the sycamore tree of dawn. Now, in one of the numerous folk-tales that were derived from the mythos, this is made a miracle of in a legend of the Infancy. It was as the child-Horus that the sun arose to create the colours ; and, as a child, it is said the Lord Jesus entered the shop of a dyer where lay many cloths which were waiting to be dyed each of a different colour. Taking them all up together he threw the whole lot into a vessel of Indian blue. The dyer cried out and said the boy had ruined them all. But Jesus said he would cause each one to come forth of the colour that was desired, and he took them out of the vessel one by one, each one being dyed of the very colour that the dyer wanted.

The story of child-Jesus in the Gospel of Thomas who, when five years old, took clay and formed the images of twelve sparrows, which turned the word into a deed when Jesus bade them fly, is a miracle manufactured from a mystery of Amenta. When the manes were transformed from mummy to spirit they became bird-headed in the likeness of Horus whose head was that of a sparrow-hawk. This in the folk-tale becomes a sparrow, and twelve sparrows created by Jesus in the miracle are the representatives of the twelve great spirits of

Horus which have the head of the sparrow-hawk in the mystery of Amenta.

When evil spirits enter swine and are driven down the mountain-side to be drowned in the lake of darkness the representation is mythical, not miraculous. The mount is rooted in Amenta. The scene is in the earth of eternity. The mount was called the mount of birth in heaven. This was ascended by the manes who had passed through the judgment-hall and come forth as the good spirits, whereas the condemned were driven back and literally sent to the devil by entering the pig of Sut, which had become a type of all impurity. The miracle begins when the avenging Har-Tema is made historical, the pig actual, and the transaction takes place on this our upper earth. We must go to the Egyptian drawings in the drama of the mysteries for the veritable fact; and once we are in presence of the real truth we learn that the argument of Professor Huxley against the miracle is just as unprofitable as the Christian belief in the miracle. Here, as everywhere, the miracle results from a misinterpretation of the mythos out of which the gospels were ultimately evolved, piecemeal, and put together in a spurious history, with a spurious version of Horus the mortal, and a spurious spectre of Horus in the spirit.

In performing his miracles with a word, in being the word incarnated or made truth in person, in wielding a magical power over the elements, in casting out devils, in causing the spirits of evil to enter the swine, in healing the woman with the issue of blood, in giving sight to the blind, in transforming and transfiguring himself, in suddenly concealing himself, in walking upon the sea, in his personal conflict and battles with Satan, in raising the dead to life out of the earth, in resuscitating himself on the third day; in all these and other things Jesus is accredited with doing exactly what was attributed to Horus in the Ritual and in the Egyptian mysteries. But these miraculous things were never done by mortal or immortal on the surface of our earth. They are other-world occurrences in the true rendering, and they can only be re-related to reality as a mythical mode of representing the scenes in the drama of Amenta. The superhuman attributes are possessed, the transformation and transfiguration effected, the waters walked, the evil spirits cast out to enter the typhonian swine; sight is restored to the blind, the dumb are given a mouth, the dead are raised up out of the earth by Horus in this divine nether-world termed the earth of eternity and not on the earth of Seb in the world of time.

The historical character of the four Gospel narratives must stand or fall by the historical facts of the miracles. From the birth derived from a virgin to the corporeal resurrection of the Christ, the sole standing-ground is upon miracle. No amount of Jesuitical dialetic or logical argument based upon false premises, can ever make right, as a trustworthy matter of faith, that which is verifiably wrong as matter-of-fact. Yet the faith was founded on the uttermost falsification of natural fact as the ground of the history. On the one hand we find a belief that these miraculous transactions, these teachings of the Christ and the Christ himself were historical. On the other, we have the proof that they were unhistorical, a proof upon evidence that has never been tampered with, and that is directly derived from witnesses that do not, cannot lie. The miracles of the virgin birth and physical resurrection of Jesus; the miracles of giving sight to the blind and of raising the dead, the descent into Hades, and the resurrection in three days or on the third day, are all Egyptian, all in the Ritual. They were previously performed by the Christ who was not historical, the Christ of the Egypto-gnostics who is Horus or Jesus, identical with the Osirian Christ who was Horus the lord by name, and who, as the records show, was also extant as a divine type or spiritual impersonation as Iusa or Iu-em-hetep many thousand years ago.

A crucial example of the mode in which the gospel history was manufactured from the matter of the mythos and the eschatology is furnished by the miracle or miracles of the loaves and fishes. In one account the multitude of men, women and children are fed on five loaves and two fishes, and the remains of the meal were sufficient to fill twelve baskets (Matt. xiv. 17-21). In the other miracle, or second version of the same, the multitude are fed on seven loaves and a few small fishes, and there were seven baskets full of broken pieces. But for the Ritual we might never have known the correct number of loaves that did suffice to feed the vast multitude. They are seven in one place and five in another, and both the seven and five are found in one and the same book. This difference, however, serves for Matthew to make out a second miracle (xv. 36). The speaker in the Ritual says, "There are seven loaves on earth with Seb; there are seven loaves with Osiris (in Amenta); there are seven loaves at Annu with Ra in heaven" (ch. 53). "Henceforth let me live upon corn in your presence, ye gods, and let there come one who bringeth to me that I may feed from those seven loaves which he hath brought for Horus" (Renouf, Rit., ch. 52). "It is the god of the sektet boat and of the maatit boat who hath brought them (the loaves) to me at Annu" (ch. 53). These seven loaves constitute the celestial diet on which the multitude of souls are fed in Annu, called "the place of multiplying bread." But those who are fed upon the seven loaves in the celestial locality of Annu are not human beings on earth; they are manes in Amenta where Horus is the bread of life as giver of food to the quickened spirits of the dead; and as the transaction occurred in the next life there was no need of a miracle in this life by asserting that about five thousand hungry men, besides women and children, were fed upon five or seven loaves of bread and two fishes.

The synoptics do not mention the incident, but according to John (vi. 9) who retains much more of the Egyptian wisdom in his Gospel, there was a lad present in the scene who had with him "five barley loaves and two fishes." "Jesus therefore took the loaves from him and distributed them to the people." We have identified the feeding of the multitude of manes on the seven loaves that were brought to Horus as distributor of the bread of life, and the lad who brings the bread to Jesus in the Gospel with the one who brings the seven loaves to Horus, or, it may be, the five loaves to Taht, in the Ritual, and who is described as "someone" who comes with the bread of Horus and Taht which is ritualistically represented by the seven loaves. A primitive concept of the infinite had been expressed in terms of boundless food and drink. Providence was the provider; and the power that provided the fruits of the earth or water was Providence. When bread was made the providing power or godhead itself was figured by the Egyptians as an illimitable loaf, the food of spirits or celestial diet for the life to come. The one great loaf was equivalent to the one supreme source of soul. Seven loaves were numerically equivalent to the seven souls of Ra. The human soul was fed from the bread of life as typical of divine source. With bread of that kind one loaf might have sufficed without the pretence of a miracle, as it was cut and come again without diminution. It was the kind of bread which keeps on rising and expanding for ever as in the German tale of Jesus and the miserly woman with her dough.

Annu is the place of bread in which the multitudes of manes are fed as men, women and children also, if the younglings of Shu are included. It is called the place of *multiplying bread*. There are seven loaves of bread with Ra in Annu (Rit., ch. 53 B) on which the manes are fed by Horus. They feed upon the seven loaves of celestial bread which were brought for Horus to feed the manes with by a divine messenger. Seven loaves were brought for Horus and there were also loaves for Taht (ch. 52), the two which correspond to the seven loaves and the five in the "historical" miracles. The manes prays that he may feed on the seven loaves that are brought for Horus, and the loaves that were brought for Taht, which shows at least that there was more than one set of loaves, when the multitude were fed on the divine diet in the place of multiplying bread. In the Gospel the multitude recline upon the grass. In the Ritual they rest upon the grassy sward beneath the sycamore of Hathor (ch. 52, 4). But when the multitudes were fed in Annu they were the souls of the departed, and the symbolical seven loaves on which they fed was Ka-bread that was neither made nor eaten on earth, nor did it need a miracle to make the food go far enough. Annu was a mythical locality which did not supply the conditions for a miracle. A miracle had to be performed only when the eschatological representation was shifted from the mount of Annu in Amenta to a mountain in Judea. One hieroglyphic sign of the mount hetep is *a pile of food*. The mount was the place of feasting for the followers of Horus, the beatified spirits of the departed. "Every feast on earth and on the mountain" signifies the feasts of the living and the dead; the living upon earth, the dead or the departed on the mountain. In the feasting on the mount "Jesus went up into the mountain and sat there. And there came unto him great multitudes, having with them the lame, blind, dumb, maimed, and many others, and they cast them down at his feet; and he healed them; insomuch that the multitude wondered when they saw the dumb speaking, the maimed whole, the lame walking, and the blind seeing; and they glorified the God of Israel. And Jesus called his disciples and said, I have compassion on the multitude, because they continue with me *three days* and have nothing to eat." (Matt. xv. 29-32.) The miracles of healing, including the casting out of evil spirits and the raising of the dead, as portrayed in the Ritual and corroborated by the "Pistis Sophia," occurred *in the resurrection on the mount*; and this shows that those who had been with Jesus having nothing to eat *for three days* had been awaiting their resurrection on the third day, and that they were the manes and not mortals.

The only reason why the blind and deaf and dumb, the palsied and the lame, including the dead, assembled in their multitudes upon the mount is because this was the mount of resurrection and regeneration, thence of healing, for the manes who had waited in Amenta for the coming of the Lord. The resurrection of Osiris was solemnized at the great Haker festival. This is one of the ten mysteries described in the "Book of the Dead" (ch. 18) said to have been celebrated "before the great circle of gods in Abydos (the place of Osiris's rebirth and resurrections) on the night of "Haker" (or Ha-k-er-a) when the glorious ones are rightly judged: when the evil dead are parted off, and joy goeth its round in Thinis" (ch. 18, Renouf). The name for this festival is rendered "*Come thou hither* or *Come thou to me*": as the call of Ra upon the mount addressed to Osiris in the valley on the day of resurrection, when the soul of Horus the mortal was blended with Horus the immortal in the mystery of Tattu (ch. 17). The Haker celebration included both fasting and feasting. The word haker signifies fasting, to be famished, as well as denoting the festival of "Come thou to me" or the rite of resurrection. Now, as the comparative process shows an "historical" version of the Haker festival is given in the Gospels where we find an exoteric account of the funeral fast and resurrection feast, in the miracles of healing performed upon the mount and feeding the famished multitude upon the seven loaves of bread. It should be premised that the raising of Osiris, the god in matter was individual, but, at the same time, the resurrection of the dead in Osiris who were the "All Souls" for the year or cycle was general. The supreme miracle of "raising the dead" suffices of itself to show that it belonged to the mysteries of Amenta, as asserted in the "Pistis Sophia," where the dead were raised; evil spirits were cast out, the blind were made to see, the deaf to hear, the lame to walk, the bed-ridden to get up and go, not by miracle but as a dramatic mode of illustrating the mysteries of the resurrection in the *Peri em hru* or coming forth to day. It is noticeable that *the miracles of healing on the mount* described in Matthew (xv. 29–31), *are immediately followed by the miracle of multiplying the loaves and fishes.* There is no change of scene, the multitude upon the mount remain the same. "And Jesus called unto Him His disciples, and said 'I have compassion on the multitude, because they continue with Me now *three days and have nothing to eat*; and I would not send them away fasting." Thus three days are allotted to the work of healing in the mount, during which time the multitude were fasting in the company of Jesus and his disciples. In the Ritual these are not only the fasting, they are also deprived of breath. They are without a mouth. They are the blind, the dumb, the motionless, in short, they are the deceased awaiting in their coffins and their cells for him who is the resurrection and the life, as the divine healer and deliverer of the manes from Amenta; he is the "divine one who dwelleth in heaven, and who sitteth on the eastern side of heaven" (Rit., ch. 25) that is on Mount Bakhu, the mount of the olive-tree, the only mount on which the dead were ever raised (*P. S.*, B. 2, 279). This healing then was a mystery of the resurrection, the same in the canonical as in the Egypto-gnostic Gospel; the same in both as in the Book of the Dead, or Ritual of the resurrection.   Three days was the length of time allowed for the burial in Amenta.   This would constitute a three days' fasting of the dead.   We must discriminate.   In the lunar reckoning the resurrection of Osiris in the moon was on the third day, which corresponded to the actual reappearance of the light in nature.   This death, described by Plutarch, occurred on the seventeenth of the month.   In the solar reckoning three whole days and nights were allowed for the burial of the sun or sun-god in the earth. Both are employed in the Gospels but not scientifically.   Neither could the complex of soli-lunar reckoning be explicated on the single line of a personal human history.   Both solar and lunar reckonings remain, but hugely gaping apart with a gulf for ever fixed between the two.   The Son of Man was to remain three nights as well as days in the "heart of the earth."   That is in keeping with the solar reckoning, whereas the resurrection is on the third day, the same as that of Osiris in the moon.   We repeat, there was a two-fold computation of time, lunar and solar, both of which are given in the gospels, but without the gnosis that explained the astronomical mythology.   Three days is the full period, and this is the length of time over which the miracles of healing were extended and during which the multitude with Jesus had "nothing to eat," because they were with him in the Valley of Amenta; the same that were healed by him on the Mount of Resurrection.   It was in the resurrection that the dead were raised to life and became spirits.   These were the good spirits which were parted from the evil spirits that were then "cast out."   Sight was given to the blind, a mouth to the dumb, hearing was restored to the deaf.   The lame were enabled to rise and walk. Then the three days' fast was ended by the feeding of the multitude on what the Ritual terms celestial diet, *i.e.*, the "seven loaves" of heaven that were supplied as sustenance for the risen dead in Annu, the *place of multiplying bread.*   In the Egyptian mysteries, all who enter the nether world as manes to rise again as spirits are blind and deaf and dumb and maimed and impotent *because they are the dead.*   Their condition is typified by that of mortal Horus who is portrayed as blind and maimed, deaf and dumb in An-arar-ef the abode of occultation, the house of obscurity, the "city of dreadful night" where all the denizens were deaf and dumb and maimed and blind awaiting the cure that only came with the divine healer who is Horus of the resurrection in the Ritual, or Khunsu, the caster out of demons, or Iu-em-hetep the healer, or Jesus in the Gospels, gnostic or agnostic.   Thus the restoring of sight to the blind man, or the two blind men, was one of the mysteries of Amenta that is reproduced amongst the miracles in the canonical gospels.

The speaker in the Ritual often makes the merest allusion to some act of the drama that was visibly performed and fully unfolded in the mysteries.   For example, Horus the avenger is described as blending his being with that of the Sightless One, who had been Horus in the flesh (Rit. 17).   In a previous allusion (same chapter) the coming of the soul of Ra to embrace and blend with the body-soul of Osiris, to give light and life to the Mummy-God is also described as the act of Horus-Tema who is blended with the Sightless God.   In either representation there is a restoration of sight to the blind; and this when written out and narrated as "History" becomes the miracle of Jesus curing the man and giving sight to him who was blind; or to the two men as Osiris and the Osiris, N., or to any number of those who were sightless in the city of the blind. When Horus the deliverer descends into Amenta he is hailed as the prince in the city or the region of the blind. That is, of the dead who are sleeping in their prison cells, and who therefore are the prototypal spirits in prison. He comes to shine into their sepulchres and to restore their sight to the blind. "Hail to Thee, Lord of Light, who art prince of the house which is encircled by darkness and obscurity," in the city of the blind (Rit. ch. 21). This picture is repeated in the Gospel of Matthew (iv. 16). "The people which sat in darkness saw a great light: and to them which sat in the region and shadow of death, to them did the light spring up." This, as written in the "Book of the Dead" was in Amenta.

The typical blind man of Amenta, then, is Horus in the gloom of his sightless condition, as the human soul obscured in matter or groping in the darkness of the grave. This is Horus An-arar-ef in the city of the blind. And the Horus who comes to restore the lost sight, is he who had been divinized in the likeness of Ra, the holy spirit. It is said of this dual Horus in the Ritual (ch. 17), "The pair of gods are Horus the reconstitutor of his father and Horus the prince in the city of blindness." The second Horus is the spirit perfected. He descends from heaven to the darkness of Amenta as *The Light of the World.* He is called the one whose head is clothed with a white radiance. His presence shines into the sepulchres and cells of the manes. He comes to the blind in the city of the blind, the place in which blind Horus was enveloped in obscurity. He shows as a great light in the darkness of the land of the dead, and is described as restoring sight to those who are blind, that is to the manes who have not yet attained the beatific or spiritual vision. This is represented as giving sight to the blind. *Amenta was looked upon as the earth of the blind.* The manes were there as blind folk awaiting sight. The human Horus Har-Khent-An-arar-ef in Sekhem was the prince of the blind, being chief amongst the manes who were sightless or without the means of seeing in the dark. For this reason the mole or shrewmouse was his zootype. The typical blind man in Amenta is the blind Horus who was deprived of sight by Sut, the Power of Darkness. But every manes that entered Amenta was also blind in the darkness of death. Thus there are two blind men, or one as the God and one as the manes; one in the soli-lunar mythos, and one in the eschatology; Horus in his darkness of night or the eclipse; the mortal in the dark of death. Miracle for mystery, this may explain the two different versions of healing the blind in the Gospels. Three of the evangelists know of a single blind man only, who was cured by Jesus, where Matthew reports the healing of two blind men in which he obviously gives two separate versions of one and the same miracle. In the Ritual, then, we can identify the one blind man with Horus in the dark, or without sight (Rit., ch. 18, as Har-Khent-an-maati); the two blind men with Horus and the manes (otherwise with Osiris and *the* Osiris); and the multitudes of blind people above ground with the manes or the dead in Amenta. There is no need of limiting the miracle of curing the blind to one or two men. Horus the light of the world in the earth of Amenta comes to cure the blind in general who are dwelling in the darkness of the city of the blind, in which the devil (Sut) was dominant previous to the second advent of Horus. The dead in Osiris were as blind mummies awaiting the spiritual light which gave the beatific vision; and Horus comes to unseal the eyes of the manes waking in their coffins.

The poor blind Horus was given eyes at the time when he became the anointed son, and the child of twelve years made his transformation into the adult of thirty years with the head and sight of the hawk, or the beatific vision of Horus in the spirit. He was anointed with oil at the lustration in Abydos, the place of re-birth. Hence one mode of making the anointed or the Christ whom Horus became in this transformation was by anointing with saliva. The lustration of children by spittle was an old Papal rite, and in the Gospel the spittle used to open the eyes of the blind is equivalent to anointing the sightless Horus in Sekhem. In acting the mystery of Amenta the "Eye of Horus," the anointed son, the light of the world, was brought to blind Horus lying in his darkness. This mystery is reproduced as miracle in the healing of the blind man. "When I am in the world," says Jesus, "I am the Light of the World." This is equivalent to bringing the eye of Horus to the benighted manes in Amenta. "When he had spoken, he spat on the ground, and made clay of the spittle, and anointed his eyes with the clay." And in this unsightly way the man is said to have attained his sight in thus becoming the anointed. Such is the puerility of the miracle-mongers who misrepresent the mystery-teachers in the Gospels. To preach the "recovery of sight to the blind" was to teach a doctrine of the resurrection and the opening of the eyes in death, such as was set forth dramatically in the mysteries of the Ritual (chs. 20–30). It was the same also in giving a mouth to the dumb; in making the dead to rise and the lame to walk; likewise in casting out evil spirits, and the powers of darkness, the associates of Sut, the Sami or the Sebau, which originated in physical phenomena, and were afterwards mis-rendered as obsessing spirits that were primarily human. When the divine healer and caster-out of demons, Khunsu-Horus, went to Bakhten to exorcize an evil spirit from the possessed Princess, the god was carried there in effigy, as the "driver away of evil spirits that take possession" of the human body, not as a divinized medicine-man portrayed in human form. The effigy is an image of the wonderful healer who originated as a power of renewal in external nature, and not as a mortal on this earth. The caster-out of demons is also portrayed as Khunsu offering up the abominable pig in the lunar disk as a sacrifice to the Lord of Light (Planisphere of Denderah), the pig being a zootype of Sut the evil one. Thus we reach a root-origin in the war of light and darkness, or Horus and Sut, that is waged for ever in the Moon. The black boar, Sut, makes his attack upon the eye, which is healed by Horus or Khunsu, Taht or Ra. The power of light was then the healer of the wound in nature that was wrought by the representative of darkness as the pig, the Apap-dragon, or the adversary Sut. Hence the eye of Horus in the moon is a symbol of healing, and of safety or salvation ; an amulet, therefore, or fetish, good against the powers of darkness. There was no miracle in the natural phenomena. There was no miracle involved or taught in the original mode of representation. But when a "human mortal" with the name of Jesus is put in place of Horus, Taht or Khunsu, he becomes the supposed to be, but for ever impossible, miracle-monger ; Jesus, the Jewish Saviour, who is described as coming into a world of blind people ; some of whom are blind figuratively, others actually. The Scribes and Pharisees are denounced as blind, " blind guides," "fools and blind," "blind leaders of the blind." Jesus restores the sight of those who are physically blind, "to many blind he gave sight." That is in fitting the canonical Jesus to the *rôle* of Horus. A form of blind Horus described by Isaiah leaves no room for doubt that the Hebrew Messiah was the Egyptian Horus. This is he who is blind ; " my servant, who is blind as he that is made perfect, and blind as the Lord's servant" (chs. xlii., xliii.). This servant of the Lord is the suffering Horus who was portrayed as the servant of Osiris the Lord, blind, dumb, and therefore deaf, but as being perfected in serving the Lord, who " confirmed the word of His servant." Being perfected marks the change from the servant, as Horus who was born blind in matter to Horus in spirit, the restorer of sight to the blind, that is, to the dead. Also the word of the servant was confirmed by the coming of Horus as the word-made-truth in Har-Ma-Kheru. But it was in the earth of Amenta that Horus came to restore their sight to the blind, and in the canonical Gospels Judea, full of blind folk being cured by miracle, is just Amenta wrong-side uppermost, with the drama of the double-earth in a state of topsy-turvydom through the conversion of the ancient mysteries into Gospel-miracles.

In arranging for the resurrection of the dead, as performed in the mysteries of Osiris, the funeral bed, called the Khenkhat, is prepared as the couch of the mummy. It is said to the deceased, " I have fastened thy bones together for thee. I have given thy flesh to thee. I have collected thy members for thee." This is in arranging the deceased upon the funeral couch, for his rising from, or as, the dead (ch. 170). "Hail N," it is said to the deceased upon the funeral couch, "*Arise on thy bed and come forth*" (Rit., chs. 169-170). Here is an instructive instance of the way in which the mysteries of the Ritual have been converted into the miracles of the Gospels. There are two chapters concerning the funeral bed. The first is " on making the Khenkhat *to stand up*" ; the other is on " arranging the Khenkhat." We repeat, the Khenkhat is the funeral bed on which the dead were laid out in Amenta, waiting for the coming of Horus, lord of the resurrection, to wake the sleepers who are in their coffins or lying breathless on their couches in the likeness of inert Osiris. It is the couch of the dead that is set up on end like the mummy-case with the body inside which is thus erected on its feet as a mode of rendering the mystery of the resurrection or *re-erection* of the deceased (Rit., ch. 169). This becomes a miracle in the Gospel, when the dead are raised, and those who were paralytic take up their bed and walk. In the next chapter (170) on the arrangement of the funeral bed it is said to the risen one "Thou settest forth on thy

3 G

way. *Horus causeth thee to stand up at the risings.*" Then the deceased, as the risen mummy, is seen to be walking off. That is in the resurrection. Here, as elsewhere, the mystery of Amenta becomes a miracle when represented on this earth. That change would of itself account for a huge falsification, to say nothing of the intent and tendency of the writers, which follow and overshadow the truth of the ancient wisdom all through as darkly as the night the day; for if ancient Egypt was the light of the world, Christian theology has assuredly been its impenetrable shadow.

As already shown, a reduced form of the mysteries that were acted in the Osirian drama may here and there be recognized in the form of parables and portable sayings. Take the mystery of Tattu in the 17th chapter of the Ritual, by means of which the Sayings of the Lord, quoted from "the Gospel of the Egyptians" by the two Clements, can be explicated. The Lord himself being asked by some-one when his kingdom would come, replied : " When two shall be one. When that which is without is as that which is within, and the male with the female (shall be) neither male nor female" (Clem., Rom.). When Salome asked, when those things about which she questioned should be made known, the Lord said : " When you tread under foot the covering of shame, and when out of two is made one, and the male with the female is neither male nor female " (Clem. Alex., *Stromata*). This is that blending of the two souls or two sexes in one which was figured and effected in the mystery of Tattu. This blending of two halves in one whole, which is a like-ness of neither, but a new image of both, is exemplified thrice over in the Ritual, when a soul was established that should live for ever. Ra is blended with Osiris ; Shu with Tefnut ; child-Horus with Horus the adult. Ra represents the divine soul, and Osiris the body-soul in matter. Shu represents the male, and Tefnut the female nature. Child-Horus is the mortal and Horus in spirit the immortal. Thus the divine soul was blended with the soul of matter ; female with male, and mortal with immortal in the mystery of Tattu. The mystery was of course performed, and in the present instance, the drama consists of three acts with six different characters which are Ra and Osiris ; Shu and Tefnut, Horus the sightless, with Horus the bringer of the beatific vision. In the saying quoted from " the Gospel according to the Egyptians" the mystery has been reduced to the male and female becoming neither male nor female in the mystical marriage, the other factors being omitted. This shows the process by which the mysteries of the Ritual were reduced and made portable in the miracles, the parables and sayings, or *Logoi*, whether as separate sayings or as miscellaneous collections. A distant echo of the doctrine is to be heard in the Gospel according to Matthew (xxii. 30) : " For in the resurrection they neither marry nor are given in marriage, but are as angels in heaven." So remote is this from the mystical marriage in Tattu that the mystery in Amenta is limited to sexual conjunction. Now we learn from the Ritual that one mode of making the change from matter to spirit and of being unified in the type beyond sex was by discarding the garb of the female in the preparation of the manes for the funeral bed at the time of the second birth (Rit., ch. 170). The garment is again referred to in " the fragments of a lost Gospel" when the speaker says "he himself will give you your garment." "His disciples say unto him, when wilt thou be manifest to us, and when shall we see thee? He saith, when ye shall be stripped and not be ashamed" (Grenfell and Hunt, *New Sayings of Jesus*, p. 40), which is the same thing as being freed from the garb of shame upon the funeral bed. This is no mystical reference to Genesis iii. 7, but to the mystery of Amenta and a ceremony that was performed in the nether-world, of which it is said "*Thou puttest on the pure garment and thou divestest thyself of thy apron when thou stretchest thyself on the funeral bed*" (Rit., ch. 172). "Thou receivest a bandage of the finest linen," in place of the old garb of shame, or the apron which was now a symbol of the flesh. Lastly, amongst the mysteries of Amenta which were converted into Gospel miracles one of the most arresting is that of the Widow and her only son whom Jesus raised up from the funeral bier at Nain (Luke vii. 14), because Isis is the widow by name in the Ritual who was represented by the disconsolate swallow as the widow who has lost her mate, and Horus was her only son. The connection of the child with the widow in Egypt is already seen in the Gospel of Thomas or Tum, which goes far towards identifying the child-Jesus with the child of Isis. Moreover, the mystery shows us how the mother as Isis became a widow. When Osiris had been put to death, the birth of the child-Horus followed the decease of his father, and his mother was consequently the widow who had an only son in Horus, the only child of his mother. In the mystery of Tattu, child-Horus was raised up from the dead when Horus in the spirit came to the funeral couch and the immortal was blended with the mortal in the mystery of the resurrection. This is repeated in the Gospel as one of the most telling of the mysteries that were Christianized in the miracles.

JESUS IN THE MOUNT.

Ascending the mountain of Amenta is a figure of the resurrection from the dead. When Jesus Aber-Amentho rises after death it is to take his seat upon the mountain with the twelve preservers of the light. The group of twelve followers was the latest to gather form upon the mount. This was preceded by the seven, the four, and the two. The Ritual of the Resurrection opens with the coming forth to day of Horus or the Osiris, who ascends the mount of glory, or Mount Bakhu, the mount of the green olive-tree, which afterwards was represented in Judea by the local Mount of Olives. In the older manuscripts of the Ritual this ascent is called "the coming forth to the divine powers attached to Osiris," which are the four with Horus in the mount, or on the Papyrus-column, the four that were his brethren first; and who are afterwards portrayed as his children. But in both the Ritual and *Pistis Sophia* the mount, the scenes upon the mount, the twelve with Jesus or the four with Horus on the mount, are all in spirit-world. As we have seen, *Pistis Sophia* opens with the resurrection of the Egypto-gnostic Jesus. The life of suffering represented on the earth was over, and the victor rose triumphant after death, to be invested with the glory of the Father on the mount.

This is the Peri-em-hru or coming forth to day with which the Egyptian Ritual of the resurrection begins. Jesus comes forth from Amenta as the teacher of the greater mysteries to the twelve disciples who are gathered together on Mount Olivet, which is the mountain of Amenta in the Kamite eschatology. Thus the mount, the scene upon the mount, the teaching and the twelve are all *post-resurrectional*, and therefore the transactions are not upon our earth. There was a double resurrection in the Osirian mysteries, just as there is a first and second death. The earliest is a resurrection of the soul that passes from the body on earth and emerges as the Sahu in Amenta. This is Amsu-Horus, who is still a mummy, but who has risen to his feet with one arm loosened from the bandages of burial. It has the look of a corporeal resurrection, for the body is semi-corporeal. But Horus has not yet attained the garment of his glory.

The typical mountain likewise had a twofold character in the mythology and the eschatology. As solar, it was the mount of sunrise or of the great green olive-tree of the Egyptian dawn. As eschatological, it was the mountain of Amenta, up which the manes climbed—the mount of glory and the glorified. It was the mount on which the human Horus was transfigured and regenerated to become pure spirit in the likeness of the Father. Hence it is the mount of transfiguration, of regeneration, of healing, and also the means of ascent into the land of spirits (Rit., ch. 17).

The second resurrection is *from* Amenta. When Horus has transformed and made his change into the likeness of his Father and become pure spirit he ascends *from* the mount and rises into Heaven from Bakhu, the mount of the olive-tree, or the Mount of Olives in the later rendering. This was the meeting-place of Horus and his heavenly Father Ra when they conversed together in the mount. It is that Mount of Olives on which Horus, or the Egypto-gnostic Jesus, met the twelve disciples after his resurrection from Amenta, which meeting-place is repeated when the Gospel-Jesus makes the appointment for the Eleven to meet him in the mountain after he has risen from the dead (Matthew xxviii. 16). The Kamite founders of the astronomical mythology had placed the equinoxes high up on the horizon, or the summit of the mount, as it was figured, at the meeting-point of equal night and day. Thus the equinox or *level place* was one with the top of the mount, and where one writer speaks of the equinoctial station as being on the mount another might assign it to the "level place" or plain, when neither of them possessed the proper clue. In this way one discrepancy may be explained concerning the delivery of the sermon on the mount. According to Matthew, Jesus delivered it upon the mount. According to Luke, he came down from the mount and "*stood on a level place*" (ch. vi. 17). Both places meet in one, but only on the mountain of the equinox, the Egyptian mountain of Amenta. According to Matthew, the sermon was delivered to the four brethren in the mount. This follows the Ritual. According to Luke, the sermon was delivered to the twelve on the mount by Jesus standing on the level place.

No rational explanation has ever been suggested why the divine healer on earth should have compelled the sick and ailing, the obsessed, the halt and maimed, the deaf and dumb and blind who besought him for a cure, to climb a lofty mountain with the cripples on crutches in order that they might come into his presence and be healed. When Jesus was followed by the clamorous multitude he went up into the mountain and sat there. "And there came unto him great multitudes, having with them the lame, blind, dumb, maimed, and many others, and they cast them down at his feet, and he healed them." The answer is that the mount was mythical, not geographical; the divine healer was no human thaumaturgist; the multitudes were manes, not mundane mortals.

The only mountain mentioned by name in the Gospels as the scene of the miraculous occurrences is Mount Olivet. There was such a mountain to the east of Jerusalem, but beyond that was the mythical Mount of Olives, which was localized in many places under various names as the typical mount of the astronomical mythos. At first the mount was a figure of the earth that rose up in the waters of the Nun, or space. Then it was a type equivalent to the horizon. To be upon the horizon in the mythos is to be upon the mount—the mount of the double equinox—the four quarters or the twelve divisions of the ecliptic. It is shown in the *Pistis Sophia* that the twelve disciples, teachers, or supporters who sat with Jesus on the Mount of Olives had originated as the twelve æons or rulers in the zodiac. As such they were the teachers of time and the pre-servers of the treasures of light. Their stations were in an aërial region. This is otherwise called the sphere or circle of the zodiac, in which the twelve seats or thrones were finally established, with the central throne of the Egypto-gnostic Jesus towering over all.

In the early Christian iconography the cross of Christ is erected on a mount. This is shown to be the mount of the four quarters, or the equinox, by means of the four rivers flowing from the summit. The Christ stands on the top along with the cross. Sometimes the ram or lamb is portrayed on the mount of the four quarters in place of the Christ; and Horus was likewise the lamb as well as the calf upon the mount. The Christ is also accompanied by seven lambs = seven rams, supposed by Didron to represent the *twelve* apostles! (Didron, Fig. 86). But the ram (Mithraic lamb) is the Egyptian ideograph for the ba-spirit, and seven rams or lambs that accompany the Christ are equal to the seven spirits which served Horus in the octonary of the mount. The ram also appears with seven eyes and seven horns, which identify it with the seven rams as seven spirits, or the seven souls of Ra. This shows an earlier stratum of the astronomical mythos in survival. It is the Egypto-gnostic Jesus, who was Horus, with the seven great spirits that were earlier than the twelve upon the mount. When Jesus has transformed, or spiritualized in his baptism, he is "led up of the spirit to be tempted of the devil" (Matth. iv. 1). He is then a spirit on the mount that is exceeding high, like the mountain of Amenta, which is said to reach the sky. To meet upon the mountain after death could only be as spirits meet in spirit-world upon the mount of re-union in the mysteries of Amenta. Thus it is obvious that the meeting-point of Sut and Horus, or of Satan and the Christ, was no earthly hill; and that the teacher and the teaching on the mountain are the same in the canonical Gospels as in *Pistis Sophia* and the Ritual, that is, they are in spirit-world, and therefore the total transactions on the typical mountain are post-resurrectional and not humanly historical.

According to John, the earliest discourse of Jesus is not the sermon on the mount as given by Matthew. In place of this, John presents the discourse upon regeneration which is the same subject as that of the sermon on the mount in the *Divine Pymander*. Jesus says to Nicodemus, " Verily, verily, I say unto thee, Except a man be born anew (or from above) he cannot see the kingdom of God." Nicodemus saith unto him, " How can a man be born when he is old ? Can he enter a second time into his mother's womb and be born ? " Jesus answered, " Verily, verily, I say unto thee, Except a man be born of water and the spirit, he cannot enter into the kingdom of God. That which is born of the flesh is flesh : and that which is born of the spirit is spirit. Marvel not that I said unto thee, ye must be born from above. The wind bloweth where it listeth, and thou hearest the voice thereof, but knowest not whence it cometh, and whither it goeth : So is everyone that is born of the spirit." Nicodemus answered and said unto him, " How can these things be ? " Jesus answered and said unto him, " Art thou a teacher in Israel and understandest not these things ? Verily, verily, I say unto thee, We speak that we do know, and bear witness of that we have seen : and ye receive not our witness. If I told you earthly things and ye believe them not, how shall ye believe if I tell you heavenly things ? And no man hath ascended into heaven but he that descended out of heaven, the Son of Man, which is in heaven" (John iii. 1–14). This is a sermon on regeneration. The sermon of Hermes is in the mount of regeneration. The subject is the same in both. Previous to this discourse Hermes had told Tat that " no man can be saved before regeneration." At a previous ascent into the mount Hermes had promised Tat that if he would estrange himself from the world and prepare his mind for this mystery to be unfolded, he would then impart it to him. " Now," says Tat, " fulfil my defects and instruct me of regeneration either by word of mouth, or secretly ; for I know not, O Trismegistus, of what substance or what *womb*, or what seed a man is *thus* born." That is, how he is to be reborn in the process of regeneration ? Hermes replies, " O son, this wisdom is to be understood in silence, and the seed is the true good." " Who soweth it, O father ? for I am utterly ignorant and doubtful." " The will of God, O son." Now, this is called " the secret sermon in the mount," on the subject of " regeneration and the profession of silence." The subject is the same, the characters of teacher and doubtful inquirer are identical, and the physical misinterpretation regarding the mode of rebirth is one and the same in both interviews. Hermes describes a form of the Son of Man who is in heaven, otherwise the heavenly man, when he says, " I see in myself an unfeigned sight or spectacle made by the mercy of God : and I am gone out of myself into an immortal body, and am not now what I was before, but am *begotten in mind*." He also says of the physical and spiritual, " He that looketh only upon that which is carried upward as fire, that which is carried downward as earth, that which is moist as water, and that *which bloweth* or is subject to blast as air ; how can he sensibly understand that which is neither hard nor moist, nor tangible, nor perspicuous, seeing it is only understood in power and operation: but I beseech and pray to the mind, which alone can understand the generation that is in God." But Hermes, who wrote the Ritual in hieroglyphics as the scribe of the Egyptian gods, did not derive his matter from the Gospels collected by Eusebius and his co-conspirators in Rome (*Divine Pymander*, B. 7).

After the prophecy of the immediate coming of the Son, who is supposed to be speaking of himself, we have the real meaning of the manifestation identified in the very next verse, which contains a representation of the entrance of Osiris and his transfiguration as Horus in the mount on the sixth day of the new moon. We are told that "after six days"—it would have been more correct if "on the sixth day"; the discrepancy, however, is but slight—"Jesus taketh with him Peter and James and John his brother, and bringeth them up into a high mountain apart. And he was transfigured before them. And his face did shine as the sun, and his garments became white as the light. And behold there appeared unto them Moses and Elijah talking with him. And Peter answered and said unto Jesus, Lord, it is good for us to be here: if thou wilt, I will make here three booths, one for thee, one for Moses, and one for Elijah. While he was yet speaking, behold, a bright cloud overshadowed them: and behold a voice out of the cloud, saying, This is my beloved Son, in whom I am well pleased: hear ye him" (Matt. xvii. 1–5). Then Jesus retires into his secrecy, saying, "Tell the vision to no man, until the Son of Man has risen from the dead." This identifies the mount of resurrection, which is one with the mount of regeneration, the sermon on which is obviously post-resurrectional. There is a scene of Transfiguration on the Mount in the mysteries of Amenta. "Ra maketh his appearance at the mount of glory with the cycle of gods about him." The Osiris deceased acquireth might with Ra, and is made to possess power with the gods —and when men or the manes see him they fall upon their faces. He is seen in the nether-world "*as the image of Ra*." So in the Gospel, the face of Jesus "did shine as the sun." The disciples likewise fell upon their faces, and "were sore afraid." Not only is Jesus seen in the likeness of Ra, the father in heaven; the voice from the father proclaims that this is the beloved son. In coming down from the mount the witnesses are commanded to "tell the vision to no man," and of the scene in the mysteries, it is said by the speaker in the Ritual, "the Osiris N hath not told what he hath seen; he hath not repeated what he hath heard in the house of the god who hideth his face" (ch. 133). The point here is the identity of the mythical mount, whether astronomical or as the seat of the teacher; and the twelve; or as the mount of the mysteries; the mount of resurrection, of regeneration and of transfiguration. It is the same mount when those multitudes that meet upon the summit are described as the blind, the halt, and maimed. The mount on which the dead were raised to life, the blind were made to see, the dumb to speak, the impotent to become virile, like the risen ithyphallic Horus; the mount upon which the famished multitudes were fed from the illimitable loaf, or loaves, was the mount of resurrection that rose up from the nether earth for the departed to ascend as spirits. Hence it is the mount on which the miracles in the Gospels are alleged to have been performed. The mount of glory in the Ritual becomes the mount of the glorified in the Gospels. This, according to the gnosis, was the mount that has been localized in Judea, to which the people were bidden to flee for refuge when the end of all things should come; not a geographical mount, but the mount of the manes in Amenta; the mount of the resurrection, which only spirits could ascend; the mount from which the swine obsessed by devils were driven down into the lake when the evil Apap and his host of fiends is hurled back at dawn from the horizon to be drowned in the bottomless pit of Putrata (Rit., ch. 39).

Horus in the solar mythos is the prototype of Jesus on the mount. He is described as the sovereign lord upon the mount = horizon (ch. 40). Elsewhere he says, " I come before you and make my appearance on the seat of Ra, and I sit upon my seat which is on the mount" (or on the horizon) (Rit., ch. 79). Horus has alighted on the mount or is lifted on his monolith, when he says, " I make my appearance as that god in the form of a man that liveth like a god, and I stand out before you in the form of that god who is raised high upon his pedestal (of the mount, or the papyrus-column) to whom the gods come with acclamation." He maketh his appearance on the mount of glory or upon his pedestal with the cycle of gods about him (ch. 133). The papyrus being a figure of the earth, Horus, on his papyrus-column or lotus-plant, is Horus in the mount. Also the four brethren, Amsta, Hapi, Tuamutef, and Kahbsenuf, who stand upon the papyrus (or column), are the gods of the four quarters with Horus in the mount. Now, when the four brothers, Simon and Andrew with James and John, are called upon to leave their nets and follow Jesus, they became straightway the four with Jesus in the mount. For, according to Matthew, the disciples were only four in number when the sermon was delivered in the mount (Matt. iv., v.). Again, the typical group of four in the mount are represented by Jesus, James, Peter and John at the time of the transfiguration (Matt. xvii. 1). Mount Bakhu having been named in Egyptian from the olive-tree of dawn as a celestial summit was localized in Olivet, the mountain eastward. This, as solar, was the one sole mount of the mythos; and in the Gospels, although the mount is mentioned several times, and apparently in different localities, there is but one name given to it, that of Mount Olivet = Bakhu the solar mount, the one typical mount, the Egyptian mount, equivalent to the horizon, as the summit of the earth and figure of the ascent into heaven.

The canonical Jesus is also shown to be a form of the son of Ra, the father in heaven, in his retiring from the world at eventide and passing the night alone on the mount. It may be worth noting that there was a temple of the solar Horus, as ancient as the time of Sebek, upon the eastward side of Mount Bakhu. As it is said in the Ritual (ch. 108), " Sebek the Lord of Bakhu is at the East of the hill, and his temple is upon it." And Sebek was very possibly the most ancient form of Horus the young solar god. Horus wars against the serpent of darkness on behalf of his father in the mount by night, and is the teacher in the temple of heaven by day. Jesus obviously makes use of both the mount and the temple, for he went up into

the mountain when "he opened his mouth and taught" the multitudes (Matt. v. 2). The devil took him up into an exceeding high
mountain when he was in the spirit. He was transfigured on a "high
mountain apart"(Matt. xvii. 1, 2). He sat upon the Mount of Olives
when expounding the consummation of the cycle and the gospel of
the kingdom to the disciples privately (Matt. xxiv. 3). Many details
are of course omitted from the "history" and there is no guidance in
the Gospels to the secret meaning of the mysteries. For that we
must "search the Scriptures" which are genuine and self-explanatory
as Egyptian ; the scriptures of Maati and Taht-Aan. Of Jesus and his
doings in the mount by night we are told that he went into the
mountain to pray ; and he continued all night in prayer to God
(Luke vi. 12). "And when it was day, he called his disciples ; and
he chose from them twelve" (vi. 13). It is said in the Ritual
that "Horus is united at sunset with his Father Ra who goeth round
the heaven." So Jesus at sunset is united with his Father in prayer
all night in the mount. The sun-god has to fight the adversary Sut
for his passage through the mount by night. Horus is said to come
at evening and "seize upon the tunnels of Ra" for making his
passage through the mount. These are elsewhere called the tunnels
of Sut; a synonym for darkness. The sun-god entered the mountain
each night for rebirth every morning. Horus came forth from the
Mount of Olives. He is portrayed in the Ritual walking over the
waters. He ascends the Mount Bakhu to enter the solar bark. It is
said that his "sister goddesses stand in Bakhu"; they receive him
there as the two mothers, they lift him up into his boat (Hymn to
Harmachis). There is a curious conjunction of the Temple and
the Mount in Luke's description of Jesus as the teacher. Like so many
other fragments it stands by itself in the Gospel. "Every day he
was teaching in the Temple ; and every night he went out and lodged
in the mount that is called *of Olives*. And all the people came
early in the morning to him, in the Temple, to hear him" (ch. xxi.
37, 38). This passage identifies the mount as being named from the
olive-tree, on which the temple of Sebek-Horus stood, and therefore
with Mount Bakhu. On coming forth from the ·mount of Amenta
Horus entered the bark that was rowed or towed round by the
twelve who were called the twelve kings in the solar mythos, and
afterwards twelve teachers or apostles who were servants to Iu the
son of Atum, the Egyptian Jesus in the eschatology.

It is Horus in the mountain with his father who says—"I am the
Lord on high. I make my nest on the confines of heaven," that is,
aloft on the mount. "Invisible is my nest." "From thence I descend
to the earth of Seb" his foster-father, "and put a stop to evil."
"I see my father, the lord of the gloaming, and I breathe" (ch. 85,
Renouf). Horus in the mount is designated "lord of the Staircase"
or steps at the top of which his father sat enthroned. In this dual
character the peripatetic Jesus is made to journey, betwixt plain and
mountain, town and country, in a vain endeavour to make the track
of Horus become historical. Horus enters the mountain by night
and comes forth by day as the "lord of daylight" divinized. On
coming forth he says, "I have ascertained what there is in Sekhem,"
the shrine in the mount, where dead Osiris lay. "I have touched

with my two hands the heart of Osiris, and that which I went to ascertain I have come to tell. . . . Here am I, and I come that I may overthrow mine adversaries on the earth (even) though my dead body be buried" as the Osiris (ch. 86, Renouf). In entering the mountain at sunset he has seen the great mystery of Osiris, his death, his transformation, and his resurrection, and he comes forth as a spirit divinized to make the experience known as a teacher of the mysteries to those that became his followers, his children who were adopted by him as the four brethren two by two, then the seven, and finally the twelve who row the solar bark or reap the harvest of eternal plenty in the Aarru paradise of the Amenta.

A specially important feature in the "history" is this retirement of Jesus into a mountain at sunset to commune with his Father. Jesus "when even was come went up into the mountain apart to pray, and was there alone" (Matt. xiv. 23). "He went out into the mountain to pray; and he continued all night in prayer to God" (Luke vi. 12). It is noticeable that he goes into the mountain, and in the mythos the sun at evening entered the mount which is a figure of the earth. The type was continued in the eschatology. God the Father as Osiris had his dwelling-place and shrine in the mount of earth and it was there that Horus interviewed the father. The speaker in the "Book of the Dead" says, in the character of Horus the son, "I seek my father at sunset, compressing my mouth." This latter phrase is Renouf's rendering of the words "hapet ru," the sense of which is determined by the ideograph of closing or enclosing. Therefore the meaning is "I close my mouth" as the synonym for silence in the mount. He seeks his father in the character of Horus with the silent mouth. "I seek my father at sunset in silence, and I feed on life," is the complete declaration made in this line. Horus feeds on life in silence when alone with the father in the mount of earth where souls were fed on sustenance divine. This is the meat referred to by Jesus when he said, "I have meat to eat that ye know not of," "My meat is to do the will of him that sent me, and to accomplish his work." Horus says, "I live in Tattu, and I repeat daily my life after death, like the sun." For he is Horus risen in Amenta, where he is the instructor of the manes in the mysteries, otherwise he preaches to the "spirits in prison."

In building the house of heaven, which was annually repeated in the mysteries, the fourfold foundation, the four supports or cornerstones, were laid in the mount. These four supports were personalized in the four children of Horus, Amsta, Hapi, Tuamutef, and Kabhsenuf, who had already been four of his brothers in the earlier mythos when they were the four sustainers of the heaven at the four corners of the mount, and also as the four who stand upon the flower of the papyrus-plant. Now we have to bear in mind that the rock is identical with the mount, and that the house or temple of Horus built upon the mount was founded on the rock. In establishing his father's kingdom of the beatified, Horus built upon the typical rock. In the Gospel Simon is told by Jesus that he will build his church upon *this* rock, and the gates of Hades shall not prevail against it. The gates of Hades or Amenta opened in the rock of the Tser Hill to let the dead come forth in the glorified train of Horus the conqueror whose temple, from the time of Sebek, had been built upon the rock with the four brethren as the pillars of support, which were finally extended to the twelve in keeping with the complete number of zodiacal signs. Peter, in the Gospels, has been assigned the place and position of the rock or mount (or Tat of stability) because in the Greek the word *petra* signifies the rock. But the rock was the same as the mount; the mount was one and the same all through; and it was the site of the building, whether this is called the Church of Rome, the temple of Sebek, or the house of Tum, that was built by his son Jesus for the divine abode, at the level of the equinox.

Horus in the character of Har-Makhu was the sun-god of the double horizon, who passed from west to east and united the two in one. These two horizons of the double earth have been a source of endless perplexity to the students of the history. The two horizons reappear in the Gospels as those of the two opposite countries, Judea and Galilee. Both have been used independently; the result is that one writer localizes the works of Jesus in the one region, whilst another places the scenes in the country opposite, as if they did not know which leg to stand on, or on which horizon to take their stand. Horus of the double horizon is reproduced in Jesus, who itinerated in two lands or two parts of the one land which takes the place of the Egyptian double earth. Horus passes from one horizon to the other by making his passage through the mount. He makes the passage in the stellar Atit, or Maatet-boat, which he enters with the seven glorious ones at sunset. Horus in the mount is one with Horus in the boat, and thus as teacher of the four, or the seven, or the twelve, he is the teacher in the boat. In this character Jesus likewise teaches in the boat. It is said that "he sat down and taught the multitudes out of the boat" (Luke v. 3, 4). Horus, with the seven on board the boat, who were portrayed in heaven as the Sahus in Orion, is usually depicted standing. The nearest likeness to the passage through the mountain in the Maatet-boat by night occurs when Jesus "withdrew again into the mountain himself alone," whereas the disciples go by water. "When evening came, his disciples went down into the sea; and they entered into a boat and were going over the sea unto Capernaum. And it was now dark." The scribe hardly dared to send them through the mountain by the boat of the mysteries, therefore Jesus comes to them by walking on the water, "and straightway the boat was at the land whither they were going" (John vi. 15–21), that is, by magic or by miracle.

At the summit of the mount the glorified deceased who came up from Amenta were now given a seat upon the bark of Ra. In one of his many characters Horus is the divine teacher called "the teller," on board the boat. He says, "I am the teller in the divine ship. I am the unresting navigator in the bark of Ra" (Rit., ch. 109). As the teacher in the boat he also says, "I utter the words of Ra (his father) in heaven to the men of the present generation (or to the living on earth), and I repeat his words to those who are deprived of breath (or to the manes in Amenta)" (Rit., ch. 38). This, then, is Horus as the teacher in the solar boat, who utters the words or sayings of his father Ra, by day and night, to the living on earth and the manes in Amenta. These are spoken of as those who are in their

shrines, but who are also said to accompany Horus as his guides.
Horus further says, " I have made my way and gone round the
celestial ocean on the path of the bark of Ra, and standing on the
deck (bekasu) of the bark."   It is in this position on the boat that he
utters the words of Ra—the word of God—to both the living and the
dead.   He says, " I come forth from the cabin of the Sektit bark, and
I raise myself up from the eastern hill.   I stoop upon the eastern hill.
I stoop upon the Maatet (or Atet) bark that I may come and raise
to me those who are in their circles, and who bow down before me "
(Renouf, ch. 77).   The boat or bark of the sun has been made
historical in the Gospels.   In the time of the celestial Heptanomis
there were seven on board the bark with Horus.   And seven is the
number on board the ship with Jesus after his resurrection.   In the
heaven of ten nomes there were ten on board the solar boat with
Horus, and there are ten on board the boat with Jesus (not twelve) in
a very early picture given by Bosio.   In this scene, Jesus with the
ten in the boat is the child of twelve years, not the man of thirty
years.   Ten in the solar boat preceded the twelve in the heaven of
ten divisions, which were earlier than the seventy-two.   (Lundy,
Monumental Christianity, fig. 56.)

Horus in the boat is another of the mythical characters assigned to
Jesus by the " sacred historian."   Jesus likewise plays the part of
Horus in the boat as the *teller* of parables.   " There were gathered
unto him great multitudes so that he entered into a boat and sat ;
and all the multitude stood on the beach.   And he spake to them
many things in parables " (Matt. xiii. 2, 3).   Four of the parables are
then told to the people by Jesus, the teller in the boat, which is a co-
type with the sayer or logos in person.   We find that the Teacher,
now become historic, also addresses two classes or kinds of people
when he utters the words of his father from the boat.   One audience
consists of the twelve disciples to whom he is supposed to communi-
cate a knowledge of the mysteries of the kingdom of heaven.   These
correspond to the glorious ones who are enshrined, and who accompany Horus as his guides.   The others are called the multitude.
To these it is not given to know the mysteries because " seeing they
see not, and hearing they hear not, neither do they understand "
(Matt. xiii.).   If the thing were historic, the supposed great demo-
cratic Teacher would be excluding the " swinish multitude " from all
knowledge of the kingdom of heaven.   They were not to be
enlightened because they were too densely, darkly ignorant.   They
are to be put off with parables, according to Luke (viii. 10), " that
seeing they might *not* see, and hearing they might *not* understand "
these heavenly stories which had for them no earthly meaning.   Thus,
in this process of transmogrifying the Kamite mythos into Christian
history, the common people, the ignorant multitude, are assigned the
status of the Pait; the breathless, non-intelligent, unilluminated dead
who were slumbering darkly in the coffins of Amenta, and these are
inevitably mixed up, in the teaching of Jesus, with the deaf and blind
who do not hear and cannot see, and may not perceive, as mortals on
this earth.

Moreover the bark in which the sun-god made his celestial voyage
was double under two different names.   " I am the great one among

the gods," says the speaker in the Ritual (ch. 136B), "coming in the *two barks* of the lord of Sau." In the morning it was the Sektit boat, in the evening the Maatet bark. "Let the soul of the deceased come forth with thee (the god) into heaven; let him journey in the Maatet boat till he reach the heaven of the setting stars" (Rit., ch. 15). Two boats are also mentioned by Luke where Matthew only speaks of one—"while the multitude pressed upon him and heard the word of God, Jesus saw *two boats* standing by them." He asks that one of these may put out from the land in order that he may address the multitude from the shore. And he sat down and taught the multitudes out of the boat (Luke v. 4). Again, we meet with Jesus on board the Maatet bark at evening. In the Gospel according to Matthew there is a scene in which Jesus is asleep on board the boat. At sunset, "when even was come," he "entered into a boat and his disciples followed him. And behold, there arose a great tempest in the sea, insomuch that the boat was covered with the waves, but he was asleep." Then "he arose and rebuked the winds and the sea, and there was a great calm" (Matt. viii. 24). The scene may be paralleled with that on board the bark of Ra at evening (Rit., ch. 108). In this conflict between Apap and Ra the evil one is in the western mountain, and it is said of him, "Now at the *close of day* he turneth down his eyes to Rà: for there cometh a standing still in the bark, and a deep slumber within the ship." Here the solar god as Ra, or Horus, when sinking to rest in the boat, is described as being asleep on board when the evil one makes his attack. There is a contest. "Then Sut is made to flee with a chain of steel upon him, and he is forced to vomit all that he hath swallowed. Then Sut is put into his prison" (Rit., ch. 108). The western mountain overlooks the lake of Putrata. "I know the place," says the speaker, "where Ra navigated against adverse winds" (ch. 107). The lake that is crossed by night amidst the terrors of the tempest is a replica of the dreadful lake of darkness which the followers of Horus have to cross in Amenta. It is mentioned in the pyramid texts (Pepi I. 332, and Merira 635) as a lake that is traversed by the glorified personage. In the chapter by which "one dieth not a second time" (Rit., ch. 44, Renouf) it is spoken of as the lake or chasm of Putrata, where the "dead fall into darkness," if not supported by the eye of Horus, their moon by night. Elsewhere it is described as the void of Apap over which the bark of heaven sails; the void in which the Herrut-reptile lurks to prey on those who fall down headlong in the dark (ch. 99). In this place the deceased pleads that he may be brought into the bark "as a distressed mariner," for safety. After crossing the lake of darkness, the solar god is thus addressed—"O thou who art devoid of moisture in coming forth from the stream, and who restest upon the deck of thy bark, as thou proceedest in the direction of yesterday, and restest upon the deck of thy bark, let me join thy boatmen." "O Ra, since thou passest through those who are perishing headlong, do thou keep me standing on my feet." That is, in crossing the water— but not in walking on it. Some of the matter may have sunk down a little too deep to dredge for, but as Herod the monster is the Herrut-reptile, the dragon-Apap, in an anthropomorphic guise, we may complete the parallel by pointing out that the murder of John by Herod immediately precedes the crossing of the stormy lake = the lake of darkness, called the void of Apap in Amenta. John is slain, but Jesus escapes to cross over and to save those who were sinking in the waters and who are described in the Ritual as " falling down headlong," and finding nothing to lay hold on by which they can be saved from the bottomless abyss, until Horus comes to the rescue of the " distressed mariners " in the " divine form which revealeth the solar orb," and with the eye that was an emblem of the moon ; the sun by day and moon by night being called the two eyes of Horus.

In the original mythos the boat is the solar bark ; in the eschatological phase it is the boat of souls. It is steered by Horus, who is called the oar that guides. It is rowed by his followers, who may be the " four paddles," or the seven great spirits, or the twelve mariners ; and it is the ark of salvation for souls when Horus the Saviour is at the look-out. This ark or bark has served for a model in the New Testament as the boat of souls distressed that is nearly swamped, and only saved from sinking by the God who is on board. On entering the bark the speaker pleads : " O Great One in thy bark, let me be lifted up into thy bark " (ch. 102). The data for comparison with the story in the Gospel are—the divine bark, which is solar in the mythos, and the boat of salvation, or of safety, in the eschatology. In crossing the terrible lake from which the Apap monster emerges, and the storms and tempests rise to overwhelm the bark, the god rises unwetted from the water to rest upon the deck of the bark and insure the safety of those on board. This is identical with Jesus, who comes on board by walking upon the water, whilst the individual speaker that makes the appeal for safety in the place of perishing headlong is equivalent to Peter, who calls for help when sinking in the lake, saying, " Lord save me," and is " lifted into the bark " (Matt. xiv. 22–33), like the rescued manes in the Ritual. Jesus on board the boat with his disciples in the storm sustains the character of Horus in the boat, who is the oar, paddle, or rudder of Ra, and who exclaims " I am the kheru (paddle or rudder) of Ra who *brings the boat to land*" (Rit., ch. 63). In this passage Horus is the oar or rudder to the boat of the sun, with the ancient ones on board, in the mythos, and to the boat of salvation for souls in the eschatology. It is he who brings the boat to the shore.

The germ of the Gospel story concerning Peter sinking in the waters may be detected in this same chapter. The speaker is a " wretched one " in the water who was to be saved by him who is an oar or a boat to the shipwrecked (cf. ch. 125, 38). In the Ritual it is hot water that the sinking manes has got into, the imagery being solar, and he speaks of being helpless as a dead person. But Horus, the oar of the boat, the rudder of Ra, is obviously his saviour, like Jesus with Peter in the Gospel. A shipwrecked spirit is the inspiring thought, and Horus was the rescuer as the pilot, or figuratively the paddle to the boat by which the sinking soul was saved from drowning in the overwhelming waters.

The Lord appears on the water in the morning watch, the " fourth watch of the night," that is, the πρωί or dawning (cf. Mark xiii. 35), at which time the Sun-God begins his march or his " walking," as it is termed, upon the waters of the Nun. It is said to the God who walks this water at sunrise, "Thou art the only one since thy coming forth upon the Nun." And here we may discover the prototype of the Gospel version. The deceased addresses Ra at his coming forth to walk the water and pleads, like Peter, that he may do so likewise. "Grant," he says, "that I too may be able to walk (the water) as thou walkest (on the Nun) without making any halt." The sun was seen to rise on the blue above, which was imaged as the water of heaven. His follower prays that he also may walk the water and make the passage successfully and without sinking, like the solar God. In another chapter the deceased exclaims "I fail, I sink into the abyss of the flowing that issues from Osiris," that is, the water of which Osiris is the source ; and in these we find the parallel and prototypes of Jesus walking on the water and Peter sinking into its engulfing depths.

Horus commands in the boat. Ra annihilates his enemies from the boat. It is in the boat of the Sun that Ra puts a limit to the power of his enemies when they pursue him to the water's edge ; that is, to the horizon of day. So Jesus takes refuge in the boat and finds protection when he perceives that he is about to be taken by force ; he likewise walks upon the water to the boat. Death by drowning in the lake was the mode of execution appointed for the evil Apap and his host of darkness who attacked the solar bark by night. The fiends of Sut are also included in this sentence of death by drowning in the emerald lake of heaven, or of dawn. Now the fiends of the evil Sut were represented as swine. And immediately after the great tempest in the sea which Jesus stills, the devils are made to enter the swine, and, like the emissaries of Apap and of Sut who "causes storms and tempests," they are driven down the mountain-side to suffer death by drowning in the lake. It was *on the mount* that Jesus met with the man obsessed with a legion of devils who "entreated him that he would not command them to depart into the abyss." "Now there was a herd of swine feeding on the mountain," "and the devils came out from the man and entered into the swine," "and the herd rushed down the "steep into the lake and were choked" (Luke viii. 33). It was by Sut, in the shape of a great black boar, that Horus was gored in the eye. It was also the Pig of Sut that devoured the arm of Osiris in the burial-place. And when the evil spirits are cast out, as represented in the judgment-scenes, they enter the swine of Typhon and are driven down the side of the mount to be submerged in the Lake of Putrata or the fathomless abyss of outer darkness.

SUT AND HORUS AS HISTORIC CHARACTERS IN THE CANONICAL GOSPELS.

The Gospel story of the devil taking Jesus, or the Christ, up into an exceeding high mountain from which all the kingdoms of the world and the glory of them could be seen, and of the contention on the summit, is originally a legend of the astronomical mythos which, in common with so many others, has been converted into "history." As legend it can be explained by means of the Egyptian wisdom.

As "history" it is, of course, miraculous, if *nothing else.* Satan and Jesus are the representatives of Sut and Horus, the contending twins of darkness and light, of drought and fertility, who strove for supremacy in the various phenomena of external nature, and in several celestial localities belonging to the mythology. In the Ritual (ch. 110) the struggle is described as taking place upon the mount, that is, "the mountain in the midst of the earth," or the mountain of Amenta, which "reaches up to the sky," and which in the solar mythos stood at the point of equinox where the conflict was continued and the twins were reconciled year after year. The equinox was figured at the summit of the mount on the ecliptic, and the scene of strife was finally configurated as a fixture in the constellation of the Gemini, the sign of the twin-brothers who for ever fought and wrestled "up and down the garden," first one, then the other being uppermost during the two halves of the year, or of night and day. The mountain of the equinox "in the midst of the earth" joined the portion of Sut to the portion of Horus at this the point midway betwixt the south and north. It was on the mountain of the equinox and only there the twins were reconciled for the time being by the star-god Shu (Rit., ch. 110) or by the earth-god Seb (text from Memphis). Sut the Satanic is described as seizing the good Horus in the desert of Amenta and carrying him to the top of the mount here called Mount Hetep, the place of peace, where the two contending powers are reconciled by Shu, according to the treaty made by Seb. Thus, episode after episode, the Gospel history can and will be traced to the original documents as matter of the Egyptian mysteries and astronomical mythology.

The battles of Sut and Horus are represented in both the apocryphal and canonical Gospels. In the Gospels of the Infancy there are two boys—the bad boy and the good boy. In this form the two born antagonists continue their altercation with a root-relationship to the Osirian mythos. Sut is the representative of evil, of darkness, drought, sterility, negation, and non-existence. It is his devilry to undo the good work that Horus does, like Satan sowing tares amongst the wheat. It was Sut who paralyzed the left arm of Osiris and held it bound in Sekhem (Rit., ch. 1). It is the express delight of the bad boy, the child of Satan, to destroy the works of Jesus, the child of light. There is one particularly enlightening illustration of the mythos reproduced as Märchen. The power of resurrection was imaged by the lifting of the arm from the mummy-bandages; Horus in Sekhem is the lifter of the arm. Whilst the arm is fettered in death, Sut is triumphant over Horus in the dark. When Horus frees his arm, he raises the hand that was motionless (Rit., ch. 5). He strikes down Sut, or stabs him to the heart. The power of darkness, one form of which was Sut, is designated the "eater of the arm" (ch. 11). This act of the Osirian drama is rendered in the apocryphal Gospels by the bad boy persistently aiming at injuring the good boy's arm or shoulder. In the Gospel of pseudo-Matthew (29) the bad boy, who is called a son of Satan and the worker of iniquity, runs at Jesus and thrusts himself bodily against his shoulder with the intention of breaking or paralyzing his arm. In the Gospel of Thomas the boy ran and thrust against the shoulder of Jesus (ch. 4). Again, the bad boy threw a stone and hit him on the shoulder (Gospel of Thomas, B. 2, ch. 4). Several times when this occurs the bad boy is smitten dead by Jesus, just as Sut is pierced to the heart by Horus. Other evidence might be cited from these Gospels to show that the bad boy who tries to destroy the arm of Jesus is one with Sut who renders the arm of Horus (or Osiris) powerless in Amenta. This being established, we are enabled to identify Judas the betrayer of Jesus, his brother, with Sut the enemy of Horus. According to "the Arabic Gospel of the Infancy," "In the same place" (with Lady Mary and her child Jesus), "there dwelt another woman whose son was vexed by Satan. He, *Judas by name*, whenever Satan obsessed him, bit all who approached him. He sought to bite the Lord Jesus, but he could not, yet he struck the right side of Jesus." "Now this boy who struck Jesus and from whom Satan went out in the form of a dog, was *Judas Iscariot*, who betrayed him to the Jews" (ch. 35).

We now have the original matter with which to compare the remains, and the comparative process will prove that these "apocrypha" are not perversions of the canonical Gospels, but that they preserve traditions derived from the Kamite mythology and eschatology. This can be determined once for all by the contests of Horus with Sut, and by his warfare with the Apap-serpent or dragon, which are assigned to the child-Jesus, as they were previously ascribed to the child-Horus.

There are two types of evil, or, according to modern terminology, the devil, in the Kamite mysteries. One is zoomorphic, as the Apap-reptile, the other anthropomorphic, as Sut, the personal adversary of Osiris. Apap is the Evil One in the mythology; Sut is Satan the adversary in the eschatology. In the 108th chapter of the Ritual there is a curious fusion of Apap with Sut, the anthropomorphic type of Satan. The serpent of darkness, the old enemy of Osiris-Ra, is portrayed in the vignette as Apap, and spoken of in the text as Sut. After the battle "Sut is made to flee with a chain of steel upon him, and he is forced to disgorge all that he hath swallowed. Then Sut is made fast in his prison." At the same time the serpent is described as "the bright one who cometh on his belly, his hind parts, and on the joints of his back." To him it is said, "Thou art pierced with hooks, as it was decreed against thee of old" (ch. 108). The battle here, betwixt Ra and Apap, or Sut, is finished on the horizon, that is, on the mount, from which the devil is hurled down defeated into the abyss. In the canonical Gospels, Jesus and Satan occupy the place of the two opponents Horus and the Apap, or Horus and Sut. The Herrut-reptile has been paralleled with the monster Herod; Satan is now to be compared with Sut. Sat=Satan in Egyptian is a name of the Evil One (Budge, *Vocabulary*, p. 268).

In Africa the primal curse was drought. Drought was a form of evil straight from nature. This was figured as the fiery dragon, "hellish Apap," that was drowned by Horus in the inundation when he came as saviour to the land of Egypt in his little ark of the papyrus plant. Sut warred with Horus in the wilderness as representative of drought, when the "father of the inundation was athirst" (Rit., ch. 97), a cry of Horus that was echoed on the Cross (John xix. 28). Drought,

3 H

as we have said, was the earliest devil. In the Osirian cult the whole of nature was expressed in a twofold totality according to the doctrine of Maati. Night and day, body and soul, water and drought, life and death, health and disease, were modes of the duality manifested in phenomena. Sut and Horus were the representatives of this alternation and opposition personified as a pair of twins, now called the children of Osiris. Osiris Un-nefer is the Good Being, but as with nature he includes both the good and the evil in the totality. In the mythos, however, Horus represents the good and Sut the bad. Sut is said to undo the good that Horus does. Hence he is the adversary or Satan when personified. As Prince of Darkness he puts out the eye of Horus, or the light by night. He sows the tares amidst the grain. He is the "eater of the arm." He dries up the water of life with the desert-drought. He lets loose the locusts, the scorpions and other plagues. He represents negation and non-being in opposition to being, and to the Good Being who is divinized in Osiris and manifested by Horus. The triumph of Horus over Sut is frequently referred to in the Ritual. In one of his battles Horus destroyed the virile member of Sut, as the symbol of his power (ch. 17, 68, 69). In another, Sut and his associates were overthrown and pierced by Horus so long as blood would flow. In his resurrection Horus comes to put an end to the opposition of Sut, and to the troubles he had raised against Osiris his father (Rit., 137 B). He says: I am the beloved son. I am come to see my father Osiris, and to pierce the heart of Sut (Rit., ch. 9). He is armed with horns against Sut (ch. 78, 42). Horus, "who giveth light by means of his own body," is the God who is against Sut when Taht is between them as adjudicator in their dispute (Rit., ch. 83, 4). In the discourse of Horus to his father he says to Osiris, " I have brought thee the associates of Sut in chains."

In the Gospels of the Infancy, which contain some remains of the more ancient legendary lore, the grapple of child-Horus with the deadly Apap-reptile is frequently portrayed, as in the Arabic Gospel of the Infancy, when the boy has been bitten by the serpent, and the Lord Jesus says to his playmates, " Boys, let us go and kill the serpent." He proves his power over the reptile by making it suck the venom from the wound. Then the Lord Jesus curses the serpent, "whereupon the reptile was instantly rent asunder" (ch. 42). But the war of Horus with the Apap-dragon, or serpent of evil, is not fought out directly by Jesus in the canonical Gospels. Sut as the power of darkness and as the opponent in the moral domain had taken the place of the old first adversary of man in the phenomena of external nature. Jesus promises to give his followers power over the serpent and the scorpion, but there is no personal conflict with the pre-anthropomorphic Satan recognized in the four Gospels. Sut, as Satan in a human form, was a somewhat less unhistoric-looking type of the devil than the Apap-reptile. Satan, however, retains his old primitive form of the dragon in " the Arabic Gospel of the Infancy." In this it is related that a damsel was afflicted by Satan, the cursed one, in the form of a huge dragon, which from time to time appeared to her and prepared to swallow her up. He also *sucked out all her blood, so that she remained like a corpse.* She is cured by a strip of the clothing that had been worn by the child, Lord Jesus (ch. 33).

This is a form of the woman with an issue of blood. Her persecutor is the dragon of darkness who is the eternal devourer of the light in the Egyptian mythology, and of condemned souls in the eschatology. In the gnostic version it is Sophia who suffers from the issue of blood and who is restrained and supported by Horus when her life is flowing away into immensity. The woman suffering from the swallowing dragon of darkness was the mother of the child of light in the moon. Expressed in human terms, Horus the bull, or fecundator of the mother, stopped her female flow and filled her with the glory of the light, and thus he overthrew the monster that assailed her in the dark, which was figured as the wide-mouthed crocodile or devouring dragon (Rit., ch. 80, 10). Horus puts a boundary round about Sophia. The child-Jesus cures the damsel with a strip of his raiment ; and in the Gospel according to Matthew the woman who is flowing away like Sophia with her issue of blood is healed by touching the border of the garment worn by Jesus (Matt. ix. 20, 21). Here the dragon is omitted. The suffering lunar lady has been humanized, together with the Divine Healer ; the cure is wrought ; the modern miracle remains in place of the mystery according to the ancient wisdom.

The conflict between Sut and Horus (or Osiris), who are represented by Satan and Jesus in the Gospels, commences immediately after the baptism in the river Jordan. One form of baptism in the solar mythos was derived from the setting of the sun-god in the waters of the west, the waters in which Un-nefer washes when he has his dispute with Sut—either in the character of Horus or Osiris. Asar in his baptism is said to plunge into the waters with "Isis and Nephthys looking on." Apuat (Anup) is present apparently conducting the submersion of the god (Inscrip. of Shabaka from Memphis, line 42). In his baptism the god Un-nefer was prepared for his struggle with Sut, the power of drought in the desert of Anrutef. So, in the Gospels, Jesus is prepared by John in his baptism for the conflict with Satan in the wilderness, on the pinnacle, and upon the exceeding high mountain. It was only after he had entered spirit-life that Horus could grapple with Sut, or Jesus with Satan, in the desert, on the pinnacle of the temple, or on the summit of the mount ; consequently the earth-life had ended when the contest betwixt Satan and Jesus first began, in the phase of eschatology. The wilderness of Satan in the Gospel represents the desert of Sut in Amenta. When Satan seized on Jesus and bore him bodily up into the mountain Jesus had just risen from his baptism and was led up "of the Spirit." Otherwise he had made his transformation from the state of manes to the status of a spirit. This was in the phase of eschatology and the transaction is in spirit-world.

When Jesus was "led up of the Spirit into the wilderness to be tempted of the devil" he is said to have "fasted forty days and forty nights," and, afterwards, to "have hungered," whatsoever that may mean. This contention in the wilderness was one of the great battles of Sut and Horus, or, in the other version of the mythos, of Sut and Osiris. As Egyptian, the wilderness is the desert of Anrutef, a desolate, stony place where nothing grew. It was here that Horus was made blind by Sut, and was a sufferer from hunger and thirst in this region of stony sterility, and rootless, waterless sand. Horus in

3 H 2

Amenta had to make way through the barren desert, in the domain of Sut, as sower of the seed from which the bread of life was made, much of which must have fallen on stony ground in the region of Anrutef. Forty days was the length of time in Egypt that was reckoned for the grain in the earth before it sprouted visibly from the ground. It was a time of scarcity and fasting in Egypt, which gave a very natural significance to the season of Lent, with its mourning for the dead Osiris, and its rejoicing over the child of promise, the germinating green shoot springing from the earth. This is represented in the Gospel as a fast of forty days and forty nights, during which Jesus wrestled with the devil and was hungry. The struggle then of Jesus with the devil in the wilderness is a repetition of the conflict between Horus and Sut in the desert of Amenta ; on the mount and on the pinnacle of the ben-ben or temple in Annu. During the forty days that Osiris was typically buried in the nether-earth as seed, from which the bread of heaven was made, the struggle was continued by Sut and Horus in the mountain. This is repeated in the Gospels as the contest of Christ and Satan for the mastery in the mount. The conflict is between the powers of light and darkness, of fertility and sterility, betwixt Osiris (or Horus) the giver of bread, and Sut, whose symbol of the desert was a stone. The fasting of Jesus in the desert represents the absence of food that is caused by Sut in the wilderness during forty days of burial for the corn, and Satan asking Jesus to turn the stones into bread is playing with the sign of Sut. Satan's jape about converting stones into loaves of bread is likewise reminiscent of the mythos. The stone was an especial symbol of the adversary Sut. Also the place of the temple in Annu, and the pinnacle, or Ha-ben-ben, was the place of the stones by name. More-over, Annu was the place of bread, or the loaves. As it is said, "there are seven loaves in Annu with Ra," the Father in heaven (Rit., ch. 53B).

As represented in the Ritual, Sut and Horus are more upon a foot-ing of equality, whether in the wilderness or on the summit of the mount of glory. Their triumph is alternate, though that of Sut is much the more limited. As the power of drought and darkness he is master in the desert, and chief of the powers called the "*tesheru* deities," or gods of the desert. The speaker in chapter 96 exclaims, " I have come to propitiate Sut and to make offerings to the God Akar and to the deities of the desert," where Sut attained supremacy over Horus for a time. The desert was the natural domain of Sut the adversary of Horus. Hence Horus at his second coming exclaims, " I am Horus, the Lord of Kamit and the heir of *tesherit* " (Rit., ch. 138, lines 3 and 4), which he has also seized. Kamit is Egypt as a mythical locality : the dark and moist, fat and fertile land. Tesherit, the red land, is the desert. So that in taking possession of the "two worlds," or the double earth, Horus has also seized the domain of Sut, the wilderness, which was a subject of contention in Amenta. Hence he says, " I have also seized the desert—I, the invincible one, who avengeth his father and is fierce at the drowning of his mother " (ch. 138).

In his resurrection Horus cometh forth as "the heir of the temple " in Annu. He is called " the active and powerful heir of the temple, whose arm resteth not " in the mummy bandages (ch. 115). That is, as the avenger of his father Osiris in Annu, where he rises with the whip or flail in his hand to drive the adversaries from the temple. Now Annu, the station of the temple, was the place of the pillar. The temple itself in Annu, or Heliopolis, was known by the name of Ha-ben-ben, the house of the pyramidion or temple of the pinnacle, and the struggle of Satan with Jesus on the pinnacle of the temple may be traced to that of Sut and Horus the heir of the temple or the Ha-ben-ben of Annu, following the contention of the twin powers of darkness and light, or of food and famine in the wilderness. "All the kingdoms of the world" are more definitely presented to view as celestial localities upon Mount Hetep. There are ten divisions of this divine domain. The three scenes of struggle betwixt Jesus and Satan are (1) in the wilderness, (2) on the pinnacle, and (3) on an exceeding high mountain ; and these can be paralleled in the conflicts between Horus and Sut. The forty days' struggle in the wilderness was in Amenta. Next, there was a struggle on the ben-ben or pinnacle in Annu. And thirdly, Horus was carried off by Sut to the summit of Mount Hetep, where the two combatants were reconciled by Shu. The mount was a figure of the horizon in the solar mythos. On this the warring twins were constellated as the Gemini, and may be seen continuing their old conflict still, as Sut and Horus in the mythos, or as Satan and Jesus in the Christian eschatology. The earth, or heaven, that was first divided in two halves between Sut and Horus in the mythology is finally claimed to be the sole possession of Horus, the conqueror and the legitimate heir of God the father in the eschatology. The triumph of Horus over Sut is denoted by his kindling a light in the dark of death for the Ka or spiritual image in Amenta (Rit., ch. 137A). He was not only the light of the world in the mortal sphere. As it is said in the Ritual, "O light! let the light be kindled for the ka !" "Let the light be kindled for the night which followeth the day." The light is called the eye of Horus, the glorious one, shining like Ra from the mount of glory, putting an end to the opposition of the dark-hearted Sut (Rit., ch. 137B).

The question of an historic Jesus is by no means so simple as the grossly simple early Christians thought. It is equally a question of the historic devil. From first to last the Lord and Satan are twin, and without Satan there is no Christ-Jesus nor any need of a redeemer. In the mythology Horus was the lord of light and Sut the adversary, or the Satan of drought and darkness, from the time when the two contended as the black bird and the white (or the golden hawk), or as the two lions (our lion and unicorn a-fighting in the moonlight for the crown), as the Rehus are described in the 80th chapter of the Ritual. As there was no Horus without Sut in the mythos, so there is no Jesus without Satan in the history. The brotherhood or twinship of Horus and Sut the betrayer is repeated in the canonical Gospels. Sut was the brother of Horus, born twin with him in one phase of the mythos, or with Osiris in another. In like manner Judas is a brother of Jesus.. Now, when Horus the youth of twelve years makes his transformation into Horus the adult, the man of thirty years, it is as the enemy and eternal conqueror of Sut who in the earth-life often had the upper hand. But the contest of the personal Christ with a personal Satan in the New Testament is no more historical fact than the contest between the seed of the woman and the serpent of evil in the Old. Both are mythical; both are Egyptian mysteries. In the earlier narrative we have the struggle between Horus and the Apap-serpent of evil reproduced as Gospel truth by a writer in Aramaic. In the later the conflict between Horus and Sut (or Satan in his anthropomorphic guise) has been repeated as Christian history. As mythos the Ritual explains both, and for ever disproves their right to be considered historical. In one of the sayings assigned to Jesus it is promised that " in the regeneration when the son of man shall sit on the throne of his glory, the disciples also shall sit upon twelve thrones, judging the twelve tribes of Israel" (Matt. xix. 28). Now, when this was said, according to Matthew, Judas the traitor was one of the twelve. Moreover, as reported by Luke, the same thing is uttered by Jesus *after* "Satan entered into Judas who was called Iscariot, being of the number of the twelve," and therefore one of those who are to sit on the twelve thrones in the future kingdom, and judge the twelve tribes of Israel. No defection of the son of perdition is foreseen, no treachery allowed for. Judas is reckoned as one of the twelve who are to sit at the table of the Lord and eat and drink in the kingdom that is yet to come (Luke xxii. 4–30). There is but one way in which the traitor could remain one of the twelve in heaven. This belongs to the astronomical mythology, not to any human history, as when the sign of the scorpion is given to Sut-typhon. In the newly-recovered Gospel of Peter there is no sign of Judas the betrayer having been one of the twelve. Immediately *after the resurrection*, it is said, the feast of the Passover being ended, " We the twelve disciples of the Lord wept and grieved, and each of us in grief at what had happened withdrew to his house" (Harris, page 56). At the same time, in Matthew, the disciples are but eleven in number when they go to meet Jesus by appointment on the mount, with Judas no longer one of them. Sut is as inseparable from Jesus in the Gospels as from Horus in the dual figure of the Egyptian twins. The name alone is changed; otherwise it is Sut the devil who is the tempter of Jesus during forty days and forty nights in the wilderness. It is Sut who carries Jesus to the summit of an exceeding high mountain. It is Sut who, as personal opponent, is seen to fall as lightning from heaven. It is Sut the betrayer who enters Judas to become the betrayer of Jesus. Also an historical Christ implies, involves, necessitates an historical devil. According to the canonical record the two must stand or fall together as realities. Both are personal or neither. And both were pre-extant as Horus and Sut, who were neither personal nor historical. Indeed, it is asserted by Lactantius (*Inst. Div.*, B. 2, ch. 8), that the Word of God, the logos of John, is the first-born brother of Satan. That is honestly spoken and true, if we re-identify the word with the Horus who was born twin with Sut. He is wrong in making Horus the logos the first-born, but that is of little importance. Otherwise, he has got the twins all right. Sut was the first-born, but the birthright belonged to Horus who was the real heir. Now the "word of God" is made flesh in Jesus, and the contention of the twin-powers of darkness and light is rendered historically in the conflicts between Jesus and Satan in the wilderness, upon the pinnacle, or the mount, or in the harvest-field. The contest is also illustrated by Luke (viii. 12): "Then cometh the devil and taketh away the word from their heart that they may not believe and be saved." This is one with Sut in undoing what Horus the Word had done, especially in sowing the seed of the logos. The contention of Sut and Horus is carried out betwixt Satan and Jesus to the last. Sut, the king in his turn, was triumphant over Horus in his suffering and death. "I go away," says Jesus, "for the prince of this world cometh, and he hath nothing in me" (John xiv. 30).

Beelzebub, God of flies, is the particular name assigned to Satan in the Gospels as the prince of devils. And as Sut was Prince of the Sebau, it seems probable that the "zebub," or infernal flies, may have been identical with and therefore derived by name from that spawn of Satan the Sebau, the associates of Sut on the night of the great battle in the Ritual. In the parable of the sower it is said, "When anyone heareth the word of the kingdom, and understandeth it not, then cometh the evil one (the adversary Sut or Satan) and snatcheth away that which hath been sown in his heart" (Matt. xiii. 19). And in "the parable of the tares" it is said, "He that soweth the good seed is the son of man"; and of the good seed, "these are the sons of the kingdom; and the tares are the sons of the evil one; and the enemy that sowed them is the devil" (Matt. xiii. 36–39). This is the contention of Horus and Sut in the harvest-field of Osiris represented in parables instead of in the mysteries. Horus sows the good seed and Sut the tares. When Horus rises in Amenta after death it is as the husbandman or harvester who comes to gather in the harvest previously sown for the father by Horus in the earth of Seb, and to vanquish Sut, the sower of the tares, the thorns, and thistles in Anrutef.

The judgment of the world by Horus and the casting out of Sut is spoken of as a present fulfilment. "Now is the (or a) judgment of this world. Now shall the prince of this world be cast out" (John xii. 31, 32). This judgment was annual in the mysteries of Amenta. Sut as prince of this world and the son of perdition was cast out and judgment passed on those who were to be no more. This was at the time when Horus as the son of man was glorified, and Sut with his associates were once more overthrown by him on the highways of the damned. In John's account of the betrayal and arrest, when Jesus declares himself, the soldiers and officers who are with Judas are "struck to the ground," or "they went backwards and fell to the ground" (John xviii. 6, 7). So when "Horus repulses the associates of Sut," they see the diadem upon his head and "fall upon their faces in presence of his Majesty" (Rit., 134, 11). Sut put out the eye of Horus. This is parodied in the Gospels when Jesus is blindfolded and then asked to tell who struck him in the dark?

We get one other passing glimpse of Sut and Horus the contending twins in the parable of the marriage feast (Matt. xxii.). The wisdom of the Kamite mysteries was memorized in the sayings, and made portable in the parables. And in this the parable represents the marriage in the mystery of Tattu (Rit., ch. 17). Horus was the king's son for whom the feast was made. He is Horus of the royal countenance in the mythos; the wearer of the Greek cloak of royalty in the Roman catacombs. The king is Ra who issues the invitation to the festival of "Come thou hither," which is represented by the Gospel marriage feast, to which those invited would not come. Sut as the adversary of Horus is the unbidden marriage guest who had no wedding garment on. The murderers who slay the servants of the king are the Sebau and co-conspirators of Sut, and the vindictive treatment that followed becomes intelligible only by means of the mythos.

The conflict betwixt Satan and Jesus attains a culmination astronomically. In the betrayal of Osiris the Good Being by the evil Sut there are seventy-two conspirators associated with the adversary. Seventy-two on the one hand as the powers of darkness imply the same number of opponent powers fighting on behalf of Horus or, it may be, Jesus on the other, the battle being in the seventy-two duodecans of the zodiac. This war of Sut and Horus is repeated once more in the Gospel when the seventy-two or the seventy "returned with joy, saying, Lord, even the devils are subject unto us in thy name." And he said unto them, "I beheld Satan fallen as lightning from heaven." "Behold, I have given you authority to tread upon serpents and scorpions and over all the powers of the enemy." The enemy was Sut, and as a symbol in the zodiac Sut was at one time figured in the scorpion-sign. Thus, the betrayal of Osiris happened when the sun or the bull of eternity, as the divinity is also called, was in the sign of Scorpio. The sign of the bull being secretly assaulted by the scorpion is well known from the Mithraic monuments according to Hyde (Drummond, *Ædipus Judaicus*, Pl. 13). In some of the Greco-Egyptian planispheres, given by Kircher, Sut is also identified as the scorpion which slew Osiris (Drummond, Pl. 13). In the Gospel, power is given for the seventy-two to tread on the scorpion and to triumph over all the powers of the enemy (Luke x. 17–20). The two different numbers of seventy and seventy-two for those whose names were written in heaven show that both belong to the planisphere which had been divided at two different periods into the heaven of seventy and the heaven of seventy-two divisions. We can now see how and why the betrayer keeps his place as one of the twelve in the Gospel of Peter, and why he has been cast out in the Gospel according to Matthew. The Gospel of Peter was not historical, which means that it was astronomically based ; and according to the gnosis the twelve whose thrones were set in heaven are zodiacal, not ethnical characters. Sut the betrayer was assigned the scorpion as a type of evil. And as the scorpion he keeps his place, like Judas in the Petrine Gospel, as one of the twelve who were to sit on twelve celestial thrones in spite of his defection, because the twelve originated as astronomical and not as historical realities.

The Gnostics maintained that Jesus was the Lord for one year only, and that he suffered in the twelfth month, as did Osiris with the sun in the sign of Scorpio. Thus, the Egypto-gnostic Jesus throned upon Mount Olivet with the twelve around him—he being a "little apart"—is a figure of the solar god with the twelve who row the bark of Ra around the zodiac.

One result of turning the Egyptian mythos into Christian history has been to inflict the most nefarious injustice on the Jews. By shifting the scene of the Mysteries from the nether-earth of Amenta to the land of Judea the ethnical Jews have been thrust into the position of the Typhonian enemies of the Good Being, the Sebau and the Sami, the powers of evil in the mythos and the condemned manes in the eschatology. The Jews have been transmogrified into the associates of Sut and the spawn of Satan. That is why the father of the Jews is called the devil, and a murderer from the beginning ; the liar and the father of all lying. That is why Judas is a devil ; and the Jews as a people figure in the same category with Herod, slayer of the innocents, with Judas the betrayer of Jesus, and with the fiends of Sut, because they were charged with doing those things on earth which had only been and could only be enacted according to the mysteries in Amenta. For this perversion of the mythos the Jews have been hunted over the earth and persecuted ever since. They have suffered precisely in the same way as the red-haired Typhonian animals suffered in ancient Egypt (Plutarch, *Of Isis and Osiris*, 30, 31), which were dedicated and doomed to be slain in an avenging sacrifice because they represented the associates of the wicked Sut, the liar, the betrayer, the murderer, who put to death and mutilated the body of the good Osiris. The sufferers on account of the mythos were the Typhonian ass, the pig, and the goat. The sufferers on account of the "history" have been and still are the children of Israel. Whereas the Jews were no more racial in the Gospels than the accursed Sebau are Egyptians in the Ritual. That they should be made to appear so is but a result of literalizing and localizing the Osirian drama in a spurious Judean history.

And here the present writer would remark that, in his view, the Jewish rejection of Christianity constitutes one of the sanest and the bravest intellectual triumphs of all time. It is worth all that the race has suffered from the persecution of the Christian world. The Jews, like the Gnostics, knew well enough that the Christian *schema* was a "fake," and, although they were unable to explain how it had been manufactured from the leavings of the past, they knew that it was false, non-natural and unnecessary. Up to the present time their victory may have been comparatively negative, in consequence of their failure to retell the story in the only one authentic way, that is, with a sufficient grasp of the data. They have not been able to reinstate the truth once confounded and overthrown, but they have borne witness dumbly, doggedly, unceasingly, with faces set like flint unflinchingly against the lie. They would not believe that their God, though imaged anthropomorphically, had become a man, and so they have remained non-Christian to this day, never to be converted now. For at last the long infernal Juden-Hetze nears its end ; the time of their justification and triumph is at hand, when the persecutor with the stone in his grasp will drop it suddenly and flee helter-skelter for his life.

THE GROUP IN BETHANY.

The canonical Gospels may be described as different collections of "episodes" and "sayings," and one of the most disconnected of these episodes is to be found in the raising of Lazarus from the tomb that

"was a cave" (John xi. 38), which contains a version of the resurrection of Osiris from the cave. The subject of all subjects in the
religious mysteries of the Egyptians was the resurgence of the human
soul from death and its transformation into an eternal spirit. This
is the foundation of the Book of the Dead or Ritual of the resurrection. So far as we know, this resurrection was originally represented in the mysteries of Memphis, where Kheper-Ptah was the
divinity that rose again in mummy-form from which the soul was
seen to issue forth as a divine hawk. On entering Amenta as a still
living being, though but a soul in matter, the Osiris, late deceased,
addresses the god in the character of those powers who effect the
triumph of Osiris over all his adversaries, the chief of whom is Horus,
in whose name he is magically assimilated to the Son of God, and
thus is one with Horus in his resurrection from the dead.

It has now to be shown that the resurrection of Osiris in Annu has
been partially reproduced as the raising of Lazarus in Bethany.
Osiris reposing in Annu is an image of the soul inert in matter or in
decay and death. Hence he was portrayed in the likeness of the
mummy called "the breathless one," also the god with the non-beating
heart, who is laid out in the burial-place as a corpse-like form lying
extended at full length, awaiting his resurrection from the funeral
couch, or the transfiguration into the risen sahu of the glorified. In
his first advent Horus is the son of Seb, God of earth. In his second,
he is the son of Ra, the Holy Spirit. It is in this latter character that
he enters Amenta to represent the resurrection of *the* Osiris in the
earth of eternity.

The resurrection of the sun from out the grave of night; the
rearising of vegetation from the grip of winter; and of the waters
returning periodically from their source; that is the resurrection in
external nature; it was, in short, the resurrection of new life from
the old, in a variety of phenomena, mystically imaged by zootypes
like the serpent of Rannut; the frog or beetle of Ptah; the shoot of
papyrus, or the green branch of endless years. The doctrine culminated in a resurrection of the soul of human life from the body
of death that was imaged by the mummy-Osiris, the god who in
his rising again united all phases of the doctrine under one type
of the resurrection, viz., that of the risen mummy defecated to
the consistency of a sahu, or a spiritual body. It is as the reconstitutor of his father in Amenta that Horus raises Osiris from the
tomb. He calls the mummy to come forth and assume the likeness of Ra the later god. Osiris is now glorified by Ra the Holy
Spirit. The mummy being an image of the earlier body-soul that
was transubstantialized into spirit. As it is said, Osiris is "renewed
in an instant," and it is his son Horus who thus establishes him upon
"the pedestal of Tum" (Atum Ra) the god in spirit (Rit., ch. 182).

The resurrection of the human soul in the after-life was the central
fact of the Egyptian religion, and the transfigured, re-erected mummy,
otherwise called the Karast, was a supreme symbol. The opening
day of New Year, the day of "Come thou to me," was named from
the resurrection, which was solar in the mythos and spiritual in the
eschatology. The mummy-type was divinized to preserve intact that
bodily form which suffered dissolution after death. This, as mummy

of the god in matter, was a type inviolate and imperishable. Osiris in his coffin does not see corruption. In him was life for evermore. And as with the divine exemplar, so was it postulated for all who died in Osiris. He was terribly mutilated by the evil Sut, and his mummy had to be joined together again piecemeal, for as it is said to Osiris, "I come to embalm thee," *thou hast existence "with thy members"* when these were put together. And again, "I have come myself and delivered the god from that pain and suffering that were in trunk, in shoulder and in leg." "I have come and healed the trunk, and fastened the shoulder and made firm the leg" (ch. 102, Renouf). This was in reconstituting the personality, which was performed in a mystery when the different parts of Osiris, the head, the vertebræ, the thigh, the leg, the heel were collected at the coffin (Rit., ch. 18). But the god in matter was also the god in spirit according to the mystery or *modus operandi* of the Resurrection; or he became so by being blended with Ra in his resurrection.

In the Kamite mythos as in the totemic sociology, the son (of the mother) was earlier than the father. When it is said in the texts "I am a son begotten of his father; I am a father begotten of his son," the sense of the expression turns on the son of the mother having been earlier than the father of the son. Child-Horus, Har-si-Hesi, is the mother's son. Mother and son, as As-Ar; Isis and child, passed into the complex of Asar or Osiris, the one great god in whom all previous powers were merged and unified at last. Isis had embodied a soul in matter or flesh, as her child, when there was as yet no God the Father, no God the Son, no Horus in spirit. This fatherhood of the spirit was founded in Atum-Ra the father of spirits. Thence followed the sonship in spirit of Horus in his second character as divine adult. Ra in spirit represented the supreme type of deity whose symbol is the sun or solar hawk. Osiris remained the god in matter as the mummy in Amenta; Ra is described as calling on Osiris in the resurrection and is also said to bid the mummy "come forth," when the deity in matter was to be united with the god in spirit. But Horus, the Son of God, the beloved only begotten son, is now the representative of Ra and the chief agent in the raising of the mummy-Osiris from the dead. He is the son who comes to the assistance, not only of the father, for the mummy-Asar is both Isis and Osiris in one body. Hence it is said in the chapter by which the tomb is opened for the Osiris to come forth, "I am Horus the reconstituter of his father, who lifteth up his father, and who lifteth up his mother *with his wand* (rod or staff)" (Rit., ch. 92, Renouf). As it is said in the Ritual (ch. 78), "it is Horus who hath reconstituted his father and restored him"—after the mutilation of his body by the murderer Sut. He descends into the funeral land of darkness and the shadow of death. He opens the Tuat to drive away the darkness so that he may look upon his father's face. He says pathetically, "I am his beloved son. I have come to pierce the heart of Sut and to perform all duties to my father" (ch. 9, Renouf). Horus the prince in Sekhem also uplifts his father as Osiris-Tat with his two arms clasped behind him for support (ch. 18). In this mythical character of the son who gives life, reconstitutes, restores and re-establishes his father, the Egyptians continued an inner African type of the "*Son who makes his Father."* Miss Kingsley called attention to a function of the Oil-river-Chief who has to observe the custom of " making his father " once every year.   The custom is sacred and symbolical, as the deceased chief need not be his own real father, but must be his predecessor in the headmanship (Kingsley, M., *West African Studies*, p. 146).   This custom of " making his father" by the son survived and was perpetuated in the mythology of Egypt, in which Horus is the son who makes, or " reconstitutes," his father once a year, and describes, it as one of his duties in the Book of the Dead.   This resurrection of the father as the soul of life in matter, *i.e.*, the mummy-soul, by Horus the son, is the great mystery of the ten mysteries which are briefly described in the 18th chapter of the Ritual.

In a later scene there is another description of the resurrection of Osiris, in which the mummy-god is raised by his son Horus from the tomb.   As it is said, " Horus exalteth his father Osiris in every place, associating Isis the Great with her sister Nephthys " as the two women at the tomb.   " Rise up, Horus, son of Isis, and restore thy father Osiris "—that was Osiris in the inert and breathless condition of the mummy.   " Ha, Osiris, I have come to thee.   I am Horus, and I restore thee unto life upon this day with the funeral offerings and all good things for Osiris."   " Rise up, then, Osiris.   I have stricken down thine enemies for thee ; I have delivered thee from them."   " I am Horus on this fair day at the beautiful coming forth of thy powers (in his resurrection), who lifteth thee up with himself on this fair day as thine associate God."   " Ha, Osiris, thou hast received thy sceptre, thy pedestal, and thy flight of stairs beneath thee."   On the coffin of Nes-Shu-Tefnut, at Vienna, it is said : " Horus openeth for thee thy two eyes that thou mayest see with them in thy name of Ap-Uat."   (Renouf, *Book of the Dead*, ch. 128, note 8.)   Horus as son of Ra the Holy Spirit in the eschatology is now higher in status than the mummy-god, the father and mother in matter.   Hence he rises in Amenta as the resurrection and the life to his own father Osiris.

Horus as the divine heir had now been furnished with the double force.   The gods rejoice to meet him walking on the way to Annu, and the hall of the horizon or house in Annu where divine perfumes are awaiting him and mourning does not reach him, and where the guardians of the hall do not overthrow the mysterious of face who is in the sanctuary of Sekhem.   That is Osiris, who is not dead but sleeping in Annu, the place of his repose, awaiting the call that bids the mummy to " come forth to day."   Horus, the deliverer of his father, reaches him in the train of Hathor, who is Meri, the beloved by name in the Ritual.   Thus Horus follows Meri to the place where Asar lies buried in the sepulchre, as Jesus follows Mary, who had come forth to meet him on the way to Bethany (John xi. 29, 33).   Jesus reaches the tomb of Lazarus in the train of Mary and Martha. Horus makes the way for Osiris.   He repulses the attack of Apap, who represents negation or non-being = death.   The portrait of Horus in this scene is very grand.   His face is glorified and greatened by the diadem which he wears as the lord of strength.   His double force is imaged by two lions.   A loud voice is heard upon the horizon as Horus lifts the truth to Ra, and the way is made for Osiris to come forth at his rising from the cave. So Jesus "cried with a loud voice, Lazarus, come forth!" and "he that was dead came forth bound hand and foot with grave-bands." In the original the mummy-Osiris comes forth as Amsu, with one arm only released from the bandages. In the "discourse of Horus" to his Father at his coming forth from the sanctuary in Sekhem to see Ra, Horus says, "I have given thee thy soul, I have given thee thy strength, I have given thee thy victory, I have given thee thy two eyes (mertæ), I have given thee Isis and Nephthys," who are the two divine sisters, the Mary and Martha of Beth-Annu (*Records*, vol. 10, p. 163). In showing that "mourning does not reach him," Jesus "abode at that time two days in the place where he was." After the sisters had sent to say that Lazarus was sick he waited until he was dead on purpose to perform the more effective miracle. He was in Bethany, "the place where John was at the first baptizing" (cf. John i. 28 with John x. 40, 41), but it took him two more days to get there at this particular time. So that Lazarus had been buried four days when Jesus arrived in the village. The tomb of Osiris was localized in Annu, the solar birthplace. Osiris, under one of his titles, is the great one in Annu. Annu is the place of his repose. "I go to rest in Annu, my dwelling," says Osiris. The deceased also goes to rest in Annu because it was the place of repose for Osiris the god (ch. 57, 4, 5). Jesus goes to rest in Bethany. The place of repose for Osiris was his sepulchre in Annu. The place of repose for Lazarus is the cave in Bethany. It was in Annu that the soul was united to its spiritual body. Annu is termed the place "where thousands reunite themselves" soul and body. The speaker says, "Let my soul see her body. Let her unite herself to her sahu"—that is, to the glorified body which can neither be destroyed nor injured ; the future body in which the soul would be incorporated to pass from out the tomb. Annu is called the abode of "those who have found their faces." These are the mummy-forms, from whose faces the napkin had been removed. The house or beth of Osiris, then, was in Annu. "He rests in Annu, which is his dwelling." The names of its builders are recorded. Num raised it on its foundation. Seshet (or Sefekh) built it for him as his house of refuge and of rest (Rit., 57, 4, 5). The house of Osiris in Annu was called Hat-Saru, the house of the Prince—that is, the abode of Horus when he came to raise Osiris from the tomb. It was the sanctuary of Osiris who was attended by the two Mertæ or Merti, the pair of divine sisters better known by the names of Isis and Nephthys. The household proper consists of Osiris and those two sisters who watch over him. Mer denotes the eye, ti is two, and these are the two eyes or two watchers over Osiris in the abode that is the place of his burial and rebirth. The two sisters as watchers are the two Mer, one of whom becomes the Mary, the other Martha, as the two merti in Bethany=Beth-Annu. The triumph of Osiris was effected over his adversaries by Horus in the house of the Prince in Annu or Heliopolis, and his supreme triumph was in his resurrection when he was recalled to life and raised up from the sepulchre by Horus (Rit., ch. 1). The raising up of Osiris the father by Horus the son is doctrinally based upon the father living over again in the son. Under the beetle-type Kheper as father transformed into the son. It was the same with Atum-Iu, in whom the father became the son and then the son transformed into the father. The mystery was deepened in the Osirian drama by superadding a more spiritual form of the fatherhood in Ra the Holy Spirit. The deceased Osiris is in possession of the funeral meals in Annu. He sits beneath the trees of Annu in the train of Hathor-Meri (Rit., ch. 68, 10). Annu is the place of provisions for the manes. Thousands are nourished or fed in Annu (89). Deceased in Annu (82) receives his vesture or Taau-garment from the goddess Tait, who is over him. This is an allusion to the mummy-case from which the left arm was not yet freed when Amsu-Horus rose up in the sepulchre. The goddess Tait is a form of one of the two divine sisters. She cooks the food and brings it to the deceased, who is either Osiris, or *the* Osiris, the God or the manes. Annu was also the place of the festivals of Osiris. One of these was kept on the sixth day of the month. " I am with Horus," says the speaker on the day when the festivals of Osiris are celebrated, "on the feast of the sixth day of the month " (ch. 1, lines 23, 24). With this we may compare the following statement : "Jesus therefore six days before the passover came to Bethany, where Lazarus was, whom Jesus raised from the dead. So they made him a supper there " (John xii.). The two sisters were present. " Martha served, and Mary anointed the feet of Jesus and wiped them with her hair."

Annu is described as a green and pleasant place, an oasis in the desert of Amenta created for the suffering Osiris, and the two divine sisters were given him there for his comfort and delight (ch. 17, 138, 139). The tree of life stood in Annu, as the sycamore, tamarisk, or persea tree, which was personified in Hathor-Meri or Isis. The manes were feasted " under the foliage of the tamarisk " (ch. 124, 6), the branches of which are described as the beautiful arms of the goddess, and the foliage as her hair, when she herself was the tree beneath which the Osiris found refreshing shade. It seems that not only the clouds of dawn, but also the foliage of the tamarisk tree may have imaged the hair of the goddess. Osiris-Ani is found in Annu with the hair of Isis spread over him (Rit., ch. 17). In another text the hair is assigned to Hathor—one of whose names is Meri (ch. 35, 1). And this is probably related to the story of Mary wiping the feet of Jesus with the hair of her head. Isis is frequently portrayed kneeling at the feet of Osiris in Annu. It is she who says : " I who drop the hair which hath loosely fallen upon my brow—I am Isis, when she concealeth herself" (ch. 17, 135). Osiris in Annu, like Lazarus in Bethany, was not dead but sleeping. In the text of Har-hetep (Rit., ch. 99) the speaker who personates Horus is he who comes to awaken Asar out of his sleep. Also, in one of the early funeral texts it is said of the sleeping Asar : " The Great One waketh, the Great One riseth ; Horus raises Osiris upon his feet." Jesus denies that Lazarus is dead. " Our friend Lazarus is fallen asleep. I go that I may awake him out of his sleep " (ch. xi., 11), which is genuine Egyptian doctrine. The manes in Amenta were not looked upon as dead, but sleeping, breathless of body, motionless of heart. The deity Osiris was not dead. And in his likeness *the* Osiris lived. Hence Horus comes to wake the sleepers in their coffins, or Osiris in his cave.

It was in Bethany that "Jesus wept." It is the place of weeping for the dead Lazarus. Mary wept, the Jews wept, and "Jesus wept." No wonder. This is the place of weeping by name in the Ritual, where the Osiris lay in his burial. It was here he was inert and motionless. The Osiris says : " I am motionless in the fields of those who are dumb in death. But I shall wake, and my soul will speak in the dwelling of Tum, the Lord of Annu." The abode of Tum in Annu being = Bethany. Then he rises from the tomb and appears at the door, and says, " I arrive at the confines of earth. I tread the dwelling of the god Rem-Rem." Rem signifies weeping : and in the Litany of Ra this god is designated " Remi the Weeper." Thus Jesus is portrayed in the character of " Remi the Weeper " in the place of weeping for the dead Osiris in Beth-Annu, who is here represented as the dead Lazarus in Bethany (Rit., 75, Renouf). Jesus comes as " Remi the Weeper " to weep for the inert Osiris, that is, as Horus who comes to the motionless Orisis on the day which is called " Come thou to me." Ra is said to make the mummy " come forth " (The Litany of Ra, 68 ; Rit., 17). Jesus cries with a loud voice, " Lazarus, come forth ! " and " he that was dead came forth, bound hand and foot with grave-bands : and his face was bound about with a napkin " (John xi. 43, 44). The picture is completed in the Roman catacombs, where the risen Lazarus is an Egyptian mummy : the likeness of the mummy-Osiris, who is beckoned forth by Horus with his staff.

According to the dramatic representation in the Mysteries, Osiris is slain by the adversary Sut, and is imaged in Amenta as a mummy. The father lives again in the son ; hence his son Horus descends into the nether-world to avenge, reconstitute and raise Osiris from his corpse-like state. He comes as a living soul from Ra the Holy Spirit, who is the Father in heaven, " to raise up the hand which is motionless " (Rit., ch. 5). " He lifts inert Osiris with his two arms " (ch. 18). He exclaims, " Ha ! Osiris, I am come to thee : I am Horus, and I restore thee to life upon this day, with *the funerary offerings and all good things* for Osiris. Rise up, then, Osiris (ch. 128). Horus hath raised thee." It is said, " Hail, Osiris, thou art born. twice " (Rit., ch. 170). In some texts it is Ra who bids the mummy come forth on the day of " *Come thou to me* " (Rit., ch. 17). Taht says : " I give Ra to enter the mysterious cave in order that he may revive the heart of him whose heart is motionless " (ch. 182). After the raising of Osiris, Taht says, " I have celebrated the festival of Eve's provender," or supper, which came to be called the Last Supper. The raising of Lazarus is likewise commemorated by a supper. " So they made him a supper there " (John xii. 2).

When Osiris, or *the* Osiris, " takes the form of a living soul " (Rit., ch. 181), it is said, " thy son Horus reconstitutes thee. Arise, Osiris, thy hands have been given to thee "—he is freed from the mummy-bandages—" stand up living for ever." " The two sisters Isis and Nephthys come to thee ; they will fill thee with life, health, and strength, and all the joy that they possess. They gather for thee all kinds of good things within thy reach " (ch. 181). Amongst other ceremonies performed in the Amenta at the raising of the mummy who is " called aloud " from the sepulchre the Osiris is freed from the bandages with which the corpse was bound. So when Lazarus was called in a loud voice to come forth, "He that was dead came forth bound hand and foot with grave-bands, and his face was bound about." In the resurrection ceremony of Osiris he is divested of his funerary garment and receives a bandage of the finest linen from the hands of the attendant of Ra, the Father in heaven (Rit., ch. 172). He eats of "the meat which has been prepared by Ra in his holy place"; he washes his feet in silver basins, which have been sculptured by the divine architect Ptah-Sekari (ch. 172). In the Gospel, Jesus, "knowing that the Father had given all things into his hands, and that he came forth from God and goeth unto God, riseth from supper, and layeth aside his garments; and he took a towel and girded himself. Then he poureth water into a basin and began to wash the disciples' feet, and to wipe them with the towel wherewith he was girded" (ch. xiii. 4-6).

Taking Lazarus, then, to represent the mummy-Osiris, we find the "raising of Lazarus" celebrated in a hymn expressly devoted to the subject. It is one of the ceremonies that were performed in the underworld. The Osiris is designated him "*who is called aloud.*" "O thou who art called aloud, thou who art called aloud, thou the lamented, thou art glorified. O thou who art raised up, thou art raised up. N. has been raised up by means of all the manifold ceremonies performed for him." The mummy-Osiris lay upon the funeral couch in the mysterious cave with the two sisters in attendance. Horus enters this cave as representative of Ra, to revive the heart of him whose heart is motionless. He says, "Hail, Osiris, thou art born twice! Arise on thy bed and come forth! Come! Come forth." Osiris or *the* Osiris is called with a loud voice. In the hymn of the resurrection, he is addressed *nine times over* in the words "*O Thou who art called aloud!*" (chs. 170-2). They call him to come forth "like a god" from the mysterious cave "to meet the powers of Annu." The resurrection is celebrated with rejoicings, "thou hearest how thou art glorified through all thy house!" There are nine verses in the hymn and each one opens with the address, "*O thou who art called aloud!*" That is for his rising up and coming forth from the cave in Annu (ch. 172). The words "O thou who art called aloud" had become the title of the hymn, as we say "the Magnificat," or "the Te Deum" (Naville, Rit., ch. 172).

The latest dynasty of Egyptian deities were born of Seb the earth-father and Nut the mother-heaven. This was the Osirian group, consisting of five persons, viz., (1) Asar, (2) the elder Horus, (3) Sut, (4) Isis, (5) Nephthys, which may be called the family in Annu and shown to be the originals of the group in Bethany. Sut, the betrayer, is the only one omitted from the Gospel. The remaining four—Lazarus = Asar; Jesus = Horus; Mary = Isis; Martha = Nephthys—are also represented sometimes in the Ritual without Sut (ch. 128). When it is said that Horus exalteth his father Osiris in every place he associates Isis the great with her sister Nephthys. Sut is not included in the group at Annu. On the other hand, Sut, in the person of the betrayer, is present at the mortuary meal in the canonical Gospels. At present we only need to identify Lazarus with Osiris, Jesus with Horus, and the two sisters of Lazarus with the two sisters of Osiris. Osiris lying as a breathless mummy in the cave, when Horus comes to raise him from the dead, is watched over and protected by the two Mertæ-sisters, one at the head and one at the feet as keepers of the body, and watchers in the burial-place. The two mertæ are mentioned in chapter 58. In this the Osiris cries, "Let the door be opened to me" as the Osiris buried in Amenta. "Who is with thee?" is asked. The reply is, "It is the mertæ," the two watchers over Osiris in the sepulchre. The deceased then asks that he may have milk, cakes and meat given to him at the house which is in Annu, the Kamite prototype of Bethany. On the way to the sepulchre in Annu Horus meets the two sister-goddesses, saying to them "Hail, ye pair of goddesses Mertæ, sister pair, Mertæ! *I inform you of my words of power*. I am Horus, the son of Isis, and I am come to see my father Osiris," and to raise him up from the sepulchre. Jesus on his way to the cave of Lazarus likewise informs Martha of his words of power, saying "thy brother shall rise again." "I am the resurrection and the life." "He that believeth on me shall never die" (John xi. 25, 26). "Now as they went on their way a certain woman named Martha received him (Jesus) into her house. And she had a sister called Mary, which also *sat at the Lord's feet* (like Isis) and heard his word." And because Mary took her place at the feet of Jesus it is said that she had "chosen the good part" (Luke x. 38, 42). The two sisters in Bethany are the Aramaic or Hebrew replica of Isis and Nephthys, who are the attendants upon Osiris; the two divine sisters of Osiris in Annu. Mary and Martha are the two sisters of Lazarus in Bethany. Horus loved the two dear sisters Isis and Nephthys, and is especially denominated the son who loves his father, *i.e.*, Asar, whom he raises from the tomb according to the dramatic representation. Jesus is said to have "loved Martha and her sister, and Lazarus" (John xi. 5).

Jesus saith, "Our friend Lazarus is fallen asleep, but I go that I may awake him out of sleep" (John xi. 4, 11). So is it in the Ritual. Horus says, "I go to give movement to the manes. I go to comfort him who is in a swoon," which is equivalent to Lazarus who sleeps (ch. 64). He goes to give life at some particular spot and in doing this he comes from Sekhem to Annu where the mummy of Osiris rested in the house there = Beth-Annu or Bethany. The Osiris does not die. The Ritual has no recognition of death, save as final extinction when death and evil die together. Osiris sleeps, he is breathless or in a swoon. He lies inert, his heart is motionless *pro tem*. Osiris thus awaits his change and resurrection; but he cannot die who is the conqueror of death and the bondage of the grave. The resurrection of Osiris at the coming of Horus is glanced at when the speaker personates him and says, "I am the great first heir (or inheritor) taking possession of Urt-hat"—otherwise the inert, sleeping, motionless Osiris. "Strength of Osiris is my name. I save him" from the impurities of matter. "He lives by me." The speaker is Horus with his father Ra, just as Jesus is with his father in the scene of raising Lazarus (John 11, 45). The resurrection applies to Osiris in matter whom Horus comes to quicken and raise up from the dead or, as it is rendered, "from the impurities of Osiris" in matter. The "corruption which befell Osiris" in his mummy-condition is mentioned in the Ritual more than once. This also befalls the corpse of Lazarus, but is more grossly stated in the Gospel. Jesus comes to raise up Lazarus when he has been in the tomb four days, and Martha saith, " Lord, by this time he stinketh" (John xi. 39). In the Ritual, when Horus comes to those who are in their cells he utters the words of Ra to raise the dead, and says, as the passage is rendered by Budge, " I am the herald of his words (his father's) to him whose throat stinketh"; that is, to the sufferer from corruption in the tomb (*Book of the Dead*, ch. 38B, line 4).

Isis not only stands or sits at the feet of Osiris, she is the Seat personified. She carries the sign of the seat upon her head. Her name of Hes signifies the seat. And Mary, who takes the place of Isis, is described as sitting at the feet of Jesus, whilst Martha is busy working about the house and left serving alone. A further allusion to the Lady of the Seat may be found when Martha heard that Jesus was coming, and went forth to meet him, whilst " Mary still *sat* in the house" (John xi. 20, 21), thus fulfilling the character of Isis, the seat, or the sitter. There is more than meets the eye in the sign of the seat which is borne by Isis. To sit is also to brood as a bird. Isis as sitter is the brood-hen, the incubator in Annu. Under this type of the sitting-hen she sits at the feet of Osiris to bring him to rebirth. Mary also sat in the house, and kept her seat at the feet of Jesus. Nephthys, the other divine sister in Annu, carries the sign of a house on her head. She is called mistress of the house. She is the benevolent, saving sister. This in the " history" is rendered by Martha being the housekeeper and by Mary sitting in the house while her sister goes forth to meet the Lord (John xi. 21). In Aramaic, Martha denotes the mistress of the house, and Nephthys, one of the two mertæ, is the mistress of the house, who carries the house as a symbol in her head-dress. The name of Nephthys in Greek represents nebt-hat, the mistress of the house in Egyptian. The two sisters are the merti or mertæ, who were the keepers of the double house in attendance upon Horus, or Jesus. They receive the Sun-God at his entrance to the mountain in the West, and stand together by him when he issues forth at dawn from Beth-Annu, or Bethany, in the East. The name of the secret shrine in which the mummy-Osiris was upraised by " the two arms of Horus, Prince of Sekhem," is " the witness of that which is raised," or the witness to the Resurrection (ch. 17). Those who are present in this scene are " Osiris, Isis, Nephthys, and Horus the reconstituter of his Father," and these, as we maintain, are the prototypes or original characters of Lazarus, Mary, Martha and Jesus in the scene of the Resurrection in Bethany.

Osiris rose from the dead to enter the little golden ark of the moon on the third day. He was buried on the 17th of Hathor and the resurrection in the lunar ark was on the 19th; that is, on the third day. In the solar mythos he rises again the day after the burial, and as the grain he rose again in forty days. But there is another mystery of Osiris, an account of which is given by Plutarch, probably from the writings of Manetho. This he calls the " Mourning of the Goddess," which began on the 17th of Hathor, the day on which Osiris was betrayed at the last supper and mutilated by the adversary Sut. He says the " Mourning of the Goddess" lasted

" four " days altogether, beginning on the 17th, the day of betrayal and death of Osiris ; and on the 19th it was proclaimed by the priests that the lost Osiris was found because he had then entered into the ark of the moon where the light was once more safe.   He tells us that amongst other melancholy things that were acted on this occasion, as the mourning of the cow for Osiris the bull of Amenta, a gilded cow, the golden Hathor, was covered with a black linen pall and exposed to public view *for four days* at the mourning of the goddess, or of the cow, for the lost Osiris.   Here, then, are *the four days of mourning* which are repeated in the one Gospel that chronicles the raising of Lazarus from the dead after " *he had been in the tomb four days already.*"   Plutarch calls this mystery the mourning of the goddess.   But there are always two mourners for Osiris, Isis and Nephthys, who are his sisters.

The process of reducing the fairy-godmother's coach-and-six to the status of a one-horse cab may be seen in the Gospel according to Luke in getting rid of Osiris.   The pair of sisters, Martha and Mary, appear in this Gospel, but without their brother Lazarus, and also without the resurrection.   After all that has now been done towards identifying Bethany with the house in Annu and the nest of the two sisters, the two sisters with Isis and Nephthys, and the Christ with Horus, it cannot be considered far-fetched if we look upon Lazarus as a form of the Osiris that was dead and buried and raised to life again.   As to the name, the Egyptian name of the Greek Osiris is Hesar, or Asar.   And when we take into consideration that some of the matter came from its Egyptian source through the Aramaic and Arabic languages (witness the Arabic Gospel of the Infancy) there is little difficulty, if any, in supposing that the Al (article the) has been adopted through the medium of the Arabic, or derived from the Hebrew prenominal stem אל, to emphasize a thing, as in *the* Osiris, which passed into the article Al for " the " in Arabic, and was pre-fixed to the name of Osiris as Al-Asar, which, with the Greek " s " for suffix becomes L-azarus.   The connecting link whereby Al-Asar was turned into Lazarus, *the* Osiris, was in all likelihood made in the Aramaic language, which had its root-relations with the Egyptian.   Hieroglyphic papyri are among its monumental remains, as well as the inscription of Carpentras.

Various representations of the raising of Lazarus in the Roman catacombs show the mummy risen and standing in the doorway of the tomb.   The figure of the supposed Jesus Christ is in front of the sarcophagus calling upon Lazarus to come forth, whilst touching the mummy with a wand or rod which he holds in his hand.   In the chapter " by which the tomb is opened to the soul and to the shade of the person that he may come forth to day and have the mastery of his feet " (Rit., ch. 92) the deliverer Horus says, " I am Horus who lifteth up his father with his staff."   This mode of raising Osiris by Horus with his staff or rod completes the picture of the re-surrection of Lazarus.   The rod that is waved by Jesus at the raising of Lazarus is the symbolic sceptre in the hand of Horus when he raises the Osiris.   In every instance Lazarus is a mummy made after the Egyptian fashion.   It is a bandaged body that had been soaked in salt and pitch which was at times so hot that it charred the bones

(Budge, "The Mummy," pp. 153–155). Seventy days was the proper length of time required for embalming the dead body in making an Egyptian mummy. Lazarus when portrayed in the Roman cata-combs comes forth from the tomb as an eviscerated, embalmed and bandaged mummy, warranted to have been made in Egypt. Now, according to the Gospel narrative, there was no time for this, as Lazarus had only been dead four days. The mummy, anyway, is non-historical; and it is the typical mummy called *the* Osiris, Asar in Egyptian, El-Asar in Aramaic, and Lazarus with the Greek terminal in the Gospel assigned to John. The coffin of Osiris, constellated in the Greater Bear, was known to the Arab astronomers as the Bier of Lazarus. Asar, or the Osiris, is the mummy in the coffin, and with the coffin of Osiris identified as the bier of Lazarus it follows perforce that the mummy-Osiris in the coffin is one with Lazarus on the bier. The gnostic pictures in the Roman catacombs suffice to prove the identity. They show that Lazarus was buried as a mummy, and that he rose again in mummy-form. Thus the dead Osiris of Egypt, El-Asar or Lazarus, as portrayed in Rome, and the story of the death, burial, and resurrection are the same wheresover and howsoever that story may be told. The bier of Lazarus, followed by the mourning sisters, was only known by that name because it had been constellated in the starry vault of the heavens ages earlier than the present era as the coffin of Osiris.

It is satisfactory to find that both forms of Asar are preserved in the Gospels, one of which was the god Osiris, the other *the* Osiris as manes. Lazarus in his resurrection represents the God; Lazarus the poor man of the parable represents the manes in Amenta who is designated *the* Osiris.

The story of the rich man and the beggar Lazarus related in the Gospel of Luke (ch. xvi. 19) is told at length in the second tale of Khamuas as Egyptian. This contains a scene from the Judgment in Amenta which is represented in the vignettes to the Ritual. Setme and his son Si-Osiris enter the Tuat as manes. They pass through the seven halls (Rit., ch. 144) into the great judgment hall. They see the figure of Osiris seated on his throne of gold, "Anup the great god being on his left hand, the great god Taht upon his right, the balance being set in the midst before them." Anup gives the word, Taht writes it down. The rich man and the poor man enter to be judged. "And behold Setme saw a great man clothed in garment of byssus (fine white linen), he being near to the place in which Osiris was," in which position he is great exceedingly. Si-Osiris says, "My father Setme, dost thou not see this great man who is clothed in garment of byssus, he being near to the place in which Osiris is? That poor man whom thou sawest, he being carried out from Memphis, there not being a man walking after him, he being wrapped in a mat, this is he." This refers to the funerals of the rich man and the poor man on earth previously described (lines 15–21). When the rich man was judged it was found that his evil deeds were more numerous than his good deeds; therefore they outweighed them in the scales of justice; consequently he was cast to the devourer of souls who did not allow him to breathe again for ever. "It was commanded before Osiris to cause to be thrown the burial outfit of that rich man whom thou sawest, he being carried out from Memphis, the praise that was made of him being great, unto this poor man named, and that they should take him (the poor man) amongst the noble spirits as a man of God that follows Osiris-Sekari (the god in his resurrection), he being near to the place in which Osiris is" (Griffith, second tale of Khamuas, pp. 149, 158). Thus the parable of the rich man and Lazarus found in a folk-tale of the first century written in Demotic is provably Egyptian and demonstrably ancient by application of the comparative process to the language. Neither the name of Lazarus nor Osiris appears in the tale of Khamuas, which is good evidence that the story was not derived from the Gospels. Thus we identify Lazarus with Osiris the mummy-god and Lazarus the poor man with Alasar as *the* Osiris.

THE FOUNDERS OF THE KINGDOM.

The elder Horus represented the wisdom of the Mother as her word or logos in the earth of Seb until he reached the age of twelve years. Then, according to the drama of the Osirian mysteries, he passed into Amenta, where he rose again as Horus in spirit. It was in this, the earth of eternity, that he made his second advent when he came again to establish the kingdom of the father. In his death and resurrection or transformation from the body-soul to an eternal spirit, he had found the father in heaven, who is Ra the holy spirit. And at his second advent Horus came to tell the joyful tidings to the manes and to found the kingdom in Amenta for the father who is now Osiris-Ra instead of the mummy-Osiris. Thus the kingdom of the Christ was founded for the father by Horus and his followers at his second coming to be represented in the mysteries of Amenta and the drama of Egyptian eschatology as the second advent which was in the spirit, now set forth by Horus the immortal Son of God.

The universe of Ptah, the supreme architect, had been divided into the three regions of Amenta, earth and heaven. In these there were three successive forms of a god the father—Seb was the god of earth, as father of physical sustenance; Osiris was the father in Amenta, where the dead were reconstituted and made to live again, and Ra the holy spirit was the father of spirits in heaven. Thus the typical seven loaves of plenty were called the bread of Seb on earth, the bread of Osiris in Amenta, and the bread of Ra in heaven. Human Horus was the heir of Seb, his foster-father, in the life on earth. At his resurrection in Amenta, Horus, as half-human, half-divine, is the heir of Osiris. In the resurrection *from* Amenta when he had become pure spirit he was Horus divinized as heir of Ra, the father on high. And on behalf of this, the newly-found father, now the supreme god, he returns to found the kingdom as the teacher of the mysteries in Amenta, and the saviour of the manes from the second death. Seb the father on earth was of the earth earthy. Osiris in Amenta was a god in matter; hence his mummy-form. The nature of these had been expounded in the lesser mysteries. Ra as father in heaven, or Huhi the eternal, is the god in spirit now, and Horus manifesting in the spirit comes to elucidate the greater mysteries to the twelve who, as the gnosis shows, had previously been the teachers of the lesser mysteries, and who now become the twelve with Horus, or Jesus, on the mountain in the phase of eschatology. Horus as the son of Ra was the representative of power superior to that of Osiris in Amenta, the god in matter, who was annually overthrown by Sut in physical phenomena, and in this character he came to the assistance of Osiris in the sepulchre. Hence he disperses the darkness from his face. He reconstitutes the body that Sut dismembered. He raises the arm that was paralyzed in death. He lifts the mummy to its feet. He is the link which unites matter with spirit, or Osiris with Ra. He brings the gnosis or word of life from the father in heaven to the previous ruling powers which include the earlier father on earth and in the nether-earth, and therefore to the men on earth and manes in Amenta. Thus, at his second coming, Horus had found his father, the father in heaven. He rises as a spirit in Amenta from the dead to tell them of this father. He repeats his father's words to those who are " deprived of breath " (Rit., ch. 38). These are the words of salvation that " bring about the resurrection and the glory to the manes " (ch. 1) by means of the gnosis.

We have now to follow Horus in his second Advent. He passed from the life on earth into the dark of death as Horus-Anaref, the sightless Horus. Death was imaged as the putting out of sight by Sut the power of darkness, the manes being the blind. At his second coming Horus is the giver of sight, or the beatific vision, to the blind. He shines into the tombs of those who are slumbering darkly in their cells and wakes them from the trance of death. At this advent of Horus " the people which sat in darkness saw a great light, and to them which sat in the region and shadow of death did light spring up " (Matt. iv. 16; also the Gospel of Nicodemus ii. 2). But this, according to the Ritual and the " Pistis Sophia," was in Amenta, the hidden earth, where the blind are made to see ; a mouth is given to the dumb ; the lame are enabled to walk ; and the dead to rise again. Amenta, as he comes, is all in motion with dead matter turning into spirit-life ; and when he rises from the sepulchre we are in the midst of those mysteries which have been rendered as Christian miracles in the Gospels.

" I am come," says Horus, " as a sahu in the spiritual body, glorious and well equipped ; and that is given to me *which lives on amidst all overthow.*" This, we repeat, is the second coming of Horus at the new birth in spirit which followed the old death in matter, or on earth, when Har-Ur, the child of Isis, was reborn, and this time begotten as the anointed and beloved son of God the father. This time he who was the Word is the doer, the word-made-truth. He comes to found the kingdom for the father in the earth of eternity or in spirit-world, not in Judea or Palestine. The work of Horus in his resurrection from the dead was to fulfil the kingdom of heaven on this foundation of the nether-earth, as foothold for eternity, the kingdom of heaven being spirit-world made palpable in the mythical representation of the mysteries.

All along the line of descent the astronomy supplied the mould of the eschatology. There was a heaven astronomically raised upon the two pillars of Sut and Horus south and north. Also on the two horizons of Harmachis, the double Horus. The Heptanomis had its sevenfold foundation. The heaven built upon a fourfold basis was the heaven founded on the four cardinal points, in the solstices and equinoxes. Lastly, the zodiac with twelve signs is the figure of heaven raised upon a foundation that is twelvefold. The mythical rulers corresponded numerically to the signs : the two, the four, the seven, the nine, and finally the twelve, at first as astronomical types, the gnostic Æons, and afterwards as spirits or gods in the phase of eschatology. Thus there are two categories in phenomenal manifestation, one being astronomical, the other spiritual or eschatological, as shown and explained in "Pistis Sophia." It now became the mission of Horus to make known the newly-found father in heaven to those who had not so much as heard of the holy spirit. It was the work of the anointed and beloved son to found the kingdom of heaven for the father in the father's name. He became the teacher of the coming kingdom, previously proclaimed by Anup the herald and forerunner who was his John the Baptist crying in the wilderness of the underworld.

When Horus in his second advent comes to establish the kingdom for his father, who is Ra in the solar mythos and the holy spirit in the eschatology, he has Two Witnesses who testify that he is verily the son of God the father in heaven and the true light of the world. These are the two Osirian Johns, Anup and Aan, or rather they are the originals of the two Johns in the canonical Gospels. They are portrayed as the two witnesses to the bird-headed Horus in his resurrection at the vernal equinox. The planisphere of Denderah shows the jackal of Anup and the cynocephalus of Taht-Aan figured back to back upon the equinoctial colure as the two principal witnesses for Horus, who are thus portrayed as supporters of the Eye which was renewed in Annu once every year (Planisphere in a Book of the Beginnings). As Egyptian, these two witnesses for Horus are Anup the baptizer and Aan the divine scribe who is the penman of the gods in the Ritual. We have seen them acting as the two witnesses for Horus in the Osirian judgment hall (see p. 705). They are also described as the two magi, or magicians.

Where John begins his preaching in the canonical Gospel Anup is the typical opener of the way (Rit., ch. 26). He is the forerunner who announces the day of reckoning ; he makes the call to judgment; he judges the world, just as John is the judge of the world who calls men and baptizes them to repentance (Rit., 31, Birch). Anup is also the educator preparatory to the advent of Horus who comes after him although he was before him in status and authority (Rit., ch. 44). Anup abode darkling in the desert of Amenta until the day of his manifestation in the heliacal rising of Sothis, the morning star of the Egyptian year, which heralded the birth of Horus. John dwelt in the wilderness till the day of his theophany or " shewing unto Israel" (Luke i. 80). The solar god was superior to either the lunar or stellar deity. As star-god, Anup had been the precursor. The moon-god, Aan, was the witness for Horus by night as reflector of the hidden sun. This, however, was but the mythical mould for the eschatology, in which Horus was no longer merely the "little sun" of winter, but the son of Ra in spirit and the typical demonstrator of immortality to the manes in Amenta and to men upon the earth. The two Johns might be distinguished from each other in the Gospels; John the Baptist from John the Divine, by means of Anup, the baptizer, and Aan, the writer of the record in the Ritual. The baptism does not actually take place in the Gospel according to John. In this there is *only a description of the scene.* And, although one John is present as the baptizer, there is no attempt made to distinguish John the baptizer from John the scribe. But John the speaker is John the scribe, and therefore to be discriminated from John the baptist, who is not named as the baptist by John the writer. John the scribe is, of course, the writer, and he likewise bears witness as well as John the Baptist. For it is he who says, " and we beheld his glory, glory as of the only begotten from the Father." This was manifested in the baptism when the heavens were opened and Jesus " saw the spirit of God descending as a dove and coming upon him; and lo ! a voice out of the heavens saying, This is my beloved Son in whom I am well pleased" (Matt. iii. 16, 17). Consequently John the scribe was present at the baptism to have beheld the glory of the only begotten of the Father which was manifested in the one particular way at one particular time, but he was *not* John the Baptist. Anup, like child-Horus, was born of the motherhood but not of the fatherhood, whereas the Horus of thirty years was the only begotten Son of God the Father. So, in the Gospel, John the Baptist is among the greatest of those who were born of woman (minus the fatherhood, in accordance with the primitive status), whereas Jesus, the Christ, was begotten of God. The first Horus was born, the second Horus is begotten. Such is the status of John and Jesus. Hence the saying " among them that are born of women there hath not arisen a greater than John the Baptist; yet he that is least in the kingdom of heaven is greater than he "(Matt. xi. 11). The characters all through are to be determined and differentiated by the doctrines. John the Baptist does not enter the kingdom of heaven, which he helps to found as preparer of the way. So Anup is the guide of ways in the wilderness of the under-world; he makes straight the path for the future life, but he does not enter the coming kingdom of the Son of God when the double earth is unified in the future heaven. His place is with the dead awaiting their resurrection. He watches, he bends over the mummy; he embraces and supports it with tenderest solicitude; he is master in the mountain of rebirth for heaven, but he himself remains in the lower earth. His *rôle* and his domain come to an end where those of the divine heir of Osiris as the son of Ra begin. When Horus rises again to take possession of his kingdom, Anup is portrayed as crouching in the tomb. He gives Horus his shoulder. He raises him up, but does not pass from out Amenta. Therefore the least in the kingdom of Horus, which is a spiritual kingdom, is greater than the highest in the kingdom of Anup or John the Baptist, who was only the precursor and proclaimer of the Christ or the Horus of the resurrection.

A glimpse of the cyclical and non-human nature of the witness, John, may be inadvertently given in the words attributed to Jesus, " If I will that he tarry till I come, what (is that) to thee? " " Yet, Jesus said not unto him that he should not die." The ending here predicated was not in the category of human phenomena, and may therefore be claimed as pertaining to the astronomical mythos, which was at the root of all the mysteries of Amenta. Once a month the lord of light, as Horus, was reborn in the moon, and Aan = John was his attendant. "*Let him stand unchanged for a month*" is equivalent to his tarrying until Horus came again.

It is said of John, "this is the disciple which beareth witness of these things, and wrote these things." Aan, in Egyptian, is the scribe by name, and he was the divine scribe as Taht-Aan, the lunar deity and registrar of time. Aan was the witness to Horus; his writings are the Ritual, and "we know that his witness is true." It was Taht-Aan = John who had power to confer the Ma-Kheru on the solar god himself, that is, the gift of making truth by means of the word, because he told time for the sun and was his true witness in the moon. "Let him stand unchanged for a month," may be read by the legend which tells us that Ra created Taht-Aan to be his lamp by night and his witness in heaven, and whether we reckon nightly or monthly, Taht-Aan = John was the witness until Horus came again at the end of the period. Anup the baptizer and Aan the saluter are the first two witnesses for the risen Horus as his helpers in establishing the kingdom for the father in heaven. Next there is a group of four, as followers of Horus and founders of his fold (Rit., ch. 97). These four were born brothers with Har-Ur, the elder Horus, in the company of the seven powers that were from the beginning in relation to certain phenomena of external nature. They are now called upon to become foundational pillars of support to the new heaven in the eschatology. In this phase the group commences as four and terminates as twelve, who reap the harvest in the fields of Amenta, for Horus-Khuti, the master of joy and lord of the spirits, who are called the glorified elect, the heirs to the kingdom of heaven, which, as Osirian always *was* but which as Christian is always coming.

The change from Horus the mortal to Horus divinized in spirit, as the son of Ra, is indicated as occurring at the time when the *four brethren* became the four children of Horus, and, as it is said, when his name became that of Horus upon his column (Rit., ch. 112, Renouf). Now Horus on his column, pedestal, or monolith is equivalent to the Egypto-gnostic Jesus with the disciples on the mount. In this position the four brethren are his four arms of support, the same as the four brothers with Jesus in the mount. In their several characters they are the servants of Horus, whether as four supports, four fishers, four shepherds, or other forms of the primordial four who are characterized as the foremost of the final twelve.

The issuing forth from Amenta on the day of the resurrection is described in the opening chapter of the Ritual as the coming to the divine powers attached to Osiris. These divine powers are Amsta, Hapi, Tuamutef and Kabhsenuf, the four children of Horus who stand upon the papyrus-symbol of the earth amidst the waters of the Nun, otherwise rendered on the mount or on the monolith. The pyramid text of Teta (270) refers to this raising of the dead. It is said that Horus hath given his children power that they may raise thee up. These children are the four who were foremost of the seven. (or later, twelve) great spirits in Annu. This did not mean that four human followers of Horus on earth had the power to raise the dead on earth. But so misrendered has the teaching been in the Gospels when Jesus bids his disciples to go forth on earth and raise the dead (Matt. x. 8). In the chapter of the baptism (Rit., ch. 97) the speaker "*propitiates*" "those four glorified ones who follow after the master of all things." They are the four supporters on whom Horus relies in founding the kingdom for his father. Speaking, as it may be, of his sheep-fold in the character of the good shepherd, Horus says, "Now let my fold be fitted for me, as one victorious against all adversaries who would not that right should be done to me—I (who) am the only one, just and true," or faithful and true (Rit., ch. 97). These four, then, are founders of the fold that is to be fitted for the good shepherd with the crook upon his shoulder as Amsu-Horus in the resurrection scenes. They are the four brethren who, in the later phase, are called his children. Hence Horus is described as coming to light in his own children and in his name of Horus (Rit., ch. 112) on his column = on the mount. To found the fold was to establish the kingdom. That was founded on the four supporters at the four corners of the mount.

There is a rebirth of Horus at his second coming. It is the same with his train of companion-powers, the four of the seven who had been with him as his brothers in the astronomical mythos. These in the rebirth become his four children, who, at the same time, are designated by him "brothers of this my own body" (Rit., ch. 112). Whether called the brothers or the children of Horus they are the same four in the two characters. These four reappear in the Gospels, also in both characters. The four as brothers are the fishers, Peter, Andrew, James and John. The other four, called James, Joseph, Simon and Judas, are represented as brothers of his own flesh and blood. At their birth Amsta, Hapi, Tuamutef, and Kabhsenuf were the brothers of Horus Anaref. These had no father. In the rebirth Horus has himself attained the status of a father or begetter in spirit. Hence it is said, "As for Amsta, Hapi, Tuamutef and Kabhsenuf, Horus is their father and Isis is their mother," in this new setting of the four. In the Gospel Cleopas and Mary take the place of Horus and Isis as the actual father and mother in the flesh. When Horus rises in Amenta he is the active and powerful one of Annu filled with might divine as the son whom the father hath begotten (Rit., ch. 115), whereas in his previous advent he was the child of the Virgin Mother as the puny impubescent impotent weakling who was born but not begotten. Horus now beseeches Ra to grant that he may have his four brothers or his children for his assistants. He says, "Give me my brother in the region of Pa; give me my brother in Nekhen—my brother for my tender affection," or give me my brothers to love. Only two brethren of the four are mentioned here, and for these Horus asks of his father that his brothers may sit with him in his kingdom as eternal judges, as benefactors of the world, as extinguishers of the Typhonian plagues and as the bringers of peace (Rit., ch. 112). The prayer of Horus is followed by the Osiris deceased, who identifies the two brethren as Amsta and Hapi, and he exclaims: "Rise up, gods, *who are in the lower heaven*, rise up for the Osiris, make him (also) to become a great god." The deceased continues : " I know the mystery of Nekhen." The mystery is that which the mother of Horus (who was also the mother of the two brethren) has done for him when she said " let him live " (ch. 113), in which we have the mother making her request on behalf of her son.

This new foundation for the kingdom of heaven was made on the night of erecting the flagstaffs (or pillars) of Horus, and of establishing him as heir to his father's property. The pillars were erected when Horus said to the four who followed him, " Let the flagstaffs be erected there," on the night of one of the ten great mysteries of Amenta (Rit., ch. 18). The two brothers first given to Horus in Pa were Amsta and Hapi (ch. 112). The other two that were given to Horus in Nekhen are Tuamutef and Kabhsenuf, the adorer of the mother and the refresher of his brethren. Thus, the kingdom announced by Anup the baptizer, and founded by Horus for his father, was established upon the four supports. These in one shape were four brothers, only one of whom, Amsta, wears *the human form*. They are adopted by him as his Shus, his servants or fishers, two by two— two in Pa and two in Nekhen, the region where Sebek was the great fisher in the marshes. The four are given by Ra to Horus as his children who are brothers of his own body, to be with him in token of everlasting renewal and of peace on earth, and these are the four pillars, flagstaffs, fishermen, or supports, on which the kingdom of heaven was to be founded in Amenta, as a spirit-world by Horus, who was the fulfiller for the father at his second coming.

We repeat that Horus had four brothers with him in the mythos who had been with him from the beginning, just as Jesus has his four brothers on earth ; and when Horus makes his change and rises in Amenta from the dead the four brothers become his children as the four supports of the future kingdom (Rit., 112), the "four glorified ones" who are foremost among the seven great spirits of Annu (Rit., ch. 97). They who were the brothers of Horus when he was the son of Seb, or, as we say, on the earth, are, after his resurrection, called his children. Coincident with this change the risen Lord, in the Gospels, addresses his disciples as his children when he has risen from the tomb. He comes to the seven fishers in the boat, and says to them, " *Children*, have ye aught to eat?" (John xxi. 5). This being *after* the resurrection. It is the only time that the disciples are addressed as the children of Jesus, and the conditions are identical with those in the Ritual where the brethren of Horus in the earth-life become his children in the spirit-life beyond the tomb. Thus, to recapitulate, Horus of the resurrection at his second coming was accompanied by Anup, the baptizer, as divine scribe, as lunar god, and the four brethren Amsta, Hapi, Tuamutef, and Kabhsenuf, one of which four was Amsta, the only brother in the human form. These four are the divine powers who were with Horus in the mount when he rose from the dead and came forth to day. They can be paralleled thus with characters in the canonical Gospels as: Horus, or the Egypto-gnostic Jesus=Jesus ; Anup, the baptizer=John the Baptist ; John, the divine scribe=Aan, the divine scribe ; Amsta, the one human brother of the Lord=James, the one human brother of Jesus ; Hapi=Andrew ; Tuamutef=John ; Kabhsenuf=Peter.

Simon Peter is the one who perceives and proclaims that Jesus is the Christ. "Thou art the Christ, the Son of the living God" (Matt. xvi. 16). The name of Peter is here identified with the Greek Petra for a rock. But if the other characters, Jesus = Horus; John = Aan; James = Amsta, are Egyptian, it follows that Peter is Egyptian also. The word Petra or Petar is Egyptian; it signifies to see, look at, to perceive, to show forth, to reveal. *Moreover, Petar is the name or title of an Egyptian god who had been already divinized as the one who discovered and made known the only begotten son of that living god*, who was Atum-Ankhu, the father of Iusa, the Egyptian Jesus (Budge, *Vocabulary*, p. 122). Probably the deified perceiver, or Petar, was the hawk-sighted Kabhsenuf, the refresher of his brethren, one of the four children of Horus, who had previously been his brothers from the beginning in the astronomical mythology.

Horus in one character is the Fisher. "Know ye what I know," saith the manes, "the name of him who fishes there, the great prince who sits at the east of the sky?" (Naville, Rit., 153B). "I know the name of the table on which he lays them (the fishes); it is the table of

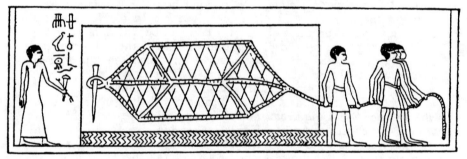

The Four as Fishers for Horus.

Horus." In this character the Osiris saith, "I shine like Horus. I govern the land, and I go down to the land *in the two great boats. I have come as a fisher*" (Naville, ch. 153A). Horus or Jesus in the Roman catacombs also comes as the fisher who at the same time is portrayed as the bringer of the grapes for the Uaka festival (Lundy, *Monumental Christianity*, fig. 54). The four as fishers for Horus are depicted as the fishers in the Ritual. They are spoken of as having been amongst the earlier elemental powers called "the ancestors of Ra." Otherwise stated, they are four of the seven souls of Ra. In fact, they are Hapi, Tuamutef, Kabhsenuf, and Amsta, now to be identified as the four children who became the four fishers for Horus, and who are one with the four fishers for Jesus in the canonical Gospels. A vignette to the *Book of the Dead* (ch. 153A, Pl. 55, Naville and Renouf) shows the four fishers as four men pulling the drag-net through the water in the act of fishing for Horus. These are they who are described as fishers for the great prince who sits at the east of the sky (ch. 153B), and who is said to *mark them as his own property*.

Horus was the prototypal fish, the same type of sacrifice that is still eaten in the penitential meal to-day as it was in On when Sebek-Horus was the Saviour as the fish that brought the food and water of the inundation. Horus as the fish preceded Horus as the fisher when Sebek, the crocodile-headed god, was the typical great fisher. It is said of the first two fishers, " These are the two hands of Horus which had become fishes," that is, as types of Horus the fisher, according to the mystery of Nekhen (Rit., ch. 113). The followers of Horus as fishers (ch. 153A) are called " *the fishermen who are fishing.*" Thus the total group who were the twelve as reapers in the harvest-field of Amenta are also the twelve as the fishers. Hence the twelve fishermen of the later legend. The two first fishes caught for Horus are then eaten at the sacramental meal. As it is said (Rit., ch. 153A), the fishes are laid on the table of Horus. They had been brought to him when the festival was founded by Ra ; " they were brought to Horus and displayed before his face at the feast of the 15th day of the month, when the fishes were produced " (Rit., ch. 113).

In the Ritual (ch. 97) there is a scene of the Seven Fishers at the boat with Horus, which can be paralleled in the Gospel of John. The scene in John's Gospel is post-resurrectional, therefore not in the earth of time. As it is said, " This is now the third time that Jesus was manifested to the disciples *after that he was risen from the dead*" (John xxi. 14). And that which follows the resurrection is in spirit-world. Therefore Jesus and the seven disciples in this scene are spirits like the seven with Horus, which were the seven great spirits of Annu, four of whom became the first fishers for Horus (Rit. chs. 97 and 153A). This view is corroborated by the appearance of Peter, "*for he was naked*," and a naked man in Sign-language means a spirit. Thus the seven with Jesus at the boat are a form of the seven great spirits with Horus at the bark in Annu, four of whom—the foremost four—become the founders of the fold for the Good Shepherd, in the same chapter of the Ritual but in another character. In this character Horus had shepherded the flocks of Ra, his heavenly father, in the deserts of Amenta (Book of Hades). In this character of the shepherd Horus of the resurrection rose up from the sepulchre with a crook instead of the later lamb or kid upon his shoulder. And it is in this character Horus chooses the first four of the seven great spirits of Annu to become the founders of his fold as well as his first four fishers. In the Gospel Jesus likewise assumes the character of the so-called good shepherd. Hence the injunctions to Peter, and the sayings, " Feed my lambs," " Tend my sheep," " Feed my sheep " (John xxi. 16–18).

According to Matthew, the four brethren first chosen by Jesus are Simon, Andrew, James and John. It is noteworthy, however, that in the Johannine account the first four followers of Jesus are Andrew and Peter, Phillip and Nathaniel. Moreover, Nathaniel was one of those who were under the fig-tree aforetime with Jesus. There is no Zebedee, father of the fishers, and there is no fishing in the opening chapter of John ; that is, as supposed in the life on earth. The fishers only appear in this Gospel *after the resurrection of Jesus*, which takes us, as does the baptism, into the spirit-world of the mythos, where the seven fishers answer to the other group of the seven in the boat with Horus.

The mysteries of Amenta show us Anup calling the world to judgment in the character of the judge. He is the precursor of

Horus in the wilderness, and the announcer of the kingdom that follows at the second coming. Under the title of Ap-Uat he is the opener or guide of roads who "makes ready the way of the Lord," and levels the path in the equinox. In the Gospels the proclamation that the kingdom of heaven is at hand was first made by John the baptizer and precursor of Jesus. The cry of the coming kingdom immediately at hand is then taken up by Jesus after the baptism in which he has become the adult of thirty years, and the co-type of Horus the anointed son of God the second born who was Horus in the spirit. Also in the Gospel of Nicodemus, John the Baptist is the teacher in the earth of eternity. The baptism and transformation of Jesus into the spirit symbolled by the dove was in the earth of eternity. The descent of the holy spirit, as God the father, in authentication of the anointed son was enacted in the earth of eternity, not in the world of time. According to the genuine mythos or gnosis which is Egyptian, and we have no other criterion, the double advent of Horus depended on his birth and rebirth, in the two earths ; the birth of a human soul in matter and the rebirth of an immortal in Amenta. The second coming of Horus is the mystery of that second birth in which the human soul is divinized from its two halves as an enduring spirit or eternal entity. This transformation follows death and burial, and therefore can only take place in spirit-world. When it does take place the second advent is accomplished as represented both in the Ritual and the Egypto-gnostic writings. But it is otherwise in the canonical Gospels, because in making out a history solely human the concocters were limited to the human life in the earth of time. For example, in the Gospel according to John, when Jesus is about to leave the disciples and is telling them of the second advent, he says, " I have yet many things to say unto you, but ye cannot bear them now " (ch. xvi. 12). These things that are to come, in some indefinite future (which has not come yet), relate to the nature of God the father. They constitute the mysteries which are to be unfolded in the future at the second coming of the son in the person of the judge, the avenger, the harvester, the spirit-of-truth, the comforter, the fulfiller who fulfils both in the Ritual and in the gnostic Gospel. Jesus had hitherto taught in parables. Now he says the hour cometh when he will tell them " plainly of the father " and speak to them no more in parables (xvi. 25). This is at the second coming *which had been already fulfilled in the Gospel of " Pistis Sophia" and in the Ritual of the Resurrection.* The Egypto-gnostic Jesus who, as the " little Iao " of " Pistis Sophia," only spoke in parables, and was not empowered to expound the profounder mysteries of the fatherhood, is a form of the child-Horus whom Plutarch called the "inarticulate discourse." At his second coming he unfolded the spiritual mysteries. The chief of these was the mystery of mysteries, namely, the mystery of " the father in the likeness of a dove" (B. 1, 1). Nevertheless, the second advent, and the mysteries pertaining thereto (according to the genuine gnosis), do *leak out* in the canonical Gospels, however carefully disguised or surreptitiously inserted. The gnostic manifestation of the first mystery, namely, that of the father as a dove, is made to the Gospel-Jesus at the time of his baptism, in the life on earth. The second coming is also illustrated in the scene of transfiguration on the mount. Likewise in the resurrection when the risen Christ has transformed into a spirit, Luke notwithstanding, with power to impart the holy spirit and share it with his followers (John xx. 22). Each of these manifestations, with others belonging to the second advent of Horus in Amenta, are assigned to Jesus in the human life in fulfilment of the history. In the Ritual the father, as the holy spirit, calls from heaven to Horus (or Osiris) the anointed son, "Come thou to me." This is Ra, the bird-headed, whose likeness is then assumed by Horus the beloved son. In the Gospel, the Father, as the holy spirit, descended on Jesus in the form of a dove, and in that guise "abode upon him." The exigency of a human history with only a single advent did not permit of the death and resurrection of Jesus occurring at the time when the youth of twelve years made his change into the adult of thirty years. Yet the baptism and ascension of Jesus from the water into the opening heavens are identical with the Egypto-gnostic resurrection. The Horus or Jesus of twelve years is the mortal on this side of death. The Horus or Jesus of thirty years is a spirit on the other side, in spirit-world. The baptism of Jesus represents the resurrection of Horus from the water. Hence Jesus in his baptism becomes a spirit. He is led up from the water "of the spirit," "in the spirit," or *as a spirit* into which he had made his transformation. When Sut put out the eye of Horus, the darkness represented death. But, in the Gospel, death, or the transformation, is only represented at this point by the baptism. If it had been actualized the history must have ended there and then, which was not in accordance with the Gospel schema. Still, the "history" notwithstanding, Jesus does become a spirit in this scene of transformation which belongs to the mysteries of Amenta. Bird-headed beings are spirits, not historical Jews. *Only as a spirit* could the foster-child of Seb, or Joseph, transform into the son of Ra the holy spirit; and only in the earth of eternity could the change occur in which the Virgin's child became the father's son by being born again of Nut the heavenly mother, one of whose names was Meri. According to the gnosis, the following are a few of the events that occur *after the resurrection*: the trans-formation of Jesus, the Virgin's child, into the beloved son of the father with the spirit of God descending on him as a dove; the contests with Satan in the spirit; the adoption of the four disciples in the mount; Jesus with the seven on board the bark; the founding of the fold; the miracles of healing; giving sight to the blind; raising the dead; casting out the devils; causing evil spirits to enter the swine; walking upon the water; founding the kingdom of heaven on the four fishers, or disciples, and conferring the holy spirit, after death, upon the twelve.

The Gospel doctrine of the Holy Spirit is true enough, according to the Egyptian wisdom, when properly applied, but only as Egyptian is it to be understood. Certain manifestations of the holy spirit in the Gospels are strictly in keeping with the mysteries of the Ritual or Book of the Dead. In the words of John "the holy spirit was not given" at the time when Jesus "was not yet glorified" (ch. vii. 39). The glorifying was by descent of the holy spirit; the spirit that was given to Horus and by him to the disciples in the mystery of Tattu upon the resurrection-day when the God in heaven called to the mummy-Osiris in Amenta "Come thou to me," when the two halves of the soul were blended in the eternal oneness, and human Horus, the soul in matter, was transformed to rise again as Horus divinized. This was in the resurrection after death, in baptismal regeneration, or in the Christifying of the Osiris-mummy.

The Ritual shows us how the apostles were established on the same foundation, beginning with the two brothers, who were followed by the four brethren, the cycle being completed by the twelve in the fields of divine harvest. The four as brothers of Horus had been figures in the astronomy. The four as his children are figures in the eschatology ; the four who are " foremost among the spirits of Annu " with the aid of whom " the fold " was constructed for him, as for one victorious against all " adversaries " (Rit., ch. 97). The two fours are thus equated in the Gospels. The four brothers of Horus=the four brothers of Jesus. Amsta, Hapi, Tuamutef, Kabhsenuf=James, Joseph, Simon, Judas. The same four in the character of his children with Horus=the four brethren, Simon, Andrew, James and John, whom Jesus addresses as his children (John xxxi. 5). At a later stage the followers in the train of Horus are the twelve who are his harvesters in the cornfields of Amenta. " Pistis Sophia " in agreement with the " Book of Hades " shows us how the twelve as followers of Horus were constituted a company that consisted at first of seven to which the five were added in forming the group of twelve. The disciples of Jesus likewise become the twelve who reap the harvest. " Then saith he unto his disciples, the harvest truly is plenteous but the labourers are few. Pray ye therefore the Lord of the harvest that he send forth labourers into his harvest. And he called unto him his twelve disciples "—who were previously but four (Matt. iv. 18, 21)— " and gave them authority over unclean spirits, to cast them out, and to heal all manner of disease and all manner of sickness." At this point the names of the twelve are for the first time given (Matt. x. 1–5). The same words are uttered in Luke concerning the harvest and its reapers, but now the number of disciples appointed and sent forth for the ingathering of harvest-home is seventy or seventy-and-two—one for each subdivision of the decans in the twelve signs, both the seventy and seventy-two being identifiable astronomical numbers.

The twelve with Horus in Amenta are they who labour at the harvest and collect the corn (otherwise the souls) for Horus. When the harvest is ready " the bearers of sickles reap the grain in their fields. Ra says to them, on earth as bearers of sickles in the fields of Amenta," " Take your sickles, reap your grain " (" Book of Hades," Records, vol. 10, 119). Here the labourers who reap the harvest in Amenta are the object of propitiatory offerings and of adoration on the earth, as the twelve disciples of Horus, son of Ra, the heavenly father. And this was ages before the story was told of the twelve fictitious harvesters in Galilee. Moreover, the Harvest is identical with the Last Judgment. Atum-Ra says at the same time, " Guard the enemies, punish the wicked. Let them not escape from your hands. Watch over the executions, according to the orders you have received from the Founder, who has marked you out to strike "—as executioners. So is it in the Gospels, where the harvest is one with the judgment at the end of the world, or consummation of the age.

As before said, when the narratives in the canonical scriptures had taken the place of the primitive drama, certain mysteries of Amenta were made portable in parables, and thenceforth the Gospels repeat the same things in parables and logoi that were represented dramatically in the mysteries. The harvest-home and judgment-day, described in the Gospels, which are to occur at some indefinite time in the future on this earth, belong to the Osirian mysteries of Amenta. The great judgment at the last day supplies an illustration of the mystery extant in parable. A first and second death occur, likewise a first and second resurrection in the mysteries of Amenta. The first is the death which takes place on earth, and the apparition of the manes in the nether-world constitutes the first resurrection from the dead. Then follows the great judgment of the righteous and the wicked. Those found guilty are doomed to suffer the second death. There is for them no other resurrection. Those who escape from the dread tribunal uncondemned pass on to the second resurrection as the spirits of the just made perfect, called the glorified. These are the inheritors of eternal life. Jesus says, " This is the will of my Father, that every one that beholdeth the Son, and believeth on him, should have eternal life, that I should raise him up at the last day," "and I will raise him up at the last day" (John vi. 40, 44). The pitiful pretence of an historical Jew being the raiser up of the dead at the last day is a miserable mockery of the actual transaction in the mysteries of Amenta with Horus as the resurrection and the life. In these, deceased is shown as Ani in the hall of judgment. He has emerged from the earth-life and risen *in* Amenta, but not yet *from* it. He must be judged in the Maat or great hall before he rises from the dead as one of the just made perfect for the life to come. If he passes, sound of heart and pure in spirit, he will enter the presence of the great god. Ani succeeds and passes pure. His resurrection from the dead and from Amenta, the world of the dead, is assured. Horus the Son of God, the Intercessor, the paraclete, now takes him by the hand as the raiser of the dead to life and introducer of the risen Ani to his father. In one scene the hair of Ani is black. The next shows him kneeling in presence of Osiris with his hair turned white. He has passed in purity. He has been raised by Horus at the " last day " or at the end of the cycle when the dead were judged, once every year or other period at the great gathering of " all souls." This took place " in presence of the gods," as one of the ten great mysteries described in the Ritual (ch. 18) when " the glorious ones were rightly judged, and joy went its round in Thinis " ; when judgment was passed upon those who were to be annihilated " on the highway of the damned " ; when " the evil dead were cast out," and the goats divided from the sheep. As it is said—" when the associates of Sut arrive, and take the form of goats, they are slain in presence of the gods so long as their blood runneth down, and this is done according to the judgment of those gods who are in Tattu," the place of establishing the soul for ever, from its two halves, as the double Horus, the divine avenger of the suffering Osiris, who at his second coming was the revealer of eternal justice. This culminating event, which was the subject of so much Old Testament prophecy that is reproduced in the New, is here fulfilled, according to the knowledge of the wise men " which knew the times " and who also " knew the law and the judgment " (Esther i. 13). The advent might be on the millennial scale of Horus in the house of a thousand years according to the cycle, but there was a Coming once a year and an ending of the cycle, the age, or the world as it was called by the Christians every year. And it is on this *one-year period* derived from the solar mythos that the second advent and *the immediate ending of the world* were ignorantly based. The end of the world or the cycle of the annual sun came once a year in the Egyptian mythos. The second advent of Horus, like the first, was also annual. He came in the terror of his glory as avenger of his father; as the great judge, as lord of the harvest with the glorious ones for reapers who were the typical twelve in number, and as the fulfiller of the heavenly kingdom in which he reigned according to the mythos for one year, whether as Horus the shoot, the fish, the fisherman, or the harvester. The gnostic Christ was likewise known to be the ruler for one year.

At the festival of Ha-ka-er-a, or " Come thou to me," the blessed ones were welcomed by Horus to the kingdom which had been prepared from the foundation of the world, or the earliest cycle of time, in the Kamite astro-mythology, if anywhere on earth, but which preparation and founding were repeated every year as a mode of the mysteries in Amenta. These mysteries were extant, and periodically performed some thousands of years ago. So ancient is some of the imagery in the Maat, that when Ani passes pure, the crown of glory placed upon his head to be worn in heaven is a form of the *top-knot*, which is still assumed at puberty by the Kaffirs and other African black races. But this great judgment, in common with the other events that were fulfilled at the second advent, still remains the subject of prophecy in the Hebrew and Christian scriptures. In the Gospel according to Matthew the last judgment is to take place at the veritable ending of the world (Matt. xxv. 31-46). " When the Son of Man shall come in his glory, and all the angels with him, then shall he sit on the throne of his glory, and before him shall be gathered all the nations, and he shall separate them, as the shepherd parteth the sheep from the goats ; and he shall set the sheep on the right hand, but the goats on the left. Then shall the King say unto them on his right hand, Come ye blessed of my Father, inherit the kingdom prepared for you from the foundation of the world : for I was an hungered, and ye gave me meat : I was thirsty, and ye gave me drink : I was a stranger and ye took me in : naked and ye clothed me, sick and ye visited me. Then shall he say unto them on the left hand, Depart from me ye cursed, into the eternal fire which is prepared for the devil and his angels." In the original, the devil and his angels are Sut and his Sami, and the goats on the left hand are also the representatives of Sut. Nevertheless, the two judgments of the Ritual and in the Gospel are fundamentally the same ; there was but one origin and one meaning for both. The great judgment in the hall of righteousness which remained the subject of Hebrew prophecy gone dateless was an annual occurrence in the

Kamite mysteries. In this the Osiris pleads: "I have done that which man prescribeth and that which pleaseth the gods. I have propitiated the god with that which he loveth. I have given bread to the hungry, water to the thirsty, clothes to the naked, a boat to the shipwrecked. I have made oblations to the gods and funeral offerings to the departed: deliver me therefore: protect me therefore: and report not against me in presence of the great God. I am one whose mouth is pure, and whose hands are pure, to whom it is said by those who look upon him, Come, come in peace" (Ritual, ch. 125, Renouf).

The great judgment was periodic in Amenta at the end of a cycle, which might be a year, a generation, or, as it was also exoterically figured, at the end of the world. The uninitiated, who had but an outside view, mistook it for the actual and immediate ending of the world. "The harvest is the end of the world" (Matt. xiii. 39). "The end of all things is at hand" (1 Peter iv. 7). "It is the last hour" (1 John ii. 18). "The kingdom of heaven is at hand" (Matt. iii. 2; iv. 17; x. 7). This was according to the literalization of the Illiterate. Paul is the only writer or speaker in the New Testament who knew better. He warns his followers amongst the Thessalonians against believing this teaching of the uninitiated. He says: "We beseech you, brethren, touching the coming of our Lord Jesus Christ, and our gathering together unto him; to the end that ye be not quickly shaken from your mind, nor yet be troubled, either by spirit or by word, or *by Epistle as from us* (*i.e.*, by a forged 'Epistle of Paul'), as that the day of the Lord is (now) present: let no man beguile you in any wise" (2 Thess. ii. 1, 3). He was the only one who knew the esoteric nature of this end of the æon, and the coming of Christ or Horus, the anointed, the Messiah in Israel, or the Jesus who was Iu the Su of Atum, whom he calls the second Adam = Atum, and who had been to him the pre-Christian Christ, the spiritual rock, from which the people drank the water of life whilst in the wilderness. When Tertullian denounced Paul as "The Apostle of the Heretics" he meant the Egypto-gnostics. Paul was epopt and perfect amongst those who knew that the historic version was a lying delusion. This we hold to have been aimed at in his "Second Epistle to the Thessalonians," when he says of his opponents, the fleshifiers of the Christ, "for this cause God sendeth them a working of error, that they should believe a lie."

The mould of the mythos being solar, once every year the heir of Ra assumed his sovereignty as Horus of the kingly countenance, whose rule was for one year. Every year Osiris, the great green one in vegetation, died to rise again in the fruits of the earth. Every year in the solar drama he was buried in Amenta to make the road that united the two earths in one, for establishing the coming kingdom on earth as it was in heaven. Every year the prophecy was fulfilled in natural phenomena, and every year the coming kingdom came. Every year was celebrated this foundation of the world that was laid and relaid by the buried body of the god; this union of the double earth in Tanen, at the equinox, this resurrection of the soul that supplied the bread of life, this completion of the circle by the sun that rose and travelled on the eternal round as representative of the author of eternity. A glimpse of this annual coming is permitted when the Christ is made to say, "Ye shall not have gone through the cities of

Israel till the son of man be come" (Matt. x. 23). "There be some of them that stand here which shall in no wise taste of death till they see the son of man coming in his kingdom" (Matt. xvi. 28). Such prophecy is in accordance with the true mythos, but for ever fatal to the falsely-founded history.

·

THE LAST SUPPER: THE CRUCIFIXION AND THE RESURRECTION.

As the legend is related by Plutarch, the death of Osiris was preceded by his betrayal, and the betrayal, which was the work of his twin brother, Sut, took place in the banqueting-room. Sut, having framed a curious ark just the size of Osiris's body, brought it to a certain banquet. As this was on the last night of Osiris's life or reign, and on the last night of the year, the meal may fairly be called the *Last Supper* (*Of Isis and Osiris*, 13). Now this mystery of the Last Supper can be traced in the Ritual as the first of a series acted in Amenta. Sut and his associates had renewed the assault upon Osiris on the night of laying the evening provisions upon the altar, called the night of the battle in which the powers of drought and darkness were defeated and extinguished. The coffin of Osiris is the earth of Amenta. Dawn upon the coffin was the resurrection; and this provender is imaged as "the dawn upon the coffin of Osiris," which shows that the evening meal, or eucharist, was eaten in celebration of the resurrection and the transubstantiation of the body into spirit. The night of laying provisions on the altar is mentioned twice: once when Osiris is in the coffin, provided by Sut and his associates, the Sebau, who entrapped him in the ark. The second mention follows the erection of the Tat-sign which denoted the resurrection; hence the "dawn upon the coffin of Osiris," which is equivalent to the resurrection morn. The resurrection on the third day originated in lunar phenomena. Twenty-eight days was the length of a moon, and this is no doubt the source of the statement that Osiris was in his eight-and-twentieth year at the time of his betrayal. The moon is invisible during two nights, which completed the luni-solar month of thirty days.

The assault upon Osiris the Good Being made by Sut was periodically renewed. This has just occurred when the first of the ten mysteries is enacted (Rit., ch. 18). The scene is in the house of Annu (Heliopolis), where Osiris lay buried and Horus was reborn. The triumph of Osiris over his adversaries is in the resurrection following the dramatized death of the inviolate god. This is called the night of the battle, when there befell the defeat of the Sebau and the extinction of the adversaries of Osiris. It is also described as "the night of provisioning the altar," otherwise stated "*the night of the Last Supper*," when "the calf of the sacrificial herd" was eaten at "the mortuary meal," which represented the body and blood of Osiris, "the bull of eternity" (Rit., ch. 1).

The second mystery of the ten is solemnized upon the night when the Tat-pillar was set up in Tattu, or when Osiris in his resurrection was raised up again as a type of the eternal. The third mystery is on the night of the things that were laid upon the altar in Sekhem which imaged the altar and the offering in one. This was the circle of Horus in the dark, the sufferer made blind by Sut, the victim in the Tat who was the prototype of Jesus on the cross, and representative of the god in matter.

As we have seen, a great Memphian festival, answering to the Christmas-tide of later times, was periodically solemnized at the temple of Medinet Habu in the last decade of the month Choiak (from December 20th to 30th), which lasted for ten days. One day, the 26th of the month = December 24th, was kept as the feast of Sekari, the god who rose again from the mummy, and this was the principal feast-day of the ten. In all likelihood the whole ten mysteries were performed during the ten days of the festival that was celebrated at Memphis (Erman, *Life in Ancient Egypt*, Eng. tr., pp. 277-9). Prominent among these was the feast of the erection or re-erection of the Tat-pillar of stability, which was an image of Ptah-Sekari, the coffined one who rose again, and who in the later religion becomes Osiris-Sekari, "Lord of resurrections, whose birth is from the house of death." The resurrection of Osiris, which, like other doctrines, was based on the realities of nature, would be appropriately celebrated in the winter solstice. At that time the powers of darkness, drought, decay and death, now personalized in Sut, were dominant, as was shown in the lessening water and the waning light of the enfeebled sun. The tat-type of stability was temporarily overthrown, by the adversary of Osiris and his co-conspirators, the Sebau. Here begins the great drama of the Osirian mysteries, in ten acts, which is outlined in the Ritual. The putting of Osiris to death—so far as a god could suffer—was followed by the funeral, and the burial by the resurrection. The opening chapters of the Ritual, called the Coming forth to day, are said to contain "the words which bring about the resurrection and the glory," also the words to be recited on the day of burial that confer the power of coming forth from the death on earth, and of entering into the new life of the manes in Amenta. Horus is described as covering Tesh-Tesh (a title of the mutilated Osiris) ; as opening the life-fountains of the god whose heart is motionless, and as closing the entrance to the hidden things in Rusta (ch. 1, 18–20). The two divine sisters are present as mourners over their brother in the tomb. They are called the mourners who weep for Osiris in Rekhet (line 15, 16). The mysteries thus commence with the burial of Osiris in Amenta—as a mummy. The mummy-making that was first applied to preserving the bones and body of the human being had been afterwards applied to the god or sun of life in matter, imaged as the typical mummy of Osiris that was buried to await the resurrection in and afterwards from Amenta. In both phases it is Osiris, as the god in matter, who is represented in the nether-earth. And the rearising of the human soul and its blending with the eternal spirit were dramatically rendered in the mysteries as the resurrection of *the* Osiris or the soul of mortal Horus rearisen in Amenta as the son of Ra.

In the Gospels, Judas the brother of Jesus in one character, elsewhere called the familiar friend, is the betrayer on the night of the last supper, and Judas " the son of perdition " answers to Sut the twin-brother of Osiris (in the later Egyptian mythos), who was his betrayer at the last supper called the *messiu* or evening meal that was eaten on the last night of the Old Year, or the reign of Osiris. The twelve disciples only are present at the last supper in the Gospels. In the betrayal of Osiris by Sut the number present in the banqueting-hall is seventy-two. These were officers who had been appointed by Osiris. The number shows they represent the seventy-two duo-decans as rulers in the planisphere, but the twelve have been chosen to sit at supper with the doomed victim in the Gospels instead of the seventy-two who were also appointed by the Lord, and are dimly apparent in their astronomical guise, as the seventy-two (or seventy) who are present in the scene where Jesus triumphs over Satan as he falls like lightning from his place in heaven (Luke x. 17).

One of the most striking of the various episodes in the Gospel narrative is that scene at the Last Supper in which Jesus washes the feet of the disciples, compared with " the washing " that is performed by the Great One in the Ritual. In the Gospel Judas is waiting to betray his master. Jesus says to the betrayer, " That thou doest, do quickly." Now it should be borne in mind that the Ritual, as it comes to us, consists to a large extent of allusions to the matter that was made out more fully in performing the drama of the mysteries. Washing the feet was one of the mysteries pertaining to the funeral of Osiris, when the feet of the disciples or followers of Horus were washed. It was one of the funeral ceremonies. As it is said in the Ritual (ch. 172), " Thou washest thy feet in silver basins made by the skilful artificer Ptah-Sekari." This was preparatory to the funeral feast, as is shown by the context (ch. 172). In the Gospel (John xiii.) the funeral feast becomes the " Last Supper " when Jesus " riseth from supper and layeth aside his garments; and he took a towel and girded himself. Then he poureth water into a basin and began to wash the disciples' feet." And here is a passage of three lines, called the chapter by which the person is not devoured by the serpent in Amenta. " O Shu, here is Tattu, *and conversely*, under the hair of Hathor. They scent Osiris. Here is the one who is to devour me. They wait apart. The serpent Seksek passeth over me. Here are wormwood bruised and reeds. Osiris is he who prayeth that he may be buried. The eyes of the great one are bent down, and he doeth for thee the work of washing, *marking out what is comformable to law and balancing the issues* " (Rit., ch. 35, Renouf). This brief excerpt contains the situation and character of the great one, who with eyes bent down in his humility does " the work of washing," and explains why this ceremony has to be performed by him in person. The " washer " is he who is in presence of the one who waits to betray him, devour him, or compass his destruction, and he beseeches a speedy burial. Osiris in this scene is a form of the typical " lowly one " who had been in type as such for ages pre-viously. But the most arresting fact of all is hidden in the words " O Shu, here is Tattu (the place of re-establishing) under the wig (or hair) of Hathor," the goddess of dawn, one of whose names is Meri. And it is here, beneath the hair of Hathor-Meri, they perfume and anoint Osiris for his burial. This when written out as " history " contains the anointing and perfuming of the feet of Jesus by Mary, who wiped them with her hair (Luke vii. 38). The two bathings of the feet are separate items in the Gospels, whereas both occur in this one short chapter of the Ritual in which Osiris is anointed for his burial, and at the same time he does for others the work of washing and purifying, "marking out what is conformable to law and balancing the issues."

Osiris also is "he who prayeth that he may be buried," and Jesus, "knowing that his hour has come," says to Judas the betrayer, "That thou doest, do quickly." And later, "Friend, do that for which thou art come" (Matt. xxvi. 50), which is the equivalent of Orisis praying that he may be buried. The wormwood bruised, or crushed, and the reeds are utilized in the crucifixion for furnishing the bitter drink, which was offered to the victim with a sponge placed upon a reed. A reed was also put in his right hand. These things were portrayed in the drama of Amenta. They were acted in the mysteries and explained by the mystery-teachers. *The* Osiris passes through the same scenes and makes continual allusion to the sufferings of Osiris (or Horus) his great forerunner, and finally the drama was staged on earth and reproduced as history in the Gospels. That is the one final and sufficient explanation of episode after episode belonging to the mysteries of Amenta reproduced according to the canon as veritable Gospel history.

The scene in Gethsemane may be compared with the scene in Pa, where Horus suffered *his* agony and bloody sweat when wounded by the black boar Sut. Pa was an ancient name of Sesennu, a locality in the lunar mythos, which was also called Khemen, later Smen, a word signifying number eight, applied to the enclosure of the eight; and the suffering of the wounded Horus in Am-Semen is, as now suggested, the Osirian original of Jesus bleeding in Gethsemane. Pa is not called "a garden," but it is described as a "place of repose" for Horus that was given to him by his father for his place of rest. Ra says, "I have given Pa to Horus as the place of his repose. Let him prosper." The story is told in "the chapter of knowing the powers of Pa" (Rit., ch. 112). The question is asked, "Know ye why Pa hath been given to Horus?" The answer is, It was Ra who gave it to him in amends of the blindness in his eye, in consequence of what Ra said to Horus: "Let me look at what is happening in thine eye to-day," and he looked at it. Ra said to Horus, "Pray, look at that black swine." He looked, and a grievous mishap befell his eye. Horus said to Ra, "Lo, mine eye is as though Sut had made a wound in it." And wrath devoured his heart. Then Ra said to the gods, "Let him be laid upon his bed that he may recover." "It was Sut who had taken the form of a black swine, and he wrought the wound which was made in the eye of Horus. And Ra said to the gods, "The swine is an abomination to Horus; may he get well." And the swine became an abomination to Horus. (Rit., ch. 112, Renouf.) It was in Pa that Horus was keeping his watch for Ra by night when the grievous mishap befell his eye. He was watching by command of Ra, who had said to Horus, "Keep your eye on the black pig." The eye was lunar, with which Horus kept the watch for Ra; and Sut in the form of the black boar of darkness pierced the eye of Horus with his tusk, the moon being the eye of Horus as the watcher by night for Ra. Sut on whom he kept the watch transformed himself into a black boar, and wounded Horus in the eye whilst he was watching on behalf of Ra as his nocturnal eye in the darkness. Jesus in the Gospels keeps the watch by night in Gethsemane, as is shown by the disciples failing to keep it. The watch by Horus was necessitated on account of Sut, who is the typical betrayer in the Kamite mythos, as Judas is in the Christian version. Sut knew the place in the original rendering and sought out Horus there when he caused the agony and bloody sweat by mutilating him. "Now Judas also which betrayed him knew the place" (to which Jesus "often resorted" with his disciples) and there the betrayer seeks him out to betray him, not in the form of a black boar that put out the eye which was the light of the world, but as a dark-hearted person befitting the supposed historical nature of the narrative. The scene of the drowsy watchers in Gethsemane is apparently derived from a scene in the mysteries. There is a reference in the Ritual (ch. 89) to "those *undrowsy watchers* who keep watch in Annu." In the Gospels Jesus asks his followers to watch with him in the garden, and on both occasions he found them sleeping. The moral is pointed by the "undrowsy watchers in Annu" being turned into the drowsy watchers who slept in Gethsemane, and who failed to keep the watch. "I know the powers in Pa," says the speaker; "they are Horus, Amsta and Hapi." That is, Horus and the "two brothers," who correspond to the two brethren James and John, the sons of Zebedee, in the Gospels, and who are here the two with Jesus in the garden. The conversation betwixt Horus the son and Ra the father, the watching by night, and the bloody sweat are followed by the glorification of Horus. Ra gives back the eye, the sight of which was restored in the new moon. In the Gospel (John xvii.) this glorification of Horus as the son of the father—Horus, who had previously been the son of the mother, *Har-si-Hesi* only—is anticipated and described as about to occur when the torment and the trial are over. "These things spake Jesus; and lifting up his eyes to heaven, he said, Father, the hour is come; glorify thy son, that thy son may glorify thee; even as thou gavest him authority over all flesh"—that was in the character of Horus the mortal—"Now, O Father, glorify me with thine own self"—in the character of Horus divinized or glorified. The temporary triumph of the treacherous Sut (the power of darkness) is acknowledged by Jesus when Judas betrays him with a kiss and he succumbs. "This," he says to his captors, "this is your hour, and the power of darkness (Sut). And they seized him" (Luke xxii. 53, 54). But when the associates of Sut saw the double-crown of Horus on his forehead they fell to the ground upon their faces (Rit., ch. 134, 11). And when the associates of Judas = Sut the betrayer, came to take "Jesus of Nazareth," and he said "I am!" (not I am he!) "They went backward and fell to the ground." Scene for scene, they are the same. One of the titles of Horus is "Lord of the Crown" (ch. 141, 9), which possibly led to Jesus being crowned "King of the Jews." In this scene the title of "Jesus of Nazareth" has the same effect on the associates of Judas that the assuming of his crown by Horus had upon the associates of Sut when it caused them to fall on their faces before him. The crowning of Jesus on the cross is as Jesus of Nazareth, king of the Jews. The crown of triumph is assigned to Horus by his father Atum, and all the adversaries of the Good Being fall on their faces at the sight of it (Rit., ch. 19).

The scene in the garden of Gethsemane, and the cry to the father from the sufferer on the cross are very pitiful—the essence of the tragedy working most subtly on account of the supplication that was all in vain, which makes all the more profound appeal to human sympathy. In the Egyptian representation there is no such cruel desertion by the father of his suffering son in his agony of great darkness. It is far otherwise in the Ritual. When Horus suffers his agony in the darkness, after being pierced and made blind by Sut, Ra, the father-God, is with him to comfort and sustain him. He tenderly examines the bleeding wound and soothes him in his great affliction. Ra charges his angels concerning Horus, or bids the gods to look to his safety and see to his welfare. Ra said to the gods, "Let him be laid upon his couch that he may recover." He also gives the eye of Horus fire to protect him, and consume the black boar of darkness. There is no sightless sufferer groping helplessly with empty hands outstretched and left unclasped in the dark void of death ; no vain and unavailing cry of the forsaken son that stuns the brain and scars the human conscience, and is of itself sufficient to empty the Christian heaven of all fatherhood, and ought to be sufficient to empty earth of all faith in such a father.

According to the synoptists, Jesus did not carry his own cross to the place of execution ; it was borne thither by one Simon of Cyrene. This is denied in the Gospel attributed to John, who declares that Jesus went out from the Judgment Hall "bearing the cross for himself." John is generally truest to the Egyptian original, and here the figure of Jesus bearing his own cross is equivalent to the figure of Ptah-Sekari or Osiris-Tat. The Tat of a fourfold foundation was the prototype of the cross, and the victim extended or standing with arms akimbo is equivalent to the victim stretched upon the cross of suffering. Sekari was the sufferer in, or on, or as the Tat, and Osiris was raised in, or as the Tat where Jesus carries the cross. The scourging of Jesus previous to his being crucified has never been explained. According to the record he was not condemned to both modes of punishment. It is probably a detail derived from the mysteries of Osiris-Sekari, Jesus scourged at the pillar being an image of Osiris or Ptah as the suffering Sekari in or on the Tat, the pillar with arms, that was superseded by the cross in the Christian iconography. In the Egyptian drama of the passion Horus was blinded by Sut and his accomplices, in suffering his change from being the human Horus to becoming Horus in spirit. The incident that is almost omitted from the Gospel account was preserved in the mysteries. It is a common subject in the passion-play and in religious pictures for the Christ to be blindfolded and brutally buffeted by the soldiers before he is crucified. This occurs in the Townley mysteries and in the Coventry mysteries, and is referred to in the "Legends of the holy rood" (pp. 178, 179, E.E. Text Society).

Christ blindfolded to be made a mockery of suggests a likeness of Horus without sight in An-arar-ef, the region of the blind. In one representation Horus has a bandage over his eyes, and the grotesque image of the humorous Bes appears to introduce a comic element into the tragedy of the blind sufferer. The blinding, buffeting and scourging, practised in the mysteries, as in passing through fire and water, was evidently continued and extended in the sports and pastimes. Still, the blindfolding of the victim for the buffeting is implied in the Gospel according to Matthew. "Then did they spit in his face and buffet him ; and some smote him with the palms of their hands, saying, Prophesy unto us, thou Christ : who is he that struck thee ? " (Matt. xxvi. 68).

It was a common popular tradition that the Christ was of a red complexion, like the child or calf which represented the little red sun of winter and also the Virgin's infant in its more mystical character. Moreover, there is a tradition of a crucified child-Christ who was coloured red like " the calf in the paintings." Among " the portraits of God the son " Didron cites one in a manuscript of the fourteenth century which answers to the red Christ as a co-type of the red calf. The manuscript " contains a miniature of the priest Eleazar sacrificing a red cow," and " opposite to this miniature is one of Christ on the cross." " Jesus is entirely naked, and the colour of his skin is red ; he is human, poor and ugly." The red Christ, equivalent to the red Horus, is here identified with the red cow and therefore with the red calf of the Ritual, which was a symbol of the little red sufferer, the " afflicted one " in the winter solstice. In some of the mystery-plays the Christ wore a close-fitting, flesh-coloured garment, through which the nails were driven into the wood of the cross. The resurrection robe was always red. Satan wants to know who this man in the "red coat " may be. And when Horus rises again, in the character of the avenger, it is as the " red god." The manes thus addresses him, " O fearsome one, who art over the two earths ; Red God, who orderest the block of execution ! " (Rit., ch. 17, Renouf). Jesus likewise appears to have been represented as the red God, or the god in red. For " they stripped him and put on him a *scarlet* robe " (Matt. xxvii. 28). A papyrus reed was the throne and sceptre of Horus, the sign of his sovereignty. In the pictures he is supported by the reed, and one of his titles is " Horus on his papyrus " (Rit., ch. 112, Renouf). The reed also has been turned to historic account in making a mockery-king of Jesus. " And they plaited a crown of thorns and put it upon his head, and a reed in his right hand ; and they kneeled down before him, and mocked him, saying, Hail, king of the Jews ! and they spat upon him, and took the reed and smote him on the head " (Matt. xxvii. 27, 29, 30). Jesus is posed in another form of the Osirian sacrificial victim. One meaning of the word "sekari " is the silent. This is the typical victim that opened not his mouth, as the inarticulate Horus. So, having been assigned the character of the silent one before Pilate, " Jesus no more answered anything."

It is possible that the crown of thorns placed upon the head of the crucified was derived from the thorn-bush of Unbu, the solar god, especially if we take it in connection with the papyrus reed, another type of Horus, "And they plaited a crown of thorns and put it upon his head, and a reed in his right hand" (Matt. xxvii. 29). The god and the branch, which is a bush of flowering thorn, are identified, the one with the other, under the name of Unbu, and the god in the Unbu-thorn is equivalent to the crucified in the crown of thorn. Moreover, Unbu, the branch, was a title of the Egyptian Jesus. "I am Unbu of An-arar-ef, the flower in the abode of occultation" or eclipse (Rit., ch. 71). And if Horus was not figured on a cross with the Unbu-thorn upon his head, as the crown was afterwards made out, he is the sacrificial victim in the place of utter darkness or sight-lessness. Horus in An-arar-ef is Horus, Lord of Sekhem—Horus in the dark. He is also "Unbu," that is, Horus in the thorn-bush. Thus the Unbu-thorn was typical of the god, who was personified as Unbu by name, and who is Unbu as Horus the sufferer in the dark, equivalent to and the prototype of the victim on the cross as wearer of the crown of thorn. It is also possible that Pilate's question, "What is truth?" may now be answered for the first time. Jesus says, "I come into the world that I should bear witness unto the truth. Everyone that is of the truth heareth my voice" (John xviii. 37, 38). And, in his second character, Horus the king, Horus the anointed and beloved son, not only came into the world as testifier to the truth, he was also given the title of Har-Makheru, the name of the Word that was made truth by the doing of it in his death and resurrection, and the demonstration of a life hereafter at his second coming.

The typical darkness at the time of the crucifixion might be nocturnal, or annual, according to the mythos. When Atum, god of the evening sun, is setting from the land of life, at the point of equinox, with his hands drooping, which is equivalent to the victim who was extended on the cross, a great darkness overspread the earth, and Nut, the mother, is said to be obscured as she receives the dying deity in her supporting arms. The figure is the same, whether the scene be on the cross or at the crossing (Rit., ch. 15). Still more express is the darkness spoken of in the Egyptian faith, or gospel (ch. 17), which contains the kernel of the credo. Here we learn that "the darkness is of Sekari." Sekari is a title of Osiris as the mutilated and dismembered god. It is explained that this darkness of Sekari, the god who is pierced, wounded, cut in pieces, is caused by Sut "the slayer," who has "terrified by prostrating." Sekari is Osiris in the sekru, or coffin; and to be in the coffin, or in the cruciform figure of the mummy, has the same meaning (with a change of type) as if the divine victim might be embodied in the Tat, or extended on the cross. The darkness of sekari was in the coffin; the darkness of Jesus is on the cross.

It is observable that the sixth division of the Tuat in Amenta, corre-sponding to the sixth hour of the night, has no representation of Ra the solar god, and in his absence naturally there was darkness. But the three hours' darkness that was over all the earth at the time of the crucifixion has no witness in the world to its being an historic event. In the mythical representation it was natural enough. As the night began at six o'clock, the sixth hour according to that reckoning was midnight, and from twelve to three there was dense darkness. This was then applied to the dying sufferer in the eschatology, and there was darkness for three hours in the mysteries. The great darkness is described in the Ritual as the shutting up of Seb and Nut, or heaven and earth, and the Resurrection as the rending asunder. The manes saith, " I am Osiris, who shut up his father and his mother when (or whilst) the great slaughter took place. I am Horus, the eldest of Ra, as he riseth. I am Anup on the day of rending asunder " (Rit., ch. 69, Renouf).

In the coming forth from the cavern the risen one exclaims, " Let the two doors of earth be opened to me : let the bolts of Seb open to me : and let the first mansion be opened to me, *that he may behold me who hath kept guard over me,* and let him enclose me who hath wound his arms about me, and hath fastened his arms around me in the earth " (ch. 68). The one who had held him fast with his arms about him in the earth, and who was the keeper of the dead on earth, is Seb ; hence it is he who kept guard over the body that was buried in the earth. The part of Seb is also assigned to Joseph of Arimathea, who took the body when it was embalmed with a hundred pounds of myrrh and aloes, and made a mummy of, and laid it in his own tomb. The tomb of Seb, the earth (John xix. 38–41), becomes the garden of Joseph ; the " bolts of Seb " are replaced by the great stone that Joseph rolls against the door of the sepulchre (Matt. xxvii. 60), and he who kept guard over the mummy-Osiris in the sepulchre is represented by the guard who watches over the tomb in the history. " Pilate said unto them, Ye have a guard, go your way, make it sure as ye can. So they went and made the sepulchre sure, sealing the stone, the guard being with them " (Matt. xxvii. 66). The guard that is set to keep watch and ward at the sepulchre may be compared with the " wardens of the passages," who are " attendant upon Osiris " in the tomb. These are the powers that safeguard the body or mummy of Osiris and keep off the forces of his adversaries. The Passages are those which lead to the outlet of Rusta in the resurrection (Rit., ch. 17). In the chapter by which one arriveth at Rusta, the deceased has risen again. He says, " I am he who is born in Rusta. Glory is given to me by those who are in their mummied forms in Pa, at the sanctuary of Osiris, whom the guards receive at Rusta when they conduct (the) Osiris through the demesnes of Osiris." In this scene of the resurrection the deceased comes forth triumphant as Osiris risen (ch. 117). The dead are there in mummied forms, and these are received by the guards as they rise and reach the place of egress in Rusta. In the Gospel according to Matthew a watch was set upon the sepulchre ; the guard is spoken of as " the centurion, and they that were with him watching Jesus " (Matt. xxvii. 54). These were watching when the graves were opened and the dead " in their mummied forms " were raised to come forth from the tomb. As nothing occurs in the Gospel except by miracle, the graves are opened by an earthquake for the passages to be made, which passages were very ancient in the geography and pictures of the Egyptian nether-world. The guards, or soldiers, in attendance on Jesus are four in number. At least it is said that they took the garments of the dead body and " made four parts, to every soldier a part " (John xix. 23). These guards correspond to the four guardians of the coffin Hapi, Tuamutef, Kabhsenuf, and Amsu, who watch by the sarcophagus of the dead Osiris, one at each of its four corners. In a German passion-play the four are invincible knights named Dietrich, Hildebrant, Isengrim, and Laurein.

At the time of the death upon the cross there is a resurrection which is not *the* resurrection. This is a general rising of the Manes, not the resurrection of the Christ. "And behold the veil of the sanctuary was rent in twain from the top to the bottom : and the rocks were. rent and the tombs were opened : and many bodies of the saints that had fallen asleep were raised." In short, a general rising must have preceded the personal resurrection of Jesus on the third day after the crucifixion. It is added, however, that the manes who had already risen came forth "out of the tombs after his resurrection" and "appeared unto many." Therefore they stayed in the open tombs a day or two longer in order that he might have the precedence. When Horus rises as a spirit, the Lord of Mehurit, the risen one, is represented by a hawk, and he says, "I am the hawk in the tabernacle, and I pierce through the veil," or, in another lection, through that which is upon the veil. To pierce through the veil of the sanctuary is equivalent to rending the veil of the temple. The hawk is a type of the sun-god in the solar mythos and of the spirit in the eschatology. Thus the veil was pierced or rent asunder when Horus rose in the shape of a divine hawk to become the Lord of heaven. In the Gospel (Matt. xxvii. 51), at the moment when Jesus "yielded up his spirit," it is said, "and behold the veil of the sanctuary was rent in twain from top to bottom : and the earth did quake : and the rocks were rent : and the tombs were opened," and, in brief, this was what the Ritual terms "the day of rending asunder," when the rocks of the Tser hill were opened, which is the day of resurrection in the mysteries of Amenta. The death of Osiris was followed by the saturnalia of Sut, in a reign of misrule and lawlessness which lasted during the five black days or *dies non* of the Egyptian calender when everything was turned topsy-turvy—a saturnalia, which to all appearance, is yet celebrated in Upper Egypt (Frazer, *Golden Bough,* i., p. 231). The mutilation of Osiris in his coffin, the stripping of his corpse and tearing it asunder by Sut, who scattered it piecemeal, is represented by the stripping of the dead body of Jesus whilst it still hung upon the cross, and parting the garments amongst the spoilers. In John's account the crucifixion takes place at the time of the Passover, and the victim of sacrifice in human form is substituted for, and identified with, the Paschal lamb. But, as this version further shows, the death assigned is in keeping with that of the non-human victim. Not a bone of the sufferer was to be broken. This is supposed to be in fulfilment of prophecy. It is said by the Psalmist (xxxiv. 20), "He keepeth all his bones ; not one of them is broken." But this was in strict accordance with the law of totemic tabu. No matter what the type, from bear to lamb, no bone of the sacrificial victim was ever permitted to be broken ; and the only change was in the substitution of the human type for the animal, which had been made already when human Horus became the type of sacrifice instead of the calf or lamb. When the Australian natives sacrificed their little bear, not a bone of it was ever broken ; when the Iroquois sacrificed the white dog, not a bone was broken. This was a common custom, on account of the resurrection, as conceived by the primitive races, and the same is applied to Osiris. Every bone of the skeleton was to remain intact as a basis for the future building. After the murder and mutilation of Osiris in Sekhem, the judgment is executed on the conspirators in the mystery of ploughing the earth on the night of fertilizing the soil with the blood of the betrayer Sut and his associates. This is done before the great divine chiefs in Tattu! In the Gospels (Matt. xxvii. 6) the chief priests take the place of the divine chiefs in the mystery of ploughing the earth and fertilizing or manuring it with the blood of the wicked: they buy the potter's field, and this was called Aceldama, the field of blood. The field of blood here bought with the price paid for the betrayal takes the place of the field that is fertilized with blood in the Ritual. In the Acts it is Judas himself, not the "chief priests," who "purchased a field with the reward of his iniquity." According to this version, Judas fertilizes or manures the field with his own blood, as does the betrayer Sut, on the night of fertilizing the field in Tattu. When, in his resurrection, Jesus reappeared to the disciples, they thought it an apparition. This it should have been if the life had been human, the death actual, the story true. In the Egyptian, however, the day of reappearance is termed the "day of apparition"; but reappearing = apparition is not necessarily manifesting as the human ghost. The Christ as Horus was not a human ghost reappearing on the earth; and Horus the pure spirit, the typical divine son of god, the reappearing one, might have denied being a phantom or a ghost, for he would not be manifesting to men, but to other characters in the religious drama. This being denied on behalf of the divinity, the carnalizers then had recourse to their human physics to illustrate the denial by making the risen Christ corporeal. In John's account, which is always the nearest to the Egyptian original, there is no denial of the ghost theory, no declaration that the risen one is not a spirit but a veritable human body of flesh and bone. He merely "showed unto them his hands and side," as Horus might have shown his wounds, and no doubt did show them, in the mysteries—the wounds that were inflicted by Sut. In fact, when Sut has wounded Horus in the eye, he shows the wound to Ra, his father (Rit., ch. 112).

When Horus, or the Egypto-gnostic Jesus, rises in the sepulchre on coming forth to day it is in the semi-corporeal form of the Karest-mummy that is not yet become pure spirit and therefore has not yet ascended to his father in the hawk-headed likeness of Ra. This figure can be studied in the tomb as that of Amsu. The scene of the resurrection is in Amenta, the earth of eternity, the earth of the manes, not on the earth of mortals. It is here the risen Horus breathes the breath of his new life into the sleeping dead to raise them from their coffins, sepulchres and cells. When the Egyptian Christ, or Karest, rose up from the tomb as Amsu-Horus it was in a likeness of the buried mummy, as regards the shape, with one arm loosened from the swathes or bandages. But this resurrection was *not corporeal on earth.* Osiris had been transformed into Horus, and although the mummy-shape was still retained, the texture had been transubstantialized; the *corpus* was transfigured into the glorious body of the Sahu or divine mummy. The mystery of transubstantiation was not understood by the writers of the Gospels, who did not know whether Jesus reappeared in the body or in spirit, as a man or as a god. They carried off all they could, but were not in possession of the secret wisdom which survived amongst the Egypto-gnostics. They wrote as carnalizers of the Christ. It follows that the risen Jesus of the canonical Gospels is not a reality in either world; neither in the sphere of time, nor as divine Horus transfigured into spirit. 'Tis but a misappropriated type; the spurious spectre of an impossible Christ; a picture of nobody. The Christian history fails in rendering Horus as an apparition of Osiris. When Horus came from Sekhem he had left the earthly body behind him in the sepulchre, and was greeted as pure spirit by the glorified ones who rejoiced to see how *he continued walking* as the risen Horus, he who "steppeth onward through eternity" (Rit., ch. 42). Jesus in this character comes forth from the tomb in the same body that was buried and still is human, flesh and bones and all. Thus, as a phantom, he is a counterfeit; a carnalized ghost, upon the resurrection of which no real future for the human spirit ever could or ever will be permanently based. A corpse that has not made the transformation from the human Horus into Horus the pure spirit offers no foundation for belief in any known natural fact. Horus in his resurrection is described as being once more set in motion. At this point he says, "I am not known, but I am one who knoweth thee. I am not to be grasped, but I am one who graspeth thee. I am Horus, prince of eternity, a fire before your faces, which inflameth your hearts towards me. I am master of my throne, and I pass onwards." "The path I have opened is the present time, and I have set myself free from all evil" (ch. 42, Renouf). But when he is transubstantialized, it is said of the deceased in his resurrection: "The gods shall come in touch with him, for he shall have become as one of them." Now let us see how this was converted into history. Jesus is the prince of eternity in opposition to Satan, Sut, or Judas, the prince of this world. In his resurrection he is supposed to have opened the pathway from the tomb historically and for the first time some 1800 or 1900 years ago. When he rises from the dead he is unknown to the watchers, but he knows them. Mary knew not that the risen form was Jesus. He is not to be grasped, saying, "Touch me not," or do not grasp me, "for I am not yet ascended unto my Father" (John xx. 14, 17). On the way to Emmaus Jesus appears and inflames the hearts of the disciples towards him, after calling them "slow of heart," and "they said one to another, Was not our heart burning within us?" (Luke xxiv. 13, 32). Horus had opened a path from the tomb as the sun-god in the mythos, the divine son of God in the eschatology, and he ascended to his father and took his seat upon the throne of which he had become the lord and master. So Jesus goes on his way "unto the mountain," where he had appointed to meet his followers (Matt. xxviii. 16). The mountain in the Ritual is the mount of rebirth in heaven, whether of the sun-god or of the enduring spirit.

The change from bodily death to future life in spirit was acted as a transformation-scene in the mysteries of the resurrection. The mummy-Osiris was an effigy of death. The Sahu-mummy

Amsu-Horus is an image of the glorious body into which Osiris transubstantiated to go forth from Sekhem as pure spirit. It is the mummy in this second stage that is of primary import. First of all the dead body was smeared over with unguents and thus glorified. During the process of anointing it was said, "O Asar (the deceased) the thick oil which is poured upon thee furnishes thy mouth with life" (Budge, "The Mummy," p. 163). It is also said that the anointing is done to *give sight to the eyes, hearing to the ears, sense of smell to the nostrils and utterance to the mouth.* To embalm the body thus was to karas it and the embalmment was a mode of making the typical Christ as the Anointed. Thus the mortal Horus was invested with the glory of the only God-begotten Son. Now this making of the Krst, or mummy-Christ, after the Egyptian fashion is apparent in the Gospels. When the woman brings the alabaster cruse of precious ointment to the house of Simon and pours it on the head of Jesus he says, "In that she poured this ointment upon my body, she did it *to prepare me for my burial*" (Matt. xxvi. 12). She was making the Christ as the anointed-mummy previous to interment. After the description of the crucifixion it is said that Nicodemus came and brought a "mixture of myrrh and aloes, about a hundred pound" and "they took the body of Jesus and bound it in linen cloths with the spices as the custom of the Jews is to bury" (John xix. 39, 40). This again denotes the making of the Karest-mummy = the Christ. Moreover, it is the dead mummy in one version and it is the living body in the other which is anointed, just as Horus was anointed with the exceedingly precious Antu ointment, or oil, that was poured upon his head and face to represent his glory.

The two Mertæ-sisters are the watchers over the dead Osiris. They are also the mourners who weep over him when he is anointed and prepared for his burial. It is said of Osiris that he was triumphant over his adversaries on the night when Isis lay watching in tears over her brother Osiris (ch. 18). But the Mertæ-sisters both watch and both weep over the dead body. In the vignettes to the Ritual one of the two stands at the head and one at the feet of the body on the bier. These two mourners, weepers, anointers, or embalmers, appear in the Gospels as two different women. According to John it was Mary the sister of Martha who anointed Jesus for his burial. And as these are the two divine sisters in historic guise we ought to find one at the head of the victim and one at the feet, as, in fact, we do so find them. In the account furnished by Luke it is said that *the woman who stood behind at the feet of Jesus weeping* "*began to wet his feet with her tears, and wiped them with the hair of her head*" (Luke vii. 38). No name is given for the woman who was "a sinner," which seems to denote the other Mary called Magdalene. Matthew also omits the name of the woman with an alabaster cruse or flask. In keeping with the mythos this other one of the two Mertæ-sisters should be Martha, but the point is that the woman with the cruse does not anoint the feet of Jesus. She poured the ointment "*upon his head as he sat at meat*" (Matt. xxvi. 7). Thus we see there are two different women who anoint Jesus, one at the head, one at the feet, even as the two divine sisters of Osiris called the Mertæ, or watchers, stand at the head and feet of Osiris, when preparing him for his burial, or watching in tears, like Isis, the prototype of the woman who never ceased to kiss the feet of Jesus since the time when he had come into the house (Luke vii. 45-6). We have identified the other sister Nephthys, the mistress of the house, with the housekeeper Martha, and as Nephthys also carries the bowl or vase upon her head, this may account for the vessel of alabaster that was carried by the "woman" who poured the ointment on the head of Jesus, whereas Mary the sister of Martha poured it on his feet. Martha is one of the two Mertæ by name. In the Egyptian mythos the two Mertæ are Isis, the dear lover of Horus the Lord, bowed at his feet, and Nephthys mourning at his head (Naville, *Totdenbuch*, V. I., Kap. 17, A. g. and B. b.).

The Karast-mummy was the body of the dead in Osiris who were prepared by human hands to meet their Lord in spirit when wrapt in the seamless vesture of a thousand folds, which was typically the robe of immortality, when they were baptized and purified and anointed with the unction of Horus taken from the tree of life. The process of preparing, embalming and Christifying the mummy obviously survives in the Chrisome or krisum of the Roman Catholic Church. The chrisome itself is properly a white cloth which the "minister of baptism places on the head of the newly-anointed child." The chrisom as ointment is made of oil and balm. In the instructions for private baptism it is charged that the minister shall put the white vesture, commonly called a chrisome, upon the child. The chrism-cloth is still the vesture of immortality, for if the infant dies within a month after birth, the chrisome is its shroud and the chrisom-child becomes an image in survival of the Karast-mummy in Amenta.

Let it be assumed that to all appearance the resurrection in Amenta is corporeal. The human Horus, or *the* Osiris, who has passed through death, and been laid out as the mummy in the Tuat, still retains the form of the mummy that was made on earth. The difference is in Horus having risen to his feet and freed his right arm from the burial bandages. Indeed, the dead were *reincorporated* in Amenta as the Sahu-mummy. The Egyptian word Sahu signifies to *incorporate*, and in this physical-looking form they were reincorporated for the resurrection *in the earth of eternity*. Amsu had made a change in rising to his feet, but was not yet the Horus glorified with the soul of Ra; therefore he has not yet ascended to the father. To the sense of sight he is corporeal still, and has not transubstantiated into spirit. When he does, the hawk or Menat will alight to abide upon him and he will assume the likeness of his father Ra, the bird-headed holy spirit. It is the body-soul that rises *in* Amenta which has to suffer purgatorial rebirth before it can become "pure spirit" as the Ritual of the resurrection has it, to attain eternal life. So far as reincorporation of the soul in Sahu-shape could go, *the resurrection is corporeal*. Yet this was only a dramatic mode of representation in the mystery of transubstantiation, which included several acts. It is in this character of Amsu-Horus reincorporated as the Sahu-mummy issuing from the tomb that Jesus is described by Luke: "See my hands and my feet, that it is I myself" (ch. xxiv. 39). In the absence of the gnosis the reincorporation in Amenta led to the doctrine of a physical resurrection at the last day *on this earth*. The power of resurrection was imparted by

Ra, the father in spirit, to the anointed and beloved son.   And Horus is said to be the "*bringer of the breaths*" to his "followers" (Rit., chapters on breathing 54, 55, 56, 57, 58, 59).   Horus as he issues forth to day, in his resurrection, comes to give the breath of life to the manes in Amenta, saying, "I give the breezes to the faithful dead amid those who eat bread."   This chapter of the Ritual follows the decease of Horus, which is equivalent to the crucifixion of Jesus.   In this the speaker says, "I have come to an end on behalf of the Lord of heaven.   I am written down sound of heart, and I rest at the table of my father Osiris" (ch. 70).   It is also said in the Rubric, "if this scripture is known upon earth he (the Osiris) will come forth to day ; he will have power to walk on the earth amid the living."   Jesus in the Gospel has "come to an end for the Lord of heaven."   He likewise manifests on earth "amid the living."   He gives "the breezes to the faithful dead" when he breathes on them, saying, "Receive ye of the holy spirit."

It is "the women" in the Gospels who announce the resurrection and proclaim that Jesus has left the tomb.   According to Matthew "the women" are "Mary Magdalene and the other Mary," who "ran to bring the disciples word" (xxviii. 1, 8).   According to Mark (xvi. 1) the women were Mary Magdalene and Mary (the mother) of James, and Salome, who discovered that Jesus had arisen but were afraid to make it known.   Here it is Mary Magdalene, who proclaims the resurrection.   It is Mary Magdalene in John (xx. 1, 2) who first announces that the Lord has arisen.   Luke xxiv. 10 has it that "Mary Magdalene and Joanna, and Mary (mother) of James and other women" first found the sepulchre empty and "told these things unto the apostles." These conflicting accounts agree in the one essential point, that it was the woman or the women who proclaimed the resurrection, and this is as it should be according to the data in the Ritual.   When the deceased comes forth from the tomb and reaches the horizon of the resurrection he exclaims, "I rise as a god amongst men. *The goddesses and the women proclaim me when they see me !*"   It is the goddesses and the women who see the risen Horus first and proclaim him to the others.   Usually the women and the female deities are identical as the two divine sisters who are represented in the Gospels by the two Marys, but in some of the scenes there are other women in attendance as well as the two sisters-Mertae.   Now, as the two Marys are originally goddesses we have the same group of goddesses and "the women" (in Luke xxiv. 10) as in the Ritual (79, 11) and both agree in proclaiming the resurrection and hailing the risen Lord with jubilation.   This chapter contains all the data necessary to construct the story of the "historic" resurrection in which the Christ arises as a god amongst men, and is proclaimed by the women.   The allusions in the Ritual are very brief.   The style of the writing is economical as that of the lapidary.   The Egyptians neither used nor tolerated many words ; verbosity was prohibited by one of their commandments.   But these allusions refer to a drama that was represented in the mysteries, the characters and scenes of which were all as well known as are those in the Christian Gospels when the play is performed at Ammergau.   And this statement, made at the moment of his resurrection—"I rise as a god amongst men. The goddesses and the women proclaim me when they see me "—contained a germ that was pregnant with a whole chapter of the future Gospel "history."

In the Gospel according to John there is but one woman weeping at the tomb. This was Mary Magdalene, who corresponds to the first great mother Apt, she who bore the seven sons that preceded the solar Horus of the pre-Osirian cult. She, like Anup, lived on in the burial-place with those that waited for the resurrection. She is called Apt, the "mistress of divine protections." Apt is portrayed as kindler of the light for the deceased in the dark of death (ch. 137, Vig. Papyrus of Nebseni). Thus the old first bringer to rebirth is the kindler of a light in the sepulchre. Mary Magdalene who takes her place comes to the tomb, "early, while it was yet dark," and finds the stone moved away and light enough to see by kindled in the tomb. Isis also was a form of the great mother alone. She is mentioned singly as watching in tears over her brother Osiris by night in Rekhet (Rit., ch. 18). So Mary Magdalene is described as "standing without at the tomb weeping" alone as the one woman. But, according to Matthew, there were two women at the tomb. "Mary Magdalene was there and the other Mary, sitting over against the sepulchre (ch. xxvii. 61). And in the Osirian representation Isis and Nephthys are the two women called the "two mourners who weep and wail over Osiris in Rekhet" (ch. 1). Isis and Nephthys, the two divine sisters, are the two women at the sepulchre of Osiris. They are portrayed, one at the head the other at the feet of the mummy. They sing the song of the resurrection as a magical means of raising their dear one from the dead. A form of this is to be found in the evocations addressed to the dead Osiris by the two sisters, who say: "Thy two sisters are near thee, protecting thy funeral bed, calling thee in weeping, thou who art prostrate on thy funeral bed" (*Records of the Past*, vol. 2, pp. 121-126). Horus rises in his Ithyphallic form with the sign of virility erect; the member that was restored by Isis when the body had been torn in pieces by Sut. This may account for the Phallus found in the Roman Catacombs as a figure of the resurrection, which, if the Gospel story had been true, would denote the phallus of an historic Jew, instead of the typical member of Horus whose word was thus manifested with pubescent power in the person of the risen Amsu.

In the Osirian legend there are three women, or goddesses, who especially attend upon Osiris to prepare him for his burial. These are the great mother, Neith, and the two divine sisters, Isis and Nephthys. It was related in the ancient version that Neith arrayed the mummy in his grave-clothes for the funerary chamber called "the good house," the house in which the dead were embalmed and swathed in pure white linen. This is described in the Book of the Dead (ch. 172) when it is said to the Osiris N, "Thou receivest a bandage of the finest linen from the hands of the attendant of Ra." The raiment put on Osiris by Neith was said to be woven by the two watchers in the tomb. In the preparation of Osiris for his burial, the ointment or unguents were compounded and applied by Neith. It was these that were to preserve the mummy from decay and dissolution. These three may be compared with the three Marys in the Gospels, thus : Neith, the great mother = Mary Magdalene, the great mother ; Isis = Mary ; Nephthys = Martha. There was also a group of seven ministrants in attendance at the birth of Horus or rebirth of Osiris. These, in the astronomical mythology, were constellated in the female hippopotamus—our Great Bear—as those who ministered " of their substance " to the young " bull of the seven cows " (Rit., ch. 141–3), which were seven forms of the great mother, seven Fates or Hathors in the birthplace, from the time when this was in the year of the Great Bear, with the seven in attendance on the child. In the legend related by Luke, the whole of the seven women who ministered of their substance to Jesus (or the sacrificial victim), appear to have been grouped together with the dead body in the sepulchre. " Now they were Mary Magdalene and Joanna and Mary the (mother) of James and the other women with them " (Luke xxiv. 10). These are called " the women which had come with them out of Galilee." They are also termed " certain women of our company " (ch. xxiv. 22). The number is not specified ; this being one of those sundries that were safest if left vague. Thus we find the foremost Great Mother at the tomb ; the two divine sisters ; the three women with Neith included, and as we suggest, the company of ministrants, who were the seven mothers, seven Hathors, seven Meri, or seven women n three different versions of the historic resurrection.

In the version given by Matthew there is but one divine visitant at the tomb, in addition to the two women here called the two Marys. As the Sabbath day began to dawn " came Mary Magdalene and the other Mary to see the sepulchre. And behold there was a great earthquake ; for an angel of the Lord descended from heaven and came and rolled away the stone and sat upon it. His appearance was as lightning, and his raiment was as white as snow " (Matt. xxviii. 2, 3). The angel that rolls the stone away from the tomb in the Gospel for the buried Christ to rise corresponds to the god Shu in the Ritual, who is described as uplifting the heaven when the god Atum or Horus comes forth from the sarcophagus and passes through the gate of the rock to approach the land of spirits. It is said the gate of Tser is where Shu stands when he lifts up the heaven (Rit., 17, 56–7). The Tser was the rock of the horizon in which the dead body of Osiris was laid for its repose when it was buried in Annu. Shu is not only the uplifter of heaven or raiser of the gravestone, he is also the opener of the sepulchre as the bringer of breath to the newly awakened soul.

The Egyptian knew well enough that his body would remain where it was left when buried. For that it had been mummified. His difficulty was concerning his soul, and how to get this freed from its surroundings in the speediest fashion and the most enduring form. The Ritual speaks of the "shade," the "soul" and "spirit" as being in the tomb with the mummy-Osiris who rises from stage to stage according to the evolution of his spirit from the bonds of matter. Chief of these are the body-soul and spirit-Ka. The deceased, when in the tomb, is thus addressed, " Let the way be opened to thy Ka and to thy Soul, O glorified one ; thou shalt not be imprisoned by those who have the custody of souls and spirits and who shut up the shades of the dead" (Rit., ch. 92). Thus the body-soul and Ka made their appearance in the tomb previously to being blended in the manifesting soul, called the double of the dead which constituted the risen Horus, and which was the only one of the seven souls that bore the human lineaments (Rit., ch. 178). The god who rises again is described in the Egyptian litany of Ra (58) as "he who *raises his soul and conceals his body*." His name is that of Herba, he who raises the soul. The body being hidden as Osiris, the soul was raised as Horus. Hence, as it is said, the mummy of Osiris was not found in the sepulchre. In one sense the body vanished by transubstantiation into spirit. The night of the evening meal on which the body was eaten sacramentally is called "the night of hiding him who is supreme of attributes" (Rit., ch. 18). The body was eaten typically as a mode of converting matter into spirit; this was the motive of the eucharist from the beginning when the mother was the victim eaten. In one of the texts cited by Birch concerning the burial of the god Osiris at Abydos, it is said the sepulchral chamber was searched but *the body was not found. The "Shade, it was found"* (Proceedings Bib. Archy., Dec. 2, 1884, p. 45). The shade was a primitive type of the soul; it is the shadow of an earthly body projected as it were into Amenta, and was portrayed in some of the vignettes lying black upon the ground of that earth, like the shadow of the human body on this earth. In Marcion's account of the resurrection there is no body to be found in the tomb; only the phantom, or the shade, was visible there. So in the Johannine version (ch. xx. 17) the buried body of Jesus is missing; the *Shade* is present in the tomb; but this is of a texture that must not be touched. Like Amsu it neither represents the dead *corpus* nor the spirit perfected. It is quite possible that we get a glimpse of the "Ka" as that personage in the sepulchre described by Mark, who relates that when the women entered the tomb they "saw a young man sitting on the right side, arrayed in a white robe and they were amazed" (ch. xvi. 5). According to the gnosis, the Ka had here taken the place of the missing mummy which had risen, or as the Egyptians said, Osiris had made his transformation into Amsu-Horus. According to Luke, when the women came to the tomb with their spices and ointments they "*found not the body of the Lord Jesus*." But, "behold, two men stood by them in dazzling apparel," who said to them "why seek ye the Living (One) among the dead?" (Luke xxiv. 5). These, in the Johannine Gospel, are "two angels in white, sitting one at the head and one at the feet, where the body of Jesus had lain" (John xx. 12). Now, if the "young man" represented the Ka-image in the human form we may suppose the "two men" to have been the soul and spirit called the Ka and the soul of the glorified, that were portrayed in the Egyptian sepulchre and which are to be read of in the Ritual. One of the numerous Egypto-gnostic scriptures which at one time were extant has lately been discovered in the fragment of a gospel assigned to Peter. This from the orthodox point of view is considered to be "docetic"—which is another name for non-historical. From this we learn that in the resurrection " the heavens opened and two men descended thence with great radiance" "and both the young men entered" the tomb. Two men entered and three figures issued forth. "They behold three men coming out of the tomb, and two of them were supporting a third, and a cross was following them ; and the heads of the two men reached to the heaven, but the head of him who was being led along by them was higher than the heavens." And they heard a voice from heaven which said, " Hast thou preached to them that are asleep?" And a response of "Yea" was heard from the cross. This has no parallel in the canonical Gospels, but, as Egyptian, it is the scene of Atum (Ptah or Osiris) rising again in or with the Tat-cross and coming forth supported by "his two hands" or his two sons Hu and Sau. Also, in the pre-Osirian mythos, Hu and Sau, the two sons of Atum-Ra, support their father when he issues from the tomb and makes his exit from Amenta. These are two young men who are in the retinue of Ra, and who accompany their father in his resurrection daily (Rit., ch. 17).

To a spiritualist the doctrines of the fleshly faith are ghastly in their grossness. The foundation of the creed was laid in a physical resurrection of the body ; and the flesh and blood of that body were to be eaten in the eucharistic rite as a physical mode of incorporating the divine. It is true the doctrine of transubstantiation was added to gild the dead body for eating. But the historical rendering of the matter necessitated the substitution of the physical for the spiritual interpretation. The founders only carried off the carnalized Horus, the Karast-mummy, for their Christ. They raised him from the grave corporeally ; whereas the Egyptians left that type of Osiris in matter, that image of Horus on earth in the tomb. Horus did rise again, but not in matter. He spiritualized to become the superhuman or divine Horus. The Egyptians did not exhume the fleshly body, living or dead, to eat it with the expectation of assimilating Horus to themselves or becoming Horus by assimilating the blood and body of his physical substance. This was what was done by the Christian Sarkolatræ. Hooker asks: " Doth any man doubt that even from the flesh of Christ (eaten sacramentally) our very bodies do receive that life which shall make them glorious at the latter day?" This was an inevitable result of making the Christ historical, and of continuing the carnalized Horus in a region beyond the tomb by means of a physical resurrection of the dead. The Christians having carried off the *Corpus Christi*, which the Egyptians transubstantiated in the sepulchre, have never since known what to do with it. But as the Christ rose again in the material body and ascended with it into heaven, leaving no mummy in the tomb, they can but nurse the delusive hope that a physical saviour may redeem the physical corpse, so that those who believe may be raised by him at the last day and follow him bodily into paradise. In this way the foundations of the faith were corporeally laid. Also in this way the pre-extant "types" of the Christ are supposed to have been realized : the fore-shadows substantialized, and Horus the Lord who had been the anointed Christ, the immortal Son of God in the Egyptian religion for at least ten thousand years, was at last converted into a Judean peasant as the unique personage of the Gospels, and the veritable saviour of the world.

It is not alleged in the Gospel history that the victim was torn piecemeal as well as crucified. And yet the bread which represents his body in the eucharistic meal is religiously torn to pieces in commemoration of the event that does not occur in the Gospels; a performance that is suggestive of those poor Norway rats which lose their lives in trying to cross the waters where there was a passage once by land. Jesus is not torn in pieces, but Osiris was. When Sut did battle with Un-Nefer, the Good Being, he tore the body into fragments, and that is the sacrifice still commemorated in the Christian eucharist. Under one of his many titles in the Ritual Osiris is "the Lord of resurrections." But this does not merely denote the periodicity of the resurrection. There were several resurrections of the god in matter and in spirit. Osiris rose again to life in the returning waters of the Nile. He rose again in the renewal of vegetation represented by Horus the branch of endless years; and as the papyrus shoot. He rose again upon the third day, in the moon; or as the sun, the supreme soul of life in physical nature. These were followed in the eschatology by the god who rose again from Amenta as Horus in spirit; as the Bennu-Osiris, or as Ra the holy spirit. Jesus is likewise portrayed as the Lord of resurrections. He is said to have risen on the third day; also on the fourth day, after being three nights in the earth; also after forty days, when he ascended into heaven from the mount; and when he rose up from the dead with power to pass where doors were shut, and to impart the Holy Spirit (John xx. 19) to his followers, the same as Horus in the Ritual (ch. 1). The first act of Horus in his resurrection is to free his right arm from the bandage of the mummy. The next is to cast aside the seamless swathe in which the body had been wrapped for burial. Now, after so much of the mythos has been established in place of the "history," it will not be so very incredible if we suggest a mythical and recognizably Kamite origin for an episode in the Gospel according to Mark which has no record elsewhere. When Jesus is arrested in the garden or enclosure of Gethsemane preparatory to his death and resurrection it is said that: "A certain young man followed him having a linen cloth cast about him over his naked body; and they laid hold on him; but he left the linen cloth and fled naked" (Mark xiv. 51). Such a statement standing alone, purposeless and unexplained, is perfectly maniacal as history; clearly it is a fragment of something that is otherwise out of sight. The Greek word sindon represents the Egyptian shenti, a linen garment which is derived from shena, a name for the flax from which the fine linen of the mummy was made. The shenti is a linen tunic. The mummy-swathe was also made from shena, and this was the garment woven without a seam. Therefore we infer that the "young man" was a form of the manes risen with the bandages about him, and that when he "left the linen-cloth and fled naked" he had made his transformation into spirit like any other of the mummies.

So soon as the risen Lord had ascended into heaven from the summit of Mount Olivet, after the space of forty days, the disciples are described as meeting in the "upper chamber" with Mary, the mother of Jesus, and his brethren who were gathered together for the purpose of prayer (Acts i. 13, 14). Now, "the upper chamber" was the cubiculum attached to the sepulchre, both in Rome and Egypt, for the meeting of the bereaved relatives and the solemnizing of the mourning for the dead. One of the inscriptions in the catacombs calls it "the upper chamber to celebrate the memory of the dead" ("Cubiculum superius ad confrequentandum memoriam quiescentium." De Rossi, *Roma Sotteranea*, 3, 474.) There were two funerary chambers in the Egyptian sepulchre; one was for the mummy and one for the Ka. Also the Ka-chamber was without a door, it being held that the risen spirit could pass through matter without a doorway. This is repeated in the Gospel according to John. When Jesus came into the room, "the doors being shut," and stood in the midst of the disciples, it was in the character of the Ka or double of the dead endowed with power to rise again, to pass through matter, and reappear to the living. The same dual figure is to be found in the pre-Christian catacombs with the subterranean sepulchre for the mummy or corpse beneath, and the chamber above which was known as the *cubiculum* or *cubiculum memoriæ*. It was the pre-Christian custom for the relatives and friends of the deceased to meet together in this upper chamber at the funeral feast, or eucharistic meal, for the purpose of celebrating the resurrection from the dead, and of making their offerings and oblations to the ancestral spirits in the mortuary sacrament.

The last scene in the personal "history" coincides with the ascent of Atum-Horus from Amenta, and the soul ascending into paradise, called the Aarru-fields. Jesus, in his final disappearance from the earth, ascends the typical mount, called Olivet, at the end of forty days. "And when he had said these things as they were looking, he was taken up; and a cloud received him out of their sight. And while they were looking steadfastly into heaven as he went, behold, two men stood by them in white apparel which also said, Ye men of Galilee, why stand ye looking into heaven?" (Acts i. 9–11). The ascent of Jesus from the mount into the clouds of heaven can be traced twice over, in the two different categories, mythical and eschatological. It was made "from the mount called Olivet." This, we repeat, was Mount Bakhu, the mount of the olive-tree of dawn. The ascent at the tree was made each day, and also yearly in the annual round, by the god in his resurrection from Amenta. Thus the sun-god in the mythos makes his ascent by the Mount of Olives, or the olive-tree of dawn, when "approaching to the land of spirits in heaven" (Rit., ch. 17). In this character Nefer-Tum the young sun-god is the Egyptian Jesus risen from the northern door of the tomb, or the northern gate of the Tuat. In the phase of eschatology it is the risen soul upon its upward journey to the circumpolar paradise "north of the olive-tree" where the eternal city was eventually attained. The olive (Bakhu) also figures in the eschatology as well as in the astronomical mythology. "He who dwelleth in the olive-tree" is a name of Horus in the burial-place; and in his resurrection the Osiris says, when coming forth from the

judgment-hall, " I pass on to a place that is north of the olive-tree."
Or it might be the fig-tree at the meeting-place of Jesus with
Nathanael. It was no earthly mount on which the typical teacher
gave instruction to the four called fishermen or to the twelve as
reapers of the harvest. It was the mountain of Amenta and the
double earth that we have traced all through the Ritual called the
mount of resurrection and of glory. This, in the mythos, was the
mount of the green olive-tree of the Egyptian dawn and a figure of
the ascent to heaven in the eschatology. Up this mount the risen
manes attained the circle of the divine powers attached to Osiris
(Rit., ch. 1 in the older MSS.). And up this mount the solar god, as
Atum-Horus, makes his ascent to heaven, termed the land of spirits ;
that is, from the Mount of Olives, the track which is here followed
by the canonical Jesus (Rit., ch. 17). Moreover, in his coming forth
to day and making the ascent to heaven, Atum was attended by his
two sons, Hu and Sau, who are said to accompany their father daily.
The copy, in this instance, is so close to the original that it may be
possible to identify the " two men in white apparel " who say to the
disciples, " Ye men of Galilee, why stand ye gazing into heaven ? "
(Acts i. 10, 11). Those two men in white apparel correspond to Hu
and Sau in the Ritual (ch. 17, 60–64) who accompany the sun-god in
his resurrection from the place of burial in Amenta. In the vague
phase, Jesus disappears into a cloud and passes out of sight. In the
Ritual of the resurrection the departed spirit is received with greetings
by the lords of eternity, who open their arms to embrace and bid him
welcome to the table of his father at the festival that is to be eternal
in the heavens.

THE RESURRECTION FROM AMENTA, OR COMING FORTH TO DAY.

In Annu shines the ray
Of resurrection on the judgment-day.

The dark Amenta quakes
As with diviner dawn Osiris wakes

And with his key [1] hath risen
To free the arm of Amsu from its prison.

Out of our mortal night
He suddenly flashed and fleshed his lance of light.

Jaw-broken lies the black
Grim Boar, mouth open, with its fangs turned back.

Egypt the living Word
Of the eternal truth once more is heard ;

Nor shall her reign be o'er
While language lasts till time shall be no more.

---

[1] The Ankh-key of life.

THE SAYINGS OF JESUS.

Of late years certain Sayings of Jesus or Iη, as the name is abbreviated, written in Greek on the leaf of a papyrus-book, have been discovered in the rubbish-heaps of Oxyrhynchus. These were at once assumed to be the sayings of Jesus, an historic Jew. The present object is to prove that all such *Logia* were the sayings of him who is here set forth as the Egypto-gnostic Jesus, who had many types and names but no individual form of historic personality.

The Book of the Dead, or Ritual of the resurrection, chiefly represents the mysteries of Amenta in the Osirian phase of the religious drama. But there is an older stratum than that of the Osirian eschatology. The Sayer of the Kamite *Logia Kuriaka* is identifiable in at least three different Egyptian religions ; in one as the Osirian Horus who predominates by name in the Ritual ; in another as Iu, the Sa or son of Iusāas and Atum-Ra ; and a third as Iu-em-hetep, the son of Ptah. Two of these titles of the typical Egyptian "sayer" are cited in the "Festal dirge" when it is said, " I have heard the words of Iu-em-hetep and Hartatef. It is said in their sayings,". some of which sayings are then quoted. These two answer to the Horus and Jesus of the Egypto-gnostics, which are two names of the same original character that was Egyptian from the root. The so-called "*Christian* eschatology" may be said to have had its origin in the mysteries of Ptah at Memphis. So far as known, it was there the doctrine of immortality was first taught ; there that the Son of God was figured in the act of issuing from the mortal mummy as a living spirit. It was likewise there the teacher of the religious mysteries was first impersonated as the sayer, Iu-em-hetep, who, as Iu the coming Su, was the son of Ptah.

Iu as a form of Tum, proclaims himself to be the Sayer in the Ritual (ch. 82). He says : "*I have come forth with the tongue of Ptah and the throat of Hathor that I may record the words of my father, Tum, with my mouth which draweth to itself the spouse of Seb.*" That is the mother on earth who was Isis in the Osirian mythos, and Hathor-Iusāas in the cult of Tum or Atum-Ra. The speaker here is Horus as Iu the coming Su, or son, who in Egyptian is *Iu-su*, or *Iusa*, the child of Iusāas, the consort of Atum-Ra. This sayer as Iu, the Su or son in one character, is Tum himself as father in the other. As Ra the father he is the author of the sayings ; as Iu the son (Iusu) he is the utterer of the sayings "with his mouth" or in person on the earth as the heir of Seb. To the Egyptians "the words of Tum" were the teachings of an everlasting gospel of truth, law, justice and right, "not to be altered is that which Tum hath uttered" (Rit., ch. 78) by the mouth of the sayer, Iu-em-hetep, or by the pen of the writer, Taht-Aan. Thus we can identify Tum or Atum-Ra as the author of the sayings which are to be spoken on earth by God the Son. Tum was the earlier name of Atum-Ra, when the character was that of child-Horus, or the infant Tum, and the sayings together with the sayer were pre-Osirian. In other words the "sayer" is Iu-em-hetep, the prince of peace in the cult of Annu, whom we trace back to the time of Ptah as the Egyptian Jesus. Hence this 82nd chapter is the one by which the manes is said to "assume the form of Ptah" in the course of becoming a pure and perfect spirit.

Upon this line of descent, distinguished from the Osirian, Ptah represented the grandfather of the gods ; Atum the father, and Iu the Su, the ever-coming son as Iu-em-hetep, the son of Ptah at Memphis, and the son of Atum at Annu. It was Ptah, the opener of the nether-earth, who made the resurrection of the manes possible that was acted in the mysteries of Amenta. And Iu the Su came to say what he had seen and had to tell as witness for the father (Rit., ch. 86), that is, as the "sayer" to whom the sayings were attributed. Hence the speaker tells us that he comes with "the tongue of Ptah" "and the throat of Hathor" to record the words of his father Tum with his own mouth, or as the sayer who was reborn at Annu as Iusu, or Iusa of Hathor-Iusãas, she who was great with Iusa, the son of Atum-Ra, and grandson of Ptah.

The "sayings" may be divided and differentiated in two categories corresponding to the two characters of the double-Horus, the child of twelve years, and Horus the adult of thirty years ; Horus the afflicted one who suffered and died and was buried, and Horus who rose again as the demonstrator of eternal life in his resurrection from the dead. At first child-Horus was the word-made-flesh as Logos of the mother. This was Hathor-Iusãas in relation to Atum-Ra (Rit., ch. 82). Next he was the word-made-truth as sayer for the father and teacher of the greater mysteries. Thus there are two classes of the sayings—those of the childhood and those of the adultship ; those that pertain to the earth of Seb and those that are uttered in Amenta the earth of eternity. It is said in the Ritual that the words of Taht are "written in the two earths," the earth of Seb or time, and the earth of eternity or Amenta (Renouf and Naville, ch. 183). So the sayings were uttered by Horus, Tum, Iu, or Jesus, in the double earth of time, and of eternity. It is also said of certain sayings in "Pistis Sophia" (or Books of the Saviour, 390, Mead), "Jesus spake these words unto his disciples in the midst of Amenta," whence they went forth three by three to the four points of heaven to preach the gospel of the kingdom. This likewise was in the earth of eternity, *versus the earth of time*. But, whether the god be represented as the heavenly father by Ptah at Memphis, by Atum-Ra at Annu, or by Osiris at Abydos, the infant was Horus or Heru the lord by name, who was the only lord as a little child. Iu, Iusu, Iusa, Tum, Aten, Sekari, Iu-em-hetep, are but titles of Horus the lord of the *Logia Kuriaka* who became the "Sayer" as the Egypto-gnostic Jesus, Iu-Su, the ever-coming Messianic son.

Now, amongst the gods of Egypt that were canonized as Christian saints the deity Tum has been converted into the Apostle Thomas. The Gospel according to Thomas is also known to have existed in several forms, some of which are yet extant in the Gospels of the Infancy, assumed to be the childhood of an historic Christ. Hippolytus cites one of these as a Gospel of the Nasseni. He says they hand down an explicit passage occurring in the Gospel inscribed "according to Thomas," expressing themselves thus : "He who seeks me (the higher soul) will find me in children from seven years old ; for there concealed I shall, in the fourteenth year (or æon), be made manifest" (Refut. v. 7).   This passage contains the doctrine of the double-Horus, the Horus of the incarnation and Horus of the resurrection, or the child-Horus and Horus the adult.   The duality of Horus as the word made flesh and the word made truth is also exemplified in the Gospel of Thomas by the boy whose every word at once became a deed (ch. 4).

In the introductory word to the " New Sayings of Jesus," found on the site of Oxyrhynchus by Messrs. Grenfell and Hunt, it is said : " These are the (wonderful) words which Jesus the living (Lord) spake to . . . and Thomas, and he said unto (them) everyone that hearkens to these words shall never taste of death " (p. 11).   The wonderful words, the words of power in the Ritual, are the words of Atum-Ra the holy spirit.   The speaker is Horus or Iu the living, he who rises from the grave and does not die a second time, or who is the resurrection and the life, that was represented as the first fruit or type of them that slept.   He is one of those to whom Nut, the mother heaven, has given birth or rebirth (Rit., ch. 1), and this power he afterwards confers on his four brethren or children that they likewise may raise up the dead (Pyramid Texts, Teta, 270).   It is in this character he says, " *I am the living soul* " (Rit., ch. 5).   That is, as Horus the lord of the resurrection from the land of death.   " I am he that cometh forth."   " I open all the paths in heaven and on earth " (ch. 9).   " That has been given to me which endureth amidst all overthrow " (ch. 10).   Thus Horus is the demonstrator of a resurrection for the human soul in a mystery of Amenta.   He says, " I am he who establishes you for eternity."   " I am he who dieth not a second time " (ch. 42).   " I am he whose orbits are of old ; my soul is divine, it is the eternal Force " (ch. 85).   " It is I who proceed from Tum "—the father of a soul that is immortal.

An original Egyptian source for the Gospels of the Infancy is recognizable in the Ritual.   In his incarnation Horus, or Iu the Su, indicates that he " disrobes himself " to " reveal himself " when he " presents himself to the earth " (ch. 71).   In his birth he says, " I am the babe " born as the connecting link betwixt earth and heaven, and as the one who does not die the second death (ch. 42).   He issues from the disc or from the egg.   He is pursued by the Herrut-reptile, but, as he says, his egg remains unpierced by the destroyer.   He escapes from the slaughter of the innocents or the Hamemmet in Suten-Khen.   On entering the earth-life Horus knows it to be in accordance with his lot that he should suffer death or come to an end and be no more (Rit., ch. 8).   He also knows that he is a *living* soul.   As such he has that within which surviveth all overthrow ; even though he may be buried in the deep, dark grave, he will not be annihilated there.   He will rise again (ch. 10 and ch. 30A).   But before quoting further what Horus says, we cite a few more of the Logoi which tell us what Horus is.   And what Horus is in the Osirian religion the same was the Egyptian Jesus in the cult of Atum-Ra, and Iu-em-hetep still earlier in the mysteries of Memphis and the cult of Ptah.

Apart from the Osirian dynasty of deities, the two chief divine personages in the Ritual are Atum-Ra and Atum-Horus, as Huhi the eternal father, and Iu the ever-coming Messianic son, who as the Su is Iusu, the Egyptian Jesus. Now Tum, or Atum-Ra the inspiring spirit, was the author of the sayings in the Ritual which he gave to Horus the Iu-su or coming son, as Sayer, for him to utter to men and manes in the two characters of the infant Horus and Horus the adult. Tum as Egyptian, is the earlier form of Atum's name; and in the Greek inscriptions Tum (or Atum) is called Tomos. We also find that the twin-totality of Tum is registered in the name of "Thomas called Didymus"; Thomas the twin being equivalent in name to the character of the twofold Tum. From this we infer that the apocryphal Gospel of the Infancy assigned to Thomas is, or was, based upon the Egyptian Gospel of *Tum*. This duality may also explain the relationship of Jesus to Thomas in the "sayings" or *Logoi*, recently recovered from the mounds of Oxyrhynchus, which are called "the sayings of Jesus," who is described as the Lord, and the living one.

Now Tum, in the Ritual, is pre-eminently "the lord." In one chapter (79) he is addressed as "the lord of heaven," "the lord of life," "the lord of all creatures," "the lord of all." Thus the Ritual contains "the sayings of the lord." The Hebrew formula "thus saith the lord" had been anticipated in the Ritual by the "so saith Tum" whose word is "not to be altered" (Ritual, ch. 78). As Egyptian, Tum is the one god called "the living." And the sayings are the words which Jesus "the living" is said to have spoken to Thomas, the son Iu here being given the foremost position of the two. The sayings of the lord, in the Ritual, then, are the sayings spoken by Tum the father to Iusa the son, who utters them to men on earth and to the manes in Amenta. It is as Atum-Horus that the son says, "I am the bright one in glory whom Tum himself brought into being, who hath made and glorified and honoured those who are to be with him," as his followers or his children (Rit., ch. 78). It is the same speaker who says, "I have come upon this earth and I take possession of it with my two feet. I am Tum, and I come from my own place." That is as Iusa the manifesting son. Thus the sayings of Horus Iu-em-hetep can be traced to Tum as Ra the inspiring spirit and to Horus as the sayer in the Ritual.

"Tum" in Egyptian was also a name for the mythical child as the inarticulate one, the little Tum, who survives in various countries. For the child Tum passed out of Egypt into Europe to become the Tom Thumb and little Thumbkin of our nursery tales. We also consider that this was the Tum who passed into India as the "historic" Thomas and who is claimed by Christians to have been the Apostle of that name. The god Tum is there identifiable in half-a-dozen features assigned to the Apostle or Saint Thomas. For one thing he is the patron of builders and architects, and his symbol is the mason's square. He is reputed to have built a superb palace in heaven for the poor of earth. Tum survives by name as the Thoma of the Indian Christians on a peninsula of the Indus this side of the gulf: also in Cochin and beyond. The so-called Christians of India who are frequently supposed to have been the followers of an historic Thomas have their own tradition which is both congruous and explicable. They say that "a certain holy man called Mar-Thome, a Syrian, first came to them with a number of beasts from Syria and Egypt" (Calmet, Thomas). That is with the hieroglyphic signs. Thome we take to be the Egyptian god, Tum. The Mar or Mer, as the surname of the holy man, is an Egyptian title for a superintendent. The "Mer-Tetu" was the superintendent of books, and also the royal mage in one person. Thus read "Mar-Thome" was one of the Egyptian Magi or Rekhi as the superintendent of a college or body of priests who went to India from Syria as missionaries and who promulgated the worship of Tum as God the Father, and Iusa as the son in the religion of Annu.

This dual character of Tum as the father and Iu the Su or son, equal to Jesus, will enable us to identify the child-Jesus in the Gospel of Thomas and that Gospel itself as a form of the Egyptian Gospel. This is one of the most ancient of the Gospels of the Infancy called Apocryphal, the origin and true significance of which are hitherto unknown. These have been denounced as idle tales, foolish traditions : pious frauds, disguised heresy, anti-evangelical representations and fables forged to supply an account of "Our Lord's History," in that infancy which the evangelists have perforce omittted. The representations, however, are anti-evangelical ; hence they are supposed to favour Docetism : in other words, they are *non-historical*. As already demonstrated, the great god Tum was the father in one character, and Iu or Horus in the other ; he is the divine son who is Iu-em-hetep the Egyptian Jesus. Tum is Tomas or Thomas in Greek, and the Gospel of Tomas in Greek is the Gospel of Tum as Egyptian. Also Tum the father and Iu the son will show why the history of the infancy should be related of a mythical Jesus in the Gospel of Tum or Thomas, and in relation to Thomas. Thus we can identify Tum as the author of the sayings which are to be spoken by Iu-em-hetep, in the person of God the Son. Tum was the earlier name of Atum-Ra, when the character was that of child-Horus, or the infant Tum, and the sayings together with the sayer were pre-Osirian. In other words, the " sayer " is Iu-em-hetep, the prince of peace in the cult of On, whom we trace back to the time of Ptah as the Egyptian Jesus. Hence this chapter is the one by which the manes is said to "assume the form of Ptah " in the course of being spiritualized. In one of the sayings ascribed to Jesus he says, " Come unto me, all ye that labour and are heavy-laden, and I will give you rest " (Matt. xi. 28). This had then become "one of the sayings." But the sayer himself had been personalized or typified in earlier ages as Iu-em-hetep at Memphis, and again at On, and later still at Alexandria. And Iu-em-hetep the bringer of peace by name was the giver of rest by nature as the Egyptian Jesus ; he who settled the matter of immortality in his resurrection from the tomb. As we have already seen, a tap-root of the Jesus legend in the eschatological phase can be traced in the Egyptian Ritual to the time and to the cult of Ptah at Memphis (Rit., ch. 82). Ptah was the earliest form of an eternal father manifesting in the person of an ever-coming son, who, as the coming one, was Iu, or Iu-em-hetep, he who comes with peace. Hence we derive the name or title of the Egypto-gnostic Jesus from Iu-Su, or Iusa, the coming son. Indeed, the question asked by the messengers of John in the Gospel,

art thou he that should come, or must we look for another ? is equivalent
to asking " art thou Iu-em-hetep, he who comes with peace as
manifester for the father ? "

It is also said of Jesus that he had compassion on the people
" because they were as sheep without a shepherd." And this has
been looked upon as one of the foundational pillars of the history,
and proof positive that he was the original Good Shepherd. But
Horus had long been extant as the good shepherd in the mythos, the
eschatology, and the iconography of Egypt. Again, it is said of Jesus
(Matt. vii. 29), that he taught the multitude as one having authority,
and not as their scribes. So was it with Horus, who claims that
authority to teach had been divinely delegated to him as the beloved
son of God the Father. Hence the sayings, " I have come forth with
the tongue of Ptah and the throat of Hathor that I may record the
words of my father Tum with my mouth " (Rit., ch. 82). " I am arrayed
and equipped with thy words of power, O Ra " (ch. 32). " I utter his
words to the men of the present generation, and I repeat his words to
him who is deprived of breath " as the manes in Amenta (ch. 38).

It was the work of Horus to exalt the father at all times and
in every place. He is exalted as Un-Nefer, the good being who
is the one alone that is good, perfect, and unique. The same mission
is assigned to the Gospel-Jesus. Hence the saying, " Why callest thou
me good? None is good save one, even God alone . . . *the Father
alone* " (Mark x. 18), who represents the same Good Being Un-
Nefer as did Osiris. This duality of the Deity as father and son
is also manifest in the saying, " Whosoever shall speak a word against
the Son of Man it shall be forgiven him, but whosoever shall speak
against the Holy Spirit it shall not be forgiven him " (Matt. xii. 32).
That is said in exaltation of the father in heaven who was the holy
spirit represented by the son on earth or in Amenta. The Ritual
likewise proves that Seb, the god of earth and foster-father of Horus,
when he was the child of the virgin mother only, is the prototype or
original of Joseph. Horus says that as the heir of Seb, from whom
he issued, he was suckled at the breast of Isis, the spouse of Seb, who
gave him his theophanies (Rit., ch. 82). Horus on earth lies down to
embrace the old man who keeps the light of earth, and who is Seb the
earth-father (Rit., ch. 84). Horus is lord of the staircase or mount of
rebirth in heaven. In his first advent as the heir of Seb Horus
says, " I am come as a mummied one " (that is, in his embodiment
when made flesh, the Hamemmet being the unmummied ones)
(Rit., ch. 9). " I come before you and make my appearance as that
god in the form of a man who liveth as a god "—otherwise stated, as
Iusu the son of Atum-Ra (ch. 79). " I repeat the acclamations at my
success on being declared the heir of Seb " (Seb was the father on
earth (ch. 82), Osiris in Amenta, Ra in heaven). " I descend to the
earth of Seb and put a stop to evil " as the bringer of peace, plenty,
and good will on earth. " I shine forth from the egg which is in the
unseen world " (ch. 22). " Lo, I bring this my word of power " from out
the silence in which the gods originated. " I am arrayed and equipped
with thy words of power, O Ra " (ch. 24, 32). " I utter his words to
the living and to those who are deprived of breath. I am Horus,
prince of eternity " (ch. 42). " I am yesterday, to-day, and to-morrow "

(ch. 64). "I am" (or, am I not) "the bull of the sacrificial herd. Are not the mortuary gifts upon me, and the supernal powers?" (ch. 105). "Witness of Eternity is my name, the persistent traveller on the highways of heaven. I am the everlasting one, I am Horus, who steppeth onwards through eternity." But Horus in the Ritual is chiefly the son of God the Father in heaven, and the subject-matter is mainly *post-resurrectional*.

After the life with Seb on earth, Horus is reborn in the earth of eternity for the heaven of eternity (78, 25). He is divinized with the flesh or substance of god (ch. 78). By means of Horus, his manifester, Osiris is said to re-live. Horus is Osiris in his rebirth. Horus rises as a god and is visible to the gods (or divine spirits) (79) in his resurrection. Horus rises as the living soul of Ra in heaven (127). Horus strikes the wakers in their cells or coffins for the resurrection of the manes in Amenta (ch. 84). "I raise myself up, I renew myself, I grow young again" (ch. 43). "Not men or gods; or the glorified ones, or the damned, can inflict any injury on me" (ch. 42). "I do not die a second time in the nether-world" (ch. 44). "I am the victorious one" (ch. 47). "I am seized (in possession) of the two earths" (ch. 50). "There hath been assigned to me eternity without end. Lo, I am the heir of endless time and my attribute is eternity" (ch. 62). "I am the heir, the primary power of motion and of rest" (ch. 63A). "I, even I, am he who knoweth the paths of heaven. Its breezes blow upon me. I advance whithersoever there lieth a wreck in the field of eternity, and I pilot myself towards the darkness and the sufferings of the deceased ones of Osiris" (ch. 78), as the deliverer or saviour of souls whose supreme concern and object is to be saved from the second death in Amenta by earning and attaining the life of the soul that is eternal. "It is I, even I, who am Horus in glory. I am the lord of light and I advance to the goal of heaven." Jesus says, "I go unto him that sent me" (John vii. 33). "I know whence I came and whither I go" (John viii. 14). "I go to prepare a place for you." "I am the way, the truth, and the life. No one cometh to the Father but through me" (John xiv. 6). "I go unto the Father" (xiv. 12). But there is nothing so striking in the Gospel as this image of Horus the saviour in the boat of souls who steers his own bark that tosses in distressful agitation over the water, whilst he carries rescue wheresoever there has been a wreck amongst the suffering and deceased ones of his father Osiris.

Horus was the sole one of the seven great spirits born of the mother who was chosen to become the only-begotten son of God the Father when he rose up from the dead. This is he who says in the Ritual, "I am the bright one in glory, *whom Atum-Ra hath called into being*, and my origin is from the apple of his eye. Verily before Isis was, I grew up and waxed old, and was honoured beyond those who were with me in glory" (Rit., ch. 78, Renouf). Those who were with him in glory were the seven great spirits, the Khuti or glorious ones. Amongst these, Horus became the divine heir of all things, the son of God who claims to have existed before Isis his mother, when speaking as manifester for the holy spirit. This is the son and heir of God who is described in the Epistle to the Hebrews as the "appointed heir of all things, through whom also he made the worlds."

He was thus exalted above the angels or great spirits through "having become by so much better than the angels" and by inheriting a more excellent name than they. "For unto which of the angels said he at any time, thou art my son?" Horus exalts his father in every place; "associating himself with the two divine sisters, Isis and Nephthys," as his two mothers. It is Taht-Ani who speaks by him the favourable incantations which issue from his heart through his mouth. Horus overthrows the serpent Apap daily for Ra. Horus unites both Osiris and Ra in one triune personality, or trinity in unity.

The sayer personalized as son of God and utterer of the logia in the Ritual says: "I am the one proceeding from the one, the son from a father, the father from the son" (Sarcophagus of Seti I.). Jesus is credited with having the magical power of being known or unknown, seen or unseen at will. When the Jews took up stones to cast at him he was suddenly invisible, even in their midst (John viii. 59). Again, whilst uttering the sayings to the multitude, he was hidden from them (John xii. 36). When risen bodily, he is the unknown one to Mary at the sepulchre. He is also the unknown one to the disciples on the way to Emmaus (Luke xxiv.). This character, like all the rest, is according to copy supplied by the Ritual. "I am he," says Horus, "who cometh forth and proceedeth, and whose name is unknown to men" (ch. 42). The Osiris has a word of power by means of which he can conceal or manifest himself. He says: "I am in possession of that word of power which is the most potent one in my body here; and by means of it *I make myself either known or unknown*" (Renouf, ch. 110), which is equivalent to becoming visible or invisible at will.

"Before the feast of the Passover, Jesus, knowing that his hour was come that he should depart out of this world unto the Father, having loved his own which were in the world, he loved them unto the end" (John xiii. 1) The end is here indicated by the feast of the Passover and the last supper. In the parallel scene Horus says: "I have come to an end for the lord of heaven, I rest at the table of my father Osiris" (Rit., ch. 70). This immediately precedes his piercing the veil of the tabernacle and coming forth as the divine hawk of soul (Rit., 70-71, Renouf). Horus when addressing Ra the father on behalf of the four brethren, his followers, says, "Be they with thee so that they may be with me" (Rit., ch. 113). Jesus says of his followers, "Holy Father, keep them in thy name which thou hast given me that they may be one even as we are." "I will that where I am they also may be with me" (John xvii. 11, 12, 24). In the same passage of the Ritual Sut is referred to as invoking the powers of Nekhen. In the same passage of the Gospel it is "the son of perdition."

In this way the canonical Gospels can be shown to be a collection of sayings from the Egyptian mythos and eschatology. The original likeness is somewhat defeatured at times in the process, but sufficient remains in the Ritual for the purpose of comparison and reclamation. When Horus returns to his father with his work accomplished on earth and in Amenta he greets Osiris in a "discourse to his father." In forty addresses he enumerates what he has done for the support and assistance of Osiris in the earth of Seb. Each line commences with

3 M

the formula, " Hail, Osiris, I am thy son Horus. I have come!" Amongst other of the assistances he says, " I have supported thee. I have struck thine enemies dead. I have brought the companions of Sut to thee in chains. I have cultivated thy fields. I have watered thy grounds. I have strengthened thine existence upon the earth. I have given thee thy soul, thy strength, thy power. I have given thee thy victory. I have anointed thee with the offerings of holy oil." This last in sign-language is, I have given thee the glory (Renouf and Naville, Rit., ch. 173). This we parallel with the sixteenth chapter of John, in which the position and character of Jesus are the same with those of Horus, and in which Jesus addresses the father at the end of his career. " I have come to thee," says Horus to Osiris. " Now I come to thee," says Jesus to the Father. " Father, the hour is come ; glorify thy son that the son may glorify thee." " I glorified thee on earth, having accomplished the work which thou hast given me to do. And now, O Father, glorify thou me with thine own self with the glory which I had with thee before the world was. I manifested thy name unto the men whom thou gavest me out of the world. I am no more in the world. But now I come to thee. I kept them in thy name, which thou hast given me. I guarded them, and not one of them perished, but the son of perdition " (xvii. 5-12). The glory of God the father was reflected by the sacred oil upon the face of Horus the anointed son, which was a sign of his divinity. This was "the glory as of the only-begotten from the father" who was Horus in spirit, Horus the adult, the anointed one with the father, and thus the representative type of a soul of life that is eternal and attainable by all as in the only-beloved son.

It is an utterance of the truth that is eternal to say that Horus as the son of God had previously been all the Gospel Jesus is made to say he is, or is to become. Horus and the father were one. Jesus says, " I and my Father are one." " He that seeth me, seeth him that sent me " (John xii. 45). Horus is the father seen in the son (Rit., 115). Jesus claims to be the son in whom the father is revealed. Horus was the light of the world, the light that is represented by the symbolical eye, the sign of salvation. Jesus is made to declare that he is the light of the world. Horus was the way, the truth, the life, by name and in person. Jesus is made to assert that he is the way, the truth, and the life. Horus was the plant, the shoot, the natzer. Jesus is made to say, " I am the true vine." The deceased says, " I spring up as a plant " (Rit., 83, 1). The deceased, in the character of Horus, or one with him by assimilation, also makes these claims for himself. Hence the sayings—the sayings which are repeated in the Gospels, more especially in the Gospel according to John = Aan. To parallel a few of the sayings in the Gospels with those of the Ritual : In the Gospel according to John, Jesus says of himself, " I am the bread of life " (vi. 35), " I am the light of the world " (viii. 12), " I am the door of the sheep " (x. 7), " I am the good shepherd " (x. 11), " I am the resurrection and the life " (xi. 25), " I am the way, the truth, and the life " (xiv. 6), " I am the true vine " (xv. 1). And Horus was the original in all seven characters. Horus was the bread of life, also the divine corn from which the bread of life was made (Rit., ch. 83). Horus was the good shepherd who carries the crook upon his shoulder.

Horus was the door of entrance into Amenta, which none but he could open. Horus was the resurrection and the life. He carries the two symbols of resurrection and of life eternal, the hare-headed sceptre, and the Ankh-key in his hands. Horus was the way. His name is written with the sign of the road (Heru). Horus was the true vine, as the branch of Osiris, who is himself the vine in person. Now the original of all these identifiable characters could occur but once, and that prototype was Horus, or Jesus in the cult of Atum-Ra. Horus says, " It is I who traverse the heaven. I go round the Sekhet-Aarru (the Elysian fields). Eternity has been assigned to me without end. Lo! I am the heir of endless time, and my·attribute is eternity " (Ritual, ch. 62). Jesus says, " I am come down from heaven. For this is the will of the Father that every one who beholdeth the son and believeth in him should have eternal life, and I will raise him up at the last day." He, too, claims to be the lord of eternity. When Horus is " lifted up " to become glorified and is " Horus in his glory " (ch. 78), " master of his diadem," he says, " I raise myself up." Then he adds, " I stoop upon the Atit-bark that I may reach and raise to me those who are in their circles, and who bow down before me " as his worshippers (ch. 77). " And I," says Jesus, " if I be lifted up out of the earth (as Horus was lifted up from out the nether-world), will draw all men after me " (John xii. 32, 33). Horus says, " I open the Tuat that I may drive away the darkness." Jesus says, " I am come a light into the world." Horus says, " I am equipped with thy words of power, O Ra " (the father in heaven) (ch. 32), " and repeat them to those who are deprived of breath " (ch. 38). These were the words of the father in heaven. Jesus says, " The Father which sent me, he hath given me a commandment, what I should say and what I should speak. The things therefore which I speak, even as the Father hath said unto me, so I speak " (John xii. 49, 50). " The word which ye hear is not mine, but the Father's who sent me " (John xiv. 24). Horus repeated to his followers that which his father Osiris had said to him in the early time (Rit., 78). Jesus says, " As the Father taught me, I speak these things " (John viii. 28). " All things that I heard from my Father I have made known unto you " (John xv. 15). Horus comes on earth to report what he has known and heard and seen and handled with the father. " I have touched with my two hands the heart of Osiris." " That which I went to ascertain I have come to tell." " I know the mysterious paths and the gates of Aarru (or Paradise) from whence I come. Here am I, and I come that I may· overthrow mine adversaries on earth, though my dead body be buried " (Renouf, ch. 86).

Horus eats the bread of Seb on earth, but he teaches the manes in Amenta to pray for the bread of heaven. Let him ask for food from the Lord, who is over all (ch. 78). In this we have the germ of the Lord's Prayer addressed to " our Father in heaven " for " our daily bread ": Ra being the heavenly father of Horus and the supplier of food to souls; the daily giver of eternal life, that was represented by the typical seven loaves of plenty. There is a prayer in the Ritual (ch. 71) which opens with an address to the Lord of Heaven who " reveals himself, who derobes himself, and presents himself to the earth " in the person of Horus his son, the divine hawk or soul that pierces through the veil of the tabernacle. It is here referred to for the refrain which occurs seven times over—" *May his will toward me be done by the Lord of the one face*," that is, by the one and only God who is the father in heaven, he who " revealed himself, who disrobed himself, and presented himself to the earth " (Renouf, ch. 71) in the person of his beloved son.

Horus who comes from heaven says, " I am the food which perisheth not, in my name of the self-originating force " (Rit., ch. 85). Jesus says, " I am the bread of life. This is the bread which cometh down out of heaven that a man may eat thereof and not die. I am the living bread which came down out of heaven " (John vi. 48–51). Horus was not only the bread of life derived from heaven and the producer of bread in the character of Amsu the husbandman; he also gave his flesh for food and his blood for drink This, however, was not in the cannibal form of human flesh and blood, but as the typical calf or the lamb. Jesus says, " The bread which I will give is my flesh." " Except ye eat the flesh of the Son of man and drink his blood ye have not life in yourselves," that is, in the human form, which is proclaimed to be the bread which came down out of heaven (John vi. 53, 58). Horus says, " I am the possessor of bread in Annu. I have bread in heaven with Ra " (ch. 53A). " There are seven loaves in heaven at Annu with Ra " (ch. 53B). Ra is the father in heaven. He is the provider of the bread of life that is given by the son, and by Jesus in the Gospel. Jesus says, " My Father giveth you the true bread out of heaven. For the bread of God is that which cometh down out of heaven, and giveth life unto the world," that is, in the person of Jesus or of Horus. " Jesus said unto them, I am the bread of life " (John vi. 32–35). Jesus, like Horus, is the giver of the water of life which likewise cometh from the Father (John iv. 10 and vii. 37). " Now on the last day, the great day of the feast, Jesus stood and cried, saying, If any man thirst, let him come unto me and drink. He that believeth on me, as the scripture hath said, out of his belly shall flow rivers of living water " (John vii. 37, 38). In passing, we may notice that the great feast corresponds to the Uaka festival by which the return of the water of life in the inundation was celebrated; and that Osiris was the lord of the water as well as of the wine. Moreover, the miracle of converting water into wine is very simply illustrated by the picture of Osiris as the vine and also as the water of renewal in which the vine springs out of the water of life that issues from beneath his throne. On the ground of natural fact, Osiris was the water of life to the land of Egypt in the inundation of the Nile. He was adored in the temple of Isis at Philæ as " Osiris of the mysteries, who springs from the returning waters." He was the water of life to the souls in Amenta; and in the eschatology Osiris is the water of life in Hetep, the paradise of peace, to spirits perfected. In the Ritual, Horus is the son of God through whom is given the water that cometh from the father, which is called the Ru of Osiris, the divine liquid that flows from him as the ichor of life. Horus speaks of quenching his thirst with the drops (the Ru) of his father Osiris. So Jesus draws and drinks and gives drink from the well of living water which is the father's; not the well of Jacob (John iv. 10, 15), but a well of water springing up unto eternal life.

Again and again, the status and character of Jesus as the Sayer in the Gospels are only to be determined by the mythical or mystical relationship. "Before Abraham was, I am," is one of the sayings ascribed to the supposed historical Christ. Abraham is of course referred to as the typical progenitor of the Jews. So in the Gospel of Thomas, or Tum, the child-Jesus says to his earth-father Joseph, "It is enough for thee to see me, not to touch me. For thou knowest not who I am. If thou knewest thou wouldst not grieve me. And although I am now with thee I was made before thee" (ch. 5). The son who existed before the father claims an immense antiquity, as a character entirely mythical, but if the statement were made a hundred times over in the märchen the meaning would be the same. It is a saying of the Divine Child who came into being earlier than God the Father as the offspring of the Virgin Mother who is Jesus the father-less Child of Mary in the Gospels, and of Neith or Iusāas in the Ritual. Joseph also plays the part of Seb, the father, to Horus on earth. "Seb giveth me his theophanies," says Horus, but "more powerful am I than the lord of time (Seb), I am the author and the master of endless years" (Rit., ch. 82) as an image of the Eternal.

In the inscription of Hatshepsu, the child-Horus is called "the elder of his mother's husband." That is, he was older than Osiris, who became the father according to the later sociology (Obelisk of Karnak, l. 4). Such is the sole ground of origin upon which the father can be later than the son whether his name is Atum, Osiris or Abraham.

The sayings involve a sayer who became the typical teacher in person as Horus in the Osirian cult and Iu-em-hetep in the religion of Atum-Ra, or Iao of the Egypto-gnostics in the *Pistis Sophia*. These are mentioned in the texts as the divine enunciators of the "sayings." Each of them is a form of the sayer, word, logos, announcer, or revealer in person, precisely the same as the Jesus of the gospels, whether Apocryphal, Egypto-gnostic or Canonical. The elder Horus was the virgin's child; he imaged the soul in matter, or, the body-soul in the life on earth. He was the teacher of the lesser mysteries in the mythology. He was solar; hence the leader of that glorious company of the twelve now stationed in the zodiac as rowers of the bark for millions of years. The primary twelve were the great gods of Egypt twenty thousand years ago as the twelve powers that rowed the solar bark for Ra around the circle of the zodiacal signs. They became the Æons of the gnostics, twelve in number. As preservers of the light, they were twelve teachers in mythology, twelve followers of Horus who are the twelve apostles or disciples of the Egypto-gnostic Christ; the seven and five being grouped together to constitute the twelve.

At his second coming when Horus of the resurrection rose again as a spirit in the image of the holy ghost—he became the teacher of the greater mysteries to the twelve who likewise had attained the status of spirits in the eschatology, and who were now the twelve to whom twelve thrones were promised in the heaven of eternity.

Horus the word in person was the sayer to whom the sayings were assigned. Hence the "sayings," attributed to Iu-em-hetep and Hartatef in Egypt: the one as child of the mother; the other as son of the father who wore the Atef-crown of Atum-Ra. Now this mystical "word" of the mother, and the word-made-truth in Har-Mat-Kheru are both apparent in the opening chapter of the Gospel according to John. "In the beginning was the word," he says; as it had been in Iu-em-hetep, or child-Horus. "And the word became flesh," which it did in the virgin-blood of the immaculate Isis or of Hathor-Iusāas. The doctrine of the second Horus follows, but is inserted parenthetically. "And we beheld his glory; glory as of the only begotten from the father." But the Jesus of the genuine legend was not yet begotten by or from the father. He was begotten or christified in his baptism. Matthew has it that when Jesus was baptized he went up straightway from the water; and lo the heavens were opened unto him, and he saw the Spirit of God descending as a dove, and coming upon him; and lo a voice out of the heavens, saying, This is my beloved son (ch. iii. 16, 17). In the original transformation scene this occurred when the child of the mother made his change into the beloved son of God the father at the time of the baptism in the Osirian mystery of Tattu (Rit., ch. 17). It was in his resurrection from the dead, here represented by the rising from the water, and becoming bird-headed as a spirit, that Horus became the beloved son of the father (Rit., ch. 9). John then proceeds to describe the transformation of Jesus in *his* baptism when "the spirit descended as a dove out of heaven, and it abode upon him," which change had already taken place before the glory of the father could have been visible in the person of the son. Now, this word that was in the beginning had already manifested as the "sayer" of the sayings in the Ritual. This is he who says, "I have come forth with the tongue of Ptah and the throat of Hathor (Iusāas) *that I may record the words of my father Atum with my mouth.*" That is, as the utterer of the "sayings" which were ascribed to the Egyptian Jesus as Iu-em-hetep, the son of Hathor-Iusāas and Atum-Ra. We have no need to go further back for the beginning of the Word, as utterer of the sayings. The canonical Gospels are based upon the "sayings" of Jesus; the Jesus that we claim to have been the son of Atum at On; genealogically, the grandson of Ptah at Memphis, and the author of the books of wisdom attributed to him as the Jesus of the Apocrypha, and Gospels of the Infancy.

Enough has been cited to show that the revelation ascribed to Jesus, the Christ of the canonical Gospels, had been previously published in the Ritual of the resurrection and uttered by Iu the Su of Atum-Ra (Iusa = Jesus or Tum = Thomas), who was and is and ever will be the Egyptian Jesus independently of any personal historical character.

The Egyptian Ritual contains the "sayings" or the words of wisdom that were attributed to Ra the inspiring holy spirit. As god the father this was Tum (or Thomas). The utterer of the "sayings" "with his mouth" was god the son, Iu (or Iu-em-hetep) the Su (son) who was Iu-Su, the ever-coming son in the religion of Annu, and *Iusu* when rendered through the Greek is Ιησοῦς or *Jesus.*

A large part of the Egyptian Book of the Dead consists of "sayings." The forty-second chapter contains at least fifty *sayings uttered by Horus in person respecting himself, his father and his work of salvation.* These are the sayings of Horus, or of the Osiris by whom they are repeated in character. And as Horus the divine word in person is the Lord whose name of Heru signifies the Lord, these sayings of Horus are the *Logia Kuriaka*; assuredly the oldest in the world, which we have now traced to Iu-em-hetep, the Egypto-gnostic Jesus as the sayer for Atum-Ra. These might be called the sayings of Ra or Horus, of Tum or Thomas, of Iu or Iu-em-hetep, of Aan, Taht or Hermes. But above all other names or titles they were known as the words of Mati.

Also, the Gospel of the Egyptians, represented by the Ritual, was the Gospel according to Mati (or Matiu, with the U, inherent). And as Mati was inculcated by means of the sayings, the sayings in the Ritual are the sayings of Mati as the words of truth, justice, law, and rightfulness, and the revelation of the resurrection. In Dr. Birch's translation of "the funeral Ritual" he has given the word "Mati" as a title of Taht-Aan the divine scribe; and from this title the present writer deduced the names of Matthias and Matthew, as the true reckoner, the just reckoner, and keeper of the tablets for Maati in the hall of Maat. Taht-Aan might be designated Mati. But, whether we take the word Mati as a proper name or title of the scribe Taht (whether called Hermes, Aan or Mati), he was the recorder of the sayings or *Logia Kuriaka* in the Ritual. But even if we do not take the name of Mati to be a title of Tehuti, whence the names of Matthias and Matthew, the character remains. Taht was the scribe in the Maat or judgment-hall, also the recorder of the sayings that were given by the Father in Heaven to be uttered by Horus, and written down by the fingers of Taht. Now, according to the often-quoted testimony of Papias, recorded in his last "commentary" on the "sayings of the Lord," the basis of the canonical Gospels was laid in a collection of sayings that were attributed to "The Lord." He tells us that Matthew wrote the sayings in the Hebrew dialect, and every one interpreted them as best he was able. This was the current *hearsay* on the subject as reported by Papias, Bishop of Hierapolis. And here we might repeat, in passing, that the sayings of Horus the lord in the Ritual were collected and written down by Taht-Mati the scribe, and that Matthew, or Matthias, corresponds to Mati both in character and by name. We have no further use for the statement beyond noting that the extant Gospel of Matthew was evidently founded on a collection of those "wise sayings, dark sentences and parables" that constituted the wisdom of the Egypto-gnostic Jesus, one late version of which has been preserved in the Book of Ecclesiasticus, entitled "the wisdom of Jesus." The present writer has previously suggested that the "sayings" collected by Matthew, which Papias had heard of as the source of the Christian Gospels, were a form of the sayings of Mati collected from the papyri of the Ritual. The Catholic Christians were sorely troubled about the Egypto-gnostic Gospels in possession of the "heretics" when they came to hear of them. These are especially associated with the name of Valentinus, an Egyptian gnostic, who came with these Egypto-gnostic Gospels from Alexandria, and to whom *Pistis Sophia* and the "Gospel of Truth" have been attributed. The "Gospel of Truth," known to the Valentinian gnostics as Egyptian, is the Gospel of Mati, or a collection of the sayings of Mati = Matthew. The Logia of Matthias was the authentic gospel of the Carpocratean gnostics. Clement of Alexandria quotes from the "Traditions of Matthias" two sayings which are not to be found in the canonical Matthew. This proves the existence of other sayings, oracles and divine words than the canonical in the time of Clement, which were assigned to Matthias = Mati. These sayings and traditions were acknowledged as genuine by the gnostic followers of Carpocrates, Valentinus and Basilides, *who never did acknowledge any historical founder*, and whose Christ was the Egypt-gnostic Jesus—he who was the utterer of the sayings and traditions first written down by the divine scribe Taht-Aan = John; or Taht-Mati = Matthew.

In writing his Gospel, Basilides appealed to a secret tradition which he had received *from Matthias*; and Hippolytus reports that this secret tradition was derived by Matthias during his private intercourse with the Saviour. But the gnostics never did acknowledge any historic saviour. Their Christ was Horus, or the non-historical Jesus, and therefore the private intercourse of Matthias with the Saviour was that of Mati with Horus the Christ of the Ritual which contains the history of that intercourse.

We are told that it was *after his Resurrection* that Christ revealed the true gnosis to Peter, John and James. (Clem. Alex. Eusebius, H. E. 2, 1). But it was only the spiritual Horus or Christ that could reveal the true gnosis, which is here admitted versus the historic personage. This revelation is post-resurrectional, the same as with the gnostic Jesus in the *Pistis Sophia* who expounds the mysteries to his twelve apostles on Mount Olivet after he has risen from the dead. The "Manifestation of Truth" is the title of the great work of Marcus the gnostic in the third century. The lost work of Celsus was the Word of Truth or Logos Alethea. In these instances the gospel is that of truth, the word of truth; the true gospel. And the gospel of Mati, we repeat, is equivalent to the gospel or the sayings according to Matthew which had been heard of by Papias as the nuclei of the canonical Gospels. Epiphanius, in speaking of the "Sabelian Heretics," says, "The whole of their errors and the main strength of their heterodoxy they derive from some apocryphal books, but principally from that which is called *the Gospel of the Egyptians* (which is a name some have given to it) *for in that many things are proposed in a hidden, mysterious manner as by our Saviour*" (Ad. Haeres, 26, 2), just as they are in the sayings of the Ritual, the sayings of Hartatef, Iu-em-hetep or the sayings of Jesus. In his tirade against gnosticism Augustine echoes the name of Mati (for truth) and shows its twofold nature in a peculiar way as "*The Truth and Truth*." He says of the gnostics: "They used to repeat '*Truth and Truth*,' for *thus* did they repeat her name to me, but she was nowhere amongst them; for they spoke false things, not only concerning thee who art the *Truth in Truth*, but even concerning the elements of this world of ours, thy creation; concerning which even the philosophers, who declared what is true, I ought to have slighted for love of thee, O my father, the supreme God, the beauty of all things beautiful. O truth! truth! how inwardly did the marrow of my soul sigh after thee even then, whilst they were perpetually dinning thy name into my ears, and after various fashions *with the mere voice*, and with *many and huge books of theirs.*" (*The Gnostics and their Remains*, King, p. 157.)

The Book of the Dead or Ritual of the resurrection virtually contains the Gospel of the Egyptians which was assumed to have been lost. This is the Gospel according to Mati or Matiu, the original, as we maintain, of that which Papias attributes to one "Matthew," and which was a collection of the sayings assigned to the Jesus whom the non-gnostic Christians always assumed to be historical. The Ritual preserves the sayings of the Egyptian Jesus who was Iu the Su, or Sa of Atum-Ra and Iusāas at On, and who was otherwise known as the Lord in different Egyptian religions. This was the sayer to whom the sayings are attributed in the " Festal Dirge " (*Records*, vol. iv., p. 115), and also in the Ritual and other Hermetic Scriptures. And now we have a form of the genuine Gospel of the Egyptians in the Ritual itself. This is the original *Evangelium Veritas*: the Gospel according to Mati = Matthew ; to Aan = John ; or Tum = Thomas. From this we learn, by means of the comparative process, that the literalizers of the legend and the carnalizers of the Egypto-gnostic Christ have but gathered up the empty husks of Pagan tradition, minus the kernel of the Gnosis ; so that when we have taken away all which pertains to Horus, the Egypto-gnostic Jesus, all that remains to base a Judean history upon is nothing more than an accretion of blindly ignorant belief ; and that of all the Gospels and collections of " Sayings " derived from the Ritual of the resurrection in the names of Mati or Matthew, Aan or John, Thomas or Tum, Hermes, Iu-em-Hetep or Jesus, those that were canonized at last as Christian are the most exoteric, and therefore the farthest away from the underlying, hidden, buried, but imperishable truth.

APPENDIX

A comparative list of some pre-existing and pre-Christian data which were christianized in the Canonical Gospels and the Book of Revelation.

Egyptian.		*Christian.*
The Mysteries	=	The miracles.
The Sem, or mythical representations	=	The parables.
The Ritual as the book of resurrection	=	The Book of Revelation.
The sayings of Iu or Iu-em-hetep	=	The sayings of Jesus.
Huhi the father in heaven as the eternal, a title of Atum-Ra	=	Ihuh, the father in heaven as the eternal.
Ra, the holy spirit	=	God the Holy Ghost.
Ra the father of Iu the Su, or son of God, with the hawk or dove as the bird of the holy spirit	=	God, the Father of Jesus, with the dove as the bird of the Holy Spirit.
Iu or Horus, the manifesting son of God	=	Jesus the manifesting Son of God.
The trinity of Atum (or Osiris) the father, Horus (or Iu) the son, and Ra the holy spirit	=	The Trinity of the Father, Son and Holy Spirit.
Iu-Su or Iusa, the coming son of Iusâas, who was great with Iusa or Iusu	=	Jesus.
The ever-coming Messu or Child as Egyptian	=	The Hebrew Messianic Child.
Horus (or Heru), the Lord by name, as a child	=	Child-Jesus as the Lord by name (Gospels of the Infancy).
Isis, the virgin mother of Iu, her Su or son	=	Mary the virgin mother of Jesus.
The first Horus as Child of the Virgin, the second as son of Ra, the father	=	Jesus as the Virgin's child, the Christ as son of the father.
The first Horus as the founder, the second as fulfiller for the father	=	Jesus as the founder, and the Christ as fulfiller for the father.
The two mothers of Child-Horus, Isis and Nephthys, who were two sisters	=	The two mothers of Child-Jesus, who were sisters.
Meri or Nut, the mother-heaven	=	Mary, as Regina Cœli.
The outcast great mother with her seven sons	=	Mary Magdalene, with her seven devils.
Isis taken by Horus in adultery with Sut	=	The woman taken in adultery.
Apt, the crib or manger, by name as the birthplace and mother in one	=	The manger as cradle of the Child-Christ.
Seb, the earth-father, as consort to the virgin Isis	=	Joseph, the father on earth, as putative husband to the Virgin Mary.
Seb, the foster-father to Child-Horus	=	Joseph, as foster-father to the Child-Jesus.
Seb, Isis and Horus, the Kamite holy trinity	=	Joseph, Mary and Jesus, a Christian holy trinity.

Egyptian.		*Christian.*
Seb, the builder of the house, the carpenter	=	Joseph, the carpenter.
Seb, the custodian of the mummied dead	=	Joseph of Arimathea, the keeper of the Corpus Christi.
Sut and Horus, the twin opponents	=	Satan and Jesus, the twin opponents.
Horus, the sower, and Sut, the destroyer, in the harvest-field	=	Jesus, the sower of the good seed, and Satan, the sower of tares.
Sut and Horus contending in the desert	=	Satan and Jesus contending in the wilderness.
Sut and Horus contending on the Ben-Ben or pyramidion	=	Satan and Jesus contending on the pinnacle.
Horus carried off by Sut to the summit of Mount Hetep	=	Jesus spirited away by Satan into an exceeding high mountain.
Sut and Horus contending on the mount	=	Satan and Jesus contending on the mount.
Sut undoing the good that Horus does	=	Satan sowing tares by night.
S'men, for Khemen, a title of Taht	=	Simeon.
S'men, who held Child-Horus in his arms as the young solar god	=	Simeon, who took the Child-Jesus in his arms.
Anna or Annit (a title of Hathor), with Taht-S'men	=	Anna, the prophetess, with Simeon.
The Petar or Petra by name in Egyptian as revealer to Horus	=	Peter, the revealer to the Christ.
The house in Annu	=	Bethany.
The group in the house at Annu	=	The group in the house at Bethany.
Horus in Annu	=	Jesus in Bethany.
Asar or Osiris	=	Lazarus.
The two sisters Mertæ	=	The two sisters Mary and Martha.
Osiris, whom Horus loved	=	Lazarus, whom Jesus loved.
Osiris perfumed for his burial	=	Jesus anointed, when the odour fills the house.
Osiris prays that he may be buried speedily	=	Jesus begs that his death may be effected quickly.
Osiris prepared for burial under the hair of Hathor-Meri	=	Jesus prepared for his burial beneath the hair of Mary.
Osiris, who slept in the tomb at Annu	=	Lazarus, who slept in the tomb at Bethany.
Osiris raised from the tomb by Horus in Annu	=	Lazarus raised from the tomb by Jesus in Bethany.
The mummy Osiris bidden to come forth by Horus	=	The mummy Lazarus bidden to come forth by Jesus.
The Great One who does the work of washing	=	Jesus washing the feet of his disciples.
The star, as announcer for the Child-Horus	=	The Star in the East that indicated the birthplace of Jesus.
The seven Hathors (or cows) who minister to Horus	=	The seven women who minister to Jesus.
Anup, the Precursor of Horus	=	John, the forerunner of Jesus the Christ.
Anup, the Baptizer	=	John the Baptist.
Aan, the saluter of Horus	=	John, the saluter of the Christ.
Aan, a name of the divine scribe	=	John, the divine scribe.
Hermes, the scribe	=	Hermas, the scribe.
Mati, the registrar	=	Matthew, the clerk.
Taht, Shu, and black Sut	=	The three kings, or Magi.
Nut at the pool of the Persea, or sycamore-tree, as giver of divine drink	=	The woman at the well as giver of the water.
Horus born in Annu, the place of bread	=	Jesus born in Bethlehem, the house of bread.
The vesture put on Horus by the Goddess Tait	=	The swaddling clothes put on the infant Jesus.

Egyptian.		*Christian.*
Offerings made to the child by the worshippers in Annu	=	Offerings and worship of the Magi.
Child-Horus with the head of Ra	=	Child-Jesus with the solar glory round his head.
The Bull of Amenta in the place of birth	=	The ox in the birthplace of the Child.
The ass, Iu, in the birthplace	=	The ass in the birthplace (catacombs).
The lions of the horizon attending upon Horus	=	The lions attending the Child-Christ (pseudo-Matthew).
Child-Horus emerging from the Papyrus-reed	=	The Child-Jesus in the catacombs issuing from the Papyrus.
Horus, the ancient child	=	The little old Jesus in the catacombs.
Horus, the gracious child	=	Jesus, the child full of grace.
Horus, one of five brethren	=	Jesus, one of five brothers.
Horus, the brother of Sut the betrayer	=	Jesus, the brother of Judas the betrayer.
Amsta, the one brother of Horus in the human form	=	James, the human brother of Jesus.
The two sisters of Horus	=	The sisters of Jesus.
Horus the lad in the country and youth in town	=	Jesus as the child in the country and youth in town.
Horus baptized with water by Anup	=	Jesus baptized with water by John.
Horus in the tank of flame	=	Jesus the baptizer with fire.
Horus in his baptism becoming the beloved Son of God the Father	=	Jesus becoming the Son of God the Father in his baptism.
Horus the husbandman with the fan in his hand	=	Christ coming with the fan in his hand.
Horus the Good Shepherd, with the crook upon his shoulder	=	Jesus the Good Shepherd, with the lamb or kid upon his shoulder.
Horus with the four followers in the Mount	=	Jesus with the four disciples in the Mount.
Horus with the seven great spirits in the Mount	=	Jesus with the seven spirits in the Mount (Rev.).
Herrut the Apap-reptile, slayer of the younglings in the egg	=	Herod, the murderer of the innocents.
Isis commanded to take her child down into Egypt for safety	=	Mary warned to take her Child down into Egypt for safety.
Horus as the typical fish	=	Jesus as Ichthus the fish.
Horus as the fisher	=	Jesus as the fisher.
The four fishers with Horus as founders of the kingdom	=	The four fishers with Jesus as founders of the kingdom.
Sebek, the father of the fishers	=	Zebedee, the father of the fishers.
Two fisher-brethren, Kabhsenuf and Hapi	=	Two fisher-brethren, Simon and Andrew.
Two other fisher-brethren, Amsta and Tuamutef.	=	Two other fisher-brethren, James and John.
The seven on board the bark with Horus	=	The seven fishers on board the bark with Jesus.
The wonderful net of the fishers	=	The miraculous draught of fishes in the net.
Horus as the lamb	=	Jesus as the lamb.
Horus as the lion	=	Jesus as a lion.
Horus (Iu) as the black child	=	Jesus as the little black bambino.
Horus as Ahi, the striker with the flabellum	=	Jesus wielding the scourge of cords as the striker.
Horus identified with the Tat or Cross	=	Jesus identified with the Cross.
The blind Horus, in two characters, as the God and Manes	=	The two blind men of the Gospels.
Horus of twelve years	=	Jesus of twelve years.
Horus made a man of thirty years in his baptism	=	Jesus, the man of thirty years in his baptism.

Egyptian.		*Christian.*
Horus (Iu), the son of a beetle	=	Jesus, the good Scarabæus.
Horus (or Ra) as the great cat	=	Jesus as the cat.
Horus as the shrewmouse	=	The mouse of Jesus dedicated to " Our Lady."
Horus, the healer in the mountain	=	Jesus, the healer in the mountain.
Horus as Iusa, the exorcizer of evil spirits as the Word	=	Jesus, the caster out of demons with a word.
Horus, born as the shoot, branch, or plant from the Nun	=	Jesus born as the Natzer of Nazareth, so rendered in the course of localizing the legend.
Osiris as the vine-plant, Aarru	=	Jesus as the vine.
Horus, the bringer of the fish and the grapes in Egypt	=	Jesus as bringer of the fish and the grapes (catacombs)
Horus, the child standing on two crocodiles which adore him	=	The Christ-Child adored by dragons = crocodiles.
Horus, the child of a widow	=	The Child-Christ who lodges with a widow in Egypt.
Horus, the child of the widow in Sutenhen	=	The Child-Christ with the widow in Sotenin (pseudo-Matthew).
The golden Horus	=	The corn-complexioned Jesus
Horus full of wine	=	Jesus the wine-bibber.
Horus, who gives the water of life	=	Jesus as giver of the water of life.
Horus in the lentils and the grain	=	Jesus the bread of life.
Horus as Unbu in the bush of thorn	=	Jesus in the crown of thorn.
Horus the just and true	=	Jesus the faithful and true.
Horus-Mat-Kheru, the Word made truth at the second coming	=	Jesus the spirit of truth at the Second Advent.
The human Horus glorified in becoming a (Khu) spirit	=	The spirit not given until Jesus is glorified.
The world made through Horus	=	The world made through Jesus.
Horus the bridegroom with the bride in Sothis	=	Jesus the bridegroom with the bride.
Horus of both sexes	=	Jesus as the bearded Sophia ; Charis, the female Christ.
Horus who exalteth his father in every sacred place	=	Jesus who exalteth his father in every place.
Horus as Remi the weeper	=	Jesus as the weeper.
Dumb Horus, or the silent Sekari	=	Jesus silent before his accusers.
Horus behaving badly to Isis	=	Jesus speaking brutally to his mother.
Horus the gladsome	=	Jesus the jocund.
Horus as prince of the divine powers	=	Jesus the prince.
Horus the uplifted serpent	=	Jesus uplifted as the serpent.
Horus as the Bennu	=	Jesus as the phœnix.
Horus who giveth light by means of his own body	=	Jesus the light of the world.
Horus the hider of himself as Har-Sheta	=	Jesus the concealer of himself.
Horus the word-made-flesh	=	Jesus the word-made-flesh.
Horus the word-made-truth	=	Jesus the doer of the word.
Horus in the bosom of Ra	=	Jesus in the bosom of the Father.
Horus the Krst	=	Jesus the Christ.
Horus the avenger	=	Jesus who brings the sword.
Iu-em-hetep who comes with peace	=	Jesus the bringer of peace.
Horus called the illegitimate child	=	Jesus called the Mamzer.
Horus the afflicted one	=	Jesus the afflicted one.
Horus the unique one	=	Jesus the unique one.
Horus the lord of resurrections from the house of death	=	Jesus the resurrection and the life.
Horus as the type of life eternal	=	Jesus the type of eternal life.
Iu (em-hetep) the child-teacher in the temple	=	The Child-Jesus as teacher in the Temple.

Egyptian.		*Christian.*
Child-Horus as sower of the seed	=	Child-Jesus as sower of the seed.
Har-Khuti, lord of the harvest	=	Jesus, lord of the harvest.
Horus the founder	=	Jesus the founder.
Horus the fulfiller	=	Jesus the fulfiller.
Horus as master of the words of power	=	Jesus whose word was with power.
Horus Ma-kheru	=	Jesus, "the witness unto the truth."
Horus as the lily	=	Jesus typified by the lily.
Horus the link	=	Jesus the bond of union.
Horus who came to fulfil the law	=	Jesus who comes to fulfil the law.
Horus as bearer of the Ankh-symbol of life and the Un-sceptre of resurrection	=	Jesus as the resurrection and the life personified.
Horus (or Khunsu) the chaser of boastfulness	=	Jesus the humbler of the proud.
Horus of the Second Advent	=	The coming Christ.
Horus the hidden force	=	Jesus the concealed.
Horus as Kam-Ura, the overflower, and extender of the water illimitably	=	Jesus, giver of the water of life without limit.
Horus, who came by the water, the blood and the spirit	=	Jesus, who came by the water, the blood and the spirit.
Horus the opener as Unen	=	Jesus the opener with the keys.
Horus of the two horizons	=	Jesus of the two lands.
Horus as teacher of the living generation	=	Jesus as teacher on the earth.
Horus as teacher of the spirits in Amenta	=	Jesus as preacher to the spirits in prison.
Horus as teacher on the Atit-bark, with the seven glorious ones on board	=	Jesus the teacher on the boat, also with the seven fishers on board.
Horus uttering the words of Ra in the solar bark	=	Jesus uttering the parables on board the boat.
Horus walking the water	=	Jesus walking the water.
The blind mummy made to see by Horus	=	The blind man given sight by Jesus.
Horus and the Hamemmet or younglings of Shu	=	Jesus and the little ones.
The children of Horus	=	The children of Jesus.
Horus the raiser of the dead	=	Jesus the raiser of the dead.
Horus the raiser up of Asar	=	Jesus the raiser up of Lazarus.
Horus, who imparts the power of the resurrection to his children	=	Jesus who confers the same power on his followers.
Horus entering the mount at sunset to hold converse with his father	=	Jesus entering the mount at sunset to hold converse with his father.
Horus one with the father	=	Jesus one with his father.
Horus transfigured on the mount	=	Jesus transfigured on the mount.
Amsu-Horus in his resurrection as a Sahu-mummy	=	Jesus rising again corporeally or incorporated.
The blood of Isis	=	The issue of blood suffered by the woman.
The field manured with blood in Tattu	=	Aceldama.
The mummy-bandage that was woven without seam	=	The vesture of the Christ without a seam.
Seven souls of Ra the Holy Spirit	=	Seven gifts of the Holy Spirit.
Seven hawks of Ra the Holy Spirit	=	Seven doves of the Holy Spirit.
Seven loaves of Horus for feeding the multitude reposing in the green fields of Annu	=	Seven loaves of Jesus for feeding the multitude reclining on the grass.
Twelve followers of Har-Khuti	=	Twelve followers of Jesus, as the twelve disciples.

Egyptian.		*Christian.*
Horus with the twelve in the field of divine harvest	=	Jesus with the twelve in the harvest-field.
The twelve who reap for Horus	=	The twelve who reap for Jesus.
Horus as the intercessor	=	Jesus as the paraclete.
Horus as the great judge	=	Jesus as the great judge.
The judgment of the righteous, who are the sheep of Horus, the good shepherd	=	Judgment of the righteous, who are the sheep of Jesus the Good Shepherd.
The judgment of the guilty, who are the goats of Sut	=	Judgment of the wicked, who are the goats of Satan.
Horus parting off the evil dead	=	Jesus parting off the accursed.
The condemned spirits entering the swine	=	The evil spirits entering the swine.
The glorious ones that wait on Horus	=	The angels that minister unto Jesus.
Horus ascending to heaven from Bakhu, the mount of the olive tree	=	Jesus ascending to heaven from Mount Olivet.

The revelation of Horus, given by Ra, his father, to make known the mysteries of divine things to his followers	=	The revelation of Jesus Christ which God gave him to show unto his servants.
The revelation written down by Aan (Tehuti), the scribe of divine words	=	The Revelation written by John the divine.
The saluter Aani, who bears witness to the word of Ra and to the testimony of Horus	=	John, who bears witness to the Word of God and the testimony of Jesus Christ.
The secret of the Mysteries revealed by Taht-Aan	=	The secret of the Mysteries made known by John.
The books in Annu	=	The book of doom and the book of life in Patmos.
The books and their bringer	=	The book and its opener.
Seven dungeon-seals	=	The book with seven seals.
The great mother Apt, the pregnant water-cow	=	The woman sitting on the waters.
The crocodile as great mother	=	The dragon as great mother.
The great mother as Hathor, the abode	=	The woman that was the great city personalized.
The great or *enceinte* mother in her lunar character	=	The woman arrayed with the sun about to bring forth the child.
Isis, who brought forth Horus in the marshes	=	The woman who brought forth in the wilderness.
Isis pursued by the great crocodile	=	The woman persecuted by the dragon.
Isis, hawk-winged	=	The woman with eagle's wings.
The bride as Hathor-Isis, with the calf or lamb upon the mount of glory	=	The bride as the lamb's wife upon the mount.
Atum-Huhi, the closer and the opener of Amenta	=	Ihuh, who carries the keys of death and Hades as closer and opener.
Atum-Ra, the holy spirit	=	The spirit.
Hathor-Iusāas the bride, with Horus the lamb (or earlier calf) upon the mount	=	The bride with the lamb upon the mount.
Anup and Aan, the two witnesses for Horus	=	The two Johns as witnesses for Jesus.
The seven Khuti or glorious ones	=	The seven spirits of God.
Horus, with the seven Khabsu stars, or gods of the lamp	=	Jesus in the midst of the seven golden lamp-stands.
Sebek-Horus the lamb on the mount	=	Jesus the lamb on the mount.
Horus the morning star	=	Jesus the morning star.

Egyptian.		*Christian.*
Horus, who gives the morning star to his followers	=	Jesus, who gives the morning star to his followers.
The Har-Seshu, or servants of Horus	=	The servants of Jesus Christ.
The seven spirits of fire around the throne of Ra	=	The seven spirits of fire before the throne.
The fathers, or the ancient ones	=	The four-and-twenty elders.
The four corner-keepers	=	The four living creatures at the four corners
The solar god of golden form	=	The form with feet like unto burnished brass, and countenance as of the sun.
Iu the son of man (or Atum)	=	Jesus the son of man.
Horus as the first-born from the dead	=	Jesus the Christ as first-born of those that slept.
Horus in the house of a thousand years	=	The Millennial reign of Jesus.
Sebek the solar dragon	=	The scarlet-coloured beast with seven heads.
Seven souls or powers of Ra	=	Seven heads of the solar dragon.
The eighth to the seven	=	The eighth to the seven.
Ten Tata-gods or powers	=	The ten horns or kings.
The war in heaven	=	The war in heaven.
Har-Tema as the avenger, the red god who orders the block of execution	=	The word of God, faithful and true, with raiment dipped in blood.
Har-Makhu	=	Michael the Archangel.
Sut the accuser	=	Satan the accuser.
Sut and Horus	=	Christ and the Anti-Christ.
The celestial Heptanomis	=	The seven mountains of earth or islands in the sea.
The seven children of the old earth-mother	=	The seven kings of the earth.
Horus at the head of the seven	=	Jesus at the head of the seven.
The last judgment	=	The last judgment.
The mount of glory	=	The throne set in heaven on the mount.
The mount as judgment-seat	=	The mount as throne of the Great Judge.
The lion-faced throne of steel	=	The great white throne.
The great judge seated on his throne	=	The Great Judge on the judgment-seat.
The god in lion form	=	The god who is the lion of the Tribe of Judah.
The god in the solar disc	=	The god with the sun-like countenance.
The god whose dazzling mouth sends forth breezes of flame	=	The god from whose mouth proceeded the two-edged sword.
Osiris-Tat, the sufferer in the Lower Egypt of Amenta	=	The Lord who was crucified in Egypt
The Apap-reptile, the serpent of evil	=	Abaddon, Apollyon, or Satan, that old serpent.
Apap, the power of evil in the Abyss	=	Abaddon or Apollyon, the angel of the Abyss.
The binding of Apap in chains and casting the beast into the Abyss	=	The binding of the dragon, that old serpent, and casting him into the Pit.
Apap and Sut bound in chains and cast into the Abyss	=	The Devil and Satan bound in a great chain and cast into the Pit.
The Ankh-key of life and the Un-symbol of the resurrection	=	The keys of death and Hades in the hands of the opener.
The first resurrection and the second death in Amenta	=	The first resurrection and the second death.

Egyptian.		*Christian.*
The Lake of Putrata where the lost souls fall headlong into everlasting night	=	The lake of the second death.
The beatified in their white garments of glory	=	The beatified spirits arrayed in white.
The name of Ra on the head of the deceased	=	The name of the Father written on the forehead.
The little column of white stone given as a talisman to the initiates	=	The white stone given to the initiated
The mount of the double earth in Hetep	=	The mountain great and high.
The eternal city at the summit	=	The Holy City.
The water of life as lake or river	=	The river of the water of life.
The two divine sycamores over the water of life	=	The tree of life on either side of the water of life.
The water of life proceeding from the throne of Osiris.	=	The water of life proceeding from the throne of God.
The great lake in Hetep upon which the gods and glorified alight	=	The glassy sea on which the victors stand triumphant.
The great white lake of Sa	=	The sea of crystal.
The calf (later lamb) of Horus standing on the mount with Hathor the bride	=	The lamb standing on Mount Zion with the bride.
The lunar goddess Hathor bearing the solar orb	=	The woman arrayed with the sun, and the moon at her feet.
The glorified in Hetep stoled and girdled and crowned	=	The angels girt about the breasts with golden girdles.
The emerald dawn around the mount or throne of Ra	=	The rainbow like an emerald round the throne.
The Ba enclosure of Aarru, in twelve measures	=	The walled enclosure of the New Jerusalem, in twelve measures.
Heaven according to the measure of a man	=	Heaven according to the measure of a man.
The paradise of the pole-star	=	The Holy City lighted by one luminary that is neither the sun nor the moon = the pole-star.
The ark of Osiris-Ra	=	The Ark of the New Covenant in heaven.

INDEX

Aaiu, the Egyptian Jews, worshippers of the Kamite deity Iu, 511, 653; —, in the Underworld, 647, 653

Aan, the divine Scribe, 691; witness for Horus, 706, 855

Aarru Garden, 196, 363, 373, 640, 658; sown with wheat and barley, 228, 460; harvest field, 239, 372; Paradise, field of papyrus reeds, 259, 304; the Upper and the Lower, 347; in the north, Paradise of the Eight Great Gods, 348, 355; allotments for cultivation, 359, 416, 447, 468, 659; Paradise repeated in Amenta, 420; the Celestial, 421; on the eastward side of Amenta, 460, 642; title-deeds of; its wheat and barley seven cubits high, 460; divine domain, divided into fourteen sections, 577; the Egyptian and the Jewish, 687

Abait : see Bee

Aber-Amentho, the Gnostic Jesus in Amenta, 772-3; lord of the Resurrection, 780, 803

Abraham, seven footprints of, 606

Abut or Abtu, a form of Apap, 714

Abyss, of waters, habitat of hideous beings, 280-2; the Mystical, 284, 302; the first, underground, 284; source of water, 282, 299, 300, 412, 446; repeated in Amenta, 446; Song sung on the steps of the, 472

Aceldama, the field of blood, compared with fertilizing the earth with the blood of the wicked, 878

Achernar, starting-point of the astronomical Nile, 286

Achor, Hebrew valley of sorrow, Egyptian Akar, 474

Adam, two wives of, Lilith and Chavvah, 78; two, the mortal on earth, Manes in Amenta, 423, 425; a dweller in the Celestial Heptanomis, 428; the first and second, 432, 442; the generations of, 435; the first, born with a tail, 436, 442

Adultery, penalty for, 85; with spirits, 174

Æsculapius, the Greek Iu-em-hetep, 755

Agapæ, Phallic festival of fertilization, 105, 108, 223, 747; Christian celebration of, 223-4

Aiu, ass-headed god, with the solar disk, 647, 653; followers of Iu, later Jews, 648; accompanying the sun-god as the "Flocks of Ra," 653

Airyana Vaêjò, Paradise described in the Avesta, 378

Ak, star to which the rope of the solar boat was made fast, 395

Akar, a name of Amenta, 396; burial-place of Gog and his multitude, 473; valley of Amenta, sepulchre of Osiris in, 474; resurrection in, 475; covert in the midst of, 476; the lowest story of the Ark, 574

Akar or Khar, an underworld presided over by the Sphinx, 337

Akerit, Goddess of Akar, 337

Akhemu-Seku, the non-setting stars, 323, 387, 627

Akilles, Sun-god, 364

Alban Hills, the seven, 609

Alcheringa, mythical past, 66; ancestors, half woman, half man, 179; no men or women in, 429

Alexander, as Ichthus, the fish, 743

Ali, the Associate Gods with Ptah, 344, 405, 409, 410, 413, 414, 432-8, 594

Altar, Coffin, the first, 221; of the Palmyrene at Rome, 343; of the Cyclops, 386; for sacrifices after the Deluge, 569; of the Pole, Mound, 587; built by Moses, 666; astronomical in the Constellation Ara, 786; night of provisioning the, 868

Amalek, compared with the Egyptian Am, 644; war of, 661

Amemit, the typical devourer, 643

Amen, the ram-headed, Constellation Aries, 302

Amen-Ra, the Egyptian Apollo, 714; the "Entire God," 717

Ame-no-mi-Hashira, Japanese divine pillar of the heavens, 351

Ame-no-mi-naka-Nushi-no-Kami, Japanese God of the Pole-star, 379

Amenta, meeting-place of sun and moon, 31; resurrection of the soul in, 152; Manes put together in, 198; mystical Abodes in, 201; Solar god in, 211; night of the great battle in; ten great mysteries on ten different nights, 220; entrance to, a movable stone, 227; traditions of, continued in Rome, 241; mysteries of, purification by fire, 247; eater of the Shades in, 318; excavated by Ptah and his Seven Ali, 344, 411, 413, 638; subterranean country of the nocturnal sun,

Monkey, prototype of Taht-Aan, 15; cause of the Arawak deluge, 572

Monotheism, foundation of, 407

Moodgeegally, first man of the Aborigines of New Holland, 377

Moon, zootypes of, 8; frog in, 10; the Crescent Bow in heaven, 562; ark of, circle of a lunar zodiac, 577

Moses, a mythical personage, 509; the rod of, 646; the Hebrew equivalent of Anhur, 658, 661, 682-3; tradition that he was a woman named Musu, 661; compared with Shu; veil of, 662-3, 665-6, 683; born from the water; adopted by Thermutis, 663; his neck made invulnerable to the sword; born circumcised; the "Crazy man"; altar built by, 666; Mount of, 678; previously Osarsiph, priest of On, 682; disappearance of, 683; Children of Israel travel through Amenta with, 686; talking with Jesus at his Transfiguration, 823

Mother, the Abode, 36-7; sons, the consorts of, 59; first founder of the Totem, 62, 64; two — s. 69; eating the —, 71, 73, 234; — and eldest daughter, 76-7; — the human and superhuman, 97; earliest, the Virgin, sacred heifer of Isis, vulture of Neith, 136; the — cast out for the god to be imaged by the father only, the goddess continued in her types of the birthplace, 674

Mother blood, importance of, 68; origin of the human race, 69; to preserve it pure, 70; descent by, 71

Mother earth, giver of food; universal great grandmother, 98-100; as Fish, 282, 289; primordial bringer-forth, 398

Mother Totems, 65, 68, 81

Mouse, type of disappearance, 16; emblem of the human soul, 136-7

Mount (Mountain, Mound), type of Mother earth, 36, 100; Mexican mother, 100; some races trace descent from, 101, 624; figure of the earth, 270, 585, 588: astronomical, 312; Shu standing on, to uplift the firmament, 314, 322; of Glory in the heavens, 330; figure of the birthplace, 340; of earth, heaven, Amenta, 347-8; two —s of the Chinese, twofold of the Todas, of the Babylonians, 349; the Pahlavi two —s, 350; — of earth, type of the Great Mother, of heaven, typical of the fatherhood, 354; the double, of the Karens, 357; the Polar, Mont Blanc in heaven, 363; Hebrew paradise on the summit, 383; means of ascent to paradise, 388-90; staircase of the Great God; heavenly Jerusalem on, 473; Zion, 473, 675; of earth, seat of the Great Mother, 538; of the Navajo Indians, 571; type of emergence from the waters, 585; figure of the Pole, 594, 624; seven —s of the Zuni Indians; of stone; of the Papyrus reed; the Ever-white of the Koreans; the Pearl, 610; the seven submerged —s, 622; — "of Mankind," 624; of the "Nations," 625; of Venus, discovered by Constantine; Horeb, 675; of Oblations, 676; of Moses, 678; of Congregation; as Judgment Seat, 703; Final Judgment on, 704; of Resurrection, where

the blind, deaf, dumb, palsied, or dead were restored, 812-3, 821, 823; Jesus in, 819; scenes in the Ritual and Pistis Sophia, on the — in spirit world, 819; solar, and means of ascent to spirit world; equinox on the top of the; Sermon on the; Cross of Christ erected on, 820, 821; meeting-place in spirit world, 821; — of the Mysteries, Miracles, Resurrection, Regeneration, Transfiguration, 823-4; Jesus taken by the devil to the; Jesus praying in, lodging in, 825

Mount of Glory, in the heavens, 330, 384; in the double equinox, 335; coincident with the Vernal equinox, 336; Solar in the east, Stellar in the north, 354; at the north celestial Pole, 360, 397; of the " never setting stars," 376; of the Esquimaux, 378; in Amenta, 420; the solar; — of God; Sinai, 536, 676, 678; Great Judgment Hall on, 537, 704; Eternal City on, 575; Crown of life given on, 602; Promised Land seen from; the summit of Amenta, 678; figured in Revelation, 702;—of the Resurrection, 819

Mount of Olives, in Amenta, 772

Mtanga (or Mulunga), god or spirit, 377

Mummy, a type of the eternal, enfolded in a seamless swathe hundreds of yards in length, 216, 887; prepared for burial covered with a golden gum as type of a spiritual body, 217; type of resurrection in the Roman Catacombs, 219; borne on the back of a cow, 387; flight of stairs, pedestal, sceptre, tat, buried with, 472; the solar god represented as a, 644; Horus the raiser of, 479, 654, 842; Jacob's, 654; mode of embalming the, 851, 852.

Mut-em-Ua, the Virgin Mother, 757-8

Mysteries, of Amenta, 186, 805; ten Great in Amenta, 220, 247, 702, 844; the seven Great, 705; the Jewish, annual, equinoctial, 737; the Ten performed at Memphis, 740; in the Pistis Sophia, 774; the Greater and the Lesser, 775; the Lesser, astronomical, 778; the Greater, spiritual, 784; Second Horus, the expounder of, 791, 901; — of Totemism, spiritual in the eschatology, 794; double baptism in, 795; the dead in the, 814; first and second resurrection in the; — made portable in parables; resurrection of Ani one of the, 865; ancientness of, 866; — of Ptah at Memphis, doctrine of immortality first taught in, 890; the Lesser, taught by the elder Horus, the Greater, by Horus in his second advent, 901

Mystery, of the Great Mother, of the Dragon with seven heads, of the Seven Stars, of the First-born from the dead, 694, 699; the Mother of, 698; the Two witnesses, the Four living creatures, the War in heaven, God, Renewal in the ancient heavens, 699; of the Woman and the beast with seven heads and ten horns, 699, 700, 707; of Messiahship, 725, 727; of the Mystical Book, 726; of the Cross, 749; of Tattu, 772, 818, 839; of Investiture, 772; the First Great, 773; — teachers, 775; of Looking Within; Looking Without, 783; of the resurrection of the dead, 784, 805-6; of

of the House of Ptah, 326 ; Two, erected by
Queen Hatshepsu ; Two, of Sut and Horus,
two Poles in Equatoria ; Japanese Two, of
Earth and Heaven ; Two, in Amenta, the
doorway from one world to another, 351 ;
Two, in a temple of Herakles at Tyre, 352 ;
Germanic Irmin ; Hebrew, " the strength
of the hill Zion," 353 ; Four, of the four
quarters, 502 ; Twelve, of the twelve Tribes,
685

Pisces, sign of, Horus of the Two Crocodiles,
302

Pisciculi, the Primitive Christians, why so
called, 734, 736

Piscis Australis, the birth of water in,
299

Pisgah, Promised Land viewed from, 678 ;
vanishing of Moses on, 683 ; the mountain
of Amenta, 685

Pistis Sophia, a means of bringing on the
Jesus Legend from its Egyptian source, 771,
773 ; matter of, post-resurrectional, 771,
820 ; the Mysteries of Amenta, of Revelation, repeated in, 772 ; twelve dungeons of,
corresponding to the twelve divisions in
Amenta ; the necessity of knowing the
magical names in, as in Amenta, 774 ; the
Mysteries in, Egyptian astronomical mythology, 775–82 ; Mystery of the Five Supports referred to, 785 ; the Saviour Twins
in, the Dual Horus, 787 ; the true version
of Horus and Jesus in Amenta, 803 ; the
resurrection or " Coming forth to day " of
the Egypto-Gnostic Jesus, 820

Plagues of Egypt, 632, 641, 645, 652

Planisphere, its starting-point, 305 ; names
of Egyptian cities in, 637

Pleroma, star of the, 709

Pole, erected at the ceremonies of puberty,
60, 76 ; two sacred —s of the Arunta, 267 ;
the greasy, in British Pastimes, 391

Pole, celestial, images of, 265, 311, 377,
607–8 ; Mount of, " Heaven's Eye mountain," 265 ; —s, two, in Equatoria, 266,
268 ; the sinking of, 302, 547 ; centre of the
starry system, 302 ; of the Thigh, 310 ;
Yoke or Bond of heaven, 311 ; " Leg of
Nut " ; " Leg of Ptah," 310, 311, 551,
605 ; Staff of Anup ; Backbone of Osiris,
311 ; cord or chain attached to the, 323 ;
Apex of the Mount, at the ; backbone a
figure of the, 352 ; two —s as two trees,
353 ; Mount of Glory at the, 360 ; imaged
as a pillar of glass, 391 ; a mooring post,
397, 553–4 ; represented by the Mount, 499,
607 ; type of fixity, 552 ; staff of Shu, 555 ;
Great Reed of the Navajo Indians, 571 ;
" Tip of heaven " ; conical huts, a figure of,
575 ; seven stations of, 580, 601 ; types of,
580–1 ; Draconis, Lesser Bear, Kepheus,
Cygnus, Lyra, Herakles, stations of, 580 ;
change of, 3,714 years, 582 ; " Peach-tree
of the Gods," 583 ; Dog-rib Indian legend,
584 ; re-erecting the, customs in connection
with, 587 ; the Great Mother and her son
Sut, founders of the, 588 ; represented by
seven trees or a tree with seven branches,
by horns, the dragon, fish, fish-men, eyes,
caves, church, city, 608

Pole-star, the Southern, 302 ; centre of the
stellar universe, 323 ; ancient deity of, 324 ;
emblem of stability, type of the eternal, type
of supreme intelligence, 330 ; Eye of Anup ;
Chinese deity of, 331 ; above the Chinese
terrestrial paradise, 349 ; Japanese god of,
379 ; Sut ruler of the primal, 590 ; guide to
the Ship of heaven ; " Star of the eagle " ;
" Star of the wain " ; " Star of the Shepherd of the heavenly flocks " ; " Key of the
crown," 597, 601 ; " Crown of heaven,"
602 ; representative of Buddha, 609 ;
change of, a star falling from heaven, 701 ;
Light of the stellar paradise, 725

Pole-stars, on the two horizons, 265

Polutu, Samoan Hades, 354

Pool, of baptism, purification, Bethesda, 236

Pope, dressed in the likeness of both sexes,
736

Prayer, modes of, 34–6, 103 ; — offerings,
144

Precession, circle of, one great year in, 423,
595 ; seven Pole-stars seven stages in, 428,
607, 613 ; reference to, in the Book of Job,
496 ; Circle of the Eternals, 581 ; Herodotus'
report on, 582 ; the Circle of Sidi, 605 ;
Creation of man in the Cycle of ; great
deluge of all at the end of the cycle of, 622 ;
changes in, changes of birthdays for Jesus
and for Horus, 739 ; Horus in the Circle
of, " witness for eternity," " he who steppeth onwards through eternity," " persistent
traveller," 730 ; " traveller of the heavenly
road," 791

Primeval Powers, " first company of the
gods of Aarru," 421 ; identified with the
Hebrew Elohim, 422

Primordial Powers, the seven, two sets of
names, 322 ; various types and names of,
422 ; seven elemental forces, 698

" Prince of Peace," Horus the, 290, 293,
424, 498, 532 ; Iu-em-hetep, 417–8, 457,
500, 516 ; Augustus in the character of, 742

Promiscuity, modification of, 84, 107 ; continued in religious festivals, 224

Promised land, Mount Hetep, 207 ; — of
the Negroes of the Southern States of
America, 382 ; the Hebrew, 383 ; of Aarru,
garden of Hetep, 385, 460, 540, 657 ;
Ammah, the Goshen of the Ritual, 652 ;
account of the abundance found there, compared with Amenta, 657 ; across the firmamental waters, 678 ; on the other side of
Jordan, 684

Prosepis, battle of, 688

Psalms, of the sons of Korah, 471 ; of " degrees " ; " sung on the steps of the Abyss,"
472–3 ; the " wicked " in, the Sebau, 478 ;
VII., XVI., XXX., LVII., references to
the Constituent Souls, 480 ; Pleas of the
speaker compared with the Pleas of the
Manes, 484–5 ; the " still waters " as in
Hetep, 488 ; Exodus of the Israelites
described in, 641

Ptah, as beetle, 2, 405, 433 ; frog, 11, 30 ;
the husband of his mother, 86 ; elemental
souls blended with the human in, 182 ; first
form of god the father ; cult of, at Memphis,
234 ; pygmy, 250 ; suspender of the heavens,

267 ; Leg of, image of the Pole, 311 ; the two horizons united in his mansion, 326 ; excavator of Amenta, 344 ; the passage through the Mount tunnelled by, 345, 407, 411–2 ; supreme craftsman of the gods, 345 ; the Kamite Vulcan, 359, 365–6 ; builder of the Hall of Truth and Justice, 359 ; a dwarf, 372 ; Egyptian first creator, 405, 407 ; Kheper and Tanen, titles of, 405 ; great architect of the universe, 406, 413 ; " Let the earth be·! " title of, 409, 410 ; lifter of the firmament of the lower earth, 410 ; types of him as worker, 411, 433 ; builder of the Ark of the dead, 412 ; former of the egg of the sun and moon, 413 ; supreme god ; former and transformer ; father of beginnings, 413, 420 ; the Put-cycle of, 422, 433–4 ; supreme ruler for 9,000 years, 422 ; his name as opener ; the one god of Genesis ; God the father and Iu the son, 423 ; link between the elemental powers and spirit ancestors ; portrayed on the Monuments as creator of the human soul, 433 ; male mother, 434 ; male and female in one, 439 ; opener of the mouth ; giver of breath, 441 ; Huhi, Ihuh, Iao, Ieou, names of, 500 ; the wise god who spoke the words of wisdom to his son, 517 ; the universe of, divided into three regions, Amenta, earth, heaven, 853 ; grandfather of the gods, 891 ; earliest form of the eternal father manifested in an ever-coming son, 894

Ptah-Hetep, Proverbs and Sayings quoted from, 517

Ptah-Sekari-Osiris, Feast of, yearly festival of the resurrection, 740

Ptah-Tanen, his land below the waves, 369 ; the opener of the earth, 404 ; maker of the earth, 406 ; hailed as creator, 410

Ptah-Tatanen, of the Lower earth, Lord of eternity, 414

Puanta or Punt, name of, land of, 262–4 ; water of the Abyss, 278 ; Atum rising from, 459 ; conical huts on piles, 575 ; land of the gods, 635

Puberty, ceremonies of, 60, amongst the Yao people, 254 ; transformation at, 61 ; seclusion previous to, 69, 135 ; opening rite, 75–6 ; running through the rain, 134 ; con-nected with mysteries of mediumship, 169 ; Top-knot assumed by the Kaffirs at, 866

Pungel, god of the Melbourne Blacks, 440

Pung-Lai, Chinese island of, brought by a tortoise, 618

Purgatory, in Amenta, 415, 480

Put, cycle or circle of the gods, 344, 422, 432 ; equivalent to the Elohim of Genesis, 420, 423 ; number nine, Egyptian plural, 421

Putrata, gulf of, 240, 361–2, 396, 613 ; Caverns of, 361 ; Lake of, 395, 418, 829 ; the Red Sea, 640

Pygmies, 249 ; the seven primal powers, 594

Pyramid, Sut buried in (Arab tradition), 266 ; of Sakkarah, seven-stepped, 391 ; artificial figure of the Mount ; tubular shaft of the — of Gizeh representative of the way to heaven, also pointer to the Pole-star, 394 ; nine —s of the Mexicans representing the sun, moon, and seven stars ; the Great, a

sign of seven, 607 ; of Medum, evidence that 6,000 years ago the dead in Egypt were buried in a faith of the Cross, 749 ; the Ka Chambers in, built on the plan of the Greek and Roman Crosses, 750.

Ra, soul of the sun, 121 ; Sun-god, 126 ; Holy Spirit, source of divine descent, 165, 853 ; seven souls of, 172, 422, 430 ; first god in the trinity of Ra, Atum, and Horus, 188 ; the Litany of, 420, 442 ; adoration of, 420 ; men, stars, souls, the children of, 630 ; the " flocks " of, 648–9, 651, 653 ; children of, 650 ; Ra revealing himself to Shu, com-pared with the god of Moses, 667 ; Huhi, the eternal, Ihuh, 668 ; the " Ancient of days," 704 ; the supreme type of deity, solar hawk the symbol of, 843 ; the father in heaven as god in spirit, 853

Rahab, survival of the Great Mother, 686

Rainbow, bridge of the gods from earth to heaven ; the snake bridge of the North American Indians ; bridge for the souls of the Maori chieftains ; the Samoan Laa Maomao, " Long step of the god," 393

Ram, Sign of, solar resurrection in, 543

Rannut, as serpent, 2, 126, 272 ; type of the Great Mother, goddess of plant life, 140, 271 ; serpent of, type of transformation, 421 ; goddess of harvest, vegetation ; — Parmuti, the eighth month, 734

Regeneration, Jesus and Hermes on, 822–3 ; baptismal, 864

Rehu, the two lions, Sut and Horus, 253, 837

Rekhit, living human beings, 385

Religion, of the Wanyamwesi, pygmies of the Ituri forest, mainly a worship of spirits, 150–1 ; beginning of, worship of providence figured as the Great Mother, 497

Religious Cult, earliest form of a, 146

Rem-Rem, the place of weeping, 373

Rephaim, valley of, 475–6 ; the dead in Sheol, 476 ; giants, 476, 658 ; King of Bashan, Goliath, 476

Reproduction, festival of, for food, 104–8

Rerit, the sow, type of the Great Mother, 97, 301 ; the suckler, 306

Resurrection, phallus, type of, 38 ; Amsu-Horus, type of, 190 ; the Ritual of, 193 ; trepanning and inserting the bones of little children ; other customs showing belief in ; carrying round the ka image ; elevation of the Host, 213 ; Mummy, type of, in the Roman Catacombs, 219 ; Arunta Mystery of, 245 ; Horus representa-tive of, 290 ; Osiris, Horus, Amsu, in Amenta, 740 ; Paul's struggle to attain, 790 ; a Mystery of Amenta, 813, 818 ; on the third day, 814, 868, 887 ; in Amenta, repeated in the Gospels, 817 ; ascending the mountain of Amenta, a figure of, 819 ; of the soul, first represented in the Mysteries of Mem-phis, 842 ; events in the Gospels which occurred after the, 863 ; the first and second, in the Mysteries, 865 ; the Annual, 867 ; a general, at the time of the Crucifixion, 877 ; of Jesus compared with that of Horus, 878–9 ; two kinds, 881 ; of Jesus, proclaimed

632, 641, 645, 652 ; Divisions, heaven of, 649, 684, 694, 713, 715 ; Commandments, judgments, 680 ; Groups of the Tata gods, 713 ; Horus of the dragon, indicative of a heaven in — domains, islands, 715

Tenait, festival, 746-7 ; measure, division of time, 747

Tepht, source, 277

Tesherit, the red land given to Sut, 419 ; seized by Horus at his second coming, 836

Tesheru deities, Sut the chief of, 836

Tezpi, the Noah of the Mexican deluge-legend, 614

Thama, the Karens' Great Judge in Hades, 358

Thermutis, who adopted Moses, 663 ; name of the Great Mother, the original of Thoueris or Tharvis, Moses' second wife, 664

Thigh : see Haunch

Thousand years, devil bound for a, 712 ; Apap bound in chains for, 713. (See "House of a Thousand Years.")

Tiamat, old Great Mother, 271, 274 ; dragon horse, 274 ; destroyed by Bel, 275 ; one of the figures first constellated in the heavens, 405

Tiavat or Thavath, form of the Great Mother, 277

Tien Ho, Chinese Milky Way, 363

Titans, giants, assistants of Hephæstus, 386

Tohil, Mexican god turned into stone, 605

Torngarsuk, Great Spirit of the Inoits, 378

Tortoise, zootype of earth ; legend of the Tuscarora Indians respecting the Great Mother and her twin sons born on the back of a, 615 ; a type of Lyra, 616 ; Arabic name of Lyra ; the Pole resting on a, in a Hindu drawing ; Pole supported by, Japanese figure ; a god with the head of, in Egyptian tombs, 617 ; Chinese island of Pung-Lai brought by a, 618

Totem, origin of the name, 53 ; ancientness of, in Egypt, 54 ; first, from one mother, 62, 64

Totemic animals, 51 ; food districts, 55 ; not to be eaten ; to be eaten, 56-7 ; relationship to totemic man, 91-2 ; men personifying the, 92-3

Totemism, founded on feminine transformation, 62-3 ; traditions of the descent of the human race, 63-4 ; primary object of, 68 ; mythology supplied with its types, 96, 270 ; types of, in astronomical mythology, 626

Totems, two Motherhoods first division, 79-81

Tower, of Babel ; symbol of the Pole ; building the, replacing the Pole, 587

Traditions, Dog-rib Indian, woman and dog ; Mangaian, mother and daughter, 86 ; Various tribes issuing from the earth, 100 ; Witchetty-Grubs transformed into men, 101 ; Manx, that their earliest people were fairies, 149 ; Arab, of the burial-place of Sut, 266 ; Aborigines, McDonnell Ranges, sky at one time inhabited by three persons ; Ainu, of their origin ; Korean, of their origin, 379 ; Badagas, of their origin, 380 ; of the Lenni Lenape Indians, their beginning underground ; Mandan, their village underground and their grape-vine, 632 ; Quiché, Ha-

waiian, Hottentot, of their ancestors crossing the waters which divided, 633 ; of the Quichés, Aztecs, Bushmen, &c., that their ancestors existed before the creation of the sun, 731

Transfiguration, of Jesus ; of the Osiris in Amenta, 823

Tree, type of earth, 4 ; of food, life, shelter, 5 ; dawn, 29, 388, 415, 719 ; sign of prayer, 34 ; type of Mother-earth, 100-4 ; gods and goddesses of, 140 ; blind man's, 246 ; of Nut, 285, 448 ; first planted in the Abyss in the South ; terebin, territory of, 303 ; of the Pole, 305, 339, 380, 591 ; figure of the equinox ; figure of the birthplace, 340 ; figures of, between two lions, two goats, two cherubs, two winged unicorns, two rams, two giraffes, two hare-headed animals, 341 ; typical means of ascent to heaven, 388, 603 ; Llagdigua, of the Mbocobis of Paraguay, 388-9 ; Bhuggu in the Rig Veda clinging to ; spirits of the Australian Natives climb to heaven by means of ; strips of bark cut spirally up a tree to make a pathway for spirits, 388 ; Yao-Miao people bind their dead to ; the — that reached to the moon, 389 ; two, in Aarru corresponding to the — of Life and — of Knowledge in the garden of Eden, 415 ; one, in Eridu ; one, in Edin, 447 ; the eternal, the Pole, 448-9 ; Chinese Fu, figure of the Pole, 448, 587 ; of eternal life ; of Hathor, earth, life ; Egyptian coffins made from the Sycamore, 448-9 ; divine drink and food from the, 449 ; Horus between two in the Roman Catacombs ; of Adam, legend of, 450 ; Nut gives the fruit of the, to the pair in the garden, 451 ; cursing the, religious hatred of the Motherhood ; the, in the upper paradise, thornless, 452 ; —, serpent and the pair ; male and female, 453 ; guarded by a flaming sword, 454 ; sycamore, of stability and safety in Amenta, 484 ; fig and vine, typical —s, 536 ; means of escape from the deluge ; the ash, "Refuge of Thor," 571 ; seven, twelve, —s ; the Asherah ; the Khabsu, 604 ; on the mount, 625 ; grape-vine, typical — of life, 729 ; sign of sustenance, foundation of the Tat-image of stability and support, 750 ; the cherry — that bowed down for Mary, 765 ; of life, in Annu ; the sycamore, &c., described as the arms and hair of Hathor, 846

Triangle, of Horus, 327, 752 ; god of, a threefold nature, 329 ; the reversed, 752

Trinity, Osiris, Horus, Ra, 184, 897 ; Sut, Horus, Shu, god of the triangle, 329 ; mother, father, son, 718

Triune Being, mother, child, and adult male in one, 717

Troy, one of the enclosures on the summit, 625

Tseret, a witch-like goddess, 382

Tsutsowt, talkers in bird-language, 50

Tua, the sun of to-morrow, 334

Tuat, walled-up doorway in, the first of twelve in the passage of Amenta, 227 ; entrance to the underworld, 268, 278 ; secret source of the Nile, 278 ; in the South, from whence the inundation came, 324 ; the birthplace of

THE END